MUSICOLOGIA

MUSICAL KNOWLEDGE FROM PLATO TO JOHN CAGE

ROBIN MACONIE

THE SCARECROW PRESS, INC.
LANHAM • TORONTO • PLYMOUTH, UK
2010

PUBLISHED BY SCARECROW PRESS, INC.
A wholly owned subsidiary of
The Rowman & Littlefield Publishing Group, Inc.
4501 Forbes Boulevard, Suite 200, Lanham, Maryland 20706
http://www.scarecrowpress.com

Estover Road, Plymouth PL6 7PY, United Kingdom

British Library Cataloguing in Publication Information Available

Library of Congress Cataloging-in-Publication Data
Maconie, Robin.
Musicologia : musical knowledge from Plato to John Cage / Robin Maconie.
p. cm.
Includes bibliographical references and index.
ISBN 978-0-8108-7696-5 (cloth : alk. paper)
1. Music—Philosophy and aesthetics. 2. Music and science. I. Title.
ML3800.M236 2010
780—dc22 2010009753

The paper used in this publication meets the minimum requirements of American National Standard for Information Sciences—Permanence of Paper for Printed Library Materials, ANSI/NISO Z39.48-1992.

Printed in the United States of America

Dedicated to the memory of

HERBERT READ

CONTENTS

Introduction vii

0 Go! 1
1 The Aha! Theory of Creation 17
2 Snake in a Tree 29
3 Error 43
4 Isolation 57
5 Notations 73
6 Wheels 95
7 String Theory 115
8 Paradox Regained 131
9 Zeno's Arrow 147
10 Path Integral 165
11 Weights and Measures 177
12 The Director's Cut 189
13 Brane Waves 201
14 Transition 219
15 Transference 235
16 Lecture on Nothing 247
17 Atonality 269
18 Sprechstimme 285
19 Multiples 299
20 A Cochlear Implant 315
21 Serialism 331

CONTENTS

22 Schrödinger's Cat 351
23 Prepared Piano 369
24 Aleatory 383
25 Satie's Captions 401
26 Minimalism 415
27 Graphic Music 429
28 Cluster Music 443
29 Fractal Music 457
30 Simultaneity 475

Bibliography 489
Index 501
About the Author 525

INTRODUCTION

ON MYTH

> The making of the sword, like all ancient metallurgy, is surrounded with ritual, and that is for a clear reason. When you have no written language, when you have nothing that can be called a chemical formula, then you must have a precise ceremonial which fixes the sequence of operations so that they are exact and memorable.
>
> JACOB BRONOWSKI

Knowledge consists in how things are done. To make music a person has to know how to handle an instrument, and, if the music one wishes to play is written down, how to read notation. Knowing how to hear and perform music requires a combination of technical and physical skills. After that comes another kind of knowledge, interpreting the music one has chosen, or been requested, to play. Simply reproducing the notes on paper is not enough. The goal of music-making, for listeners as much as performers themselves, is understanding why a piece of music exists, what music itself is for, how it communicates, and what it is capable of meaning. Until what music means, or how it makes sense, is clearly understood, any interpretation is a matter of faith. According to some authorities, the message of music is something we can never know, a puzzle we can never solve. All the same, music exists. Since instruments for making music survive from the dawn of civilization, there has to be a reason for it.

Reasoning from limited evidence back to a probable cause is called *reverse induction*, which means "thinking backwards." Invented in the nineteenth century (or possibly earlier: one could argue that when Descartes declared "I think, therefore I am" he was guilty of reverse induction) the technique is familiar today as the basis of television crime scene investigation or medical emergency dramas where the plot consists in working back from a set of instantaneous clues or symptoms to the precise cause and sequence of events leading up to the opening presentation.[1] Reverse induction is associated with a cluster of sciences that inquire into the nature and origin of things, from the ancestry of plant and animal species to the history of civilization, the evolution of language and culture, and the big bang of creation. The science of ethnomusicology applies techniques of deduction and analogy to surviving customs and artifacts to assist in the classification and analysis of endangered folk traditions of song and dance. Oral traditions live and are passed down not in written documents but in the collective memory of a community, the poetry of its songs and rituals, and the shapes and sounds of its musical instruments.

Since western classical music is written down, its interpretation is traditionally viewed as a matter of "reading the text" accurately and with conviction. The idea of inquiring into classical music from the environmental perspective of folk or ethnic music is alien to many present-day observers who have been trained to regard classical music as a field of expertise having nothing to gain from the kind of scrutiny applied to the arts of earlier or more primitive cultures. A transformation in understanding and perception of European early music since the 1970s has shown this attitude to be a mistake. When music from the pre-classical European tradition is viewed from the perspective of ethnomusicology, its focus is broadened, as it were, from analyzing the content or message in a bottle to considering the information contained in the age and manufacture of the bottle, and flow of the tides—that is, to environmental clues that would previously have been ignored.

Evidence of musical thinking and analogy is exposed to view in artworks and cultural traditions, as well as hidden in accounts of ancient myth, mathematics, and cosmology, in places where a musician is unlikely to look, and expressed in terms a nonmusician is unlikely to recognize. A widespread use of musical metaphor in ancient mythology is of value to music historians as an indication of the priorities, methods, and ulterior concepts of western classical music. As interesting is the contribution of music-related reasoning to the social and scientific development of western culture. Through studying music in more general terms, an opportunity is created, for musicians and nonmusicians alike, of obtaining new perspectives on the history of civilization and culture, for the appreciation of which a foundation in music is desirable, indeed essential.

The Pythagorean School studied music as an essential part of their cosmology, even though the contribution of musical analogy to mathematics and philosophy is seldom directly mentioned in the literature of Greek science. We can be reasonably confident that the followers of Pythagoras were practical scientists who experimented with a variety of musical instruments that they knew how to play, even though they may not have conceived or performed art music in the sense we recognize it today. Music-related concepts to be found in the speculative writings of Philolaus, Pythagoras, Parmenides, Zeno, and others have nothing to do with entertainment and arise from practical experiment rather than theory or aesthetic invention, and for that reason we can understand them as essentially grounded in reality.

Present-day cosmology continues to grapple with the same fundamental issues of space, time, and creation that preoccupied the ancient Greeks, and to look for answers, or at least, for illumination, in musical analogy. From Pythagorean paradox to the elusive ramifications of string theory, musical imagery is routinely invoked to throw light on some of the most problematic and paradoxical ideas human ingenuity is capable of imagining, from the origins of the universe to concepts of time travel, multiple dimensions, action at a distance, and the limits of human knowledge.

That musical analogies continue to be employed by scientists in this way is a matter of cultural significance in itself. The challenge for musicians is to decide whether such analogies make sense from a musical perspective, since if they do not make musical sense, doubts arise over whether or why they should make sense in logic or astrophysics—if their musical implications are recognized at all. Some musicians are not entirely comfortable with the use of music imagery by science writers in popular accounts of cosmology. Irrespective of whether we agree with Plato's purported views on music, or Zeno's on continuity, at least their acoustical analogies are real and to the point. Modern cosmologists do not inspire the same confidence that they understand music, or that they regard it at all seriously. At one point in *The Universe in a Nutshell*, his illustrated sequel to *A Brief History of Time*, Stephen Hawking depicts a black hole in the image of an ancient disc gramophone drawn in the style of Rowland Emett, but a machine that works backward in time, so that instead of music passing from the rotating disc via the stylus out of the horn, the reader is asked to imagine information spiralling back down the horn to be trapped on a rotating accretion disc —and from thence presumably to vanish forever down the hole in the middle.[2] That the author's imagery is fanciful is clear not only from the charmingly tongue-in-cheek style of the illustration itself, but also in the inaccuracy of the author's analogy, since in the antique but real world of Fritz Kreisler the hole in the center of the gramophone record is not a black hole from which music appears, or down which it disappears. In fact there is no way for the music to get there: *it stays engraved on the disc*—which ironically we learn to be the fate of information confined on an accretion disc as well. The inconsistencies are suggestive in their own way. As it happens, in the years since *Nutshell* was published, debate has reignited at the highest level over whether the information trapped in an accretion disc, or sucked down a black hole, is in fact lost and destroyed, as the theory proposes, or remains potentially recoverable, as is required by the law of conservation of energy.

It is hardly up to musicians to adjudicate in such matters, but surely of interest to observe that what we seem to be dealing with here is less like science and more like a modern equivalent of myth, an expression of knowledge in coded form to be interpreted in the same terms as ancient myth and legend. Like the ritual of crafting a Samurai sword, myth encapsulates complex and subtle knowledge in arresting and memorable imagery that is outwardly arcane, but to those in the know, meaningful and internally consistent.

Myth has the additional merit of revealing its hidden meaning only to those sympathetic to the knowledge it represents. Oral cultures rely on myth to store information that is otherwise too secret, too abstract, or too complex to publish or commit to writing.

Aesop's fable of the cicada and the ant is a case in point: a tale suggesting that the idea of music as an unproductive activity was well established and propagated among the ancient Greeks. That may be true, but it does not necessarily follow that the message of the tale is prejudicial to music and musicians. To interpret the fable as saying that music is a futile pursuit, as La Fontaine is assumed to have intended, is to taint the historic fable with the prejudices of a French working class who regarded art music as élite entertainment and its practitioners as social parasites. That this version of the story is not true, *in fact is precisely the point*. What is true in the tale and its moral are the parallel inferences (a) that musicians are indeed hardworking members of society who can count on no sympathy from the revolutionary classes, and (b) that working-class revolutionaries who would do without music are condemning themselves to a boring and joyless existence.

A similar message can be read into the slow movement of Beethoven's Piano Concerto No. 4, depicting the relationship of a graceful and eloquent solo piano facing an oafish, uncomprehending string orchestra representing collective might. If the conventional interpretation of Aesop's tale is superficial, then perhaps his readers are to blame and not Aesop, whose parables purport to be based on direct observation of animal and insect communities. A less clichéd and more interesting interpretation would take into account the solitary nature of the cicada and its cheerful disposition, expressed in music, in stark contrast to the regulated social organization of an ant community having no tradition of music-making. The tale makes sense as a reflection on the benefits, obligations, and pitfalls of being born to the solitary life. We make essentially the same point in contrasting the politics of freedom and socialism.

To interpret the messages of Aesop's stories, or myth and fable in general, as necessarily *resolved*, is a mistake. They have a different purpose. Rather, they are designed to *provoke a moral tension* that the listener is obliged to resolve somehow, either by meditation or discussion, or even by actual observation of how insects actually live. Viewed dispassionately, the fable of the cicada and the ant is a morality in the image of a divided community in revolutionary France, a contest of values in which nobody wins. To the philosopher, the underlying issue is "why then should cicadas exist, if their lives are of no practical account?"—the answer being, not only that their existence is a value in itself, but that even if the cicada's only purpose in life were to make the ant community think twice about the value of a dreary and regimented existence, that would be enough. To contemporary society in late seventeenth-century France, La Fontaine's version of Aesop's tale implies that for human life to have value, it has to be more than a life of mere survival within a structured community that exists solely to perpetuate itself. The same is the lesson of Soviet realist art, here clearly spelled out a century and a half before the fact.

To the natural scientist, cicadas are musical creatures able to communicate with other cicadas across great distances, whereas ants have powers neither of speech, nor of music, and thus no sense of personal integrity or happiness. Like birds, cicadas have distinct songs representing species and individuals, and therefore distinct messages to communicate. Aesop's intended meaning may be that if cicadas were accepted by the ant community their skills could be available at little cost to enhance the well-being of the community and help to protect it. But alas, ants are deaf and communicate by direct contact, scent and touch. They neither sing nor dance. They produce no honey. Sex is prohibited. Though science may applaud the ant community, along with termites, as a successful example of a harmonious society, the life of the ant is directed entirely to the wellbeing (such as it is) of the queen.

To Aesop's Greek audiences, the difference in livelihood between a cicada and an ant would be even more stark, as between a free citizen and a slave. The condemned Socrates would certainly have identified his accusers as a committee of ants, and himself with the cicada, endorsing the virtues of living a life, however short, packed with stimulation and the communication of ideas, and dedicated to the promotion of happiness. For eighteenth-century European readers the message of the fable may have appeared brutally direct, but nevertheless inclined in favor of the rural working class. The revolutionary working classes stood for group solidarity and identity. They did not appreciate or understand the role of classical music as it had shown itself to be in the age of exploration: a diplomatic asset and mode of communication for European merchant enterprises keen to establish and maintain good relations with their oriental hosts, not only on the borders of Europe but as far away as India, China, and Japan.

Oedipus encountering the Sphinx must rank among the earliest prototypes of the television quiz game. On the surface, the riddle "What goes first on four legs, then on two, then on three?" seems innocuous enough. But the key to the riddle is not the correct answer (a man) but what the question implies, which is movement in space. For the answer "man" to be correct requires a perception of motion as a defining characteristic of a humankind considered to be curious by nature. In order to understand the question, a listener has to be familiar with *going* as synonymous with movement in space, a concept of *movement* in the sense of directed and thus purposeful action, and for the human tendency to explore to be so ingrained that it persists through a succession of altered states any one of which may be ideal, and the others less than ideal. The thread embedded in the original riddle, of doing the same thing in different ways, has the effect of emphasizing a lifelong compulsion to move among human beings, whatever the means employed. To think in such a way implied by the answer to the question one has to be a person for whom movement and change are natural aspects of the human condition. This is only going to be true of active, non-lethargic cultures who are intellectually curious.

Another trick in the question is the idea that speed or efficiency in movement may be related to the number of legs one has. To understand that speed may require fewer and not more legs one needs to be observant and have compared the speed of a centipede, for example, to that of a roach or a chicken. (Or indeed, the two legs of Achilles in competition with the four of the tortoise, in Zeno's paradox.) That a being chooses to move first on four legs, then on two, then on three, suggests a progression in skill. But in reality the reasons are different, mastery of balance the reason for the change from four to two legs, and the onset of age and incapacity for the change from two legs to three (the third leg being, of course, a walking stick). So in order to answer the riddle correctly, Oedipus has to understand the idea of *progression in skill* related to *movement in space* as well as *movement in time* (ageing). Along with the answer comes an appreciation that movement on three legs, while less efficient than on two legs, may well be preferable to movement on four. Acquiring mobility is a consequence of learning to stand upright, and entails a purpose in life of learning to move on two legs, and a conception of the world as a dynamic environment to be explored. The message can also be read as reinforcing the moral of the persistence throughout life of the impulse to continue moving and exploring, despite progressive and eventual failure of the body. Oedipus's encounter with the Sphinx is of an emblematic human *traveler*, on a quest for knowledge, with a mythical figure representing the power of knowledge and also guardianship over access to knowledge. Though it has the body (power) of a lion and the head (cunning) of a human being, this creature is rooted to the spot, and thus has no desire or freedom to seek out knowledge for itself. Its role in guarding access to knowledge is thus to *prevent* others from acquiring a power that might otherwise destroy it or both. A fateful symmetry connects the riddle of the Sphinx and the riddle of Schrödinger's cat.

Art and music, even a music of silence, is ultimately indefensible in the sense remarked by Plato because it makes the observer or listener think. To think raises the possibility that something new is being said, either about the artist, or about the world, or about the individual in relation to the world, something that ought to be brought into active consideration, or was not known before. The musical implication of a "quest for knowledge" exists in the formal implications of music-making (either with or without a text) as encouragement to action, and endorsement of the principle of individual freedom of movement, and by association, of freedom of thought. (Movement in this sense is understood as any action having the effect of disturbing the status quo.)

Oedipus's answer to the riddle was not new knowledge, but discovered knowledge. The answer was inherent in the question. That is the fiction of all such quiz questions, that there is nothing new under the sun. That a person may discover something about the world does not change anything, though it may make the individual life easier to bear. A knowledge of facts, however (that is, access to facts enabled by learning to read) acknowledges a world consisting only of facts. During the eighteenth century, European folk-song was being gradually liberated, and acknowledged in print, as part of a process of assigning a value to rural community life and a shared humanity to country people. In the nineteenth and twentieth centuries, the same folksongs were enlisted to promote nationalist agendas and suppress individual freedom in music and art on the ground that the latter was privileged, elitist, incomprehensible, and subversive of public order. Since the ideal of a fixed and unchanging social order was bound in with a belief in literacy as a social unifier and specific against social revolution, the same prejudice against change was bound to emerge in de Saussure's philosophy of language (*la langue*) as fixed and objective, and individual speech (*la parole*) as subjective and tending to disorder. The music market, governed by bourgeois taste, continues to reject new classical music even in the twenty-first century on the implicit grounds that new experiences and new ideas are injurious to collective security. Underlying that rejection is the same truly ancient prejudice against a dynamic of social change brought to a focus in the encounter of Oedipus and the Sphinx. That Oedipus's aspiration to full disclosure would eventually lead him to murder, incest, infertility, and self-harm is a destiny reserved for those committed to a dynamic of instability and unstable relationships.

Myth transforms even prosaic events. Livy's account of the death of Archimedes at the hands of a Roman foot soldier reads today as a plausible factual report of a historical event. The great man is said to have been disturbed while working out a problem, immersed in thought, studying a diagram scratched on the dusty ground. Challenged to identify himself by a trooper of the occupying Roman forces, he waved the questioner away, and was struck down. Hearing word of Archimedes' death, the captain of the regiment realized a mistake had been made, and gave orders that the body be buried with the honors due to a famed engineer and longtime friend of Rome.

As the report of a real event, Livy's account makes perfect sense. We could take it as a true account and leave it at that. That Archimedes died is a fact. That he was killed is a contingent fact. That he was killed, *unrecognized*, by a Roman soldier, for disobeying an order, is the stuff of myth. The interesting point is that the story makes more sense, and is more truthful, as myth. One only has to reflect on the aesthetic and poetic symmetries of a face-off between an elderly philosopher and an army recruit, and its consequence in a rash act of youthful devotion to the idea of physical strength rather than wisdom as the agency for solving human problems. The discipline of a foot soldier is founded on action in preference to independent thought, ideology in preference to knowledge, and being answerable to the regiment, the state, and the sword rather than personal conscience. The symmetry is perfect for myth, and too perfect to be real.

Archimedes is interrupted while drawing a diagram in the dust. He is challenged by the soldier to give his name: that is, to identify himself as a citizen, as a name on a list. He is not recognized by the guard, despite his familiar reputation as a master engineer among the Romans, because to the military, personal identity is a meaningless concept. Furthermore, the diagram drawn in the dust can also be interpreted as the old man "drawing a line in the sand"—a line dividing the world of science and reason from the world of unthinking obedience, militarism, and vested interest. The line says, step over at your peril. It declares that the truth can be discovered even in the dirt, or planted in the soil, by a simple act of drawing a mark with a stick. It is a way of saying that inspiration is fragile, comes unbidden and must be pursued with whatever means are to hand, to the exclusion of all other considerations, even life itself. Most profoundly of all, the line in the dust is a metaphor of the act of creation itself. To the ancients, sand or dust represented the infinite, and the line the power of divine intellect.

Notes

1. Detective stories—and Greek tragedies too, I suspect—are about death, not because death is a popular subject, or because their authors are a species with a death fixation, but because death is a finality, hence a *defining point* of an event located in time, space, and *dramatis personae*. In myth, as in tragedy, the game consists in establishing the process of which the story is the conclusion. Any such process demands that the objective is the same throughout, that there is no uncertainty about the body, only about the possible motive, which in turn involves the uncertain behaviors of the suspects, and tests the skills of the detectives and forensic experts, which are both psychological (interpreting how people think) and evidential (interpreting the traces they leave behind).
2. Stephen Hawking, *The Universe in a Nutshell*. New York: Bantam Books, 2001, 62.

ZERO

GO!

> Silence can be realized only through music, which should be the "music of silence" and not an actual cessation of sound.
>
> LEONID SABANEEV

Despite interpretations to the contrary, Plato did not disapprove of music. Rather, he was insisting that music was about more than just pleasing yourself. Plato's affirmation of the power of music to arouse emotion spontaneously in a listener has been interpreted rather too readily by philosophers of the romantic era as the equivalent of saying that music is immoral, and should therefore be banned, or at least kept under strict control by the state.

Why would Plato say such a thing? Because along with others he saw a connection between the harmony implicit in music and the loss of self-control to which music-worshippers and their revels were disposed to resign themselves under its influence. We recognize the same spirit of abandon in the pop music arena, and the same attitude of skepticism in governments and religiously motivated ruling classes who legislate against popular music, or ethnic music, or music expressing allegiance to a particular religion or class, and even, on the grounds of unintelligibility, against modern music that is disliked by a majority. Fear of music is not restricted to the Axis of Evil, or socialist regimes in their crusades against "degenerate" or any other music that does not conform to official standards of modesty, optimism, or loyalty to officialdom. The same prejudices are embedded in advanced democracies, disguised as teaching standards for qualification in aesthetics, marketing, media studies, music therapy, social psychology, and the rest. All chant to the mantra that the basis of music lies in human nature, and that music that appears unnatural or offensive to anyone, is inexplicable, or simply does not fit, must be contrary to nature.

Nor did Plato say that music should be banned. What he said has been taken all too literally by educational moralists to suit their own agendas. Plato was a disciple of Pythagoras. He was trained in acoustics and aware of the explanatory power of musical knowledge to connect subjective emotions and intuitions of motion and harmony with absolute properties of nature, from the vibration of a string or air column to the cycles of human life, the planets, and the universe. It was exciting but dangerous knowledge, since it had to do with the most profound mysteries of nature and existence, control mechanisms traditionally assigned to the gods. To speculate in such matters risked offending the gods, not to mention the priestly class, who in ancient Greece were a powerful group.

Nineteenth-century educationists adapted the classic stories of Greece and Rome in terms suitable for training the middle classes. The industrial age was an age of specialist disciplines, each with its own rules. Classicists and historians were fascinated by war and the logic of war, and relatively indifferent to music, interpreting Plato's definition of the art as a lethal distraction from reality and moral integrity. Eighteenth-century educationists were attracted to the cultivation by ancient Greeks of the arts of music and rhetoric, and persuaded of their powers to influence and communicate states of mind, but these experts had little grasp of acoustics, or indeed of music, and they lacked the skills necessary to interpret the symbolisms of oral cultures. It suited those in power to interpret Plato's views in authoritarian terms which, given their employee status, endorsed the doctrinaire agendas of the government in power. In turn, it suited governments to pursue an official line that the approved practice of music should be limited to ritual forms of art, public ceremonial, and religion, regarding private or unapproved music-making as potentially indecent, immoral, or prejudicial to public order.

In the twenty-first century classical music has been reinvented as a plaything of philosophy, and in portable guise, as a constant refuge from the noisy distractions of reality. Aside from the fact that for an increasing number of listeners music has become a stimulus all but inserted directly into the brain by wires from an acoustic pacemaker carried round the neck like a religious token, not much has changed since Plato's time. Older people cling to the principle of setting limits to freedom of thought and expression, young people continue to push the boundaries of the permissible, and music of all kinds, classical as well as popular, and modern music most of all, continues to bear the taint of original sin.

Plato's exclusion of entertainment music from the ideal state as a distraction from the important concerns of life in general, and philosophy in particular, is all the more perplexing coming from a school of thought that regarded musical knowledge as the key to understanding the mysteries of the universe. The paradox is easily resolved if his caution against the perils of being taken in by the superficial attractions of music is construed as actually *defending* music against charges of superficiality and encouragement to lewd behavior. For those who were prepared to study music seriously, he is suggesting, there are layers of more profound significance to be read into the properties of an art of sound signals that for some mysterious reason has the power to arouse feelings of pleasure, harmony, proportion, clarity, and repose in the minds of those who listen.

The Platonic concept of essences is routinely interpreted as a morality of local and personal imperfection. We are encouraged to believe in an ideal world of circles, squares, and triangles, in relation to which mere human or natural representations are invariably imperfect. No tree or branch grows perfectly straight. No one face or leaf is identical to any other face or leaf. The inference that we should all strive for ideal perfection is out of keeping with Greek science, but typical of the evangelical fervor of philosophers in the early romantic era of Schopenhauer and Hegel. The oppressive morality with which Plato's reputation has been burdened has more to do with the formation of middle-class educational doctrine than an understanding of Greek. Put simply, terms of resemblance are figures of speech, and figures of speech correspond to figures of the imagination. Thus, a circle is what something resembles and not what it is, but to describe something as "a circle" also provides a pretext for inquiring into other aspects of circularity. In the same way we recognize other people as "human," though their dress and skin colour may be different from our own.

However to focus on essences as ideal rather than real is to miss the point that in music, unlike other manifestations of nature, essential relationships are demonstrably real, and repeatable, and altogether reliable. When two voices sing in unison, as a child sings in tune with its mother, or as slave cotton pickers in the field sang the blues to get the job done smoothly and synchronously, that unison is a demonstration of agreement of a kind transcending personal suffering and individual difference.

For music to exist, let alone survive, it must have something of intellectual interest to attract the attention of the philosopher and historian of science. Since music played an important role in the development of ancient philosophy, and has influenced scientific thinkers of the quality of Oresme, Buridan, Kepler, Mersenne, Newton, and Helmholtz, it is perhaps of interest for musicians to understand what aspects of musical knowledge could possibly have been of interest to the intellectual giants of the past, and for what reasons. Since the disciplines of philosophy and music share a very similar technical knowledge, differing only in the directions to which the knowledge is applied, the things musicians do by instinct or design invariably have philosophical implications, just as the ideas of cosmologists have musical implications.

As I attempted to show in *The Way of Music*,[1] whatever value it may have as entertainment, music is also a medium of inquiry into fundamental issues of individual and social consciousness: a sense of being, the nature of time, the transfer of energy, relations of chaos and order, ratio and proportion, structure and resonance, perception and illusion, attention and communication, measure and recurrence, discord and agreement, gesture, time and motion, operational management, and conflict resolution. Sheet music in symbolic notation is available to be studied as structures of thought embodied in musical instruments, systems of notation, a vast repertoire of compositions in written form, and recordings of acoustic performance. In most of these studies language plays only a small and possibly peripheral role: as text set to music, or instructions to a performer in a musical score. That music is effective in communicating is generally acknowledged: people download and buy recordings, and go to concerts. That music communicates without language is at the same time highly problematic to many of the same listeners, who have been brought up to respect the mantra that without words there can be no thoughts. And of course, there are those among us, including philosophers of music and some musicians, who have a vested interest in preserving their authority by reinforcing the mystique that music is ultimately unknowable. Communication without language, though limiting in some ways, can be considered advantageous in other respects. The chemical messages exchanged by insects and animals are truthful and undisguised. In the absence of language, instrumental music is naturally limited as a human activity to statements and formulations of a wholly explicit kind, which being uncompromised by language are therefore true in an absolute sense. Along with the Latin language, the Holy Roman Empire employed music as a means of unifying authority, and assuring consistency of doctrine, across and beyond Europe. After 1500 music assumed an alternate secular role as a medium of international diplomatic relations, in which role it continues to function today. The argument that there can be no communication without language is typically employed by those who do not understand how it is possible for anything other than language to convey intelligence, no doubt in order to persuade themselves and anybody listening that music by its very nature is incapable of thought. They are aided in that opinion, alas, by the reminiscences of many eminent musicians.

SILENCE

The Germans have a saying, "Der Weiser schweigt" (The wise man holds his tongue: or literally, the philosopher is silent).[2] I was delivered this gentle reprimand over a glass of beer by a respected music critic (I think it may have been Carl Dahlhaus) at the 1965 Darmstadt Festival of Contemporary Music, an annual celebration attended that year by Pierre Boulez and an ailing Theodor Adorno. The advice was well-intended and, coming from the music correspondent of a major newspaper, probably prudent as well, given that visitors were already subject to ambush by enemy forces in the person of an amiable Belgian sociologist, clipboard in hand, an individual driven with evangelical fervor to persuade one and all that modern music of any kind (atonal, twelve-tone, graphic, serial, aleatoric, improvised, intuitive, electronic, computed, or composed by chance procedures), having been shown by numerous polls to be unacceptable to a majority of the music-loving public, was thus a pursuit contrary to reason and public morality.

This was modern music being condemned because it *wasn't* popular or entertaining. The opposite position from Plato, who saw popular appeal as a sign of triviality and lack of intellectual content. It follows the bizarre logic of Aesop's anthill for a novice sociologist to declare that the ideal city state should disparage or exclude as morally unacceptable not only music that a majority dislikes or does not understand, on the grounds that it is unrepresentative of the community will, while simultaneously repudiating music that is popular and entertaining, on the grounds that it encourages immoral or antisocial behaviour and the pursuit of pleasure for its own sake.

In his own terms, M. Caraël of the Brussels Free University was perfectly right to be perplexed at the existence of a school (or schools) of a modern music that not only sounded incomprehensible and unpleasant to the ordinary listener, but was opposed to every rational convention of melody, harmony, reason, order, technique, and acceptable musical and social propriety. As a twenty-something student and Webern adherent, I agreed with him. I was just as baffled as he about most of the music I had journeyed all the way from New Zealand to absorb and talk about. I listened to their lectures and found Boulez's message oblique and elusive, and Adorno's tired and impenetrable. I thought that a fair proportion of the music performed at Darmstadt in the summer of 1965 was dull, mediocre, poorly argued, and in the case of some (though not all) graphic music, pretty jejune. All the same, the experience was exciting and authentic. The sheer incomprehensibility of avant-garde music had always been one of its main attractions. For that reason alone I was surprised, indeed offended at the suggestion that adherents of a modern music that intrigued and excited me, a music that had been endorsed, not just in principle, but also in imitation, by as great a composer as Stravinsky, should be blacklisted simply because an alleged vast majority of listeners (or even a small minority of sociologists) did not share my excitement, or could not be bothered.

I was equally taken aback at my mentor's suggestion, or so it appeared at the time, that it could ever be right for a wise person to keep his or her mouth firmly shut. This was Germany still in the Cold War. Was there a moral or political component? My counsel was old enough to have lived through the 1939–1945 war. Would that be the reason? In other circumstances, if a person discovered something exciting or important, how could one not want to share the information with someone else? How could silence ever be justified? Lacking a classical education, I was naively unaware of the historical resonances of such a caution—an echo of Socrates smiling quietly to himself while his pupils argued heatedly among themselves—and oblivious to Wittgenstein's dictum about silence being the only option when there is nothing more to be said, or nothing to be said. If a person is silent, I angrily wanted to know, how can you possibly know he is wise? In my awkward German I protested that surely what a person says is the only evidence we have of whether that person is wise or foolish, or anything of consequence that can even be debated. I was not thinking about books in medieval times that used to be locked away, still less of hard drives, which did not exist in 1965.

Silence is absence of speech (and music), but not the antithesis of speech (or music). In silence we understand absence of speech, the potential for speech, and the moment of speaking, all rolled into one. We experience this kind of silence in the upbeat to any piece of music ever written. Music may be the variable, but silence is universal. It was there before music began, and will still be there, just as powerfully, long after the music ends.

That music will end is a foregone conclusion. Sounds emerge momentarily into being and fade back to nothingness. The defining experience of all sound is transience. That is the point. In that crucial respect, oral cultures from the dawn of time are bound to evolve distinctive schemas of knowledge—mythologies, religions, or philosophies—very different from the confident legislations of literate and numerate societies, and predicated on the certainty that all is change, nothing lasts. In our own times, the case against modern music has as much to do with a clash of eye and ear cultures, I think, as between notional elite and working-class attitudes and values. It seems to me now that the antagonisms and conceptual difficulties arising from the music of the twentieth century, and brought to a head by the avant-gardes of the fifties and sixties, are not only fascinating in their own terms, but arguably related to many paradoxical views of ancient philosophy, derived from an oral, listening-grounded worldview, and expressed in the symbolic language of myth and legend, the information storage and retrieval systems of nonliterate cultures.

Among the most often talked about compositions of the twentieth century is the *4' 33"* (four minutes and thirty-three seconds) by the American composer John Cage. The work consists of a measured period of silence, or alternatively, silent actions on the part of the performer or performers. Composed in 1952, the work has been described as the zero point of classical music, and a response to the imminent possibility of nuclear annihilation. The 273 seconds of negative activity were later said by the composer to correspond to the –273 degrees Celsius of absolute zero, the (in fact unattainable) temperature at which all movement ceases. For such a bold gesture to have exerted an influence so far out of proportion to its ostensible musical content has something to tell us about the power and persistence of oral modes of thought in a largely visual postwar industrial civilization. "Nothing will come of nothing: speak again!" says King Lear to Cordelia, in a Shakespearean parallel moment that, as Marshall McLuhan observed, is also about a generational clash of oral and literate cultures.[3]

Cage's formal silence carries an unexpectedly potent negative charge. In practice a performance of *4' 33"* is likely to provoke audience murmurs of disbelief, embarrassment, even anger. Inside the concert hall we expect to hear music as a matter of course, forgetting that a performance of music is only possible thanks to the fact that sounds disappear into the void almost as quickly as they emerge into the air. To be conscious of silence as eternal and universal, and music as ephemeral and transitory, is bound to throw the subjective qualities of conventional music into sharp relief. The remark attributed to Bishop Berkeley, that if there is nobody present to hear it, a great tree falling down in the midst of a forest makes no sound, implies that the world of sound as we understand it is entirely an internal byproduct of the sense of hearing, rather than an effect of real actions taking place elsewhere. That sensory impressions are only knowable as mental constructs is certainly arguable, but it does not follow that they arise from nothing, or are imaginary, or depend upon the observer for their existence in the first place. Whether Cage's silence will continue to resonate when there is nobody left to hear it is a separate, and equally metaphysical issue to be determined at another time, if at all, and by other forms of life. The more relevant point is that, as guardians of an oral culture as universal and old as humanity itself, musicians are attuned to the idea of silence as a necessary condition for music, and therefore recognize an essential truth in Cage's paradox of a music consisting only of silence, especially when the silence is intended, as *4' 33"* certainly is intended, to draw attention to the intimate relationship of acoustic activity and hearing to a comforting sense of our own continuing existence. Since by convention we listen to classical music in silence, in doing so we hand over our sense of existence to the performers of music, adapting our sense of self to the harmoniously ordered acoustics of a musical imagination from another time. When that expectation is met by silence, an audience is left with a sense of what exactly it has handed over, and is now missing.

Cage was a student of western and eastern philosophy, a one-time disciple of Daihetzu Suzuki, an admirer of Zen, and reader of Wittgenstein, McLuhan, and Buckminster Fuller. We can take from this and other evidence in his published writings and commentaries that whatever difficulties a reader may have in understanding Cage's intellectual or aesthetic positions, the latter are all the same sincere, serious, and grounded. Even if the musical statements and associated ideas of Cage and a great many other twentieth-century composers seem deliberately provocative and in conflict with what we expect of music, the possibility remains that the objectors have got it wrong and the composers are right, notwithstanding the conventional mantras of freedom of speech and the duty of art to stimulate thought rather than be merely entertaining.

Silence as a performance event is already a reality, if that is the word, in small but serious social rituals that take place on significant days in the life of most civilized communities. Their meaning is understood without question. That societies observe a minute or two minutes of silence in memory of the dead on special days of remembrance is part, though perhaps only a minor part, of the reason why Cage's time-specific composition of silence has such troubling and deepseated resonances. Only a few years ago a British composer of light music incorporated a track of silence on a recording of his own works, ostensibly as a gesture in tribute to Cage. The duration of the track was not equal to, indeed a great deal less than Cage's four minutes and thirty-three seconds; all the same, his publisher threatened legal action, alleging breach of copyright, and the matter was eventually settled out of court. On reflection it was a good outcome: not so much for copyright attorneys, as for ideas and values.

There is a respect due to silence as the voluntary cessation of movement, a respect that is different from the helpless irritation experienced at an involuntary break in transmission, or as a deliberate gap introduced into an otherwise continuous flow of music or speech. Silence as a programmed event during a concert of serious music is different again from a public rite of remembrance, where the public mind is properly focused on the duty of the living to honor the dead. Cage's silence is a challenge to our understanding of the concept of absolute absence, and draws its magnitude of implication from the music and culture within which it is situated.

In context, a rite of silence is a rite of cessation. It is not like a silent movie of olden times which presents to us as a stream of accelerated activity—funny, or pointless, or both—unaccompanied by any sound. It is not like a Greta Garbo closeup, a silent movie moment of intensely emotional indecision that is impressively speechless as well—though that is not at all far from the point. Most people, even if they are not religious, know what it is to pray, and how hard it is to contemplate the paradox of non-existence within the context of a lifetime of activity, the meaning of which, to musicians at least, is expressed in the highest degree in the interactions of live classical music. Cage's silence has meaning, and the meaning of its silence is acknowledged in the reality that this work cannot easily be performed on air, even for as short a period as four minutes and thirty-three seconds. There would be too many listener complaints.

The message of silence embraces paradox. War and the Bomb are only shadows. Beside the metaphysical challenge of expressing a consciousness of "that which is not," even Wittgenstein's peculiarly central European take on the necessary inarticulateness of the ultimately inexpressible pales into an aesthetic pose. Books are silent, though print is a constant presence. Art works are silent, but persistently available. The perpetual worlds of vision and the text have conditioned western cultures to perceptions of time and existence as continuous, ongoing, and inevitable. Silence belongs to the other reality, not vision, but hearing: a reality of emergence and absence, of constant reformulation and constant renewal. The reality of silence connects the paradox of modern music with some of the strangest beliefs of ancient philosophy and modern science.

THE PRACTICALITY OF SILENCE

> The cessation of music in the cinema always produces an impression of dissonance, unless it is promptly and directly replaced by other sounds.[4]

Whatever its poetic or philosophical implications, the saying of Leonid Sabaneev cited above arises from purely practical considerations. Like his compatriot Sergei Eisenstein, Sabaneev was a pioneer movie-maker and theorist. Eisenstein's interpretation of the poetics of montage drew on literary antecedents—Shakespeare, Dante, Leonardo, Milton, Pushkin—to converge on the editing practices of the movie medium and the stream of consciousness dynamic of symbolist poetry, surrealist art, and modern psychoanalysis. Eisenstein and Sabaneev are writing in the mid-1930s: a time when the aesthetic implications of the medium were still under intense scrutiny. Whereas Eisenstein's theory of music and silence is firmly grounded in the visualizations of the silent era, treating music in terms of a silent movie accompaniment, his compatriot Sabaneev, a composer, is more acutely aware, both musically and from a sound recording perspective, of the respective roles of synchronized sound, speech, and music in the composite new art of sound film.

Sabaneev's depiction of silence as substantive, an acoustic "white space," is a conceptual insight of a kind often provoked by the impact of new technologies, encapsulated in McLuhan's epigram "the medium is the message." Before the arrival of radio, and live concert broadcasts, nobody had reason to consider the aesthetics of background noise, audience murmur, or the expectant hush. Before the gramophone era, nobody thought about surface noise as a condition of listening to classical music, or music of any kind. But by the 1930s, when Cage was a young man, the art of the microphone, in the movies, and broadcast music and drama, had already led to a raft of regulations governing the nature and quality of silence, from the length of time allowed for a break in transmission before a standby announcement had to be made, to the appropriate length of silence before, after, and between movements of a work of classical music, to deciding the optimum length of a pause in radio drama (an inspiration to writers as different as Samuel Beckett and Harold Pinter). After 1945, with the emergence of tape and electronic media, and the replacement of noisy shellac 78 rpm discs with high fidelity vinyl pressings of greatly reduced surface noise, the aesthetics of silence acquired additional nuances of meaning. Today the scale or hierarchy of degrees of silence familiar to ordinary listeners extends from accidental dropouts and the dead silence of leader tape (an experience of total absence), to recorded ambience of a concert hall inserted between movements of a classical recording (a sound of emptiness, but the emptiness of a real space), to the ambience of a live broadcast (colored by audience murmur, page turns, and discreet incidental noises), to anticipatory pauses (as between a radio announcer ending a voice-over introduction and the music beginning, or between the ending of a performance and audience applause), to momentary silences within the flow of the musical work or dialogue. In the context of an increasingly sophisticated culture of silence management, Cage's measured period of deliberate inactivity begins to assume more of the character of a radiophonic "happening" than a philosophical reflection on the threat of nuclear extinction.

Perhaps the most successful exponent of measured silence to date has been Karlheinz Stockhausen, in the composition *Trans* of 1971. In a scenario resembling an imaginary soundtrack to Edgar Allan Poe's story *The Pit and the Pendulum*, a dense fog of orchestral music is sliced into segments by what sounds like sweeps of a sinister guillotine passing overhead. Toward the end the music succumbs completely to silence for periods of up to a minute, as if knocked out cold by a slow-motion left hook. By Cage's four-and-a-half-minute standard, equivalent to the duration of one side of a 78 rpm disc, at a minute or so apiece Stockhausen's silences are not long at all, but they are still long enough to give the impression of a Grand Canyon-like void, and in the live recording available on cd, they provoke a noisy reaction in an audience already wound up to a high degree of tension by the overwhelming scale and relentless pressure of the preceding music. In the premiere recording these moments of silence are gradually filled by audience sounds of disbelief, dismay, and ridicule. For listeners today, a generation later, the musical effect of a door sliding open into another dimension and plane of existence is powerful, undeniably poetic, and certainly in keeping with the composer's intention to evoke an experience of connection across space and time.

Cage acknowledges a visit in 1951 to the anechoic chamber at Harvard University, in which he discovered that even a totally soundproofed environment is not a place of total silence. An anechoic chamber is a laboratory lined with foam rubber wedges that absorb rather than reflect ambient sound. Musicians dislike performing in an anechoic or highly sound-absorbent chamber because the lack of reflection or reverberation is acoustically and psychologically stifling. Cage went into the chamber expecting an epiphany of pure silence, but was disappointed to hear two sounds, a hiss subsequently identified as random activity of his own auditory nerves, and a low-frequency pulsation that turned out to be the sound of his circulatory system. He went on to declare in print that absolute silence does not exist. On its own terms that is merely a truism, even though it may provide an excuse for coming up with the idea of an anechoic composition in which all that can be heard is the sound of an audience listening. The same message of a contemplative silence in which only the human presence of a listener is audible, is delivered in slightly different terms in the resonant breathing of the astronaut that forms the coda of Stockhausen's tape composition *Hymnen* Region IV (1967), and in the final scene of Stanley Kubrick's movie *2001: A Space Odyssey* (1968).

Unexpectedly, the notion that absolute silence is invariably contaminated by the presence of an observer listening, or the apparatus of listening, can also be read as a statement either of the anthropic principle (that the universe we know is a mirror-image of our capacity to know it), or even the uncertainty principle (that the act of observation interferes with the behavior observed). Cage's exercise in spontaneously animated silence may even echo Casimir and Polder's 1948 theory of empty space as a quantum vacuum in which virtual particles spontaneously pop in and out of existence —making *4' 33"* the musical equivalent, so to speak, of creation itself, or at least of thermal radiation around a black hole.

Not forgetting Harry Truman's defeat of Dewey in the 1948 presidential election, when the new science of opinion polling had predicted otherwise. This is relevant because an opinion poll is silent speech, and furthermore it is about defining leadership issues by consulting the views of the *silent majority* rather than the will of a leader or interpreter. A powerful image to be drawing on, at a time when composers were seeking alternatives to the prevailing paradigm of music as an instrument of leadership in industry and war, and medium of war propaganda and nationalist sentiment. As early as 1937 the utopian Cage had written (incorrectly, as it happens) of Schoenberg's method of composing with twelve tones related only one to another as "analogous to modern society, in which the emphasis is on the group and the integration of the individual within the group." Writing in 1952, the same year as *4' 33"*, Boulez's polemic "Schoenberg is dead" takes a similarly uncompromising stand against neo-classicism, even in twelve-tone music, as an aesthetic of tyranny. This may not have been wholly coincidental, since the two composers were in close contact at the time.

The seemingly impossible task of extracting music from a normally silent majority to create a new aesthetic of "music by consent" (of which the "happenings" of the 1960s appear to be the logical outcome) suggests a long-term goal for Cage's exercise in constructive meditation of arriving at an environment in which any unintentional sound is perceived as beautiful in itself and part of a greater totality of sounds in accidental harmony. On the surface that seems ineffably pious, were it not for the fact that the same goal could be said to underlie the reverberant acoustic of a gothic cathedral, softening and harmonizing the respectively deliberate and random acoustic behaviors of celebrants and congregations, muting the more chaotic and enhancing the more musical sounds among them. An analogous intention to harmonize the sounds of everyday activity through acoustic design can be observed in the domestic architecture of Palladio, where rooms are proportioned to harmonious musical intervals, in order for random actions, speech, and musical performances to resonate in harmony. It makes sense to imagine a performance of Cage's *4' 33"* taking place in a cathedral rather than a concert hall or anechoic chamber. Furthermore, it gives the experience another layer of meaning.

In the west we pursue the fantasy that knowledge is about having an answer for everything, and that winning a quiz show is the same as being knowledgable. Other ages and cultures did not share the eighteenth-century European fantasy that literacy confers wisdom, or that being able to read a how-to book makes a reader instantly an expert. In addition to being a fundamentally troubling principle of artificial intelligence, a belief in correct answers as demonstrating knowledge, as well as manifesting an ability to deliver appropriate responses, attributes the power of prediction to the person answering, since the posing of a question evokes a situation in which no-one else has the answer, and where progress is impossible until an answer is delivered. Quiz games and karaoke are role-playing exercises in simulated leadership. A quiz however maintains the simultaneous fiction of a world in which crises that arise can be resolved by a combination of guesswork and intuition, and a world in which no crisis arises for which the appropriate answer is not already known. In order to claim the reward of survival a successful candidate of a quiz game *progresses* through a series of questions that mimic a world of personal aspiration in which a knowledge of facts is the key to wealth and status. Paradoxically, to put oneself forward as a candidate is also perceived as an act of defiance expressing a view of the world as capable of being changed, a perception philosophically at a tangent to the television audience for whom the world never changes, a simulacrum of a society of couch potatoes existing in a timeless limbo from which there is no prospect of escape.

THE WISDOM OF SILENCE

Of course I was wrong all along. The wise man is silent because he already knows the answer. Knowing that doesn't alter the point that the student has no way of knowing that the wise man is silent for a reason, or even if he is wise at all. But the solution introduces a typically central European twist to the story, by making the wisdom of the wise man's position (or even his wisdom in saying nothing, like the silence of the Tar Baby in the children's story of Brer Rabbit) dependent on the actions arising from the frustration of those around him who want to know. What the twist implies is (a) that the answer is to be found in contemplation rather than talk, and (b) when the answer is found in the future, it will still have been true from the moment of silence in the present. It also signifies that the answer to a question is inseparable from the formulation of the question itself, so that when we ask a question, we are simultaneously answering it, if we only knew.

Notes

1. Robin Maconie, *The Way of Music: Aural Training for the Internet Generation.* Lanham MD, Toronto, Plymouth UK: The Scarecrow Press, 2007.
2. *Apocrypha*, Sirach 20 v. 7: "A wise man will be silent until it is time for him to speak."
3. H. Marshall McLuhan, *The Gutenberg Galaxy: The Making of Typographic Man.* London: Routledge and Kegan Paul, 1967, 11–18. (Citing Shakespeare, *King Lear*, I. 1, lines 85–90.)
4. Leonid Sabaneev, *Music for the Films: A Handbook for Composers and Conductors* tr. S. W. Pring. London: Pitman, 1935, 29.

ONE

THE AHA! THEORY OF CREATION

Is the big bang an act of creation, or the consequence of an act of creation? If the act is creative, then it is coterminous with the thought, but if the consequence, then it implies an antecedent impulse. One is then faced with the question, to what extent is the big bang (or any creative act) the intended consequence of an original impulse? The *authority* (authorship in action) of a painting by Jackson Pollock, or a signature, or perhaps a jazz improvisation, may not have to rely on conscious intention at all, and yet convey an identity sufficient to satisfy an art or jazz connoisseur, or the bank. Art is described as "creative" to distinguish it from the routine activity of everyday life. The term is of interest for a number of reasons. Art not only documents the world, but the way we (through the artist) think about the world. Artists (Leonardo da Vinci, J. M. Turner, John Constable, Picasso) are trained in human physiology, optics, and the biological sciences as well as skilled in expressing themselves in pigment on canvas. And yet the view persists among the non-artistic community that artistic creativity is different from knowledge based on observation or experience, or that it is not knowledge at all. Why is this? Perhaps because art, and abstract art in particular, challenges conventional ways of understanding the world by creating images that are unrecognizable or inexplicable in ordinary terms.

In a number of ways, art is closer to myth than science. Among scientists art tends to be regarded as descriptive rather than innovatory or philosophical, and knowledge about art as expertise specific to the craft, not universal in implication, but limited to technical knowledge about the process. The interpretation of art imagery may occasionally be referenced as factual knowledge, for example the plant life shown in detail on the lawn in the foreground of Sandro Botticelli's *Primavera*, or to be read into the textures and freshness of a Dutch still life of flowers or vegetables. Art can also be discussed as evidence of the human condition, not only in the subject depicted, in varying degrees of emotional and physical health, and even in death, but in the manner in which the subject is visualized, as El Greco's elongation of the human body is interpreted by some as evidence of the artist's alleged astigmatism, or Picasso's *netsuke*-like contortions of the female form as studies in four dimensions rather than the two or three of classical art. That some visual artists were accurate observers of the real world, and depicted optical effects with great fidelity, often with mechanical aids, is perfectly true: indeed, it was an important part of their role. Among scientists after 1950, however—perhaps in reaction to the rise of photography and surrealism, the imaging of the unconscious —art is most often employed as a means of visually reinforcing a particular message, whether or not the image makes sense in real-world terms. Among science writers, optical illusion and visual paradox are accepted as legitimate visualizations of difficult concepts. Underlying the message of Douglas Hofstadter's *Gödel–Escher–Bach* is the proposition that mathematics, art, and classical music are equivalent means of representing aspects of the world that hover on the edge of unknowability. That the teasing visual games of Maurits Escher appeal more readily to science writers Roger Penrose and Stephen Hawking than the artworks of Leonardo, Rembrandt, or Vermeer, tells us something of how philosophers of science regard art, and also their readership.

The customary term for embedded cultural knowledge is myth. Among oral cultures, myth is the storage of useful information in condensed form. It survives, in "urban myth," as spontaneous cultural invention. The messages of myths such as flying saucers are less about real events than about attitudes and beliefs, and they often play on the difference between the imaginative life and the perception of a life of thought control associated with industrial society (government, the intelligence services, etc.). Industry and administrative bureaucracies are not particularly hospitable to creativity among the workforce, since new ideas and innovation have the potential to disturb the smooth running of normal operations.

Under such regimes creativity and personal initiative are often reduced to survival anxieties affecting the private morale of corporate individuals. Karaoke, alcohol, substance addiction, staged paintball weekends, and charity marathon runs are currently available as identity therapies to compensate for the suppression of personal creativity in professional life. The anxieties of a routine existence may be summed up in two questions, "How can I be certain about anything?" and "How can I possibly understand what anybody else is talking about?" The cultivation of art and music in industrialized communities offers, if not a solution, at least a remedy. If people are unable to agree on a practical, moral, or philosophical issue, they may nevertheless be reconciled to the possibility of agreeing about a work of art they know nothing about, while at the same time envying the freedom of art to speak its mind.

Creativity is a loaded word. As Stravinsky remarked, "Only God can create." To speak of art as a metaphor of creation imputes a spark of divine intelligence to the activity of making art. Use of the term in this sense is instructive in its own way. In a musical context, creativity is a term of praise invariably applied to virtuoso performers, hardly ever to composers. It reflects a perception of the *act* of performance, in the presence of witnesses, as the essentially creative gesture, rather than the imaginative act of composition, or the labor of writing a musical score. Rather than dismissing such a perception as ignorant, we need to understand it, in western culture at least, as the lingering residue of an eighteenth-century middle-class opposition to the music of an oppressive aristocracy, along with a romantic perception of the performing artist as the heroic personification of freedom, a people's leader and inspired genius with the power to redefine the world. Attributing divine authority to virtuoso performers and conductors says something about how ordinary people perceive music as a rhetorical art, just as popular reverence toward live performance as a rite of creation, is revealing of culturally embedded attitudes to creation itself.

Creation is the act, creativity the impulse. Creation is the ultimate act. It signifies superior existence, intelligence, motivation, and power—qualities withheld or suppressed in routine corporate life. For a musical performance to be creative entails a perception of the composition as a statement of the creative process.

Because sound emerges from silence and disappears back into silence, speech and music acts are especially potent metaphors of creation. The act of creation in Genesis is a speech act, not the wave of a magic wand. For visual thinkers creation is not the same. Visualists assume a steady-state universe that has always existed. To them, the act of creation is like opening a book, or switching on the radio, or accessing information on the web, or being born, or simply waking up. All of these are individual acts of emergence into consciousness of a reality that is already there and will continue to exist after the individual has forgotten about it or is no longer here to imagine it. That is the visual way. John Cage liked to cite the Chinese sage Chuang Chou saying he dreamed he was a butterfly and, waking up, wondering if he were a butterfly dreaming he were a man. Since Chou presumably could not imagine, or is otherwise unconcerned with what it would be like, either to see the world as a butterfly, or explain the world in terms of a butterfly's consciousness to a human audience, the moral of his story is bound in with a cultural convention that to speak of "being" is the same for a man as for a butterfly, hence that a person's identity as a living being remains the same whether it is assigned to a human or butterfly body container (a view more or less consistent with Buddhist beliefs). The other point of the story (whether Cage grasped it or not is uncertain, but he must have had a reason for being drawn to it in the first place) is the frankly exquisite (i.e., kitsch) but unreal conceit that dreaming is as real a state of being as wakefulness. Romantically, it implies that a butterfly might like to dream of being a human being because a human life is more interesting, or fulfilled, or lasts longer than the lifespan of a butterfly. One senses in any case that part of the sage's point is that the dream state is a form of parallel existence with the physical life admitted by sleep, and not a distortion of reality experienced in sickness, or as a consequence of imbibing too much rice wine.

In practice, the visual world is perceived as a continuum within which elements are persistently in motion. Shadowy objects are sensed moving in the visual field, and since our eyes also move and change focus in order to explore the latter and reveal the former, the visual field is constantly changing in orientation as well, though human processes of seeing are adapted to filter out any distortions related to personal eye or head movements and for that reason we do not notice them. We blink and turn our heads, unaware of any break or smear of visual continuity. The visual memory even of a sophisticated and trained observer (as distinct from the imagery recorded by a handheld movie camera, for example) offers no procedural basis for conceptualizing creation, other than as a sudden appearance of light in darkness, or indeed as a butterfly, a beautiful spirit of the air, waking up as a human being, a creature of the earth given to self-reflection.

The routine task of visual discrimination for an observer in motion consists in registering essential distinctions between global movements of the visual field (produced in consequence of the self as an observer in motion) and isolated movements within the visual field (moving objects against the backdrop of the visible world of experience). Indeed, many stories of creation have to do with discriminating self-identity from sense impressions of a more or less coherent external reality: silence and sound, air and water, darkness and light, etc. The same fundamental impulse (no pun intended) to distance oneself from possibly unwelcome environmental affects as dazzling lights and ear-splitting noises lingers on in the behaviors associated with the taboos of breaking wind or swearing in close society. Visual accounts of creation are invincibly introspective, since (as provided in Descartes's dictum that thinking precedes being) they arise and are construed *within consciousness*, and for that reason imply conscious awareness of an external reality as a precondition of awareness of selfhood, which all the same is not entirely logical. To observe a transition from chaos to form requires a prior awareness of chaos, and of the emergence of a world of forms as an external process refracted and resolved in the mind of an observer, who at the same time is embedded in the same world of forms. That awareness of forms as arising from an original chaos makes sense for the reason that chaos describes the original sense impressions as much as it does the world that gives rise to them. An *Aha!* theory of creation also implies that such accounts are necessarily retrospective, since chaos or darkness cannot realistically be differentiated from light until light has actually dawned.

The musical analogy works differently, since every new note of music implies a new event and thus a new moment of creation. As

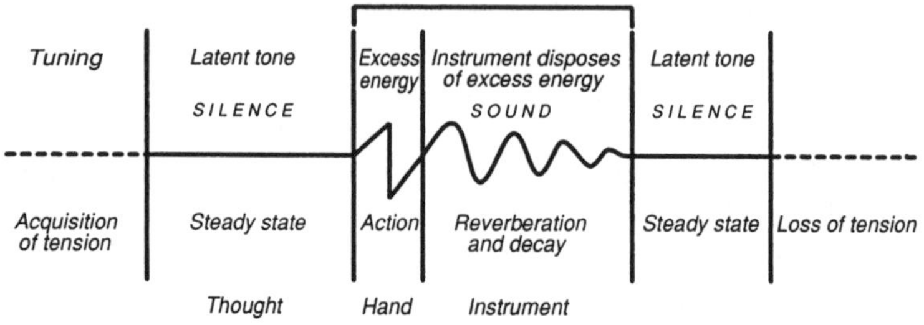

The history of a single note

the figure shows, every note in creation is preceded by a structure (the instrument), an intention, and an action of which the acoustic event is the outcome. The energy released in a momentary act of creation is followed by a period of expansion and reverberation, during which it is stored and radiated from the vibrating element into the surrounding atmosphere. Afterward the instrument reverts to silence, but remains for an indefinite period in a state of readiness to produce the same sound again, or a different sound. In the long run, the string loses its tension and eventually the instrument itself decays, along with the last human being. Any moment of creation articulated in musical terms implies a lengthy prehistory of instrument manufacture, performer preparation, and compositional intention, as well as an indefinite aftermath, all of it implied by every single note.

Modern cosmology tends to favor the idea of creation of the universe as a spontaneous event from a singularity. Such a belief was not always in fashion. An alternative view is of an oscillating universe in a perpetual cycle of expansion and contraction. In the first case, the "big bang" conjures up an image of creation as a stroke on an immense tam-tam, a burst of energy applied to the centre of a vibrating body, radiating out to the edges, and resolving into a more or less coherent tone complex as the energy is radiated or dissipated internally. An oscillating creation, on the other hand, resembles a pendulum whose motion appears intermittent rather than continuous, swinging first to the left, then to the right, separated by periods of apparent motionlessness. Significantly, in this alternative version of events, the energy driving the oscillation is necessarily greater than the energy expended in any one cycle of motion back and forth.

The creation myth as an ordered world arising out of an initial chaos is also true of music in the obvious sense that music is designed to impose order on the chaos of a noisy environment, whether a cathedral, a concert-hall, or a market square. And we are speaking of imposing order on chaos not only in the acoustic sense of controlling crowd murmur, but also in the ability of music to coordinate the actions of a group, and even their thoughts as well, since the response to music can be emotional as well as physical. The moment of anticipation when the conductor's baton is raised, when the house lights are lowered, when the audience murmur suddenly quietens to a hush immediately prior to the first notes being heard, is as good an image of the moment of creation as we are likely to find, one that provides a basis for understanding the creation myth, and music as an image of creation, as the triumph over chaos of order and organization, expressed acoustically in the superior audibility of musical signals over random noise, and gesturally in the structured organization of human activity. Famous musical images of creation include the majestic "Deus in adjutorium" of Monteverdi's *Vespers*, a huge noise of life and activity marching to a renaissance beat, triggered by divine incantation; or the hammering alarm motif of Beethoven's Fifth Symphony, breaking the silence to beat the world into action; or the Introduction to *Also sprach Zarathustra* by Richard Strauss, a classic image of bursting sunrise. Corresponding images of chaos are found in Ligeti's seething *Atmosphères*, the primal scream of the opening to Prokofiev's second *Romeo and Juliet* Suite Op. 64, and the third movement of Berio's *Sinfonie*.

THE LOGIC OF CREATION

A visual culture is naturally linear, or goal-directed. We look ahead in order to see where we are going. An oral or listening culture by contrast is self-centered and omnidirectional in attentiveness. Aural awareness is instantaneous, whereas visual awareness implies motion, thus direction in time. To imagine a creation outside of consciousness, but subject to alteration all the same (and in that sense, having a life), hearing is a more appropriate sense analogy than vision. The sound a person makes, like the sound a person hears, is an instant of creation, calling (recalling) into being something that was not there before, or had momentarily ceased to exist. The sounds of music and speech are capable of influencing the environment at a distance, and are directly identifiable with objects or actions. Every other sound is a byproduct. Sounds are invisible. They arise, in the main, from sources that are out of sight, are first located in a personal memory of sounds, in the imagination, and thereafter in an external reality that, in the scheme of things, is a world in constant renewal. The visual field available to a person at any one time is only a small segment of the world contained in the sphere of hearing. The world of vision is continuously available and what is seen is subject to personal choice. We decide when to open our eyes and what to look at. With certain exceptions, such as exposure to continuous music at dangerous saturation levels at a rave party enhanced by party drugs, the world of sound, by comparison, is normally only intermittently available to hearing. By and large we have no choice in what we hear, since we cannot "close our ears" as we can our eyes (so in response to sensory overload we shake our heads, cover our ears, and run away). Because sounds by and large are stimuli of limited duration from which recovery is rapid, human hearing is adapted to remain continuously alert, even while the listener is asleep. The mental task of hearing is of recognizing recurrence: making connections between past and present events—that is, between events imprinted in memory and those happening in the present moment. It therefore follows that whereas the visible world exists in a continuous present, the intermittent world of hearing exists in the intervals that connect a sense of before and after, construed in the detection of spontaneous change.

In the music of most cultures, leading instruments are designated—for example the voice, the flute, or the violin—that embody continuous processes, while others, for example bells, plucked strings, and percussion, express random or discontinuous events in nature. In speech itself, vowels are continuous, can be drawn out indefinitely, and are therefore capable of expressing change, whereas consonants tend to be short, sharp, and percussive, suitable only for accentuation and segmentation. A perception of continuity in speech and music relies on consistencies of tone and emotion to convey integrity and logical connection; in practice however the communication of meaning in the terms of a precise text requires an attention to distinctions and segmentations, largely articulated by consonants, which break up the continuous flow of vocal tone into a succession of discrete phonemic units and pitches. In Japanese traditional music, for example, the role of maintaining continuity of meaning is assigned to the flute, and punctuation to percussion and sharply plucked strings. Western music in general tends to emphasize continuity of experience, though exceptions arise: for example, the echo effects of renaissance polyphony, which tend away from order toward the dangerously chaotic.

Whereas the *Aha!* theory of creation is reactive (Yes!) or retroactive (Did you see that?), the alternative *Let be!* theory (as in "Let there be light!") can be read as proactive, the idea preceding the act. Musical creativity can be understood either way, whether one is involved as performer or listener. The name assigned to a piece of music gives a name, perhaps a description, and maybe even a location to the act of performance. *Let be!* precedes or coincides with the creative act, making the performer a virtual creator, whereas the *Aha!* gesture is implicitly after the event, as it would occur to an audience member who had no idea what was happening or for what reason (or indeed, to Descartes, to whom the conclusion "therefore I am" can be rationalized as an *Aha!* reaction to a spontaneous epiphany of the act of thinking).

Any account of an act of creation is bound to take into consideration prior conditions of which the creation is the outcome. For that reason, a spoken word is not only meaningful in itself, but also as a declaration of the prior possibilities of speech (as a localized act), of language itself (as a system preexisting the speech act and assigning meaning to it), of the existence of an atmosphere, of an intention to speak, and of the presence of a listener—the anthropic principle. How did Chuang Chou *know* he was a butterfly in his dream? Or was he simply aware of himself flying? If he had the mind of a butterfly, how would he have dreamed he was a man? The story entails a belief that one can *know* who one is without necessarily *being* who one is, a level of moral detachment not available to most people, except perhaps the injured and the guilty.

The *Aha!* response speaks of two things: (a) self-awareness (or disengagement from the experience); and (b) awareness of the possibility of a different outcome (relief at judging that the creation is good). Note that in the old testament account, creation is a *Let be!* acoustic act of *speech* but the goodness of creation is a *visual* judgment ("He saw that it was good"). If expressing satisfaction at the goodness of creation is a coded way of saying that the outcome is precisely what was intended, then the threatened fall of mankind can be read as another way of saying not only that people do not always behave as originally intended, but that you are only as good as what you know, and that a good outcome is not invariably guaranteed, even for a supreme divinity.

Aha! articulates a disconnection, a distinction between having the idea of something, and awareness of its existence as a thing apart. The word itself is a gesture of separation. The act of creation is completed by the thing created assuming a material existence independent of the imagination of the creator (though it remains a creation in the image (*sic*) of an original idea, person, or plan). The creative or musical outcome is entailed by the gesture, and confirms or modifies the performer's expectation at the moment of making the gesture. The timing and quality of execution of a creative gesture are therefore crucial if the result is to accord with the creative intention. (The paradox of a performer in control of a reproducing piano is another matter, since creativity in this special case resides not in depressing the keys, which is effected by a machine programmed by perforated tape, but in modulating the pace and dynamics of the reading process, like a television studio technician in charge of an announcer's autocue.)

Cage's prepared piano interferes with the consistent timbre and pitch sequence of a normal instrument in order to confound the expectations of both player and listener alike. At the same time, the composer's instructions (in the musical score) remain completely intelligible and easy to execute. The dissociative impact of preparing a prepared piano is therefore aural rather than visual. To all intents and purposes, a prepared piano performance is a regular musical process. In his chance music for unprepared piano, Cage retains some features of a regular music score (ink, paper, time and space coordinates), while removing or diminishing others (rhythm, tempo, tonality, stems, barlines). Nevertheless the performer has still to rehearse the score, and form an intention to be realized in performance, so a result that may appear totally spontaneous to the listener will still be consciously imagined and deliberately executed by the performing artist.

Anybody learning to play the flute or violin has to make an initial transition from making uncontrolled or unpleasant sounds (or no sound at all) to producing a steady and controllable musical tone. That transitional moment of creation represents the attainment of positive feedback, a harmonization of action and reaction, player and instrument. Only after that harmonization is achieved can the player go on to create or reproduce music. A musical tone emitted in response to continuous action, breath or bow, invariably relies on positive feedback, a dynamic coupling of player and instrument in which the energy process feeding into the system is matched by the energy radiating out of the system as musical sound.

The musical outcome may or may not *conform* to, or *justify* the act or intention of a performer, raising the interesting moral question whether the intention of creation is decided by the act, or if the act is justified by the intention. Western classical music is predicated all the same on the idea of a harmony of continuous execution, from intention to gesture to sound, to give the appearance of a seamless act of continuous creation. This implies that the act of making music (a) is necessarily a statement of the inevitable, or (b) is necessarily open to diversion or error, including accident, random choice, or delegation of control to the performer (as in a cadenza), or to a mechanism such as a computer or tape (as in *Répons* by Boulez).

The *Let be!* theory of creation weights the balance in favor of prior intention, hence toward the meaning of calling something into being for the first time, but *by name* (so one already has the idea of it existing). Of course, that still leaves open the possibility of an *Aha!* reaction to the name (or prior conception), as one might say "so that is what you mean by an elephant?" in reaction to a child's drawing—leaving aside the possibility that the child has made the drawing *in order to discover* what an elephant looks like.

Naturally there is a difference between an act of creation understood as "bringing something or a living thought into being," and one of merely "generating a response in a reactive substance" in the sense of a stand-up comedian "playing an audience." Even a *Let be!*

creation is open to contain an element of surprise, of novelty. For a performer, the uncertainty—and thereby the element of creativity—resides in the gap between the notional ideal performance and the actual performance which is subject to factors any of which may arise on the night. This distinction comes into play in comparing a flawed live performance with a recording edited from multiple takes that though technically perfect is emotionally uninspired (and factually discontinuous). That the word "inspiration" alludes to the breath of life, is of interest given that the value assigned to an inspired performance attributes an appearance of independent life *and continuity* to the music itself, *as well as* crediting the effort with which the work has physically been brought to life as the action of a single inspiration. A conductor gestures a symphony into life even though the music is performed by others, and in a larger sense is already living.

The appearance of life in western music can vary from a perception of movement, as in a ballet where dancers translate music into actions that describe a story evolving in time, to an aria in opera, where the music and lyric take time out from a narrative to fix the impression of a moment in the audience's memory. In the instrumental field, a prelude or fantasy is a sort of improvisation that reveals itself in time without necessarily describing or imitating actions in time, but an event articulated as a stream of consciousness. A complicated canon or fugue, on the other hand, is an intellectual structure that, like a work of architecture, exists outside time but is necessarily experienced as a temporal process. For many listeners, the various time processes implicit in a musical composition are of less immediate concern than the act of performance itself, which occurring in real time is therefore easier to digest than the temporal complexities articulated in the music itself. There are exceptions, such as the Pachelbel canon, or certain works by Arvo Pärt, in which a descending bassline circulates indefinitely at its own pace with the benign imperturbability of a shopping mall escalator, carrying the performer and listener along.

TWO

SNAKE IN A TREE

As a musician I am attracted to the idea that music is a meaningful activity. Most people, I think, enjoy working out riddles, puzzles, and hidden messages. A majority adhere to religion or are at least familiar with religious precepts, which are coded infomation about how to live. Everyone who logs onto the internet is aware of the danger of viruses whether or not they know how they work or what to do about them, and everyone who uses a computer understands the significance of machine code whether or not they know how to read or write an operating system. For most people, coping with reality and getting on with life are somehow separate from morality, belief systems, relativity, and other abstract principles. And for most people music is just another mystery to be packaged as entertainment along with the movies, crossword puzzles, and science fiction.

Personally I find the idea that music is no more than entertainment to be picked up and discarded rather difficult to accept. Since a great many professional musicians of my acquaintance feel the same way about music, I am not so much offended as perplexed and intrigued. It just beggars belief that an art as old as religion, as involved in the philosophies of ancient Egypt, Greece, and Rome, as fundamental to the development of astronomy and mechanics, as influential on the classic architecture of Vitruvius, the Gothic cathedral builders, and Palladio, as crucial to the evolution of industrial Europe, as necessary for the development of modern data processing, and as rich in implication for present-day cosmology, can be seriously believed to have no significance or meaning other than as public entertainment.

The story of original sin is a version of the story about snakes and ladders. In other words, a story about the possibility of meaning that lies in myth, legend, philosophy, nursery rhymes, indeed all counterintuitive narratives that for all their apparent lack of sense have persisted in cultural memory to the present day. The longevity of statements that have no meaning is a paradox in itself. Paradox cannot be explained away by simply drawing a line between fact and fantasy, separating the bits that are easy to believe from the bits that are difficult or impossible to believe, for example the claim that Newton was a genius but also crazy because he took alchemy seriously, or that the school of Pythagoras was responsible for stunning and fundamental insights but in other respects was just a vegetarian religious cult. Somewhere there is a real meaning in every counterintuitive statement made by a serious thinker. Finding that meaning is the challenge. For a musician it is a particularly interesting pursuit, since so much that is paradoxical in human and cultural belief either originates with or is echoed in music and acoustics. And since music is a human activity connecting all times and cultures, to begin to understand the paradoxes that underpin musical activity, is to begin to appreciate the common origins and connections embodied in human myth and legend.

Snake related mysteries are a frequent occurrence. One tradition that comes to mind is the snake charmer, enticing a cobra by the sinuous music of the oboe, to rise vertically from a basket and sway hypnotically before a watching crowd. A variant of the same formula persists in belly dance, which interestingly enough in recent years has acquired renewed popularity among modern women in the west as an assertion of feminine consciousness: music = sinuous movement = beauty = enchantment = temptation = danger (and so on). Note that in belly dance the same qualities of sinuous vitality and allure associated with the serpent are referred to the female dancer, thus to the female of the species. We will come back to that.

These mysteries all have elements in common. First, a wavy line or undulating structure; second, a tree or high place from which the undulation descends to earth; third, a degree of temptation associated with desirable beauty, influence, or high value; and four, the idea of traveling up the wavy line element into a realm

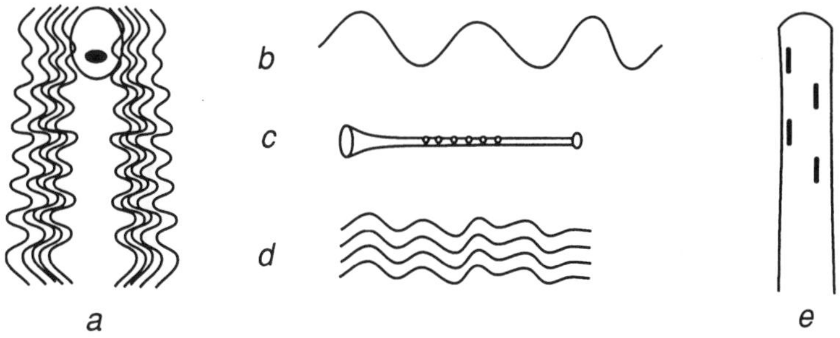

The elements of snake related myth: (a) desirable beauty; (b) a wavy line; (c) a musical instrument; (d) the sound of music; (e) a structure reaching up to the heavens

above ground where the beauty or value resides, in order to capture the beautiful or valuable item and bring it back down to earth. There is danger involved. The desirable item is forbidden to leave its airy abode, so stealing it is a dangerous undertaking.

These stories involve an adventure taking the (usually masculine) hero from solid ground, which is the realm of tangible reality, into the heavens, the world and medium of sound and music. In some mythologies the creation of the world tells of an initial separation of earth and sky, dividing the world of people and solid objects from the airy world of the gods. It provides a setting for numerous myths and legends, among them the flying dragon of oriental legend, and the story of Icarus, an inventive human being and his doomed attempts to rise above ground and conquer the air on artificial wings, and not forgetting the biblical legend of Jacob's ladder, a vision of a staircase linking earth and heaven up and down which singing angels are seen moving, like the fingers of a player up and down the fingerboard of a guitar or violin. In the present case, however, the link connecting earth and sky is a wavy line up which the hero climbs, or by which access to forbidden power is attained.

Still another version of the snake in the tree formula is the Indian rope trick, whereby on command a rope coiled on the stage rises up like a cobra and disappears "into the clouds" and out of view. The magician climbs the rope and also vanishes; after a pause, an assistant armed with a knife follows him up the rope and he too disappears. Screams are heard. Drops of blood fall to the

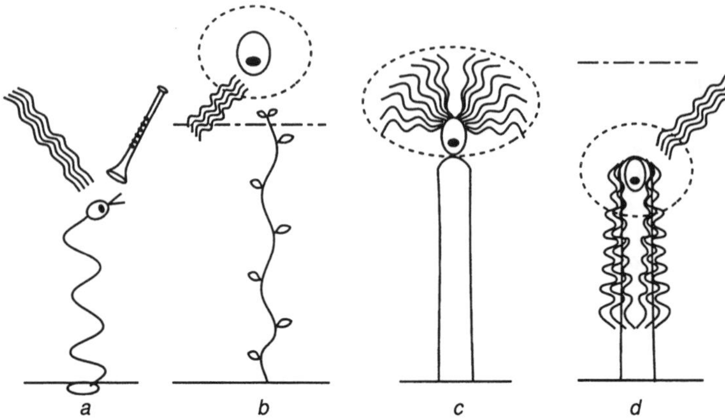

(a) Snake charmer; (b) Jack and the beanstalk; (c) Medusa; (d) Rapunzel

stage, the rope falls, and the magician and his assistant reappear onstage to take the applause. This is a message in which the virtual snake, a cord endowed with magical properties as a consequence of being stretched vertically to connect the real world on solid ground with the heaven of clouds above (the world of sound, or vibrating air), is cut in two by the magician's knife, and revealed as a harmless length of rope. The master demonstrates his power over the rope (or stretched string, that is, the monochord—of which more later) as a means of inquiry into the connection between the earth of imperfect material objects and the Platonic heaven of ideal types. He makes his way up the rope and disappears from view, and is only brought down to earth by actions involving severing the cord, which has its own symbolism.

The same illusion persists in the folk tale of Jack and the Beanstalk, in which the rope has turned into a sinuous vine reaching into the world of the clouds, the abode of a jealous ogre and also the world of musical sound, as we learn since Jack on this occasion succeeds in confronting the danger and stealing the source of the ogre's riches, a golden singing harp. Once again, the story ends with the vine or stringlike connection linking earth and sky being ritually severed. The fairy tale of Rapunzel is yet another variation: this time a story of beauty in the form of a beautiful woman trapped in a high tower and pleading for release. Her melancholy song attracts a young knight; he offers to assist, she lets down her long wavy golden hair, and he climbs up.[1]

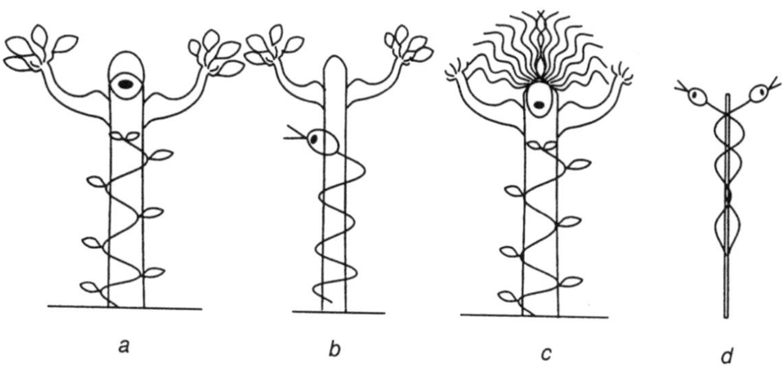

(a) Adam and Eve; (b) the Serpent in the Tree; (c) Samson; (d) Caduceus

The fatal attraction of Medusa's hair neatly conflates a fear of snakes and fascination with tumbling locks, both of which are symbols of the insoluble problem of accounting for fluid undulating motion in a world of steady-state facts and data points.

Yet another variation survives in the biblical story of Samson, whose influence (power, strength) resides in his long wavy hair, a metaphor for the strings of a harp and the power of music (also encountered elsewhere in the legend of King David and his harp). Samson's wife, the beautiful Delilah, is jealous and conspires to have his hair cut off. When Samson's hair is cut, like the strings of a musical instrument, all that is left is an empty frame. That Samson is blinded is a double symbolism, signifying loss of power, but also emphasizing that this is a story about the power of sound and hearing. That his hair grows back, so that he regains his strength, is a way of saying that the power and influence of a musical instrument also return when the strings are replaced. (Samson does not regain his sight, however.)

The snake in a tree, to return to our first story, is about Adam and Eve and what happened in the Garden of Eden. We know the story. At least, we think we know. It is a story about loss of innocence. The happy couple have been warned against "eating the fruit of the tree of knowledge." The serpent, a talking serpent, in wheedling tones persuades the woman to disobey. She eats the fruit and persuades Adam to eat. They are found out, confess, and are banished, the woman condemned "to bear children in pain," while the serpent is doomed, despised, to crawl on its belly for ever (that is, to be confined writhing to the ground, forbidden to connect with the heavens).

Like many people I have issues with this story. It seems unfair. Why should Adam and Eve be banished? Where is the sin in aspiring to knowledge? Surely human beings were created to be curious?—while in the meantime closet Freudians shake their heads and say, oy vay, it's all about sex. Well, perhaps it is, up to a point, since childbirth and teenagers are among the consequences of original sin. But surely the ancients must have realized that sex is as natural and pleasurable a part of life as eating, and also good for you, in its own way? What sort of moral message is being handed down here? Perhaps the underlying issue is not so much crime and punishment, the relative triviality of female willfulness leading to anger and retribution, as much as a statement of higher ultimate purpose over and above the point that self-gratification is not the best excuse for making a decision, or can lead to misunderstanding. There are intimations here of Plato's strictures on music. Original sin is surely not that simple.

In an earlier chapter of the Garden of Eden myth Eve is cloned out of Adam's rib while he is asleep. This is a charming botanical metaphor. It has something to do with the location of the ribcage protecting and embracing the heart and lungs like the branches of a tree, is perhaps related to the fact that rib cartilage is regenerating, and almost certainly to the fact that the ribs are a flexible part of the body frame. The image that springs to mind of woman created out of a male rib is of the male body as the trunk of a tree, and the female as a vine girdled around it. The relationship is of a pliant and decorative acanthus or grapevine that is supported by a tree. Again, the feminine image is of a naturally curvaceous *line* that depends on (*de-pends*: i.e., hangs from) a sturdy frame, and the clinging nature associated with the female of the species.

Here is what I think. The Garden of Eden temptation is a story relating to scientific and musical knowledge, rather than simple disobedience or carnal knowledge. Its message is that there are some things in life the truth of which is not self-evident, for example, why the world was created, why we are here, what we are here to do, and within what limits. The story is set in a primeval eternity, or timeless present. The serpent in the tree is part snake, part pendulum, part musical instrument, like a one-stringed aeolian harp. The snake part is the string and the tree is the frame. The string is represented as a snake or serpent for a descriptive reason, because it *talks* (makes meaningful sounds), because it *moves of its own accord* (undulates), and finally because it enchants the victim by its undulatory powers (like a vibrating string, or the pendulum of a hypnotist). Ask a small child or a bushman to draw a snake in the sand and what will be drawn is a wavy line. That the snake is discovered lurking in a tree in the Garden of Eden is not impossible, but is significant. This is no ordinary snake. It does not threaten or bite. Instead, it makes beguiling conversation about the forbidden mystery of creation itself, which is exactly the power the sound of an acoustic guitar wields over an impressionable young male or female listener as it sings of the entrancing knowledge and power of love. And what exactly are the fruits of the tree? They are the sweet sounds of music that soothe the spirit, stir the appetite, and sway the emotions of the listener.

This is not a tale of the serpent acting on its own. It is the serpent in combination with the tree, and in relation to an earlier prohibition. Like a honey tree, the tree is a hollow resonator and the buzzing bees the strings. The frame of the musical instrument is a tree because it is made of *wood*, because it is *rigid* compared with the serpent (the string) and because it provides not only a firm structure to sing from, but also a hollow space in which to live, a resonator to make his voice and message sing more sweetly and persuasively to the listening ear.

Here now is the interesting bit. Think of a snake and you think of a snakebite. Snakes bite: that is the danger. But this serpent does not bite. Rather, it is the victims Adam and Eve who bite. They take the offer, eat the apple, and are found out, as a consequence of digesting or (as we say) *ruminating* over what they have eaten, and so they suffer the consequences: a stomach ache, flatulence. (If the apple signifies a green apricot, as it would have done to a reader in Elizabethan times, Eve's stomach ache can be construed as a first sign of morning sickness.) Where is the sin? Well, the couple disobeyed strict instructions. But that is surely not enough. Their sin, the story goes, is not just of eating an apple, but of consuming or taking in "the fruit of *the tree of knowledge*." The tree of knowledge also signifies a musical instrument such as a lyre or harp; the serpent its strings; the forbidden fruit the music sounded by playing on the strings. The moral here is reminiscent of Plato: that music played for pleasure and without understanding is a sin against the divine laws of ratio and proportion revealed in the modes of vibration of the strings themselves, a knowledge unfathomable to all but an intellectual elite who have presumably renounced the pleasures of the flesh. The apple itself does not have to be a real piece of fruit, nor is it poisoned, so therefore different in kind from the witch's apple in the story of Snow White. Adam and Eve's discomfort is spiritual rather than physical.

Here is how it works. Eating is taking in food. Taking in food is taking in physical nourishment. In olden times reading aloud and eating were considered equivalent behaviors, since both involve the mouth. Here the act of eating from the tree corresponds to reading the book of life and taking in knowledge. Knowledge that is taken in can also be given out, in the words we speak. Speech uses the same orifice as eating, but outwardly, for delivering spiritual or moral nourishment. The Garden of Eden is a microcosm divinely created of reason, *ratio*, or *logos*, "the word." Among oral cultures, the act of speech (speaking in *words* about *things* rather than crying, bleating, or grunting) is equivalent to an act of creation. The world has come into existence by word of mouth of the Almighty. You might say the myth continues even today. According to current thinking in cosmology, the story of creation is also enacted "by word of mouth," in this case a mouth transformed into a null-point of zero dimension and infinite power, radiating a stream of information out of which has condensed our universe in a four- or more-dimensional spacetime.

Myth deals in verbal pictograms. The most difficult concepts of modern cosmology are expressed in terms of a children's story. The story of The Fall of Man is one such story. It connects the traditions of ancient religion with the countercultures of ancient Greek science and contemporary physics. This is not a fairy tale for cultural tourists, and its moral has nothing to do with disobedience, and everything to do with disappointment. In the biblical story, the serpent corresponds to a self-propelled undulating body *without legs*: thus an expression of a natural but unquantifiable continuity

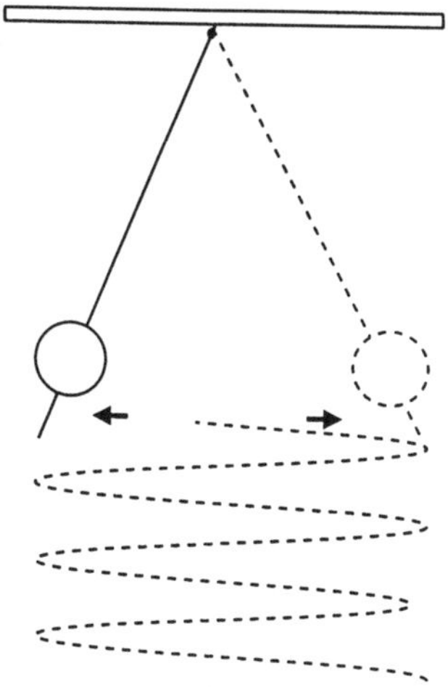

Pendulum motion as continuous over a moving surface

of motion in space and time. The story turns on an act of eating, which stands for knowledge of the real world by ingestion. Since our knowledge of the world consists in internalized sense impressions, we infer external reality on the basis of evidence we take in, whether by touch, smell, hearing, or sight, or all of these. So the meaning of *knowledge* in this context refers to a claim of dominion over, and certainty in the existence of, an external reality purely on the internalized evidence of our senses. This is no laughing matter. The serpent swinging from a branch with an apple in its mouth is also a pendulum, a object in motion that mysteriously keeps time even as its back-and-forth motion decreases. The serpent's words are an incitement to disobedience, well enough, but it is not only the content of the speech that leads the listener astray, but implicitly the power of speech to lead astray and influence the actions of others at a distance, these being mysterious attributes of sound and hearing in general.

It is always a mistake to assume that the target audience of myth is essentially naive or uninformed, or that because it is told in comic-book images, the terms of myth are necessarily imprecise. Among oral cultures—especially children—myth is a reliable way of presenting complex information in concentrated and memorable form. The child memorizes the story of Chicken Licken without fully understanding it, but is nevertheless able to return home from school and tell it to the parents, who then are in a position to confer with the child over what the story means. The role of myth is not to explain, but to package compressed information about essential relationships in unforgettable terms that stay in the mind.

The serpent is initially a pendulum, swinging with an apple in its mouth. A pendulum is a mystery because it moves back and forth, at an even pace, although it also stops moving as it changes direction. The issue is first, how does a pendulum continue to swing, when its movement stops at intervals (i.e., where does its momentum go?), and second, how does it happen that the rate of swing remains constant, even though the distance of swing diminishes as it loses momentum (why does it not slow down?). That is one temptation. It relates to geometry through the fact that a weighted cord is an instrument used in surveying, and to music, because the string of a musical instrument is also weighted (held in tension) and vibrates at a constant frequency even while losing momentum. A pendulum always points toward the earth and thus describes a straight (or vibrating) line the weighted end of which is always inclined toward the earth, and the other end always directed toward the heavens.

The ancients are likely to have discovered, from experimenting with slingshots and weighted fishing lines, that the back and forth motion of a pendulum is the same as a circular or orbital motion, but reduced to a single plane: thus what appears to be intermittent motion with periodic changes of direction, is in fact an expression of continuous motion in a circle, compressed to a vertical plane. This ties in with the mystery of snakelike motion across the surface of the ground, which is also a description of pendulum motion in relation to a moving surface. In music the same motion corresponds to the oscillation of a string after it has been plucked, or the stylus movement of a recording device.

But why the sinister construction? What is sinful about a vibrating string? I think the implication is moral in the Platonic sense, that to contemplate the nature of sinusoidal vibration is a challenge to anybody's intelligence. In its alternative guise as the monochord, the serpent in the tree is reconfigured as a musical instrument just as liable to sow confusion among the learned as

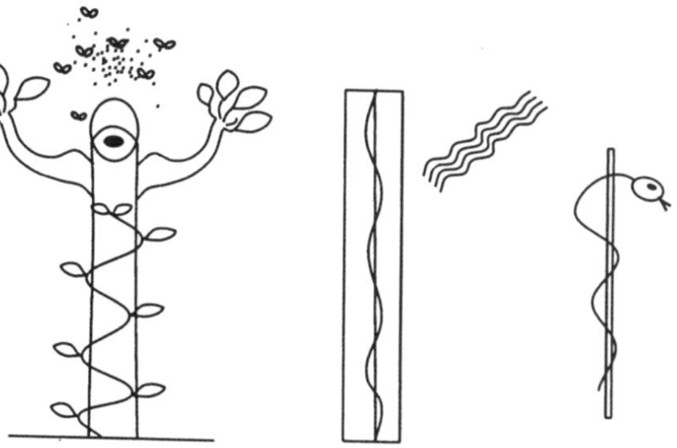

a b c

(a) the honey tree; (b) the monochord; (c) staff of Aesclepius

lure the impressionable young into abandoning decorum for song and dance. The message is thus not about error as avoidable sin, but of uncertainty as a necessary consequence of inquiry into the nature of time and motion. Such a reading of the Adam and Eve myth in my opinion makes better sense, is more morally defensible, and attributes greater intelligence to the reader than the more familiar view of it as a cautionary fairy tale or warning against the dire perils of merely being curious, disobedient, or trying to work things out for oneself. The tree, after all, is the tree of *knowledge*. The orthodox view, that knowledge is harmless as long as we stick to socially acceptable categories and don't go hunting for laws, is an all the more cynical interpretation that, in seeking to eliminate confusion and error, ends by delivering Socrates to death by hemlock, and Galileo to the terrors of the Inquisition. It means quite simply that confusion is bound to arise when we dare to observe and try to explain change and connection in merely human terms. The underlying message of loss of innocence is that to seek after knowledge carries the risk of courting the irrational, and suffering painful consequences.

What this account does not explain is the core of the story, which is to understand why knowledge has to involve temptation in the first place. Once again, the answer is musical as well as philosophical. It changes our definition of sin from simple wrongdoing and disobedience, to the realization that our own efforts to explain the world lead inevitably to an accommodation with the irrational and the uncertain. The message of sin is, that reason has its limits. Not what we should not, but what we ultimately cannot do, like work out the exact value of π, or the square root of 2.

You might wonder, if that is the case, why our mythical ancestors created in the divine image are set a test that is evidently designed to condemn them to an eternity of pain and suffering for having employed the same faculties of curiosity, observation, and analysis with which they were endowed. It doesn't seem right. We associate temptation with the serpent, but on reflection there are two temptations. The first temptation is being told not to eat of the fruit of the tree of knowledge. As a divine command, it is therefore morally good. But the command not to do something provokes tension and resistance in the victim, just like tension in the string of a musical instrument. It destroys forever an initial state of blissful ignorance by offering the victim a choice between not doing something that one is able to do, and being consumed by curiosity for the rest of one's life, or disobeying the command and risking the consequences.

So the first temptation is divinely inspired and consists in the realization that knowledge is possible. The complementary role taken by the serpent converts temptation from an intellectual possibility into physical action. The first creates tension, the second anchors it. The image is of a string drawn tight and anchored at both ends. Only when you allow yourself to be pulled in two directions do you begin to vibrate, test yourself, and become aware of your own mettle. It all makes perfect sense. When a person is stretched simultaneously in opposite directions, the tendency to pull away from sin and toward virtue is countered by an equal tendency to pull away from virtue and toward sin. Human nature, it says, is like that. We are all simply caught in the middle.

In the tale of St George and the Dragon, the dragon is winged. It is sinuous. It is stabbed through the mouth. All of which suggests the lure of a musical voice leading the young and innocent to their doom. Uccello's dragon is two-legged. The version of the story in which the dragon is stabbed through the throat, then led meekly by the belt of the young lady in question to the public square and then despatched by St George, is a none too complicated parable of the sound of music flying through the air, being grounded, and silenced by the lance of the saint, then humilated by being led by the girdle of the young lady, then being put out of its misery. It is a classic metaphor of an adolescent girl being lured out of her safety zone by the sinuous song of an unseen admirer wafting through the air; of her infatuation with the song and its maker, of the saint arriving in the nick of time to *kill the sound* and thus reveal the awful nature of the predatory beast, for the silent dragon to be revealed as easily tamed. The dragon's power is in the incendiary flames of sound emitted from his open mouth and throat. Once silenced, he is made helpless by the belt, presumably the one which protects the young lady's chastity, and led away to death. The image of the dragon is an outward visualization of the power of song. It is scaly (*sic*), undulating, and it flies through the air, but is also a substantial and overwhelming presence.

The forked tongue of the snake is associated with deceit. However even though forked it is still only one tongue. That the serpent cannot say two things at once, but says one thing that can be taken in two ways, is what it means. That the message can be taken in either of two ways is an issue for the sinner who is led astray by his (or her) preconception of what he (or she) *wants* to hear; that the possibility of a misleading interpretation is intended by the serpent in the first place, is the association of the double tongue, a natural attribute of the serpent. So the serpent is naturally guilty of speaking to young women in a way that is capable of misleading them, and the young women are culpable (in so far as a young woman in the medieval era can be held responsible for her actions) in yielding to the blandishments of the serpent.

There is little difference between the serpent, who is an animation of a vibrating string, hence of music, and the maze in which the Minotaur is trapped, which is a representation of the undulating motion of sound radiating in air. Both are images of a real but intangible and seductive force that cannot easily be pinned down, one that can turn submissive young women into volatile and dangerous Sirens or groupies, a distracting and potentially violent sisterhood addicted to music and sex.

The forked tongue does not signify disunity of speech, but rather ambiguity of intention that can be read into one speech. That ambiguity is symbolized in melodic uncertainty and sinuousness.

The temptation is dealt with by pinning it down to one place, action undertaken by a hero with a lance. The same anxieties and remedies are in place in computer games where contestants enjoy complete liberty to destroy anything that moves, since according to the mythology of such games, anything that moves is a potential threat, and the object of the game is to eliminate any potential threat.

A dragon's fiery breath is just another picturesque image of the potentially seductive and also destructive power of song or speech. It can raise the temperature, but also burn. And flames also flicker in the air, and their heat is sensed through the air. The twin snakes of medical symbolism likewise signify the power of life and death, even when administered for the best of motives.

Finally, the moral. (1) Don't trust the snake; (2) Don't trust your feminine side. You will only get into trouble.

Note

1. Examples of classical music based on imagery of magical ascent include the slow movement from the *Concerto in D major* for trumpet by Michael Haydn, and the first movement of the cello concerto in B flat by Boccherini arr. Grützmacher.

THREE

ERROR

> Scientific theories are not just the results of observation. They are, in the main, the products of myth-making and of tests.[1]
>
> KARL POPPER

This is a morality about snakes and ladders. Its meaning lies in the rules of the game: a ladder takes you up; a snake brings you down (for musicians, like the enharmonic minor scale, which goes up by one course of notes and returns by another route). The snake is the naturally undulating string that vibrates uncertainly, and in the game it signifies failure or loss. The ladder is the alternative reality, a humanly created step structure for articulating space that replaces the slippery and sinuous oscillations of a vibrating string with a system of countable and repeatable units. The ladder allows the novice to quantify and negotiate space in discrete steps, just as footsteps on the ground measure distance. Space and time (length and frequency) come together in the monochord, in which the undulations of a stretched string are put on the rack and their partial vibrations revealed as equal divisions of a fixed straight length.

The moral implications are interesting. Vibratory motion is a process of continuous change, and continuous change involves uncertainty. The philosopher Parmenides controversially claimed that time and motion do not exist, seeming to imply that the evidence of our senses is misleading, but perhaps intending that time and motion are *distortions* of reality introduced by external forces. Said Stravinsky, paraphrasing Augustine, "Things do not change. *We change*." Karl Popper interpreted the pre-Socratic challenge to explain change in the image of a green leaf turning brown, the problem being to reconcile a perception of the leaf changing color with the fact of it still being the same leaf. For all his musical training, Popper evinces no interest in the fact that, as a Pythagorean, Parmenides was also a musician, and that his claim may have been founded, among other things, on the impossibility of exactly determining the frequency of vibration of a note of a stringed instrument, perhaps on the basis that the act of plucking or bowing it stretches, and therefore distorts the string.

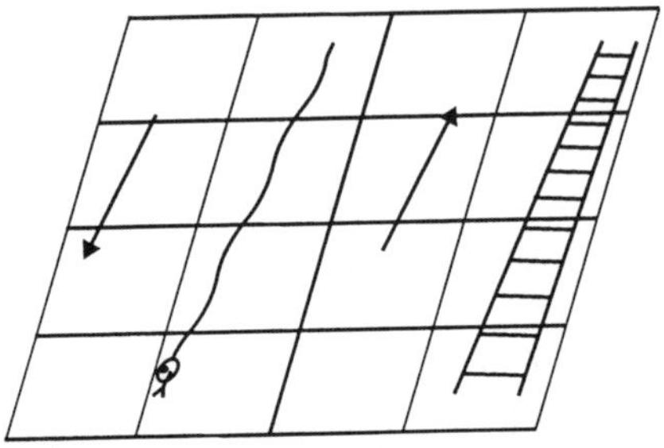

Snakes and ladders: ladder goes up, snake comes down

Popper interprets Parmenides's belief in an essential world of no change as a statement that change and motion are illusory. To an average person this does not make sense. To a musician, moreover, it is not a true statement of the problem. It makes more sense to distinguish *evidence* of change (e.g., sound as an effect of motion, arising from the string being in vibration), from *explanation* of change (in this case, as a consequence of applying force to the string causing it to undulate in space). From observing a snake, or eel, or serpent, the ancients are likely to have appreciated that such a creature moves by extension in width (thus increasing its purchase on the ground) and contraction in length, forming an S-shape, and moving forward by transferring energy from head to tail, at the same time exploiting lateral resistance from the ground (or water) to propel it forward. The ability to move by reducing size in one dimension and increasing in another is rather ingenious on the part of the serpent (though it does not account in a literal sense for the dragon having legs and being able to walk, still less the Chinese dragon's ability to fly).

The bending of a snake to allow it to move forward is directly comparable with the bending of a bow in order to propel the arrow, a change of shape which can be interpreted in the same way as compressing the line of the bow at rest and extending its area in the lateral dimension in order to propel an arrow forward. In both cases potential energy associates with curvature, and curvature in turn with conversion of a line object (the snake or bow as an object having only length) to a curve occupying a space of two dimensions. Extension in a second dimension entails a contraction in the

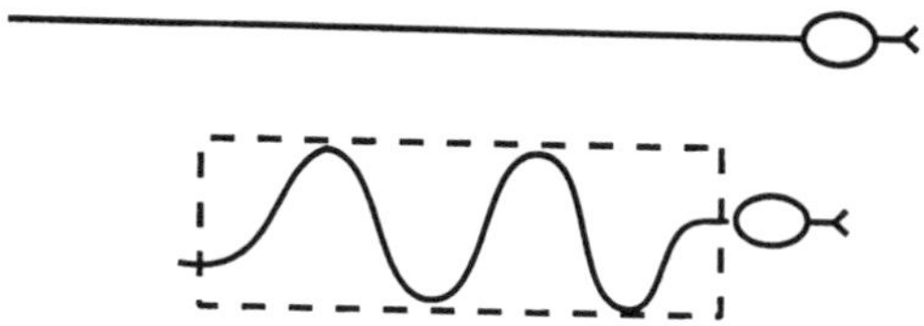

In order to move forward, a snake contracts in length and expands in width

primary direction. There are dark intimations here of the theory of relativity and increase in mass of an object accelerating at a speed approaching the speed of light. The bow and string of a bow and arrow separate the resistance and conservation of energy functions of curvature from the impulsive consequence of the flight of the arrow. Whereas the bow bends in a simple arc, the impulsive force is expressed in the straight lines of the extended string and the flight of the arrow.

According to myth the Pythagoreans were a secretive sect who forbade initiates from divulging the mysteries on which their reputation depended. The fate of Socrates is a reminder of the risks in discussing, let alone divulging, knowledge that might be construed as seditious or contrary to religion if leaked into the public domain. The world then was as dangerous a place as it is now, and if what you are saying runs the risk of giving offense to the religious beliefs of your hosts or neighbors, it makes sense to disguise what you know so the message is available only to yourself and those others who respect where your ideas are coming from.

On the question of original sin, when Parmenides cautions against "putting one's trust in erring sense-organs," the word *erring* is intuitively understood as "tending to mislead" when there are other equally important layers of meaning attached to it as well.

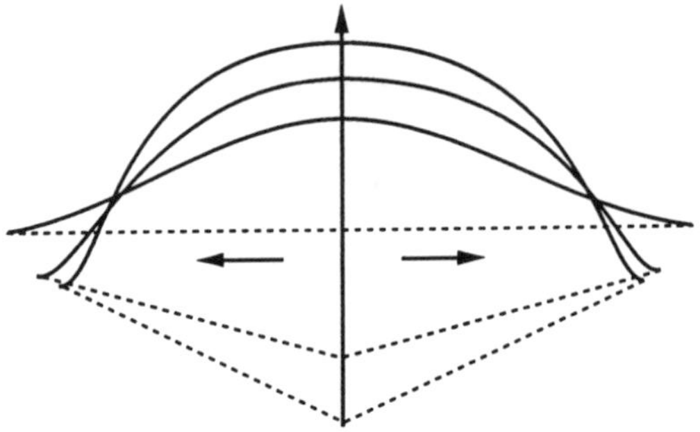

Trivially, to err means to sin. An error is regarded as an incorrect choice or assumption, and also the result arising from acting on it. We think of an error as simply a wrong, as a negative. But in its mathematical or statistical usage, however, error is understood as an inevitable and acceptable deviation from total accuracy in measuring something, for example the popularity of a politician, or how much house prices are likely to rise in the coming year. An element of error is inherent in the method of calculation, and is perfectly acceptable within limits. It signifies that the likely result will be a value somewhere within certain extremes or margins. For Parmenides to speak of the sense organs as *erring* is to make the additional point from everyday experience that the world a person discerns with two eyes and two ears is a necessary approximation of conjugated images that do not exactly coincide. The third dimensions available to vision and hearing inhabit a zone of uncertainty created by the overlapping of two-dimensional impressions, just as the movement of a vibrating string occupies an indeterminate space bounded by two fixed points.

The meaning of error as uncertainty or deviation applies with particular force in music, since the acoustical knowledge derived from plucking a musical instrument involves distortion both of the string's length, and also of the instrument's steady state, which is silence. A harp standing on its own does not emit a sound, so ironically we cannot know of its musical state of readiness (that is, whether it is in tune or not) or usefully make calculations of ratio or proportion, without causing its strings to vibrate, action which distorts the picture. That is perhaps one aspect of the meaning of Parmenides' claim that truth or reality lies in absence of motion. As Popper observes, it is remarkably close to the familiar uncertainty dictum that one cannot ascertain the position and momentum of a particle at one and the same time. The very act of observation of plucking a string and causing it to vibrate introduces a margin of error to our perception of its location in space, just as introducing a stretch to a string under tension distorts its true length as well as its fundamental frequency at rest. Nevertheless, in the case of a length such as a harp string we know the limits of error fairly precisely, since as far as we can tell the endpoints are fixed and do not move. And it follows that the tone made audible by plucking the string will tend to oscillate around the fundamental frequency represented by the string at rest. It is impossible all the same to know the exact frequency of the string without causing it to move, and thus altering its frequency, and that is paradoxical. (There is, to be sure, a certain wit in acknowledging the inevitability of error on the pathway to truth.)

From such fanciful constructions of original sin what emerges is the moral that attaining knowledge requires three things: (1) action or motivation on the part of the observer; (2) resistance from the thing observed; and (3) uncertainty as a direct result. Popper believes that Parmenides has no confidence in the evidence of the senses. I think Parmenides is saying something more subtle, that the evidence of the senses is all we have, and results are necessarily approximate. Our perception of space is founded on awareness of discontinuities in the aural field between what the ears individually hear, and in the visual field, between what the eyes separately see. To the extent that all observation is dependent on vision and hearing, the assertion of uncertainty may simply be a projection of an internal lack of precision in the way we see and hear, and indeed, measure. Only through the uncertainty arising from the disparity in evidence registering on our eyes, and ears, do we in fact see and hear the world with the added dimension of depth. Without awareness of depth we would not be able to navigate in space with certainty, or be willing to believe that the world existed in continuous extension beyond the reach of our organs of touch. In this respect the messages of hearing and music coincide with the discoveries of J. J. Gibson in the field of visual perception.

Given his commitment to falsifiability, it is perhaps surprising that Popper appears to overlook the paradox of a vibrating string, a system in unpredictable motion, giving rise to exactly measurable quantities: pitch (frequency), division (harmonic segmentation), and ratio (relative length), as a direct consequence of the constant frequency and wavelength of a vibrating string. From the evidence of which one may conclude with Parmenides that abstract knowledge may aspire to absolute knowledge but can only tend toward it through testing or experimentation that for any one result may be uncertain, but cumulatively lead toward the truth.

THE MYTH OF CREATION

Just as a line is defined as the extension of a point, so the image of a snake can be regarded as the extension of a mouth. A mouth is a point. A point has location but no dimension. The mouth of a snake is a point having extension like a black hole in astrophysics: anything edible in three dimensions that comes within its event horizon is liable to be sucked in and lost for good (or, if it is a genuine *wormhole*, to be crushed out of existence and expelled as waste product at the other end). In the case of a talking snake, as in the Garden of Eden, the mouth is also a source of radiant energy in the form of words. Words are matter converted to energy in the body and released as information from the mind. The mind of a snake, like the mind of a human being, is an alternate universe of compacted sense impressions and relationships expressed in symbolic form. Given that ancient cultures were just as interested as we are in the mysteries of creation and how the beginning and end of time are to be explained, in depicting creation as issuing from the mouth of a divine intelligence, the old testament story is using the same reverse induction technique as modern astrophysics to reach a surprisingly similar conclusion, an account of the origin of everything as a spontaneous ejaculation (utterance) in four or more dimensions of data configured in the ostensibly dimensionless mind of a transcendental observer. The ancients also recognized a symmetry between eating and speech—nourishment goes in, and information comes out—arising from the fact that both actions employ the same orifice.

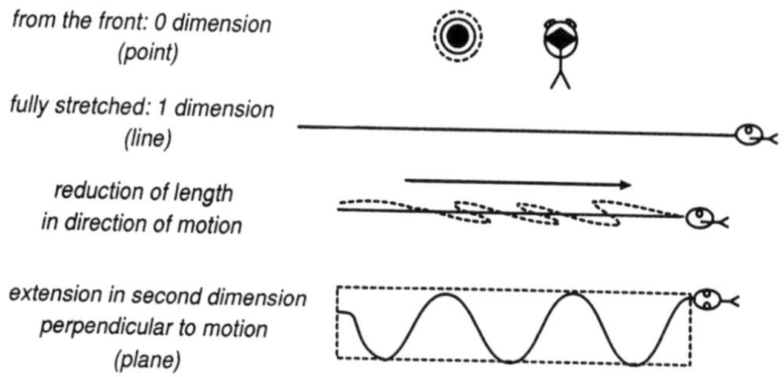

Dimensions of a snake in motion

An extension of a point is a line. The snake is a line. The line has ends, and the ends define a length. If one end of a line is fixed, the other end moving freely, the totality of possible locations of the snake is all points within a sphere; however if the snake is rigid and unable to bend, the totality of all possible locations of the free end is limited to the surface of a sphere.

A ray of light issuing from a point is defined as a line of energy radiating in time and space in three dimensions. In the movies, when a torch is pointed toward the camera, the viewer in the audience is dazzled, because the torch beam broadens as it penetrates space; but when we look up at the stars on a cloudless night, what we see are points of light that follow us around. How are points of light (a different point for each eye) compatible with the radiation of light in every direction? Why do stars twinkle? Why is starlight not diffused by the earth's atmosphere? Surely what we ought to see is an indeterminate haze, but what we do see are distinct points of light, described by some ancient observers as "pinpricks in the fabric of the heavens." To earlier cultures who would presumably have recognized that the stars were light sources and not simply light-reflecting, like the moon, the finitude of starlight may have represented a mysterious specificity of location, like the sound of a distant voice. What we understand by a star in the sky is a unique ray or line of light extending between the source and the observer in person. The point of light in fact is that point on the retina where an observer connects directly "down the line" to the source. The totality of illumination radiated at any one point in elapsed time is a sphere whose radius is the maximum expansion of starlight from the time and place of emission to interception, and the degree of illumination at any point on the sphere, to the attentuation of light energy at that distance and moment. Finally, in order to see a star as a point of light, of course its light has to be brought to a focus, even though the focal length involved is as good as infinite.

Unlike starlight, a ray of coherent light, as from a laser, suffers fewer losses of internal energy in transit from phase cancellations and, because its energy is better organized, is capable of penetrating greater distances, and may be modulated to carry information. The ancient Greeks and Mesopotamians may not have entertained any concept of radio, or radar, or laser interferometry, or paintball games that employ a laser direction finder. But they did grapple with the realities of the stars, and they did employ musical instruments to act in the role of acoustic lasers, generating internally coherent signals that penetrate the atmosphere more effectively, and can be heard at a greater distance, than incoherent speech or noise.

Whether one thinks of them as distant suns or simply as pinholes in the fabric of space, stars are points of light that maintain a fixed relationship with a moving observer. The larger moon and sun, despite radiating light in every direction, are visible from every point on earth as discs of finite magnitude. That an incident sphere of radiated light, whether the flickering light of a distant fire or star, or the steady light of the moon, is perceived nonetheless as a multiplicity of point sources by observers in different locations is a mystery to be explained by the fact that for every observer the possibility of the light source being smeared over the entire visual field is collapsed to a cross-section of a line of direct radiation in one dimension. The presence of an observer establishes a fixed, albeit arbitrary, endpoint for the ray of light in space and time; in turn, that establishes a line of connection between the observer and the distant star.

The same is true for musical sounds. The ancients invented structures, like the bow and the sling, that make sounds of coherent if variable pitch as a byproduct of the forces incorporated in their preparation and use. The ancients also knew that rigid human and natural structures, such as the weaving frame, stone, bone, hollow log, hollow reed, or earthenware jar, were apt to resonate at specific pitches upon being struck or in the presence of wind currents. By accident, or out of curiosity, in order to discover more of the properties of musical sound, they modified and combined these structures to create instruments that could be modulated in pitch by varying the tension or modifying the vibrating structure in exactly controlled ways. Through the fact of their very existence, early musical instruments offer clear evidence of ancient cultures having a grasp of sophisticated concepts of energy, radiation, coherence, direction, and dimension, of which surviving mythologies are available to provide clues or other evidence of their conceptualization in abstract terms. It implies, for example, that the maker of a horn or trumpet understood the nature of a signal and had the means to conceptualize Schrödinger's equation of the collapse of the wave function in the presence of an observer, even though he or she probably did not choose to formulate it in such a way.

Musical instruments generate coherent waveforms by means of self-organizing processes that operate within structured limitations of movement. These instruments are normally mute. They sound in consequence of the addition of excess energy, and when the excess energy is appropriately managed, an oscillatory feedback develops between the input of raw energy and the radiation of an equivalent energy in processed form. Like light, sound radiates in spherical shells, packets or pulses of fluctuating energy. Unlike light, sound requires a medium, and its velocity of propagation varies with the density of the medium, usually air. The steady tones produced by a musical instrument are evidence of consistent and continuously variable solutions of energy conversion equations that are relatively (though not totally) independent of the energy source, a mystery of which voices and instruments sounding in unison are a manifest proof. The function of a resonating body, as of a guitar or violin, is not merely to amplify the vibration of a plucked string, but also to maintain its steady state by feedback. Most primitive instruments require a consistent input of energy from the performer, through breath control or steady bow movement and pressure, and deliver consistency of tone in return. In turn, these controls amount to skills (focus, a steady hand, etc.) that have survival value to the community and can be exhibited in abstract—non-functional—art or ritual. We tend to regard instruments of fixed pitch from prehistoric times to the present, from panpipes to pipe organs, pianos, xylophones or synthesisers, as self-evidently designed to produce steady-state vibrations of constant frequency, and more or less controllable amplitude and decay. Since the classical era, however, the age of the violin, some of the more sophisticated instruments of a modern symphony orchestra—including the grand piano in the nineteenth century—have been deliberately engineered and tuned to generate *unstable* sounds sensitive to delicate variations in playing technique. Related performance innovations have included *vibrato*, a rapidly undulating intonation designed for greater penetration in large concert halls, and sanctioned by the uncertainties of equal temperament. An immediate consequence of introducing tonal instability to the performance of a musical instrument is that it allows a greater density of information to be carried on the radiant tone by continuous modulation of energy input (amplitude), timbre (tone color), and operating length (wavelength or pitch). A local indeterminacy of pitch conveniently disguises imperfect consonances and harmonic relations in equal tempered music of changing key. The musical aesthetic of J. S. Bach is predicated on unstable pitch relations. Since the voice is a naturally unstable instrument, vibrato allows an instrument to be perceived as voice-like, and baroque music in the eighteenth century to become more rhetorical or gestural in expression, and thus richer in implication. In performing the music of earlier periods, as for viol consort, the requirements of uniform tone quality and exact intonation rule out expressive uncertainties of intonation as wilful distractions from perfect harmony.

A musical instrument converts chaotic energy into structured energy. With the aid of a bone flute or bow fiddle, ancient seekers after knowledge were able to inquire into the mechanism of energy conversion as a metaphor of creation. The lesson of creation by music involves three components: (1) a *will* or intention on the part of the musician who is the source of energy; (2) the *impulse* of creation in which energy is released; and (3) a conception of the *instrument* as a transducer or set of resisting boundary conditions by means of which the added energy is organized, radiated into three-dimensional space, and modulated in time. We can add (4) a perception of the act of emitting a musical note as simultaneously a declaration of the reality of space and time.

The characteristic feature of structured energy is cyclical motion, as of a pendulum or vibrating string. The moving parts of a flute, trumpet, or clarinet cannot be seen, hence wind instruments are open to be construed as sacred or spiritual rather than material objects. Whereas the human voice is naturally unstable and apt constantly to modulate in tone in an unpredictable fashion, a wind or string instrument by virtue of its construction tends to vibrate in a consistent manner producing a distinctive and readily recognized tonal impression on the ear. The more rigid construction of a musical instrument sets limitations to its flexibility of expression; these drawbacks however are offset by greater efficiency in energy conversion, resulting in greater clarity and penetration of tone. The ideal compromise to ensure clarity of vocal expression is for a vocalist to adopt a rigid, tense, and uniform style of utterance in situations of ritual formality, improving control over alterations in pitch or tone that may occur. The alteration of personality implied by the adoption of a stronger and more focused style of voice is recognized throughout history as expressing strength of character and moral resolution.

The definition of a successful creation is of orderly structure emerging more or less spontaneously out of chaos. The definition of original sin, in art as in politics, is of deliberate intervention that seeks to gain authority over an organized but static creation by reintroducing an element of chaos and unpredictability to the mix.

TRANSLATION

The *Timaeus*, Plato's account of the world in Pythagorean terms, is difficult to "read" in terms of everyday experience. Indeed, it is often described as dealing more in theology than physics, more about pious speculation than hard observation:

> The work constitutes the high point of the Pythagorean tradition of theological philosophy. . . .

Theology is often used as a term of abuse for unintelligible speech. In situations of this kind it is not enough to be able to read Greek: one has to have some idea of what the Greek author is trying to say. Translation involves concepts and ideas of which words are merely pointers. If a translator has no inkling of what an author has in mind, his meaning is likely to remain obscure.

> *A priori* arguments are adduced for the opinion that the world is one, that it is in the form of a perfect sphere, that it is necessarily made up of the four elements Earth, Air, Fire, and Water, and that it has a soul. . . . The purpose of God in endowing men with sight and hearing was that they might learn the lesson of law and order from astronomy and music and apply it to their own lives.[2]

To say "the phenomenal world is an image of the eternal world" amounts to saying that the world of experience—and by world he means the heavens as well—conforms to an ideal structure of laws, and in saying that "the world is one," that these laws are the same for heaven and earth. A "perfect sphere" could be saying that the universe is spherical in extent, but is also a way of hinting that the laws of rotary motion that govern organized power and guarantee stability of motion to the wheel, the tides, the seasons, the planets, and the rhythms of human life and activity, apply in time and space and not just to actions on a plane. If "matter, vapor, energy, and fluid" are substituted for "Earth, Air, Fire, and Water," there is little to distinguish the Pythagorean universe from the Newtonian. That the world has a soul is simply a way of saying that the world is dynamic and self-governing, properties that are self-evident.

> My reasoning will be unfamiliar, but those schooled in the branches of knowledge needed for the explanation of my propositions will be able to follow. We begin with the obvious, that energy, matter, fluidity, and air are properties of bodies, and all body has volume [i.e., extension in three dimensions]. Volume is enclosed by surface [two dimensions], and rectilinear surface is composed of triangles [i.e. the area of any surface can be computed by triangulation]. . . .

The Pythagoreans identify *fire* with radiant energy and light, and the constitution of the universe as *fire and earth*, or matter and energy. That interactions of matter and energy—for example, to create sound and combustion—are mediated by the dynamics of air and water, is also a noncontroversial statement.

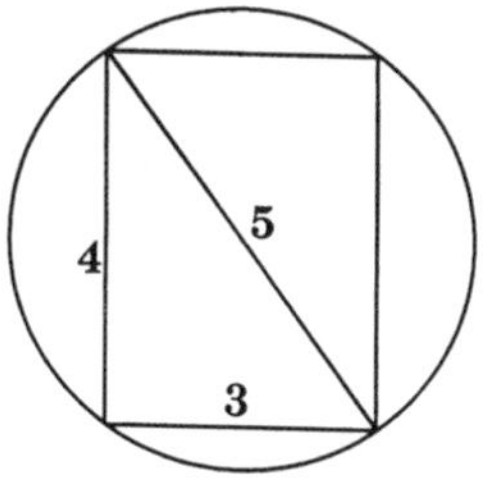

Every right-angle triangle fits into a semicircle

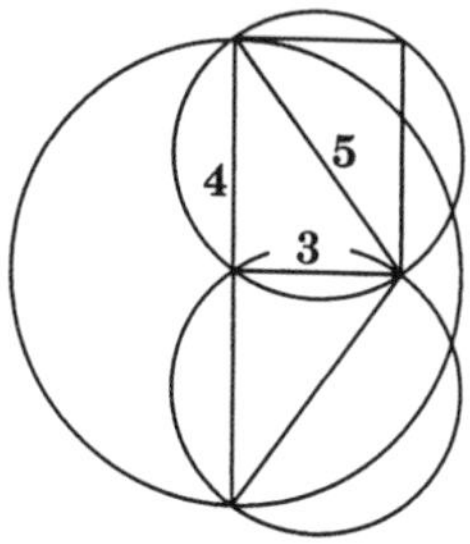

Every triangle is derived from two

In the following obscure but essential statement Plato defines the integration of the four elements. When Plato refers to triangles, he is alluding to the Theorem of Pythagoras as an equation of Einsteinian significance that applies not only to the geometrical conundrum of squaring the circle (a problem of force in two dimensions) but also to the conversion of energy into motion in three dimensions.

> All triangles are derived from two, and each of these has one right angle and two acute. One of them has, on either side, half a right angle, subtended by equal sides [its hypotenuse the square root of two]. The other has, on either side, unequal parts of a right angle subtended by unequal sides [e.g., the 3, 4, 5 triangle of the Theorem]. So we postulate this as the source of fire and of the other bodies, as we pursue our argument which combines necessity with probability. . . .[3]

"Thus the nature of fire is explained by the properties of the scalene triangle," Benjamin Farrington sardonically comments. Plato is saying nothing of the kind. Rather he is talking about *firing* an arrow from a bow (fire = conversion of energy) and referring to the remarkable discovery by the Pythagoreans that the law of the square on the hypotenuse is not limited to two dimensions, but can also be seen to account for the force that drives the arrow as a function of the bow being extended. That "all triangles derive from two" is shorthand for saying (among other things) that all triangles can be bisected in two right triangles, that every right triangle fits into a semicircle, and that ideally there are always two similar triangles formed when a bow is drawn, one above and one below the line of the arrow. This is the Pythagorean key to reconciling cyclical force (the bow), resistance (drawing the bow), and impulsion (the arrow in flight). The same duplication of the triangle appears in the Mesopotamian diagram of the bow in a circle.

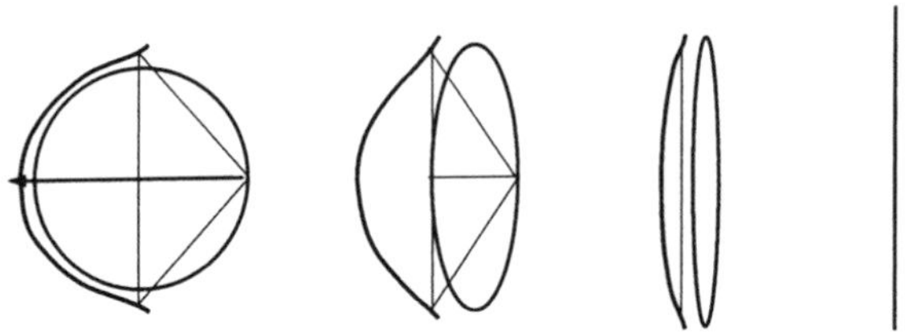

1 : 1 : √2 3 : 4 : 5

When an arrow is drawn, the bow is compressed in one dimension and expanded in another into a two-dimensional plane bounded by a semicircle (the bow) and an angle (the drawn string). The transference of impulsive (expendable) power is expressed by the line of the bowstring and arrow forming a pair of right triangles in relation to the line of the bowstring at rest. The increase in tension of the bowstring as it is being drawn is audible as a change in pitch. The added force exerted on the string at the hypotenuse is the square of the interval change in pitch as the string is pulled back. The added force is equivalent to increasing the weight tensioning the string of a monochord, and the same law applies. As the frequency increases, the tension ratio also increases as the square of the change of frequency. Thus, to raise the pitch of a string by an octave (2 : 1) the increase in tension is 4 : 1. As the bowstring forms the hypotenuse, the added force is exerted on the hypotenuse of the triangle formed by extension.

Notes

1. Karl R. Popper, *Conjectures and Refutations: The Growth of Scientific Knowledge*. 4th edition. London: Routledge and Kegan Paul, 1972, 128.
2. Benjamin Farrington, *Greek Science* rev. ed. Harmondsworth: Penguin Books, 1963, 117.
3. Benjamin Farrington, *Greek Science*, 119–20.

FOUR

ISOLATION

> At the moment of birth, or at the moment of consciousness of the first thought, every human being is an exile. JANET FRAME

Birth is a separation. Cells divide and change. Physical separation is absolute. How to deal with it determines the kind of person you are and the life you lead. The options are stark. Go it alone and sort out your own destiny; take the lead and conquer the world; or join the tribe, accept the rules, and take your chances. For most people, to escape the roar of everyday life is an occasional luxury and a necessary antidote to the stresses of dealing with others, whereas the reclusive life carries implications of being cut off from reality. A condition of self-willed isolation is often perceived by society in negative terms as antisocial, elitist, or mystical, whence derive the stereotypes of the dreaming poet, hermit, mad scientist, wandering exile, leper, castaway, or prisoner locked in solitary confinement.

Social fear of isolation is a fear of having nothing to say as well as having nobody to talk to. By definition, a life without people is a life without interaction and thus without language. A life without language is a life of isolation, as of one lacking the gift of speech. A life of isolation is denied recognition or empathy, and incapable of showing feeling—adding up, for an eighteenth-century readership, to the primeval human condition experienced and observed by Defoe's fictional castaway Robinson Crusoe.

Interaction has its rewards. To the castaway, the natural environment is passive and changeless. One interacts with the natural environment through touch, sight, hearing, and smell. The rewards of interaction are the securities of difference between the self and the world, of continuity from one moment to the next, and of control ("dominion") over the sensory environment. Control arises in the first place not by action or dialogue but rather by stillness. The first rule of the hunt is to stop moving, and thereafter to move with caution. The aim of not moving is to observe without being noticed, since if you are moving yourself you are not only more exposed to predators but also less sensitive to movement elsewhere in the field of vision or hearing. A comparable interaction of the cautiously moving individual against the steady backdrop of an environment is expressed musically in the moving relationship of a melody against a fixed reference or drone, and in the case of an unaccompanied instrument, such as a flute, in the constant features of the acoustic environment revealed to hearing by a continuously modulated melodic signal (a technique employed more discreetly and in reverse but to equal effect by the visually impaired, who navigate with the aid of vocal clicks or by tapping a stick).

Controlling personal movement as an aid to orientation has the beneficial effects of reducing unwanted judder in the visual and aural fields; thus improving visual and aural definition within the environment, and making the detection of target objects easier. In music, the symbolic function of melodic movement is monitored: (1) in relation to absence of body movement of the performer; (2) in relation to starting and finishing notes corresponding to positions of rest; and (3) as a tension gradient or pattern of excursion within a pitch space articulated as a scale or mode. (For such reasons a solo musician who makes great play of moving about, in order to draw attention, is behaving counter-intuitively; a music that ends in a different place from where it began has lost its way; and a style of performance that prioritizes panic responses—extremes of speed, range, and loudness—is missing the point.)

Musical models of stillness and contemplation, perceived as unfolding against an unchanging accompaniment (examples include Tibetan Buddhist chant, "Farben" from *Five Orchestral Pieces* by Schoenberg, and Stockhausen's *Stimmung*) tend inevitably to imply absence of head movement. Equally, and for the same reason, since microphones are fixed in place and orientation in a recording studio, the contemplative mode is implied for listening to a radio transmission or recording, invariably monitored from one or more fixed locations, or, in the case of electroacoustic music, virtual locations. In an auditory figure-ground relationship the ground or unchanging accompaniment constitutes the background acoustic, or constants of natural reverberation in response to a variable signal.

Every musical concert is a ritual of invasion and conciliation. The space in which a concert takes place belongs to the audience, either in fact or by convention. The invader is the visiting performer. The concert in effect is an interview. It asks, Do you belong here? Do you have abilities the community appreciates, that are better than those we already have, or of a new kind we might be able to use? Should we respect you? What level of education and culture do you represent? These are more or less subliminal issues, but they are all addressed in the choice and manner of music to be put on display, and in the audience's response.

Since an enclosed environment of regular shape and proportion responds preferentially to music of specific keys and related wavelengths, a solo performance, whatever its cultural, emotional, or expressive content, is bound to function as a *procedure* to survey an acoustic environment, and in communication terms as a *rite of self-disclosure* to any other person who may be listening. Even though the audience at a formal concert knows that the performer is going to appear, and who that person is, and the kind of music that person is likely to make, the underlying meaning of any formal music presentation (the same is equally true of animal vocal gestures) is to advertise the presence and character of the alien performer. The formal guise of an initial statement or signal of greeting, following the tuning ritual, may convey hostility (I am in charge, I am taking possession), respect (I am comfortable being here, and interested in dialogue), or indeed, invitation (I need help). In turn, for a performer to be received in silence or acknowledged by polite applause carries its own message of endorsement or otherwise of the presence of the newcomer, and authorization to remain and move freely within the alien environment. Exactly the same message obtains for an opening prelude by Scarlatti as for the answering grunt of a wild animal to an intruder or potential predator, or the natural echo or reverberation of an alien enclosure to the cry of the newcomer. The primeval hunter-gatherer interpreted the ambient reflection of his own vocalizations from a cave or cliff face as a gesture of endorsement by the spirits of the location.

Dialogue, as between the intruder and the natural environment, is the typical basis of rituals of consecration, formal procedures that ask permission of the spirit of the place to occupy the place or harvest provision from it, for example to cut down a tree.

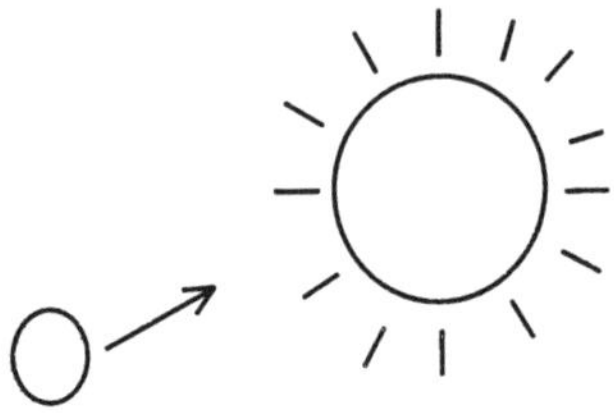

Invocation and response

Since the combined acoustic and psychological purpose of incantation is to provoke a measured response from an imaginary occupant of the space—a reverberation identified with the space itself—the ritual function of a melody launched into the environment naturally requires the text always to be delivered in the correct form and intonation. A musical instrument such as a pierced flute allows the correct form to be memorized in a pattern of finger-holes, while ensuring that the associated sequence of notes is always correctly reproduced. The invocation may also be constructed as a particular hierarchy or range of frequencies so that a clearer acoustic picture of the environment is revealed, along with qualities indicating the presence of wood, water, or stone, or the presence of life. In the movies (which are viewed in darkness for precisely the same reason) the same primitive anxieties and rites of expiation are routinely recreated in scenes and dialogue that take place at night, or in the dark, in unknown and potentially hostile and often labyrinthine settings. In the concert hall, on the other hand, even the tranquil bucolic setting of a work like Debussy's *Prélude à l'Après-midi d'un Faune* is ritually invoked by a solo flute playing a plain up-and-down whole-tone scale, a gesture of inquiry in an alien musical tongue, intended literally as well as figuratively to alert one and all to the presence of an observer, and to tease the orchestral wildlife into graceful animation. Wilder and more distant is the mysterious Introduction to Stravinsky's *Le Sacre du Printemps*, a wailing wake-up call by solo bassoon provoking a dawn chorus on a far grander scale. By implication, the silent world includes other intelligences.

Musical dialogue between an active melody element (the self as observer) and a passive harmony element (the revealed world, or reverberant space) expresses a purpose of self-declaration and self-location in relation to a silent, and potentially hostile world. The pace and formality of such a music is designed to convey respect and a sense of occasion, is naturally geared to a human scale, and may vary in solemnity from a grand event to an intimate function such as the domestic rite of checking the tuning of a guitar or violin in front of an audience before a concert begins. Preliminary actions even of so modest a kind are equally open to interpretation as a preparatory greeting and testing of the waters of a space invaded by a stranger and about to be occupied by music. The unmeasured prelude in improvisatory style that announces a suite of dance movements for harpsichord solo enacts a similar double ritual of sounding out the instrument and asserting control over a performance space. The opening gesture is perhaps less prescriptive in baroque and classical practice, if only because the performance protocols in place already imply respect for the guest status and authority of the musician. In Beethoven's era, however, a time of social upheaval when the per-former can no longer be sure of the respect of a newly liberated proletarian audience, the opening invocation may tend to be more aggressively rhetorical, as for the Fifth Symphony. The notional show of superior force persists to the present day in the inten-tionally deafening chord of welcome of a heavy metal pop concert.

An unresponsive audience, like an anechoic environment, is as good as dead. Since music has always operated as a communal event, rhetorical tactics to establish and retain audience attention have traditionally helped to determine the form and style of musical expression. Silence—that is, absence of response, whether of ambience or audience participation—is also absence of resistance or hostility allowing a soloist, at least for the time being, to operate with the authority and freedom of action implied by a Bach solo partita for cello, a lute invention by John Dowland, or indeed an improvisation or cadenza in western or ethnic traditional music. In the twentieth century, the change of primary locus of execution and performers alike to the concept of alienation in music, the idea of doing what one likes without regard to a performance acoustic, or concern for the traditional formalities of audience engagement.

The moral issue arising from absence of dialogue is what to do next, since if there is nobody to control or with whom to negotiate, and therefore no restraint on invention, there is also nobody to help or talk to, or to offer resistance. What to do next implies a situation of making a statement and receiving no response. If the purpose of making a statement is to seek permission to continue, then absence of response can mean either no objection, or nobody to object. In which case you either stop and go away, or carry on and do what you came to do, until you reach your goal or somebody turns up to talk to, a recurrent situation in plays by Samuel Beckett—plays incidentally devised for radio, a medium where actors and audience alike are suspended in a limbo of isolation. The moral challenge of a play like *Waiting for Godot* is how to survive with morale intact, and organize life in the meantime, in the hope that somebody or something might turn up, or of being rescued, or relief arriving in the form of divine intervention.

There are musical idioms that evoke isolation. They include mechanical processes in music from which the human component is excluded, such as music for musical box, the impersonal music of Erik Satie, the metronomic style of J. S. Bach, or neoclassicism in the player-piano sense of Stravinsky's 1924 Piano Sonata, through to the structuralism of Webern or the philosophical abstraction of Cage's *Music of Changes* for piano, music to be processed optically as though by a machine, perhaps one of Percy Grainger's photocell contraptions. The moral message of mechanical music from the first programmed carillons of the fourteenth century to sampling software in the present is its air of divine indifference and self-sufficiency, of not having to acknowledge the existence of an audience or the private sufferings of the performer. Abstraction sends a message of the merits of sticking to a routine task for its own sake even at times when there may be nobody there to appreciate it. We respond in such a way to the private devotion to technique expressed in the solo partitas for cello of J. S. Bach.

Romantic era art and music also defend a power relationship of natural authority and indifference toward the listening audience, as the storm clouds of a John Constable landscape convey a sense of the majestic indifference of nature to the trivial apprehensions of a suffering humanity. Just as the rise of instrumental music in the seventeenth century eliminated the voice, and by implication the human presence, so too the development in the eighteenth century of the symphony, music for ensemble doing away with the leading role of the soloist, also had the effect of eliminating the symbolic figure of ancient ritual delegated to intercede with the gods of the environment on an audience's behalf, a role not easily assumed by a conductor with his back turned away from the audience, gesturing in silence. In the absence of an audible interlocutor, a music for massed voices such as Thomas Tallis's *Spem in Alium* threatens to become an overwhelming chaos, equivalent to a cluster work by Ligeti in modern times, obliterating any sense of personal space, and leaving the listener nowhere to turn. Absence of melodic leadership or harmonic orientation also contribute to the delirium associated with the dense polyphonic textures of Scelsi, Penderecki, Feldman, and the Stockhausen of *Trans*. Panic reactions of intimidation and indifference are evoked in the revolutionary symphonies of Mozart, Haydn, and Beethoven, though modern audiences no longer understand how to recognize them. Today we suffer having to negotiate with the authoritarian indifference of voicemail customer service interfaces (often to the accompaniment of elevator music) of major corporations.

In the long run, musical representations of chaos can normally be tolerated, if not at the time of performance, certainly in retrospect as experiences of natural disorder ultimately bounded within impermeable limitations of time, instrumentation, pitch, loudness, density, and so on. The warming up of players before a concert is a familiar example of chaos in real life in which a multitude of uncoordinated actions neutralize one another until silence is imposed by the tapping of a baton. In fact, the most powerful expressions of chaos in music are those that have to be most perfectly coodinated. To achieve the highest level of perceived disorder ironically requires the greatest discipline among the players, as can be heard in certain compositions of Berg or Edgar Varèse, or the inspired cacophony of Tibetan Buddhism.

As social constructs, both language and music presuppose a

community and audience of other people, and a culture of cooperation in the sharing of information. For the individual, interaction with others is an essential part of a life process of developing an identity and role within the group. For the group, the actions and protocols of sharing speech and music are primarily rites of bonding and cooperation, and only secondarily exercises in information sharing, irrespective of whether they are hostile or friendly in intention. The goals of personal development, in a musical context as in a beauty contest, are linked with actions that draw attention to the soloist, demonstrate skill and intricacy of movement, inspire admiration, and demonstrate leadership through controlling the responses of others, not only within the group, but among the audience as well.

Had John Donne written "Every man is an Island," in principle nobody would have been able to understand what he was saying, even though the meaning of his original words is perfectly clear. Identifying isolation as a fundamental human condition allows us to recognize a universal tendency toward social bonding and cooperation that at one level drives the evolution of language, and at another level finds an outlet in musical activity. Without exception, music of every culture or tradition embraces the principle of declaring and sharing information. That means that all music, of whatever age or culture, is open to evaluation in the same general terms of locating the individual within the group, outside the group, or in opposition to the group; and is also prescriptive of the dynamics of social relationship that apply at a particular time and place. (These conventions may also change and be lost over time, so that modern performers are no longer aware of, nor audiences attend to, the sexual dynamics of baroque dance forms, for example, or the subversive erotic implications of Brahms's *Hungarian Dances*.)

From studying music as information sharing it is a short step to identifying structural features that are common to the music of all cultures (e.g., melody, dialogue, rhythm, pattern), and that express universal human traits (i.e., of speech, movement, work). Musical traits indigenous to the human species are easily distinguished from variations in cultural expression that arise from the circumstances of a particular locality, for example the 7, 11, and 13-unit rhythms of classical Indian music, or the subtle intonations of Chinese art music, elements customary to the language and culture but difficult for western audiences to hear, let alone appreciate.

Western music in its present form is an art grounded in the geometry of ancient Egypt and the mathematics of ancient Greece. Over a period of five hundred years, from the end of the Dark Ages to the late Middle Ages, music theorists across Europe evolved an efficient and stable symbolic notation enabling the music of ritual to be fixed in written form and thus to unify the practice of religion throughout the Holy Roman Empire and to the far east. By 1500 written music had evolved to a point of coordinating multilayered musical processes of great imaginative complexity. The intellectual achievement expressed in musical process planning mirrored the development and publication of written civil command and control systems within principalities, along with sophisticated diplomatic and economic information networks throughout greater Europe and beyond, of which the development of mapmaking is an outstanding example. The complexities of information exchange made possible by standard music notation constitute a triumph of abstract thought that allowed European culture to move on from the Gothic era of cathedral building and secret knowledge, parodied in *The Da Vinci Code*, to a dynamic baroque era of cross-border cooperation, scientific progress, and private enterprise based on the free exchange of information.

That music is largely social in practice does not mean it is inevitably or exclusively a social activity by nature. There is no reason in principle for music to conform to tribal protocols of social interaction and cooperation—though even John Cage's unstructured musical happenings conform to, and rely on, surviving cultural protocols of musical performance (the concert hall, the respectful attention, the fee, etc.). Nature itself is not always well-organized, which is why we understand the task of science and art as embracing disorder in nature as it appears to our limited comprehension, and exploring ways of coming to terms with it that are often difficult for a majority to understand. The conceptual difficulties attached to the music of a great many twentieth-century composers, from Schoenberg and Berg to John Cage and beyond, acknowledge an identical spirit of inquiry into the nature and meaning of a fundamentally disordered reality.

A focus on confronting and mastering the unknown is entirely normal in medical science, or economic planning, or the visual arts. Disorder and disharmony are arguably more suitable objects of musical inquiry than the regular and repeatable work patterns reflected in the popular majority of classical and traditional idioms. Chaotic or disorderly experiences are more frequent occurrences in everyday life than harmony and order. Sitting among the crowd in a stadium at a ball game, for example. Waking up to the sound of birdsong. The roar of a waterfall. Peak hour traffic. The sporadic explosions of fireworks. Rain pattering on the roof. An afternoon chorus of cicadas. A summer's evening chorus of frogs. Applause. These images from life are real, evocative, at times inspirational. In fact, people tend to prefer chaos to structured sounds in the natural world, for the reason that chaotic sounds are easier to digest—are processed in a different way—and, more importantly, because the absence of structure signifies absence of danger. Since structure and pattern are no more self-evident in the natural environment than in a chance composition by Cage, it is possible to argue that Cage's chance music is (a) more realistic, since it presents sounds unfettered by cultural meaning, and (b) more akin to nature (though in turn that presupposes a concept of nature as chaotic at every level, when in fact it is only chaotic and unstructured on a human scale of auditory awareness). Among Asian cultures, the rustling sound of garlands of bells woven into the costumes of dancers brings graceful movement to audible life, reflected in the nursery refrain "with rings on her fingers, and bells on her toes, she shall make music wherever she goes." The aesthetic case in favor of the sublime naturalism of documentary against fictional movies, made by early pioneers Pudovkin and Grierson, then reinforced by the arrival of tape after the war, is likely to have directed Cage's attitude toward chance music in mid-life.

Tone and noise are the *yin* and *yang* of music and speech. In language, the noise elements are consonants, the musical elements the vowels. Until very recently in the history of western music it was customary to associate noise, and percussion instruments like drums and cymbals, with confusion, disorder, disharmony. Musical noises are used to signal alarm, as in the fearsome thunder of drums. The more tranquil associations of natural disorder are also cultivated in the gentle random melodies of bamboo chimes hanging in the breeze that bring peace to the garden, and the mobile of tiny bells suspended over a baby's cot that acts as a soothing reminder of the benign presence of other spirits. That random effects in western music, despite being pleasant and soothing to the ear, tend to be perceived as disruptive, tells us perhaps more about a tradition among western cultures of identifying order with coordinated actions and a moral preference for the discipline of synchronized actions. The existence of bell garlands, wind chimes, and aeolian harp also tells us that ancient cultures sought ways of discerning shape and pattern in natural processes such as dance and wind currents, by interposing structures to act as filters and tuning agents. The strings of an aeolian harp may be of different thickness and tuned to the same frequency, or of similar thickness and tuned randomly. An airflow across the strings sets up an alternating pattern of vortices that will either be in tune with the natural frequency of the individual string, and therefore amplify it in vibration, or out of tune, in which case the string will resist. Since the speed of the wind is inconstant, the frequency of turbulence is bound to vary correspondingly and create an audible fluctuation of tone of a voicelike, singing quality. The scientific principle is the reverse of a jaw harp, in which the harmonic characteristics of real vowels are resonated in the mouth from a free reed waveform of fixed pitch; by contrast, in the aeolian harp voicelike sounds are stimulated in a multi-string resonator by an inconstant airflow.

Noises from real life are routinely captured on tape or disc and inserted into a movie sound track, or sampled and shuffled to be inserted into a song composed on a computer. The conventional view that music is primarily about creating harmony and definitely not about the imitation of random effects in nature, can be read as an example of converting a technical difficulty in describing nature into a moral injunction to avoid anything difficult, explained in part because such effects are too subtle or complicated to write down, partly because they would be too difficult to perform accurately in any case, and residually because of a lingering prejudice against complexity *per se* (similar to prejudices against irrational numbers, infinity, zero, etc.). Similar moral objections have routinely been directed against the technically difficult music of composers like

Boulez, Xenakis, and Stockhausen. But the bureaucratic objection that complex, random or unpredictable effects are unmusical in principle, or culturally unacceptable, and therefore to be avoided to preserve the harmony of the state, is illogical in principle as well as being morally indefensible.

That most music conforms to what a majority of human beings enjoys listening to and is able to play is—even if untrue—a defensible statement, but one that has no moral authority. It is no more a value judgment than saying that most of the world's books conform to what a majority of the public wants to read. To argue on such a basis that music is *neither permitted nor intended* to imitate random effects—as some musicians are disposed to say of some twentieth-century music—is clearly absurd. For a long line of cultural authorities from Hegel and Schopenhauer in the nineteenth century to Schenker and Adorno in the twentieth to have attempted nevertheless to set limits to what music *should be allowed* to express, on the basis of what they have mistakenly perceived it to have been limited to expressing in the past, introduces a spurious moral dimension to the debate. A tendency toward order, harmony, and synchronized action, no matter how impressively persistent in history, does not equate to a moral imperative for music to avoid representing what the nineteenth-century romantic imagination was only too eager to identify as the chaos and disorder of the natural world. (The reality, as we shall see, is that classical and traditional musics of every culture *already* imitate random and unpredictable phenomena. It is like saying that doctors ought not to study disease, or engineers the debris of a mechanical failure. Only by addressing chaos and disorder in musical terms on our behalf are composers ever going to understand harmony and order.)

Having to cope with isolation as a condition of existence establishes a dynamic in human behavior toward group formation and cooperation. In turn the feedback of group cooperation assists in the development of acceptable terms of information sharing and social management. In music also. We relate to melody as an expression of individuality, and interpret harmony, rhythm, and tonality as cooperative responses designed to reconcile the concerns of the individual with the identity of the group. In addition to managing personal solitude, language and music are also strategies for managing other people with whom the individual is already associated. These reciprocal objectives, of reaching accommodation with the majority, or alternatively imposing one's will on the group, are as visible in the hierarchies of musical idioms and ensembles, as they are audible in the music they play. The relative status of the individual and group is not always clear-cut. Arguably, leadership consists in imposing the individual will on others for the sake of group unity as a means of group survival. But for a spokesperson, the same role just as easily implies subordination of personal will to the interests of the collective. If the objective of a speech act is to manage other people, or simply keep other people out of the way, its text content does not actually have to make sense, or be understood. Nor is it either in certain varieties of garage band music, the words of which are unintelligible against the overwhelming noise of an amplification system. On the other hand, in order to gain the active cooperation of others, a message has to be expressed in intelligible and acceptable, though not always rational terms. Rational content and meaningful agreement are only mandatory in situations involving teamwork directed to a specific objective. Only in a task-orientated, cooperative sense may language, even momentarily, be properly defined as a social construct, with coherence and precision as essential components. At a personal and private level, however, from composing a prayer, to nonsense, to poetry, to a symphony, language and music operate with a freedom that allows individuals to talk to themselves in a private language under the guise of exchanging information, in the sense of "bouncing ideas off other people." The ideal listener, as Stravinsky conceded, is the composer in disguise.

THE CONTRADICTIONS OF LANGUAGE

The art of western classical music is implicated in language both at the private level (as a medium of self-expression), and at the social level (as a system of names and performance instructions). Since the meanings of the words we use are not our own but those of other people, the paradox of language as a social construct is that the "off the shelf" formulae we are obliged to use are (a) inevitably a compromise with the exact feelings we may wish to express, and therefore (b) invariably open to misunderstanding. That people continue to talk all the same indicates, though it does not prove, that on balance, and at a certain level of precision, language communication actually works. More to the point, it defines the conversational speech act primarily as a personal gesture of sensory and social affirmation, and only secondarily as a social act or information transaction. At the very least, the compromises of everyday conversation oblige us to take other factors, such as posture, facial expression, and the transactional environment into account (office, restaurant, the dentist's chair, etc.) in the process of deciding what socially relevant meaning is likely to have been intended.

It follows that for the content of a speech act (or poem, or musical score, or classified advertisement in the local paper) to be intended or construed as accurate information requires some reorientation toward what language itself is supposed to do. In biology and medicine, commonplace names are replaced by highly specific titles in a fossilized Latin; in law and religion, the truth content of the testimony of an individual witness or preacher is measured against a cumbersome apparatus of written precedent; while calculations in algebra, mathematics, and physics reduce statements of ordinary language to concise, abstract, and infinitely manipulable formulae. One would expect western music notation, given its objective precision and longevity, to be accorded at least equal status to algebra. Surprisingly, the question continues to be raised whether in principle music is a language at all.

That music is not a language in the sense recognized by linguistic science is a truism equivalent in some circles to saying that music is empty of meaning, a charge leveled at music by non-musicians perhaps to divert attention from the embarrassing possibility that music may actually have something interesting to say of which they are unaware. That music all the same has language-like properties we already know. To say that music of all kinds tends toward harmony is a noncontroversial, if incomplete, statement that applies equally to language, with the difference that in music, local precision is sacrificed for the sake of direct communication across language boundaries.

The term *harmony* describes collective agreement in the larger sense of unity of place and time, unity of purpose, and coordination of action, from starting and stopping together to underlying structures of pulse, melody, and key. A tendency toward harmony sets music apart from language. Although language as a system (termed *la langue*) embraces a vocabulary representing consensus (and thus harmony of a sort), the practical applications of language in everyday life (termed *la parole*) naturally tend to articulate change, disturb, provoke action, and in other ways contribute to the dynamic flow of human commerce. Unity of purpose implies other people and a mutual understanding that agreement is possible. In tending toward harmony (that is, literally, *intending* harmony), music and language alike are open to interpretation as expressing an instinctive predisposition toward agreement in order to escape a condition of existential isolation. There is ample evidence of such a predisposition. It is easier to sing in unison with another person, than to sing a completely different melody. Babies come into the world already equipped to impose order on the environment of other people through spontaneous vocal gestures that some would call enthusiastic breathing, and others of more poetic frame of mind, discern as the first indications of language and music.

Those for whom language and music are primarily exercises in social bonding are fated all the same to perceive the individual speech act or performance of music as fundamentally disruptive. That at least is the morality adopted by classical linguistics from de Saussure to Chomsky, and embodied in such iconic works of art as Kafka's *The Trial*, Munch's *The Scream*, and Orwell's *1984*. Any ideology seeking to prescribe that music is *and ought to be* responsible to the identity needs of society as a whole, is fated to perceive works of abstract or nonrealistic art and literature as deviating from their socially appointed roles. The imperialistic (and not so new) mind-set which perceives music as vague and nonspecific, and therefore lacking in meaning, is doomed to wrestle in perpetuity with the chimera of language as exact, precise, and invincibly elusive.

FIVE

NOTATIONS

> Our consciousness of space is a consciousness of coexistent positions. . . . However, since a position is not an entity, it follows that the coexistent positions are not sensible existences but rather the blank forms or abstracts of coexistences . . . experiences of individual positions as ascertained by touch.[1]
>
> HERBERT SPENCER

A philosophy, observed Alfred North Whitehead, is best characterized by the assumptions it takes for granted, assumptions "so obvious that people do not know what they are assuming because no other way of putting things has ever occurred to them."[2] The Ionian philosophers proceeded on the basis that things available to the senses exist in substance and are located in space and time. This is like defining everything—every ultimate point—in the world as a note of music, in so far as it has position, magnitude, and timbre (material qualities), and coexists to some degree in harmonious relation with everything else. The problem with such a view of the world is explaining movement and change, the qualities that make a work of music come to life.

The modern idea of "a work of music" relies on a sophisticated notion of "the work" as an abstract procedure to be executed in a particular way, rather than a character reference to be attached to a particular performance in the here and now. To achieve this degree of separation of the procedural ideal from the actual execution, the process is imagined as a series of stages or steps to be memorized and executed in a particular order. In order to remember each step (which in isolation may not constitute a meaningful action) a form of notation is often necessary: for instance a description, number, mnemonic, or formulaic expression of the task. In classical music, notation ranges from the full score of data points positioned on a register of five-line staves, through short score of outline melody and bass-line with chord indications (figured bass), to graphics representing finger positions (tablature), or decorations (trills and turns). To meet the objectives of primitive ritual and execute a series of tasks smoothly and in the correct sequence, an over-arching formula and rhythm may be devised to integrate and maintain the sequence while preserving the distinctive patterns of specific actions. Alternatively, a rhythmic sequence might be invented to assist in memorizing a text complete with its necessary inflections and emphases (as with scansion in classical poetry, and conducting in classical music). In practice, rhythmic action and music form a mutually helpful partnership. Formulae for coordinating repetitive teamwork activities, in which the task alternates between executing a new stage and reviewing the entire process, are standardized in the additive structure of improvised verse and repeated chorus of song, for example the medieval *rondeau*, and also the blues.

The Greeks had little idea of a notated music, in the sense of marks on a surface—though they clearly did have a concept of pitch identity being embodied in the tension of a string, or the hole location of a flute, which is notation of a sort. Eighteenth-century explorers, and nineteenth-century scholars such as Alexander Ellis, the English annotator of Helmholtz, were disposed to consider the fingerhole positions of ancient wind instruments as exact notations of particular scales, since the length of a tube and thus its frequency are permanent features, and a set of panpipes cannot be retuned except by altering the length of the pipes. By contrast the tuning of a string instrument such as a lyre or violin is impossible to determine exactly since strings are made of organic dried animal tissue, and are therefore flexible, perishable, and liable to alter in tension as the ambient temperature or humidity changes. As instruments of naturally inconstant pitch and therefore adaptable to a variety of tunings, stringed instruments such as the lyre or kithara are better suited, and by inference *intended*, to vary in tuning according to chosen modes or scales conforming to different personality types or emotional states. The ancients were well aware that the personality expressed in tone of voice, tessitura, and range of tonal variation, is typically altered in direct response to stress.

Wind and string instruments are modeled in the image of a speechlike conception of music, one that recognizes the range of permitted pitch levels in a scale or mode as expressing a given temperament corresponding to an unequal but very specific pattern of intervals rising to an upper level of maximum tension. The emotional gradient defined by a given temperament is expressed in a particular mode, or order of interval steps. That gradient can be memorized, preserved in the tuning of a musical instrument, and called into service at an appropriate time by an appropriate person. The art of manipulating modes of expression is cultivated by persuasive speakers including priests, politicians, diplomats, and door-to-door vendors and evangelists. Over time the temperament (or "sales pitch") associated with a particular rhetoric will tend to harden into a scale or mode ("mood"), trading the immediacy of natural inflection for the authority and formality of artistic expression. By structuring the appropriate scale of degrees of pitch into the tuning of a musical instrument such as a flute, musical box, or pipe organ, a musician can be confident of reproducing the meaning of a lyric with an exact and appropriate degree of emotional inflection. Through eliminating gliding tones, and reducing the infinite variety of nuance of ordinary speech to a scale of seven or eight distinct pitches, the musical mnemonic of a spoken text is not only made easy to follow but also reduced to a formal outline that can be readily committed to memory as a dynamic shape. The contour of a voice reading is necessarily exaggerated in the public arena for the sake of clarity and intelligibility. However stylized or mannered a delivery, the underlying purpose of reproducing a mode of speech or song is to trigger a latent emotion, and thereby impart a spirit and meaning to a statement aspiring to social significance, in terms that are ultimately realistic. Since meaning in this instance is conceived in human terms—unlike the speech of dolphins, birds, or humpback whales—the wellsprings of meaning that emerge in varieties of incantation have at least something to do with the emotional connotations of rising and falling inflections in everyday life, as well as meeting the information sharing requirements of clarity and audibility. Naturally the tuning and temperament of a musical instrument will tend to influence the emotional nuance of a song or verse, as well as the sharpness of definition of its syllabic content.

For understandable reasons of maintaining tribal integrity and discipline, as echoed in Plato's strictures, the ancients conceived of music, as they conceived the universe, as the expression of ideally stable structures disturbed by external forces, and not as dynamic complexes of independent motivations. A person's tone of voice, or the tuning of a musical instrument, was understood to correspond to a coherent world of experience, and the individual performance, to an executive strategy aiming either to assert control over, or reach an accommodation with, the limiting conditions of the poet's personal world.

A belief in predestination can be rationalized as a response to an intellectual difficulty in explaining or justifying continuity and change, in general terms that include free will. What is admired in Greek tragedy is a sense of inevitability arising from the clash of constitutions of the protagonists of the drama, spelled out in actions that on the surface give the appearance of freedom of choice, but nevertheless are bound to conform, like musical instruments, to the way individual personalities are made and "performed," and the temperaments (tuning and tone of voice) assigned to them at birth. We may think of the inevitability of Greek tragedy only as a poetic device, but on its own terms the artifice affirms a belief in predestination as a consequence of the way human characters are made, behave, and respond to temptation.

Continuity implies a perception of time in continuous transition, whereas change implies a reciprocal perception of personal continuity of being, as well as establishing dramatic conventions of physical and emotional transformation. Most of us take continuity of being for granted, not realizing how difficult a concept it has always been to justify, both philosophically and mathematically. To imagine that the world exists as an agglomeration of people and things each of whom is self-motivated, manifests free will, and is individually responsible for its actions, represented anarchy for ancient cultures; not that these ideas were unbelievable but because they led to essentially destructive perceptions of society and social relationship. The same *horror vacui* has been expressed by scholars in the late twentieth century toward John Cage and his advocacy of a music of indeterminacy. The ancients looked up to the heavens as a structure of ideal perfection and order, in which the planets following independent paths represented minor divinities, and one-off events such as novas, comets, and meteors, portents of doom. Compared to the serene order and predictability of the heavens, the uncertain realities of life on earth, including war, pestilence, death, and the weather, implied forces of incoherence, moral deviation, disobedience, and disharmony, all difficult to reconcile with the ideal of an orderly and efficient world community in which everything has its place, and all cooperate in perfect harmony.

In order to define a relationship one has first to establish the context within which the idea of relationship has meaning. Part of the definition of context embraces the notion of a more or less uniform continuum within which items to be related may be located and differentiated in time, space, and essential nature. For example, the conceptual leap implied by a transition from multiple panpipes to a single pipe with multiple fingerholes, can be understood as a paradigm shift from a ligatured collection of different voices to the advanced conception of a unified voice (the single pipe) embracing an allowable variation of pitch and tone qualities (the fingerholes). Extrapolating from the concrete artifact of a single instrument of multiple voices, to the abstract idea of society as a unity embracing multiple personalities, tribal cultures are led to the elegant image of a controlling intelligence, a divine musician whose breath animates society, and one who nevertheless "thinks like us." In Greek drama the multiple dynamics of a clash of relationships are resolved and witnessed onstage and in real time on the assumption that character types and motivations are inherently unable to adapt to stress, and therefore bound to follow through to a point of crisis, at which the scheme of relationships suffers irreversible change, as we see for example in the fatal attraction of Oedipus and Jocasta.

In music a distinction is made between fixed relationships or temperaments tuned in advance to specific scales or modes, and performance actions that operate with some degree of freedom of inflection within those constraints. A lyre or harp tuned to C minor, for example, is set up in advance to produce music in C minor, expressing a particular mode or state of being, and at one time it may well have been considered inappropriate, and even irreligious, to attempt to perform music within that range of intervals that was not a genuine expression of the C minor spirit or genie. A scale or mode is a set of rules of behavior, and the art of being a musician consists in discovering those rules and pushing them to the limit, or even beyond the limit of conventional acceptability. Similar perceptions persist across the world: in the classical music of India, for example, or other eastern cultures where a choice of mode provides the framework on which a musical invention is destined to germinate and flourish.

The ability constantly to fix one's position during the course of a continuous movement in relation to an absolute frame of reference is easily recognized as a navigational skill, and it comes as no surprise that the adventures of Columbus and others in extending the map of the known world into new and distant regions should have occurred at the same time as music stave notation (and to a lesser extent, tuning) was achieving a degree of precision still valid today. We understand perspective drawing in the world of art, and the development of scientific mapmaking for navigation in travel and commerce, as elements of a phase of exploration, invention, and discovery in European history characterized by a freedom to venture into unknown regions embodied literally in the travels of Columbus, Vasco da Gama, and Francis Drake, morally in the plays of Shakespeare, mathematically in the challenges of equal temperament and planetary motion, and figuratively in the development of a new style of music for instruments only, a music unencumbered by a text and dedicated to exploring the implications of freedom of extension and modulation in musical space and time represented by the great stave.

The breakthrough achieved by the Europeans as a direct consequence of developing a stave notation of visual signs was a new ability to map the trajectory of a music evolving continuously not only in time, from moment to moment, but equally in temperament, from major to minor, and from key to key, by altering the centers of attraction of an evolving tonality, and thereby varying its emotional location. The perfection of seventeenth-century notation liberated composers from earlier constraints of tonality and fixed tuning, to a point where a key such as C minor could be perceived as simply one location in a greater universe or circle of key relations, a metaphor allowing innovative thinkers like Galileo to envisage the earth itself as a small planet orbiting in a larger solar system also in continuous motion, not to mention the morally daring madrigals of Gesualdo, for example, which meditate on the consequences of unfettered freedom of modulation and altered states of affection.

"By reality," wrote Herbert Spencer in the nineteenth century, "we mean *persistence* in consciousness." He was writing at a time when the world map was virtually complete.[3] Knowledge of space, the philosopher added, is based on experiences of *touch* and *resistance*, the author defining a person's understanding of motion rather blandly as of "a something that moves" in relation to "a series of positions occupied in succession." Spencer is relying on the navigator's or composer's conventional representation of movement as an imaginary line connecting a succession of reference points marked out on a chart or musical stave. Movement in musical terms is perhaps best defined in this context as the sensation of continuity of gesture or transition realized in the execution of a sequence of notes corresponding to locations in pitch, and spelled out in order like a join-the-dots picture. The English philosopher's stubborn adherence to the seventeenth-century definition of a line as a journey of points marked out on a two-dimensional surface is anachronistic at a time when conventional notions of continuous motion and extension in time and space are increasingly challenged by a new dynamic of force fields (magnetism, electricity) and constant change. In the same way as the arrival of stave notation in the renaissance era inspired a new Machiavellian freedom to maneuver and dissemble between states of being, the publication of Charles Darwin's *On the Origin of Species* in the mid-nineteenth century had the effect of retrofitting radical concepts of a world of continuous change into a classical philosophy of knowledge classification hitherto regarded as static, discrete, and local.

The new paradigm of continuous transition impacted decisively on popular understanding of time, logic, the elements, the animal kingdom, and even the class system. As the implications of Darwin's revolutionary study began to sink in, the Belgian inventor Léon Scott made the first baffling graphic recordings of the sound of a living human voice, visual representations of speech as fluctuating lines of energy totally undecipherable to the naked eye as words, melody or even rhythm. Scarcely a decade after Scott, the English photographer Eadweard Muybridge would embark on an epic documentation of human beings and animals in motion, research destined to revolutionize scientific, artistic, and natural perceptions of a dynamic real world no longer content to be perceived as a still life, but rather revealed as an unpredictable stream, even a torrent, of events in continuous and constant change in space and time.

For the Greeks the difference between continuous motion and motion by intervals was the difference between wheels and feet: the wheel representing the reality of a continuous motion which was all the same uncomputable (involving irrational numbers), in contrast to movement on foot in discrete steps, the latter being both real and quantifiable (countable in real numbers, and measured in relation to a standard imperial foot or pace). During the eighteenth-century age of reason, an age defending causality in logic as well as continuity of movement in real space, composers cultivated an imagery of sensibility and leadership in the rhetoric of the long line, or leading melody. This secular form of ritual incantation maintains continuity and momentum by means of a connecting tissue of transitional tones, hesitations and ornamentations applied to a dominant melody typically executed at a high pitch over a firmly grounded and regular pulsation in the bass.

By the late eighteenth century, a period of accelerated scientific progess and increasing moral and social unrest, the uncertainty of motion normally associated with melody alone begins to migrate into a normally stable bassline, giving rise to tempestuous tidal surges clearly audible in the symphonies of late Mozart and Haydn, spectacularly in Beethoven, and fading out in the time of Mendelssohn. Images of instability on a global scale evoke a world out of control, a civilization whose connection with the steady-state hierarchies of classicism was fated to be abruptly severed by the guillotine. The new dynamic of continuous melody suited a revolutionary era coming to terms with a machine age of steam-powered motion on land and water, and having to adjust in the 1820s to the immanence of electricity and magnetism. It also coincides with the invention of the steerable bicycle. In converting stepwise motion into continuous wheel propulsion, the bicycle introduced the concept of dynamic instability to personal locomotion as a basis for superior speed. Like a spinning top or stealth fighter, the bicycle is conceived on a presumption of imbalance. In other words, in order for the bicycle to be invented, the culture had to embrace the principle of a stability achieved by continuous forward motion rather than by standing still. In the piano music of Chopin the melody line is the uncertain component, reflecting a conception of the voice as by nature unsteady and liable to waver, against which the underlying beat proceeds in stable and regular rhythm, in imitation of walking.

Before the arrival of high-speed photography, artists had difficulty in visualizing objects in motion, such as a waterfall or a galloping horse. Until Léon Scott de Mandéville made his first graphic recordings of the human voice—wavy-line traces scratched onto a moving lamp-blacked paper surface by a bristle attached to a diaphragm stretched across the end of a barrel-shaped speaking trumpet—it had been widely assumed that the visual appearance of recorded speech would bear some resemblance to notated music or the printed word, as a visually intelligible segmented configuration of shapes representing consonants and vowels. Voice recording might have had considerable potential for the world of commerce if only the recorded trace had been easy to read. But from the earliest attempts it was clear that the oscillograms were simply impossible to decipher, and that the actual sound of continuous speech was very different from the strings of pearls of wisdom we consciously hear. It became clear that the only way a voice recording device could be made to work as a dictaphone would be for the process to be reversible, allowing the recorded voice to be recovered as sound from the marks engraved on the surface. Such reverse thinking prompted the French poet Charles Cros to imagine a recording process engraving onto a wax-resist coated copper or zinc disc from which the bare metal exposed by the recording stylus would be eaten away by acid to create a permanent groove from which the original sound might be played back. Cros's vision of recognizable voice reproduction would later be depicted in Francis Barraud's sentimental and idealistic image of Nipper the dog cocking an ear to a cylinder recording of "His Master's Voice." In the meantime, alternative methods of speed writing were introduced, the earliest among them, Pitman's shorthand, under the name *phonography*, meaning "sound writing."

Scientific interest in voice recording centered on the medical and psychological diagnosis of personality through analysis of the dynamics of voice production and intonation. The spread of Italian opera across Europe in the eighteenth and nineteenth centuries had reflected a long-standing interest among the intellectual community in the power of rhetoric as an instrument of leadership, and on the complex interrelationships of tone and manner of speech in relation to perceptions of intelligence, selfhood, and cultural identity. After coming to terms with the Newtonian model of the solar system as a system in dynamic equilibrium, eighteenth-century science was led to examine the possibility of explaining the natural diversity of human affairs in the world order in similar terms, as a dynamical system of interacting bodies individually motivated by natural self-interest rather than responding to divine will. A rearguard devotion among the ruling Viennese elite to the Cartesian notion of a clockwork universe populated by working-class robots was laid to rest with the invention by Wolfgang von Kempelen of a programmable speech synthesizer, a device based on the reduction of speech to a permutatable series of speech actions assembled from a treasure trove of tone-generating modules to create an industrial fantasy of Heath Robinsonian ingenuity that all the same actually worked.

The notion of a clockwork universe so dear to the old aristocracy, resuscitated in recent times as the philosophy of intelligent design, can be seen as a way of coping with an uncertain future by eliminating both the future and the uncertainty at a stroke, a stroke of the clock. There is a certain irony in the coexistence of an upper-class belief in a static universe and the rise of an eighteenth-century maritime culture dependent on artificial timekeeping, aware of time as a negotiable continuum, and increasingly adept at programming the movement of goods in space and time with a precision and certainty never possible before. When an organic growth process is reconfigured as a sequence of operations, time enters the equation as an objective dimension. In consequence, a process previously construed as organic and continuous suddenly reemerges as a programmed succession of individually abstract operations, located in different places, and each point introducing a new set of choices. Once again, it was up to music, this time instrumental music, to develop the templates for a new style of corporate organization in which operations traditionally assigned to a single individual were dissected into an ordered succession of stages allocated to different specialists. This new distributive framework is exemplified in the pre-symphonic repertoire of the mid-eighteenth century Mannheim School and after, and would be destined to influence the art of war as well as the spread of mass production.

The development of psychoanalysis as a discipline is conventionally attributed to Sigmund Freud in the early twentieth century, and the stream of consciousness as a literary genre, to the novels of James Joyce and the poetry of Gertrude Stein. Though the image of life as a moving line was crystallized in popular consciousness by the spidery trace of the first optical sound recordings, and further reinforced by early online imagery of speech communication by telephone and teletype, both the science of psychoanalysis and the literary concept of life, experienced as a perpetual transition rather than a steady state, connect with ideas current in the eighteenth century and reaching back to Augustine of Hippo in the late Roman era and Parmenides in ancient Greece. Voice recording, as distinct from voice synthesis by mechanical means, is a natural development of the invention of the stethoscope at the time of the Battle of Waterloo. The familiar doctor's stethoscope is an aid to diagnosing a patient's state of physical well-being by monitoring the body's internal rhythms. Physicians in the early nineteenth century studied language, music, and the physiology of speech as joint aspects of cultural and mental temperament, based on an established scientific belief in the relationship of physical characteristics (lungs, throat, tongue, teeth, and nasal cavity) to accent and ability to articulate speech, and associated intellectual performance, mental health, and tone of voice.

Sound recording as originally conceived was certainly intended as a speech diagnostic aid for patients with psychological issues. The theory conformed to long-established perceptions, in relation to women, the mentally unstable, and working classes, of speech as the involuntary expression of physiological and psychological conditioning, irrespective of whatever factual information a patient might have in mind to communicate. In March 2008 an original Scott-Koenig phonogram of a female voice (said to be the daughter of the inventor) reciting a couple of lines from the rhyme "Au Clair de la Lune" was successfully digitized and reproduced as an acoustic recording, showing a remarkable absence of distortion of the original voice. As a visual aid to voice analysis, however, the new equipment by Léon Scott and Rudolf Koenig quickly proved that voice recordings in graphic form could not be read spontaneously, lacked the distinguishing regularities of cardiac rhythms, and were too short-lived in duration to convey any reliable information about the subject's state of health. It soon became apparent that permanent engraving of longer samples of speech, in a medium allowing the recorded wave traces to be reproduced acoustically, would be the way forward.

The idea of recording body rhythms for diagnostic purposes would continue to circulate within the medical profession, leading to the cardiogram and electroencephalogram electronic life-support systems that have since become staple items of television medical soap operas. Self-regulating brain and body rhythms such as respiration and blood flow tend to oscillate in relatively stable patterns, whereas speech waveforms, being the expression of a naturally volatile individual will, are inherently unstable. Bodily systems tend toward regularity, so the role of the clinician is not to interpret a constantly changing signal, as with a voice recording, but to recognize a basic repertoire of waveforms and be on the alert for any significant deviation from a healthy waveform. The development of speech transcription technology was taken up by Alexander Graham Bell as a diagnostic aid for the hearing impaired. Its role as a diagnostic tool in mental health was taken over by a Freudian analyst sitting unobtrusively at the head of the analyst's couch, taking down a patient's free flowing prattle in real time in a form of scientific shorthand.

Spencer's conventional formulation of space as manifesting an ordered consciousness of coexistent points has features in common with the classical Greek definition of a line as a succession of points. That he describes these points as "ascertained by touch" (i.e., by *pointing*) suggests that in his mind they are not notional or theoretical locations but actual and tangible markers to be sought out by touching a line at different locations along its length. This is arguably no different from the Greeks describing the perimeter of a wheel as a line of studs. When a freely vibrating monochord or violin string is touched with the point of a feather along its length, however, one discovers a number of privileged points where the string spontaneously resonates at a tone corresponding to a harmonic. To the ancients, the existence of privileged locations implied a meaningful distinction between adjacent points expressing length in an additive process, and points expressing a hierarchy of divisions of a continuum, organized in a hierarchy of proportions. The idea that continuous space itself might be organized hierarchically and discontinuously, though not easy for a layperson to imagine, resonates in a curious way with Einsteinian relativity, of a space shaped and warped by the objects within it.

When we use touch to navigate in total darkness, we touch only one object at a time and have to build up a picture of the environment cumulatively, mapping the surface appearance of objects into memory. When Herbert Spencer speaks of space as "a coexistence of individual positions experienced by touch" the analogy of vision and touch is understandable in the sense that the eyes, working as a pair, focus clearly on only one object at a time, or part of an object, in the field of vision. Lacking the dimension of depth, paintings or movies—both of which are scanned onto a flat plane—allow the viewer to "read" foreground and background elements simultaneously as "a world in relation," even though it is a world reduced to two dimensions, like a printed page or television screen, a very different experience from viewing the real world in three dimensions. The comparison leads to a conclusion that in order to come to terms with "a world in relation" it is necessary to eliminate depth as a variable, and map an entire field onto a single plane, either in the form of a diagram or, more abstractly, as a text. A conventional text is read in continuous lines from left to right, and top to bottom, a specifically western mode of organization. A text displayed as a map, on the other hand, is less rigidly organized and encourages the eye to explore. Examples include Egyptian hieroglyphs, Roman numerals, Arabic and surrealist calligrammes, Chinese and Japanese pictograms, the layout of George Herbert's poem *Easter Wings*, the rebus, Mallarmé's poem *Un coup de dés*, futurist, dada, and concrete poetry, John Cage's mesostics, certain types of music notation, and the daily newspaper.

Hearing supersedes vision in the sense that all the information in a local sound field is constantly available, in depth, and in focus, from points in every direction. Music in sheet notation represents space and time in two dimensions. A line of music describes a movement in time, whereas a path or line of sight in a picture is a trajectory in space.

To demonstrate the connectedness of a path considered as a succession of points, of course you need a physical line, and a monochord is the device that comes immediately to hand. In the context of Pythagorean science of determining the harmonics of a stretched string, a distinction is made between points representing arbitrary divisions of a string, defined by shortening its sounding length with the aid of a moving bridge and organized in a linear sequence, and privileged divisions corresponding to natural modes of vibration revealed by touching the string lightly with a feather along a string without altering its tension or length. There is an ethereal disembodied quality to natural harmonics, a very different quality to the change of pitch effected by stopping the string against the fingerboard.

In seeking out the harmonics of a vibrating stretched string one is actually seeking out points of rest or nodes that when touched with the tip or feather edge of a quill isolate the harmonic while allowing the string to continue vibrating along its entire length. We begin with the first harmonic, located at the center of the string, then progress to the second, third, fourth and higher harmonics, noting their respective divisions on a paper laid under the string and over the soundboard. In the diagram, the fixed endpoints of the string are designated alpha and omega, and the nodes as zeros.

The reader will notice that the nodes form a pattern corresponding to the Pythagorean triangle of real numbers. I do not think this is mere coincidence, because the similarity of configuration between the formal triangular array of dots and the actual positions of successive nodes on a string suggests a number of fascinating ideas that would not otherwise arise, and that are likely to have attracted the thinkers of the day. According to the conventional literature, the triangular arrangement of dots is a mainly aesthetic convention with a number of interesting numerical implications (e.g., the series of natural numbers 1 + 2 + 3 + 4 + 5 etc.; the series 1, 3, 6, 10, 15 etc.; the series 1, 3, 6, 9, 12 etc.). But if there is a

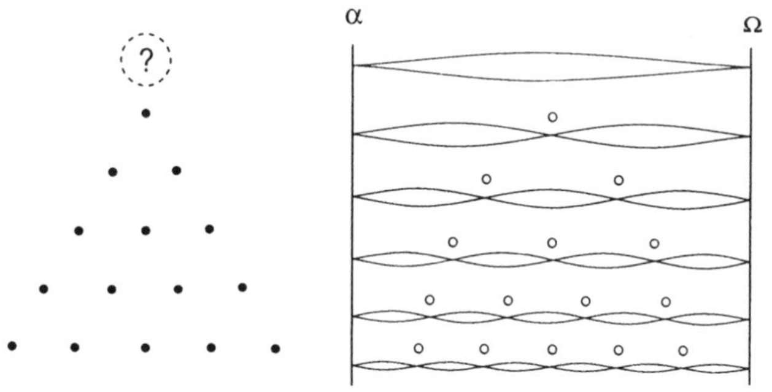

The Pythagorean triangle of real numbers compared to the harmonic nodes on a stretched string

meaning to be discovered in the correspondence between the triangular formation representing number and quantity, and the actual locations of successive harmonic divisions of a vibrating string, what it indicates is the undoubtedly provocative possibility of a connection between the intellectual laws of number and geometry, and the physical laws of time and motion.

In other words, the basis of a Theory of Everything. The triangular formation visualizes a hierarchy in numbers that just happens to correspond to the pattern of successive harmonic divisions of a stretched string, representing a physical hierarchy (of which the first harmonic is the strongest, and subsequent harmonics progressively weaker). Since the dots on the left correspond to sensible units such as counters or beads, whereas the harmonics on the right correspond to locations of *absence* of motion, or gaps in the flow of energy, there is already an intriguing symmetry suggesting itself between positive and negative objects, being and not-being, along with the intriguing promise of reconciling quantity and motion, digital and analogue, number and continuity in space and time.

A musician is intrigued by the triangle formation of these points, which have practical as well as mystical attributes in a musical sense. The rational number hierarchy 1, 2, 3, 4, 5, etc., with 1 as the first real number, is easily mapped onto the disposition of nodes at successive harmonic divisions of a stretched string. For a musician, however, the nodes are perceived not as independent points like frets on the fingerboard of a guitar, but rather as negative locations along a continuous string held in tension between fixed endpoints. For example, in the diagram above, dot 1 on the left triangle corresponds to the first harmonic on the right. But there is no corresponding dot to represent the fundamental vibration of the string. The idea that there may be a "number" higher than 1 is a mystery that would only occur to a musical observer theorizing number relations from a monochord. The non-existence of a higher number is explained in the trivial sense of there being no division and therefore no node to the string at the fundamental. In other words, the ultimate quantum or fundamental vibration corresponds to the totality of motion (or "living force") from which the ordinal numbers (harmonics) arise. To a musician the nodes (a term meaning "knots," by the way) refer only to locations *within* a string in vibration, between the two ends, and not to either extreme (the boundary conditions). In actual fact, though when touched at nodal points the string appears not to be vibrating, at those locations it is in fact vibrating not perpendicularly [out and back] but longitudinally [end to end].

The deeper and more interesting consideration arising from all of this is how or whether a Pythagorean may have read the diagram as indicating an unstatable or inexpressible value higher than one. The Greeks, we are told, had no concept of zero. And indeed, the missing quantum does not correspond to nothingness, but rather to everything. Nor, in string terms, is *everything* the same as *infinity*. It has limits: *alpha* and *omega*, a beginning and an ending. In turn, the "everything" of the fundamental vibration expresses not just the length of the string (which is arbitrary), but more particularly the opposing forces holding the string in tension and driving the vibration.

Paradoxically, it is only when the string is held in tension and in vibration that harmonic divisions can be located by ear. However, if the same locations are marked—for example, by tying a colored thread around the string at each nodal point—the string may be relaxed and tightened afresh, to any reasonable tension, and the same threads will indicate where the nodes are to be found, since their location does not vary with tension or mass of the string. (By contrast, the strings of present-day string theory are described in terms that make them seem loose and wobbly, like rubber bands, so that a musician wonders how, in the absence of any defining tension, different modes of vibration corresponding to distinct particles can possibly arise.) From the example of a stretched string it follows that measurement is only possible where tension already exists, and even then, only by the addition of excess force. By the same definition, a world "full" of measure and relation is a world already primed with radiant energy and momentum while existing "without form and void." William Blake's celebrated image of creation shows the globe being measured from on high with a giant pair of dividers. Readers of a religious disposition may find added theological implications in the fact that the *fundamental* vibration of a stretched string (between the two fixed compass points of alpha and omega) is itself *indivisible*, the first harmonic dividing the string in two, the second, in three, the third, in four, and so on.

The fundamental vibration of a string is the source and sum of movement of all its harmonic divisions, and is open to be construed as a metaphor for a prime mover in a religious sense. One might ask in that case what role or divine purpose is assigned to alpha and omega, the two fixed endpoints of the string, limits determining the fundamental and all harmonics, whose resistance to extension and lateral motion provides the feedback that divides the vibration symmetrically into standing waves of harmonic frequencies and equidistant locations of rest. Understanding the role of the endpoints of a string in tension is almost as challenging, in its own way, as theorizing about the beginning and endpoints of time in modern cosmological theory, and it leads among other ideas to the challenging hypothesis that *time* cannot be a division of itself, but is rather the totality of motion between the beginning and ending of creation, impelled by an external force, and maintained in tension. It implies a radical conception of a cosmology in constant vibration back and forth between the beginning and end of time, and the speed of light as the tension. The history of a single note is construed as a model of creation itself. Similar perceptions of time as a physical dimension, and human life as a vibration between fixed points, also underpin the message of Greek tragedy.

The concept of limiters in Greek science is clearly understandable in terms of fixed points of no motion, as in a stretched string, and in the sense of an object having a definable boundary, such as the surface of a sphere, or the outline of a human face or body.

However there are other forms of musical vibration that are "limited" in the sense of a monochord string or bowstring. As the name indicates, the panpipes are an early musical instrument associated with the god Pan, as the lyre is associated with Apollo. Pan is a creature of nature and the panpipes are hollow reeds of various lengths tied together in a trapezoid and played by blowing across their aligned top ends. The different lengths of pipe determine the extremities of the air columns contained within, and it is the air column that can be felt vibrating in such an instrument, rather than the substance that contains it.

The music of panpipes is a music of vibrating air pressure, and the mystery of a vibrating column of air is not just that the air is perceived as an absence or vapor rather than as a solid, but also in the fact that, unlike a string, a column of air in an open pipe is unbounded at either end. Since any higher pressure at each end of the pipe is sucked away by the surrounding atmosphere, the nodes or zones of maximum pressure and minimum movement are of necessity located within the tube. Ripples of higher pressure pass down the tube and are released at the other end, causing pulses of lower pressure to flow back up the tube at the same rate. Positive and negative pressure flows meet and interact to create a stable back and forth oscillation with zones of maximum pressure at equidistant points. The paradox is that the same effects of limitation occur for an air column unbounded at either end, as for a string secured at either end. The forces holding a string in tension are exerted longitudinally along the string, whereas those holding the air column in compression are exerted perpendicular to its axis of propagation.

DOTS ON A LINE

Ask whether the notes of music correspond to states or measurements of a process in continuous transition. There is no easy answer. It is difficult to imagine music without notes. Without notes there can be no harmony, nor any idea where to put one's fingers. On the other hand, to position notes on a gridwork of lines brings dimension and consistency to the otherwise intangible continuities of musical space and time, without which the complexities of western music would not be conceivable, let alone performable.

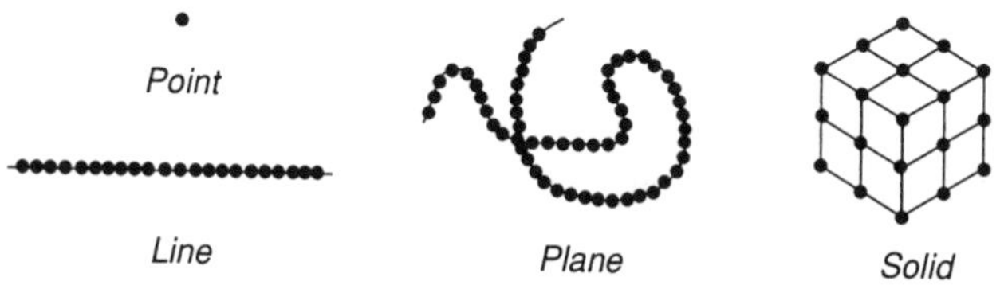

Music notation attracted a great deal of attention outside music for the very good reason that it introduced a standard procedure for representing dynamic processes in real time, including navigating in real space with the aid of a map. Without it we would not have graphs of economic or population dynamics, such as share prices in the financial pages. Although some scientific graphs are drawn to resemble organ pipes (to show precision), financial statistics are typically displayed as curves rather than successions of data points, though we accept that the curves are only approximations based on sample values taken at specific intervals. Descartes did not invent the graph: he adapted it from music notation. The rise and fall of share prices disguises the musical origins of data management while at the same time drawing attention to the reality of a process in continuous evolution. Representing share prices as a moving line assigns a prior truth value to the reader's perception of movement, and a lesser value to the sample data obtaining at any one moment. Indeed, it is only through representing successive data points as a line that the reader is helped to form an opinion on where the share price is likely to go next.

Western classical music is exactly the same, though confusion remains within the profession over the relative importance of notes as data points, and as transitional values. On one hand, "joining the dots" is the task of every musician: to express the line connecting the notes as a continuous flow. On the other hand, certain kinds of music depend on the treatment of note values as exact quantities to be delivered precisely as written. That kind of thinking is embodied in a range of western instruments, from the Greek harp and African xylophone to the piano and modern synthesizer, instruments designed to eliminate ambiguity and inflection in musical affairs and promote a perception of exact precision in the representation of musical movement. There is even a subtle distinction in classical diatonic music between melodies that move from one partial to another, like the notes of a natural trumpet, and melodies that flow continuously up and down the scale. In the former case, the trumpet melody expresses a sequential pattern of transitions between permitted energy states within the same stable tonality, so is essentially static in implication, whereas a movement up and down the scale incorporates transitional pitches that do not belong to a prevailing key, and therefore represents a dynamic movement or trend in tension relations that introduces passing distortions of an underlying tonality. The emotional distinction between the two types of melody is exactly and poignantly illustrated in alternating phrases of the solo melody of the slow movement of Mozart's concerto for clarinet in A.

The idea of a line being measurable in points of no length appears counterintuitive on the face of it. Especially for musicians, who are taught from an early age that scales and modes are like steps or ladders (*scala* means ladder, after all): aids for moving up and down in pitch, and essentially discontinuous, just as walking at ground level is movement by discrete steps and not continuous motion like a wheel (or indeed, a snake). Young musicians are aware from an early age of the importance of singing and playing *in tune*, which means by default that the notes of a scale are particular locations in a continuum of pitch, that finding the right pitch is a matter of making the right choice, and in consequence that there is an indefinite number of wrong notes to be avoided. Since wrong notes are more numerous and easy to find than correct notes, we should perhaps be surprised that the *necessary* existence of wrong notes as locations "between the notes" should ever be regarded as unthinkable, along with the idea of a continuum of pitch. A tendency to avoid gliding tones and rising or falling inflected tones is a peculiar feature of western classical music, almost certainly related to its origin in ratio and number, and the values attached to exact quality and proportion. Many nonwestern cultures recognize gliding, wavering, and bending tones as expressive devices and as representations of bending in nature.

A disdain for transitional tones and glissandi connects, it seems to me, with a historic perception of the notes of the musical scale as rational numbers. An ongoing commitment to the conception of a line as a sequence of points not only emerges in Herbert Spencer's image of continuity in a string of musical notes or rosary beads, but is seemingly confirmed by the capture of living motion on film as a succession of instantaneous stills.

Aristotle attributed the phrase "all things are number" to the Pythagoreans implying a belief that the universe and everything in it could be expressed in terms of exact quantities. More recently Professor Huffman interprets Philolaus as declaring in significantly different terms that "Nature in the world-order is fitted together out of *limiters* and *unlimiteds*, both the world-order as a whole and everything within it."[4] If we understand limiters and unlimiteds as not quantities but boundaries and divisions then this new definition accords with a conception of the world in the image of a stretched string, which is a fascinating musical concept. The limiters in that case are the fixed endpoints, alpha and omega, at which the string is held in tension, along with the subsidiary nodal points, where motion is suppressed, which divide the string into equal vibrating segments. The *unlimiteds* in turn embrace noncomputable relations, such as π and the square root of 2 or 3, that account for cyclical motion, and also the nonquantifiable behavior of the string at extremes of motion (the antinodes). The term *limiters* applies to the physical terminations of a tube or string that define its length and associated frequency of vibration, and *unlimiteds* to the latent energies holding the string or air column in tension, as well as the impulsive energies stirring them into audible motion. The nodal points of a stretched string are determined to be independent of the tension at which the string is held, or the force with which it is set in motion, energies strictly unquantifiable in relation to the frequency of oscillation, and affecting only the amplitude of vibration.

So when, for example, we describe a woodwind as a clarinet in A, we are identifying it as an instrument of a certain length and bore that sounds a scale of pitches based on a fundamental wavelength of A. They are the limiting conditions describing the instrument. These limiting conditions are only present to hearing, however, when the instrument is played by blowing into it and introducing the non-quantifiable (i.e., "unlimited") element of force necessary to make it sound. Nothing is measurable that does not have limits, and therefore what is measured is actually resistance. For anything to have length, size, elapsed time, area, latent tension etc. involves setting boundaries. With fixed boundaries comes resistance, but again, only when they are pushed by the introduction of excess energy or force, which brings us back to Herbert Spencer's equation of touch and resistance (and perhaps even an intimation of the uncertainty arising from the act of measuring itself).

The musical and acoustical analogy allows us to distinguish creation on one level as structures potentially capable of sound (though not sounding), on another level as structures in vibration (motivated by some external force), and both of the above from absence of structure (the void). In doing so we make a further distinction between latent energy, retained in a musical instrument that is in tune but not being played, from applied energy which is introduced by the act of playing and is lost as radiation. The concept of a creation existing in potential and only intermittently manifest to the senses (or "tangible" in Spencer's term), is central to acoustic experience, but alien to visual experience, which takes continuity of being largely for granted.

Notes

1. Herbert Spencer, *A System of Synthetic Philosophy.* Vol. I. 5th rev. edn. London: Williams & Norgate, 1884, 160.
2. Alfred N. Whitehead, *Science in the Modern World.* Cambridge: Cambridge University Press, 1926, 61.
3. Herbert Spencer, *A System of Synthetic Philosophy* I, 160–64.
4. Carl A. Huffman, *Philolaus of Croton, Pythagorean and Presocratic.* Cambridge: Cambridge University Press, 1993, 58.

SIX

WHEELS

> Looking back over the long struggle to make the concepts of *real number*, *continuity*, *limit*, and *infinity* precise and consistently usable in mathematics, we see that Zeno and Eudoxus were not so far in time from Weierstrass, Dedekind, and Cantor as the twenty-four or twenty-five centuries which separate modern Germany from ancient Greece might seem to imply.[1]
>
> E. T. BELL

The great imponderables of infinity, continuity, real numbers, and limit are among the lessons of childhood that emerge from playing with familiar toys: among them, the spinning top, the wheel, the pendulum, and the bow. These simple objects behave in mysterious ways. Defying reason, yet they work. The principles of motion and number arising from these devices come together in the monochord, a single-string musical instrument employed as a teaching aid by the School of Pythagoras, that as the sonometer remained an item of laboratory equipment until well into the twentieth century.

Take a pencil and stand it on its point, and it will fall over. Spin the pencil and it may stay upright for a moment, but it will still fall over. Fit a disc to the pencil and spin it, and everything changes: you have a spinning top. The pencil shaped axis of a spinning top remains upright on its point. The mass and spin of the spinning disc give stability so that the pencil can defy gravity and remain standing. A spinning top stays upright "because it does not know where to fall down"—or rather, because falling down means to fall in one place, and a rotating object is unable to fall down in more than one place at once. A spinning top is not unbalanced in just one direction but unstable in every direction. The instabilities cancel out. If the base of the pencil is rounded, the top will wander randomly across the table, but if the pencil has a strong and sharp point it will tend to spin in one place, where its weight is concentrated on a single point. The message of a spinning top is that stability in the vertical dimension can be obtained by adding mass and spin in another two dimensions (the plane of the horizontal). When the spinning top is elevated to the status of a gyroscope, however, and is enclosed in a casket and at liberty to rotate in any direction, its orientation tends to remain constant despite movements of the external structure in which it is carried, such as a boat or airplane. In a mysterious way its spin orientation becomes absolute. This sends a message about stability. We regard a stable object, such as a load on a cart, as one that stays in place when the cart begins to move, and a load falling off the back of a cart once it began to move as unstable or insecure. In fact, a load will always tend to fall off a moving cart unless it is strapped down or otherwise held in place. The tendency for a load to fall off a moving cart is in fact a tendency for it to remain in the same place, the "same place" being in relation to the ground rather than the cart. The real meaning of stability is inertia, or resistance to movement, a term that takes the mass of the object into account.

A child learning to walk does not have to read books about mass or inertia, but is all the same instinctively having to solve the same universal equations that govern a spinning top, in order to acquire mobility of a much more complicated kind. A small child cannot rely on an air sac, like a fish, or a spinning disc like a tutu around the diaphragm, to stay upright. What a child does have is a middle ear, a motion sensor in three dimensions and a natural balancing aid that can be trained to orchestrate a constant interplay of muscles in response to involuntary tendencies of the body to fall forward, or sit down. In industry, the use of a gyrostat governor to maintain a rotary engine in operation at a constant optimum speed is an idea taken from eighteenth-century watchmaking and scaled up during the industrial revolution to regulate heavy machinery. The rather more radical idea of designing structures that are naturally unstable at rest and have to be constantly corrected by an overseeing intelligence in order to remain under control may have started with the bicycle in 1819 but came to fruition in the electronic age. Because its shape, designed to be undetectable by radar, is aerodynamically inefficient, a stealth fighter is impossible to fly without computer assistance. The argument for dynamic instability in military aircraft is that an unstable platform, like a spinning top, is apt to tumble in a number of directions at any moment, instead of being forced by its own aerodynamics to follow a predictable trajectory that can be easily tracked by an enemy missile. Such a vehicle is better adapted to take evasive action in response to any threat. The tradeoff of constant instability is freedom to move in any direction, to change direction on impulse, and evade interception. Learning to control and exploit a natural instability is a source of primal pleasure and delight among young animals of any species. Once they learn to walk, youngsters run, chase, bound, and play. The more a child masters the art of moving on two legs, the more freedom it has to explore its surroundings.

Schoenberg is alluding to instability when he distinguishes a melody from a theme. A complete melody is simply a datum: it has no momentum of its own, it is simply a pathway to be traversed. A melody takes energy but does not generate any energy. A theme is necessarily incomplete. It is asymmetrical, like the "dit-dit-dit-dah" theme of Beethoven's Fifth Symphony. It demands a response, but is open not just to one but a whole variety of responses (it can fall in many different directions). The more laid-back refrain of Debussy's rondeau *L'Après-midi d'un Faune*, drifting downward, then up, is presented in the same way, as a gust of wind at liberty to blow in any direction it chooses. Stravinsky transforms Debussy's theme into a remote wake-up call in *Le Sacre du Printemps* stirring the primeval world into life. Like the wobbly legs of a child learning to stand, the natural unsteadiness of a theme generates forward movement: not because of a need to move in a particular direction, but because forward motion eliminates the imbalance of standing still. As a bonus, in addition to dynamic stability, forward motion introduces the moving child or melody to a world of larger possibilities, including options of choosing where to go, and changing direction.

Bach's Brandenburg concertos are prime examples of mechanical impulsion. The dotted rhythms of a French overture imitate the regular swing of a pendulum rather than the ticking of a pocket watch. The keyboard dance suites of baroque music are inquiries into the different patterns of human movement embodied in dance, but translated to keyboard instruments that have no inherent sense of flow or connection, relying instead on the gesture of the player to move forward and hang together.

In ballet the pirouette is an interesting technical device transforming a living human being into a spinning top. The British humorist Gerard Hoffnung famously portrayed a haughty prima ballerina performing a pirouette and drilling herself into the stage, ending up bemused, stuck fast, and surrounded by wood dust and shavings. In effect the cartoon asked why anybody would be interested in a dancer of high culture and technical ability spinning in one place, what aesthetic value a pirouette may command, and what merit might attach to being able to execute it. The answer is that ballet in the abstract is an art of balance and control, allied to a natural tendency to instability combined with exceptional physical fitness. For a dancer to be able to move erratically and at speed, *and* spin like a top, are admirable achievements: in a physical sense, since the whole weight of the body is concentrated on the point of one foot; in a balance sense, because the dancer has to be able to control the speed of rotation without succumbing to dizziness (requiring skill in head movement control); and intellectually because in a pirouette the normally fluid dynamics of narrative movement in ballet—telling a story in lifts, leaps, turns etc.—are stripped away to expose the abstract laws and bare mechanics of continuous motion in space. Unlike a whirling dervish, or tarantella, rites of rotation dedicated to the mind-altering, ecstatic, or therapeutic experiences of dizziness, the pirouette transforms a leading dancer of either sex from a person into a compass point or spinning top, and the character of ballet from human romance to outwardly irrational behavior of no narrative value. A pirouette is simply a reminder that the art of movement, even among human beings having free will, is ultimately governed by universal laws. The eighteenth-century European culture of ballet responsible for introducing the pirouette was looking beyond athletic prowess to the science of motion control, just as the original Olympians cultivated track racing and javelin throwing, not just as expressions of strength and endurance, but as manifestations of superior grace and efficiency in movement, qualities usually interpreted as aspects of beauty or strength, but to a connoisseur the purest embodiments of natural law.

Objects able to move of their own accord do so on a presumption of instability, and those that move in a predictable manner, as naturally unstable items subject to internal or external direction. Individual unpredictability of action is commensurate with freedom of choice, of which erratic behavior can be understood as either a sign (of constantly changing one's mind) or a symptom (e.g., of having had too much to drink). In normal life things do not move of their own accord, but stay in one place. Movement presupposes intention, and also resistance to staying in one place. To the extent that the dynamics of a behavior are internally consistent, an intention can be assigned to it and described in general terms. For music it is the same. The name assigned to the common features of a dynamic system—say, a human being—in constant movement, is an *emotion*. In music the terms *mode* or *key* allude to character and freedom of movement, *tempo* to the unit of change (or degree of instability), and *rhythm* the quality of movement. Human behavior is logically unpredictable from one moment to the next, and functionally predictable to the extent that human actions are self-evidently goal-directed. Goal-directed activity tends to energy-efficiency leading to cyclical repetition and economy of gesture. Completely random or purposeless activity is pathological behavior in both the human and the animal kingdom. Having no goal, random actions waste energy, and tend to self-destruction and exhaustion. Such behavior is routinely considered immoral.

In addition to the practical advantages of efficiency and economy in action, there is thus a moral component to acquiring and maintaining good posture and balance. To exhibit self-control is a virtue for the simple reason that it allows a person to perform other useful actions. The same applies to intellectual activity. For a philosopher or mathematician, problem-solving may involve balancing the two halves of an equation, or syllogism. Solving a problem is pleasurable in itself and raises the issue of continuity of being allowing for a *progression* or change of habits of thinking from an earlier confusion of unresolved ideas into a new and stable condition of harmony, clarity, and pattern. For a philosopher to decide whether to rate the solving of a problem as an instantaneous epiphany, or alternatively as a product of direction toward a particular goal in intellectual space, may be a difficult issue. In classical logic a syllogism is revelatory but not an alteration: it expresses a truth that is already implicit in the statement of its terms, rather than a change in the terms themselves. This idea of the nature of reality as unchanging is a tenet of religious belief. It is among the ironies of history that Galileo's offense against the ecclesiastical authorities arose directly as a consequence of his scientific interest in continuity of movement. Readers of Descartes are invited to construe the observation "I think, therefore I am" as a statement of apposition rather than causation, since the act of thinking and the state of being are supposed to coincide, each buttressing the other. Solving a problem, or new discovery, on the other hand, is open to consideration as an example of intellectual progression or change of state, since finding a solution may also entail an intention to find it (by virtue of recognition of the solution as an answer)—even though by definition the answer is previously unknown and thus cannot have been anticipated.

Live and mechanical actions tend to differ in predictability. The cultivated followers of Descartes believed that freedom of action was an intellectual trait unavailable to the working classes and the animal kingdom, who were considered little more than animated machines. The same ideas continue to influence marketing strategy in the present. Accordingly, the behavior of a predator or consumer is defined by habit-forming appetites directed to a limited number of goals; drives that in the longer term can be seen to follow predictable patterns and routines. In human society the creation and marketing of addictive or appetite-driven behaviors can lead to socially and physiologically undesirable consequences, even when defended on the ground that routine in the execution of everyday tasks is healthy and tends to promote longevity. A healthy individual whose life is organized in cycles of activity is usually better equipped to resist and deal with external influences that may otherwise represent a threat. The same drama translates in music to a tension between a tendency toward meeting and accommodating new information, and resistance to disruption by unpredictable and destabilizing forces. Twentieth-century minimalist music evokes mindless stability and reliance on mechanical processes, whereas improvised or chance music draws attention to the impulsive and unpredictable elements in life, and their management.

Spinning tops and other such familiar devices are of interest to scientists and musicians first of all, in what their behavior appears to tell us of the way the world works; second, in how the same principles of dynamic self-regulation are addressed in the abstract terms of art, philosophy, and elsewhere; and third, how the same concepts may be hidden in myth, allegory, popular belief, and cultural practice. Music is both part of that allegorical resource, as well as a direct expression of the original science.

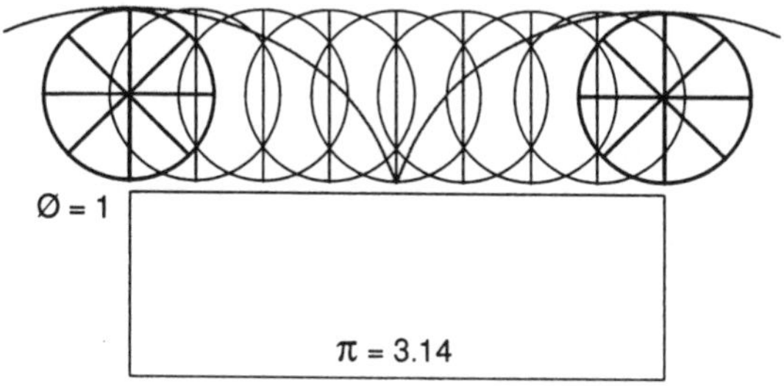

A cycloid traces the movement of a point on the circumference of a wheel

THE IMPOSSIBLE WHEEL

"If the tire don't grip, the wheel will slip." Getting stuck can be a messy business. A drive wheel that loses traction rotates aimlessly and sprays mud in all directions. A wheel is a rotating structure attached to a cart that allows an otherwise inert load to be moved by reducing its area of contact with the ground to a point where its relationship with the ground becomes unstable. As a result, when sufficient energy is applied the load on a wheeled vehicle can be moved along the ground.

Inventing the wheel is one thing. Explaining the behavior of a wheel in motion is something else. The wheel could never have been invented by a philosopher. The concept is much too difficult. It begs too many questions. Fortunately inventing the wheel, as of the spinning top, was left to practical people to achieve by trial and error from observation of spinning and wheeling processes in nature, long before intelligent people got into the act to cast doubt on whether any of it was actually possible.

Rotating or cyclical processes are everywhere in nature, from the movement of the sun and stars in the sky, to a Swiss cheese rolling down a slope, or a sycamore seed spinning as it glides to earth. There is a relationship between the perfect roundness of a ball, or the circularity of a spinning weight at the end of a sling, and their predictability of motion. The tick of a clock is different from the flow of sand in an hour-glass. The former divides time into equal units, the latter expresses it as a continuous stream of countless particles. In practice objects that move in the real world do so with less than complete regularity. Surfaces are never perfectly frictionless, and natural objects seldom totally symmetrical. That the movements of celestial objects in the night sky are absolutely predictable gives them ideal, divine status by comparison with objects in the material world. A wheel is a human prototype of continuous motion that aspires to the ideal smoothness and regularity of motion of the orbiting sun and moon. The word *divine* carries the implication of predictable as well as godlike behavior. The sometimes backward (epicyclic) motion of the outer planets led them to be assigned human traits of willfulness or disobedience, a fate also reserved for unpredictable elements on earth.

Rationalizing the measurements and explaining the motion of a wheel are intellectual tasks out of which the classic definition of a continuum as a succession of points—or in music, a succession of notes—can be seen to have emerged. As a wheel converts stepwise motion to continuous motion, so the execution of a musical performance converts a succession of data points into an impression of continuous movement, a line of melody.

> Aristotle's distinctions between motion up, down, and in a circle, and between natural and violent motion, were based on a direct classification of what bodies are actually seen to do. . . . The "natures" that were supposed to be the explanatory sources of the behaviour of different things were characterized simply by a direct description of what things actually did. . . . Medieval "Platonists" looked, like Galileo, for explanations not in immediate experience but in theoretical concepts at a remove from it and capable of quantification.[2]

When a wheelbarrow is pushed from point to point, outwardly there is no question that both the load and the person pushing it

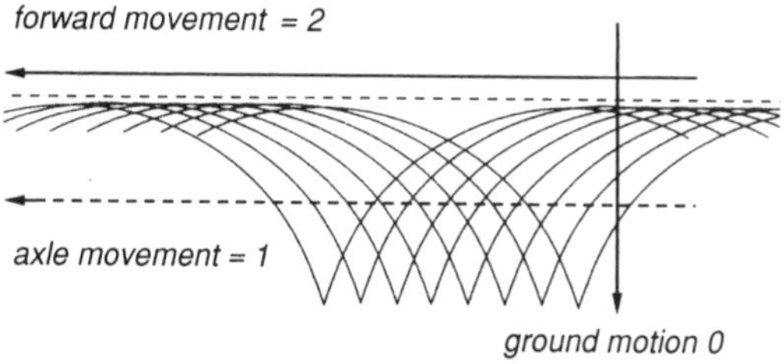

Every point on the circumference of a rotating wheel is moving vertically at the moment of contact with the ground

cover the same distance in the same time, or that both move continuously through space, despite the fact that the barrow is moved on a wheel that is in continuous contact with the ground, whereas the human being progresses in stepwise motion, on alternate feet, having only intermittent contact with the ground. For most people there is a degree of commensurability of wheels and feet. Whether continuous motion involves an infinite number of infinitely small steps, or a whole number of measurable steps, is an esoteric, not to mention difficult and controversial question that hinges on how displacement in space is defined, and thus how it is measured. The ancients believed in a necessarily harmonious relationship between the diameter and circumference of a wheel. As the circle is an image of divine perfection, they were concerned to reconcile the measurements of the circumference of a wheel and its diameter. They ran their own tests, commissioned their own wheels and rolled them on soft ground with studs inserted into the rim to leave a line of impressions that could be counted and the distance between them measured. Their aim was to divide the length of the circumference into the lowest common denominator of units which also measured the diameter of the wheel, and thus arrive at a ratio of diameter to circumference. To their great chagrin, it did not work out that way. The formula proved to be "irrational," the ratio unknowable. No matter how many studs were fitted around the circumference of a wheel, and how small the unit of measurement between them, the diameter of the wheel could never be measured with complete accuracy to a whole number of the same units. This was a paradox.

From experiments summarized, among others, by Aristotle,

another paradox came to light. It seemed that in order for the stud on the rim to make a distinct impression on the ground—and for the wheel not to be slipping at the point of contact with the ground—the stud would have to be moving not in a forward direction, but straight up and down. On the surface this is highly counterintuitive. As the diagram shows, when a wheel rolls along the ground the axle and cart move forward relative to the ground at the average speed of every point on the circumference. On closer inspection, however, we see that points on the upper rim of the wheel are moving forward at twice the speed of the axle, whereas points opposite on the lower rim at the moment of contact with the ground are moving *not at all*. To an observer, furthermore, each point on the wheel rim executes a similar curve consisting of an acceleration and a retardation between successive points of contact with the ground; thus each point represented by a stud on the circumference travels a considerably *greater* distance in each rotation than the distance between successive impressions left by the same stud on the ground.

When the circumference of a wheel is viewed as a succession of points and not as a closed surface in continuous motion, the paradoxical inference arises of parts of the circumference of the wheel moving at different speeds relative to one another and in relation to the ground. Medieval scholars wondered how to account for a solid object like a wheel to be simultaneously moving and not moving, or for parts of the wheel to be varying in speed even though the wheel itself was a palpably solid object moving at constant speed. In the course of rotating about a common axis, opposite points on the circumference of a disc move in contrary motion, points on the lower moving backward, and on the upper rim forward relative to the axle. Hence every point in contact with the ground, relative to the ground, at the moment of contact with the ground, is by definition motionless.

Cyclical processes in nature tend to involve noncomputable numbers. Like the circumference of a wheel, the duration of the cycle of a calendar year is also an irrational number, not divisible into a whole number of days, or even hours. One can imagine the Greeks drawing a parallel between rationalizing rotational motion at ground level and in the heavens. Relics of Greek scientific

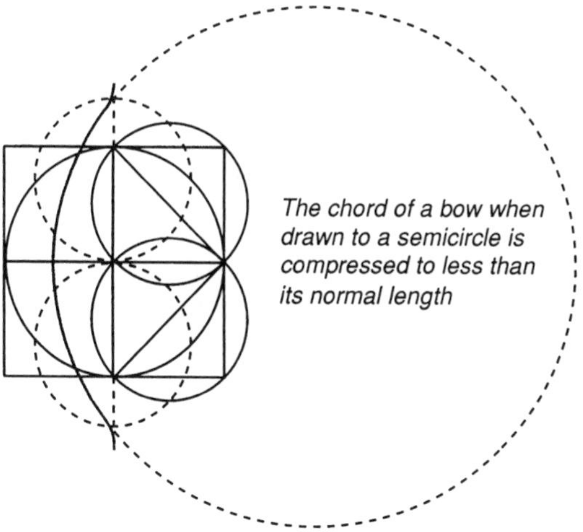

method survive today in simple musical instruments and children's toys, but it may be that the Pythagoreans came to abandon the idea of seeking a connection between abstract knowledge and direct experience as intellectually insuperable, morally suspect, or at least politically unsafe; and it is interesting to see the same problems recurring in medieval Europe more than a thousand years later. By then of course the purpose of scientific knowledge had altered from explaining the world in terms of direct experience, from experimenting with solid objects such as wheels and musical instruments, to constructing theoretical models of a idealized universe in terms reconcilable with religious doctrine.

The chord of a bow when drawn to a semicircle is compressed to less than its normal length

That medieval scholars were less interested in explaining the real world of objects in motion, and more interested in abstract essences, does not mean they avoided musical experimentation using the pipe organ, recorders, or viols as experimental devices for observing the interaction of tones of different frequency. Sound is among the most tenuous of realities, and musical sound even rarer. Pipe organists have some justification for insisting that the organ is the king of instruments, even though they fail to explain why such a marvel was created in the first place, which if not for musical purposes would necessarily have involved motion studies.

The science of motion developed at Oxford in the fourteenth century by Thomas Brawardine and his followers, and by Nicole Oresme in Paris, attempted to address the issue of reconciling uniform and intermittent motion, otherwise known as instantaneous velocity and acceleration, without reference to the wheel, the pendulum, or the vibrating string. Instead they devised occult terms *quality* and *quantity* for movement, *uniform* for continuous or sinusoidal motion, *difform* for cycloid motion, and *longitude*, *latitude*, and *extension* for additional dimensions.

> The "intensity" or "latitude" of a form, for example velocity, changed in relation to an invariable form known as the "extension" or "longitude," such as distance or time. Velocity was said to be "uniform" when equal distances were covered in equal successive intervals of time, and "difform" when unequal distances were covered as in accelerated or retarded motion. . . .
>
> In Paris Nicole Oresme represented the "extension" of time by a horizontal straight line and the intensity of velocity at each instant by a perpendicular raised at a corresponding point. The height of the perpendicular represented the intensity or "quality" of a velocity, whereas the area of the whole figure . . . was its "quantity" or "total" velocity.[3]

These terms are at some remove from the Greeks' hands-on study of objects in motion, but look ahead nevertheless to the development of a graphic notation for motion in space. Such descriptions would eventually lead to the graphic conventions of seventeenth-century astronomy, and just as explicitly to the development of a *music notation* suitable for describing images of continuous motion in terms of a succession of points on a graph that are equally definable as momentary steady states. Every note in a melody corresponds to a location, but at the same time the location of an individual melody note in pitch and time implies neither movement nor direction. The imagery of motion available to music notation is based on relationships in time and space, and not on quantity or value. That individual notes in a melody lack inherent momentum, and in principle can go up, or down, or anywhere, is explained as a necessary consequence of cyclical motion, in that each data point, whether a musical note or the observed location of a prominent star, is unmoving at the point and moment of contact with the observer's field of reference.

All of a sudden Parmenides' contention that movement is an

illusion begins to make sense, since a wheeled vehicle appears to move in relation to the ground, and yet in order for it to move and not slip, each successive point on the wheel in contact with the ground is required not to be moving. (It could also mean that Parmenides' use of the term *illusion* might be better translated as *imaginary* in the sense of "an imaginary number.")

Since it is not strictly measurable, another complication arises as to whether the circumference of a wheel of any size is thus of indefinite length, and perhaps even infinite length. Again, the issue comes down to what is implied by "length." For length to have significance, it has to be measurable. To the ancients, the distance traveled by a wheeled vehicle is measured in paces or wheel units, each unit corresponding to the distance covered in one rotation. To calculate linear distance in terms of rotations of the circumference of the wheel (already a noncomputable ratio) is strictly irrational since the actual distance covered by each point on the circumference of the wheel is more than the distance covered on the ground. Rationally, the track left on the ground by a rotating wheel is the only way the movement in space of the axis, representing the vehicle, can be measured, since a measurement is invariably in relation to an external frame of reference, in this case the ground, which is assumed to be flat. But because the distance traveled by a stud on the circumference is greater than the distance between successive points of contact of the same stud on the ground, the ground distance cannot logically be said to correspond either to the path taken by the stud or indeed, to the movement of the vehicle. And since a wheel track is of indefinite length, it is at least arguable that the circumference of a wheel, being endless, is also of indefinite, and potentially infinite length.

Why does this matter? Why is it so confusing? Because there is a clear and obvious analogy between wheel motion and periodic events (periodic, that is, in relation to life in general) like walking, or the phases of the moon, the tides, and seasons (recurrent events assumed to be the intermittent expressions of continuous processes in nature). Not for nothing are the seven ages of human life depicted as a cycloid between fixed points of birth and death consisting of an acceleration peaking at maturity and followed by a decline. As the circumference of a wheel, so too the span of an individual life cannot be exactly predicted from its pace of forward motion. We cannot tell from the periodic motion of the planets and stars how long they will continue to move in their orbits. We cannot tell from the motion of a vibrating string (its frequency of vibration) how long a tone will continue to sound. The ancients' conflation of musical vibration with the motion of the celestial spheres is significant because the science of musical acoustics is grounded in the study of periodic motion, and the laws of music are in principle laws of relationship and not quantity. The steady tone of a musical instrument is a cyclical event of fixed frequency, a periodicity related in turn, among other considerations, to *two* fixed lengths: the string or pipe length (which is visible and material) and the wavelength (which is invisible and immaterial), in addition to mass and tension (of a string) or pressure and density (of an air column). While the frequency of a plucked string is a cyclical event having extension in time, the frequency in itself is no indication of how long the tone will last.

The cycloid described by each point on the circumference of the wheel can be seen to occupy a rectangle the height of which is the diameter of the wheel, and π, the length of the circumference, approximately 3.14 times the diameter, an irrational number. We see that the ratio of diameter to circumference is irrational, thus unresolvable. This is not good. If wheel rotation is cyclical in a universal sense it is reasonable to anticipate an analogous inharmonicity of motion in related cyclical events such as the vibration of a string. The implications of inharmonicity in the motion of the celestial spheres are deeply alarming, suggesting that the universe is governed by laws that are not only dynamically unstable but irrational in principle.

When the properties of wheel motion are compared to those of of a stretched string in vibration, the same relationships obtain:

1. The length of a cycle describes the vertical back and forth motion of a point on the circumference between successive points of rest, or contact with the ground. Likewise the endpoints of a vibrating string are points of rest that determine the frequency of vibration, the vibration at any intermediate point moving perpendicular to the line of rest.

2. The greater movement is the length of a cycle: i.e., in each case the fundamental vibration is equivalent to the least distance between the two endpoints.
3. At a point of maximum vibration midway between the two endpoints (the midpoint of the cycloid, or of the vibrating string), the associated movement (velocity, frequency) is doubled.

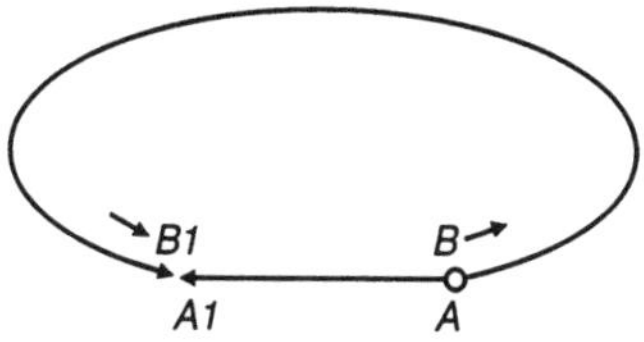

The twins paradox in a wheel: A moving with the axle, B on the circumference

(An ingenious medieval flight of fancy based on an assumption that the fundamental frequency of a vibrating string corresponds to the lowest common denominator of all possible movements of the string between its fixed endpoints, and thereby to the shortest movement, or direct line, of a wheel track between successive stud marks. If so, the frequency of the first harmonic, at the midpoint of the string, an octave higher, is analogous to the forward speed at the midpoint of the cycloid—the upper rim of the moving wheel—moving twice as fast as the wheel as a whole.)

In 1851 Foucault demonstrated that a pendulum of substantial length and mass continued to oscillate in a fixed direction relative to the celestial spheres while the earth rotated beneath it. A decade later, Herbert Spencer was still unable to explain pendulum motion, that is, how a movement could be both continuous and intermittent at once: a cycle of acceleration and deceleration between points of apparent rest. (It is explained overleaf as continuous motion in four dimensions of which two are reduced to zero.)

In the early twentieth century Albert Einstein returned to the paradox of relative motion of points at the center and circumference of a wheel. Einstein's relativistic arguments are peppered with fashionable modern imagery of elevators, trains, wind up gramophones, and airplanes. The twins paradox compares the experience of a person on earth, whose frame of reference is constant, like the center of the wheel, with an identical twin who travels away from

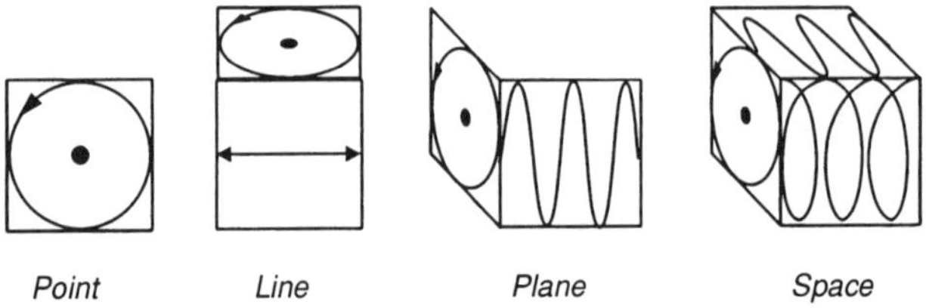

The same rotation in a space of 0, 1, 2, and 3 dimensions (plus time)

the earth, accelerating to a velocity close to the speed of light, then decelerating and returning to earth to discover that his earth twin is considerably older than himself. The traveling twin has experienced a dilation of time, and slowing-down of the ageing process, in consequence of taking the longer route involving an acceleration and deceleration, in comparison to his brother, whose frame of reference has remained constant. This could be construed as saying that time moves more slowly for the point on the circumference of the wheel in relation to the point in the center, on the basis that it travels a greater distance in the same time period as a point on the axle. Even if that were shown to be true—as indeed a number of experiments involving astronauts and twin clocks tend to endorse such a conclusion—such a proposition appears nevertheless to sidestep the issue of accounting for the continuous motion of the wheel *as a whole* as an accumulation of discontinuous motions of every point on its circumference.

From drawing circles with a string or compass, the ancients understood the radius as defining two boundaries of a circle, one at the center (absence of motion), the other at the limit of extension in every direction (maximum acceleration). Whether they believed or not that the dimensions of a perfect shape like a circle ought in principle to conform to a simple ratio, they already knew that the length and frequency of a vibrating string and the cyclical motions of its harmonic vibrations did actually conform to simple ratios.

As illustrated earlier, when the cycloids of successive points on the circumference of a rolling wheel are plotted onto a graph, the resulting diagram of rotational motion resolves into a succession of discrete points at ground level, tending toward a continuous line at the upper extreme. The merging of discrete points into a continuous line goes some way toward validating music notation as the discontinuous expression of continuous motion or intention, and also to explaining the various modes of a vibrating string as locations in a continuum of vibration. How the shift in perception is made from considering the line as a succession of discrete points to calculating its behavior as a continuum is clearly relevant to plotting the movement of the planets in their orbits on the basis of observed changes in position from one night to the next over a period of time. Mariners and astronomers alike from Ptolemaus to Galileo, Kepler, Huygens, and Newton based their calculations of planetary motion on an implied continuity of momentum between successive observations. A significant complication of their joint endeavors was the inconstancy of planetary epicycles appearing to contradict the principle of continuous rotary motion.

Einstein's twins paradox, and the puzzle of accounting for the movement of a wheel as a continuum of overlapping accelerations and retardations of an infinity of points on the circumference, surface yet gain in the intellectual sleight of hand of Richard Feynman's sum over histories, according to which a particle traveling between two points may take an infinite number of routes. This is the physicist's shorthand way of accounting for the arrival at endpoint B of a hypothetical particle journeying from point A, as a necessary consequence of it having started its journey at point A. On the one hand, the theoretically infinite possibility of movement of the invisible particle resembles the "sum over histories" average of the distance traveled by an infinite number of points at the circumference of the wheel. On the other hand, it may also be analogous to defining the string of a musical instrument as vibrating simultaneously in every possible mode between two endpoints, while pretending that the endpoints are completely arbitrary and have no influence on the movements between them.

Understanding the wheel, and how rotational motion may be translated to horizontal or vertical (piston) motion, is crucial to the industrial revolution in mechanical engineering, beginning with mechanical timekeeping. The conversion of rotation to frequency of vibration entails continuity and consistency of resistance, translating into material qualities. When loose objects such as pebbles are placed on the upper rim of a freely rotating wheel, they are projected forward with force like a missile from a slingshot. Objects such as a bowstring or straightedge, when held against a moving wheel rim, are subject to friction audible as a screeching or rasping sound, giving rise, in instances where the speed and pressure are continuous, to a tone of constant pitch. In the action of playing a violin, a rosined bow moving at right angles across a string initiates a cyclical movement along the length of the string, perpendicular to the direction of bow motion, and made audible by cavity resonance as a musical tone. Rotational friction is the secret of grindstones and also the hurdy-gurdy, a distant relative of the violin in which the external bow moving across the string is replaced by an internal abrasive disc.

That a vibrating string is in continuous oscillatory motion is indicated first, by the fact that it produces a tone of constant pitch, and second, by the fact that the tone is prolonged. That a tone is constant and prolonged shows that its movement is distributed and organized along the string's entire length between two fixed points, and not confined to the point where it is initially agitated. Thus the musical tone of a vibrating string is evidence of time and motion as well as of continuity of line (the physical string). After plucking the string, the burst of excess energy introduced at a single point is propagated (extended) and reflected along its entire length. Extension is understood in a technical sense as accounting for continuity of movement by introducing additional dimensions, in this case exciting a one-dimensional string at rest into vibrating in three dimensions, with time as the fourth.

The Pythagoreans' use of the monochord can be understood as a scientific device for quantifying, and ultimately perfecting, the formula for conversion of force in a longbow. The bow is a tension mechanism for converting impulsive or chaotic motion to orderly motion, with the difference that the excess energy of drawing the bow is converted entirely to propulsive motion in a forward direction, in a manner analogous to a wheel. The Greeks distinguished an *alteration* (linear motion) from a *locomotion* (cyclical motion, "motion about a point"). Because the accelerated motion of an arrow from a bow is associated with bending the bow in the arc of a circle, its explanation is in terms drawn from the study of cyclical motion, in particular the accelerated motion of the upper surface of the wheel, or a missile shot from a sling. One might even attempt to explain the direct, straight-line propulsion of an arrow from the center of the bow arc—by analogy with the continuous forward direction of the axle at the center of a rotating wheel—as in accordance with the ratio of the circumference to the centre, or arc of the bow to the mid-point of the arrow. In other words, the force that moves the cart forward in a straight line warps the movement of every point in the circumference of the wheel into a bow shape.

Limit is a concept musically expressed in the endpoints of the string, also known as a *course*. The mystical "added dimension" is time. If the term *lifeline* has meaning, one meaning is the "course" of a person's life, another the rescuer's line that lifts an accident victim to safety. Closely related is the abstract notion of a *timeline* as the necessary order of events in a job to be done, or the history of a criminal event deduced by investigators after the event. In each case time is represented as a physical dimension, a line (by implication a physical *substance* through which energy is conducted and dissipated); and the motivating force, what drives the life, or course of events. An interesting gloss on the lifeline analogy is to regard moving events, even free will, as determined in advance, as the vibration of a string is determined by the bow arc holding the bowstring in tension. If time is indeed stringlike, stretched between a fixed beginning and a fixed ending, then the events of a person's lifeline are predetermined, which is what Greek tragedy is about. The bowstring or monochord as a line is symmetrical, since the same measurements and tensions obtain in either direction. All the same, the arrow moves in one direction only, and does not fly back to the center of the bowstring.

Notes

1. E. T. Bell, *Men of Mathematics* Vol. 2 repr. Harmondsworth: Penguin Books, 1953, 634.
2. A. C. Crombie, "Quantification in Medieval Physics" (1961). In *Science, Optics, and Music in Medieval and Early Modern Thought*. London: Hambledon Press, 1990, 75–90.
3. A. C. Crombie, "Quantification in Medieval Physics," 82–83.

SEVEN

STRING THEORY

Music has to do with managing change. We all know what change is. Some change is organic and involuntary. Things grow. Some change is systemic and self-perpetuating. The sun rises and sets. Some change is imposed by force, on impulse. The wind blows and the tree bends. Some change is catastrophic, as when lightning strikes, or you crash.

Whether arising from growth or instability, change is inherent in nature and while some change is orderly and other change is destructive, all change, even in personal character, is accountable as a consequence of natural action or agency. The task at one level is to reconcile the different kinds of change as aspects of the same nature, and distinguish them from misunderstandings or illusions contrary to nature.

We deal with change defensively by setting limits to what it can do. We make houses to manage changes in the weather, and we make laws to limit the freedom of action of those nearest to us. We also manage change in a more positive way by creating instruments to take advantage of its effects.

Change may involve a transfer of energy and a transformation in nature, space, and time. To understand change it is necessary to form the concept of continuity in existence, time, and space, so that you recognize that what has been changed is identified with its previous existence as well as being not the same in some respect. This is not as simple as it appears. That something changes means that what and where it was before is not altogether what and where it is after the event, but more importantly, that it is nevertheless perceived as the same thing and not a substitution. In some cases, for example anger management, it may be more important to understand that under the effects of strong emotion or stimulant, a character can be radically altered and may have to be understood as a different person even though the outward appearance remains the same as before. The idea of continuity in existence, space and time is important for human sanity because without an assurance that the world continues to be, there is a danger of becoming lost in a world of inconstant reality. The paradoxical idea of a world without change —or in which change is unverifiable—was advanced by Parmenides in the fifth century BC. How to define continuous change has always been a controversial topic, since it involves reconciling issues of space, time, and identity. For classical musicians, continuity is expressed in the actions of singing, dancing, or performing, even indeed in the continuous groove of a gramophone recording, and change in the movement of a musical line between data points notated in the score, or syllables in the text of a song.

A PIECE OF STRING

The question "How long is a piece of string" is an old and familiar puzzle. That a string has length we don't doubt. We can see the string and that it has length. Whatever it is made of and however long a string it is, it still has length. A piece of string is both an illustration and a demonstration of the concept of length, which is also a demonstration of continuity in space and connection between two points.

The length of a piece of string is established by it having two ends. The length of a string is the distance between the two ends, measured by a convenient unit of length. (From Mandelbrot's revelations of fractal dimension we understand that the smaller the unit of measurement, the longer the string is likely to be.) Distance, direction, and continuity inhere in the string having length. How the ends are defined is another matter. The ends of a piece of string are the points at which the string terminates or ceases to exist. The existence of the end of a piece of string could actually be regarded as problematic, since it involves attributing thingness and location to an absence of string. Absence of string could signify (and to some observers does, in fact, signify) location *anywhere else*, hence the ends of a string are at the same time specific (finite and located) and nonspecific (everywhere else).

A string may be interpreted as the physical embodiment of a line. A line is straight or curved. To illustrate his special theory of relativity, Einstein imagined a line as a passenger train traveling at speed along a straight track, a subtle compound metaphor in which the line as a preordained trajectory (the railway) is superimposed on the line as extension of a point (a train as a number of carriages joined together), a measure of length (the length of the train), a vibration expressing energy, amplitude, and velocity (the train moving along the railway line), and as a partial frequency (the guard moving back and forth along the train as it travels at speed).

Meditating on the inconstancy of length in a newly relativistic age, the artist Marcel Duchamp dropped three meter-long lengths of thread onto the floor and transferred the resulting curves to three straightedges to make the work *Three Standard Stoppages*, included in the collection *The 1914 Box*. Because the resulting edges are curved rather than straight, they are no longer of any practical use as rulers, though they remain interesting as indications of length in the domain of fractal geometry. Straightness is not a requirement of length, but a convention of length that allows measurements to be made to the same scale. A straight line also implies a plane surface. If the paper on which it is drawn is rolled into a cylinder, a line becomes a curve, or even a loop. So a straight line implies a condition that space is flat.

To make a string straight it has to be put under tension. The same is implicitly the case for a drawn straight line. Even though a line on paper, a finishing line, or a line drawn in the sand has no substance of itself, its straightness may be understood as an expression of tension in one or more dimensions. (As we know from the example of a stringed instrument, the precise degree of tension is immaterial, providing the line is sufficiently straight for our purposes.) When a string is held in tension, energy is stored. The more tension, the straighter the string and the more resistant it is to deviation from straightness. A railway line is attached to the ground and describes a fixed trajectory between destinations. The implied tension of a line drawn on paper is its fixed position in relation to the paper. Operations calculated on a drawn line are actually calculated with respect to the stability of the paper surface.

A stretched string model of a straight line is of a line maintained in tension by a resisting frame: for example, a bow. The state of tension of a string is audible as a tone of constant pitch, which also signifies a potential to drive an arrow, and thus to catch food animals, or repel an enemy. The power of direction stored in a bowstring is manifested in peculiar modes of vibration that, when one end of a bow is touched to a shield, or hollow gourd, or tortoise shell, or empty earthenware pot, can be heard resonating as a compound tone of constant pitch (the tuning fork test).

The question "How long is a piece of string?" is self-evidently a question about length. To answer it rationally suggests that the string is held in a straight line for ease of comparison with whatever may be used as a measure or standard. It may be exactly the same length as something else, or it may be shorter, or it may be longer. Length implies a standard for measuring length: a palm, a thumb, a foot. As we are asked when buying shoes, "What size are you?" signifying that length is relative to the individual. Absolute length, for a piece of string, may rely on frequency, so that two strings cut from the same reel, stretched on a resonating frame, and weighted by equal weights, one after another, ideally sound in unison, at the same fundamental frequency. Or that, suspended from the same crossbar and equally weighted, they will swing back and forth synchronously.

The question "How long is a piece of string?" may also be understood as asking "How long is a line between two points?" or "How long does it take to go from one end of the string to the other?" These are subtly different questions for which there are different answers. The length of a line considered as a succession of points is the sum of the distances between all adjacent points. Defined as the shortest distance between two points, however, the length of a line is the longest distance between its two ends. If space itself is warped, for example by laying the line on the surface of a globe, the distance between its two ends may be less than the sum of the distances between adjacent points (i.e., along its length). An unstraight line, as Duchamp demonstrated, can only join points that are closer together in real space "as the crow flies." In fractal geometry the shortest distance between two points—reformulated as the greatest distance measurable by a string of given length—is determined by the curvature of the surface articulated by the string, and the choice of unit or scale of measurement. (By this definition, a vibrating string is also a continuously varying curved surface.) Scale transposition, when the unit of measurement is made smaller or larger, is inherently musical, corresponding to an alteration of *key*, meaning fundamental frequency or *wavelength*. The same melody harmonized in two different keys represents a different set of measures and interval ratios in each case, not all of which may be harmonious in the same way. In the time domain, an alteration of tempo may also lead to a difference in the perception of elements in a continuum. The eighteenth-century sonata convention of varying the tempo of successive movements without altering the unit pulsation (heard for example in Beethoven's "Moonlight" sonata for piano) is an extension of baroque inquiry into the nature of movement related to human activity (the dance suite), into the domain of abstract or mechanical timing unrelated to human mobility or measures of time. Hence the footnote to Stockhausen's *Piano Piece I* saying that "The tempo of the piece, determined by the shortest note, is 'as fast as possible'."

On the issue of length as duration, meaning the time elapsed in traveling the distance between two points, things start to get complicated. Since the fixed ends of a string in tension are the determinants of its length, and when in vibration the string is vibrating at every point in between, it follows that the act of measuring the distance between the two ends involves an assumption that the relationship between them is both instantaneous and simultaneous. We understand the two points connected by the string length as occupying a uniform space and time. That this is not inevitably the case is part of the message of Zeno's paradox of Achilles and the tortoise, which involves a race over a fixed (though arbitrary) length in which the longer and fleeter steps of the athlete Achilles, though "naturally faster," are unable to overtake the distance covered by the shorter and slower steps of the dependable tortoise. It is a way of saying that no matter how fast you run, you can't change the distance, only the time, which is a valid point. It is also saying that the fewer steps you take (i.e., the larger the unit you apply to measuring the distance) does not influence the straight-line distance traveled, only the elapsed time. That a faster speed is normally associated with a greater stride and thereby fewer intermediate steps is another valid conclusion, but one of secondary importance.

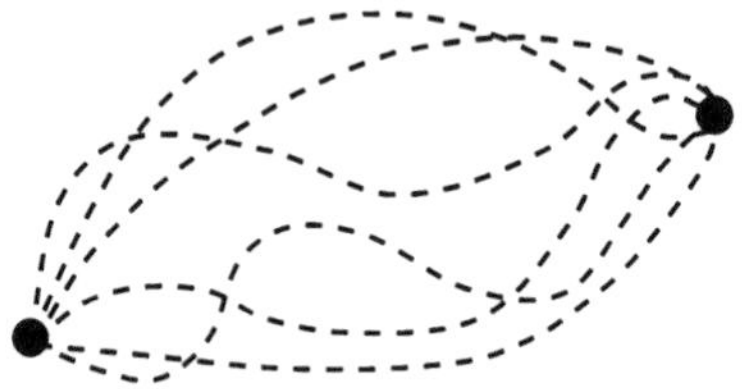

A Feynman diagram of multiple paths between two points

That the issue of movement between two points is nontrivial is indicated by Einstein's use of a moving train to illustrate relativity. A moving train is a convenient analogy of movement in a straight line in relation to observers both within the train and also outside it. The observer within the train is also moving, but can only move toward the front, in the direction the train is moving, or toward the rear. In the case of a vibrating string, the equivalent consideration is the nature of movement within the string, which is simultaneously longitudinal and lateral, moving back and forth and side to side all at the same time, at different through related frequencies. (In this respect its potential to carry information resembles the groove of an analogue gramophone recording.) The string vibrates in response to energy applied at an arbitrary point or zone along its length (usually near the interval of a seventh, which is a problematic partial in a musical sense), and because the vibration is a traveling wave, the string is set in vibration along its length in a plurality of modes. It follows that if the vibrating string in question is viewed as a line of force, the force is expressed throughout its length, and is not confined to a point along its length, or determined by considering the movement at only one point.

Einstein's train paradox refers only to relative movement past a stationary observer (an external single point occupying a larger frame of reference). The twins paradox, for comparison, compares the trajectories of two particles between the same starting and end points, one moving in space and time, in the process undergoing an acceleration (to light speed) and a retardation, the other moving at a constant speed through time. The proposition is startlingly similar to comparing the motion of a point located on the circumference of

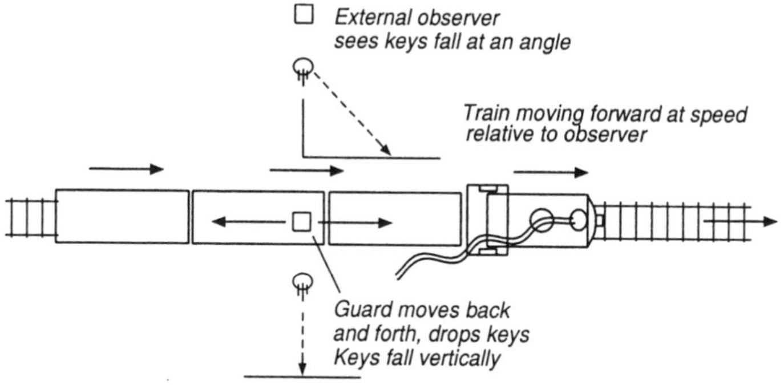

Einstein's relativity train

a wheel, which undergoes an acceleration and a retardation between successive points of contact with the ground, compared with a point at the center of the wheel, which covers the same forward distance while taking a shorter line and moving at a constant speed. It also has features in common with Zeno's paradox of Achilles and the tortoise, since in all but name the twins paradox is also a race over a predetermined course between equivalent points in space and time. In Aesop's fable of the hare and the tortoise—a variation—the hare loses the race because it travels at an inconstant speed, whereas the tortoise moves forward at a slower but steady pace. Aesop's fable is supposed to be about dogged persistence, but it is equally about comparing the trajectories of nonequivalent particles covering the same distance between the same two points, one of which (the tortoise) moves through time and space at a constant speed, while the other (the hare) alternates running and resting, acceleration and retardation, rather than moving at a consistent pace. At the end of the race it is the steadier partner who prevails, by covering the minimum distance between the two points in the shortest time. But the philosophical message is that the race is won in time as well as space. Applied to the twins paradox, it signifies that the hare or faster twin, has not saved time by being younger at the finish line, but has lost time by traveling faster and over a greater distance. We are supposed to think that the faster traveler has the advantage, by being younger at the end of the journey than his stay-at-home twin, when in fact the stresses imposed by the faster journey have left him less time to achieve his goals in life and may indeed have compromised his health. Here as in Zeno's paradox, the counter-intuitive conclusion relies on the two endpoints being fixed in space and time. The twins start together and finish together, but are vastly separated in between.

That the ends of a vibrating stretched string of a traditional longbow or musical instrument are fixed, is an essential condition of the string vibrating in a coherent manner. (The alternative is a whip, where energy is transferred in one direction only, and dissipates explosively.) In other words, when a string is in motion it is only possible to locate the two ends with absolute certainty. The center of a vibrating string is visible only as a blur and it is not possible to determine with any accuracy where it is located in space at any one moment, though of course it remains the midpoint of the string. The uncertainty of location of any point within the vibrating string increases to a maximum at the center, tending to zero at either end. It is as though, in Feynman's terms, the motion of a string follows all possible routes between two points, and it is only the arbitrary determination of the endpoints that collapses the uncertainty of motion to zero at either end, a sophistication that would not be necessary if the endpoints were assumed to exist as a prior condition of the string vibrating, and not as the effect of a spontaneous decision by an external observer.

The number of points within a line is assumed to be large but not infinite. Infinity is contentious because if a given string is shown to contain an infinity of points, it may follow that any string of whatever length also contains an infinity of points, implying that every piece of string is the same length, which is contrary to sense and observation. How then is length exactly computed, if not by the number of points within it? In the macro world of miles, feet, and inches, we do it by choosing a unit of length and counting the number of times the unit length is incremented to cover the distance from one end, which we may call the starting or alpha point, to the other end, the omega or endpoint. The accumulated number of units at the omega point determines a value for the distance covered. For the invading Romans, relatively long distances of several miles were measured in paces, a mile equaling a thousand (*mille*) paces. Smaller lengths like a cricket pitch are measure in steps, foot to

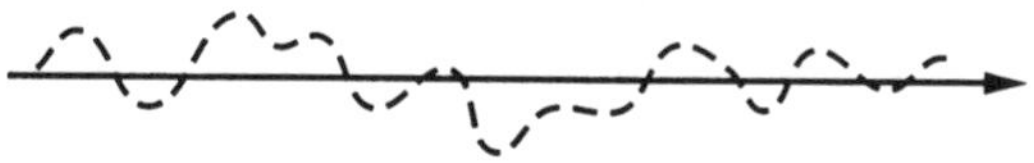

Failing the breath test

foot. In my childhood this step measure was known as "granny steps" and being asked to walk a line in this fashion is still a test of drunkenness if you happen to be caught by a traffic officer with the smell of alcohol on your breath. (It is curious to reflect that sobriety and good citizenship are monitored at the side of the road in the twenty-first century to standards laid down by the ancient Greeks: by the ability of a person to move steadily along a straight line path, and by implication to measure the arbitrary distance of a straight line accurately in feet.)

Accurate measurement on the micro scale however depends on establishing an agreed unit of measurement, and this the ancients found hard to do, practically and perhaps intellectually. We know from efforts to establish the value of π by approximation, from triangulating the circle into smaller and smaller wedges until the base of each triangle approached a point, that the principle of dividing the circumference of a circle into a fixed number of unit lengths was taken seriously. That a similar method was applied to computing linear measure would make sense, and it is not out of the question that the ancients understood that problems in measuring curves had to do with the fact that they were not ideally flat.

The special status of a stretched string, however, is that when set in vibration *it measures itself*, signified by the fact that it gives out a tone of constant pitch. The length of a vibrating string organizes itself in consequence of the tension that renders it straight, and in disposing of the energy input of plucking it. The excess energy is dissipated, while the original tension is conserved. Since the two ends of a bowstring in tension are held fast, the length of the string does not change (at least, not to the naked eye). What an observer discovers from examining a vibrating string is a complex of simultaneous vibrations in equal divisions ranging from the entire length to the very small: 1/1, 1/2, 1/3, 1/4, 1/5, . . . etc. For a string to vibrate in more than one mode simultaneously it has to be straight, and in tension, and in motion—that is, under the influence of an external force (not alcohol in this case). The various modes of vibration can be observed by coating the string with fine particles, placing paper spurs along its length, or applying a quill feather or tip to different points along the length and noting any change in the pitch of the tone. All lead to the discovery that the vibration of a stretched string is compounded of many vibrations of lesser length, each an exact division of the fundamental. These smaller divisions are available as tangible measures only when the string is held in tension above a minimum threshold.

Intriguingly, the locations of these points of division remain the same even when the tension of the string is varied without becoming slack or breaking. Providing the tension sustains the string in vibration, the nodal points at which a string vibrates at a harmonic are always at the same relative locations, independently of the thickness and tension of the string, and determined only by the distance between the endpoints. This corresponds to the truism that the midpoints and finer divisions of the open strings of a guitar, as indicated by the frets, remain perfectly aligned, depite the fact that individual strings are tuned to different pitches. Higher tension and thinner strings allow progressively more partials to be selected by touch, indicating measurement to a higher degree of precision. That the frequency of a string in vibration persists even while its radiant energy dies away is further proof that the energy being dissipated is independent of the force holding the string in tension.

THE MONOCHORD

The second question is, is the length of a vibrating string any different from the length of the same string at rest? Well yes, it is, since the string is organic and flexible, and therefore stretchable. How do we estimate the difference in length? Indirectly as a consequence of the force applied to make it vibrate. In vibrating that force is transferred to the surrounding atmosphere and some is converted to heat. For this to make sense the string has to be able to recover from being stretched, meaning it has resistance. If a string had no resistance it would simply get longer every time it was stretched, like a string of bubblegum. Making a violin string out of catgut (or any other gut) involves organic matter that is drawn into a stringlike shape and allowed to dry out, which has the effect of

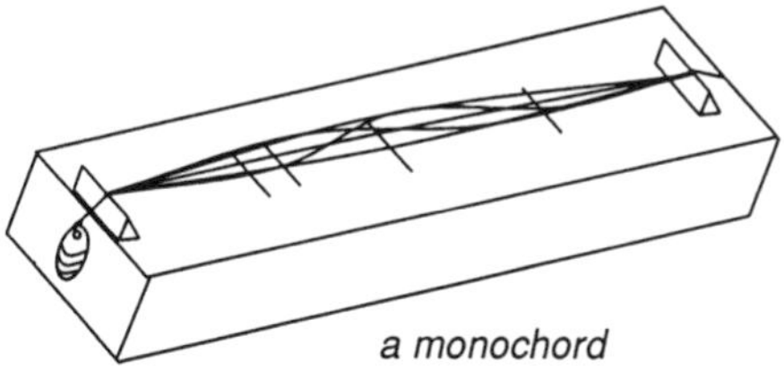

a monochord

fixing its length. So one answer to the question "How long is a piece of string?" is "I will tell you once it is cured, but not before." Being organic, gut strings lose tension in conditions of humidity. Losing tension is another way of saying that the string gains in length and elasticity by absorbing moisture from the atmosphere. But the very act of setting the string in motion also changes its length by a minute amount, making the act of verifying the length by plucking the string a logical and practical impossibility. The modern idea that the act of measuring interferes with the object being measured and its actual measured value thus has a classical precedent.

A monochord is a string stretched over a box. The string is the best kind, a gut string like the string of a harp or cello. It has been made to be stretched tight and to maintain its tautness. It is not like a rubber band. If you stretch a rubber band between two pencils and get somebody to pluck it while you pull it tighter and tighter, you find that it reaches a plateau of tension, audible as a musical tone, beyond which the band gets longer until it reaches breaking point, but the tone does not get any higher in pitch. The added length compensates exactly for the added tension: the two forces balance out, and the pitch remains the same. For a stringed instrument the ideal tension is somewhere within that plateau.

A flexible string like a rubber band is of no use for a musical instrument or for archery, because it lacks the tensile strength to resist stretching, or power an arrow. A bowstring holds its length when pulled back. The bow does not stretch, instead bending in the arc of a circle. The power of the bow is a power of resistance, and is recursive or circular in nature (retained in the bow). The power propelling the arrow is expressed in a complementary geometry of straight lines, and is impulsive in nature, the result of an external agency pulling the string.

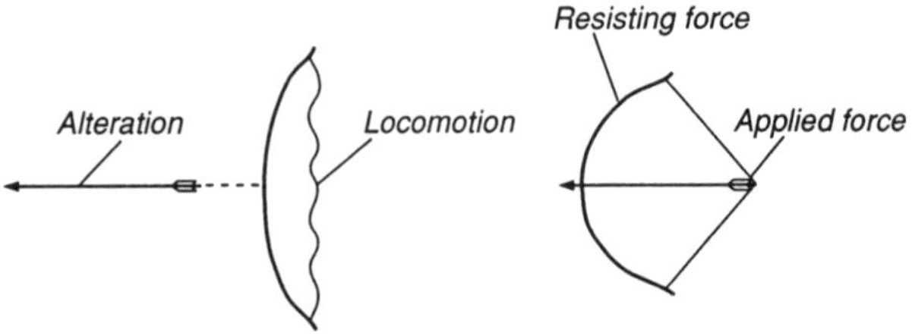

The bow powers a deadly missile through the air at a faster speed than it can be thrown by hand. A slingshot propels a stone at superhuman speed by harnessing the power of rotation, but the string of a slingshot is normally slack and held in tension only by the weight of the stone and the speed of rotation, audible as a whirring tone of variable pitch. In a bowstring, however, the power retained in tension by the bow is expressed in the musical tone that sounds in the string when the bow is drawn, and dying away when the arrow is released. A musical vibration is cyclical in nature, and expresses a relationship of dynamic tension. As long as the tone is constant, the relationship is also constant. A sling has no inherent tension and has to be powered up every time a missile is thrown, a bow however maintains the string in tension after the arrow is fired. Because its energy potential is constant, a bow is more efficient and energy-saving as a propulsion device, as well as more consistent in performance, than a sling. The basic requirements of a bowstring are that it does not stretch or break when pulled back to fire an arrow, and that it revert to its former state of tension after the arrow has been fired. The return to its former state implies that the force expended to propel the arrow is to all intents and purposes the same amount of force employed to draw the bow to the firing position, so there is a minimum of waste. That too makes the bow more efficient a weapon than a slingshot (or ball and chain).

The inner strength of a bowstring—or the string of a guitar, koto, violin, sitar, fiddle, or any musical instrument incorporating a string held in tension—is expressed first, in the fact that when plucked, it sounds at a *frequency* that remains constant as it loses energy and dies away; second, that the *tension* remains constant during and after the tone dies away; and third, that *the same pitch returns* when the string is plucked again after an interval of silence. This means that the coupled system of bow and string mysteriously "knows the difference" or is able to distinguish between the energy applied when the string is plucked, or the bow drawn, and the latent energy stored in the bow and arrow at rest. It also "knows" that the latent energy persists during periods of inaction between firing one arrow and the next. We could say that the bow retains a memory of its original tension. This may seem obvious to us, but to a novice is actually quite mysterious. Like a human being, with advancing age and wear and tear the string is bound to lose strength and in consequence its power and memory also begin to fail, but the fact that the material of a string is perishable does not alter the fundamental principle of persistence of energy. Indeed, the fact that the power source of a bow, or of a musical instrument, is *renewable* —that a worn out or broken string can be replaced—can be interpreted as a metaphor of the persistence of energy independently of the material through which it is expressed, and by analogy, the persistence of life after death, since the vitality that one might assume to be inherent in the string itself, can be restored after an old string is discarded by a new string being fitted. A distinctive voice can be brought back to life, in effect, by substitution of a new string. In human terms it implies that the elements of an active individual personality (energy, influence, tone of voice, strength in action) are properties somehow distinct from the physical body, and result from an externally applied tension. The moral implications of such an analogy of music with human life are extremely rich and powerful.

Trivial though it may seem, the mere fact that a bow, a violin, or a guitar stays in tune, or maintains its tension, so that its tone quality and pitch can be relied upon to remain the same (or rather, to reproduce the same) during a reasonable period of performance time, and also between playings, is hugely significant. It allows these instruments to be regarded as information storage devices, and as means of information exchange, since the same tone quality and pitch can be transferred to another person by handing over the instrument. It is not the same as handing over a spear, since despite its strength and constancy the spear does not imply latent energy or tone of voice. Furthermore, the information in a stretched string can be manipulated, is invisible, is about storing and releasing power, and ultimately about relationships that connect the real and tangible world of perishable things with the eternal realm of unseen forces.

It follows that, in its role as a guide to speech or song, a lyre, or harp, or other stringed instrument, acts as an important adjunct memory for the retention and reproduction of culturally significant information (namely, pitch as an expression of dynamic tension, and alteration of pitch as an effect of altering tension). The same understanding of tension relationships transfers to emotional or grammatical alterations in pitch of the human voice in delivering a text, even as the instrument leads a natural voice inflection toward an artificial melody in abstract intervallic steps. Human memory is shape-orientated, reliable when it comes to words and for recalling the general inflection of a verse, speech, or sacred ritual, but less certain (unless the speaker has perfect pitch) in recalling exact pitches or interval relationships. Unlike ordinary speech or conversation, where intonation is casual and approximate, public speaking in a ritual context is designed to be heard at a distance, and for that reason tends to be more formal in delivery, hence more musical and rhythmic. Musical qualities inevitably become an essential part of the meaning of a public speaker's message, and when delivered in accordance with the scale of pitches of a musical instrument, allow the same speech to be reproduced years afterward by later generations of speakers, with the guidance of the same instrument (or one tuned to the same mode or scale), and with virtually the same intonation, melody, and rhythm, thus enabling the content of the message to be expressed with the same *meaning* as before. Musical instruments and their scales embody a range of notes representing pitch levels of a voice and expressing varying degrees of intensity or emotional tension. The notes of a scale or mode are more than just counters on a musical string. They correspond to a scale of energy states in the speaker (though not of the string, whose energy states are harmonics), preserved in the tuning, and reproduced with the aid of a reliable external measuring device, which is the instrument itself. Strings sing naturally and spontaneously in harmonics, but human beings do not. The non-commensurability of harmonics and scales or modes has something to tell us about the difference in nature between wayward living things and inert structures; or, in the hierarchy of living creatures, between those who lead—self-motivated members of the tribe—and those who are content to respond passively to external direction. The same character distinction is made between the unstable dynamics of human action revealed in a musical performance, compared to the precise and consistent response of a musical instrument.

What we are interested in is the knowledge that can be derived from a plucked string, and how if at all that knowledge relates on the one hand to music, and on the other hand, to other areas of knowledge. The motive for developing research devices such as a monochord is first, in order better to understand the ratios of force to tension in the bow as a weapon, and second, to discover whether the laws governing bows and arrows are of wider or more universal application. For the ancients, a vibrating string was a mediator between earth and sky, linking the plain world of material objects with the divine heavens above. Strings and plumb-bobs have been employed for surveying from the dawn of civilization. The ancient Egyptians used a weighted string to find the vertical, and because the weight invariably tends toward the center of the earth, associated the weighted end of a string on the monochord with the earth, and the retaining end with the heavens, and movement along the string with a rise or fall in pitch space.

Ancient civilizations also knew how to obtain a right angle with a string knotted in lengths of 3, 4, and 5 units. In this case, however, the string is simply knotted in four places and can be transported loose, is used only for the sake of obtaining a right angle, and is not attached to any frame or employed for any higher purpose of inquiry into power and motion ratios. Since for surveying purposes only length is required, and not tensile strength, any nonstretching string will do for surveying purposes. The Greeks saw meaning of a different kind in comparisons of the ratios of pitch and tension, for the study of which unusually strong and stable strings, like bowstrings, are required to make them audible, and that require reliable and rigid structures to hold them in tension.

Only when a string is held in tension, in a frame, are the ratios of 1/3, 1/4, and 1/5 audible as tones: miraculously forming the second inversion of the common chord of western music.

harmonics

Whenever a stringed instrument is played, the music is sending out significant underlying messages. These include (1) persistence of being (constancy of the reverberating string tone, and by inference, of the listener); (2) a perception of pitch as moving up and down in its own space, a dimension at the same time real (string length) and imaginary (frequency); and (3) continuity of tension, of length, and therefore of time itself. Since proof of continuity has been a vexed issue in philosophy from ancient times, the necessary continuities of line, pitch, tension, and time demonstrated in early music for stringed instruments are clearly significant. The tension of a string in a stringed instrument is invisible, but its length is clearly visible. For that reason the tones associated with successive strings of a lyre or harp are identifiable as locations in an energy continuum, and musical intervals as energy relationships, perhaps in the same way that an astronomer identifies the absorption lines in the spectrum of a distant star with the light frequencies of different elements. The rising tone of the bowstring as it is drawn back prior to firing, or a wailing voice rising and falling under emotional stress, are real world expressions of continuity and extension in time and space, to which the discretely tuned strings of a musical instrument bring a sense of quantity and relation. Unlike the surveyor's plumb-bob or knotted string, which are passive surveying aids with implications only for measuring space, a stringed musical instrument is a tension device allowing the dimensions of space, time, and energy to be reconciled.

EIGHT

PARADOX REGAINED

"Greek city states varied appreciably in their measures," observed O. A. W. Dilke with masterly understatement.[1] In olden times, counting was for sheep, not for measuring the universe. The smallest linear measures in ancient cultures were based on the human body: thumb joint, palm, foot, forearm etc. Naturally they varied from place to place, often according to the physical stature of whomever was in charge: in other words, the *ruler*.

In a world of inconstant units, measurement by division and ratio takes precedence over measurement by aggregation. The standard measures of ancient Europe related to the average height of an individual citizen. To present generations, who are better nourished and taller than their ancestors of a century and more ago, the cityscapes and dwellings of earlier times appear cramped and unliveable. As architect Le Corbusier observed, the compensating merit of basing the measurements of a building on a local, standard human being is arriving at a harmony of inner proportion, or scale of measurements, often missing from more recent architecture. The Vitruvian figure of Renaissance Italy, most famously realized in the image of a standing male figure by Leonardo da Vinci, represents the human body and its parts as a construction of harmonious proportions, reconciling the square and the circle, and incorporating equilateral and 3 : 4 : 5 triangles.

In contrast to the inconstant measurements of the human body, varying from person to person, music (proportional relations in sound, verified with the monochord) offered the ancients a reliable system of generating harmonious proportions by division, and also of fine-tuning measurement into smaller units than the average thumb or finger's breadth. Proportion deals in scale relationships,

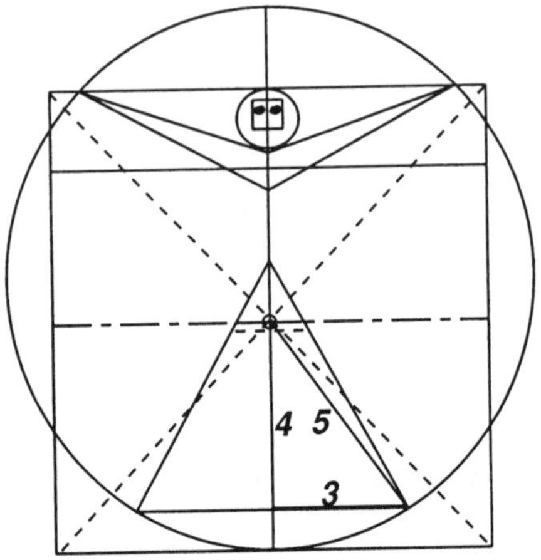

Schematic of Leonardo's Vitruvian figure incorporating measures of the bow and pace

and harmony with internal ratio or proportion rather than multiples of a unit measure.

Counting units up and down the string of a monochord is as unnatural as it would be for a guitarist. The string of a monochord, or its portable equivalent, *tromba marina* (an obscure term for a real instrument, the name possibly signifying *wave trumpet*, hence "waveform generator"), is all the same a measuring device. By touching the vibrating string along its length with a feather or quill tip, a series of privileged and inherently harmonious proportions is found in the locations of harmonics or nodes of a fundamental length. These do not however form a stepwise scale from low to high like the player's fingers pressing on the fingerboard. Pressing on the string changes its sounding length, so what a listener hears is a pattern of changing lengths. Touching the vibrating string while it continues to vibrate over its whole length reveals a series of partial tones corresponding to aliquot divisions of the whole length, first in descending order of pitch, as a harmonic series 1/5, 1/4, 1/3, 1/2, to the midpoint of the string, then ascending 2/3, 3/4, 4/5, 5/6 etc. The physical wavelength of a cello low C string (*c.* 64 hertz) is about 17 feet 6 inches, roughly 5.5 meters, from pressure peak to pressure peak. Proportions based on the larger divisions of such a fundamental unit, 1 : 2, 2 : 3, 3 : 4 etc., are appropriate for determining

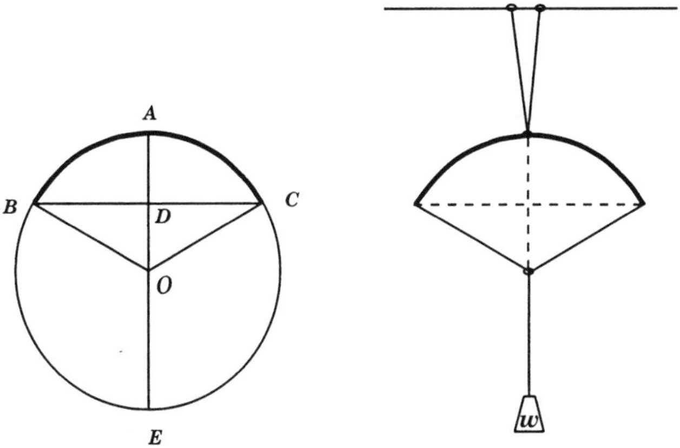

Babylonian diagram (left) for computing the diameter of a circle. It can also be used to derive the ratio of extension to force powering an arrow (right). The same triangulated arc is concealed in Leonardo's Vitruvian figure opposite

the greater structural dimensions of a house or public building. Lesser divisions 8 : 9, 9 : 10, 15 : 16 etc. can be used to determine the sizes of floorboards, pipes, ornaments, and decorations, arriving at a scale of rational divisions, like the *Modulor* of Le Corbusier, instead of multiples of a unit foot or inch. In calculating by divisions of a greater length rather than arbitrary multiples of a smaller unit, an overall harmony is preserved that conforms in turn to the harmonic language of music, based on divisions of a fundamental wavelength.

The poet Apollodorus records that Pythagoras offered "a splendid sacrifice of oxen" to celebrate his discovery of the theorem bearing his name. Pythagoras was a vegetarian, but more to the point, the theorem had been discovered as a geometrical proof long before. That there is more to the theorem than mere geometry is suggested by the above diagram from ancient Mesopotamia showing that the general theorem was known to the Babylonians of about 1700 BC. Tablets of this date discuss how to calculate the diameter *AE* of a circle when the *chord BC* and the *sagitta DA* are known, the result obtained being simply an expression of the Pythagorean theorem

$$(OC^2 = OD^2 + DC^2).$$

The Babylonian diagram is on the left.[2] (The term *sagitta* is the word for *arrow*.) It is interesting for a number of reasons. Firstly, it resembles the shape created by a bow suspended at its center and with a weight suspended from the center of its string. The purpose of such a diagram might be to calculate the diameter of a circle, but it might also be intended to show the degree of curvature imparted to the bow when a bowstring is pulled back, and that a symmetrical pair of right triangles is formed as a consequence of correctly drawing a bow. The diagram can also be interpreted as the logical way of setting up an experiment to measure the force required to draw a bowstring back to a certain angle, in order to calculate the compression of the arc of the bow as a consequence of the added weight, and to relate the added force and angle produced to the alteration in pitch of the string as it varies in tension. What the diagram also demonstrates is a perception of the bow as an arc of a circle, which has power as well as aesthetic and geometrical implications. It may be taken as signifying that the nonrenewable force associated with bending the bow is different in nature from the renewable force associated with the straight lines of a string held in tension, and the triangular forms associated with it.

The Pythagoreans worshipped Apollo, the god of archery as well as music. The connection of archery and music expresses an understanding of the power implications of the stretched string. The Pythagoreans are credited with the breakthrough discovery that reconciles the ratio of lengths of the 3, 4, 5 triangle with the frequencies of harmonics 3, 4, 5 of a stretched string, and associated tension ratios. These harmonics are significant in western music as the major triad in second inversion.

FROM FRETS TO SLIDE RULE

The Egyptian and Babylonian method of computation by fractions is musical in implication. The following equation is recorded in the Rhind Papyrus in the British Museum:[3]

$$2/97 = 1/56 + 1/679 + 1/776$$

It can be reformulated as:

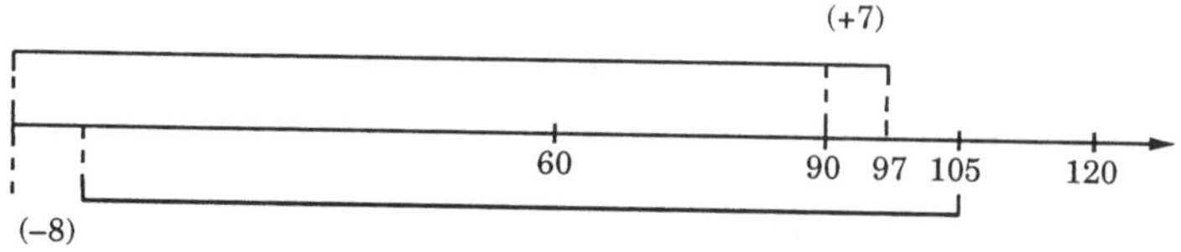

Hypothetical calculation by monochord

$$2/97 = 1/(7 \times 8) + 1/(97 \times 7) + 1/(97 \times 8)$$

of which the derivation of 7 and 8 suggests a scale marked up in the manner of a monochord in divisions of 60 (as above):

0	60	90	105	112.5	. . .
60/0	+60/1	+60/2	+60/3	+60/4	. . . etc.

from which it can be seen that the location corresponding to 97 falls between cardinal points 90 and 105, i.e. is 7 greater than 90 and 8 less than 105. At times they approximated, for example the answer

$$1/13 = 7/91 = 7 \times (1/91) = \text{approx. } 7 \times (1/90)$$

where 91 is rounded to 90, the harmonic 3 : 2 of 60.

Counting in minutes and seconds, and degrees of arc, connects arithmetic with geometry, time measurement, and music, all divisions of a cycle. The Pythagoreans interpreted the harmonics of a stretched string as divinely preordained and cyclic in nature. The knowledge that a fundamental length between the fixed endpoints of a stretched string is equal to 2 halves, 3 thirds, 4 quarters etc., is trivial when only one string is considered, but nontrivial when two strings of the same frequency but different length and tension are compared, or unisons and harmonic ratios between two voices, or voice and instrument, or strings or tubes of similar or proportionate length. Such comparisons of length and pitch are essentially music-related, and would lead in due course to the development of logarithm tables and calculation by slide rule by John Napier in the sixteenth century. (Interestingly, the first slide rules were circular in shape.)

Although we know little of the musical repertoire of ancient civilizations, it is possible to infer from surviving examples of harps, lyres, kitharas, bow fiddles, and similar instruments, that an art of musical ratios was cultivated by ancient cultures for ritual purposes of which music may conceivably have been regarded as a form of mnemonic. The knowledge base to devise and operate such instruments is available for mathematical calculation as well as for popular entertainment. Indeed, the instruments themselves constitute the significant knowledge, the music played on them being simply demonstrative. The relationship of ancient mathematics to music can be compared in this respect to the development of computers for warfare training in the modern era, and subsequent proliferation of violent and warlike computer games for public sale and entertainment purposes.

The ritual of a violinist or guitarist tuning up onstage at the start of a concert is a reminder of the computational practices of earlier times, based on concordances of unisons, fifths, fourths, and other harmonic ratios. Finding the same note on two strings of different length, as when a violinist stops A on the D string to sound in unison with the open A string a fifth above, is computing the same frequency and wavelength as a ratio of different scales. The fundamental frequency of an open A string on a violin (440 hertz; wavelength 30 inches) is asserted to be equal and in unison with the fifth on the D string (293 hertz; wavelength 45 inches), and the ninth (double fifth) on the G string (196 hertz, 66 inches). Thus

$$A^{1} = D^{3/2} = G^{9/4}$$

Whole families of instruments have been created in harmonic proportion in the past, notably the violin, viola, and cello of a string quartet, scaled musically in the ratios 1/3 : 1/2 : 1.

For a musician, the question "How long is a piece of string?" involves a consideration of the wavelength of the tone produced as much as the physical length and tension of the string. The physical length is sufficient to determine harmonic divisions, however the wavelength or fundamental frequency can only be worked out from the length and tension of the string, and the distance between peaks of the fundamental frequency as a relation of the two. Musical ratios are demonstrated in ways that tend to be instrument-specific: between strings of different length and the same tension, as with the harp, or between strings of similar weight and length, but differing

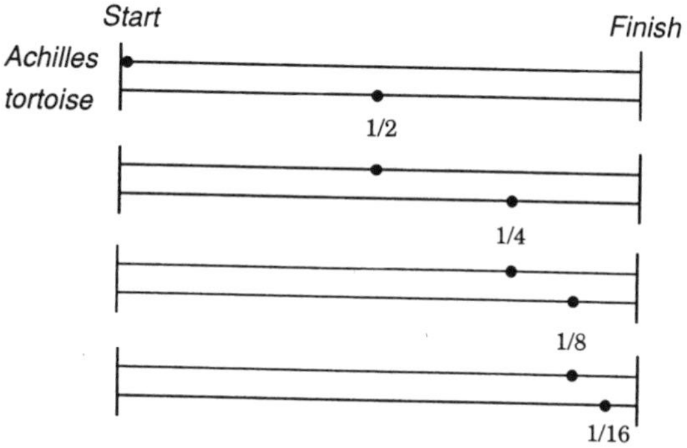

Zeno's paradox of Achilles and the tortoise. When demonstrated on a string instrument, the tortoise is given a lead of 1/2 (an octave) and remains an octave ahead in pitch terms

tension, as with the lyre; or of similar length, but differing weight and tension (the violin family).

PARADOX REGAINED

Orthodox sources (Aristotle among them) tend to disparage Zeno and those who worry over his paradoxes as mischievous, mystical, or easily confused. If the tale of Achilles and the tortoise is told with the aid of a monochord, the race becomes a comparison of two positions moving in pitch along the string (or *course*) toward the bridge. According to this scenario, not only does the tortoise stay ahead of Achilles, but in pitch terms the interval between the pair remains constant. Thus if the tortoise has a lead of half the length (first harmonic position) and moves up the string at half the pace of Achilles, at the start of the race the tortoise is an octave ahead, and by the time Achilles has reached the halfway point, the tortoise is still half the remaining distance ahead, so still an octave ahead.

The paradox is a necessary consequence of the initial conditions. Achilles can never overtake the tortoise because the relative positions of both are determined by the overall length of the course, so for Achilles to win would involve breaking the initial terms, either by moving the finish line, or allowing him free will. (A *course*, by coincidence, is also the name of a string or pair of unison strings on a lute.) Contradictions arise when methods of geometry (ratio) are applied to problems involving measurement (arithmetic). Since the Pythagoreans were musically aware, we can assume that Zeno's paradoxes are based on musical observation and not just thought experiments, even though the results appear contrary to reason. Given the reality of irrational numbers in computing the circumference of a circle and the diagonal of a square, Zeno's demonstration of the reality of irrational ratios in related applications of monochord string theory make sense, as extensions of his teacher Parmenides' thesis of a changeless or motionless world, indicating that the terms of a comparison exercise affect the results obtained, and proving furthermore that any formulation of such a kind presupposes a universe at rest.

Zeno's paradox makes a great deal more sense for all involved if the story is read as a legitimate criticism of how the ancients computed length, and how the concept of length or distance was supposed to tally with the concept of motion. In the seventeenth century a number of leading scientists, among them Zarlino and Vincenzo Galilei, the father of Galileo, labored with only limited success to devise an ideal scale of twelve equal divisions of the octave that preserved the perfect ratios of the harmonic series, to allow modulation from one scale of reference to another in musical terms, in a manner consistent with the scale modulation of spatial relationships in the perspective theory of art. In the early twentieth century, Einstein's special theory revisited the challenge of reconciling measures of distance, time, and relative speed. Einstein was a violinist, so he understood the intimate relationship of string length, tension, mass, and frequency. That the puzzle of Achilles and the tortoise continues to entertain readers in the present day suggests that it still has a message to deliver.

Modern authors tend to describe the contest between Achilles and the tortoise as a race of unspecified but finite length in which the tortoise has a fixed advantage, expressed as a fraction of the total *length*, but can only move at a commensurate fraction of the *speed* of Achilles. When demonstrated on the monochord, the distance between the two contestants is expressed aurally as a ratio of two frequencies, and visually as a ratio of distance in space, the point being made is that the two measures, sound and vision, are not commensurate. In this instance the gap between the two contestants can never be closed *within the endpoints of the string*. Although

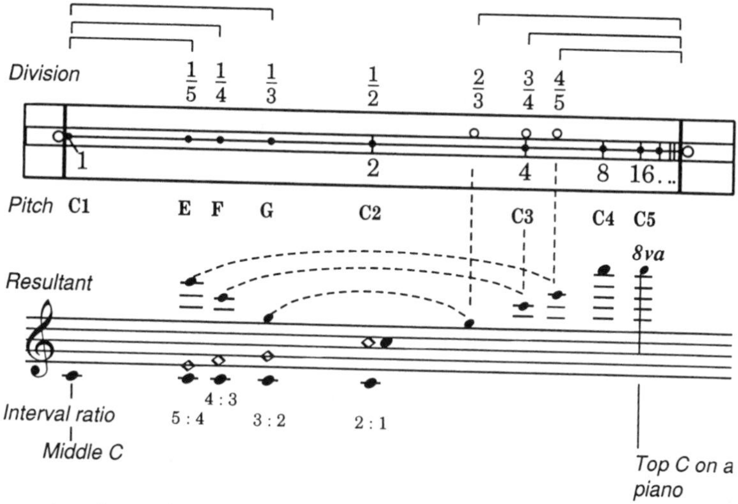

Location and ratio of natural harmonics to their audible frequencies. The harmonic at the major third (5 : 4) sounds at the seventeenth, two octaves and a third higher

Achilles gets closer and closer to the tortoise in visual terms, the interval between them in pitch terms remains exactly the same—one octave, 1 : 2. And while the length of the string appears finite and measurable in visual terms, in pitch terms its length tends to infinity, given that length is computed by the number of discrete points from end to end, and the number of points in the string is more than can be counted.

> The Greeks could not do sums on paper. . . . The immense difficulty which the mathematicians of the ancient world experienced when they dealt with a process of division carried on indefinitely, or with what modern mathematicians call infinite series, limits, transcendental numbers, irrational qualities, and so forth, provides an example of a great social truth. . . . Whenever the culture of a people loses contact with the common life of mankind and becomes exclusively the plaything of a leisure class, it is becoming a priestcraft. It is destined to end, as does all priestcraft, in superstition. [4]

A traditional aversion to paradox for the sake of it has been used by scholars in the past as an excuse to beat up Zeno and his followers

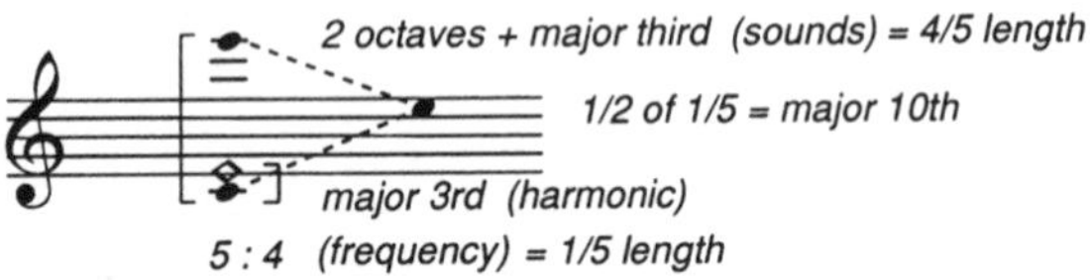

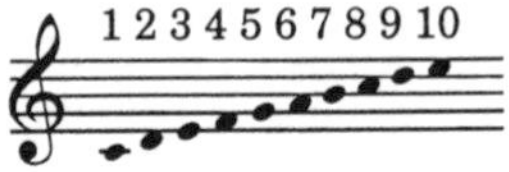

The interval of a tenth can be expressed as 1/2 of 1/5 of the length of a string, or as a distance of 10 notes counting up the fingerboard

as social parasites, which is frankly unfair. An alternative version of the paradox is a great deal more subtle. Here again the course length is unspecified, only in this version the tortoise is said to move at one-tenth the speed of Achilles and has a "100 yard" start. The puzzle hinges on the meanings to be assigned to "speed" and "yard" in this context, the inference being that at whatever point Achilles reaches, the tortoise maintains an advantage or lead of "one-tenth" the remaining distance.

This is a puzzle in which Achilles has position and the tortoise has momentum, and as long as the comparison remains in these unequal terms, the tortoise will always hold the advantage. As a contest of position versus momentum, it can be seen to resemble Zeno's related paradox of the moving arrow. The interval of a tenth has peculiar properties that may be used to confuse an audience, as indicated above. To satisfy the terms of *any* interval, however, the mystery of the tenth can be set aside.

For a distance of one-half, in pitch terms an octave, the story works for Achilles and the tortoise to be moving along the *same* course or string. For the tortoise to win at any other interval, two strings side by side are necessary. They are the same length, and thus correspond to the same distance. Since the tortoise is heavier than Achilles, the tortoise's string invariably implies *added weight* (tortoise = added weight = added tension = higher pitch). The amount of added weight, in other words the precise difference in pitch between the two strings, is immaterial: what matters is that the string associated with the tortoise is necessarily tuned to a higher frequency than the string of Achilles, and that interval is

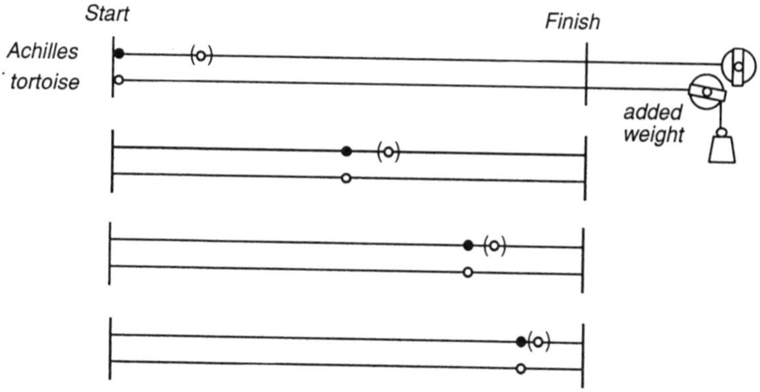

In the alternative version of the paradox, two different strings of the same length and thickness are compared. The string representing the tortoise is set at a higher tension (is pulled by a greater weight), thus at a higher pitch. At every point along the length of the course, the frequency of the tortoise string is ahead of Achilles by the same interval. This is only a mystery to nonmusicians

constant for comparable distances along the entire length of the two strings, meaning that as one follows the movement in pitch up the "lighter" string and compares its pitch at successive locations to the adjacent "heavier" string, the same location will always be as far ahead in pitch as it was at the beginning of the course. If frequency is construed as *velocity* then the paradox, acoustically speaking, is that by making something carry more weight it will go faster. (This sounds like relativity theory in reverse; we are more used to reading that the greater the velocity, the greater the mass.)

Needless to say, the Pythagoreans were not interested in calculating the limit point at which Achilles passed the tortoise. For them, the limit is the length of the string, and shortening the length of the string (e.g., by moving the bridge on the monochord) makes not the slightest bit of difference to the terms or to the outcome of the puzzle. That Zeno was not stupid is equally clear. The terms of the paradox are that the course is raced over *a fixed distance* expressed either as twice or 10 times the (pitch) interval between them, the tortoise being given a lead of the reciprocal of the distance, hence 1/2; 1/10, and moving at a speed (i.e., *frequency*) corresponding to the reciprocal of the pace (i.e., stride) of Achilles. This could be read as an allusion to the reciprocity of tension and frequency between strings of unequal length. The incongruity of staging a match between a human being and a tortoise can also be explained if one interprets the contest as between the relative priority of *velocity* (change of length) against *weight* (change of tension) in determining the same alteration of frequency.

The squat tortoise, in other words, is the *weight* holding the string in tension, and Achilles corresponds to the *movement* of energy along the string, and the exercise is properly speaking a *contest* rather than a *race*, focusing attention on the key issue of frequency as a resultant of movement rather than inertia, which is the same in distinguishing the force driving the arrow from that holding the bowstring in tension. The paradox is further complicated from the finesse of an observer not knowing the exact distance of the course (which in musical terms is irrelevant anyway) and thus of having to calculate the relative distance between the contestants in terms of divisions of a total length and not as the sum of fixed intervals of length, a complication dramatically enhanced when the course is represented by a stretched string, and the relative positions of the two contestants, in terms of audible harmonic divisions of the string.

Zeno is playing on the idea that in pitch terms the string of a monochord is infinitely long. This is a perfectly valid observation, and not a trick based on noncomputable numbers. Furthermore, it situates his paradox in a real world of musical instruments in which measure and frequency are calculated by division and weight, and not by simple addition. So the point of the Achilles paradox is that if you start with a finite length and base your calculations of speed and distance covered on ratios of that original length, you may end up with a logical contradiction. And for the paradox to make sense at all, even as a paradox, it is bound to refer to existing conventions of computing distance (elapsed time and space) in terms of relative speed—both of which are related to wavelength.

To claim that the Greeks were unused to division is highly presumptuous. The ancients did not enjoy the luxuries of standard measures of time or space, and had to work round them. Zeno could hardly have avoided learning about division, since musical ratios are divisions, constant whatever the length or tension of the string. They are true universals. The nodes of a stretched string are the

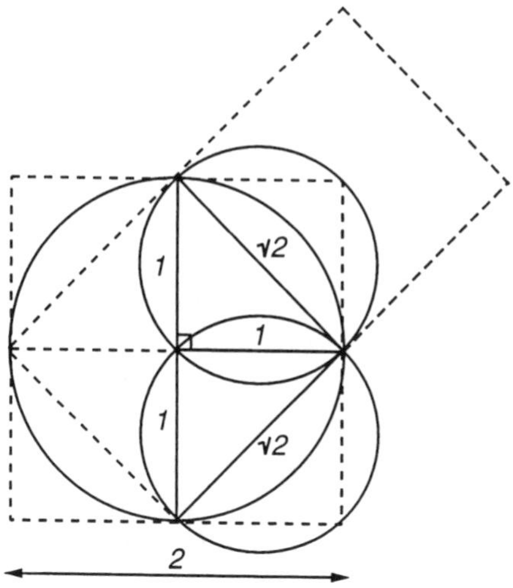

Squaring the circle: the arc of the circle left representing the bow, and superimposed squares to the right governing the angle of the drawn bowstring. The square on the hypotenuse is half the area of the square enclosing the arc. These ratios correspond to octaves in music and are basic axioms of Gothic architecture and the tempered scale

measure and basis not only of harmonic proportion, but of classical tonality in music as we know it.

The Pythagoreans saw significance in the fact that a stretched string, such as a bowstring, stored energy; that the energy inherent in its tension at rest could be increased by the action of drawing the bowstring; that drawing the bowstring increased the tension from its rest state (audible as a rise in pitch); and that only the surplus energy of drawing the bow was transferred to an arrow, since once the arrow was set in flight the bowstring reverted to its initial state of tension.

The paradoxical inferences to be drawn from the example of the bow as a weapon include the following: (1) There is an optimum tension for a bowstring at rest for it to function as an agent to propel an arrow. (2) There is also an optimum added tension in drawing the bow to propel the arrow with greatest control over the greatest distance. (3) The added tension is audible as *a change in pitch* of the bowstring, hence there is a measurable interval in space corresponding to the added force in drawing the bow, and also to the change of pitch. (4) The added energy is almost totally converted to propulsive force at the moment of release of the arrow (the residue causing the string to vibrate). (5) So it is possible to measure the propulsive force applied to an arrow at the moment of release by comparing the first harmonic of the bowstring at rest (where the arrow is placed) with the tone of the string in its drawn state at the moment of release of the arrow. And (6) the two triangles subtended by drawing the bow prior to releasing the arrow are similar right angle triangles, the squares on the hypotenuses of which correspond to the ratios of added force driving the arrow in flight. The solutions of these classic problems: doubling the square, "squaring the circle"—or rather, reconciling the power in the drawn bowstring, calculated as twice the square on the hypotenuse, with the resistance of the bow, bent into the arc of a circle—and finding the ratio of the smaller circle (diameter square root of 2) to the larger (diameter 2) are all subsumed in the solution to the greater problem of the force driving the arrow.

The Greeks recognized a difference between an *alteration* and a *locomotion*. Alteration is what happens when the string is released and its stored energy is transferred to the arrow. The arrow flies away, in a direct line, and its energy is used up in the process. An alteration is an *expenditure* of energy. A locomotion, as its name implies, is motion around a point, or *cyclical motion*. It is associated with bending in the arc of a circle, or rotation, or a vibrating string audible as a musical tone of constant pitch. Circular shapes or tendencies are products of tension and resistance. To draw a circle, the string between the chalk and the center has to be held tight. Where there is resistance, there is conservation of energy. When the bowstring is released, the bow takes up the slack and restores the tension to its former state. So in the working of a bow there are two types of force: one, resistance, associated with curvature and conservation of energy (the bow); the other, impulsion, associated with straight lines, added force, and expenditure of energy (the string and arrow).

A further complication arises from the fact that two different forces are involved. One is the tone associated with a stretched string "at rest," before the arrow is inserted. The constant tone of a bowstring in vibration represents the degree of tension maintained by the bow. (How long the string is, is not the issue here, but rather its constancy of tension, which is partly Zeno's point.) The motion of a stretched string oscillates back and forth until the superfluous energy of plucking it is dissipated as sound, but its underlying tension remains the same. The ancients associated cyclical motion (such as the energy contained in a circle or arc, such as a bow) with conservation of energy and stable dynamic processes such as the orbital motion of the planets. The energy released in drawing the bow and shooting an arrow, on the other hand, was recognized as an *alteration*, associated with straight line motion, and distinguished as impulsive, finite, and directed to a limited and local goal. Thus, the action of firing an arrow made use of stored energy of a cyclical nature to convert excess energy of an impulsive nature into directed motion. The Greeks distinguished dynamic processes and relationships in nature that were self-perpetuating, like the days, the phases of the moon, tides, seasons, and motion of celestial bodies, from one-off events that were terminal. The former, constructive, are associated with harmonic ratios, the latter, destructive, with nonharmonic ratios.

Notes

1. O. A. W. Dilke, *Mathematics and Measurement*. London: British Museum Press, 1987, 26.
2. Sir James Jeans, *The Growth of Physical Science*. Cambridge: Cambridge University Press, 1950, 29.
3. Sir James Jeans, *The Growth of Physical Science*, 10–11.
4. Lancelot Hogben, *Mathematics for the Million* 3rd rev. edn. London: George Allen & Unwin, 1951, 17–19.

NINE

ZENO'S ARROW

Zeno is said to have wanted to establish the existence of an indivisible continuum between points in time and space.[1] This only amounts to an achievement in a situation where continuity is either unquantifiable or practically undemonstrable, as in calculating the circumference of a wheel, or the "note-length" (frequency span) of a stretched string. If matter resolves into atoms, it is natural to wonder if space and time also resolve into fundamental particles. The higher up the scale the violinist's fingers move, the shorter the distance between adjacent notes. It suggests an ultimate point of convergence toward the end of the fingerboard where successive locations (notes, quantities, or ratios) merge into a seamless continuum. The proposition that only what can be measured is knowable and real, and hence reality and measure are the same, is remarkably persistent in human affairs. Just as a perception of the rainbow as bands of color does not alter the fact that the visible spectrum is a frequency continuum, so a musician is bound to protest that the existence of harmonics as privileged divisions of a stretched string determined by its endpoints in no way alters the continuity of frequency between them, and go on to prove the point by playing a gliding tone, gipsy style, from high to low. Intellectual devotion to the reality of measurable (hence, computable and standardizable) objects, is all the same in conflict with a real-world experience of continuous change, not just in pitch, but in space and time as well (we move about, we grow older).

It is easy to imagine an elderly Parmenides presiding over a debate over the ideal compatibility of length, frequency, and tension ratios of strings in vibration, suddenly experiencing a moment of epiphany that vibrations in air perceived as musical tones do not exist in themselves but are only audible as the consequence of energy imparted to the strings and disturbing them from their natural rest state, which is manifestly still and silent. The pitch ratios under discussion are therefore representative of human actions and not of the strings themselves. That the eye cannot see the movement of a moving string other than as a blur can therefore be taken as a divine indication of the "invalid" nature of movement as a distortion of reality rather than a true state of being. Such a view would be consistent with the "invalid" or noncomputable ratios of π and the square root of 2, both of which relate to movement, the former of a wheel, the latter of a bowstring.

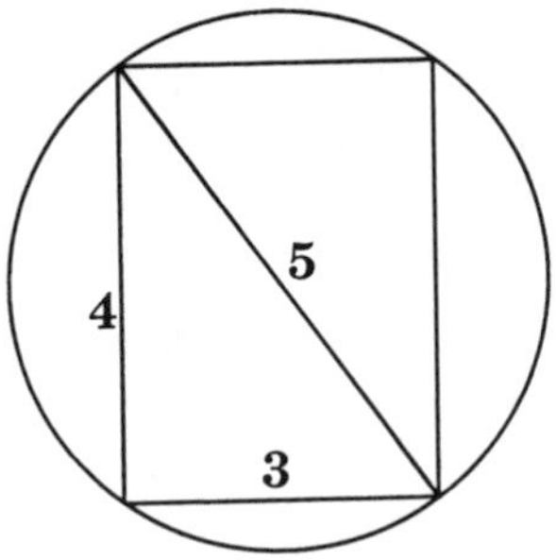

The hypotenuse of a right triangle is inevitably the diameter of a circle

On the other hand, having established the 3 : 4 : 5 triangle as a harmony in geometry reconcilable with the circle, with rational number values, with the inverse square law as tension ratios, and with the musical triad, the Pythagoreans would take confidence in their belief in the ultimate unification of the dynamic forces of nature with the timeless perfection of a universe in harmonious proportion.

Adding excess energy to a passively resonating body (or string, or column of air) has the effect of converting chaotic (inflicted) motion into structured (resonant) motion. In Greek terms, the bow or monochord converts an *alteration* or impulse, energy which can only decay, into a *locomotion* or cyclical motion, a form which is continuous and self-renewing. This is so obvious and significant a difference, not even a barbarian could have ignored it. In order to make a stretched string or a pipe produce a sound, you have to add energy to an instrument that is silent in its undisturbed state, like the wise man of the proverb. In adding energy you discover the acoustic quality and response of the string or tube, eventually achieving by a process of feedback a state of dynamic exchange between the distorting energy being added (by bowing or blowing) and the natural resistance of the instrument structure, producing an oscillation radiated as a musical tone. In addition to being pleasant to listen to, a musical tone is the sign of a dynamic compromise, and an efficient mode of vibration (or energy dissipation) by a resonating structure. Where you have an integrated structure of fixed length (even an air column open at both ends is a structure) the continuous addition of energy must be absorbed or dissipated; if absorbed, the structure is likely to heat up, if radiated, it vibrates in alternate phases of absorption and radiation. That vibration, moreover, can be transferred to the air cavity of a pot or hollow vessel, or to a sounding board, hollow log, or membrane. A musical tone is mysterious in several ways. It is a consequence of energy being introduced, stored momentarily, and then released in a structured form. A reverberation outlives the impulsive energy that set it in motion, storing and releasing it economically in a vibrating process audible as a tone of constant pitch. Not all vibrating bodies emit a constant pitch, only those of a certain hardness, tension, or harmoniousness of inner structure. The stability of a musical tone is open to be interpreted as a metaphor of human life, physical status, and moral constitution—in other words, as indicative of personal integrity, or integrity of the entire structure.

A constant tone, as of a bowstring in vibration, is not only a sign of consistency in relations, as of tension and length, but also easier to hear analytically, for example in the sound of a digeridu. A modulated monotone is easier to hear at a distance than an inflected speaking voice, (a) because the energy of the tone is focused on a single modulated frequency, like a laser, and (b) because a steady tone is unlike any other sound in nature, and thus stands out from the background even though it may not be loud. Modulations of the monotone are perceived as changes of balance within the resonant spectrum of a constant fundamental. The speech content of monotone chant, mouth music, or a robot voice is modulated timbre, or formant resonance, of the constant tone functioning as a carrier frequency. Constancy of the fundamental is an expression of unity and continuity; modulation of the tone, the variable that carries information. It is the same for radio transmissions. What the listener discerns as information is expressed as spectrum variation of a fundamental carrier frequency. That the principle of transmitting information on a modulated drone was well understood is shown by the worldwide distribution of drone instruments and jaw harps among folk cultures. Singing voices in harmony show unity (empathy) by virtue of their close harmony, and emotion by individual or collective distortion of an existing stable harmony; on that basis emotion is indicated by variation in harmony, or dissonance. That voices singing at pitches other than the unison or octave can still be understood as singing the same words indicates an empathy that transcends considerations of pitch identity or unity. Formants are cavity resonances within a certain bandwidth unaffected by the pitch of a singing or speaking voice. The same lyrics sung simultaneously in high and low registers by male and female voices, or in harmony, are no less intelligible for being sung at different pitch levels. Heterophony, where the same words are intoned in rhythm, but out of unison, is a way of demonstrating unity without any sacrifice of personal identity.

Two paradoxes associated with Zeno involve a stretched string. In the paradox of Achilles and the tortoise, the hidden allusion is to a monochord; in the motionless arrow paradox the allusion is to the bowstring. On the surface, the arrow paradox alludes to the flight path of an arrow from a bow: Zeno's point (so to speak) being that the arrow does not move because it cannot occupy a space greater than itself and therefore must be motionless to have an exact location at any one moment. If the paradox of a moving arrow is one of impossibility of definition of movement, other than as a succession of arrows at a succession of locations in space and time (like frames of an animated movie), then we have to wonder whether the riddle is actually referring to a real arrow, which manifestly moves continuously in a continuous space, or is intended as a metaphor for some other phenomenon in nature that is not normally visible. Such a paradox also arises as a logical extension of defining a trajectory in time and space as a succession of points.

Apollo is the god of music and also of war (archery); the two roles are connected, involving expert knowledge of the behavior of a stretched string. Hence, imagery in myth of archery and hitting a target is also about music and its influence. At a deeper level the arrow is not from Apollo's but Cupid's bow: a metaphorical arrow, the tone of a plucked musical instrument (a harp, for instance) that flies through the air to excite sympathetic vibrations in the heart-strings of the target listener and render her helpless. The underlying

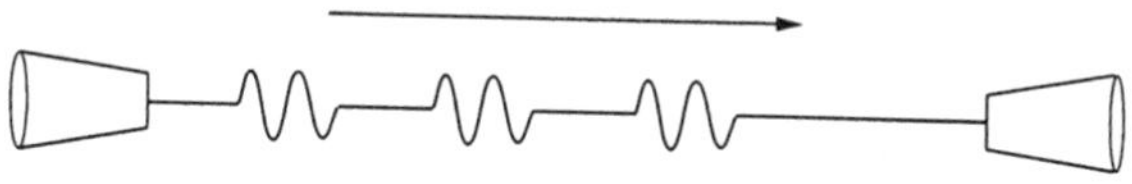

Sound travels along a stretched string from paper cup to paper cup, and yet the string does not move

question is really about sound and how it travels invisibly through the air. Zeno's paradox gains in potency from the fact that it was of interest to his contemporaries to reflect that the air through which sound is carried does not itself move. If sound, a physical disturbance, is carried through the air, one would expect the air to move as well. So the question arises, if the air does not move, what then is sound and how does it travel? Commentators tend to interpret the puzzle literally and be baffled at what Zeno appears to be saying: that for every instant in its flight a new arrow comes into existence, since there is an arrow at the moment of launching, and an arrow that strikes the target, and we presume at all intermediate points in between, even though it is impossible to determine precisely where it is at any one moment, or how it is possible for it to move instantaneously from one point to the next. The analogy with movement of energy along a vibrating string is apparent since we know the string's exact location at either end, but are unable to determine the exact location of any intermediate point in the energized string for as long as it continues to vibrate. And because sounds in air are invisible, a listener can only intuit their existence at the point of departure (the voice or instrument) and arrival (the listener) but is unable to verify their position and movement at any intermediate point.

So perhaps Zeno is not talking about a physical arrow at all, but the movement of a shock wave through the air. That sound consists of shock waves is understood from the familiar experience of a clap of thunder, the impact of which can be felt as a palpable blow to the skin. To be struck by such a sound raises the issue of where it came from, and how it got there. That a person can feel the impact suggests a substantial body, and since sound is invisible, it raises the issue of the nature of an invisible substantial body. A substantial body traveling through the air with the speed of an arrow and striking a person, would normally create a rush of turbulence in its wake. However, a clap of thunder does no such thing. It is invisible, palpable, but somehow insubstantial. It is as though nothing has moved. If anything, the air is "electric" and unnaturally still.

Zeno's arrow metaphor is apt because a real arrow normally delivers a blow to a recipient by overcoming the resistance of the intervening atmosphere and without creating any shock wave along the way. That the sounds of music represented by Cupid's arrows, launched from the strings of the lyre, are fatal blows in their own way is a charming but incidental fancy. Zeno's suggestion that the arrow in flight is regenerated from moment to moment is a perhaps enigmatic, but not altogether fanciful way of describing how a sound wave is actually propagated. Given that energy passes in a straight (or perhaps, curved) line through the center balls of an executive toy, or the intervening beads of a string of beads, without appearing to disturb them, Zeno's self-reproducing arrow can be understood as a poetic metaphor for a sound wave passing through successive layers of the atmosphere. From that viewpoint, the image of a succession of arrows forming at every point along its trajectory makes sense. We observe a cork bobbing on expanding ripples of a pond into which a pebble has been thrown. That the cork bobs up and down, but is not carried away on the ripples, leads to the conclusion that the wave motion is passing through the water, rather than corresponding to a tidal movement of the water itself.

Explaining the propagation of sound through the air is not an easy task. Zeno uses the convenient and poetic image of an arrow in flight, but only to demonstrate that the conventional use of poetic analogy (the image of force as an arrow, or solid projectile) leads to paradox, and the truth is elsewhere. But the paradox is remarkably persistent. Nineteenth- and twentieth-century textbooks of musical acoustics continue to explain the propagation of a sound wave by impact from point to point in terms of a line of falling dominoes. The alternative image of a zone of compression passing along a spring, while more difficult to visualize, more readily expresses the dynamics of sound propagation, since it conveys the idea of the atmosphere as a compressible medium. Another popular demonstration is of speech waves transmitted through a taut length of twine connecting a pair of empty tin cans or waxed paper cups. This is closer to a model of a vibrating string, with the difference that a plucked or bowed string is stretched beyond its rest length, whereas

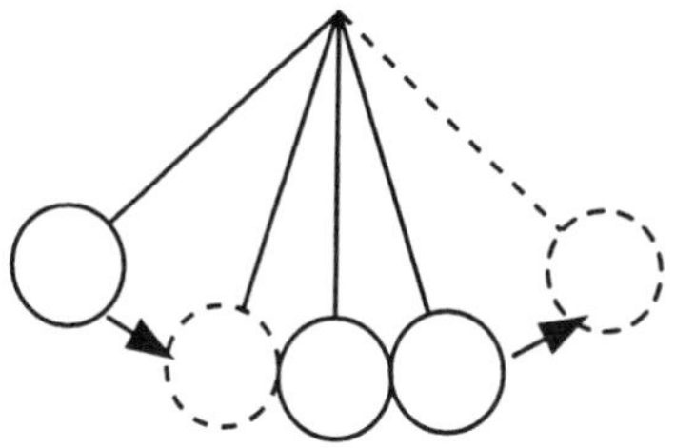

Zeno's arrow paradox: a fable of the transference of energy. The ball in the middle does not move

a voice speaking into a paper cup mouthpiece tends to propagate as compression waves (waves of reduced tension).

An alternative to a set of dominoes readily available to ancient cultures was a string of uniform beads of good quality, shall we say glass (in deference to the *Glass Bead Game* of Hermann Hesse), that is, beads of consistent size strung on a fine wire allowing them freedom of movement. In theory, the impact of a blow to the bead at one end passes through the whole string and causes the loose bead at the other end to move away, the intermediate beads remaining in place. The conceptual difficulty of the image of beads on a string is that beads are physical objects, whereas sound is immaterial and travels through the air, making arrows in flight a more appropriate, if more mystifying analogy.

The notion of transference of force from domino to domino, or bead to bead, harmonizes rather well with the definition of a line as a succession of points, since a theory of sound propagation requires a succession of points or zones in contact through which to pass. Although in theory a hypothesis of motion reduced to a potentially infinite succession of impacts suggests infinite force and thus infinite heat, in practice it lends itself to be reconciled with the theory of motion of a wheel, each point on the rim striking the ground vertically in succession, like a miniature piston. It is curious to think that a string of beads or pearls, considered as a fashion statement, also implies a susceptibility to a transfer of emotional energy, amorous or otherwise. The pearls are sounds.

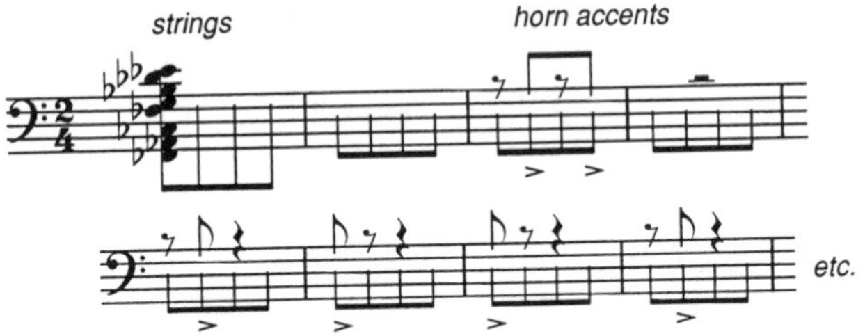

Stravinsky: "Danse des Adolescentes" from
Le Sacre du Printemps

A familiar musical illustration of motion in stasis is heard in the pulsatile "Danse des Adolescentes" of *Le Sacre du Printemps* of 1913 by Stravinsky, a music largely consisting of a single repeating chord, each one a downbeat, played by the string orchestra in close harmony and accented by eight horns. This is a music of immense energy and movement—the image of an express train comes readily to mind—and yet at the same time it does not appear to move at all. Nijinsky's original choreography of the ballet, described by the composer in later life somewhat derisively as "a bunch of knock-kneed Lolitas jumping up and down" reinforces an impression of piston motion.

Like a line of beads or dominoes, an arrow travels in only one direction (directed or impulsive, straight-line motion), whereas a sound spirals outward in every direction (locomotion: motion about a point). All the same, an individual listener can only be aware of a sound as moving in one direction, the line between the listener and the source, hence the image of Cupid's arrow as directed motion is a transformed epithet: we imagine the sound to be directed at ourself, even though it propagates in every direction. That the ancients understood that sound propagates spherically is evident in their construction of outdoor auditoria as segments of a hollow sphere, demonstrating the spread of sound as equal in every direction and not directed preferentially to one target, and not linear, but radiant. That the ancients were concerned on occasion to limit the spread of sound and focus its energy in a single direction is indicated just as clearly by the design of early trumpets as signaling instruments. A bow and arrow concentrates power in one direction. It is selective, it expresses choice: it also leads to the metaphor of the chosen one. That ancient cultures also understood the direction of flight of sound as a problematic conversion of cyclical motion (undulatory vibration) into linear or plane motion (sound projection) is often acknowledged in the mythology of the times, including the paradox of Achilles and the tortoise. It may even be inferred from the design of the early military trumpet or buccina as a tube either straight or formed into a circle, in the latter case as though to project sound like the movement of a sling.

The mystery here concerns the relationship of musical vibration, which is "centered on itself" (the vibrating string or air column, which does not go anywhere) to the radiated signal heard at an infinity of points near and far. The "string" or source of vibration that strikes the consciousness of the listener does not move bodily through the air, which remains to all intents and purposes at rest, and yet the sound radiates in every direction simultaneously. The paradox is real and not a figure of speech. Since we cannot speak of sound traveling from point to point, perhaps it is also incorrect to speak of a physical arrow traveling from point to point. Or that even if an arrow did travel continuously it would not be possible to visualize it, because the eye is unable to perceive movement as continuous, but only as a series of saccades, or momentary snapshots (after the manner of the movies, though the movies did not exist in Zeno's time). Here the sticking point concerns what it is possible for human observation to infer of the real (external) world on the basis of internal sensory processes, which consist only of imperfect and momentary impressions.

Identical questions exercised medieval science. In the absence of certain knowledge about the eye, scholars imagined a parallelism of process between vision and hearing. Robert Grosseteste was a lover of music and a student of the physics of music and interval relationships. It is tempting to imagine Grosseteste and his Oxford contemporary Roger Bacon agreeing on the definition of sound as a wave process conducted through the atmosphere, and from there exploring the idea of visual impressions transmitted and received through the atmosphere in an analogous wavelike fashion.[2] That the word *speculative* is understood as referring to an educated guess and not exact observation, may lend residual support to the idea that musical and acoustic knowledge referred to hearing and the monochord was considered more reliable, because more exactly demonstrable by ear, than knowledge based on visual measurement alone.

A wave or particle theory of vision acknowledges the experience of vision as intermittent and voluntary, rather than continuous and passive-receptive, on the basis that people blink and their eyes move spontaneously, change focus, and suffer fatigue. In contrast, our ears do not move of their own volition and our experience of hearing is of a continuous and effortless process.

All of which underlies the broader issue of measurement and definition of processes exhibiting continuity in space and time as a matter of protracted controversy in ancient times, one that recurred in medieval Europe at the rebirth of the science of optics, again in the early baroque era in relation to equal temperament and accelerated motion, yet again in the late nineteeth and early twentieth century in relation to time, motion photography, the wave-particle theory of light, and harmonic discontinuities of subatomic energy states in the era of Niels Bohr and Erwin Schrödinger, through to string theory in the present day. That western music notation persists in recognizing pitch and time as particulate, and continuous change (gliding tones, accelerations, and retards) as local aberrations, only reinforces long-term cultural and intellectual difficulties in handling continuity and continuous change in any dimension of human experience. A hereditary inability to quantify change without lapsing into irrational or noncomputable numbers may account for the mysterious reluctance of many nineteenth-century intellectuals to concede the reality of a world in dynamic motion captured in moving pictures and sound recordings. The pioneer psychologist Hugo Münsterberg, a Harvard colleague of William James, declared that "films, by their nature, observe the laws of the mind rather than those of the outer world"—a very German use of the transferred epithet, as if to suggest that a mechanical representation were able to observe anything, let alone see into a person's mind.

That Greek science was concerned with universal answers links its goals with today's quest for a Theory of Everything, along with the irrational but tidy anticipation that nature's laws of vision are bound to harmonize with those relating to the sense of hearing. In *The Dream of Scipio*, Cicero supposes that the more distant a planet is from the earth, the faster it travels through the heavens, a flight of fancy interpreting frequency as speed of orbital motion, by analogy with the acceleration of a whirring slingshot as it stretches out to its maximum spin.[3] Aristotle is more reliable, correctly identifying the Doppler effect (a rise and fall in pitch of a moving source of sound, approaching then receding) as not intrinsic to the source but an effect of its movement in relation to a stationary observer. Galileo's celebrated experiment of rolling marbles down a slope, to measure acceleration in physical space, correlates precisely with efforts by his contemporaries to harmonize alterations of scale in frequency space, in musical terms the newly fashionable seventeenth-century practice of modulating from key to key.

Today we account for continuous change by appealing to abstractions such as momentum and the transfer of energy. In former times, as we now appreciate, the same abstractions or "natural causes" were personified and given the names and characters of gods or heroes. Having godlike status simply means that the forces or laws represented by them operated consistently and impartially throughout the observable world and not as a consequence of local and individual decision-making or magic. That musical instruments were devised and employed to inquire into natural laws makes sense. Indeed, the uniquely verifiable nature of musical inquiries into harmony, force, ratio, and tension—the fact that music deals in demonstrable phenomena—accorded music a privileged status among the sciences that endured at least until the late seventeenth century of Isaac Newton, a status that continues to resonate in the most abstruse and difficult areas of speculation of the twenty-first century, despite the fact that the contribution of musical reasoning to modern science has long since been discarded from serious consideration.

INFINITE SETS

Prior to the work of Georg Cantor in the mid–nineteenth century, a number of leading mathematicians denied the existence of real

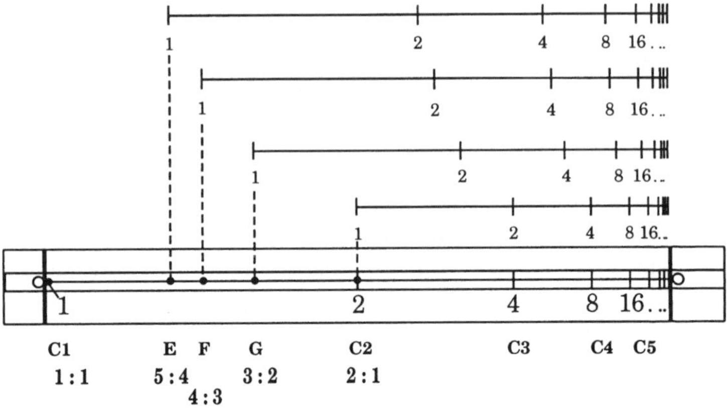

Shown here on a monochord, the set of harmonics of a given fundamental is infinite, as is the set of any division of the fundamental

infinities. According to Karl Friedrich Gauss, the infinite was an abomination, a mere figure of speech. Cantor is credited with proving the existence not only of infinite sets, but orders of magnitude of infinite sets, to which he assigned "transfinite" numbers, the smallest, *aleph null*, comprising the integers (. . . –5, –4, –3, –2, –1, 1, 2, 3, 4, 5 . . .). This or any infinite subset of objects that can be put into correspondence with the integers (1, 2, 3, 4, 5 . . .) is called *countable*. Cantor was able to show that the set of all integral fractions (for example, musical intervals) is countable, but the set of irrational numbers that cannot be expressed as integral fractions (such as π and the square root of 2) is not countable. The transfinite number that counts real numbers (rational together with irrational) Cantor called *aleph one*, or C (for *continuum*), because it counts the number of points on a line segment.[4]

A musician confronted with a series 1/2 + 1/3 + 1/4 + 1/5 . . . recognizes straight away that it is musical in implication, since it corresponds to the successive harmonics of a stretched string, and the conclusion that the series is infinite, as equivalent to demonstrating musically that in principle the finite physical length of a string contains an infinite series of harmonics.

With the aid of an open string (monochord or violin, or cello), a musician can both demonstrate the existence of an infinite number of rational and irrational fractions, and also explain Zeno's paradox of Achilles and the tortoise. In fact, it is hardly possible to solve the older paradox without at the same time introducing the concept of infinite sets.

Consider what the ancient Greeks understood by a *race*. We think of a race as a contest between ostensible equals to find which of the group is the most perfect athlete, which may be in terms of speed, explosive strength, or endurance, all of which in the long run are effects of harmonious interaction of body parts in motion. The remarkable difference in the case of Achilles and the tortoise is the obvious physical inequality between the two. As in the fable of the cicada and the ant, when two very different creatures are compared, we are meant to understand that they are not being compared as like for like, even though the notion of a contest seems to presuppose a degree of equality between the two. The reader who assumes that the contest between Achilles and the tortoise is simply a race has not understood the fine detail of the scenario, which is structured to ask not which candidate is the winner, but what is the relationship between weight and velocity in a vibrating string. Such a question makes sense because the fundamental *frequency* (i.e., pitch, often mistakenly identified as the *velocity*) of a stretched string can be increased by either shortening the string, or adding weight and thus increasing the tension on the string. For the pitch of a string to rise when encumbered with extra weight, is counterintuitive. It begs the question: how can the speed of vibration of a string be increased by putting more weight on it, since in the real world if you pile extra weight on a runner he will run more slowly.

The string of a stringed instrument is understood as a fixed length at a preset and constant tension. That tension can be varied by the addition or subtraction of weights, the length remaining the same. A change in tension accounts for a change in audible pitch of the unstopped, freely vibrating string. However the string may also be stopped at any point along its length, the tension remaining the same, to create a different pitch, exactly as the fingers move up and down a guitar or violin string to create a melody. Since the string along its length is manifestly continuous, so in the same way pitch is also understood as a manifest continuum, since a specific pitch can be stopped at a specific point, and only at that point. However, we make a distinction between integral divisions (1/2, 1/3, 1/4, . . .) and compound fractions (2/7, 4/9 etc.) of a string, because the former are generated at integral divisions of the length of the string, and not at any other locations. Though the same occur equally in pipes, the coincidence of harmonics and rational fractions is more convincingly demonstrated in stretched strings, where harmonics and their locations are simultaneously audible, visible, and tangible, than for pipe instruments where the relationship of harmonics to divisions of a fundamental length is less easy to discern and harder to verify.

Recognition by the ancients of the implications of infinite sets or scales (in all but name) can be inferred from the absence of universal standards of linear measure in the ancient world. Arithmetic dealt with quantities, geometry with ratios, and the problem for the ancients lay in finding ways of reconciling the two. The invention of money in the trading of goods came about, at least in part, in order to allow the values of different goods to be reconciled. One can understand the desire of early civilizations to achieve an equivalent harmonization of standards in the physical domains of area, volume, material, and force. It is a matter of significance that all of the above dimensions are reconciled in the characteristic sound of a stringed instrument: its surface area radiating sound energy, the volume of air contained within the sound box enhancing the tone at particular frequencies, the relative contributions of weight and density of material of the sound box, and ultimately the tension of the string itself. The search for universals is an old problem that will not go away. It is the basis of an ongoing quest in the world of science for a Theory of Everything.

THESEUS AND THE MINOTAUR

The story of Theseus and the Minotaur is a legend about what today we would call chaotic motion and the strange attractor. It tells of the periodic (annual) sacrifice of a virgin to a man-bull (a metaphor for an untamed energy source) held captive in the center of a circular labyrinth. It tells how the hero Theseus finds his way into the center of the labyrinth, despatches the bull, and finds his way out again with the aid of a harmless thread. Like other legends of sacrifice with musical implications, such as Stravinsky's ballet *Le Sacre du Printemps*, the structural features of the story draw attention to cyclical processes in nature, including the shedding of blood, sexual violence, and the death of innocence, as rites of passage associated with spring and rebirth. In Picasso's lithograph, the Minotaur is depicted as blind, like Samson, as well as trapped within the labyrinth, a way of saying that the strength of the bull represents a *blind*

This optical illusion resembling a spider in a labyrinth is a moiré produced by the superimposition of patterns of concentric circles in white and black. According to the Greek myth, Theseus sought the Minotaur trapped in the center of a maze, a concentric labyrinth representing a cross-section of a vibrating string

natural force confined within a tangled maze that cannot be navigated by sight by ordinary mortals, only by *touch*, and from which the beast cannot find its way out.

A labyrinth can be imagined as a connected maze of concentric circles, an unmistakable image from acoustics, of waves of sound radiating outward in space, forming a complex pathway that ordinary mortals can neither see nor penetrate unaided. Theseus's task is not just to find his way to the center of the maze where the power is greatest, and neutralize it, but also to avoid being trapped himself, and find his way out again. The task is symmetrical: a rite of death or conquest, leading to rebirth or restoration of peace, one of painstakingly tracking down and neutralizing a force of nature, and surviving to tell the tale by retracing one's path. Today's world is accustomed to constructing labyrinths like beltways around the centers of power, and equally having to deal with labyrinthine bureaucracies on the way to reaching the sources of power at their center. Since the Minotaur is part human, part bull, one might expect to find it charging about in all directions in the center of the labyrinth like any angry bull at a rodeo or bullfight. This bull however is a figure of tragedy. The Minotaur is clearly not an image of arbitrary political authority but a living force owing its existence ultimately to Zeus (who himself was also not averse to assuming the form of a bull from time to time). It is thus open to be construed as the equivalent of a rock star today, an uncontrolled, possibly predatory, energy of a kind that demands and receives sacrificial offerings of young virgins. In other words, the Minotaur represents the power of music, or more specifically, the power visible as the chaotic motion described by the cross-section of a vibrating string. At the center of the labyrinth is a rock star; the labyrinth itself, the sound of a guitar (or perhaps even the bony labyrinth of the cochlea).

When a guitar string is plucked and allowed to vibrate freely its power is clear to the ear as a highly resolved tone of constant pitch, but contradictorily to vision, as a chaotic motion unresolvable to the naked eye. One can see nevertheless that the blurred outer shape of the moving string is invariably symmetrical. Unlike a hurricane, the eye of which is a menacing calm, the region of greatest uncertainty in a vibrating string is always the center. Once the power center of a vibratory labyrinth is reached, there remains still more complexity to be negotiated to pass through and reach the other end. The indirect route in and out involves finding a way through the undulations of a strange attractor without getting lost. Theseus is aided in his quest by laying down a thread, the gift of Ariadne, along his path. After silencing the Minotaur, he finds his way back to safety by following the thread. The original maze is transformed into a complex of boundary conditions, while the intricacy and uncertainty of the task are reduced to following a simple length of slack string. There are hints of a spiderweb as well, and not just in the graphics of overlaid concentric circles. From a single thread, a spider weaves a maze that no other insect can negotiate, and lurks at the center to wait for its victims to blunder into its sticky labyrinth. The message is that in order to dispose of the power vested in the sound of the guitar, simply cut the string and all of that passion and grief is suddenly reduced to a limp thread. Freudian exegetes take note. We have already encountered the motif of cutting the cord in the stories of Samson, Rapunzel, and Jack and the Beanstalk.

As with all myths, this one operates on more than one level.

The power at the center of this labyrinthine structure—the Minotaur—cannot be liberated or dealt with in isolation. By a divine irony it resides, like the power of a bow or a guitar, in the constraints placed on its movements, in the same way as a bow or guitar has no power or influence except when its string is held fast at either end to so great a tension that it resonates at the slightest touch. Since the shape and power of a vibrating string in tension also resemble the physical shape and intrinsic power of a muscle terminating in fixed tendons at either end, it may not be too far-fetched to interpret the mythical death of Hector and humiliation of his corpse by a triumphant Achilles, dragging Hector's corpse through the city by a rope tied to his heel, as a metaphor for the loss of power and eloquence of a bow- or lyre string once it has been cut and rendered speechless and slack.

Much the same point is made, if with rather more wit, by the Elizabethan poet Thomas Wyatt in his lyric "Blame not my lute," a song of unrequited love that brings together in exemplary fashion Zeno's image of the darts of love and the vibrating strings of a lute played none too well. Clearly a classical scholar, Wyatt cautions the reluctant object of his affections that cutting the strings of his lute will not make his music—or the love that drives it—go away. New strings can always be found, and lo! there the music is again to remind her of his undying passion.[5]

Farewell, Unknown! For though thou break
My strings in spite with great disdain
Yet have I found out for thy sake
Strings for to string my lute again!

Hidden in this gentle message is a deeper meditation on the persistence of energy. The coupled system of lute and string is merely a vehicle of the motivation or directed energies of the poet. In turn the poet is energized by his attraction to the beauty of the lady. This is an image of a renaissance universe in which the power represented by the Minotaur is inextinguishable and can only be passed from body to body. That his fair lady *resists* the message of the poet's music is paradoxical proof that she is all the same *touched and influenced* by the energies transmitted across the space between them from the vibrating strings of his instrument. "My lute and strings may not deny" he sings, in effect saying that the laws of motion being invoked are universal and not subject to denial by objects or mere mortals. The poet identifies his feelings with these eternal laws, which remain constant through time and space.

Notes

1. A. C. Crombie, "The Mechanistic Hypothesis and the Study of Vision." In *Science, Optics and Music in Medieval and Early Modern Thought*. London: Hambledon Press, 1990, 177.
2. A. C. Crombie, "Avicenna's Influence." In *Science, Optics and Music in Medieval and Early Modern Thought*, 105.
3. Robin Maconie, *The Concept of Music*. Oxford: Clarendon Press, 1990, 85–87.
4. John Barrow, *Theories of Everything: The Quest for Ultimate Explanation* (London: Oxford University Press, 1990). New edition. London: Vintage, 1992, 33–34.
5. Robin Maconie, *The Second Sense: Language, Hearing, and Music*. Lanham, MD: The Scarecrow Press, 2002, 147–48.

TEN

PATH INTEGRAL

> The Ionian tendency was to see motion everywhere; it was rest that had to be explained, or rather the appearance of it. [1]
>
> J. BURNET

> If you don't know where you are going, any road will get you there.
>
> THE RED QUEEN

It is a matter of wonder to reflect that our most gifted physicists are now able to speak with confidence about the state of the universe some 16 billion years ago, 10^{-35} second after the big bang, whereas their colleagues seeking to determine the weather two weeks ahead are open to frustration by the equivalent beating of a butterfly's wings. (It is not the butterfly that is to blame, but rather the need to establish starting conditions to an impossible degree of precision. Not that precision is impossible, but because to establish *any* starting condition with absolute precision is impossible.)

Of passing interest to musicians is the ostentatious reemergence in theoretical physics of concepts relating to music of which string theory is only among the more notorious. The development is interesting for two reasons, first, that the physicists themselves are coming forward with musical analogies for imaginary processes that are difficult to explain in any other terms, and second, because most of the time, musically speaking, they do not make any sense. Whether the musical analogies of modern cosmology are intended to be taken seriously, or are simply designed to make the accompanying theories more palatable to a wider readership, is not always clear. The "butterfly effect" of chaos theory is a statement to the effect that because one can never define the starting conditions of a system in continuous evolution with absolute precision, one can

Feynman's multiple path (sum over histories) diagram accounts for gaps in the recorded trajectory of an accelerated particle

never predict its subsequent condition with complete accuracy, since a numerical error corresponding to the *order of magnitude* of a butterfly's wings flapping in a weather system can generate a cascade effect in subsequent computation equivalent to generating a tropical hurricane in a matter of weeks on the other side of the world. This is a myth of computer modeling. In real life there is no definable initial steady state. That was Laplace's little joke.

Feynman's path integral (we have seen it before) is another case in point. Here it concerns the probable movement of a particle through space from a given starting point to an endpoint, both of which are exactly defined albeit arbitrary locations. In practice it also accounts for the unseen path of a subatomic particle between origin and reappearance points in an image from a particle accelerator, and is thus the mathematical description of an invisible jump between two endpoints. In other words, it askes the opposite question to "How long is a piece of string?"—which is, "How big is the gap?" On the one hand, the solution is equivalent to calculating the line of least resistance taken by an electrical discharge across the gap between two electrodes. In the present case, which involves a disappearance and reappearance, the route taken between exit and reentry points is treated as the continuation of a point into another dimension, rather than (or in addition to) a succession of points that imply increments in time. Writing for the general reader, Stephen Hawking defines the *string* of string theory as "a one-dimensional object having only length," a definition that while appearing to be the same as a line or a path, crucially fudges the time dimension.[2] Whereas we would normally consider a line as an extension or pathway connecting points of departure and arrival, along which information travels in time, a line defined as a one-dimensional object having extension only in time, assuming time to be a space-like dimension, is one in which the information at every point is simultaneous with the information at every other point.[3]

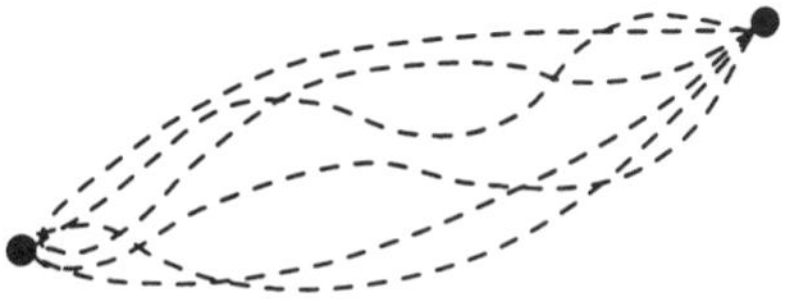

The trajectory of a particle *in motion* has wavelike properties, in accordance with the principles of quantum electrodynamics. To a musician, it resembles the movement of an imaginary peak—back and forth, but mainly forth—between the fixed ends of a vibrating string. Hawking explains, "Feynman disputed the classical assumption that a particle follows a fixed trajectory, suggesting that particles travel *from one location to another* along every possible path through spacetime. With each trajectory Feynman associated two numbers, one for the size—the amplitude—of a wave and one for its phase—whether it is at a crest or a trough. The probability of a particle going from A to B is found by adding up the waves associated with every possible path that *passes through* A and B."[4] The conventional illustration provided by Hawking and reproduced above shows points A and B as fixed, and the path integral as a superposition of possible paths, resembling a Marey photogram, or futurist painting of the early 1900s of the movement of a skipping rope.

To a musician the diagram is open to be construed as a careless image of the movement of a vibrating string. There is nothing in the author's summary to suggest that the fixed locations of the start and endpoints have any influence on the particle's choice of trajectories, despite the fact that all of them meet at the same two fixed points. Hawking's form of words, saying only that the particle is "passing through" points A and B, implies that their joint locations in imaginary space and time, while fixed, are not only arbitrary, but of no consequence. To a musician, this is about as logical as saying that the movement creating the note E on the bass string of a guitar is also just "passing through" the two endpoints and their locations have nothing to do with it. The scientists' tendency to focus attention on the trajectory as a wavelike movement between two points, while ignoring the limiting contribution of the two endpoints to the possibilities of motion between them, is completely antithetical to how a musician would interpret such a process.

The Pythagoreans were aware of an equivalent mystery, which we know as sympathetic vibration, observing a mysterious influence or transference of energy from a moving pendulum to other pendulums of differing length suspended from the same structure, or from harp strings to other strings on the same instrument. To them the induced vibration was evidence of action at a distance communicated across empty space. The Greeks also observed that the passive pendulums or strings excited into sympathetic motion at a distance were only those whose natural frequencies were in harmony with the active element. They perceived sympathetic vibration both as an intellectual and as a moral challenge. Intellectually, the task was to explain the transfer of energy and influence through the air or framework connecting active and passive vibrating strings; morally, the phenomenon could be seen as similar to the power of rhetoric, accounting for the transfer of information from teacher to pupil, or speaker to listener, exciting a positive resonance only in those listeners who were already mentally tuned to the same wavelength. (This analogy would later become the basis of the dubious science of rhetoric in the seventeenth and eighteenth centuries, and the basis of a psychology of leadership as residing in the speaker's power to excite a harmonious response in others in passive attendance, not so much by quality of argument as by the energy, rhythm, and melody of the speech itself.)

In the nineteenth century much the same conundrum emerged with the discovery of radio waves radiating through the ether and capable of exciting a response in a receiver tuned to resonate at the transmitting frequency. The subsequent employment of radio as an instrument of propaganda in the early twentieth century seems to tap into ancient mythical implications of action at a distance and the power of rhetoric. Poetically, sympathetic vibration is a phenomenon requiring the transmitter and receiver to be attuned to the same frequency, or to be vibrating in sympathy with one another.

The musical equivalent of Feynman's path integral is relatively trivial. What Feynman appears to be saying is that between every pair of locations A and B representing an interval or interruption in the path of a particle in motion (which we are invited to consider as a *line*), it is impossible (indeed, unnecessary) to specify a precise trajectory. The particle can be assumed notwithstanding to take every possible path between A and B, and the sum of all possible trajectories is always the same.

The probability of a particle going from A to B is determined by the precision with which A and B, and the time elapsed, are measured. If A and B and the time elapsed are fixed—which by implication they have to be—then the sum of all possible trajectories is the same as the sum of all possible waveforms intersecting these exact two points in space and time. They therefore correspond to the sum of possible vibrations of a stretched string. Since the sum of all possible vibrations of a stretched string is audible as the behavior and tone of a bowstring or harp string, or the string of a musical instrument, it is familiar musical knowledge. To a musician, such curves are invariably harmonic divisions of the distance between the two endpoints, and adding them all together is equivalent to modeling the oscillatory behavior of a vibrating string: there is certainty at either termination and a probabilistic antinode of maximum uncertainty midway between A and B, but certainly no tangle of unrelated possibilities.

To allude to a "collapse of the wave function in the presence of an observer" sounds like a rather grandiose, even mystical, term of last resort to acknowledge the power of the endpoints, even of a thought experiment, to determine the path that may be taken between them. But the point of the mystification is surely that the path of the particle is a movement in elapsed time, beginning at A and ending a moment later at B. If A and B on the other hand coexist simultaneously the problem is solved at once, since the location of B is bound to influence the movement of the particle. This is not entirely fanciful, since much the same imagery in nature has been captured on camera, of lightning strikes where charges are seen rising from the ground to meet discharges descending from above.

For a particle to travel from A to B requires energy. A particle traveling an infinite number of routes from A to B would require infinite energy. Since however the moving particle is identical with itself, the issue is not that it exists in every part of the universe at once on its way between A and B, or that we don't know or are unable to predict exactly where it is along the way, or even that the contributing energy may be surplus to the requirements of travel between these two points. The energy of the particle at point A is measured, likewise at point B. The question remaining is whether it can pick up any more energy in between. Presumably there are no filling stations on the way. From a musician's perspective of a stretched string, there is no need to know how much energy is involved in order to make the string vibrate, since we know the vibration travels from A to B, and in order to go from A to B it is bound to have had at least enough energy to make the one-way trip. Whatever the tension of the string, the sum of all possible modes of vibration in between is bound to conform to the same rules (expanding to maximum uncertainty in the center, converging to fixed points at either end). Furthermore, the totality of movement is symmetrical whether the movement is forward or backward in time. Only after the transition is complete does the question of accounting for any surplus energy arise, assuming that the particle does not end its journey at point B but intends to carry on.

To readers who play the guitar or violin an additional mystery in all of this is that the *same* degree of improbability obtains for calculating the movement of the *same* particle *between any two points on its imaginary journey* from A to B. (It is the equivalent of stopping an open string on the fingerboard: the action of stopping the string creates a new fundamental and new mode of vibration attuned to the new distance between endpoints.) The only limiting factor is fixing the points. If you play a scale passage up the string of a guitar, the movement of the string vibration between finger and bridge does not get any simpler, or more or less predictable, as the finger approaches the midpoint, because stopping the string invariably creates a new endpoint and new midpoint. The difficulty is more likely to arise in tracking the line of an accelerated subatomic particle on a photographic plate, from the point where it disappears from view to the point where it reappears. Where the path cannot be seen and may be anywhere, establishing the location of any two intermediate points is not going to be easy.

WHAT PARMENIDES SAID

Parmenides' reported insistence that "Being is changeless, eternal and motionless; change, transitoriness and motion are non-Being and are unreal and illusory" may simply be a modern misconstruction of what he actually intended to say.[5] Let us assume that by "Being" the philosopher means anything the existence of which is *construed* as the same for every observer. This reads like a variation on the Platonic enigma of essences: that no two things in the real world are exactly the same, a consideration difficult for more recent philosophers to entertain, perhaps, especially in an industrial age of manufactured objects all of which are supposed to be alike.

> In a hexameter poem, he describes, in mythological, physical terms (the only terms possible) his experience of rapture. He was swept up from earth in a divine chariot to the closed gates of 'the paths of night and day.' The goddess Dikë—Justice, 'who punishes,' but also more than justice; the Way and the Truth, almost the Chinese Tao—opened to him and taught him that IT IS, and there is no beginning and no end, nor past nor future, but an unchanging present; nor anything outside it, nor any not-being (identified with empty space).
>
> . . . If the senses give impressions contrary to reason, so much the worse for the senses.[6]

If there is no Beginning and no End, then all of time exists in an instantaneous present. Furthermore, if beginning and end are simultaneous—a variant—then time is a spatial dimension. In such a case you do not speak of a particle or wave moving from A to B, since it is already at A and B, and any amplitude or uncertainty of vibration, or direction of movement, is naturally conditioned by the relationship between the observer and the two endpoints between which the motion of a particle is simply demonstrative—a momentarily visible cross-section—of a string in spacetime.

Here, as in music, you cannot speak of vibration as a little local disturbance traveling along a string, since the whole of the string is in vibration. You cannot speak of the metaphorical arrow (of sound) traveling by air, because the air itself does not move. The arrow also does not move *of itself*, but only in response to an external force. Likewise the person drawing the bow is not acting of himself (exercising free will) but is motivated by an external force acting on him (or her). And so on. By motion Parmenides means "life force" or energy. Energy is not consumed, it is merely transferred. All of creation is not in motion in the sense of being independently self-motivated, it is simply engaged in an ongoing exchange of energy: resonating, as a surface resonates in the presence of sounds which in turn are the byproducts of actions of others. What we observe as motion is illusory, since motion cannot be measured. And since we cannot track back to the source of all being, we can never know directly the source of any movement, other than the gods who, being eternal and everywhere at once, paradoxically have no need of movement. By "illusion" Parmenides means empirically unverifiable, subjective, unproven. The evidence in our eyes or ears is located only in our eyes and ears; we cannot know for sure, under our present terms of reasoning, that an observed event correlates in any way to an independent external event, either in location, time, or nature—or even to the perception of others who are by definition "not there" at the point of the observer. Here Parmenides connects with the philosophy of Karl Popper.

Perhaps what Parmenides really wanted to say was more along the lines of the laws of the conservation of energy: "All that exists, and all that we know is the consequence of vibration. Vibration is energy expressed in regular oscillatory motion. What we attribute to change is a consequence of a transfer of energy. Motion (as of an arrow in flight) is not inherent in the arrow but is a consequence of energy applied to it. A transfer of energy is not a loss of energy since energy cannot be lost, only redistributed. Therefore change is energy redistribution, since at a fundamental level the elements of which all creation is constituted remain the same. Movement is not a property of an arrow or missile or planet, but is always the consequence of an external force applied to it." All of which sounds reasonable and consistent with the musical model. It follows that if movement is not inherent in any one *thing* it is invariably the consequence of (or the expression of) energy transferred to it from elsewhere. So it might be concluded, for example, that when we walk it is not ourselves who move, rather it is the energy transferred through our feet that moves the world.

Insistence on permanence of being can also be understood as a statement of the obvious taken to an extreme: that all statements about anything are necessarily descriptions of states, and necessarily instantaneous (in that they are statements of the reality of a given moment of time that is ideally the moment at which the statement is formulated). If so, they can only be true or relevant of the reality of a given instant, and in consequence do not allow us to predict the future, or infer the past. (Much the same sense of entrapment of being is conveyed in the plays of Samuel Beckett.)

However, Parmenides' thesis, in his own words, is the gift of a supernatural agency, the goddess Dikë. That can be read as a way of acknowledging the reality of a world beyond space and time. His message is addressed as a cautionary tale to those among his contemporaries who have shown themselves to be too easily distracted by irrelevant considerations of locality and temporality, of which movement is merely a sign. In order to describe a movement, one has to assign a starting point and an endpoint to the thing moving or moved. These terminations are locations in space and time, and movement is a transition from one to the other. But for the ancient Greeks, neither time nor space is strictly measurable: thus the only way of describing movement is by saying "what and where something is now is not what and where it was then," which is strictly speaking a nonsense since what *was* is no longer available to our senses, and the word "now" is superfluous since no other time is available to us. The question to be decided is whether this is a statement about reality, or the inability of language to formulate universal propositions, or perhaps even that universal propositions are invariably contaminated by human expectations that in turn are either manifestations of the transience of human existence, or evidence of the fallibility of human perceptions. There is for sure a striking congruence of outcomes, in terms of what conclusions it allows us to draw, between the notion of an essentially static universe and the equally crippling definition of language as static —to be used to enforce the perception of a stable and unchanging universe—that surfaced in the wake of Darwin's evolutionary hypothesis, a time coinciding with the invention of new technologies for capturing motion on film and wax, and the concurrent emergence of a new science of relative motion entailed by the concept of a universe in continuous evolution.[7]

PREDESTINATION

Striking evidence is found in Greek drama of a general perception among the ancients of human destiny directed along a lifeline (or in modern physics, a *timeline*) stretching between fixed points of past and future, birth and extinction. Fate is a wire along which the individual is inexorably drawn, not a path the individual discovers for himself or herself. The message of Greek tragedy is that our predecessors were just as preoccupied with the destiny of their heroes, and in the same way, as Feynman and his contemporaries with the life of subatomic particles, and their freedom of motion.

> The earliest Greek philosopher that we know of—Thales—asserted, so Aristotle tells us, that the world is full of *theoi*. Thales was certainly not being religious; he was doing his best to be what we used to call a natural philosopher. His idea seems to have been that the world, the physical world, was not composed of inert matter operated by some external power but had within it its own life, forces, laws. Such *theoi*, clearly, have nothing to do with religion.[8]

The characters of Greek drama are emotional archetypes whose actions under stress are predetermined by the kinds of people they are, in very much the same way as the behavior of elementary particles is explained in terms of their mass, spin, and electrical charge. We do not expect elementary particles to have thoughts or feelings, or indeed that they believe themselves to have free will; rather, we interpret the overwhelming tragedy of the atomic bomb in the twentieth century as a human morality affecting the scientists in its development as much as the victims of its use as a weapon of war. We do not ascribe guilt to uranium 235 or radioactive decay. They are elements whose behavior is preordained, to be manipulated by higher intelligences for good or evil. The ancient Greeks saw their heroes in precisely the same terms.

That human actions are guided both by the constitution of the individual character, and according to the stresses to which the person is subjected, is evident from the perception that still obtains between the timbre of the voice as a statement of character, and the degree of motivation associated with the rise and fall of speech in response to the promptings of others, or of circumstance. The ancients believed that an individual being has no control over its own destiny but can only respond to external pressures in accordance with its nature (what it is made of) and inner strength (how it is made and to what scale or mode it is tuned). In the same way as for a bow in archery, or a musical instrument, a distinction is drawn between intrinsic tension (tuning of the string) and applied force (drawing the bow or plucking the string).

Tragedy arises from the fact that, unlike an atomic particle, a person has self-consciousness, and arising from a sense of having the power to act, a belief in personal freedom of action. In reality, however, decisions are merely local manifestations of the forces that hold a person's lifeline in tension and in readiness to respond to external disturbance. Oedipus may think he has a choice, but his actions are already determined by the pull of destiny.

> We are not to concentrate on the character, motives, psychology of Agamemnon, Clytemnestra, Aegisthus themselves, except in the second degree. . . . The function of the human characters is to exhibit the violence in sharp, and as it were, local terms; the function of the *theoi* is to add a further dimension, to universalise the particular. . . . I will risk my neck by suggesting that what we find time after time in these plays smacks more of the scientific than of the religious mind.[9]

The characters of the drama are recognizable as personalities only on the surface. What they in fact portray are transitional expressions of elemental states of being of which the human dimensions, or *emotions*, movements in time, are ultimately local and transitory affects. Like the excitement of Feynman's sum over histories, the drama of Greek tragedy lies in the observer's contemplation of the fate of a pure and elemental character as embracing an infinity of possibilities on a predestined jouney from point A, inexorably to end at point B, but by what route we do not know exactly.

ON ABSURDITY

The Pythagoreans are said to have been embarrassed at discovering non-computable numbers such as the square root of 2, realizing that "they made havoc of their doctrines that every line consists of a chain of equal finite units, and that nature is dominated by integral numbers."[10] But were they really so deluded? Since Pythagoras and his followers Parmenides and Zeno were trained in music, we might expect to find some hint of an answer in musical acoustics. Unfortunately, many leading scientists have little experience in musical matters. Sir James Jeans concludes that Zeno's paradox was devised to point up the absurdity of the Pythagorean position. "If they were right, Achilles could never catch up the tortoise, all of which is, of course, absurd." By a curious irony, the original meaning of the word *absurd* relates to out-of-tuneness and irrational numbers as well as simple impossibility.

Notes

1. J. Burnet, "Philosophy." 57–96 in R. W. Livingstone ed., *The Legacy of Greece*. Oxford: Clarendon Press, 1921.
2. Stephen Hawking, *The Universe in a Nutshell*. New York: Bantam Books, 2001, 54.
3. John Barrow, *Theories of Everything: The Quest for Ultimate Explanation*. New edition. London: Vintage, 1992, 33–34.
4. Stephen Hawking, *The Universe in a Nutshell*, 82–83, 152.
5. Colin A. Ronan, *Cambridge Illustrated History of the World's Science*. Cambridge: Cambridge University Press, 1983, 79–80.
6. A. R. Burn, *Pelican History of Greece*. Harmondsworth: Penguin Books, 1966, 142.
7. Stephen Hawking, *The Universe in a Nutshell*, 150–51.
8. H. D. F. Kitto, "That Famous Greek 'Wholeness.'" In R. B. McConnell ed., *Art, Science, and Human Progress: The Richard Bradford Trust Lectures given between 1975 and 1978 under the auspices of the Royal Institution*. London: John Murray, 1983, 54.
9. H. D. F. Kitto, "That Famous Greek 'Wholeness,'" 58–59.
10. Sir James Jeans, *The Growth of Physical Science*, 33.

ELEVEN

WEIGHTS AND MEASURES

Commentators on Boethius's *De institutione musica* are not very helpful at conveying what they think he is trying to say in his account of Pythagoras and the blacksmiths. The problem is only partly due to the elliptical way in which ancient sources expressed themselves—for good reason, as the information was top secret—and ensuing difficulties in translation. A great deal more has to do, I fear, with a lack of concern for practical musical experience, and ignorance of basic acoustics, on the part of scholars of all ages, ancient, medieval, and modern. The ordinary musician's understanding of basic doctrine is hampered from the outset by the term *musica speculativa*, evoking a mystical world of speculation, of mirrors and appearances, rather than a coherent body of knowledge based on acoustic observation and testing. Boethius's account is a rare and valuable surviving record of how the ancient Greeks may have thought about music, but it appears his disciples were more interested in its theological potential than its scientific implications. In our own time, Claude Palisca observes "Boethius needed to be repossessed as an authority on ancient music, to be reclaimed from medieval theory, . . . [and] his image altered from that of a universal musical lawgiver to that of a transmitter of ancient learning."[1] It is an oddly deliberate distinction to make, and one that speaks of a scholarship more at ease with the forms and procedures of ancient learning than the acoustical and musical information it may have been intended to convey.

The author's skepticism is brought to bear especially heavily on the late Roman scholar's famous account of Pythagoras passing by a smithy and hearing a number of hammers ringing on anvils at different pitches. Imagining the differences in pitch to be caused by variations in the force with which the hammers were swung, Pythagoras examines them and surmises that their differences in pitch are related to their respective weights and not to the strength of the blows.[2] The implication that this is something Pythagoras wouldn't have known already should alert the reader that this is a story with an underlying didactic purpose and not the account of a historical event. By giving prominence to the role of the hammers, Boethius is contriving to draw the reader's attention to the role of raw energy or brute force in creating musical sounds. Returning home, the philosopher performs a number of experiments in pitch relations using a range of different materials: (1) a scale of glasses filled to different levels of water (closed, tapered air columns), (2) a scale of open pipes of different lengths (open, parallel air columns), (3) a scale of bells of different size, and (4) an array of stretched strings of the same length, but tensioned to varying degrees by weights over a rectangular frame. The story is illustrated in Franchino Gaffurio's *Theorica musice,* by a famous woodcut of a number of panels, in one of which the blacksmiths and their hammers are depicted in action, and the other three panels indicating consistent intervallic ratios audible among pairs of strings stretched over a frame, water glasses, bells, and (with Philolaus assisting) between pairs of flutes or whistles of varying sizes.

Palisca is a leading expert in renaissance music theory, but he completely fails to get the message:

> In both Boethius and Gaffurio, the legend is introduced to show that, given the inadequacy of the hearing when confronted with a multitude of sensations, only the reason coupled with accurate observation and measurement can establish the true relationships of tones. Yet neither author gives evidence of observation or measurement, or reasoning thereon.[3]

What he says does not make sense. This is not a demonstration of the inadequacy of human hearing. Quite the reverse. Given that a newborn can recognize the harmonic features of its mother's voice, a complex timbre, we already know that human hearing even in infancy is adequate to recognize tonal and harmonic relations, and for our purposes is bound to be the final arbiter on such matters. The true mystery is that human hearing is so reliable in the absence

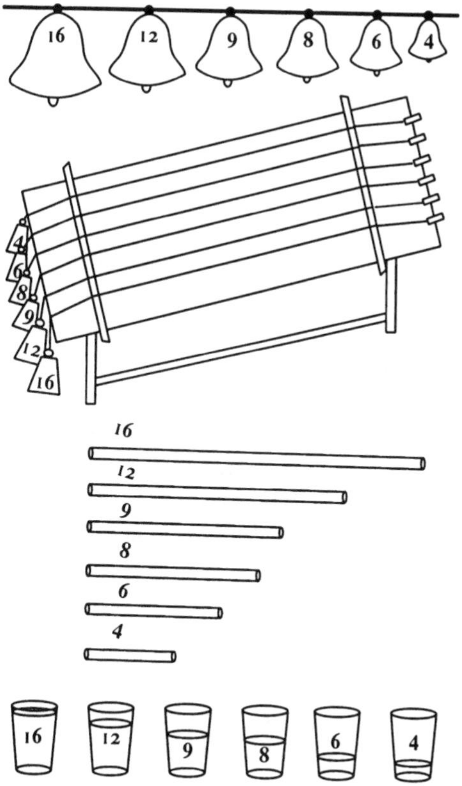

The four categories of instrument examined by Pythagoras and Philolaus: bells, tensioned strings (a multiple monochord), open-ended pipes, and water glasses (after Gaffurio)

of a prior knowledge of acoustics. In denying any "evidence of observation, or measurement, or reasoning thereon," Palisca is missing the point that the octave and other interval relationships represented by the numbers 4, 6, 8, 9, 12, and 16 in the Gaffurio illustration apply to tonal relationships *as they are actually heard*, and not to the relative weights or dimensions of individual sounding objects. Since the range of numbers, corresponding to classic ratios, is the same for each set of objects, the only rational interpretation of Boethius's account and Gaffurio's illustration is that both are statements attesting to Pythagoras's proof *by audition* of the same harmonic ratios obtaining among vastly different materials: solid metal, gut strings, cylindrical air columns in wooden tubes, tapered air columns bounded at one end by water, and domed air cavities bounded by metal. Boethius is indeed acting in the role of lawgiver, and what he is declaring here is that the observed ratios of harmony are universal and independent of the vibrating material substance.

The evidence of the blacksmiths' hammers is not to be taken literally. Rather it is the author's way of saying that the same ratios are invariably *and only* made audible as a consequence of added force, symbolized in this case by the physical act of wielding a hammer. (The reader is thereby invited to infer that the musical frequencies resonated from these devices are also *independent of the weight of the hammer or amount of force applied*, a fact obvious to a trained musician, but of didactic significance in the present context.) Boethius's message is literally identical, one might conjecture, with René Char's and Pierre Boulez's *Le marteau sans maître*, a twentieth-century masterpiece composed 1,450 years after Boethius, in which the composer's careful choice of instrumentation follows Gaffurio's example to represent the art of music as unseen force made audible as harmony.

> Of the four woodcuts in Gaffurio's figure, only the last represents phenomena that are verifiable. If pipes 4, 6, 8, 9, 12, and 16 units long are alike in other respects, the sequence of intervals that Gaffurio aimed to illustrate, a series comparable to A E a b e a', will result when they are blown. In the other four cases . . . the intervals will not be the same.[4]

Since the numbers in the Gaffurio illustration refer to pitch ratios and not to relative sizes, weights, or capacities, their agreement in the woodcut amounts to precisely the verification Palisca is looking for. (Incidentally, the interval series cited by the author is stated back to front, the correct *descending* order of pitches for pipes of increasing length being a' e b a E A.) The presumably widespread assumption, that numbers in the illustration refer to objects rather than frequency ratios, is manifestly improbable. As Palisca rightly notes, the illustrations in that sense would be inconsistent. In the case of bells, flutes, and weights the numbering 4–16 is evidently related to size, and for the water glasses (erroneously, as it happens) to the weight of water and not the volume of air in each, from 4 being almost empty, to 16 almost full. For flutes and bells, the larger the number, the lower the associated fundamental frequency, but for weighted strings and water glasses, larger numbers signify higher, not lower tones. The greater the weight, the greater the tension of a string, raising the pitch, and the greater the amount of water in the glass, the lesser the air cavity, and higher the pitch. When there is a perfectly adequate interpretation available it seems perverse as well as prejudicial to opt for a reading that is confused and also inconclusive. Far better, one would think, to interpret the given numerical values as signifying a congruence of tone ratios obtaining among a diversity of instruments and materials, than as indicating differences of physical and material scale among the objects themselves.

When even the best scholars do not know what they are looking for, it is perhaps not surprising if they fail to find it. Palisca reproaches Gaffurio for not including a monochord in his illustration, "the one medium with which he had direct experience, the single stretched string, the division of which would support the series of ratios he wished to demonstrate," the author going on to disparage the entire exercise as "a transparent appeal to authority and legend"—not scientific exposition at all, but a concession to a literary convention.[5]

What modern readers are urged to conclude, namely that the ancients were deluded, others may interpret as a reflection on the shortcomings of more recent scholarship. The image of a monochord is plain to see, the fact that there is more than one string illustrated being simply a device to show that different weights applied to the same string produce different tones. Once again the essential point of the story is that the same pure tonal ratios of theory obtain for a diversity of vibrating materials and shapes in nature, and for the natural world as readily as the artificial world of music, sounding in air, water, wood, metal, in *any* combination, and *always* as a consequence of external force being applied. The notes of a xylophone are in tune with those of a flute or piano. The underlying mystery to which the reader's attention is being brought in this case is therefore much richer and more subtle in implication than the story appears on the surface. We can express its message in three parts: (1) *The instrument as transducer*, expressed in the conversion of impulsive energy (the hammer blow) into structured periodic vibration (the tone); (2) *Positive mutual interference*: tone reinforcement *at a distance* (through the intervening air) between instruments resonating in unison or at harmonic pitch ratios; and (3) *Universal harmonic ratios*: illustrations proving by experiment that the same laws of ratio apply for all resonating materials. One could go further and adduce (4) the very powerful inference of *Universal musical laws* revealed by a connected three-stage process of energy transference between invisible and substantial worlds, evident in the application of unstructured, inaudible, and invisible *force* (the hammer blows) to structured, tangible, and visible *material resonators* causing structured, invisible and harmonious *vibrations* to be transmitted into and through the air and to the hearing of the listener, there becoming audible.

There is an element of idealism in Boethius's account, since bells in particular are not designed to sound, nor do they always sound, in exact accordance with simple harmonic ratios, and not all materials or structures respond spontaneously to applied force with precise musical tones. But that is arguably part of the message Boethius intends: of a visible and differentiated material world of the senses stirred into action by unseen external forces, out of which emerges a potential for harmony transcending differences of material substance within the group, sustaining energy within the group, and projecting an influence extending beyond the physical limits of the group.

On reflection, the conversion of impulsive (percussive, hence unstructured) hammer blows into resonant musical tones amounts to a remarkable transformation of indeterminate brute force into periodic, quantifiable, and potentially sustainable motion. As we know, the Greeks associated cyclical phenomena with renewable energy, stability, and order, in contrast to impulsive or unstructured energy, which is both nonrenewable and associated with destruction and portents of doom, like arrows and comets. The story of David and Goliath delivers the same message in an earlier account of the superiority in combat of a lesser force with access to cyclical motion (David and his slingshot) against the giant Goliath, a physically larger and more powerful warrior restricted to impulsive action, such as thrusting a spear or sword. The young David, like the mythical Apollo, is also a musician whose skill with the harp (or lyre) signifies a mastery of string power in cyclical motion (the tuneful vibrations of the harp evoking the musical tone of a rapidly rotating sling). And as we learn from the biblical sequel to the story, the same power over strings that can be used to vanquish the king's enemy can also be applied, in playing music, to touch the emotions and ease the suffering of the old king himself.

TEMPERAMENT

In Greek mythology Apollo is the god of war, and also the god of music. The arts of war, represented by archery, and of music, represented by the lyre or harp, are connected through the agency of the stretched string. As complementary arts, one touching the physical body and destructive of life and movement, the other touching the seat of the emotions and enhancing the will to live or to create life, it is understandable that they should be supposed to work in similar ways. Both archery and music operate at a distance by projecting influence through the air. The arrow, a material object, is limited by its substance to moving in one direction only, whereas the sound of the harp, which is immaterial, radiates in every direction at once. To fire an arrow, you must first select and aim for a target, and operate with a steady hand and eye; music, on the other hand, is released into the open air to seek out a target for itself. There are further correspondences. Just as a straight shot with bow and arrow requires a perfectly straight and balanced arrow, and correspondingly steady nerves and a high degree of tension and focus on the part of the person taking aim, so too for music to reach its mark and have the desired impact, a musician must cultivate a steady tone, sounding at a high tension (for clarity and penetration), matched with physical strength and endurance, an acute sense of timing, and other heroic qualities. From a comparison of the two arts it seems reasonable for the ancients to have inferred a correspondence between the laws governing physical and moral systems. After all, we still employ figures of speech that refer to a person as highly strung, or dull, or slack.

As a figure of speech, the arrow of time introduces a further correlation of movement in space with elapsed time. Parmenides said that without movement there is no time, however because defining movement in time and space involves noncomputable numbers, what the Pythagoreans may have really been saying is that change itself is an irrational (not nonexistent, merely insoluble) concept. There are other options, for example comparing the movement of objects in space with the movement of information in speech, which is a modulation of energy in time issuing into three-dimensional space from a point of zero dimension. (Though zero in mathematical terms did not exist for the Greeks, the mouth was their real enough equivalent of an event horizon in modern cosmology). Considering that the source of speech is the mind, a place of no dimension, the commonplace act of translating mental energy into speech becomes quite a plausible explanation for spontaneous movement, or change, or creation itself issuing as more or less coherent acoustic information from a null-dimensional point—the mouth—like the trickle of sand in an hourglass, or Hawking radiation from a black hole. At a more fatalistic level Parmenides may be arguing that what we perceive as volitional movement of solid objects in space and time, along with free will and all the complicated motivations normally assigned to human actions, are simply illusory byproducts of an individual's passage through time along a preordained lifeline.

ESCAPE MECHANISM

A person cannot count the grains of sand falling in an hourglass, or track the moment to moment movement of a shadow across a sundial, but a clock is a counting and measuring device, powered and operating to a timescale independent of the activity taking place in relation to it, whether moving, chanting, working, or dancing. Once a civilization possesses a mechanism to separate timing from activity, it has the conceptual basis for creating a time notation that can be adjusted to match the timing of real life activities and situations.

The builders of thirteenth-century Beauvais cathedral marked its completion by commissioning an elaborate chiming clock to signal, not the hours of the day (which were not yet conceptualized), but the daily offices of religious ritual. In fourteenth-century Paris, taking the mechanical clock as his model, the scientist Jean Buridan theorized that the motion of the stars and planetary bodies in the heavens might also be due to *impetus* (applied energy) rather than a divine guiding intelligence. His pupil Nicole Oresme went further, suggesting that the heavens were kept in motion by a mechanism analogous to the drive of a clock (a surprisingly insightful view, given that mechanical clocks at the time were driven by weights, hence by gravity). The same new ways of perceiving the real world, replacing the plainchant era theory of time as movement based on intellect (i.e., reading a text), with a new theory of time driven by external force and measured in accordance with physical action, are conceptualized in the *ars nova* ("new art") compositions of Philippe de Vitry and pupil Guillaume de Machaut, settings of sacred texts that break with the old convention of timing directed by speech, to accommodate models of physical action and recurrence already current in the secular rhythms of popular song.

The break with closed religious observance provoked a new interest in musical imagery drawn from real life, as expressed in the music of Clément Janequin (*c.*1485–1558), in imagery of birdsong, market cries, and sounds of battle that looks ahead not only to the pastoral landscapes of Antonio Vivaldi and Messiaen, but even to movie music today. If the Beauvais clock's daily puppet show enacting the Day of Judgment helped to set in motion Buridan and Oresme's conjectures of a mechanically driven universe, it also prefigured the arrival of opera, secular ritual human drama guided inexorably by a music that in turn is driven by a notation expressing mechanical time.

A perception of human affairs as mechanically driven supersedes the message of Greek tragedy as driven by fate, and signifies that the human drama lies as much in the inevitability of time's onward march, as in the action unfolding within it. If all drama is meditation on the inevitable, then the critical issue is how well the *action* works (meaning the driving mechanism), as much as what the puppet characters are required to do. It is exactly the same for computer games in the present, one reason why gamers feel no particular sympathy for the story characters, but are completely focused on mastering the underlying software mechanisms. That computer games are largely possessed by plotlines and imagery of death and cruelty is simply another manifestation of the medieval Day of Judgment ethos in contemporary terms.

With the arrival of the movies, an invention coming into being without the assistance of nineteenth-century philosophy, the same paradoxes of time and motion that engaged the school of Pythagoras magically resurfaced, having lain dormant for 1,500 years.

> Put into a logical form, the supposed impossibility of moving pictures rests on some such argument as this: if an object moves from point A *in a picture* to point B, then it must occupy in doing so an infinite number of positions between A and B. Accordingly, an infinite number of pictures would be required to represent even the simplest bit of movement. The argument breaks down because the human eye cannot tell the difference between the infinite series of positions involved in actual motion and a set of samples selected from the series at sufficiently short intervals.[6]

Feynman, here we come. The joint authors of the above passage are technical experts in sound film, writing in the late 1930s, and they know exactly what they are talking about. The element of surprise is that they are talking about it at all, and are constrained to do so because of a prevailing intellectual view that the impression of movement in moving pictures is irrational. One notices an interesting symmetry with Parmenides and Zeno on the impossibility of motion, a comparison doomed to be lost, alas, on a younger generation today for whom sound and vision are digitally encoded and inseparable. One of the ironies of originally adding sound to silent movies in the 1930s was that to do so, engineers were forced to confront the same distinction, between continuous recorded sound and intermittent recorded vision, that so fascinated and confounded the Pythagoreans, when one might have imagined the problem to have long since died a natural death.

In a traditional movie camera the mechanism reproducing visual motion dissects the temporal process into a succession of instantaneous frames, recorded and reproduced at a speed just below the flicker threshold of human vision. By contrast, audio information has to be recorded and reproduced continuously, rather than frame by frame, for it to make sense and sound realistic. A conventional movie projector for that reason first "reads" the visual recording, by an ingenious flicker mechanism that stops each frame momentarily, the film strip then passing via a holding loop to an optical sound or tape reading mechanism through which it is fed continuously.

That an intelligent public in the twentieth century could doubt the reality of motion capture on film is a paradox in itself. The movie mechanism yokes together two completely different ways of managing time: the visual, which represents movement as a succession of time points in line, and the soundtrack, which represents movement in time as a dynamic continuum. That the two mechanisms are necessarily incompatible as well as distinctly different casts light on what seem to be equivalent incompatibilities in earlier accounts of time and motion, reality and continuity, throughout the history of western science.

Public disbelief in the reality of motion pictures resonated with a broader intellectual unease in 1939 at the rise of a new philosophy of indeterminacy in nature, a belief in the fundamental impossibility of pinpointing events simultaneously in space and time.

Notes

1. Claude V. Palisca, *Humanism in Italian Renaissance Musical Thought*. New Haven CT: Yale University Press, 1985, 226.
2. Palisca, *Humanism in Italian Renaissance Musical Thought*, 226–27.
3. Palisca, *Humanism in Italian Renaissance Musical Thought*, 227–29.
4. With the development in 1900 of the touch-sensitive reproducing piano the relationship of force to tone quality and amplitude could finally be measured with certainty.
5. Palisca, *Humanism in Italian Renaissance Musical Thought*, 229.
6. D. A. Spencer and H. D. Waley, *Cinema Today* (1939). 2nd edition. London: Oxford University Press, 1956, 1–2.

TWELVE

THE DIRECTOR'S CUT

> Imperceptibly shots would start to sort themselves, migrating from film-can to film-can and gathering like molecules round a nucleus. But there was no conscious thought directing it. . . . Flaherty would suddenly realize that he was looking at a sequence. It was a peculiar sensation. One day a mere collection of shots joined up together, the next, a perceptible semblance of a sequence, seemingly self-generated, organic, belonging.[1]
>
> ARTHUR CALDER-MARSHALL

Problem solving takes a number of forms: one, looking ahead, reasoning from A to B; two, looking back, reasoning from B to A; and three, the big picture, reasoning from the center to the edges. In the great scheme of things, we are all in the middle, caught in an uncertain present.

Letters are connected to make words, words to make sentences, sentences to create images and describe actions, and images assembled together in a certain order to tell a story. At every stage there are rules to be followed. To make words from letters you need spelling; to make sentences from words you need grammar, and to tell a good story you need a plot that makes sense from start to finish.

Movie audiences prefer happy endings. In a happy ending the good person wins out and earns the respect and affection of the community, while the bad person is found out, obliged to leave town, or locked up for an indefinite period. How the story ends is the moral message of how it was meant to be, what the story was about, and how life in an ideal world should turn out. So you look in at the video warehouse and the movie you enjoyed back then has been rereleased, but in a different version, the "director's cut."

This is a movie you know and love. By definition, the director's cut is different. It is not the movie you remember, but the movie the director originally intended to make. The implication is profoundly disturbing. It means that the message of the movie that meant so much to you all those years ago is not the message the director actually intended. The original story ended differently, but at the time the studio objected. Audiences like happy endings, they said. And so they made it have a happy ending. But it wasn't really a happy ending. The director never originally intended the story to have a happy ending. The rereleased version tells the real story: the same characters, the same sequence of events, the same dialogue and situations—only this time it's not a happy ending but a tragic conclusion. And that changes everything.

What do you do? Do you want to revisit a significant experience in your life, a moral experience, an experience that taught you the meaning of living a decent godfearing life, that despite everything the good guy or girl will win out in the end, only to find out that in reality life is more complicated, good deeds and virtuous intentions do not always lead to good results, and sometimes you lose? Do you feel cheated? (If you do, think how the director must have felt.) It is not just that the ending is unexpected. It is that the whole point of the story, and how you interpret each and every line of dialogue, has been changed. For most of us the version we first saw and loved is the real movie, while the director's cut belongs to some parallel universe. It might even make you wonder whether you would be the same person you are today if you had seen the director's cut the first time round, with its tough moral lesson that virtue does not always triumph over the forces of adversity, which is an unnerving thought.

A director's cut forces everyone to reevaluate the story and the message. A substantial part of the new message (or meta-message) is: "never trust the message." Like a detective story, a movie is a work of fiction. By assembling events in a certain order a message can be made to emerge spontaneously, and only one message, implying only one possible outcome. By revisiting the same events, and ordering or interpreting them differently, you may come to a completely different conclusion. This dilemma is not just about the movies. It is also about how people store and retrieve events in real life, about the fact that history is colored by what people want to remember, and ultimately how they want to be remembered: as heroes who triumph over adversity, are successful, and are loved.

Movie-making is the art of connecting events so that they tell a story. The documentary filmmaker Robert J. Flaherty traveled deep into the icy landscape of Alaska to make *Nanook of the North*, and years later to a remote fishing community off the Irish coast to make *Man of Aran*. As an observer of the real world in a new medium he wanted his movies to tell the truth about the lives of ordinary people in extraordinary situations, stories largely unknown to the rest of the world, but presented in a narrative form that would have to omit, since a movie is unable to reproduce real life in real time, the long stretches of waiting between events that correspond to how life is actually experienced. Flaherty's method of "composing" a movie (assembling the story from unedited takes, like a piece of music) while remaining true to its subject matter, was to begin by viewing the unedited takes over and over again until they were impressed in his memory.

For Flaherty the art of montage was an art of intuition: patient observation of materials until a hidden pattern revealed itself. Intuiting the truth is recognizing a pattern of events to be faithful to how things really are, even if the final composition of images is not in the order they actually happened at the time. Documentary filmmakers in the early days tended to be social moralists with a highly developed sense of obligation to tell the truth. They looked askance at the rest of the movie industry, especially in the depression era, as cynical dealers in escapist fantasy and dreams.

Objects or experiences in memory can be juggled at will. In the movies, as in the novel, and indeed for a witness in the courtroom, the recall and juxtaposition of real events can be manipulated under cross-examination to create or suggest false memories. For this reason the art of montage is invariably an art of creating occasionally nonfactual but essentially plausible narrative connections that reinforce the perceptions of a particular person or audience. In *Film Form* Sergei Eisenstein recalls the dramatic effect of two tiny edits and an altered subtitle on audience perception of a scene from the German movie *Danton*, a story of the French Revolution starring Emil Jannings.

> Camille Desmoulins is condemned to the guillotine. Greatly agitated, Danton rushes to Robespierre, who turns aside and slowly wipes away a tear. The subtitle said, approximately, "In the name of freedom I had to sacrifice a friend." Fine. But who could have guessed that in the German original, Danton . . . ran to the evil Robespierre and . . . spat in his face? and that it was this spit that Robespierre wiped from his face with a handkerchief? And that the title indicated Robespierre's hatred of Danton![2]

In detective stories the possibility of multiple histories is laid bare, as part of the plot. In fact, the underlying premise of detective fiction is that the same end situation can be reached by an indefinite number of different routes. Reality becomes a crime scene. You can't change what has happened, instead the game lies in accounting for an outcome in different ways, of which only one will be the truth, dealing satisfactorily with all the circumstantial evidence. The second point is this: whoever turns out to be the guilty party, the outcome remains the same. The body is already dead, and that is that. A director's cut might conceivably change the guilty person, but even a director's cut is not going to bring the corpse back to life. Despite that minor detail, however, finding out that somebody else is responsible can still change everything.

LIFELINE

Life and death are two ends of a lifeline, and the subtext of a happy (or even a sad) ending is that the moral a reader takes from the story of a life, and message of the quality and value of the life itself, are by convention determined by how the story ends. (Note that the word *determined* already connects the meaning of "making a decision" with "reaching a conclusion.") In a classic detective story a number of ideas are joined: one, that the death of the victim is a deliberate act; two, that the act arises from a relationship; three, that only one relationship out of many satisfies the moral and logical requirements of the plot; and four, that the correct answer is only obtained *because an outside expert happened to be present at the time as an observer and arranged the events in the correct order*. We face the same kind of mystery in Erwin Schrödinger's cat in a box paradox, a cat that may or may not be dead but is assumed to be in both states simultaneously, a mystery from the world of quantum physics, the answer to which is that both outcomes are possible, but there is only one that can be determined for sure—and then only by opening the box.

Like so many myths, Schrödinger's thought experiment has surprising cultural resonances. As with the Adam and Eve myth, it is a cautionary tale about knowledge and choice; like a detective story, it holds the reader in suspense over a superimposed plurality of possible outcomes; in the spirit of Wittgenstein, it implies a moral dilemma over whether it is right to predict an outcome when the prediction itself may be the catalyst for the outcome. This was 1935, remember, the early days of Nazism. Schrödinger's casket is a more up to date version of *Pandora's Box*, the title and subject of a silent movie by Pabst dating from 1929, on the cusp of the arrival of the sound film.[3] (In turn, the movie is based on the *Lulu* plays by Franz Wedekind, on which Alban Berg would base his opera of the same name, a work unfinished at the composer's death—in 1935.) The original story of Pandora's box tells of a gift by Jupiter of a box supposed to contain all of the world's ills—or alternatively, all of the blessings of the gods. The gift was accompanied by a caution that the box should on no account be opened. Like Eve in the temptation of Eden, Pandora's curiosity got the better of her and she opened the box, and its contents escaped.

Magic caskets had taken on a new lease of life in the thirties, in the form of radio and the portable gramophone, so there is also a slight but palpable frisson of contemporary angst in a story from the rise of National Socialism hinting at the dangerous knowledge that might be released—indeed, information that might change your life—if a person were to follow government orders, boldly plug in the radio and switch it on. The original Pandora's box, as the name clearly reveals, was also a source of music, the *bandoura*, a type of lute, a historic connection which adds the revealing gloss that the information locked in the mysterious container is none other than all the music that ever was or will be, having the power to comfort and please, or equally to rouse a listener to anger and violence, or indeed, reveal the secrets of the universe in ratio and harmony. By "opening the box" one is not merely playing the instrument, but dicing with knowledge and the power of life and death. All of those outcomes, including life and death, are simultaneously present in potential. (Today's ultimate version of Pandora's box, of course, is the internet.)

The concept of "lifeline" implies inevitability of the outcome of a story, and—since the story is about a life—the inevitability of a real life as well. The fatalist tradition of Greek tragedy, the modern novel, even implicit in biography itself—which says that in life there is no free will and individual fate is predetermined, though we don't realize it or necessarily accept it—is a routine aspect of oral cultures, though for reasons that are not altogether clear (I suppose they have partly to do with the perception that we are trapped in a continuous present and cannot see into the future). The fanciful or mystical interpretation of a fate which asks either to be taken on trust or simply ignored, has a firmer grounding in reality once the imagery of the monochord and its vibrating string is taken into account, from which we can conceive of the dynamics of a person's *lifespan* in terms of the note and tension of a stringed instrument, and the timeline of a person's life, extending and vibrating continuously between the fixed points of birth and death, as movement along the length of the string.

The string of a musical instrument is an image of physical and temporal continuity, and vibration of the string, a pattern of audible and coherent deviation that is continuous throughout the entire length of the string. Like a human life, the movement is less powerful or wayward at either end, and most agitated at the center (the midlife crisis), in total describing an arch that corresponds to the growth and decline in power of a normal life history, and a demonstration of continuity and connection through time.

Fatalism is musically inspired, if we imagine that the evolution of a person's life is predetermined in the same way as the sound of a melody is predetermined by the tuning of a musical instrument. For such an image to make sense, it has to signify that the lifeline is gripped in tension between the point of birth and the point of death, and for that reason the tone quality *at every point in between* is connected to a fundamental vibration that carries through from birth to extinction. In turn, the quality and *temperament* of a life (the analogy is telling) are determined by a combination of a tension (or emotional character) and a length (the duration of life) that are already in place at the moment of birth.

If that were so, one might object, how come a person's end is not totally predictable? The answer is that the note of a tuned string is the product of tension in relation to length, and we do not know tension exactly, so cannot tell from the note of a given string how long the lifeline in fact may be. In human terms, all we are invited to know is that the fate (or ultimate termination) of a person's life is intimately related to the degree of tension in the person's character.

Life involves risk. We take chances with money, jobs, education, religion and health. The lesson of life is how to cope with uncertainty. Under the guise of entertainment, art and literature (including the movies) offer guidance in how to manage risk and maximize personal security. Be careful whom you trust. Invest in these stocks and you could win big. Take these tablets and get rid of your heartburn. Study computer programming and you will never want for well-paid employment. Follow this person's example and be successful. Put your trust in religion and be sure of life in the hereafter. The traditional method of dealing with life's uncertainties is to form attachments to persons or ideas that reinforce certainty, such as widely held beliefs, proven medication, solid precepts, good advice, *and stories that come to a definite conclusion.* Art, literature, and the movies are a part of that trust. Music as well. A work of art is a statement. It says: this is how it is. And you go away and think about it and you come back and measure your experience against it. And it always says the same thing. You can count on it. That way you know. You know what you think for the reason that the statement against which your thought is measured never changes.

Unless and until you revisit the video store and find the movie is now the director's cut with the scene between Tony Curtis and Laurence Olivier restored and the ending changed. Or the cd reissue of your favorite vinyl lp has been remixed. Or your Shakespeare edition has been revised to show that Hamlet was in fact gay. Or the Sistine Chapel frescoes have been cleaned and now tell a completely different story. They no longer look old, and because they no longer seem to belong to the past they suddenly speak to people of the present, which is not what tourists on vacation are led to expect. Increasingly we are having to come to terms with the fact that the certainties we grew up to trust are no longer certain any more, which is why television series like *The X-files* are so popular, or documentaries that keep asking Who killed the president? Have flying saucers really landed? If OJ didn't do it, who did? The legal profession and news media thrive on uncertainty while cutting-edge science plays with the notion of convergent multi-path timelines and the possibility of traveling backward in time. Like the augurs of ancient Greece, news experts ritually slaughter headline events, fuss over the entrails, and issue oracles that change the next day, and again the day after that.

For the rest of us the notion that the facts of life are no longer as certain as they used to be can be disconcerting. In the long run however it has the effect of refocusing a reader's attention away from the expected outcome to understanding the process. Not just what the shares are worth, but how the company performs. Not just the love interest, but the character development. Not just the verdict but the evidence. After acquiring a feeling for the process you no longer depend on the outcome as a moral justification. The facts of the case can always be used to negotiate a different outcome. A new ending is just another possibility.

Eisenstein also said, "A work of art directs all the refinement of its methods to the process."[4] For example, Chaucer's *Canterbury Tales* is a sequence of stories connected in time expressed as a journey in space, from London to Canterbury. English storytelling from John Bunyan's *The Pilgrim's Progress* to Charles Dickens's *Nicholas Nickleby* follows the model of a person's life expressed as a journey, meeting challenges along the way, and ending with a moral. The detective story introduced the radically new idea of an uncertain outcome to be reconciled with circumstantial evidence by a visiting intelligence thinking retrospectively. Today, computer games take the paradigm even farther away from literature as moral example to storytelling as an interactive environment, a morally neutral process combining an often dystopian virtual reality with escapist entertainment in a hybridization of realism and fantasy that may appear to have begun in adventure movies of the 1930s, but whose roots are deeply embedded in ancient myth and legend.

A computer game is a distinctive environment and situation in which the outcome is not predetermined, or rather where there may be a variety of outcomes to be attained by one of a variety of narrative pathways selected by the reader. That makes it interesting from a technical point of view. Most artforms do not have variable outcomes, though Tarot, poker, and chess are exceptions. The immediate predecessor of the computer game is the cybernovel, a story form ill-adapted to print media where the reader is invited to make decisions that affect the order and sequence of chapters to be read, and thereby the outcome of the story. In the 1960s a number of attempts at composing variable form opera were undertaken by avant-garde composers. They include Stockhausen's *Momente*, *Votre Faust* by Henri Pousseur, and other titles by Mauricio Kagel and Luciano Berio. In these, too, the action unfolds in a series of episodes that may be shuffled in order from performance to performance. The Alain Resnais movie *Last Year at Marienbad* played with the idea of an episode in memory repeating itself in the present, a conceit parodied by Hollywood twenty years later in the *Terminator* series with Arnold Schwarzenegger, and comedies *Groundhog Day* and the *Back to the Future* trilogy. We admire the ingenuity of such inventions and are curious in the way they explore and attempt to subvert the convention of time as linear and continuous. Naturally there are exceptions: the newspaper, magazine, encyclopedia, or dictionary, representing collections of data existing somehow perpendicular to the arrow of time, to be sampled rather than reviewed continuously. Such sources don't pretend to tell stories or trade in moral virtue. (Or rather, any story or moral is for the reader to decide.)

Compared to the novel in print, the website and cd-rom are ideal environments for creating stories of multiple directions and logical alternatives. The designer of a computer game has to develop a schema that allows for multiple narrative pathways and a variety of possible outcomes, to which the associated artwork is bound to adapt. If the artist Paolo Uccello were to recreate his painting *St George and the Dragon* as a computer game he would have to account for the background events leading up to the binding of the princess, the arrival of St George and the slaying of the monster, while leaving open the possibilities that the princess might escape on her own, or that St George might arrive late and find a contented dragon dozing at the stake alongside a small neat pile of bones. Such entertaining conceits make present-day conjectures of multiple parallel universes sound rather too much like astrophysics reinventing reality as a computer game.

Why are computer games studied as narrative processes, and yet not as literature? I can think of several reasons: one, that the open form concept is still too new, which I doubt; two, that the writing is not of a high enough quality to rank alongside Homer or *Beowulf*, which is probably true; and the main reason, three, that such stories ask for, but don't have, a definite ending. That is not the same as saying that art and literature and religion do not deal with uncertainty and choice and the possibility of error, because of course they do deal in these matters. It is just that the mindset of western cultural and religious traditions, not to mention the traditional narrative forms available to artists and storytellers—poem, song, the book, painting, sculpture, sonata—while recognizing the possibility of variant endings, are all the same geared philosophically and technically to reinforce the idea of there being one and only one legitimate outcome to a particular set of circumstances and possible actions. A maze would not be a maze without false leads and dead ends, but there is only one ultimate goal and only one way to get there. The convention that there is only one outcome gives rise to the more general perception that in any given set of circumstances there is only one correct course of action to take, which though it may be true in even most cases does not mean that it is true in every case, and even if it were to be true in every case, would not necessarily make alternative outcomes invalid, or the concept of variant outcomes immoral, as some legislators in education and public morals sometimes appear to believe.

In his comic novel *The Life and Times of Tristram Shandy* the author Laurence Sterne apologizes for the digressions of his plotline from the straight and narrow. The English novel reinvented narrative fiction in the image of the straight-edge and the clock. In this example Sterne, who trained as a parson, uses humor to make the philosophical point that a real life does not travel in a straight line, neither in real time, nor in the telling of it. The Feynman-like "timeline" of the hero's fictional life is clearly capable of traveling backward as well as forward in time, as well as moving through time by a variety of different routes, and leading toward more than one possible outcome.

An attitude of focusing on the process and leaving open the outcome is typical of the world of science. An eighteenth-century parson of liberal education such as Laurence Sterne understands the challenge to old-fashioned literary determinism represented by the new outlook of the Age of Reason. Science is exploratory. It imagines goals or desirable outcomes and then sets about finding how these goals are to be achieved within the rules we already know. There is by definition no guarantee of success or correct course of action to follow, and indeed no way of knowing if a chosen course of action will lead to the intended goal or instead branch off and go somewhere else. The scientific path is not predetermined, so one cannot be blamed for not following a particular line, only for not following procedure. Unlike fiction, science does not promise that if you are virtuous you will get the answer you are looking for, or offer any guarantee you will get an answer at all. The interest and excitement of science, unlike conventional art and literature (or music, for that matter) lies in the dialogue that arises when prediction is tested against real-world results. The culture clash between religion and science that we associate with the historic trial of Galileo by the Inquisition, and that continues to make small headlines in the popular science press, can best be understood as a conflict of interest between those who believe in the original story, and those who understand the message of the Director's Cut. On the side of religion you have a structure of understanding in terms of a storyline where the real-world outcome—the world we know—is all-important and self-evident and the inevitable consequence of a history known only to a privileged few. And on the other side, a science representing a dynamic of continuous clarification where the world we know is perpetually uncertain and the task of understanding the process is available to anyone.

Computer games are interactive narratives in which the reader assumes a fictional role as a hero whose actions and decision-making abilities are tested in the course of a journey that aspires only to completion, usually at speed, not to achieve anything in particular other than the triumph of the individual and elimination of anybody standing in the way. (Since the real test of the game is understanding the process of the game, any moral component of the game narrative, however repulsive, is arguably only a distraction.)

The superficial resemblance of game narratives to bloody ancient epic tales is striking, obliging the scholar to consider the interactive implications of the old tales of Ulysses and Odysseus, the lives of the Saints, and the *Mahabharata*, along with their medieval counterparts Sir Lancelot and the *Chanson de Roland*. The attractions of epic form to computer game authors are both procedural and philosophical. Epic form fits the principles of game software design, creating a dynamic environment where choices are made, problems encountered, and life-threatening challenges overcome as elements of a personal growth process. The individual interacts with epic narrative as a player in a fictional game controlled by the gods (the original software designers). The point of the story is ostensibly self-improvement; the reward of success, winning the intellectual battle; and the price of failure, momentary annihilation. It is not real life. You can always try again. That is the difference.

Notes

1. Arthur Calder-Marshall, *The Innocent Eye: The Life of Robert J. Flaherty*. New York: Harcourt, Brace & World, 1963, 159–60.
2. Sergei Eisenstein, "Through Theater to Cinema" (1934). 2–17 from *Film Form: Essays in Film Theory* tr. ed. Jay Leyda. New York: Harcourt Brace & Company, 1949.
3. Georg Wilhelm Pabst, *Die Büchse der Pandora* (1929). Silent movie starring Louise Brooks ("Lulu").
4. Sergei Eisenstein, *The Film Sense* tr. ed. Jay Leda. London: Faber and Faber, 1943, 17.

THIRTEEN

BRANE WAVES

> When I am in the company of scientists I feel like a curate who has strayed into a drawing-room full of dukes.[1] W. H. AUDEN

Cosmology has a childlike fascination with loops, waves, sheets, and hidden dimensions. In such a world a musician may be excused for feeling like an alien. A poet or artist has no way of knowing if the cosmologists are right. All one can do is marvel at the weirdness and feel uplifted at the enthusiasm with which brilliant minds pursue the truth about reality into ever stranger imaginative realms. And yet loops, strings, waves, columns, and vibrating sheets (drums, tam-tams) are the stuff of music, and not abstractions but real. To a musician they are not strange at all, even if most find their behavior impossible to account for in mathematical terms. The question arises whether this fascination with abstractions that have musical implications is an extension of Pythagoreanism, with the difference that the ancient Greeks based their mathematical abstractions on the observed behavior of real musical instruments, or whether today's theoretical physicists are attempting to reconcile existing abstractions with reference to objects in higher dimensions. For instance, the ancient myth of the Minotaur in the center of his maze, the Lissajous curve, and the strange attractor of chaos theory, can all be interpreted as variations on the theme of a seemingly random but in fact lawful movement of a point around a center, and its explanation, that the pattern corresponds to the vibration of a string in cross-section, as the consequence of a third dimension arising from excess energy being introduced to a normally static object of only two dimensions. The rosette carved in the center of a lute is another version of the maze encircling the Minotaur.

For musicians there is an added complexity in that the surreal world of cosmology is not only drawing on imagery that has musical or acoustical implications, but is largely *unaware* of the musical implications of their imaginative ventures, and is employing such procedures in ways inconsistent with musical knowledge. That the postulation of loops, strings, and branes has led to simplifications or resolutions of otherwise intractable theoretical problems leads a reader to suppose that these prescriptions may correspond in turn to four-dimensional cross-sections of higher dimensional realities. The Occam's razor objection that we have no evidence of higher dimensions may give way in due course to the conclusion that they are all the same real, only that the human mind is unable to conceptualize them in any other way. We may in fact be dealing with a way of thinking about such matters that remains locked in mono (to take an analogy from recording) while attempting to account, *in mono*, for relationships in stereo or surround-sound: that is, lateral, vertical, or longitudinal motion. If philosophers find it difficult to reconcile the reality of continuous motion with the theoretical convenience of clock time, and if mathematicians also find it difficult to reconcile the theory of multiple infinite series with the reality of multiple infinite harmonic series available on a stretched string, perhaps we should not be surprised to find the issue of multiple dimensions turning on a problem of adapting the method of calculation, and the expectations associated with the calculation, to a higher conceptual framework.

For example, the limitation of calculating on a whiteboard, a two-dimensional surface on which symbols representing objects in a multi-dimensional mind space are arranged to converge and resolve on a one-dimensional point represented by the blank space to the right of the last equal sign. Everything on the board is part of a process spiraling toward that one point. If one wants to think metaphysically, the solution of such a problem is also a point of conjunction with the mind space of the passive observer, the point where the problem leaps from the two-dimensional surface of the whiteboard to lodge in the multi-dimensional brains of at least some of the assembled audience. In the musical world, a point (where a microphone is located) occupies one of an infinity of possible locations in an acoustic space extending in four dimensions, and every point in the continuously fluctuating voltage it transmits during a music recording is the reconciliation of a uniquely distinct equation of phases and amplitudes.

Acoustic information from a single microphone at a single point in space is not enough however for a listener to infer the relative locations of sounding bodies in three-dimensional space. We all have two ears for a reason. When somebody taps a spoon on a glass to call the party to order, everybody with two functioning ears can tell where the sound is coming from, but since everybody is in a different place, each individual calculation of that location is based on completely different sets of data. For a spider sitting in a web, the shock wave will be intercepted at eight different locations, and for a fly on the wall or ceiling, motion sensed in six channels, one for each leg. The perceived orientation and movement in space of an acoustic event are decided by processes of approximation, reconciling multiple coincident inputs, each of which is equally "true" and "authentic," but none of which, taken in isolation, contains precise location information.

Whether religious or scientific in origin, appeals to transcendental dimensions beyond space and time as a means of accounting for the universe are as old as recorded civilization. Whether these hypotheses "work" in accounting for the universe is not the issue in question, and certainly not one for a musician to determine. That they lead to outwardly baffling pronouncements about reality as we know it is certainly true. Cosmologists are by no means united in their views of the efficacy of theories many of which are by definition untestable. That making baffling pronouncements in their role as cosmologists that are nevertheless justified because they lead to correct predictions is also, one suspects, true. That making pronouncements that are deliberately baffling is a marketing device to ensure that the public is kept in a state of constant fascination, so that the funds keep rolling in, even if not true, would have to be accounted extremely persuasive. Irrespective of their truth content, prevailing doctrines of cosmology and the manner in which their enigmatic messages are traded in the public domain inevitably suggest parallelisms with the social role and mystical utterances of soothsayers and augurs of ancient times.

To a lay reader the strangeness of present-day cosmology is a large part of its fascination and (dare I say it) its charm. There is an aesthetic dimension. The appeal of aesthetics lies in the intuitive recognition of pattern. What is particularly appealing about the paradoxical or controversial imagery of cosmology may arguably have nothing at all to do with what cosmology is attempting to prove, or even what it intends to say. It is just that these images, now so widespread in the popular literature of science, are at times congruent in scope and pattern with musical concepts, and that the latter are not speculative but real, and may have been around for several thousands of years. And yet these cosmologists give the impression that they thought of them first; they appear to have no interest in prior intimations of the same ideas of coexistent multiple dimensions in the history of music and acoustics, and the reader who goes looking for "music" in the index is disappointed to find no mention of the subject.

A musician is forced to conclude either (1) that the scientist's use of musical imagery is impressionistic, that is, not intended to be taken seriously because it has not been thought through; (2) that its significance, if anywhere, lies in a *subconscious intuition* of relationships that may obtain between visual and aural metaphor; or (3) that what we are speaking of in any case are figures of speech and not descriptions of reality, in the equivalent sense that to speak of infinity was regarded by some mathematicians at one time as a figure of speech. In that case, we seem to be dealing with a Popperian dilemma of statements that are neither verifiable nor falsifiable, never intended to conform to reality but simply to be consistent with cosmological theory.

PARTICLE–WAVE DUALITY

That light, gravity, and other radiant phenomena exhibit wavelike properties when measured in one way, and particle-like properties when measured in a different way, may be compared to a musician identifying a note of music—on paper or in performance—either as a steady state datum or as a transitional moment in a continuum. If a note is considered in detachment from a melody, then it has frequency and duration, perhaps also tone-color, and maybe even a tension ratio in relation to an associated harmony or key. In classical western music, however, a single chord can be identified not only in itself as a pitch datum or harmonic component, but also as a transitional element in a much larger work. Fifty years ago, on a good day, John Amis, a stalwart team member of the BBC radio music quiz *My Music*, was able not only to identify the opening chord of Mendelssohn's "Wedding March" from a snippet of tape of less than a second in duration, but from the acoustical evidence make an educated guess at the orchestra and conductor performing it. A musician needs only to hear the upbeat in G octaves to recognize the start of Beethoven's Fifth Symphony. Among musicians, knowledge of the classical repertoire involves not only a memory for instantaneous data but also for data as cross-sections of complex processes extending in time.

More to the point, perhaps, is that full knowledge of the particle, slice, sample, or point source—in the case of the Mendelssohn opening chord, that it is a diminished ninth on the dominant chord of E minor in the third inversion—is true of the instant but does not allow even the most knowledgeable musician to predict with certainty the development of that information in time. The pronoun "I" does not imply the sentence, let alone the identifying voice, of "I have a dream," any more than the letter I implies termination of the word "Peccavi" (I have Sind) of Sir Charles Napier's mythical telegram from the Indian wars of 1842. All the same, one would certainly not feel it necessary to propose the existence of parallel universes in order to account for these two possibilities.

That composers of classical music were aware of the possibility of their notes on paper being interpreted either as particles or waves is evident as early as the composition of late medieval plainchant, in the graphic setting of a text. There are at least three options of reconciling text and intonation in plainchant. In one, a text is set to music syllabically, so that every syllable is allocated to a different note. This may be done for expression, emphasis, or alternatively for clarity of articulation, since changes of pitch add useful distinction to every syllable of a melody to be sung without expression in a resonant environment such as a stone cathedral.

A second option, melisma, is the setting of just one extended syllable to an elaborate sequence of notes; part of the purpose of the melodic extension may be to convey expression, and for a syllable of significance, such as the first syllable of "Do - - - - - minus," to invest an entire word with a sense of magnitude and extension in time, like the decorated initial letter in a medieval manuscript. In the context of orthodox plainchant unfolding at recitative pace, for the voice to dwell on a single syllable has the effect of delaying the flow and thus drawing and sustaining the attention of an audience, like a rhetorical pause. Alternatively, to intone multiple syllables on the same pitch without melodic variation is to *eliminate* expression as a variable, and perhaps also rhythm, in order to focus attention on distinctions of timbre within the flow of syllables themselves, after the manner of mouth music, jaw harp music, or synthesized speech for robots, and anticipating the *klangfarbenmelodie* (tone-color melody) of Webern's music. Prolonging a single syllable on one note is rarely encountered for obvious reasons, and when it is encountered (in Perotin's settings of *Viderunt omnes* and *Sederunt principes*, for example) is interpreted as a representation of eternity.

Daniel Ling has written cogently of the functional utility, as distinct from the aesthetic value, of pitch variation in speech:

> To the extent that intonation carries information provided in parallel by the segmental stream, it is redundant; but this is not the case when intonation may be used to modify the meaning of an utterance. . . . Voice patterns that vary in pitch . . . appear to facilitate acquisition of both speech reception and speech production skills. Intonation patterns apparently provide a framework within which the segmental components can be better remembered, aid in the segmentation of an utterance, and indicate underlying grammatical construction and semantic content. Voice produced at an optimum pitch for the speaker and with intonation is far more pleasant to listen to than speech which is poorly pitched and monotonous, probably because it carries more information on the personal qualities of the speaker.[2]

What has any of this to do with wave-particle duality? At the very least it demonstrates a consciousness of variant approaches to melody information (snake or ladder, continuous melody or syllabic succession) that have distinctly different implications for the unity and intelligibility of a text, and for consciousness of time and space, existential time in the instant as distinct from the concept of being in relation to a nominal eternity. The corresponding implication for physics is that to speak of light either as a wavelike continuum or as a succession of photons may ultimately have less to do with the nature of light than with the kind of information required at a particular time, and how that information is obtained. That being the case, a reader is curious to discover why wave and particle interpretations need to be reconciled in the first place, and where the mystery lies.

The same distinction emerges afresh in rational eighteenth-century Europe, a period when skilled watchmakers competed to build mechanical automata to imitate human actions, for instance playing the violin, signing one's name, or reproducing an outline drawing in pen and ink. Writing and drawing devices were programmed after the fashion of a musical box, sequential processes secured by pins on an internal rotating cylinder, employed here not to pluck notes of music, but to position a pen on a paper surface and engage eccentric gear trains to move it about. On the Cartesian principle that children amount to programmable robots, the same basic schema is still published today in follow-the-dot picture puzzles, and in movement capture for computer animation based on successive locations of a limited number of key reference points recorded from reflective dots on a prototype live moving body. In all such methods of modeling movement in space a distinction is made between the grid reference points representing successive locations in space and time, and the effect of movement created by the process interpolating, or being dragged, from point to point.

The opening of the third movement of Beethoven's "Pastoral" Sixth Symphony is an illustrative deliberate comparison of melody defined alternately as a succession of points or steady states, and as locations within a continuum. The opening phrase, beginning high in pitch and moving in a downward direction, consists of a spiky succession of upbeat staccato "points," each note distinct and the whole phrase difficult to perceive as a shape or a line. Returning upward in direction, the answering *legato* phrase emphasizes the continuous line. The symmetrical relationship of staccato and legato adjoining phrases is typical of Beethoven (it is a feature of the opening measures of his Fourth Symphony) and makes good sense as a meditation on the relationship between measured time (in the sense of time-point data) and the experience of continuous

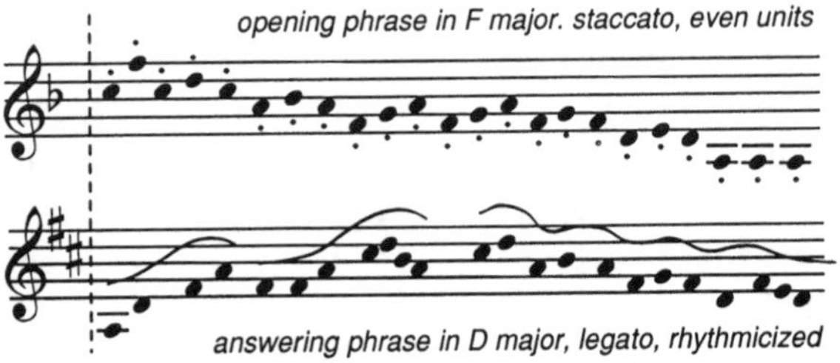

Beginning the third movement of Beethoven's Sixth Symphony, a descending staccato line in F and answering legato in D make an intelligent distinction between point and line (or rain and wind)

motion. Beethoven was well aware of mechanical automata and, along with Haydn, an associate of Maelzel, inventor of the classic pyramid metronome and other mechanical music devices. Beethoven well understood the intellectual and practical challenges of representing organic movement as a succession of programmable discrete states.

It might be objected that classical music is all about "programmable discrete states" and nothing more. Most notated classical music is intended for live performers and not for mechanical dolls. But that simply means that as long as music is performed by live musicians, the element of continuity is taken care of by virtue of the fact that the performers themselves are living beings; it is only when notated music is executed by a mechanical keyboard or automaton that the absence of organic connection inherent in notation emerges as a perceptual or interpretative difficulty.

The mechanical implications of the keyboard itself are sufficiently strong to influence audience perception of a performance for piano, whether it is a piece by Chopin in imitation of a mechanical keyboard, on the one hand, or by Cage or Stockhausen on the other. They imply that to play like a machine can invest a performance with the appearance of prior intentionality even if it does not exist. For example, a player piano rendition of Chopin's "Minute Waltz" can reveal that all the factors normally associated with virtuosity in a live performance (speed, precision, lightness and evenness of touch, etc.) are no more than mechanical characteristics transferred to a human being, and therefore involve no "soul" as such; on the other hand, a performance by player piano of Cage's *Music of*

Changes, or Stockhausen's *Piano Piece IV*, would possibly be *more* impressive than a live performance, by virtue of the listener knowing that a mechanical performance is necessarily programmed in advance by a real person, in contrast to a live performance that might just as well be made up on the spur of the moment. From Scott Joplin to Philip Glass, the mechanical style of piano music is typically uninflected in either tempo or dynamic; it is a music relying on speed, invariance, and precision to avoid generating a sense of boredom. The contrasting attraction of a reproducing piano aesthetic, from Satie's *Gymnopédies* via Stravinsky's 1924 Sonata to Cage, Boulez, and Stockhausen, is closer to the classical automaton of the Mozart era, its appeal a mix of transcendent calm, precision, intellectual complexity, and total absence of vulgar rhetoric. Such is the power vested in a live performer that audiences have come to rely on the continuity of performance in a live concert as guarantor of integrity of the music itself. The performer is esteemed in fact as the guarantor of life.

Perhaps the most abstracted example of point and line interface is the Turing test of artificial intelligence, saying in effect that if an observer cannot tell the difference in intelligibility between a live input and an automated prompt then there is no difference in intelligence (as a manifestation of consciousness) between the two. Here intelligence is defined as giving the appearance of logically continuous thought.

CASIMIR EFFECT

The Casimir effect is an attractive (or more accurately, negative-repulsive) force between parallel surfaces at submicroscopic distances. Its discovery seems to have arisen from a thought experiment translating cavity resonance in microphones to the world of subatomic physics. In 1948, while researching the cohesive properties of viscous fluids (a group including the atmosphere on a microscopic scale), Philips Electrical Industries scientist Hendrik Casimir was led to speculate that empty space is not empty at all, but a constant flux of virtual particles popping in and out of existence. It led him to redefine the zero point vacuum of empty space no longer as a perfect vacuum but rather an energy state or cavity resonance in constant fluctuation above and below zero in consequence of the constant creation and annihilation of virtual particles. For an audio industry scientist the cavity resonance associated with adjacent parallel surfaces is an irritating artifact of electrostatic microphones and reproducers. In the acoustic domain, in much the same way as thermal energy in the atmosphere can be made audible by holding the cavity of an empty seashell to one's ear, parallel surfaces tend to ring or resonate *eigentones* of corresponding wavelength as a consequence of feedback of random thermal motion in the air space between them, causing a series of harmonic resonance spikes to color any intercepted sound. The Casimir effect corresponds in the subatomic domain to an analogous resonance presumed to obtain between hypothetical parallel surfaces, arising from spontaneous particle creation and annihilation at the most fundamental level. In subatomic physics, a particle is associated with a particular energy state and spin, and thus with a frequency and wavelength. Reasoning that a measurable fluctuation of specific frequency should be produced in a similar manner between parallel facing surfaces of a suitably designed resonant cavity, Casimir fabricated a microphone-like cavity of 1 cm^2 parallel metal plates suspended at a distance of a few microns. On the basis that only a limited number of emergent particles will be of wavelengths conforming with the gap between the plates, the experiment tested the proposition that there will be more virtual particles pressing on the external surfaces of the plates than those resisting between the gap, creating a tiny but measurable pressure differential forcing the plates toward one another. The Casimir effect also implies that the resultant energy state between the plates converges to a value *less than zero* by a factor increasing in magnitude as the distance between the plates reduces to nanometric scale.[3]

Wherever there are opposing parallel walls, there are acoustic effects. A musician considers the Casimir effect in acoustical terms. Parallel reflecting surfaces are acoustically tuned cavities that enhance wavelengths and aliquot divisions (frequencies and their multiples) conforming to the shortest distance between them. In the macroscopic world of sound and music, paradoxical influences of flat, curved, and irregular surfaces have been exploited for thousands of years. In the Australian Northern Territories, natural stone outcrops sacred to the Aboriginal people from primeval times have been found to act as acoustic lenses, focusing and projecting the voice. Prehistoric caves in Europe famous for their paintings of hunting scenes and wild animals are now considered to be sacred in implication, and there is evidence that such paintings tend to be clustered at locations of acoustic significance. During the 1939–1945 war, large sculptural concrete aerials were erected along the

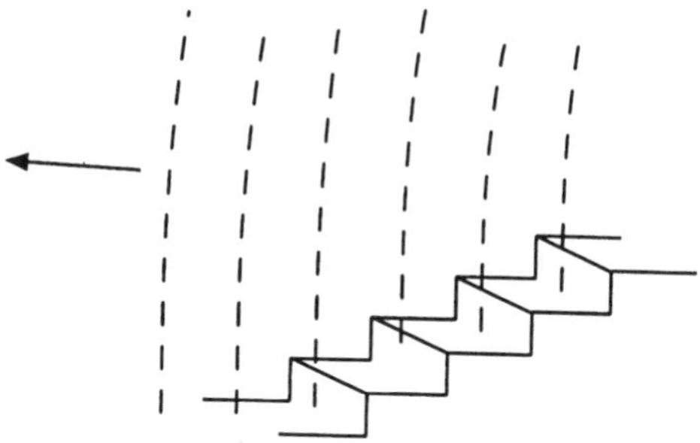

Sound reflected from regular steps is "tuned" to the wavelength of the step depth

English south coast to detect and amplify the sound of approaching bomber squadrons.

From the time of Vitruvius, the Roman master builder whose treatise on town planning is among the profession's oldest surviving documents, builders have understood and exploited the close relationship between acoustics and surfaces in constructing buildings for popular entertainment and public debate. The seventeenth-century Dutch astronomer Christian Huygens observed by chance that a stone stairway of regular step depth tuned incidental sound to an audible wavelength related to the periodic reflections of successive risers. What he discovered by accident, it is fair to assume others before him may have known and thought about. Acousticians in the twentieth century have noted the same tuned filter effect in Greek and Roman stepped amphitheaters, assuming it to be an indication of faulty design, and ignoring the more likely inference that such a feature would have been deliberate and would have led to adaptive behaviors, for example that dramas were chanted rather than spoken, and in a tonality in harmony with the wavelength reflected from the stepped seating.

The Casimir effect is yet another example of a familiar acoustic effect in the macrocosmic (human scaled) domain, reinvented as a new discovery in the microcosmic realm of subatomic particles. Perhaps it is no more than a coincidence. Experiments to test the effect have been focused so far on the detection of cavity resonances between surfaces that are ideally parallel and flat. In the macrocosmic world of acoustics, however, interesting discoveries have long since been made, and tested musically, in relation to the acoustic implications not only of flat and negatively curved walled cavities, but also of complex fractal surfaces such as the interiors of gothic and baroque churches, complex curves that reflect sound differentially at different frequency scales.

BRANES

Out of knot theory and string theory emerges an ultimate reality of multidimensional surfaces called "branes," in some accounts called "P-branes," which is self-deprecating and rather witty.[4] Branes are to strings seemingly what the parallel walls of a corridor are to wavelengths of sound—or indeed, to stretched strings, since the clap tone standing wave generated between the walls of a corridor twangs exactly like the metallic string of a harpsichord. There is a curious symmetry connecting brane theory and baroque era acoustics. Brane theory reasons from *branes* (strictly, *2-branes*), surface or membraneous resonators of waveforms, via *strings* (*1-branes*), conductors of waveforms, to string *harmonics* as energy states corresponding to particle constituents of atoms and macroscopic solids. To an outsider it is somewhat like reasoning from the motion of a drumskin back to the drumstick as a solid object. A brane is like the vibrating surface of a pond, where water meets air. Newtonian era music on the other hand reasons from the metallic-sounding eigentones of a parallel walled corridor to the sound of an actual harpsichord string, and from there to a note of musical manuscript defining a location in the frequency continuum and its associated time value. Whereas brane theory appears to reason in a direction leading from abstract mental representations to physical realities, in Newtonian acoustics the thought experiment leads in the opposite direction, from concrete to abstract. It leads from a physical *reverberation* arising from the conversion of random to structured motion (the clap becoming audible as a tone in the presence of parallel walls), to a laboratory *simulation* of the same effect in a theoretical context (the action of plucking reorganized as an audible tone by the tension of the string), thence to the *graphic representation* of the same tone in a music notation that allows the same information to be manipulated in complex ways.

Branes are singletons; they do not come in pairs with a resonant gap, like Casimir's parallel plates, or ringing like the airspace between the plaster walls of a narrow corridor. The equivalent of a pair of 2-branes interacting as independent carriers of information calls to mind the pressure waves issuing from the vibrating membranes of a pair of electrostatic loudspeakers, combining in the listener's hearing to recreate the appearance of acoustic objects in a virtual two-dimensional space. Or, even more vividly, Bridget Riley moiré images of the sixties, op art transparencies printed in regular wavelike patterns in black and white that, when viewed by both eyes at once create illusory interference patterns in the brain, sometimes as fringe color effects, corresponding in the visual domain to eigentones or string harmonics in the acoustical domain. (A random example of moiré interference pattern is the fanciful illustration of a maze accompanying the story of Theseus and the Minotaur in chapter nine, in which the interference pattern of black and white concentric rings resembles a giant spider.)

Transparent moiré sheets also have an acoustical history in practical endeavors to represent, combine, and reproduce musical waveforms graphically. These initiatives date from the 1930s, early years of optical sound, research undertaken by Rudolf Pfenninger, Oskar Fischinger, and others partly to allow for the optical synthesis of complex waveforms, and in part to improve the musical quality of movie soundtracks.[5] Optical movie sound had arisen in the early years of the twentieth century, combining techniques of high-resolution microphotography with advances in the detection and conversion of fluctuating luminance to electrical current.

The interest of such developments can be appreciated in the context of a scientific mind-set newly distracted by the implications of wave-particle duality. Theories of waveform analysis, synthesis, and interaction on a musical scale correspond in their fashion to theories of particle identification and interaction at subatomic scale.

By painstakingly combining and superimposing optical waveforms on transparent sheets, experimenters succeeded in creating and combining organ-like synthetic tones to produce simple music tracks. Following an outwardly similar line of reasoning, present-day brane theory adduces a world of particle combinations from a theory of waveforms corresponding to energy states. Viewed from the sidelines it looks just like another version of the Turing test, the rough and ready justification being if the simulation sounds like a sheep and looks like a sheep, then to all intents and purposes it is a sheep. There is, let us admit, a historic predisposition in the western world to identify artificial waveforms with the sound and corresponding nature of real musical instruments, including the human voice (*vox humana*). The same propensity to identify particles and waves in the subatomic domain can be seen extending from the weak correlation of real instruments and organ stops, to the more bizarrely influential strong correlation of Fourier Theory synthesized waveforms with natural sounds, along with correspondingly inadequate theories of analogue and digital music synthesis in the twentieth century. One is hardly surprised therefore if cosmologists are inspired on occasion to identify waveforms and their interactions with substantial phenomena. (Perhaps what it all boils down to is a neo-Platonist view of physical bodies as local manifestations of idealized ratios.)

In choosing to approach reality in terms of waveforms interacting in hypothetical space, cosmologists are allowing themselves to be drawn, either wittingly or unwittingly, into a representational schema that overlaps in a number of areas with sound recording. Sound recording involves the replication of a three-dimensional acoustic process in real time through technology that superimposes a virtual three- or four-dimensional spacetime on the real spacetime of the observer. The information from which this virtual spacetime is reconfigured, at will and out of historical spacetime (that is, independent of the spacetime the listener currently inhabits), has effectively been sucked out of the atmospheric disturbance of a real event in the past by virtual "black holes," known as microphones, registered on a moving "2-brane," otherwise known as magnetic tape, and subsequently transferred as a recoverable impression to analogue vinyl or digital disc.

In *The Concept of Music*, reflecting on the gold-plated analogue disc transported aboard the *Voyager 2* spacecraft on its journey beyond the solar system, I wondered how an alien intelligence might distinguish how to read the information contained in the line drawings of nine-inch high human beings, and associated graphics of the solar system, from audio information on the disc recording, including voice clips of Elvis and JFK and orchestral music by Beethoven. After all, both kinds of information consist of lines engraved on a more or less flat surface. The pictures are naturally read by eye, whereas the audio information is read by touch, using an appropriate stylus. We know that, but how does the alien work it out? It occurred to me that the alien intelligence would more readily understand the audio than the visual illustrations and text, since the continuous spiral groove of a stereo disc is a tangible expression of continuity in space and time, more logically suited to convey what it is to be a living and thinking entity existing in time, as well as conveying the human and cultural terms and priorities of communicating the experience of being alive, as music reveals them.[6]

MULTIPLE DIMENSIONS

Just at the time when many in the world of physics are wearying of the concept of an eleven-dimensional spacetime, the world of audio recording steps up with a convenient analogy. Accounting for the seven hypothetical dimensions that are necessary for string theory to work, in addition to the four dimensions of regular spacetime, involves a leap of faith that from time to time imagines the hidden dimensions as somehow curled in on themselves, a puzzle perhaps easier to digest in the more familiar terms of a dvd-audio disc. Enjoying a movie or classical music in surround sound in effect superimposes the three virtual spatial dimensions and one of time of the recording, on the three "real" spatial dimensions and one of time of the listener's spacetime, along with added dimensions of pitch (frequency space), color (timbre), and phase space (direction and relative motion), making eleven dimensions in all. An early illustration of multiple dimensions in music is found in Monteverdi's anthem "Deposuit potentes" from the *Magnificat*, composed in 1610, a remarkably up to date lesson in audio perspective that extends to additional polarities of eternity and chronometric time, internal feeling and external sensation, and internal (the world inside your head) and exterior space (the physical world out there).[7]

One can even discern a conceptual trajectory leading from a Newtonian universe modeled in the image of the harmonic ratios of a stretched string, through to an Einsteinian universe where the string is reinvented as a groove on a gramophone disc (though as Stephen Hawking observes, there are relativistic advantages to the timeline of a universe conceived as a groove on an Edison cylinder recording than on a disc). The groove of a 78 rpm disc is an informational string expressed as a timeline. It incorporates vibratory information that evolves in time from a starting point to an end point, but with the added complication that the original frequency information once embedded in the disc is no longer independent of the time dimension, but mechanically geared to the speed of motion of the disc past the pickup head. Such a recording can be adjusted to go faster or slower relative to the original timescale and that of the listener, the relative pitch of the music rising and falling in relation, and making its duration shorter or longer in comparison.

A relativistic worldview in which an individual's experience of reality is dependent on the speed at which the observer moves through time, if not triggered by the the arrival of music recording, would certainly receive a tremendous boost from it. The theoretical attraction to astrophysicists of being able to travel backward in time appears to consist largely in speculation over the possibility of doing away with one's grandfather, which seems to be missing the point. Western polyphony, from children's rounds to the *canon cancrizans* of Bach and the multiple timescales of high renaissance masses, has a great deal to say about the harmonious coexistence of past and future, and even about time wrapped around on itself in an unending cycle, most famously perhaps in the medieval round "Sumer is icumen in," and the fifteenth-century rondeau *Ma fin est mon commencement* (My end is my beginning) by the French master Guillaume de Machaut.

That time goes in cycles is perhaps a natural conclusion for cultures who are conscious of time as motion but are otherwise locked in the present. The art of canon, which flourished from the sixteenth to the early nineteenth centuries, is a development of the rondeau where the subject element is subjected to shifts in both frequency space and time, a sophistication reflecting the new sensibility of renaissance perspective, as well as exploiting the freedoms afforded by standard notation to manipulate time as a spatial dimension. In the fugues of Bach, themes are not only superimposed but transposed in pitch, on occasion inverted and reversed in time. These are purely intellectual conceits, but they also make acceptable music. In one sense they are statements about the eternal coexistence of time and space in every direction (even upside down and backwards); in another sense, however, the fugue (meaning *flight*) is simply saying that time flies.

That time is an internal process and not an objective measure is another matter, one that connects to a perception of time or timeline in the image of the traveling wave in the vibrating string of a musical instrument. Accordingly, and echoed in the fatalism of Greek tragedy, events are predetermined and human fate is held in tension between fixed points of origin and departure, and influences are capable of moving in either direction to affect a life in the present.

Notes

1. W. H. Auden, "The Word and the Machine." *Encounter* Vol. II, No. 2 (April 1954), 3–4.
2. Daniel Ling, *Speech and the Hearing-Impaired Child: Theory and Practice*. Washington DC: Alexander Graham Bell Association for the Deaf, 1975, 216–17.
3. J. Richard Gott, *Time Travel in Einstein's Universe: The Physical Possibilities of Travel Through Time*. Boston: Houghton Mifflin, 2001, 134–36.
4. Stephen Hawking, *The Universe in a Nutshell*, 54–55, 126–27.
5. Kurt London, *Film Music: A Summary of the Characteristic Features of its History, Aesthetics, Technique; and possible Developments* tr. Eric S. Bensinger. London: Faber and Faber, 1936, 197. *See also* Roger Manvell and John Huntley, *The Technique of Film Music*. London: Focal Press, 1957, 170–77.
6. Robin Maconie, *The Concept of Music*. Oxford: Clarendon Press, 1990, 4–5.
7. Robin Maconie, *The Second Sense: Language, Music, and Hearing*. Lanham MD: The Scarecrow Press, 2002, 106–10.

FOURTEEN

TRANSITION

The opening measures of the *Chromatic Fantasy* by J. S. Bach give the impression of a wizard waving a magic wand. Composed for clavecin, a keyboard edition (if you like) of a Hungarian zither or dulcimer, the introduction sounds as though the composer has lifted the lid and is gliding his fingernails back and forth across the strings as if to check the tuning. And since the piece is a fantasy or improvisation, it could even be taken as a European homage to Indian classical music for sitar. We associate the practice of demonstrating the mode or scale at the beginning of an improvisation with the classical music of north India. It is an intriguing if unlikely thought that in this example Bach might actually be recalling an encounter with music for sitar. In his lifetime, European trade in India was well established, and merchants and their families who traveled and lived in the subcontinent were people of high culture. Since Bach and other keyboardists of the era were accustomed to tuning their instruments every other day, and we know Bach was interested in "fine tuning" his instrument to give increased mobility in modulating from one key to another, there is no reason to doubt that the opening flourish as illustrated is an equivalent gesture to demonstrate the tuning of the instrument and define the scale—a *chromatic* scale, as the title says—for the music to come.

That despite the reality of continuous transitions in everyday speech and song, western notated music is firmly attached to fixed pitches, and ill-equipped to deal with intermediate or gliding tones, is symptomatic of a larger tradition of superstition in Europe toward transitions of any kind. The feminine mystique is implicitly a mystique of uncertainty: the smile on the face of the Mona Lisa the subtlest of distortions of ideal composure, signifying that the young

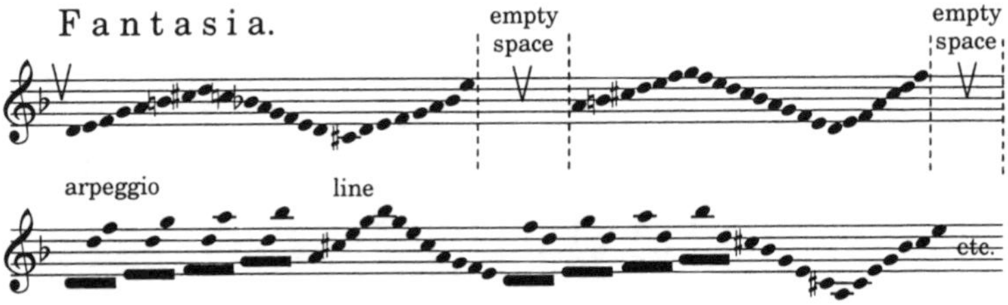

J.S. Bach: opening "magic wand" flourish of the Chromatic Fantasy in D minor *for harpsichord. Structure emerges out of chaos*

lady in question is pregnant, has just found out, and wants to keep it a secret, or her expression a demure response to the artist making conversation, putting her at ease, asking if she has a boyfriend. Religion, magic, and occult science—alchemy, witchcraft, all the way through to psychiatry—are all connected with the control of processes of continuous change: life, time, fertility (female), mood swings (also female); the mystery of converting base metal into gold; and effects of poison, liquor, and disease. Galileo's pioneering studies of acceleration attracted public and expert ridicule, but led to the invention of golf as a recreation; Zeno's paradox of the moving arrow is dismissed as a fantasy, but computer games are still firmly based on firing a gun and hitting a target. Individual skill in controlling the flight of a missile, as in English football, or golf, is regarded today as a show of magic to be rewarded. By contrast, an art of dissonance, as a condition of musical expression, or pretext for atonal music in general, continues to be demonized by clerical minds in the twenty-first century as behavior contrary to reason and the psychological health of the community. Today even the study of history has come under attack as unscientific:

> Descartes . . . denied to history any claim to be a serious study. Where were the definitions, the logical transformation rules, the rules of inference, the rigorously deduced conclusions? . . . If only we could . . . establish a coherent system of regularities, . . . we could perhaps afford to ignore, or treat as secondary, such intermediate phenomena as feelings, thoughts, volitions, of which men's lives seem to themselves to be largely composed, but which do not lend themselves to exact measurement.[1]

Isaiah Berlin writes of history as "a confused amalgam of memories," but the case he outlines against a science of history, which came to a head in the mid-nineteenth century of Herbert Spencer, rests on a much older and broader issue of the impossibility of quantifying continuous processes in nature, observing "the methods and concepts of the mechanists were not adequate for dealing with growth and change." Publication of Darwin's *Origin of Species* had not only extended the timeframe of biological history into an incomprehensibly distant past, it introduced a radically new perception of biological evolution as a scientific study involving the location of evidence in time as well as space.

The new nineteenth-century culture of continuously evolving processes is vividly conveyed in Wagnerian opera and its abandonment of classical set piece construction in favor of a new melodic fusion of aria and recitative, harmonic development by continuous modulation, and depiction in real time of emotional transitions. Building on the romantic conception of a remote, mythical past, Wagner's operas are dramas in which signature melodies or *leitmotives* assume the role of archetypal forms or DNA markers in a continuously evolving tribal and harmonic landscape, codified in the names of protagonists: Siegfried, Siegmund, Sieglinde, Brünnhilde, Gerhilde, Flosshilde, etc.

THE DYNAMICS OF SPEECH

A gliding tone, portamento or *glissando*, is a continuous movement between notated pitches. Classical music is not well-equipped to handle gliding tones, though they are plentiful in nature: in the wind, mostly as signals of animals, in the howl of wolves, the wail of those in pain, the squeak of bats, and the call of the whale. All gliding cries have powerful emotional connotations. A variant of the gliding tone, more commonly found in music, is the sequence, a repeating figure ascending or descending in pitch. To renaissance composers working within a tonal framework of *just* (that is, pure but unequal) intonation, the musical interest of a sequence lies in the subtle changes of internal harmony that arise from shifts in key, or transpositions within the same key, within a compromised system of tuning. Such experiments in transposition led to the perception of different keys as differently stressed, and thus as

A L-le lú- ia.
℣. Ado- rá- bo ad templum san- ctum tuum

Plainchant notation. Each note-group or neume *corresponds to an inflected syllable that is prolonged until the next syllable*

expressing different emotions or degrees of inner harmony, in an extension of the classic Greek interpretation of the modes.

In speech, bending or gliding tones within the syllable or phrase are commonplace. We call them *inflections* or bends as distinct from intonation or exact notes. The connotations of "informal instability" are generally positive, if one considers the alternative of steady-toned and uninflected speech, conveying a contrasting impression of distance, authority, even robotic indifference toward the listener. To counter an impression of insensitivity and bring life back into music, French baroque composers developed an elaborate system of graces or ornamentation, elevated to a high art by the generation of Lully and quite possibly transferred or related, via the French connection with Scottish royalty, to the Scots tradition of pipe music as a form of heightened speech employing ornamentation as syllabic accentuation. Graphics assigned to accent notes in a melody incude the trill, mordent, turn, acciaccatura, and appoggiatura—the last named a true inflection or "bending the note." While baroque ornamentation is often misconstrued, ignored, or mistaken for superfluous decoration, its original purpose in certain areas—the trill, for example—can still be clearly discerned.

Ornamentation allows a classical performer to introduce realistic qualities of inflection, or expressive instability of tone, to an outwardly strictly notated and impersonal score. In turn, the uncertainties of these deviant signs—derived from, and analogous to, the accents and diacriticals of a printed text—bring emotion to bear on an otherwise clinical musical line. Scholarly interest in the natural instabilities of speech coincides with a growing attention, during the baroque era, to the description and composition of movement in

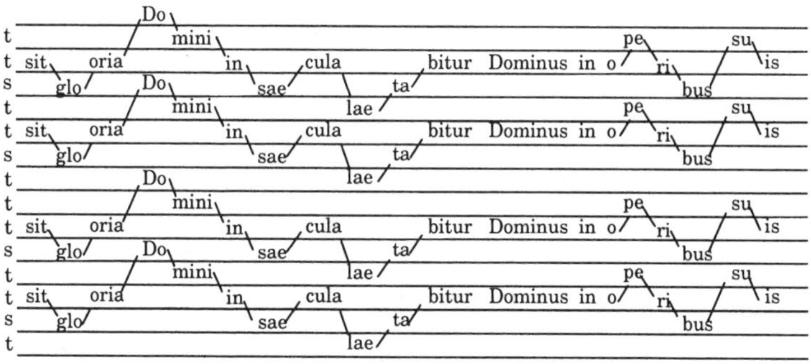

Polyphonic notation of Hucbald (tenth century)

time, away from the cyclical formalities of courtly dance and rustic dance toward a more liberal or contrived art of spatial attraction and dialogue. Led again by the French, the trend developed a highly ingenious notation *in three dimensions* of step patterns, courtesies, and leaps in dance. Revived in the late twentieth century, today the art and science of movement in space is associated with computer animation, but in seventeenth-century Paris it was implemented in a ballet of multiple dancers, governed by double-dotted rhythms imitating the periodic swing of the pendulum, a choreography also alluding to the sublime complexities of planetary circulation under the benign influence of the sun king Louis XIV.

On the graphic evidence of the signs themselves, and considering the history of medieval notation, its evolution into spacetime notation, and subsequent elaboration by the epicycles of gracenote ornamentation, it is possible to infer the original function of music notation as a code of voice accentuation and inflection, assigning a value to the melody and stress patterns of speech as inflections essential to expressing the meaning of a text. Such a view conforms to the medieval convention that the totality of meaning of a written text is only conveyed in the dynamic process of reading aloud. Learning a language and learning to read aloud—as in acting from a script—are processes wherein ordered sequences of static terms are fused into coherent lines of dynamic thought. If the first music notations seem to consist mainly of accents written above words to indicate how they are inflected in context, that is already evidence of an intelligent appreciation that meaning resides in the movement between pitches, and not in the pitches themselves.

Precise intonation is required specifically for the harmonization of multiple voices, a consideration which helps to explain the slow progress of harmonic development in medieval times. Hucbald's prototype notation from the tenth century indicates pitch movement conforming to a preexisting scale of pitches (presumably of a pipe organ) by writing the syllables of a chant higher and lower on the page, like musical notes, and connecting them by lines (a style Stockhausen returns to in 1968 for notating the verse interpolations

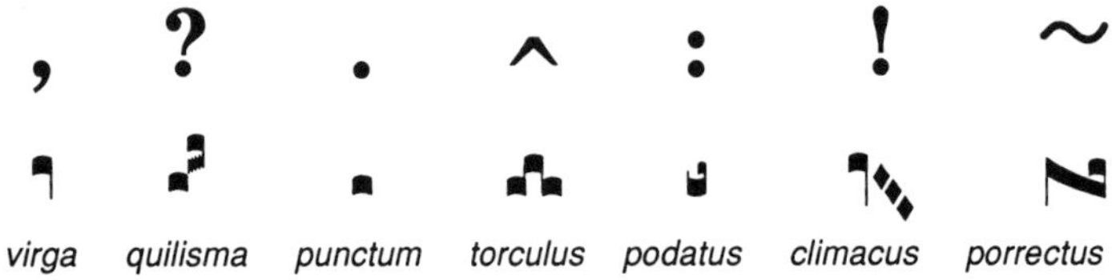

Medieval neumata and their equivalents in modern punctuation

of *Stimmung*). Such a notation demonstrates a grasp of pitch space but not of pitch information (or inflection) as qualities independent of a text. An ability to distinguish the visual meaning of a text from the physical speech act (or melody) did not arise, and was not exploited in music, at least until the fourteenth century. The singer of Hucbald's era would have had difficulty interpreting text and musical notations at the same time, or recognizing note values as transitional elements rather than fixed locations.

Pitch values in plainchant are grouped in shapes corresponding to modes of inflection: for example, rising (scandicus, quilisma), falling (clivis, climacus), or both (torculus, porrectus). The ligature or diagonal of a porrectus, and the tail of the climacus written as a descending line of lozenges, are usually explained away as stylistic conventions to be interpreted as discrete notes. However, given the manifest relationship between a quilisma (a rising inflection) and the modern question mark, or between the torculus (an up and down inflection) and the modern circumflex, it is not out of the question that these notations or *neumes* (from the Greek *pneuma* implying "in a breath") were originally intended to be inflected as units gliding between pitches, and not as distinct pitches. The grounds for thinking so are that if a notation is intended to preserve a natural inflection of speech, since natural speech involves continuous transitions within syllables, a neume is open to be interpreted in appropriate circumstances as syllabic incantation embodying continuous transitions. If, on the other hand, the notation is interpreted as pitch data, more related to formal speech, or if the singer is unsure in interpretation, it will tend to be sung as discrete pitches. The case for a more flexible interpretation rests on the fact that living speech is the example on which notation is based, not the other way around; reasons for the more flexible interpretation eventually dying out arising from authority being transferred from the speech act to the written form.

As notation evolved from plainchant to the standard form of dots on a stave, we recognize a perception of the dynamics of voice movement drawing away from syllabic unity and continuity of line to focus on accuracy of location (and by implication, tonal stability within the frame of reference represented by the stave). Just as astronomical observations of planetary positions from night to night required the development of graphics to record precise locations in spacetime from which their orbital motion could be computed, so the evolution of music notation from Hucbald through to Machaut evolved from graphics representing dynamic syllabic shapes toward a system of fixed points within an ordered pitch spectrum and time frame, each note the tick of a clock as it were. The two converge on schemas of visualizing motion and temperament that reach a peak with Kepler and his symbolic representation of planetary motion in music notation.[2]

When multiple voices are singing together, it also makes sense for them to converge on exact values in pitch and time. The opening "Hallelujah!" of Handel's "Hallelujah Chorus" from *Messiah*, to take a famous example, is a figure of musical speech from the Greeks, showing a learned appreciation of the Aristoxenian tetrachord or bisected perfect fourth. The shout of praise is articulated as disjunct syllables of distinct timbre: "Ha – lle – lu – jah!" in a figure or musical callsign in broken intervals expressing energy and boundless optimism after the manner of a trumpet fanfare. A solo singer, on the other hand, has the freedom to inflect: thus in the equally famous aria "Where e'er you walk," from Handel's opera *Semele* to a libretto after Ovid by Congreve, with additions (as here) by Alexander Pope, liquescant vowel lines alternate with stepwise, percussive consonants:

Where e'er you walk
Cool gales shall fan the glade;
Trees where you sit
Shall crowd into a shade.

In the second verse of the same aria: "Where e'er you tread/The blushing flow'rs shall *rise*. . ." a dissonant major seventh leap—expressing growth—reaches upward on the word "rise" to a telling equivalent upward glide of the audible second formant [ra–eez]. The poet's deliberate symmetry of alternating phrases of vowel and consonant, and perfect marriage of verbal and musical line and step—for example the rustling [sh] and [ff] sounds to accompany "cool gales shall fan the glade"—indicate that poet and composer alike are fully aware of the abstract qualities of continuous and disjunct speech and their emotional (and possibly gender) implications. A listener in the twenty-first century may even be disposed to hear the lines as an effect of alternating slow motion and normal speed, in the manner of a tape recording.

Inflections, like accents, and indeed like the original shapes of neumes in plainchant (not to mention their antecedent forms) are indications of personality as well as signs of transition. Apart from their usefulness as indicators of meaning, stresses and accents conspire to suggest that the syllable is not a steady state but a moment in a process, surreptitiously implying that it is the process or inflection that carries the meaning, not the steady state or the word itself (bringing the argument back to the commonplace proletarian view of the musical performance as the creative act, rather than the notated composition). We know from Vitruvius and his reading of Aristoxenus that the Romans were aware of words and syllables as compound entities with a beginning (usually a consonant), a middle (usually a vowel) and a termination (usually a consonant).[3] Early in the twentieth century cryptologists were surprised to discover that the written language of the ancient Sumerians also recognized the

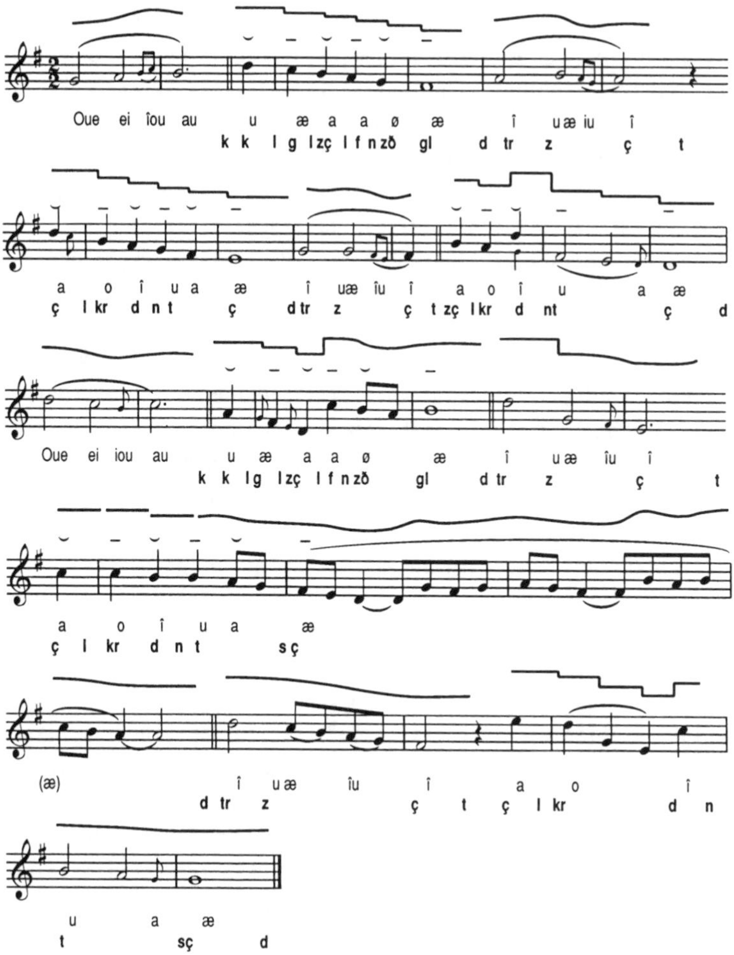

Handel's aria "Where'er you walk" from the opera Semele *alternates gliding vowel phrases with crisp stepwise (implicitly scalewise) consonantal formations*

syllable as a three-stage process consisting of an onset, a steady state, and a decay. Ancient graphic languages such as the Egyptian hieroglyphs had previously been assumed to be letter codes, like the typographic alphabet. A written language that conforms to the way people actually speak is more likely to incorporate nuances of inflection that tend to be left out of consideration by mainly visual (i.e., silent) readers. As with medieval plainchant, the evidence of attention to vowel terminations speaks of a culture that understands the dynamic evolution of a fundamental particle of speech and, by extension, speech itself as a dynamic continuum rather than an ad hoc juxtaposition of discrete sound objects. Recognising a syllable as a *gestalt* or dynamic shape creates its own possibilities of the syllable taking on different meanings as its onset is varied, or inflected ornamentally, as for example in the tone languages of Asian countries. Despite having to notate her emotional sacred songs in the austere terms of plainchant, Hildegard von Bingen succeeded in organizing the musical flow of her text settings in ways making her emotional subtext absolutely clear. The ornamental superscriptions of French baroque tell much the same story of a local perception of standard notation as deficient in a human dimension of expressive nuance, and as a corollary, of the significant contribution of inflection in conveying meaning.

Nobody sets out to invent a defective system, but a collective enterprise such as a written language is bound to conform to collective standards rather than personal traits and local usages. It follows that a perception of writing as a *defective* representation of the richness of natural speech (entailing the need for punctuation marks and other guides to inflection) is at the same time an understanding of the role of a written language as embodying standard protocols of communication. The same shift applies to a perception of music notation as deficient in expression, in other words, as mechanical in nature and lacking the natural cadence of a real human being. Conveying the richness and ambiguity of natural speech was not a top priority at the time music notation was invented, rather the aim was to base a utilitarian system of writing on common features of language and pronunciation in a world of multiple accents and dialects, in much the same way as BBC standard English pronunciation emerged as a priority in the early years of British radio. For such reasons the implications of baroque ornamentation go way beyond imitating the artificial courtesies of aristocratic discourse to imply a subtler trend away from the mechanistic concept of a clockwork universe introduced by Oresme and Buridan toward more refined and volatile forms of expression associated with a newly evolving philosophy of consciousness and free will. Paradoxically, the Cartesian corollary of such a trend is that the freedoms of expression sanctioned by ornamentation are doomed to mutate, like the inflections of plainchant, into the dead formalities of classical notation.

Much of the emotional poetry of western classical music arises from a tension between "masculine" characteristics of discipline, endurance, and order, expressed in stepwise motion and steady-state pitches and harmonies, and contrasting "feminine" expressive characteristics that glide, warp, bend, and otherwise express uncertainty, inconstancy, and unpredictability. As a system, classical western notation is clearly biased toward masculine qualities of standardization and definition, and noticeably deficient in indications of nuance or feeling, most of which survive as clip-on words and signs, in French or Italian, superimposed on the score.

A wit observed that the renaissance Italians invented joined-up writing at the same time as Machiavelli invented joined-up thinking, introducing a new consciousness of continuity or implication in thought and action. Originating from the same culture as Machiavelli, the violin family was developed specifically to mimic the ebb and flow of the human voice, in order to convey the volatile human emotions celebrated in the new operas of Peri and Monteverdi. The penetrating, unsteady tone of the violin family inexorably took over the role of the older viols, instruments of even tone employed not for expression but to suit an older aesthetic aspiring to mastery of perfect steady-state harmonies by imperfect human beings working in concert. A giveaway feature of the violin family is their absence of frets or ridges on the fingerboard, allowing the player's fingers to *portamento* or glide continuously from note to note, not only to inflect a solo melody in the manner of a human voice, but also to fine tune the pitch and ensure perfect harmony. The violin became key to a new music of continuous movement in pitch and key relations in the very same era that Kepler sought to measure the inconstant elliptical motion of the planets, and Galileo the acceleration of a ball, rolling down a slope, or dropped from a high tower.

Unlike classical music, oral cultures have no inherent prejudice against gliding tones. Male leadership figures invented western notation and it is natural that the latter should embody masculine values of precision and objectivity. The culture changes with the arrival of secular opera, a genre shift in which a musical writing originally designed for technical and scientific applications became diverted to the service of popular entertainment on dramatic themes of a deliberately uncertain and emotional character.

Classical music is largely known and discussed in terms of its pitch notation, which is an international system of signs. In purely notational terms the glide or extended continuous inflection is a rarity, for the simple reason that it is difficult to draw precisely. Or rather, we might conclude that classical notation embodies an unstated set of priorities that considers gliding tones as in some way defective. The Princeton-Columbia digital synthesizers designed by Harry Olson in the 1950s did not incorporate glissandi, and the serial theories of Boulez and Milton Babbitt likewise avoid them. Gliding tones were first introduced to the synthesizer vocabulary by Yamaha and other Japanese manufacturers in the 1980s. Traditional Japanese music, on the other hand, has always recognized a variety of tonal inflections.

All the same, gliding tones are an essential ingredient of European and western speech. In speech there are two distinct types of glide. The first is a melodic transition, where the voice intones a rising or falling inflection. The second, more subtle, is a transition of formant resonance from vowel to vowel, or diphthong. A diphthong has gestural implications. In English, "I" and "You" refer respectively to the self and to the other person, and that distinction is subtly reinforced by dynamic tendencies within the sounds themselves: upward in "I" [ah-ee], and downward in "You" [ee-oo]. These audible transitions in vowel tone arise from changes effected in the mouth cavity that cause the associated resonances to rise and fall. The French *oui* (yes) typically has a rising inflection [oo-ee], conveying uncertainty, expressed in the formant resonance. The German *ja* (yes), on the other hand, and American colloquial *yeah*, are typically intoned with a falling inflection [ee-ah], suggesting certainty. These gliding movements within the syllable are just as clearly audible when whispered rather than spoken.

In music notations for dance, steps and beats correspond to positions and momentary points of repose, while glides are transitions between them. An extended glide in classical music can be expressed as a scale passage, interpolating degrees of the scale between points of repose, in much the same way as animated movie is based on human or software expertise to interpolate between pivotal moments a number of frames apart to create the impression of graceful continuous movement, which in a simulation corresponds equally to an impression of continuity in space and time.

The gestural content of vowel transitions in casual speech, being dependent on a choice of vocabulary usually dictated by sense, is more or less out of the control of the speaker. An obvious exception is swearing, which is verbal gesture intended to give offense and having little or no other communicative function. In polite conversation gestural meaning is exchanged in otherwise superfluous interjections or ejaculations (. . .Yes. . . . Really? . . . Oh . . . Wow! etc.). In the extreme formality of speech associated with public ritual, royalty, the legal profession, and classical acting, it is noticeable that spoken inflections or glides of any kind, including diphthongs, tend to be suppressed in favor of fixed temperaments and steady-state vowels, whence derive the clipped accents of British imperialism, and the ringing nasal resonances of classical French drama. The difference between upper-class "correct" speech and demotic "slovenly" speech is typically identified with the presence or absence of gliding tones—inflection and the modulated diphthong. That the pronunciation of imperial speech in England may have been deliberately cultivated from the time of William the Conqueror, to avoid diphthongs and emphasize stable vowel formants of diatonic harmonic content, cannot be entirely ruled out.

We are left speculating by George Bernard Shaw's ingenious transliteration of flower girl Eliza Doolittle's speech in Act I of *Pygmalion*, familiar to most as the movie musical *My Fair Lady*. Shaw's fable of Eliza Doolittle is a fairy tale of the power of cultivated diction to transform an uneducated working-class girl into an aristocrat:

> Ow, eez ye-ooa san, is e? Wal, fewd dan y' dee-ooty bawmz a mather should, eed now bettern to spawl a pore gel's flahrzn than ran awy athaht pyin. Will ye-oo py me f'them? [4]

"Here, with apologies" (the Irish playwright adds in an aside), "this desperate attempt to represent her dialect without a phonetic alphabet must be abandoned as unintelligible outside London." A reader is forced to decipher acoustically the diphthongs and run-together syllables of a natural cockney speech delivered in a continuous stream without regard to the separations of print. As the stage directions make clear, the playwright and his alter ego Professor Higgins are able to transcribe local accents with spectacular accuracy with the aid of wax cylinder recording. Shaw's witty exercise in the ethnography of demotic speech would anticipate by some twenty-seven years, and may well have inspired, the stream of consciousness of *Finnegans Wake*, by his compatriot James Joyce.

PORTAMENTO

Abundant evidence survives in early phonograph recordings of the employment by classical musicians of techniques of *vibrato* (frequency and amplitude modulation of sustained tone) and *portamento* (continuous transition between notes) for expression. Both devices are rhetorical rather than ornamental in the French sense. Vibrato introduces a dynamic and calculated instability to tonal relations historically valued for precision and accuracy; portamento is an authentic tradition in fiddle music for the expression of melody as a continuous, speechlike line. Prior to the mid-nineteenth century, the introduction of trembling or uncertain intonation for expressive effect, like the momentarily wavering balance of a circus tight-rope walker, was relatively infrequent and regarded as a special effect for special occasions, as an attention-seeking device to be applied, randomly and intuitively in a live concert situation, and not a predictable feature of the composer's score.[5]

That standard notation is not designed with gliding tones in mind does not mean that glides are to be avoided at any cost, only that they are latent in the phrasing and contour of a musical line, in the flow of normal speech, and in ornamental effects such as the appoggiatura (leaning into a note), the turn (hovering around the note), and the mordent (biting the note: a word suggesting grinding one's teeth). On the evidence of historical recordings of the pre-electric era, performers cultivated a discreet art of sighing, gliding, wavering, and related inflections. That portamento was discontinued as an aesthetic device, after the arrival of electrical recording, only serves to confirm that a sighing inflection was a widely acceptable mode of expression prior to that change in practice.

With the arrival of electric recording in the 1930s the older, softer style of portamento declined, to be replaced by a new, hard-edge aesthetic of straight lines and relatively stable pitches. The change of aesthetic coincided with the rise of a new and troubling uncertainty over where an elementary particle might be, or where it was going next.

Notes

1. Isaiah Berlin, "The Concept of Scientific History" (1960). In *Concepts and Categories: Philosophical Essays* ed. Henry Hardy. Oxford: Oxford University Press, 1980, 103–6.
2. Owen Gingerich, "Kepler, Galileo, and the harmony of the world." In Victor Coelho ed., *Music and science in the Age of Galileo*. Dordrecht: Kluwer, 1992, 45–63.
3. Vitruvius (Marcus Vitruvius Pollio), *Ten Books on Architecture* tr. Morris Hickey Morgan. Cambridge MA: Harvard University Press (1914) repr. New York: Dover, 1960, 140. *See also* Robin Maconie, "Musical Acoustics in the Age of Vitruvius." *Musical Times* Vol. 146, No. 1890 (Spring 2005), 75–82.
4. *Oh, he's your son, is he? Well, if you had done your duty by him as a mother should, you would know better than to spoil a poor girl's flowers, then run away without paying. Will you pay me for them?*
5. Robert Philip, *Early Recordings and Musical Style: Changing Tastes in Instrumental Performance, 1900–1950*. Cambridge: Cambridge University Press, 1992.

FIFTEEN

TRANSFERENCE

> What makes it possible that a second tone should follow a first, a beginning tone? How is this logically possible?
>
> ARNOLD SCHOENBERG

In his treatise *On the Unity of the Intellect*, written in 1270, Thomas Aquinas criticized two contentions arising from the new Aristotelianism of Averroes. As his title suggests, these criticisms have to do with what knowledge is, how it is transferred, and what happens to it on the way. In modern terms, how information passes from person to person and whether it can be trusted. Aquinas objects:

> First, that the possible (or potential) intellect was a separate substance and not the form of the body, and secondly that it was one for all men. . . . A principal consideration advanced is the difficulty otherwise of explaining how it is that the individual understands.[1]

What is he saying exactly? It has to do first with a view of knowledge as information that is simply poured into a person. We encounter the same attitude today that small children are empty vessels waiting to be filled up with learning in order for them to become functioning members of society. Aquinas is objecting that such a view of knowledge as separate from the individual suggests (1) that knowledge is unaffected by the processing abilities of the person possessing it, and (2) that it is the same knowledge for everyone. If individuals are simply containers of knowledge, how do they "know" how to use it, he asks, and furthermore, how do people "know" that they know something new when they learn something?

Aquinas's criticism is targeted on a controversial passage in Aristotle's *De Anima* Book III, chapter 5, "On the intellective soul," wherein the philosopher appears to draw a distinction between knowledge expressed in anticipation of a possible future event, something that is not yet happening, and knowledge that resolves information that is already present to the senses (he uses the example of "making light into colors," as when a ray of white light passing through glass is refracted as a spectrum). Whereas an act of knowledge recovery (for example, reading) is necessarily contemporaneous with the data available to be known (which is present on the page), potential knowledge on the other hand is separate from, and independent of, anything that may have happened in the past, as well as untouched by any event that may happen in the future. Aristotle appears to be using the ingenious argument that every new event is different, in support of the larger proposition that the memory of a past event offers no certainty of application to any future event. This would appear to be one implication of the philosopher's elliptical contention that "potential knowledge in the universe as a whole is not prior even in time."

Aristotle is defending the point of view of a new visual science emerging out of a long tradition of acoustical reasoning. The essence of aural science is that sounds die and are reborn: that is their nature. In a world (or universe) of sound, things continue to exist even though they are only audible from time to time. Aristotle's alternative viewpoint is based on a new, visual perception of a world in constant change, the contrary implication of which is that things experienced intermittently are *never* the same from one appearance to the next. Such a view seems like a recipe for anarchy, unless a way is found of explaining the continuity of events in terms that can be reconciled with common sense. Aristotle does so by proposing that knowledge is a kind of external resource that is tapped into by individuals at different times, much as a computer database today is available to be accessed by different people on different occasions. What this entails is whether the knowledge acquired by different people is the same for all, which comes down to whether knowledge consists in information in the identical state in which it is acquired, or as modified by actual use. Aquinas is attacking Averroes' interpretation that true knowledge is the same for everyone, the individual use of it being merely a limited application open to error. There are interesting parallels with the view of contemporary linguistics, that language is the universal authority, and speech the subjective variable. The interesting complication is whether the employer of knowledge is entitled to claim the infallible authority of eternal knowledge, or is invariably laid open to charges of merely trivializing or perverting knowledge for personal ends. An analogous doctrinal controversy continues to rumble over the truth or otherwise of what Igor Stravinsky is supposed to have said in his published conversations with Robert Craft, and whether or not he actually held the opinions attributed to him. (Confirmation of which of course may lie in the evidence of the late music itself, which is typically left out of the equation.)

Aquinas's point is nominally theological, but also pragmatic. He is all for the notion that knowledge acquired is shaped by the person who acquires it, and that person's expectations and needs. His phrase "the form of the body" is a musical metaphor, recognizing that as the song passes from voice to voice, or instrument to instrument (the fingering and phrasing remaining the same), its tone and expression change, and therefore its precise meaning changes, because every sounding body is different. As real or virtual instruments, we are individually gifted with greater or lesser capacities to extract meaning from the information provided to us. That it is morally objectionable to pretend that people are not responsible for the things they say or do, on the ground that they are merely the instruments of a higher authority, is one of the rather more startling implications of Aquinas' asking how individual understanding is to be explained or otherwise excused. The Nuremberg defense that one is merely following orders is entailed by acceptance of the principle that people are empty vessels into which knowledge is poured, and that they are not required to understand—or question—what they have been told to do.

Writing a decade before Nuremberg, and under the shadow of a rising national socialism, Schoenberg distinguishes a theme from a melody. He is mindful enough of the use of folksong as material for symphonic treatment by composers as various as Brahms, Debussy, Bartók, Stravinsky, Milhaud, and Shostakovich, a practice at the time increasingly geared to the service of aggressive or defensive nationalist posturing. Schoenberg aims to distinguish the function of melody in such cases from the exposition and development of a theme in his own music, and that of the classical tradition of Bach, Mozart, and Beethoven. A melody, he says, is a gestalt, a complete statement; it stands alone, and when incorporated in a symphony it behaves like a passive object that has things done to it that tend in practice to transform its identity into something more grandiose than the tradition to which it originally belonged, or the function to which it was originally assigned. (A traditional working class song aggrandized into a symphonic statement is still a statement about peasant workers, but a statement invested with the appearance of power and authority ascribed, not to the workers themselves, but to a governing elite.) In the manner of a "found object" of *musique concrète*, a folk melody comes laden with a cargo of associations and meaningful connections that would normally be taken apart, turned over, examined, tested, and measured in traditional first-movement form. In the late medieval tradition of more distant times it was also acceptable, and intellectually daring, to treat a common-place melody, a "found object," as the basis of a sacred work, for example a mass (of which there are many) on the popular song *L'Homme Armé*.

A theme, on the other hand, is defined by Schoenberg as memorable but incomplete. The best themes are those asking to be resolved, and open to development and elaboration in a variety of ways, taking advantage of the full range of treatments available to a symphony orchestra, like the "fate knocking at the door" motif of Beethoven's Fifth symphony.

In between theme and melody lies the *leading motive* of Wagnerian opera, a formulaic musical character embodying distinctive personality traits that undergoes changes in mood as an indicator of narrative and character development, and is subject to recombination with the motives of other characters as an expression of the same relationships and interactions in the drama. A melody can also be the "Theme," in the technical sense, of a "Theme and Variations" where the interest is less in developing the structural or logical implications of the found object, and rather more to do with timescale elaboration and decoration—originally *divisions*—of an otherwise anonymous formula.[2] At the end of a set of variations the primary melody reappears, as if nothing has happened. And indeed, that is what it means. Nothing has happened.

To read Schoenberg's criticism of melody simply as a criticism of a tendency in early modern music to adopt popular or folk melodies to serve nationalist or populist agendas, is to miss his other point that the tactic overlooks, ignores, or distracts attention from the deeper concern of classical music for the nature of musical logic and connection, a question that, the composer says, "to my knowledge . . . has not previously been raised. . . . No one has yet asked: How, after all, can two tones be joined one with another? . . . Logically, we can only join things that are related."[3] He is not talking about combining tones into chords or multiple layers, but about employing notes as stepping stones in the progression of an idea, and musical dialogue as an exchange of ideas, implying the recognition and development of a statement of potential meaning from voice to voice—most clearly exemplified perhaps in the delicate exchanges of Webernian *klangfarbenmelodie*. To base a symphony on a melody instead of a theme is to trivialize, indeed contradict, the symphonic tradition, as Schoenberg sees it, of the exposition and development of a musical idea. A theme, in other words, ought to be a leading question, whereas a melody, by contrast, is merely a mission statement.

Ideas can be worked out in isolation, which is fine. But for the working out of an idea to be verified, which is a moral and social, as well as an intellectual issue, involves an exchange of information with a second party, not just the audience. Ideally a theme should be developed in partnership; if so, there is always the possibility of it leading in more than one direction, so that the conclusion may also be understood not as an arbitrary choice, but the consequence of a process leading to an agreement or accommodation. Part of the meaning of classical theme-and-development music is captured in what might be called the thrill of the chase: the pleasure of following a musical idea as it passes from the grasp of one instrument to another, eluding resolution until the very last. In joining in the chase, as it were, classical ensemble music, and especially music for symphonic forces, can be understood as representing as well as endorsing the virtues of cooperation and dialogue in everyday social life.

TRANSMUTATION

The old meaning of "translation" is of an object or person being moved without alteration of its nature from one place to another, as in the removal of a bishop from one region of influence to another, or a saint going straight to heaven ("a better place"), or an arrow flying from a bow toward a target. In the more usual sense it signifies a movement of ideas from one language to another, retaining the concept of object relocation to another environment without intrinsic change. In its earliest and most basic sense, transmutation alludes to an alteration of context without alteration of role. The deeper implication of such a concept (remembering Aquinas) is the notion that *identity* in this special case is independent of location, meaning that who you are as well as what you are saying does not rely on kinship or the society of other people among whom you live, of which the language you speak (say, Yorkshire dialect) is the outward and obvious sign. A visiting bishop who speaks Latin represents a higher state of being untouched by the business of daily life, committed to a world of Platonic essences, perhaps, in keeping with the cultivated perception of a spiritual leader or authority as "not of this world"—or indeed, "out of this world." [4]

When a melody is transposed from a home key to a foreign key its general shape remains the same although its context is altered. For the intervallic relations that define a melody to remain exactly the same in transposition usually requires a change of key (that is, a change of the notes of the scale); if on the other hand the melody is transposed within the same key, its internal ratios are sure to change to some extent. It is no coincidence that the challenge of freely modulating a melody from key to key without loss of shape and associated meaning arose at the same time as kingdoms of renaissance Europe and a newly powerful class of merchant entrepreneurs were actively seeking to extend trade and diplomatic relations into new markets and remote areas, and forging treaties and agreements to make such relations legally binding. Expansion of trade between communities of different language fostered a Machiavellian subculture of acquiring political and economic influence by language, through manipulation of the terms of a binding agreement or treaty, rather than through wasteful military conquest. Four hundred years before the European Common Market, a combination of social changes, including the arrival of print technology, abandonment of Latin as the language of international relations, and a desire for increased traffic in both goods and intelligence, led expert minds to sharpen their focus on the potential for translation of documents of agreement into another language to influence, surreptitiously or otherwise, their legal interpretation, and thereby tip the balance of profitability of trade and diplomatic relations in favor of one or other of a group of ostensibly equal partners. The dramatic possibilities of textual and contextual misrepresentation provided fertile ground for Shakespeare's Elizabethan dramas, which are located in the fashionably alien environments of Scotland, Venice, Denmark, Rome, and France, as well as England, and their associated cultures of moral and legal betrayal, political and financial opportunism, and disintegration of family codes and loyalties. Translation as a concept unites the movement of goods and the sharing of ideas with the preservation of respective identities and relationships.

Transmutation is different. It involves action upon an object or substance in ways that have the effect of changing its identity and relations without altering its outward appearance or function, or removing it from its natural context. The mysterious powers of transmutation are associated, among others, with medicine (treating functional and behavioral change), magic (effecting change in the nature or behavior of objects in the world at large), and religion (social protocols devised to reconcile human behavior with the reality of change). Examples from ritual traditions include the practice of animal sacrifice, which is ceremonial action depriving a creature of life, independence, and identity; and rites of eating and drinking aimed—either metaphorically or in real terms—at restoring health and social functionality (a sense of caring and sharing) to the sick or weak in spirit. It can also mean bringing inanimate objects to life, from voodoo tradition to the story of the sorcerer's apprentice (a magic extending, in Disney's animation, to the life-giving influence wielded over a symphony orchestra by a conductor and his baton). Changing the behavior of things is the mystery at the heart of chemistry and witchcraft (the making of potions), and alchemy, the power to turn base metals into gold. In the sense recognized by renaissance intellectuals, the power also relates to rhetoric, diplomacy, music and poetry, all of them arts of converting others through the power of argument or suggestion so that those influenced appear the same as before, but are in fact permanently altered in their choices and relationships. For transmutation to be recognized as an alteration of identity involves a definition of identity in terms of relationships, so that what a thing is, is defined not by how it looks or where it is located, but by how it behaves. This is very different from translation. A religious conversion is not the same as a trip to Lourdes.

The story of King Midas is about a person of influence with the unfortunate knack (or mania) of perceiving everything in terms of his own advantage and profit, even his own daughter. Nothing is seen or respected for what it is, and to be touched by such a person is to lose what individual identity, value, and function one originally possessed. The king is oblivious to the effect he has on other people. The metaphor of authority is compelling. That the story hinges on turning things and people to gold is a way of saying, not only that they are rendered as objects of merely monetary value, but rendered to the point of being altered beyond recovery of any sense of individuality. The value of gold is that it shines and is incorruptible. An object turned to gold loses its utility and intrinsic value to become an item of currency. This is of course part of the broader moral objection to alchemy. Once something is turned to gold, it cannot be changed back, or turned into any other substance. (Gold is also a metaphor, incidentally, for human waste.)

Transmutation experiences rank high in the pantheon of tribal life and values. Religious conversion, ecstasy and epiphany, the acquisition of knowledge, falling in love, guilt, mental illness, and, until recently in human history, mysteries of pain, pleasure, and disease, have all been understood as alterations of personal being expressed in changed patterns of behavior. Such experiences and their causes are bound to attract alarm, in part because they are unaccountable, in part because they appear irresistible, and in part because the alterations of personality that arise with them are so complete. Music is traditionally of interest because it too changes the behavior of an audience in mysterious ways, though its effects, like those of drink or narcotics, are fortunately reversible.

Of concern is the persistence across cultures of a sophisticated, widely recognized, and articulate but superstitious anxiety toward inexplicable behavioral change as a manifestation of hidden agencies of change having the potential to affect the integrity of the individual or the group. Since growth and change in human life are inevitable, the challenge is not to eliminate, but to control them. We make a distinction between learning a skill and taking instruction, for example, induced alterations that are personally and socially useful—and going mad, falling ill or falling in love, the effects of which tend to be socially and personally destructive. Much of art and culture, including disaster movies, has to do with anticipating, identifying, controlling, and adapting to the effects of invisible influences on human consciousness. Among these invisible influences, speech and music (and not forgetting the printed word) are especially prominent, not because they are inevitably corrupting, but in the role of constant reminders of the power of unseen threats to affect personal well-being.

When a singer sings in tune, or a dancer dances to music, it is fair to ask whether an information transaction is taking place, and if so, of what kind. The voice acquires definition in pitch from an instrument, as a dancer's movement is given shape and gestural definition by an accompanying music. We might conclude that singing and dancing are alterations of normal behavior involving a transference of influence from a musical source to an executant, though in practice an accompaniment is available to be matched against a pattern of actions in the performer's internal memory, making it more of a feedback process than a one-way transaction, —and more satisfying too, just as ballet is more accomplished and satisfying than karaoke. The subtext of unnatural behaviors (or idealized actions) such as music and dance, is that ordinary human beings are susceptible to outside influences that enable them to execute abstract but internally consistent and aesthetically pleasing actions, lasting over an extended period, in a manner oblivious to reason and conveying a sense of inevitable or transcendent grace and formality, comparable (for example) to the celestial movements of the sun and moon. There is an abstract, transpersonal beauty to the musically guided expressive arts that in addition to enhancing efficiency in action and relieving the stress of decision-making, send a socially useful if morally questionable message of aspiration to superhuman status through submission to external guidance.

An accompanying instrument, such as a lyre or piano, has no "intention" and therefore no motive for altering the behavior of a solo performer; if on the other hand a performance is perceived as dialogue and the accompanist as a double or partner (or indeed, *doppelgänger*), the relationship is transformed into one of mutual influence. Wherever the effect of music is to harmonize (and therefore, to check) the actions of participants who would otherwise be acting independently or chaotically, there is bound to be ambiguity over who is influencing whom (whether the accompanist is leading or following, for example). Such considerations come especially to mind in the context of jazz.

In music and dance, as in artificial intelligence, dialogue is both retroactive, affirming an ongoing relationship, and proactive, anticipating changes in relationship in the immediate future. Mere imitation, like rote learning, is not enough. The idea that dialogue evolves through a mutual exchange of accurate status reports is a quaint residue of early AI theory, and today a practice no longer taken seriously even by psychoanalysts. Using the cooperation and trust of a patient, a consultant is trained to initiate and sustain the appearance of dialogue by judicious prompting, without actually disclosing any information of substance.

In a truly transactional relationship, as in flamenco dance for instance, the largely improvised interactions of one partner provoke responses of a coherent but all the same unpredictable nature from the other. In such instances we may speak authentically of inspiration passing back and forth from person to person, in a ritual confrontation of a range of meaningful polarities, male and female, instrument and human being, as well as juxtaposing a fixed schema of tonal relationships embodied in the music, against the flexible and momentary response expressing the humanity of the singer or dancer. The character of any such transaction—quite apart from the symbolism that may be attached to it—is of a dynamic exchange that feeds on the energy generated by tension and friction between opposing tendencies, on the one hand toward mutual harmony, and on the other, toward individual freedom of expression.

Where a change of behavior is introduced, the question of a transfer of influence is bound to arise. Imitation is one thing, but acting independently (for instance, improvising) quite another.

Society assigns a value to education as a means of licensing or regulating individual behavior. When a person learns a language or a skill, it extends the person's range of permitted, available, and hence predictable actions. That the acquisition of knowledge may lead to unpredictable actions or socially destabilizing beliefs is a paradoxical consequence of the rise of secular education in the sixteenth century, of which the persecution of Galileo by the Inquisition is a benchmark example. That technical knowledge is apt to lead to uncertain moral consequences is also a lesson of nuclear physics and modern art, a consideration that continues to ring alarm bells in the new millennium.

Musicians and the public harbor a greater suspicion toward composers, who are independently creative, than the executants who interpret their music (whose creativity is exercised within idiomatically controllable limits). To assign creativity to a performer's role is to assign a higher, or at least different, value to the conversion of symbolic information into audible actions, which is the same authority assigned to legislators and the executive branches of government on the basis of their ability to convert an inscribed text into speech, and from speech to action of a kind. Creativity in that limited sense is revealed as just another reading superstition.

The Lady Lovelace test of a benevolent (and real) creative intelligence is whether the thing created is capable of independent life and action, of which endurance is a major criterion, and disobedience a vital secondary consideration. In robotics the difference between a merely labor-saving device and artificial intelligence is whether the item can think for itself and adjust to changes in its surroundings, rather than simply execute a preordained task. The test of independent intelligence is whether the object can learn, and through learning, take actions to meet unprecedented situations that represent a threat to its continuing existence.

Notes

1. Michael Haren, *Medieval Thought: The Western Intellectual Tradition from Antiquity to the Thirteenth Century*. London: Macmillan, 1985, 197–98.
2. Revived in the eighteenth century as an interpolation procedure to simulate movement of a mechanical automaton, the practice

can be traced back to *divisiones* in the late middle ages, which is more about measuring time. See Curt Sachs, *Rhythm and Tempo: A Study in Music History*. London: Dent, 1953, 186.

3. Arnold Schoenberg, "Problems of Harmony" tr. Adolph Weiss. In Merle Armitage ed., *Schoenberg*. New York: Schirmer, 1937 repr. Westport CT: Greenwood Press, 1977, 269.
4. Stockhausen's claim to originate from the star system Sirius can be regarded as a restatement of this viewpoint.

SIXTEEN

LECTURE ON NOTHING

Consider the following:

1. If you cannot read, you are not reading this.
2. If you can read, but not English, the meaning of this statement is that you cannot read it.
3. If you can read English, this statement is a tautology.
4. The significance of this statement is the significance of this statement.[1]

The presumptions a reader brings to bear on any statement and dialogue are of interest because the existence of language implies a precondition that language is possible, so that for communication to take place presupposes a sharing of language as well as of information (or rather, that every act of communication is simultaneously a rite of verification of the language itself and its ability to convey information at all). For information to be shared, it has to be understood—at least, up to a point. Imitation is not only the sincerest form of flattery, it is also a fundamental indicator of understanding. The issue here is the limit of understanding implied by direct imitation. Whether the purpose of communication is to enable the recipient either to act independently, or merely to obey: whether information is understood with reference to understanding the language, or the information content of language. For example, the statement "I am in pain" may appear incomprehensible to a person who does not speak English, meaningless or incomplete to a philosopher for whom pain is inexpressible, hence nonexistent, or a genuine cry for help. Understanding the process of information exchange is a fundamental consideration of artificial intelligence, and also of philosophy. How we understand the operation of dialogue in speech has a bearing on music as well. The case against music, and modern music in particular, is founded on a misconception that information can only be shared by means of a language, that language communicates spontaneously, and that because music, especially modern music, does not communicate anything specific, it is not a language. The analogous case against poetry is that it does not qualify as language use for the purposes of communication science or linguistics because its use of language is invincibly subjective and its information content is either trivial, or negligible, or at best unreliable. Arguments from communication science, as from incomprehension, further imply that statements in language are *morally bound* to convey useful information, making philosophers to that extent obligated to avoid bringing language itself into disrepute by raising doubts over the reliability of terms or the efficacy of language as a medium of communication. The assumption that to deal with language is to deal with the whole of communication is only one of the more startling misconceptions of modern day linguistics and linguistic philosophy.

In 1950, when information science and artificial (machine) intelligence were exciting and new subjects of inquiry, a British biologist declared that "The function of language is to tell each other as much as possible that is useful, so that we may help each other to live," adding that pleasure and pain, which are indefinable, do not therefore "exist."[2] Such a statement is highminded rather than true because in real life people use language in a variety of nonproductive ways. The biologist is focused on how the neural pathways and waystations of the brain actually process information —how the brain separates, processes, and reintegrates the various layers of *affect* conveyed in pitch, rhythm, intonation, and text—in order to provide information science with a natural framework for a theory of artificial intelligence.

However, too utilitarian a definition of language is likely to exclude a great many uses of language in everyday life, including poetry and the expression of human feelings that arise from inner conflict or absence of certainty. That language is often employed in imprecise ways is a criticism, not of language, but of our imperfect understanding of how language works and its limitations. What we identify as emotions are perhaps more appropriately explained as stresses brought on by a combination of inadequate vocabulary and defective communication skills.

In 1950 John Cage delivered a *Lecture on Nothing*, celebrated for the remark "I have nothing to say, I am saying it, and that is poetry."[3] (Today we might be tempted to describe a statement of having nothing to say as appropriate for a press release after a trial hearing, but not as poetry, but that would be unfair to press releases, many of which are poetry of a high order.) Out of context, Cage's statement appears either pointless or needlessly enigmatic; but in the context of the era, both in relation to contemporary thinking in information science, and to today's culture of text messaging and internet discourse, Cage's epigram and lecture do in fact make interesting sense and are intelligible as reaffirmations of the natural, indeed, essential ambiguities of language, and the value of poetry and the poetic impulse. In saying so in different ways here and elsewhere in his writings, Cage's style of multi-level, hermetic utterance draws attention to the underlying philosophical, not to mention political, implications for freedom of speech of a strictly utilitarian view of language (meaning the printed text, the visual recognition of which is ostensibly beyond dispute, rather than acts of speech whose words may be misheard, and whose rhythm and inflection are apt to convey alternative layers of meaning).

That music presupposes an audience even though it may be performed for its own sake, in isolation, is understandable for the reason that music by definition is a distracting and organized invasion of a listener's auditory space. That language presupposes an audience is more controversial, since speech or writing by any definition cannot be imposed on the casual passer-by without the participation or encouragement of the person reading or listening. A text, even of poetry, is nowhere near as attractive to ingest as music, nor as spontaneously meaningful, requiring thought as well as a grasp of language. In the course of daily life, therefore, there is no irresistible aesthetic or profit motive for a listener to pay attention to, or believe, or obey just anything at all that somebody else has to say, merely because it is said aloud or available in print. (At least, one would hope not.)

Underpinning the biological argument that language is useful for living is the unspoken assumption that useful information implies a response, or action of some specific kind, like a traffic signal that tells a driver to go left or stop. (The idea, that is, that meaning is intrinsic to the information, i.e. that the traffic light is red, and that its meaning is validated by the actions of the driver having to stop.) It assumes a prior disposition to act upon external instruction that is implicitly advantageous to the person acting as well as from the fact that the information is unobtainable in any other way or form. Such a theory of natural disposition, in assigning authority to the information being delivered, imposes a duty on the person reading (1) to understand the language, and (2) to act on the message *in an acceptable way*. It evokes a real if Kafkaesque scenario of social management by way of information management in which the rest of us are supposed to be constantly seeking new information and for that reason unable to question, and permanently in thrall to, the providers of information and the values they hold.

The tyrannical implications of authoritarian intelligence constructed after such a model are exposed in Eugene Ionesco's play *The Lesson*, dating from 1951:

> *Professor*: How does it come about that while the lower classes talk without knowing what language they're speaking, while each person actually believes he is speaking a language that, in fact, he is not, they all somehow manage to communicate satisfactorily with one another?
> *Pupil*: Wonders will never cease.[4]

In Samuel Beckett's equally droll *Waiting for Godot*, from 1952, Estragon and Vladimir engage in a Laurel and Hardy dialogue on the uncertainty surrounding the instruction given to them to await a meeting, an obligation that must be obeyed, and the manner in which it is to be obeyed, in the most famous of a lifelong series of radio-inspired plays for voices that meditate on the meaninglessness of dialogue among characters depicted as conditioned to take instruction, but unable to act (unable to make up their minds about what to do). Their dialogue takes on new meaning when considered not as absurdist or shell-shocked, but as a pointed critique of post-war information theory: a dystopian impression of intelligent discourse between characters reduced to robots.

Published in 1950 and part of the same discourse is the paper "Computing Machines and Intelligence" by Alan Turing, a major contribution to the burgeoning science of machine intelligence.[5] Turing's paper endorses the classical French school of Descartes and La Mettrie (author of *L'Homme Machine*) in stipulating that a machine may be said to think like a human being if it responds in a manner indistinguishable from a human being. Turing's paper has since been described in apologetic tone by philosopher Daniel Dennett as a thought experiment in human-machine dialogue the purpose of which is to discover the ground rules for communicating with a computer. It is somewhat more than that. Since agreement—or, *in extremis*, arbitration—is needed to establish meaningfulness (not the same as intelligence), Turing is also saying that mere obedience to rules of grammar and syntax alone is insufficient to assign meaning to a statement. This makes sense for the equally compelling reason that people make mistakes and use words incorrectly even though their intention is to convey meaning, and an incorrect statement may still in that sense be meaningful. People also make misleading statements, which are correct but untrue.

Turing concedes all the same that "most of the programs which we can put into the [at the time, fictitious] machine will result in its doing something that we cannot make sense of at all, or which we regard as completely random behavior." This is a way of saying language is limited and for that reason unpredictable (a) because language is inexact, (b) because rules of grammar do not guarantee content (the meaning of what is said), and (c) because in real life people have free will (know that language is sometimes inadequate to express what they have to say but persist in trying to say it all the same). Concidentally, Turing's remarks on intelligence signal the arrival of aleatoric thinking in art and music.

Intelligence, says Turing, is a matter requiring the adjudication of an external (and for some reason, human) assessor. For a computer to be assessed as thinking in a human kind of way requires a special kind of validation unprejudiced by the knowledge that what is being assessed is the response of a computer and not of a human being. Since human beings make mistakes and produce unintelligible (or simply wrong) answers, whether the answers a machine delivers are right or wrong, or even plausibly human, comes down to the subjective evaluation of an allegedly independent observer of the answers of a human being and those of a machine: a judgment based neither on tone of voice (the machine does not speak), nor on facial expression through eye contact (the machine is concealed from view), nor even by handwriting (answers are printed).

In the world of twentieth-century music the issue of human intelligence was already raised in relation to written-out as distinct from improvised performance. Jazz is based on familiar musical stereotypes that imply melody, harmony, and rhythm, reproduced indirectly by participants in the form of spontaneous dialogue. The comparison of reading music with reading from a script is clear. At the classical extreme an ideal performance is word-perfect and the performer's personality totally sublimated, allowing the composer's "intention" to emerge. In a Beethoven or Schubert quartet moments arise where the listener senses that the composer is pausing in mid-thought, as it were, wondering where to go next, or whether to take another path. In order to achieve that clarity of communication, a performer has to learn to think like the composer and not impose a persona on the notes.

At the other extreme, a jazz performer has to sublimate the original theme so completely that neither the audience nor other members of the performing group is completely sure of where they are at, giving the impression of a free-for-all that even so, manages to stay together and follow a plan.

A musical version of Turing's Game asks the question whether a performance of music from a printed score is mechanical or intelligent. Conventional wisdom holds that a performance is *intelligent* by virtue of being executed by a living person who knows how to respond appropriately to notational instructions, and *human* by virtue of incorporating performance traits that emulate emotion or trigger an emotional response in a listener. Turing might well have questioned whether the interpretation of an actor (Olivier as Hamlet, for example) could be described as intelligent. Whether or not a machine is assessed to behave with intelligence is surely contingent on whether a human being is capable of being assessed as intelligent. If we cannot do so for a performer of music, then how can we hope to do the same for a machine?

In another version of Turing's "Imitation Game" the question and answer interaction is imagined as a contest in which the human participant posing the questions attempts to trick the computer into revealing that it is in fact a machine and not a woman or man.[6] Accordingly, the computer is set up to simulate convincing replies, for example:

> Q. Will X please tell me the length of his or her hair?
> A. My hair is shingled, and the longest strands are about nine inches long.[7]

Charitably, Dennett interprets Turing's thought experiment as the reflection of a mathematician on what a mathematician is doing when he is going about solving a mathematical problem or performing a computation.[8] That is far too easy: it amounts to saying that mathematicians have their own way of thinking that differs from everybody else, and from which large areas of normal human ambiguity are excluded. At the same time, however, Turing is creating a scenario where misleading information may validly be offered and must therefore be open to detection. Intuition and deception do not normally figure in a routine mathematical operation. More to the point is the British scientist's attempt to contextualize person-to-person dialogue, or person-to-machine interaction, within a culturally revealing set of conditions and assumptions, along lines such as the following:

1. *A statement requiring an answer is incomplete.* (The requiredness of incompletion. A factual statement is either superfluous or a question.) Agreement is repetition from a secondary source, so redundancy is agreement: the echo effect. Agreement in the one part is not a condition of agreement in the second or any subsequent part.
2. *Incompleteness is signified by the statement itself*, e.g., "Please insert your card." Any statement inviting a response calls into question the external reasons for the statement and not the truth content of the statement itself.
3. *For an answer to be given the machine must be active* (has to be switched on and ready to go), hence, any answer is evidence of activity (consciousness).
4. *Not responding is inadmissible or an error.*
5. *An error is a fault of input not of software.*

> 6. *A dialogue is ended when the user logs off.* Logging off is an answer of a sort.
> 7. *A machine does not know the person but only asks.* And so on. *The very existence of the machine is predicated on a service to be performed, expressed as a request for information.*

We recognize the last of these in the old joke in which the caller asks "Well, if that is the wrong number, why did you answer the phone?" Or the even older joke, "Operator: What number do you want? Caller: I don't know: what numbers have you got?"—a way of characterizing the act of communication as independent of the connection as well as the content. This is Cage's point as well.

PAIN AS MOTIVATION

Since a computer does not feel pain, and language is supposedly inadequate to determine pain, it is somewhat disconcerting to discover that among the earliest applications of AI are interactive programs designed to assist in the diagnosis of medical and psychological complaints, according with the view that the purpose of exchanging intelligence is to bring coherence and definition to human suffering—defined as a lack of understanding—of which a primary symptom is indeed physical pain. As Ionesco's play *The Lesson* moves to a climax, the female student's responses to interrogation are increasingly hampered by the onset of a crippling toothache, and the lesson ends with the student being stabbed to death by violent repetition of the word "knife." This is to characterize the victim as a programmed intelligence that, having been trained to respond to language according to inflexible rules, cannot withstand an instruction to crash. In the guise of a Greek Chorus, the serving maid, who has seen it all before, sagely observes "Arithmetic leads to Philology, and Philology to Crime."

Ionesco's use of the word *knife* as a virtual weapon in a drama of ideas is distinctive and interesting, but it is not the first time. The Alfred Hitchcock thriller *Blackmail*, first released in 1929, tells of the inadvertent stabbing with a bread-knife of an artist in his studio by a girl acting in self-defense.

> At breakfast she is nervous, distraught. . . . A gossiping woman neighbour comes in to talk to the girl's parents. She is full of the

> details of the murder spread across the morning newspapers. In her harsh, metallic voice she speaks of the knife which has been found. Again she mentions the word "knife." The girl is asked by her father to cut some bread: a close shot shows the look of terror staring from her eyes. The woman's gossip has become a continuous mumble in which only one word is heard clearly at intervals: "knife . . . knife . . . knife." The girl stretches out her hand for the bread-knife, and as she touches it, the word "knife" is suddenly shouted out, and she drops it with a clatter; in the silence which follows, everyone stares at her in amazement."[9]

It would be easy to imagine that Ionesco has simply copied from Hitchcock and exaggerated the unreality of the device for surrealist effect. The Rumanian playwright may be using the stage and its artifices (assuming the genuine humanity of the actors, and the realism—or at least, intellectual coherence—of the text) to critique the artificiality of the movies. The comedy of surrealism resides in an ironic presentation of movie reality as stream-of-consciousness fantasy by removing its imagery from a movie context. In doing so, however, it is creating a new subjective art of dream and coincidence that by virtue of its detachment from the film medium reinvents art as myth.

Hitchcock's use of the word "knife" as a guilty motif is of particular interest because his original movie was made in 1928 as a silent movie, then revised to incorporate sound. The use of sound in all movies, but noticeably in the earliest sound movies, is highly selective. One only hears sounds that are germane to setting the scene or setting up action and relationships. The same is true of sound effects. Only those sounds that contribute to the drama are incorporated in the sound track. This is psychologically realistic, in that in real life people hear what they want to hear. Despite being surrounded at times by a chaos of sounds, a listener can decide which is meaningful and which not, ignoring the rest. Human ears register everything audible at a given time, and the information is processed in short-term memory by a mental map that is preactivated to particular profiles and combinations of frequencies. That ability to discriminate is not available in a microphone.

Hitchcock's imaginative touch, to use the word "knife" as a refrain that stands out accusingly from a neutral or indeterminate background of noise or desultory conversation, is psychologically astute and the kind of insight a dramatist newly acquainted with microphones and their characteristics is likely to identify and exploit. The unfortunate girl is reinvented as a microphone, her hearing a condition of sensitivity or pre-existing tension, like the diaphragm of a microphone, the word "knife" being portrayed as an effect of resonance, like the cavity resonance of an early microphone. This resonance is precisely the quality that Ernest Lindgren identifies in the "harsh, metallic voice," of the local gossip, a personification of the newly sinister presence of radio broadcasting in everyday life. Like a microphone, the gossip hears and relays every item of news in the same flat, impersonal, and uncomprehending manner. The difference between the cavity resonance of a real microphone and the mental resonance of its human equivalent is that cavity resonance is frequency- rather than word-specific: it is responsible for the hard, indifferent, metallic quality of early microphones along with the vocal mannerisms associated with their use. As a poetic device, however, it illuminates the drama with the kind of insight often encountered in artists coming to terms for the first time with new technology.

The larger message of Hitchcock's poetic device is not that certain words echo hypnotically in the minds of the guilty, but that the sound movie is a portrait of subjective experience, and not of any real world. In conventional stage drama it is always possible to imagine that the dialogue corresponds to real actions in a real world, even though we are perfectly aware that dialogue is artfully composed to convey a great deal of information on a number of levels in a very short space of time. Simply excluding extraneous words and conversation does not make stage dialogue less real, since the audience experiences the action as a silent participant and the drama is conveyed as much in relationships as in what is actually said. However a movie sound track incorporating dialogue and sound effects is immediately and obviously artificial, for the most part because the audience is now in a situation of relying on the microphones for what it hears, and thus emphatically aware that every sound or word of dialogue that is audible, is audible for a reason and in consequence of prior conditioning. What this means in turn is that the film drama, like radio drama, is reconstituted from a public event in which mass perceptions take priority, to a private and personal exercise in which the drama is played out not in real life, but in the mind of the observer. Naturally such a transformation in the psychology of performance has an effect on the genre of drama. It gives rise to new varieties of entertainment: among them comedy, jazz, crooning, psychological drama, and the thriller, that are intimate and personal rather than public and tribal. Among the consequences of that reorientation from the collective to the personal are computer games predicated at the most primitive level on the elimination, not just of a particular adversary, but of the whole of society, a society reinvented as hostile and predatory.

When Ionesco rediscovers the word "knife" as a psychological weapon in 1951, once again it can only make sense as a fable of perverted magic, an ironic (generically Eastern European) commentary on an invincibly subjective experience of a collective real world fashioned by language and government rather than genuine feeling. One could label the Rumanian playwright an opportunist, or accuse him of missing the plot. Whereas in Hitchcock the fearful message of the word "knife" lies in its suggestive capacity just as a word—part of the language—for Ionesco the word has become invested with objective reality. We all know words are capable of wounding, but the wounds are psychological rather than physical. For Ionesco, however, the characters are already verbal stereotypes and not real people, so this is a flatland where words can only kill other words, and nobody is the wiser. In Hitchcock, the repetitions with emphasis of the word arise spontaneously out of a realistic fabric of dialogue by virtue of the special sensitivity of the character whose mind is being portrayed. In Ionesco, the repetitions of the word are deliberately abusive behaviour initiated by an authority figure to inflict suffering on a defenseless target whose sensitivities to language are thereby held up to ridicule by an audience implicitly representing collective endorsement of the authority of language. You be the judge.

That ignorance, anxiety, and suffering are fundamental reasons for seeking relief in dialogue in the first place is an irony not entirely lost on Daniel Dennett who, citing Winograd's innovative but crude 1972 SHRDLU program for the interrogation of medical patients, is quick to reassure readers (not for the first time) that the software is merely intended "to explore some of the information-handling tasks faced by any interlocutor, not to model human speech production realistically."[10] (Dennett defines the act of speaking, rather than the mechanism of vocalization, as "speech production," an indication that his priorities are intellectual rather than biological, a principal reason why some species of anatomist and philosopher continue to regard pain as not a valid subject of discussion.) Dealing with pain is also the subtext of Roger Penrose's citation in *The Emperor's New Mind*, under the rubric "Can machines think?" of a classic dialogue between a computer "virtual therapist" and a patient, taken from a program by K. M. Colby after Joseph Weizenbaum's ELIZA software of 1965:

T: How can I help you
P: I don't know
T: Try to tell me something about it
P: No
T: Can you elaborate
P: I am sick and tired today
T: Do you have any idea why
P: Yes. I'm old (. . .)[11]

Of Charles Babbage's analytical engine Lady Lovelace objected "The Analytical Engine has no pretensions to *originate* anything. It can do [only] whatever we know how to order it to perform."[12] Much the same prejudice against novelty underlies the outdated AI definition of new intelligence as a rearrangement of old data to new locations and configurations. The sophisticated objection to such dialogue as the sample above is that in order to respond like a real human being the program is doing little more than prompt the patient with affable interjections that have no content, and are simply designed to keep the patient talking, in the style of "*Really? Well, well. Dear me. Uh-huh. Is that so? Go on.*" etc. Although some intelligent professions (lawyers, psychoanalysts) converse in such a way, such interactions have more to do with attention cues and responses than about an intelligent exchange of information (and whether the technique works is not the point either). Such promptings are not intelligent in any real sense, but act simply as reminders to the patient that the analyst is still awake.

Cage followed up his 1950 *Lecture on Nothing* by reading prepared answers to the first six questions from the audience "in keeping with the thought . . . that a discussion is nothing more than an entertainment." (One of his prepared answers, incidentally, was "My head wants to ache.") Describing discussion as entertainment casts a shadow over the broader AI claim of information exchange in dialogue form as a test of intelligence, for instance describing a television quiz show as a test of knowledge rather than a test of memory and retrieval of facts. In more sinister guise, Cage's topic of nothing as poetry may be taken as a covert response to the inquisitional style of the Un-American Activities Committee, on the rampage at the time.

> Q. Mr Cage: are you, or have you ever been a member of the communist party?
> A. I'll take the fifth.

The tactic of responding to questions by answering from a prepared statement is usually associated with the interrogation of prisoners of war. In 1950, when Cage delivered his *Lecture on Nothing*, it was also about defending oneself against allegations of treasonable association. Both Cage and his audience would have been all too aware of the rise to power of the junior Senator from Wisconsin and his manipulation of question and answer techniques to lure public figures, many of them artists, to condemn themselves out of their own mouths. For several years in the *I Love Lucy* era McCarthy as prosecutor made riveting television entertainment until a famous media confrontation with newscaster Edward R. Murrow led to his political demise in 1954. (Fifty years on the same events, reenacted in George Clooney's movie *Good Night, and Good Luck*, would be characterized by right-wing critics as a news story driven more by ratings than political conscience.) [13]

Responding to questions with readymade answers makes better sense, however, for a suffering patient whose condition provides the motivation for asking questions and delivering plausible answers. The tactic also resonates with the readymade artworks of Marcel Duchamp, works about which the questions "Is it art?" and "Is it beautiful?" express a conditioned disbelief that a utilitarian object such as a bottle rack, a snow shovel, or a bicycle wheel mounted on a stool should ever be able to acquire altered significance and aesthetic value when exhibited "out of context" in an art gallery among other works of art. (Not to mention its corollary, that the pleasure derived from high art is also functional and utilitarian from a sensory perspective.)

A prisoner of war under interrogation who responds to every question with name, rank, and serial number is actually refusing to answer any other question than "What is your name, rank, and serial number?" That of course is all the information a captured uniformed member of the military is obliged to divulge. When Cage responds to audience questions with prepared answers, in the aftermath of an intellectually diverting lecture on nothing, he is engaging in a similar form of play, not exactly refusing to answer the question, but refusing to allow his answers to be construed as acknowledging the legitimacy, or the terms of reference, of the question asked, as though to say "I will tell you what I have in mind to tell you, not what you wish me to say, and you have to work it out for yourself." For a libertarian like Cage, the refusal to answer directly also comes across as an oddly authoritarian trait. It is also curiously reminiscent of the Möbius strip logic of E. M. Forster's quip, quoted by Marshall McLuhan, "How can I know what I think till I see what I say?"—though in the sense of "How can you know an answer is the information you want when your question shows you don't know it already?" Which brings us back to square one, with Schoenberg, asking how one note can follow another.

Cage's fortune cookie approach to dialogue is trivially read as a deliberate intrusion of chance into real life, and philosophically speaking as intended to provoke a questioner to reflect on what kind of answer was initally expected, and thereby partly or wholly to eliminate the question. (There is a degree of affectation in deliberate enigma that I find faintly irritating, if only because it seems to be based on a romantic misconstruction of Zen.) If an unexpected question is disconcerting, there is poetic justice in responding with an unexpected answer, because it is always the unexpected that is fresh and new and most likely to provoke thought. It is not the same anticipation as the unexpected juxtapositions of montage in the movies, because any accident of logic or appearance of connection arising in the movies is created editorially by a deliberate act of an external intelligence, and not by either party to the dialogue. Often what a listener encounters in a movie or opera is not dialogue in the normal sense at all, but rather an engineered coexistence of monologues representing different states of mind and trains of thought, connected only by accidents of time and place.

Cage's stance unexpectedly recalls Stravinsky's remark, in *An Autobiography,* that music is powerless to express anything at all, and therefore uninterpretable. A reader can even detect the same political conscience linking Stravinsky's denial of interpretation in relation to his own reputation in 1935, the era of rising Fascism, with the benign detachment advocated by Cage in the era of Joseph McCarthy, the subtext in each case being that a potentially hostile interpreter should not seek to force a meaning on music but accept the truth of what is written in a dispassionate manner. Cage had uttered a similar caution the previous year, that "the responsibility of the artist consists in perfecting his work so that it may become attractively disinteresting."[14]

James Pritchett picks out two quotations from Cage's *Lecture* that make particular sense in relation to the communication of meaning in dialogue. "Our poetry now is the realization that we possess nothing. Anything therefore is a delight." By *possession* we construe Cage to mean *prior knowledge*, evoking a childlike delight in novelty while at the same time seeking protection in the solipsism that what he is enjoying is knowing and contemplating his own innocence. In response to the Lovelace conjecture, Turing also compromised by saying "there is nothing new under the sun"—that new data is just recycled old data—implying that the correct (or only viable) definition of new information is old information presented in new relationships.[15]

In a particularly revealing anecdote Cage speaks of tonality as an integrating convention, but strangely in terms of what he darkly describes—as though he were reading from a student textbook—as the "deceptive cadence." What he may mean is that every cadence is deceptive, in the sense that no statement is ever true, or complete, or final, since the world goes on. But in saying so, the reader is also being invited to perceive the tonality of finality as a Machiavellian invention for misleading or alienating the listener, an astonishingly slender pretext for defending an aesthetic of no hierarchies at all, of letting sounds be free and relate only to themselves. There is no deception, he claims. "What is being fooled?" he asks rhetorically. "Not the ear but the mind. The whole question is very intellectual."[16] In fact Cage is making the very point that for a cadence to be deceptive involves an assumption by the listener of a music of logical inference being possible, and in the present instance, even probable. The logical argument is stronger perhaps for English and German harmonic practices, which are tonally goal-directed, than for modern French music, which is harmonic and expository.

That anything new is a delight, in Cage's phrase, is also a way of saying that more attention is brought to bear on the unfamiliar, and for that reason we are disposed to learn more from dealing with the new than the familiar. The sound neurological basis for such a view is that information that cannot be referred to memory is either discarded or evaluated, and if evaluated, by definition experienced more richly.

Pritchett is equally impressed by another enigmatic remark of Cage's: "Continuity today, when it is necessary, is a demonstration of disinterestedness." By *continuity* we understand persistence or extension of meaning considered from a neutral perspective. For Cage the saving grace of disinterestedness in the communication of meaning is guaranteed by his technique of using secondary sources, in anecdote delivered without comment, involving real people, and told from direct personal experience. For Stravinsky, on the other hand—or indeed, Boulez—disinterestedness is embodied in the dispassionate and accurate performance of an impersonal notation. Cage's allusion to continuity is open to interpretation as a criticism either of the idea of dialogue as a transfer of data, or of achieving agreement (unison or unanimity), or perhaps even agreement to differ (harmony), ideally through the intervention of a third party, in the form of a citation, anecdote, or text that is free of contaminating associations of personal motive and objectively the same for both speaker and listener.

So what is dialogue in the normal sense and how does it apply to music? Rationally speaking, dialogue implies a continuity of thought pursued by alternating voices and leading to a change of attitude or mental state on the part of either or both. The hallmarks of dialogue in this sense are agreement on the subject coinciding with differences in interpretation and point of view. In a formal debate there are rules of engagement and the outcome is decided by majority vote.

Two issues are in contention here: one, of understanding, and two, of continuity of thought. Both are necessary for a viable theory of strong AI applying to music. In the era of Thomas Aquinas, music was less complex than it is today. Unison singing, alternating solo and chorus, was standard practice. Harmony consisted in singing in parallel octaves (in the ratio 1 : 2), or in parallel intervals of the perfect fourth or fifth (3 : 4; 2 : 3). Unison singing is prima facie evidence of agreement, since everyone is singing the same melody line at the same pitch; and also of continuity, since agreement is expressed, not in a kiss, but in a performance of unbroken continuity. Unison *singing* invariably means there is a script, which rationally must have originated with somebody else in another time. Therefore, unison signifies understanding between parties, not merely as one with another, but both in relation to a third, common model—and thereby with a past existence. Unisons reinforce one another at the same pitch, whereas parallel fifths or fourths interfere to create a third, difference tone audible at the fundamental or lowest common denominator.

The solo mime of Stockhausen's *Inori* (1977) was criticized for appearing to be improvising gestures to the music. A second mime was added, the two gesturing in unison. In medieval plainchant the solo voice may be perceived as improvising, even when the chant is well-known. Subtly varying the meaning of a solo line by inflection is available to every soloist, hence the aura of magic associated with being a soloist. A unison chorus on the other hand cannot improvise and sing in unison at the same time. There is bound to be a script. The tonal discrepancies among members of a chorus cancel out to leave a fuzzy consensus that nevertheless signifies majority agreement with only a marginal residue of uncertainty or dissent. Organum or parallel singing at the octave, fourth, or fifth corresponds to unison among voices of naturally higher and lower pitch, indicating the possibility of agreement between nonidentical voices. Renaissance polyphony extends the concept of multiple relations to voices individually orientated toward a guiding tenor *cantus firmus* like planetary bodies orbiting around a common center.

ROLE OF AN AUDIENCE

Much of the power of Greek tragedy and classic drama consists in the *audience's* awareness of its superior knowledge of the outcome, compared to the protagonists. By convention, an audience witnessing onstage dialogue is in a better position to monitor a flow of understanding from character to character, both in relation to the fate of the individual, and in relation to a global outcome, than the characters themselves, each of whom is engaged in pursuing a personal agenda and to that extent ill-disposed or unable to read the purpose of others. In the mechanics of a play the flow of intelligence is further compromised from the protagonists' point of view by devices such as characters having to leave the stage, soliloquy, plots within plots (the play within a play), injury, disease, and divine intervention. We understand these conventions in a stage setting and deal with them in real life, but we are a great deal less familiar with the same conventions in relation to music.

In music as in real life the test of intelligent and meaningful dialogue is not agreement in the content of information exchanged at any one point, but rather cooperation over the long term as evidence of a real or virtual third-party script to which the participants conform, in doing so achieving the appearance of mutuality.

In a movie, the visual narrative of which is typically fragmented, music and dialogue actively cooperate to sustain a perception of organic continuity of plot and dialogue. In this connection, the accelerated pace and violent actions of classic animated movies, in drawing to the narrative surface a fractured continuity that is normally subliminal, can be read as statements about the artificiality of continuous discourse in the movie medium, an artificiality that might potentially be true of narrative in general. Accordingly, the first and second subjects of classical sonata form are reborn as Tom and Jerry, or Ren and Stimpy, and the working out of their relationship as an ongoing chase. By an interesting coincidence, the speed and concentration of animated movies, as well as their underlying theme of constant variation, are elevated to high art in Stravinsky's late serial music.

Time passes. Fifty years on, Marvin Minsky declares that there is a place for emotion in machine intelligence. Interviewed in 2007, the cofounder of MIT's Artificial Intelligence Laboratory counters suggestions that a half century of AI research has not brought robots any closer to thinking like human beings, with the proposition that modeling emotional states is the key to making AI "more human." In Minsky's terms, to be human is to think in ways that are human and not AI.[17] What that appears to mean is an approach to modeling decision-making in ways that do not follow orthodox AI pathways. Minsky's approach to emotion is resolutely AI. He does not speak of the dynamics of human emotion, but only of emotional "states." "Each emotional *state* (he observes) is a different *style* of thinking" (my italics). Minsky does not appear to realize that to describe a state of being as a style of action is a contradiction. It implies that what a person is at any one moment determines how that person thinks and acts in the future of that moment, when in reality a person's inner thoughts and consequent actions are expressions of a dynamic of adjusting to changing external circumstances, both acting in response to inner promptings, and simultaneously reacting to the unforeseen behavior of other people. According to Minsky, an emotional state is what is produced when parts of a person's mental resources are shut down, allowing for faster, and possibly more efficient, but inevitably less accurate responses. Not much has changed in fifty years. Different emotional situations and levels of crisis trigger different configurations of problem-solving machinery. He no longer regards human intelligence as reflecting a single unified consciousness, but instead a capacity for coordinating multiple personalities, each equipped to handle a specific kind of task. It is the cosmologist's many-worlds hypothesis applied to the human mind. Agreeing with Daniel Dennett that "there is no single meaning for consciousness" allows Minsky to give an impression of alignment with current opinion that consciousness is a distribution of functions, but one which in AI terminology amounts to no more than a declaration that the term "consciousness" embraces a variety of options, some of which are more exacting than others.

Notes

1. The meaning of any statement is that any statement is self-affirmative at the very least. In this case its only meaning is that a statement has meaning. The same can be extended to encompass

nonsense statements as well.

2. J. Z. Young, *Doubt and Certainty in Science* new edn. New York: Galaxy Books, 1960, 118.
3. John Cage, "Lecture on Nothing" (1950) repr. *Incontri Musicali*, (April 1959). In *Silence: Lectures and Writings*. Cambridge MA: M.I.T. Press, 1966, 109–27.
4. Eugene Ionesco, *The Lesson*. In *Plays Volume I* tr. Donald Watson. London: John Calder, 1958, 30.
5. Alan M. Turing, "Computing Machinery and Intelligence." *Mind* Vol. LIX No. 236 (1950). In Alan Ross Anderson ed., *Minds and Machines*. Englewood Cliffs: Prentice-Hall, 1964, 4–30.
6. A. M. Turing, "Computing Machinery and Intelligence." *Minds and Machines*, 29. *See also* Keith Gunderson, *Mentality and Machines: A Survey of the Artificial Intelligence Debate* 2nd edn. London: Croom Helm, 1985, 39–59.
7. "Shingled" is wavy hair, alluding perhaps unconsciously to the role of wavy hair (or wave motion) in temptation myth from the serpent in the garden to Samson and Rapunzel.
8. Daniel C. Dennett, *Consciousness Explained*. Boston and New York: Little, Brown, 1991, 212–13.
9. Ernest Lindgren, *The Art of the Film*. London: George Allen & Unwin, 1948, 108–9.
10. Daniel C. Dennett, *Consciousness Explained*, 92. *See also* Gunderson, *Mentality and Machines*, 185–92.
11. Roger Penrose, *The Emperor's New Mind*. London: Vintage, 1990, 15–16.
12. A. M. Turing, "Computing Machinery and Intelligence," 20–21. The gifted daughter of Lord Byron, Lady Ada Lovelace was a mathematician and colleague of Charles Babbage. Her friend Mary Shelley is remembered as the author of *Frankenstein*, a fictional meditation on the creation of artificial intelligence out of unrelated body parts reanimated by electricity.
13. Arthur Spiegelman, "Clooney takes on Joe McCarthy in new movie." Syndicated column October 3, 2005 (Reuters).
14. James Pritchett, *The Music of John Cage*. Cambridge, Cambridge University Press, 1993, 55–59.
15. Turing, "Computing Machinery and Intelligence," 21.
16. John Cage, "Forerunners of Modern Music" (1949), 62–66 in

Silence: Lectures and Writings. Cambridge MA: M. I. T. Press, 1966.

17. Marvin Minsky. "Once more with feelings." Interview with Amanda Gefter. *New Scientist* Vol. 193 No. 2592 (2007), 48–49. It relates to the launch of Minsky's book *The Emotion Machine*. New York: Simon and Schuster, 2006.

SEVENTEEN

ATONALITY

Atonal music is music whose sense of tonality appears distorted or obscured, a music of no apparent key. In contrast to chromaticism, which applies to a music of extended but conventional key sense, as for example in jazz, atonality is perceived as a use of dissonance to suppress the vertical or harmonic sense in order to emphasize the horizontal or leading tendency of a musical line or argument. In conventional tonal music a leading dissonance at a cadence creates a moment of suspense and uncertainty that the listener recognizes as the cue for a resolution to a terminal harmony. In atonal music the suspense or irresolution is prolonged indefinitely in a process of ongoing and unresolved harmonic flow, or stream of consciousness: the emotional equivalent of Wagner's "endless melody." Avoiding closure holds an audience in suspense over where the music will go next. It is ideal for evoking a sense of isolation in a soloist or leading solo voice, for example the female lead in Arnold Schoenberg's psychological monodrama *Erwartung* 1909, and the doomed characters of Wozzeck and Lulu in Alban Berg's operas of the same name.

Like abstraction—the avoidance of figuration—in painting, avoiding harmony is an aesthetic choice. Both genres focus on the uncertain process of divining reality, rather than contemplating the object relations already presented to view. Avoiding tonality is not an easy task, since listeners are predisposed to hear all tonal relations as actually or potentially harmonious. An awareness of the danger of free atonality falling into cliché led Schoenberg in 1921 to develop the system of melodic-harmonic controls that he called twelve-tone music, the subject of a separate commentary.

Tonal instability is not new. In the baroque era it is associated

Dido's Lament
HENRY PURCELL
When I am laid, Am laid in earth, May my wrongs cre ate No
trou ble, no trou ble in thy breast;
Re mem ber me!

The poignant lament from Purcell's opera Dido and Aeneas *(1689) employs a constantly recycling descending bassline to convey the inevitability of the heroine's fate and the instability of her situation*

with a moving bassline. In the aria "Dido's Lament" from Purcell's opera *Dido and Aeneas*, the constant decline of a descending bassline—an impression of being on a moving escalator—reinforces a dramatic perception of inexorable doom. An unsettling sensation, or "sinking feeling," of having no firm tonal ground to stand upon, is the composer's way of expressing Dido's moral anguish at losing Aeneas, who must leave her to fulfill his mission to found Rome. Addressed to an English audience coming to terms with a new age of maritime exploration, the underlying message of the opera examines the consequences of embracing a life of exploration that is bound to cause grief to loved ones, and of a culture itself coming to terms with an intellectual and political environment in which nothing is stable anymore. The metaphor draws not only on an original Greek tragic theme of masculine restlessness of spirit and urge to explore in conflict with a feminine desire for stability and a lasting relationship, but also alludes in a musical sense to a new urge to travel to distant new keys and become acquainted with new and exotic key relationships.

One definition of atonality is "managed instability." Atonal music is like a tightrope walker, in constant imbalance, that is, constantly adjusting orientation while moving toward a resolution. We associate managed instability with a spinning top, learning to walk, and riding a bicycle, but not normally with music. Walking and riding a bicycle increase the range and speed of movement, and thus enlarge the territory over which a person has the freedom to move and claim ownership. As in learning to walk or ride a bicycle, the composer of atonal music trades the security and stability of a fixed key location for the excitement of carrying the body forward into new and unknown places. The striding statues of Rodin and Giacometti are studies in the same dynamics of movement. Underlying the process of J. S. Bach's "Vom Himmel Hoch" Variations is a narrative of progression from the anchored harmonic columns of the initial harmonization (mostly root position chords) into ever more elaborate networks of contrapuntal tissue.

G–B–D	*dominant (fifth above)*
C–E–**G**	*tonic (home key)*
F–A–**C**	*subdominant (fifth below)*

In the Galileian era, instability acquired cosmological as well as musical implications. In earlier times, the rotating universe of different planets was analogized to the ringing timbre of a bell, a stable but oscillating harmony of partial tones rising and falling in amplitude. Conflict arose between astronomers and the church after new technology, the telescope, revealed puzzling loops or epicycles in the orbital motion of planets that could only be accounted for by proposing that the latter moved around the sun and not the earth. It gave rise to new ways of thinking about motion in general that would lead in due course to the theory of relativity.

In tonal music, directed movement or progression is expressed by chord changes, linked by a common tone. For example, in the key of C, the tonic triad consists of the notes C–E–G, permitting a change to the F triad a fifth below (F–A–C, called the subdominant, linked by the note C), or to the G triad a fifth above (G–B–D, called the dominant, linked by the note G).

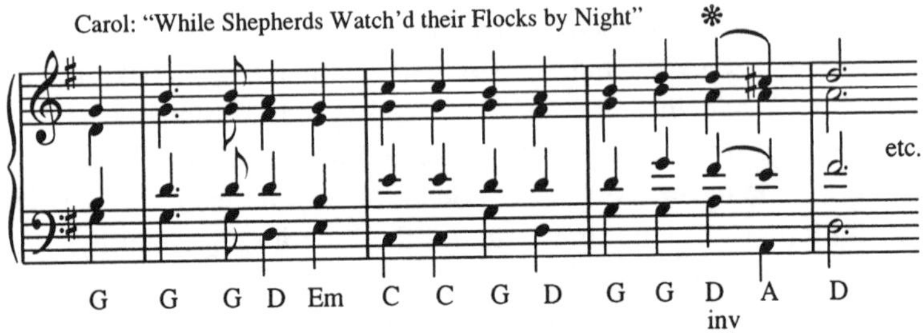

Harmonization of a melody in static chords. The starred (inverted) chord is the only unstable harmony

Influenced by astronomy in the Galileian era, music sought to rationalize the behavior of a universe in constant motion. Galileo measured the motion of accelerating bodies; others like Zarlino sought to rationalize the twelve semitonal degrees of the octave—divide the octave ratio of the square root of 2 : 1 into twelve equal steps—in order to accommodate a music of changing scale while preserving essential harmonic relationships. This was shown to be an impossibility. It led in the seventeenth century or baroque era to a new music and architecture of warped and curved surfaces and voids, an aesthetic of dynamic uncertainty to be reclaimed two centuries later by art nouveau and the architecture of Antonio Gaudí. Baroque architecture, created in the image of a violin, is suited to a music of constantly changing key, since it avoids the box-like shape and parallel walls of the Palladian era that reinforce specific wavelengths and associated fixed key relations. During the baroque era classical music in Europe began to embrace the map-maker's and surveyor's concept of a *sliding scale*, or variable unit of measure, for plotting the movement of music on the great stave, like ships on the ocean. Scale modulation within a *movement* superseded the older concept of a fixed *mode* as the governing principle of melodic and harmonic expression (even though *temperament*, the tuning or choice of key, continues to imply a relationship between the scale of a piece of music and its emotional character).

The innovative maps of Mercator, which project the outlines of land masses from a spherical earth onto a flat plane, are effectively drawn to a relativistic scale that is constantly changing with latitude from unitary at the equator to infinity at either pole. The madrigal composer Don Carlo Gesualdo, a contemporary of Galileo, used the

The same melody harmonized in neo-Bach style, in which simple static chords are replaced by a dynamic cascade of dissonances

technique of enharmonic modulation to dramatic and disorientating emotional effect in expressionist settings of his own love poems, in a close harmony verging on the atonal. Keyboard composers like Girolamo Frescobaldi—the software designers of their era—were equally interested in mapping the movements of a musical figure as a sequence of positions across a uniform pitch space. A famous example of sequential invention is the familar Prelude No. 1 in C of J. S. Bach's *Well-tempered Clavier*.

Increased sophistication of key modulation in the baroque era implies a new awareness of chord change as relative motion. By convention, a change of chord is perceived as a change of state. The anthem *God Save the King* ("My Country 'tis of Thee") and the carol "While Shepherds watched their flocks by night" are examples of music progressing from static chord to chord as though switching from one stable state to another. The purpose of tonic or root position harmonization is to establish a sense of permanence and security, which in turn makes a song appear to lack movement and grace. Absence of movement is an understandable consequence of a music that conceives each moment or chord as a situation of repose; in the absence of a drive mechanism it is just as difficult to visualize a succession of frames in a movie strip as transitional elements of a dynamic process. Bach's skill in transforming humble chord progressions into a continuum of unfolding and resolving dissonances was rediscovered by Mendelssohn and adopted as a style cliché for an industrialized nineteenth century. In the above example of harmonization in the Bach style, an earlier succession of static chords is transformed into a domino effect of unstable harmonies, each leaning on the next to steady it, and the whole sequence creating an impression of movement.

Until interrupted by the social revolutions of the late eighteenth century, the art of continuous modulation (movement in pitch relations) evolved in parallel with studies in the dynamics of dance (movement in spatial relations). It stimulated a flurry of parallel researches into the simulation of human and animal movement, including musical boxes, dancing figurines, mechanical birds, and violin-playing automata. Formal dances and their music are usually ignored as relaxing entertainment for the well-to-do, but in a musical sense they double as covert studies in motion dynamics, the symbolic connotations of partnership relations, processes of fluid flow and weaving, and the dynamics of cyclical motion after the manner of a pendulum or piston. During the nineteenth century, ballet came to the fore as a specialist art of narrative dance, requiring exceptional movement skills and physical strength, expressed in extreme feats of balance (points) and managed instability (leaps and lifts), applied to storytelling rather than abstract patternmaking.

Marshall McLuhan has drawn attention to Byron's celebration of the waltz, an unskilled but dynamic rotational dance based on managed instability and adopted by a sophisticated public in the Napoleonic era at the time of the bicycle. For the first time, partners in waltz were permitted to hold one another steady—a novel and daring form of public intimacy and expression of equality among the sexes, previously confined to the peasantry—while moving in rotation about a personal center, and at the same time describing a larger orbital motion within the ballroom. The association of rotational motion with motion stability, and a new freedom of movement within a floor space previously strictly zoned in accordance with dancers' rank and class, helped set the tone of a nineteenth century intoxicated with the dynamics of nature, power generation, and wheeled transport, and newly fascinated by images of time and motion represented in the flow dynamics of great rivers (the Danube, the Rhine, the Moldau).

In the field of opera and the novel, not to mention the medical sciences, the same dynamics of continuous evolution are explored in terms of human motivations of passion, suffering, and ambition. In the concert arena, they embraced an aesthetic of speed, technical precision, and fluidity of tempo; in art song and opera, the trend shifted away from the rigid and stereotyped formalities of Rameau,

Handel and Mozart, toward informal and unpredictable character studies and relationships, often depicted as evolving within the drama, onstage and in real time, and often out of control.

Public fascination with the implications of continuous change was enhanced with the arrival of Darwinism, a science of constant evolution which in addition to locating human society within an extended biological and planetary history on a scale impossible to comprehend, also introduced a survival of the fittest morality to a civilized western world in the throes of growing political instability arising from a newly assertive and militant nationalism.

The term "atonal" is usually associated with a small but influential body of compositions by Schoenberg, Berg, and Webern, composed in the era of expressionist and early abstract art. Like a number of terms of modern art—for example, "impressionism" and "pointillism"—atonality began as critic's shorthand for a music that sounded as though it ought to be in a key, but wasn't. The term relates to a charge of continuously unresolved dissonance, a crime against public morals even though it could easily be defended as an extension of ongoing suspension and resolution in classical tonal music such as Bach's. In other respects—contour, rhythm, form—atonal music resembles conventional tonal music, though it tends to be somewhat denser in texture and argument.

To sum up, there are two points of departure for atonal music. One is exposed, the other implied. The first is the accented dissonance of baroque music, resolving on the weak beat only to lead in to a new dissonance on the next strong beat, a procedure employed with great cunning by Bach to create a dynamic of constant tension and uncertain resolution. It embodies the idea of continuity, of instability, of evading closure, or emphasizing the arbitrary nature of closure (the cadence or resolution). At the personal level it implies that there is never a satisfactory end to your endeavors, and at the universal level, that the world is in constant motion.

Emotional realism, or truth to nature, is a defining goal of the romantic aesthetic. A classical set-piece opera by Handel is less interested in individual drives and emotions than archetypal responses provoked in characters of fixed temperament to externally imposed crises, including falling in love. The idealized nature of classical emotion is reflected in the formulaic way in which human

The voice of Florence Nightingale, transcribed from an 1890 recording

characters are determined, and responses to crises depicted. The typology of emotion underpinning classical opera drew on ancient Greek theory, edited and refined by the French philologist Joseph Sauveur under the influence of Descartes' theory of human beings as programmed machines. The eighteenth-century theory of people as machines, and consequently lacking free will, came increasingly under attack in the lifetime of Mozart, as the bourgeoisie began to revolt against the aristocracy, and the literati themselves began to consider the dramatic implications of disruption and dysfunction in the dynamics of human nature. In the nineteenth century, themes of psychological dysfunction are overtaken by themes of social and natural disaster: war, the shipwreck, the tubercular heroine.

Wagner broke with classical tradition. His characters are out of control. Their goal is self-determination, their motives uncertain, and they express themselves in a musical language of perpetual indecision. You never know what they are going to say, where the narrative is going to go next, or in which direction, and that is the point. After Wagner, atonality takes the aesthetic of driven intuition to a higher level of complexity, based on a fresh understanding of how single and multiple strands are able to coexist in real life, triggered in part by the narrative complexities of Charles Dickens, and in part responding to the introduction of new film, telephone, and voice recording technologies.

When emotions are uncertain, so too are voices. This is more than just about having feelings. It is about reality. Harmony is not real but imposed. Normal people do not speak in C major, carry on a conversation in diatonic mode, walk collectively in step, or talk all at once in strict counterpoint. That such things don't happen in real life is simply another way of acknowledging that the rules of harmony in classical music conform to a preexisting, and by implication, socially determined intellectual and emotional script. In real life people not only have a natural tendency to speak in their own individual *tonality* (a system of tonal preferences, more than just an individual tone of voice), they also have a vested interest in preserving that tonality as a fundamental datum of personal identity, but at the most basic level, as a way of showing that the speaker is in control and not a zombie. To a majority of people, free will and freedom of speech are embodied in independence of intonation and inflection, freedom to speak at your own pace and in your own rhythm. The paradoxical subtext of a great deal of currently popular music, by contrast, is the appearance of freedom to say what you like, in the tonality of your own voice, achieved as a practical consequence of unnatural limitations on other forms of self-expression (total submission to management, loss of movement on the stage, and conformity to a rigidly enforced beat).

Music of fixed states or temperaments is perfectly appropriate for ritual situations or narratives that require emotional detachment as a matter of course. The entertainment value of the masque, a predecessor of opera taking the form of a themed concert party, does not require a storyline involving the continuous emotional development of a human subject. With courtly dance it is the same. The challenge of expressing emotions directly in musical terms begins to surface in music dramas of the early baroque era, starting with the first Italian operas and leading on to Bach's dramatizations of the Passion as well as the secular and political moralities of Mozart and his contemporaries. Since a change of emotion is an alteration of state or personal temperament experienced in real time, a music restricted to stable states is inadequate to convey the dynamics of natural emotion. Classical composers could deal with momentary transitions and fluctuations of emotion through dissonance and ornamentation of the musical flow, especially at cadences marking

Beethoven's "Moonlight" sonata Op. 27 No. 2 for piano. Introductory measures from the three movements, showing the same pulsation uniting all three tempos

points of repose and transition, such as falling in love, or making a decision. The suspended dissonances of "Ach! Golgotha" in Bach's *St. Matthew Passion* speak of excruciating emotional tension, just as the dissonant refrain "Mein Vater!" of Schubert's *Der Erlkönig* conveys the mounting fear of the boy. To express momentary emotional transitions within an aria or recitative, composers resorted to temporary modulation to an alien key. In that sense these and other conventions of western tonality might be said to embody a philosophical resistance to the idea of uncontrolled emotion in addition to putting practical obstacles in the way of expressing emotional change.

Compared to vocal music, which is conditioned by a text, music for instruments allows for greater abstraction of expression and freedom of movement. In imitation of Royal Society rules of chemistry (regulations designed to standardize, and by the same token, *legitimize*, a science of transmutation previously associated with magic and the occult), the first-movement form of classical abstraction arose as a procedure of inquiry into the dynamic of continuous change, and musical description of processes expressing continuity and identity. This was very much to the point at a time in the eighteenth century when the concept of a hierarchically organized and ideally harmonious world was coming increasingly under challenge by unseen forces of nature—natural forces leading to the great social revolutions of 1776, 1789, and thereafter.

In the romantic era, partly in response to Franklin and Faraday, and a new scientific theory of life as an electrical force, and partly driven by public interest in real-life subject matter in preference to the abstractions of classical music, new forms of musical and narrative drama arose in which both the physical and emotional states of the protagonists are depicted as inherently unstable. The Cartesian fantasy of the human being as a machine is superseded in the early romantic era by Mary Shelley's *Frankenstein*, a romantic fantasy of recreating a living person from assorted body parts, reanimated by electricity. Echoes of both the classical and romantic are revisited after the 1939–1945 war in attempts to program a computer to compose melodies, and to engage in meaningful dialogue with a human being. If the folklore of robotics is anything to go by, such attempts tend to reinforce, even now, a perception that not only the process of manufacture but also the creatures arising from an assembly of specialized talents, or abstracted body parts, are denied integrity, or lacking a sense of wholeness or conscience.

Further groundwork for atonality was laid in the early romantic era in works as familiar as Beethoven's "Moonlight" sonata, a piece perfectly acceptable to listeners who would never dream of listening to a piano work by Schoenberg. Beethoven's sonata is the expression in music of a spirit unable to find rest. Its fashionably nocturnal title evokes a feeling of claustrophobic isolation tempered by popular fear of the dark. The first movement *Adagio sostenuto* could be described as less about contemplating nature at night than trying to sleep while suffering a toothache. The key of C sharp minor is remote and darkly resonant. No chord in this key is ever completely resolved, since the tuning of black keys is never perfect, leaving ghostly tremors and resonances lingering in every harmony. There are two elements to Beethoven's somnambulism: a restless accompanying triplet figure that refuses to go away, and an insistent, jabbing "Nevermore!" motif in the melody, prefiguring the haunting refrain of Edgar Allan Poe's poem *The Raven*, itself a morse code motif that cries out for closure.

The same refusal of the accompanying figure to lie down and rest reappears in a more upbeat *Allegretto* second movement, in the major mode. This is a dialogue reduced to a play of slightly manic phrases in left and right hands that move in and out of synchronization. The theme of dislocation returns yet again in an explosive third movement, *Presto agitato*, returning to the minor mode, and featuring turbulent gestures rising and detonating aloft like fireworks, alternating with tremolo octaves that simulate the jangle of jangling nerves, like the effects of a bad hangover. In all three movements the same two elements recur in opposition: a rhythmic motif that will not go away, pitted against a resisting harmonic tendency to rest, achieve stability, and bring matters to a close. We can understand the sonata today as Beethoven's way of discussing the mind-body paradox, pitting the body's motor rhythms against the will, in a play dramatizing the tension of human instinct (or human nature, or physical suffering) against regulation by morality, propriety, forethought, indeed even raw fatigue. At the sonata's end it is not the will or the mind that prevails, only exhaustion.

Beethoven's formulations are simple and repetitive in all three movements, and deal with the same question from different perspectives. The music asks, who is in charge, the mind or the body, reason or instinct, intelligence or human nature? After digesting the "Moonlight" sonata, a listener should have little problem coming to terms with the more volatile temperament of Schoenberg's Op. 11 *Three Pieces for Piano*, which cover much the same emotional territory but in a more impulsive manner, without the constant hassle of an unremitting beat. Beethoven's inflexible pulsation, metronomically identical from movement to movement though perceived as sometimes faster, sometimes slower, is also the elder composer's way of addressing the implications for suffering humanity of an industrial age dominated by mechanical time, a spirit sympathetic with Goethe and William Blake.

Along with Haydn and Mozart, Beethoven collaborated with a number of inventors of mechanical musical instruments, such as the Maelzel metronome and panharmonicon, and was well aware of the mysterious and paradoxical inhumanity of mechanical reproduction of music. We hear its influence equally in Mozart's lightweight *Eine kleine Nachtmusik* as in the epic first-movement introduction of Beethoven's Symphony No. 4, an awareness of clock time as a mechanical motive force that, once set in motion, cannot stop of its own volition.[1]

Out of this trend Wagner emerges as a master of emotional realism allied to larger than life character types. In his operatic dramas, based not on set pieces but on a form of continuous recitative, the listener is all too aware of processes of unrestrained emotional development happening in real time, and reflected in a music of deliberately wayward and unpredictable modulation from key to key. Wagner's naturalism is all the same faithful to the older baroque tradition of representing emotional change and character development in terms of harmonic suspense and resolution.

Because the human voice is naturally uncertain both in tone and in timing, the management of uncertainty and its emotional implications is most effectively confronted in music for the voice. Early examples of atonal melodies are Alban Berg's *Altenberg Lieder*, Schoenberg's *Das Buch der Hängenden Gärten*, settings of Stefan George, and interpolations of lyrics by Richard Dehmel in Schoenberg's Second String Quartet Op. 10, poems expressing the strangeness of breathing the (quite possibly noxious, and certainly mind-altering) air of other planets.

The romantics were fascinated by states of consciousness and the inner workings of the mind. With a notebook and pencil at hand, in 1799 Humphry Davy put his head into a box containing nitrous oxide to breathe in the gas and observe its effects for the cause of science. His experiments led to the use of nitrous oxide as an anesthetic. Davy's friend, the poet Samuel Taylor Coleridge was addicted to opiates, which inspired the visionary poem *Kubla Khan*, conceived in 1797 and published in 1815; a trend reinforced in 1822 with publication of Thomas de Quincey's *Confessions of an English Opium Eater*. Dehmel's ecstatic image of inhaling an alien atmosphere inspired Schoenberg's breakthrough into atonality in the Second String Quartet, and is brought to earth with a bump by Oliver Wendell Holmes's famous attempt at recording the transcendental visions reported by patients after experiencing anesthesia by nitrous oxide, or "etherized upon a table," in T. S. Eliot's surrealist phrase. After ingesting gas under medical supervision the American jurist (after whom Arthur Conan Doyle's fictional detective Sherlock Holmes is named, incidentally) wrote, in trembling hand, that the universe smelled strongly of turpentine.[2]

Stimulated by early cylinder recordings of famous voices such as Florence Nightingale, atonality peaked in the early years of the twentieth century. In 1912 Schoenberg composed *Pierrot Lunaire* for female speaking voice and chamber ensemble, the same year in which W. C. Handy made his debut as the composer of *Memphis Blues*. Born in Alabama, Handy was a classically trained musician in tune with black consciousness at a time of rising ethnic awareness among musicians in Europe. A century later, Schoenberg's transcription of the melody of a speaking voice in melodramatic mode is still regarded as an aberration by musicologists, and even Boulez, whereas Handy's ethnic version of *sprechstimme* in blues style (notably the 1914 hit *St Louis Blues*: "I hate to see the evenin' sun go down") passes without disparagement. Both Schoenberg and Handy distort the traditional tone relations of classical music in deference to naturalistic expression, for the Austrian Schoenberg the menacing sing-song cadences of a cabaret artiste in decadent Vienna, and for Handy, the authentic tone of stoic resignation of African Americans working in the cottonfields.

The association of freedom with "natural" disharmony is a constant, if neglected, presence in western music. In atonal music shape and contour become more important expressive indicators than relationship to a key. This is how it is in everyday speech, which is perceived as gesture rather than tone. Rules of tonality are rules of corporate expression and agreement, whereas atonality ushers in a new era of individual self-determination and corporate relativism. In everyday life it is more natural to attend to the up and down cadence of conversational speech, than be distracted by the twists and turns of tonal relationship of adjacent syllables. With the arrival of Edison cylinder recording on the scene, anthropology and the market raised public awareness of speech and songs as indicators of personality and charisma to be captured on phonograph cylinder or disc. The attraction of voice recording was not so much the content of what was spoken or sung, but the mystery of a machine capturing the personality of a real voice. Hence the advertising plan based on Barraud's painting of Nipper the Dog, and G. B. Shaw's comedy, *Pygmalion*—also dating from 1912—on the subject of elocution training as an indicator of good breeding, social class, and education. It is no coincidence that the Vienna where Schoenberg received his musical training was also the birthplace of Freudian psychoanalysis, and thereafter of the music psychology of Theodor Adorno.

What distinguishes Schoenberg's and Webern's atonal melodies even from Berg's, whose musical impulses are more romantically stylized, is their evident truthfulness to natural speech, revealed with startling clarity in those rare cases where a singer performs with a sense of recovered natural speech rather than an artificial "art song" diction. I am thinking of Marni Nixon and Phyllis Bryn-Julson's recordings of Webern songs, and Martina Arroyo's of *Momente* by Stockhausen, a work in which the vocal and dramatic elements of *Pierrot Lunaire* and American gospel music are ingeniously reconciled. Stravinsky's opera *The Nightingale*, conceived in 1910, and based on Hans Christian Andersen's fairy tale, makes the same point that the melody of a mechanical bird (one programmed to sing in diatonic scales and precisely notated rhythms) is never the same as the song of a real bird, the living creature being able to express emotions that cannot be reduced to mechanical states or settings, including keyboards and the tempered scale. The message of Schoenberg's atonal music is that the emotional meaning of speech, or its analogue in instrumental melody, lies in its abstract contour and not its relationship to a key, with the implication that by eliminating key one is able to enlarge the emotional truth of a musical setting of a poem or text. As he was later to say of twelve-tone composition, the new art is based on a perception of note to note—that is, intervallic—relationships.

Notes

1. Robin Maconie, *Second Sense*, 275–81.
2. Oliver Wendell Holmes Sr., *Mechanism in Thought and Morals*. Phi Beta Kappa address, Harvard University, June 29, 1870. Boston: J. R. Osgood and Company, 1871. (www.druglibrary.org/schaffer/Library/studies/cuCU43.html) (06. 07. 2006).

EIGHTEEN

SPRECHSTIMME

All singing resembles speech in the obvious sense that it involves the voice and delivery of a text. That singing is higher in cultural significance than ordinary speech has to do with several factors:

1. The text is of greater consequence than ordinary speech;
2. The vocalist is an important or charismatic figure;
3. The message is delivered to a group of people and requires skill in interpretation, both mental and physical;
4. The occasion is a significant public event and affirmation of community values.

A comic opera, a presidential press conference, the movie *My Fair Lady*, a high profile murder trial in front of television cameras, or a hiphop contest may not all rate as high culture, but as examples of charismatic public figures affirming public values (however transient) they serve well enough. And they all involve musical speech. The patter songs of Gilbert and Sullivan are not high art, they are a person talking to himself.

The distinction between recitative and aria in opera and oratorio alike is not only between the function of a narrator and participant in the drama, but also arguably a distinction of vocal style, the one tending toward speech, the other to song. Rex Harrison as Professor Higgins in the movie *My Fair Lady* is also talking to himself, and for the very good reason that he cannot sing; instead the actor recites his lyrics with the extravert cadence of sung speech, relying on the orchestral accompaniment to convey the melody and harmonic inflection of his words. Imagine the drama and added realism of effect if the Evangelist of Bach's *St Matthew Passion* were to declaim his lines in heightened *sprechstimme* rather than song. Shaw's serio-comic message in *Pygmalion* is interesting in another way, satirizing a perception of culture and status as a matter of simple voice training, qualities to be imprinted on the blank sheet of an uneducated flowergirl by military-style practice in imitating aristocratic speech. Today the technique survives as method acting. Shaw's comedy is firmly grounded in the intellectual realities of the day, and the magic of Higgins's makeover of Eliza, as the Act 1 stage prescriptions make resolutely clear, is firmly grounded on the Svengali-like professor's adoption of the new medium of cylinder recording.

The rich and varied acoustic qualities of speech are of constant interest to language scholars as nonverbal indicators of meaning, to computer science as a programming challenge for speech recognition, and to electroacoustic composers as templates for sound synthesis and modulation. Speech is an extraordinarily rich and totally natural manipulation of tone and noise combinations for communication purposes. We train ourselves to ignore the textures and complexities of spoken language in order to focus on word recognition, but when encountering a foreign language for the first time it is the external range of sounds, their patterns and tonal preferences, that have to be sorted out before the terms of the language are absorbed and can be imitated to exchange information. This initial process of noting the characters and limitations of a new language is essentially musical in nature, focusing on voice melody, rhythm, accent, tonal (vowel) priorities, and gestural implication. All languages and modes of speech involve essentially the same mechanisms: the vocal folds for tone generation, the teeth, lips, and tongue for articulation, and mouth and nasal cavities for resonance. In imitating and learning a new speech—as distinct from learning to read a foreign language from books—the learner is bound to acquire a sense of the functional association of speech actions with speech sounds and their meanings.

The history of western music—of music as a cultural practice, as distinct from musical acoustics as an adjunct to philosophy, that is—is intimately connected with speech transcription as a memory aid, and recognition of layers of meaning and implication in speech over and above those implied by a written text. The postmodernist doctrine of the essential privacy or inaccessibility of meaning, in

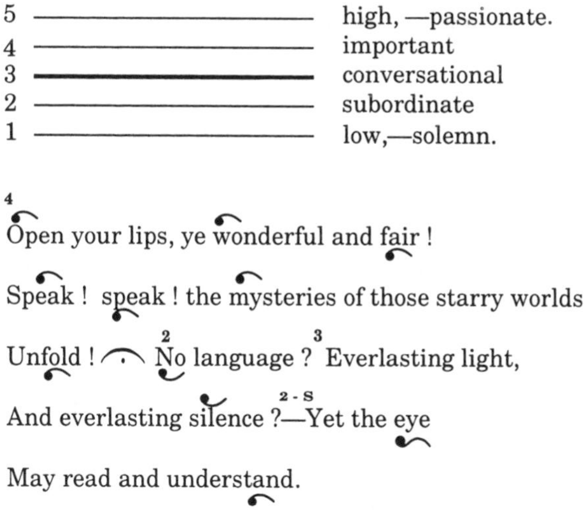

5 high,—passionate.
4 important
3 conversational
2 subordinate
1 low,—solemn.
4
Open your lips, ye wonderful and fair !
Speak ! speak ! the mysteries of those starry worlds
Unfold ! No language ? Everlasting light,
2 3
And everlasting silence ?—Yet the eye
2 - s
May read and understand.

Excerpt from Bell's Standard Elocutionist *(1892) by David Charles Bell and Alexander Melville Bell, showing the stave of emotion, and below, a practice excerpt of poetic declamation, with inflectional notations. Note the expressive punctuation marks in the text, which also have inflectional implications*

art, or literature, or music, or even the movies, can be understood as a natural consequence of signing up to the dogma that the meanings inherent in the sounds of speech cannot be codified. And yet it was precisely in order to overcome the inadequacies of a written or printed text that the artifices of poetry—rhyme, rhythm, and punctuation—were developed in the first place so many centuries ago. It is because they did not understand the history of music as speech science that nineteenth-century speech and language experts were forced to devote so much effort to reinventing the wheel.

The voice is naturally versatile. Vocal expression embraces the whisper, undertone, the gestures of conversation, song, incantation, formal speech, wail, and cry of alarm. They are common to all cultures and share the same contextual and emotional implications in every language. The highest form of communication is also the most limited. Of British and American English it is said that a common language is a great divider of the two peoples. Music for voice is conventionally understood as a delivery system for a text, its function to enhance meaning by simplifying and formalizing the normally wayward modulations of speech, so as to fix both text and meaning firmly in the mind of a listener as a fusion of words and vocal gesture. On the operatic stage a singing voice may contrive, for example, to give an impression ranging from the shriek of anger of Mozart's "Queen of the Night" aria from *The Magic Flute*, to the intimate conversation of Debussy's *Pelléas et Mélisande*, but in the live non-dramatized concert setting, where most classical music is performed, the room space and distance between singer and listener are normally such that in order to be clearly audible a vocalist is obliged to adopt a particular tone of voice that is natural to singing but alien to ordinary speech.

To understand the expressive component of intonation, one only has to compare normal with whispered speech. Whispering is speech without tone. In whispering the vocal cords are inactive. A whisper uses the noise of forced breathing out to excite cavity resonances in the mouth and nose that occupy the same frequency zones as vowels in normal speech and are modulated in the same way. In whispering only vowels are affected, because only vowels are intoned. Consonants are unvoiced bands of noise controlled through the combined movements of the tongue, lips and teeth interfering with the outward flow of air.

As long as an audience is silent, a stage whisper is surprisingly easy to hear. Consonants are the sense-givers of speech and the human ear is particularly sensitive to sounds in the frequency band associated with consonants. Lacking tone, however, a whisper has little scope for expression, power, and penetration. The upper frequency region is easily masked or blocked by objects or people standing in the way. By contrast, a speaking or singing voice is not only more clearly audible over a greater area, but thanks to the power of the lungs, is also strong enough to fill a space and be reflected from surrounding walls and ceiling, which means the voice can be heard even from behind a door. Unlike a whisper, a singing or speaking voice can be modulated in *pitch*, up and down the scale; in *loudness*, by varying the level of energy; and in *timbre* or tone quality, by varying the manner of speaking or singing through changes of facial and body posture. These modulations bring their own cognitive associations to the interpretation of a spoken text.

Speech is therefore a more versatile and preferable mode of communication than whispering. Whispering is what you do when you have a sore throat, or do not want to be overheard. Speech is preferable because people who have something to say in general like to be listened to, and because the powers of speech are added controls over the attention of an audience, over the meaning of the words a person intends to convey, and over the urgency of the message. Whispering is associated with loss of well-being, exhaustion, or sickness, and situations of danger, intimacy, secrecy, and the need to avoid discovery. Nevertheless, it also signifies that the person *remains determined* to communicate a message despite the personal difficulties loss of the ability to speak might imply. By contrast, speech clearly signifies relative health, a sense of freedom to speak openly, confidence in speaking, a sense of identity, and, in a majority of cases, motivation to impart a message that is all the more effectively communicated with the addition of melodic and dynamic cues.

When a person whispers in the dark, or out of view, it is often difficult to tell who is doing the whispering. By contrast, a person who speaks or sings out of view is clearly a distinct and recognizable individual. Recognition of a person's voice depends on a combination of active and passive features of voice production. The active component relates to tone qualities specific to the individual vocal mechanism—the length and condition of the vocal cords, the energy level of the voice, and the tessitura or normal range of variation of the speaking voice. The passive component relates to the resonant structures of the throat, mouth, and nasal passages, features as distinctive to a particular individual as a person's fingerprints. Tone and resonance profiles in combination make up the individual voice. The skills applied in identifying a voice with a person are applied equally, and with varying degrees of success, to identifying a room, an animal, and a foreign language.

Outside the realm of electronic music, examples of whispering or muttering in classical music are rare. An example is Stravinsky's sacred cantata *Threni*, where the choir is instructed to emphasize and draw out the opening and closing consonants of letter names of the Hebrew alphabet that punctuate the text: *Aleph, Samech, Coph, Zain, Resh, Sin, Tsade*. Another is *Circles* by Luciano Berio, a setting of verses by e e cummings in which the lines of spoken text are dissociated and re-formed as if on tape, into fragmentary vowel and consonant groups, echoed and imitated by a mixed group of melody and percussion instruments.

In intimate conversation the voice is relaxed and flexible in pitch and dynamics, from low chest tones to high head tones. Professional singers work to focus more power at these extremes of range. Flexibility without precise pitch control is a recipe for a form of expression where what matters is the *contour* of speech, that is, the pattern of movement up and down, rather than the exact position of the voice at any one moment. During the 1970s a cataloguer for the British Library, Denys Parsons, discovered that the *incipit* or opening ten or twelve notes of a familiar melody, when expressed simply as a sequence of movements up or down, without any reference to interval, pitch, tempo, rhythm, or prevailing key, was quite sufficient for the melody to be identified.[1] That we remember melody as a contour rather than as a sequence of exact pitches is the explanation behind the mystery of how anyone can recognize or reproduce a favorite melody in whatever key it is heard. A memory of shapes rather than values not only gives added credence to the ancient tradition of computing by ratio in preference to exact quantities or measures, it also helps to explain the high priority accorded to modulation (shape translation) in the history of western music since renaissance times.

The difficulty of reconciling small-scale utterance with large-scale surroundings is of making oneself heard, without the help of a microphone, often against a large body of instrumental sound. A great deal of contemporary music involving wide leaps and outwardly dissonant intervals, such as the *Altenberg Lieder* Op. 3 of Alban Berg, and the monodrama *Erwartung* by Schoenberg, can be interpreted as heightened but essentially intimate musical soliloquy to be performed however as though the singer were singing to herself, but on a scale commensurate with a concert-hall acoustic. Schoenberg's *Herzgewächse* and Boulez's *Le marteau sans maître* and *Improvisations sur Mallarmé*, and Berio's *Circles* for soprano and chamber ensemble, belong to a genre of post-1950 music for female voice and chamber ensemble in which the instruments echo and imitate the sounds and natural inflections of speech, vowels, and consonants. It is surprising to note that authorized recordings of these works, those supervised and conducted by the composers themselves, are not performed with a more appropriate intimacy.

Because *sprechstimme* tends to be associated with the inner life of the imagination, it is arguably unnecessary to employ the rhetorical mannerisms of a large auditorium, including vibrato. One would prefer the theater of cabaret, even the untutored realism of a Lotte Lenya or Marlene Dietrich, tone qualities closer to an instrument. A *sprechstimme* delivered without vibrato in the manner of a cylinder-recorded voice can be dramatic, as in *Pierrot Lunaire*, diverting, as in the megaphonic verses of Edith Sitwell for William Walton's *Façade*, and even attain a sublime musicality, as we know from recordings of Webern. It is possible to negotiate the angular melodies of Schoenberg, Berg, and Webern with a lightness and precision that not only makes them sound completely natural but is even able to draw out a latent accent and timbre, so that a listener is able even to sense the composer's personal tone of voice. A Webern performance is by definition an intensely private affair, a Boulez or Berio performance less so. Webern and his aesthetic of transparent intimacy belong to the era of acoustic horn recording and the shellac disc; Boulez and Berio by contrast belong to a generation enjoying access to noise-free tape and vinyl, along with unlimited amplification, an intimacy already adopted into the mainstream of western radio culture in the 1930s by Piaf, Chevalier, Jourdan, Crosby and Sinatra. The challenge of singing to a microphone is of scaling the voice, so as to convey the privacy of the lyrics without sacrificing audibility. A microphone style exploits the full frequency range of the voice, including consonants that tend to be lost in the atmospherics of an opera house. Such a style is arguably more appropriate for atonal and *sprechstimme* items than the amplified rhetoric of grand opera.

Scale distinctions are also spatial in implication. The pentatonic mode of folk music throughout the world represents a standard of pitch discrimination for voice communication in the open air, such as for workers in the cottonfields. The diatonic scale of western music involves greater refinement of perception, and the assistance of an acoustic enclosure such as a concert chamber. By the same token, atonal and twelve-tone idioms are naturally geared to the close intimacy of a microphone and studio. From the simple acoustics of vocalization we learn that singing is a formalization of natural speech designed for distance communication. In turn, the fixed and variable conventions of voice melody, specifically in the case of folksong, but by implication for composed song as well, are open to interpretation as templates of natural inflection patterns *within the language*. Scots bagpipe music, for example, is pentatonic, hence music for outdoors, intoned over a drone tonality and overlaid by a melody composed in imitation of speech and articulated in syllabic or wordlike segments by gracenote figurations. It is no surprise to discover that, prior to its adoption of classical stave notation in the late eighteenth century, the traditional method of memorizing pipe music was phonetically based, with melody notes corresponding to vowels, and the embellishments to consonants.

TRANSLATION

When a lyric is translated into another language, the characteristic rhythms and intonation applicable to the original text are overlaid on an alien form of words, which is the translator's nightmare and a major reason for performing opera for preference in the original language. Given that the function of singing is to articulate the features that make a spoken text intelligible in the first place, a policy of singing opera in the original language would seem to make emotional (and indeed, anthropological) sense, even while rendering the actual meaning of the composer's libretto inaccessible to a majority of listeners. Mussorgsky, Stravinsky, Bartók, and Janáček are among a number of composers of Central and Eastern Europe whose melodies as a whole are affected by identifiable traits of the national language. The double-stress feminine endings in Bartók melodies, for example, are a feature of Hungarian speech rhythm. Janáček was quite open about his determination, for reasons of national identity and pride, to embed the distinctive forms and patterns of his native tongue in his music. Much the same goal of reproducing the natural flow of speech can be determined from the songs of Satie and Debussy, and even Francis Poulenc, though in general the French style tends more toward the neutrality of near-monotone plainchant than the excitable cadences of natural Parisian speech.

To the degree that they rely on instruments to remain in tune, chant and song alike are bound to conform to regular scales or modes of these instruments—or at least, to be *heard* as the volatile partners of regular scales or modes. Today we distinguish fidelity to a script (song) from an authentic (personally deviant) expression of personal experience or conviction (speech). Crudely expressed, the underlying implication of words set to music can only be *false* because the message and its inflection are essentially scripted and not the spontaneous expression of the singer's actual feelings. By that definition, the speech-song of Jimi Hendrix, or rap of Eminem (the artist, that is, not the chocolate drop) are more truthful because their lyrics are delivered in a virtual speaking voice and in a manner seemingly improvised on the spot. Both conjure an appearance of authenticity and intimacy with the assistance of microphone and amplification ensuring they do not have to raise their voices and thus formalize their style of delivery.

Authenticity has fascinating implications. Did the Greek audience think that the messenger bringing the news that Oedipus has put out his eyes was not telling the truth, or less convincing, as a secondary source speaking of an event that takes place out of view? The idea that an intermediary is obliged to give the impression of having suffered the experience in person, in order to convince a listener of the truth of an experience, is recognized in the difference between US method acting and European traditions of Shakespeare and Racine. Similar distinctions separate comedy, supposed to be informal and improvisatory, and tragedy, which is more schematic. A lead actor or star is idealized as a performer who remains recognizable as the face behind a particular role, whereas a character actor is enjoined to virtual anonymity in a supporting role.

In musical terms similar differences of perception affect public attitudes toward classical (formal) art song and popular (informal, hence more real) song, between classical (scripted) music and jazz or improvised (unscripted) folk traditions, and between orchestra concerts, which are about exact reproduction of a script, and pop concerts, which deviate intentionally from the versions released on record in order to prove their authenticity (that the players are real and not miming).

Despite conforming to musical conventions of firm pitch,

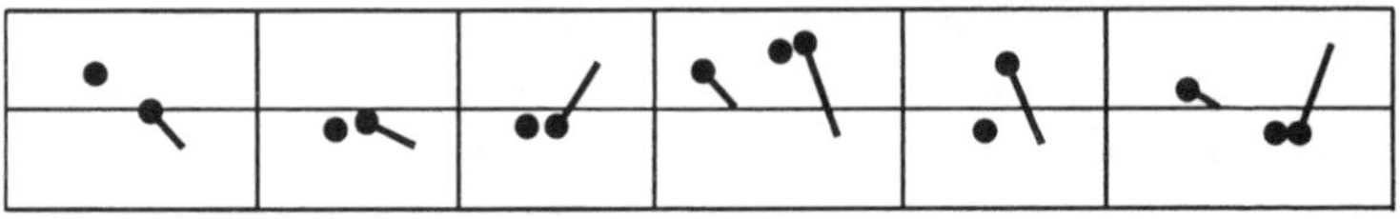

You do. *Okay.* | You do. *Good.* | You do? *What?* | Ah. You do! *Exactly.* | You do?! *Gosh.* | Ah. You do? *Are you sure?*

Varieties of inflection

steady rhythm, and carefully modulated melody, rhetorical speech is distinguished from song or ritual incantation by taking care to avoid lapsing into a recognizable key, into verse, or employing musical instruments as backup. Formal devices of any kind are bound to compromise an appearance of sincerity. These devices include repetition and cliché. The most skilled orators and their most memorable utterances are those steering as close as possible to music while retaining the natural imperfection and tone of voice of the average speaker. Examples of speech remembered as music tend to be sound-bites such as Winston Churchill's "We will fight them on the beaches," John F. Kennedy's nicely symmetrical "Ask not what your country can do for you—ask what you can do for your country," and Martin Luther King Junior's iconic "I have a dream." An especially compelling twentieth-century equivalent of live-action recitative and aria, one that has still not lost its power to move the listener, is Herbert Morrison's radio newscast covering the *Hindenburg* disaster.

As speech is converted to music its context of meaning changes from spontaneous and immediate to historic and formulaic. That is what music does to a text, and the singing style itself is transformed from a rhetorical appeal for agreement, asking the audience to accept the idea, into a statement of doctrine to which agreement is assumed to obtain, at least in principle. In practice the meaning of a classical song is subject to subtle alteration or transformation in meaning by an interpreter of genius whose understanding of the text breathes new life, from an audience's perspective, into a familiar item of memory. To achieve that degree of control over the perceived meaning of a song, a speechlike style is invariably an advantage.

From exactly notated speech it is a short step to abstract word and syllabic invention. The most famous setting of Gertrude Stein's verse is the opera *Four Saints in Three Acts* by Virgil Thomson, employing a form of abstracted scat singing. Stein's own recorded readings reveal an original rap artist with interesting linguistic connections to the Italian futurists, jazz, the German speech scientist Hermann Ebbinghaus, and her Harvard mentor William James. Since the nonsense poems of Lewis Carroll in the nineteenth century, abstracted speech is associated in twentieth-century culture with Tolkien, inventor of the metalanguages of the *Lord of the Rings* series, the dadaist poets, the playful Kurt Schwitters, the gnomic mesostics of John Cage, and not forgetting Klingon and the other invented languages of flying saucer civilizations of post-1945 science fiction movies and television series. The present-day higher consciousness of the musical features of speech or nonsense speech has been driven partly by science and partly by increased exposure to nonwestern cultures through travel and international media. In the operas of his *LICHT* cycle, Stockhausen plays with abstracted glossolalia as a precursor language imprinted in the genetic code and favored by visionaries and the mentally distracted, out of deference both to the irrational speech of ancient priesthoods, and in memory of his own generation's encounters with exotic cultures in newsreels and movies of the Buck Rogers era.

Historically, the black American tradition of gospel worship is a form of part-improvised, part-composed religious theater in which heightened and emotionally driven recitative blends in and out with choir and congregational harmony. That tradition emerges afresh in hiphop, a music of rhythmicized speech with instrumental backing in which verses of an individually assertive nature alternate with affirmative choruses.

Situated in elegant Boston—the modern equivalent of Mozart's Vienna—the television series *Boston Legal* is today's version of a Mozart opera, an opportunity for viewers to delight, in closeup and in court, at the artistry with which highly sophisticated and experienced actors representing the legal profession, one that wins or loses on verbal skills, demonstrate their powers of suggestion and persuasion through their exact control of intonation and inflection, skills exercised as much in outwardly casual dialogue and intimate relations as in the conventionally artificial environment of a courtroom. Though expressed in speech, these are musical skills. They involve the manipulation of pitch, timing, accentuation, and rhythm to influence an emotional response and the desired outcome.

In all of the above familiar examples, the emotional subtext of employing heightened speech rather than song is to demonstrate realism through artlessness: that is, by *absence of art*. It implies that song is false, but speech is genuine, the feelings are authentic, and there are no tricks. However, intellectually we all know that it is in fact art, and we are being persuaded. The court in the play is just a front. In reality the courtroom is the public arena, and the jury, the public.

For a Schoenberg to be interested in accurate transcription of the inflections of speech, whether in the interests of documentary realism, or in the clinical representation of an emotional condition for dramatic purposes, is neither bizarre nor eccentic, but a mainstream artistic objective expressed with unusual clarity at a time when new portable technology allowing the sampling and transcription of speech had emerged on the scene. The atonal dimensions of twentieth-century music have gone largely unnoticed by generations of musicians and a general public whose preferences have remained locked into classical emotional and harmonious stereotypes, more interested in the art object as an elegant creation than in art as a vehicle for authentic human experience.

Shakespeare employs neutral or meaningless phrases at the beginning of scenes: "What ho!" "Make way!" "My Lord!"—often as devices to quieten the audience and call attention to important information about to be delivered that might otherwise be lost in the hubbub. Here again, the verbal content of the interjection is of little significance compared to what might be called the musical function of such phrases in employing distinctive tone, loudness, and rhythm (a) to call attention and interrupt the continuity of the event, and (b) through melodic contour or inflection to express affirmation, doubt, grief, alarm, or whatever other nuance of emotion might be appropriate to set the scene. In classic European theater, great acting consists in applying an appropriate accompanying inflection to a preordained text to convey an impression of real motivation and emotion, even on occasion at the cost of obscuring the meaning of the words. Method acting, by contrast, employs immersion techniques in order to release spontaneous and apparently authentic emotions through improvisation involving only approximate adherence to a script. Equivalent techniques are employed in jazz.

Like the plays of Shakespeare, classical vocal music is bound to words as well as inflection. There is little room for "um" and "ah" in classical music, lied, opera, or oratorio. Toward the end of the nineteenth century, symbolist poets recognized an emotional truth latent in pure inflection, a transcendent emotion exemplified in the wordless vocalise of Ravel's *Daphnis et Chloé* and the spiritualist fascination of the theremin. Symbolism alleged the singing of pure melody to be more authentic emotionally than any words being sung, since words are bound to follow their own rules of association and bring only a spurious surface definition to more complex human motivations that are mostly hidden from view.

Freud felt the same way about his patients, and so in their own way did the surrealists. It doesn't alter the fact that in music for words not only the text but also the inflection is usually a given, sometimes to a degree of precision that allows a performer very little room to maneuver. The question remains, how to articulate a given text within a given melody and rhythm and still manage to convey an impression of an authentic personality. The simple and easy answer is for a singer to go completely with the flow and endeavor to discover the meaning within by submitting to the will of the composer. All too frequently that policy leads to a kind of automatic singing that ultimately reflects technique rather than attempting to convey any authentically human character. The more difficult and challenging task for a singer interpreter is to develop the personality within the musical pattern of text and inflection as it is indicated in the nature of the written cadence (and language, of course), in the conviction that what the composer has set down is based on the speech of a real person, and not simply assigned to high or low notes at random.

In reality most songs of the classical and romantic eras conform to easily recognized and stylized melody types: the issue of dealing with manifestly stock gestures in song is that they are likely to do little for the text and are employed as cliché to please an unsophisticated audience. Conventions of theater quickly deteriorate into empty rhetoric. Dissonant intervals and hesitations are all the same features of authentic and sincere speech. In real life people do not speak in tune. To convey realism in singing it may be advisable to sing as if one were really speaking, which is not an easy task, because it brings the added burden of understanding in depth what one is speaking or singing about. Avoidance of vibrato and perfect control of the voice over all registers are preconditions of a naturalistic style in a formal setting. It means, for example, that Boulez's setting of "Le vierge, le vivace, et le bel aujourd'hui" sung amid the tinkling and chiming of metal percussion and harps, should come across as a delicate, birdlike frisson of exquisitely Parisian delight, set amidst the musical equivalent of a jeweller's or clockmaker's shop. There is very little place for vibrato in avant-garde twentieth-century music, or (to be honest) in classical music of any period.

That Boulez remains so emphatic that the vocal part of *Pierrot Lunaire* should be sung is of added interest given the angular vocal lines he himself has composed for female voice, which also reflect a blend of symbolist and expressionist sympathies. That does not alter the fact that a realistic or appropriate interpretation of Schoenberg's intentions in notating speech should take into account a wider context of speech expression and representation.

Schoenberg continued to experiment with speech notations for the rest of his life, and his notations vary in interesting ways. In *A Survivor from Warsaw* the speaker's part is notated in relative pitch, in contrast to *Pierrot*, where the pitches are exactly notated but inexactly reproduced. Boulez has recorded *Survivor* with a bass-baritone taking the voice part; a more recent recording by Robert Craft has employed an actor to speak the part, whose lighter voice is more in the tenor range. A few recordings survive of Schoenberg speaking, among them a 1930 German radio recording of the composer speaking in rather urgent tones about his *Variations* Op. 31 for orchestra, and a much later interview conducted in English. On the admittedly scant evidence of these archive recordings I am inclined to the view that the voice part of *Survivor* is modeled on the composer's own voice, and distinctive Austrian lilt.

Note

1. Denys Parsons, *A Directory of Tunes and Musical Themes*. Cambridge: Spencer Brown, 1975.

NINETEEN

MULTIPLES

> The power to apply a brake or accelerator at will to the visible universe can take us beyond the realm of science into a world of fantasy. By giving to vegetable growth the speed normally associated with animal action we give it also an appearance of consciousness, and even intention. An opening rose seems to "flaunt" its petals literally, not merely by poetic licence, and the dodder, a parasitic plant, has every appearance of attacking its neighbours "with malice aforethought." This suggests that the bases on which we are prepared to found moral judgements are sometimes a little insecure. SPENCER AND WALEY

Traditionally, music is about unity and integration. The conventional function of music is to model patterns of integrated activity, either by direct imitation, like a chorus line, or by choreographed coordination of related but different functions. During the twentieth century a number of composers are seen to inquire into the possibility of a music representing multiple actions pursued independently. The interest of a music expressing multiplicity—or disintegration—is simple: it is the way the world works in practice. Teamwork and uniformity are the exceptions rather than the rule.

To achieve musical images of multiplicity or absence of coordination might appear to be simple, but in fact is unusually difficult. In the music of oral cultures a listener recognizes a striving, indeed a moral tendency, toward integration that we can understand as a fundamental human need to unite the family and the social group. Like all moralities, it is a convenient fiction rather than a trait in human nature. We approve of orderly behavior because it is easier to understand and to manage than chaos, and because orderly activity is predictable and can achieve useful results.

Perhaps it begins in the modern era with Stravinsky's fairground in *Petrushka*, and the symphonic studies of Charles Ives. Exuberant multiplicity is synonymous with jazz, especially dixieland, in the conventional freedoms and associated limits exercised by players to do as they like and express their individuality. The downside of freedom of expression, in jazz or anywhere else, is that freedom to do what you like is obtained at a cost of submitting to common formulae that remain discreetly in control and coordinate individual players, like the *cantus firmus* (basic melody) of renaissance polyphony, to guarantee discipline and consistency within the ensemble. In classical music multiplicity is a perception of voices or instrumental parts acting independently, in terms of their spatial location, their tonal orientation, and also their timing. In reality the art of composing a music working simultaneously in different timescales has been cultivated since notation was invented. Medieval and renaissance music recognized an art of proportional tempi, different divisions of a common beat corresponding to different tempi, but harmonically related like the partial wavelengths of a string. A baroque fugue is a composition in which the same figure is depicted at different locations in pitch space (up and down), in normal and inverted attitudes, forward and reverse orientations, and even in different timescales (augmentation and diminution).

A music of multiple tempi is one where several layers of music of different speeds are combined and can be freely monitored by the audience either as a complex totality, like a crowd effect, or as individual layers standing out against a complex background. The "cocktail effect" of perception psychology is usually described as the curious ability of a listener to identify and follow a particular voice or sound from a sea of conversation. The world of psychology tends to present this ability as a twentieth-century discovery arising from the study of recorded complex sounds in real life. Audiology studies from the mid-twentieth century have suggested a maximum of between seven and ten separate voices in music that the human ear and brain are able to monitor simultaneously. By that definition Thomas Tallis's mighty *Spem in alium* for forty voice parts should be both mentally inconceivable and aurally unimaginable. From the scores that survive as evidence of western musical practice, however, we can be certain that interest in manufactured

Sixteenth-century polyrhythms: Sumite Carissimi *by Magister Zacharias*

complexity arose in music along with the development of a viable notation, in the fourteenth and fifteenth centuries. Notation enabled complex multipart music to be designed and visualized on paper even though it may not have been aurally verifiable in advance. What that suggests in turn is that composers were fascinated by complexity, despite or even *because* it exceeded the bounds of the humanly conceivable, for the very reason that graphic notation provided a means of rendering previously unimaginable complexity in audible and harmonious form.

Organization of music of multiple tempi is not a simple matter, even though the concept of a music subject to alteration between mechanically geared tempi in simple ratios, e.g. 3 : 2, 4 : 3, goes back a thousand years to the time of the invention of the clock. A counterpoint of superimposed tempi that maintains separation of individual lines and avoids congestion or "clotting" requires technical skill in notation and also considerable skill in execution. Examples are the studies for piano roll by Conlon Nancarrow, the string quartets of Elliott Carter, and Stockhausen's *Zeitmasse* for woodwind quintet, in all of which complexity and multiple timescales are identified with notational approaches and methods that are difficult to acquire visually as well as to execute.

A somewhat more provocative question is whether the same or similar complexities of time relation can be discovered in the classical repertoire. Hitherto scholars have assumed a uniformity of timescale in the music of Bach, Chopin, or Beethoven, based on a notional uniformity of notational style, even where layers of overlapping timescales are clearly audible, for example, Bach's choral "Durch Adams Fall" prelude for organ, which articulates different

Mozart, *Don Giovanni*

The Ballroom Scene from Mozart's Don Giovanni. *Three stage orchestras play simultaneously at different tempi*

pulsations for pedals, left, and right hand respectively. Nineteenth-century performers were aware of the conceptual complexities of music such as the *Grande Valse* Op. 42, and the "Minute Waltz" Op. 64 No. 1 for piano of Chopin, in addition to the difficulties of execution they entailed (often reduced to a play of variable tempi in the right hand, in opposition to a regular beat in the left hand). A modern aversion to the visual complexity of some recent scores has led some readers of contemporary music to ignore analogous complexities in renaissance and *galant* idioms, perhaps on the ground that because the various time layers look as if they share a uniform pulse, they should be performed to a uniform pulse.

They are answered in evidence of aural complexity that has come down to the present disguised in simpler notation. Nobody objects to the celebrated ballroom scene in Mozart's *Don Giovanni* in which three dance orchestras perform simultaneously in 3/8, 2/4, and 3/4, which looks more complicated on paper than it sounds in practice. As Curt Sachs observes, the 2/4 orchestra shares all of its bar lines with the 3/8 orchestra; and after every two measures of the 3/4 orchestra, all three orchestras synchronize on the first beat. But the challenge in this case is to celebrate Mozart's daring conception of a multilayered musical chaos by contriving to make the different tempi more clearly audible, and this is not easy to do on an opera platform of limited size. But it can be done. Think of Ives, whose symphonies ingeniously superimpose incompatible layers of music in different keys, characters, tempi, and at times even different tuning systems.

Since actions at different speeds frequently coincide in the real world, and rarely interact, the achievement of a music of different coexistent timescales is of interest in itself, and amply justifiable as imitation of nature. The eighteenth-century development of mechanical devices and their associated time controls for reproduction of music, instruments such as the musical box, panharmonium, and pianola, has been crucial in developing the conceptual and notational skills for musical multitasking. Even those clockwork instruments lacking speed controls, such as the musical box, are all the same able to convey an experience of "time fading away" as the mechanism winds down.

There are two ways of defining multiple tempi. The American tradition of Charles Ives, Conlon Nancarrow, Elliott Carter, and John Cage is characterized by superimposed timescales that remain resolutely indifferent to one another; the older tradition dating from the European renaissance and associated in the twentieth century with the music of Berg, Schoenberg, Stockhausen, and Stravinsky, involves superimposed timescales that are different but related to a common fundamental pulse. The Emersonian tradition, if we may call it that, conceives music in the image of nature; the European tradition in the image of the Music of the Spheres. An interest in overlapping periodicities of nature can be traced back appropriately to astronomy, a science aiming at reconciling the differing motion of the planets, along with the domestic cycles of the day, the phases of the moon, the solar year, and the seasons. It is exemplified in the famous musical notation by Kepler of the orbits of the planets in their differing periodicities and orbital speeds. Such a view of the harmony of different periodicities conforms to a scientific interest in reconciling not simply the fact but also the underlying dynamics of complex orbiting processes, driven by a philosophical or religious conviction that the only way the multiple periodicities of the universe are able to coexist in mutually supportive relationship is by orbiting in harmony with a common fundamental, associated with a divine motivating force of supreme power.

A person is unable to count the grains of sand falling in an hourglass, or track the moment to moment movement of a shadow across a sundial, but a clock is a counting and measuring device, powered by nature and working to a humanly quantifiable timescale independent of the activity taking place in relation to it, whether the action is marching, chanting, working, or dancing. Once a civilization possesses a mechanism to distinguish timing from activity, it has the conceptual basis for creating a time notation that can be adjusted to match the pace of real life activities and situations.

To conceive a music of multiple tempi, a composer requires an idea of tempo: not just a sense of time as constantly slipping away, but a time controlled and directed either by human activity or divine intelligence. There are two components of a sense of tempo: one, a perception of continuity or connectedness from one moment of awareness to the next, as for a melody, and two, a perception of consistency in the flow of time, associated with a uniform pulsation or beat. The evolution of western music notation from the time of Hucbald to the time of Monteverdi outlines a clear progression in the way time is perceived, from a starting-point of controlling the syllabic movement of a sung text from beginning to end, within the context of a recycling melodic shape; through to plainchant, articulating a text as a continuum of meaning unrelated to an external timeframe; finally to the *ars nova* concept of a music based on a notional clock time independent of the material articulated. The breakthrough, coinciding with the era of exploration of da Gama, Columbus, and Drake, enabled continuous movement in music to be conceived, mapped and navigated in relation to external coordinates of time and space. Only where external frames of reference are in place is it possible to imagine a music of multiple timescales working in harmony, like the turning gearwheels of a clock driven by a common weight.

Composing with mechanical musical instruments in mind changes how one thinks about time. Clockwork or gravity-powered mechanical instruments operate at a constant speed: they cannot in principle do normal expressive accents (hesitations), ornaments, or accelerandi or ritardandi (speeding up or slowing down) without running the risk of sounding broken down or dilapidated, which is how old musical boxes perform that have become worn and unfit. A composer of music for mechanical reproduction is bound to consider musical time and its emotional correlatives from an altered perspective. We observe this attitude to mechanical pulsation in arrangements of his own works by Haydn for mechanical organ, in Beethoven's "Moonlight" sonata for piano, and more recently in music for movies by twentieth-century composers from Honegger and Korngold to John Barry and John Williams, professionals who also have to work to clock time rather than in accordance with their natural impulses. Spurred on by the Cartesian doctrine of a universe driven by clockwork, and the human being as a machine, European inventors of the late eighteenth century applied their watchmaking and musical box skills to building a range of automata that imitated human actions, and which by implication could be said to imitate human consciousness. They were the forerunners of artificial intelligence research in the twentieth century. The generation of Goethe, Beethoven, Blake, and Coleridge was certainly aware of the implications for free will and human destiny of an industrial philosophy that regarded human thoughts and feelings as simply programmed responses to essentially mechanical drives.

Big Ben and the grandfather clock in the hall tick somberly and slowly, while the ormolu clock on the mantelpiece or alarm clock on the bedside table swing and tick at a more rapid pace. Faster or slower, all timepieces measure the same time passing at the same rate. That of course is what we mean by "keeping time," and therein lies the mystery. The different speeds at which human beings appear to live their lives (compared to giant redwood trees, insects, or goldfish) have no effect on the hours of daylight or the pace of universal time. For all these and other reasons music is an ideal forum for inquiring into the nature of time, the varieties of temporal experience, and their corresponding psychological or emotional associations. Among a number of indicators of such a philosophical objective in the work of a composer are: (1) a common pulsation for fast and slow tempi, encountered in Beethoven's "Moonlight" sonata for piano and Symphony No. 4; (2) spontaneous changes of pace and density within a uniform pulse structure, as in the *Eine kleine Nachtmusik* of Mozart, and movie scores by Hollywood composers; (3) a music of strictly invariant tempi, such as Bach's "Brandenburg" concertos and Messiaen's piano studies; and (4) a fluid melodic impulse offset by a rigid beat, as in the aria "Dido's Lament" by Purcell, or a waltz by Chopin.

That most performers of the Beethoven sonata, let alone their listeners, fail to get the message of mechanically geared tempi in classical western music is not our main problem. What matters is how to bring the intended opposition of free and mechanical tempi into clearer view, so that the three movements of the "Moonlight" sonata, or the three orchestras in Mozart's *Don Giovanni* are able to make the point that the same pulsation can cover a multitude of time experiences (as in the Beethoven) or differences in time management (as in the Mozart). To understand the task of harmonizing the tempi of all three Beethoven sonata movements to a common timescale attributes a philosophical interest in the nature of time to the composer and his contemporaries. The performer who recognizes a deliberate intention and purpose in Beethoven's paradoxical timing is persuaded into an interpretation intuitively more satisfying than treating tempo relations as trivial or optional. So in the first movement of the "Moonlight," for example, the unit pulse is expressed as a triplet, in the second movement the triplet becomes an accentual measure, again in triple time, the pulse falling on the downbeat, and in the breakneck last movement finale the identical pulse is subdivided in eights.

The same historical trend that produced the calliope, panharmonicon, and elaborate musical boxes for domestic use in the late eighteenth century, also invented the barrel organ of the street organ grinder, and the coin operated nickelodeon or player piano. Both instruments began life as pin cylinder programmed devices styled in the manner of a musical box. After the importation of new and stronger paper from China, these devices were adapted to play from perforated paper rolls. These allowed for the performance of musical works of longer duration, were simpler to manufacture, and allowed the purchaser to draw on a much larger repertoire. Music boxes of all kinds allowed the owners of such instruments (1) freedom of access to music at any time, (2) the advantage of not having to pay live musicians, and (3) guaranteed accuracy of performance (at least, as long as the drive mechanism was properly maintained).

Mechanical instruments also afforded the user unaccustomed control over the speed of performance, removing tempo from the judgment of the composer or artist, and allowing a performance to be pushed to extremes of speed and accuracy beyond the limitations of any living concert artist. In the interest of faster speeds of execution, piano-roll keyboard mechanisms preserved the classical fashion for a light and agile key response. The characteristically brittle fortepiano timbre of the Mozart era would survive in the cliché honky-tonk player piano of classic Western movies long after the classical keyboard had morphed into the heavyweight concert grand of the nineteenth-century idioms of Brahms and Tchaikovsky. The mechanical piano's lightness of touch and aesthetic of speed influenced the rise of a distinct breed of romantic era pianists and composers, from Chopin, through Liszt and Moszkowski, to Ravel, Scriabin, Busoni, Stravinsky, and even Boulez.

The very first paper voice recorders of Léon Scott had no governor or speed control. These devices were manually operated, not driven by weight like a clock. They were succeeded by a first generation of movie cameras and sound recording devices which were also manually rather than mechanically powered. Many decades were to elapse before either the record industry or the film industry could be persuaded to agree on standard speeds of sound and moving image recording and reproduction.

There is something enormously significant about so strange an omission at so particular a time, in the decades leading up to Einstein's special theory of relativity. It seems to say that the inventors and engineers who imagined and perfected these motion recording devices believed that the time information of human speech and actions was somehow embedded in the speech and actions themselves. These inventors appeared to have no concept of time flowing independently of human actions, and for that reason saw no necessity to ensure either that the speed of a recording was constant throughout the duration of the recording, or that it should be played back at the same speed as it had been recorded.

Aristotle's "things are not in time, time is in things" may be cited in justification of what we regard today as essential time control mechanisms. To record morse code and replay it at a different speed, which was Edison's original purpose in inventing the tinfoil phonograph, is one thing: when the information is in morse code, a change of speed simply changes the density of information. It is the same for a musical box, or a piano roll. But to apply the same reasoning to a recording of music, or the voice, is an obvious mistake. When a voice or music recording is accelerated, time itself is compressed: the pitch rises, and the pace of delivery rises to a gabble. The fact that inventors and audiences alike were initially unconcerned to ensure that the speed of music reproduction conformed to the speed at which it was recorded, tells us perhaps that the public enjoyed the thrill of superhuman speed in a reproduced performance, and did not complain as long as the music stayed in tune. At a more fundamental level, however, it suggests that the general public had no conception of time relative to performance, and no idea that the authenticity of recorded speech or music depended on it being reproduced at the same speed as it had been originally recorded.

That neither musical boxes nor player pianos change pitch as a consequence of varying in playback speed helps to explain the absence of strict time controls on early sound and vision recorders. All the same, many European philosophers and biologists of the mid- to late nineteenth century continued to view chronological time as an illusion and real time as a property embedded in the actions and metabolism of living things. A similar view persisted until well into the twentieth century, and is defended even today by some artists and philosophers. In other words, the idea prevailed that the correct tempo of a movie or piano roll performance somehow inhered in the performance itself, and not in the mechanical speed of a recording or playback device. It was not until the third decade of the twentieth century that manufacturers reached agreement on standard recording and playback speeds for movies and gramophone records. Curiously, the moment of industry-wide acceptance of standard frames of reference for time and motion in the entertainment world coincided with international acceptance of Einstein's general theory of relativity in the world of science, and recognition of the speed of light as a universal constant.

Though the rise of an art nouveau aesthetic of layered complexity and multiple tempi in the early decades of the early twentieth century—in the music of Berg, Schoenberg, Ravel, Debussy, and the Stravinsky ballets—might suggest a fashionable interest in relativity theory, perhaps a more prosaic reason is modern music's emergence from an era of chaotic and dynamic motion captured for the first time in photography, sound recording, and the movies. Picture postcards survive from the nineteenth century in which a sharply delineated townscape of buildings and telegraph poles is populated by blurred shapes and shadowy intimations of a ghostly and unstable human presence. Movie audiences a century ago tolerated the distortions of involuntary fast and slow motion because the effects were stimulating and gave a pleasing impression of dynamism in human and natural affairs (as they still do).

From the silent movie era to the nature documentaries of the thirties, the presentation of natural movement at unnaturally slow or high speeds (the growing plant, the slow-motion bullet, etc.) fed a public appetite for altered motion effects, both slower and faster than normal, of rushing floods, city traffic, pursuits, rioting crowds, and stampeding cattle, outwardly chaotic events that, when filmed from an elevated vantage point by D. W. Griffith, revealed coherence and pattern. The science of turbulence owes its existence to the silent movies. At the same time as American movie pioneers Griffith and Mayer were creating epic movies featuring images of crowd turbulence and multiple actions in real time, Charles Ives was creating music on a symphonic scale which sought in a similar way to depict the clash of simultaneous events on different timescales that had inspired him as a child.

POLYTONALITY

Polytonal music is a music that achieves a degree of separation into multiple parts by isolating them in different keys. The genre is associated with the French composer Darius Milhaud, whose miniature movements of the *Serenade* for orchestra combine up to six major keys at once. More frequently encountered is a music of two superimposed tonalities. A typical example of bitonal music is the *Duo Concertant* for violin and piano by Stravinsky.

The technical origins of polytonality can be traced back to Thomas Edison and his concept of the harmonic telegraph for increasing the capacity of telegraph lines by sending multiple messages in monotone morse code simultaneously along the same wire and assigning each sender a different frequency, the receiver filtering out all but the desired message with the aid of a mechanical reed sensor tuned to the appropriate frequency.

Decades later much the same principle was employed by RCA-Bell to control the amplitudes of multiple speaker arrays of the "Fantasound" surround-sound system, a technological breakthrough developed for the Disney movie *Fantasia*. The varying amplitudes of left, center, and right principal tracks were governed by separate tones of fluctuating intensity, optically recorded on a dedicated film strip, and synchronized with the three music tracks. In playback the fluctuating voltages of the control strip were filtered and routed to the appropriate audio channels to reproduce the appearance of movement in three dimensions. In an analogous process, radio allows the user to tune into the information specific to one carrier frequency out of a vast range of available transmissions. Shortwave radio manifests a real-world polyphony of tonalities and idioms that would inspire, even if it did not quite justify aesthetically, Cage's *Imaginary Landscape IV* for twelve radios, an experiment that did not quite work out as intended. Stockhausen's 1967 composition *Hymnen* could perhaps be classified as borderline polytonal on the ground that the national anthems acting as thematic signposts are largely tonal and easily identifiable against a broader radiophonic background. The composer's interest however is not so much polyphonic as contrapuntal, in the modulation of anthems in time, and composing transitions between them, in the manner of a pilgrimage from place to place.

Polytonality in the classical sense is a technique permitting the simultaneous exposition and discrimination of more than one melody in an otherwise rhythmically integrated and coherent musical structure. Rhythmically, the strands intermesh, but tonally, they are perceived as independent. Milhaud would go on to develop the idea of total independence of coincident melodies as a teacher of composition at Mills College, San Francisco, from 1940. His advocacy of an aesthetic of coincident but separate multiple strands was in tune with Ives, and may have assisted the rise of a similar aesthetic in a younger generation of composers including Cage, Henry Brant, and Mauricio Kagel. Since the art of soundtrack multitracking had been evolving continuously from the late 1930s to meet the increasingly sophisticated demands of radio and the movies, it may be closer to reality to attribute most of the impetus in this direction to actual experience of the media rather than divine inspiration.

Milhaud was a prolific composer and the power of his ideas on occasion seems to outrun his musical invention. His Op. 333 *Étude poétique* of 1954 deserves comment all the same as a serious and relatively coherent precursor of the "Happening" or Sonic Circus

Bernstein: "I Want to be in America"

Gershwin: "I Got Rhythm"

Burt Bacharach "Trains and Boats and Planes"

As a consequence of long exposure to mechanical piano rhythms such as ragtime, US composers have a flair for adapted polyrhythms that flow naturally. A medieval hemiola (3 against 2) is heard in Bernstein's song I Want to be in America *(top) from* West Side Story. *In* I Got Rhythm *Gershwin plays with 4 against 3. Burt Bacharach studied with Milhaud, a master of multiple layer music. In his song* Trains and Boats and Planes *Bacharach sets 5 against 3 and converts both to a lyrical swing rhythm in 4 time*

events associated with Cage and others in the 1950s and sixties. Inspired by encounters in Paris with *musique concrète*, an aesthetic of superimposed loops of melody of different duration recycling indefinitely, the *Étude* draws on radiophonic mixing techniques applied to tape recorded materials including a setting for mezzo-soprano and two alto saxophones of a poem "La Rivière endormie" by Claude Roy—a title suggestive of flow and timelessness—and four prerecorded Cadenzas for chamber octet of flute, clarinet, bassoon, trumpet, violin, viola, cello, and double bass. While the song setting is through-composed, each of the Cadenzas consists of eight instrumental parts repeating and recycling independently.[1] In one respect Milhaud's multi-layering technique could be said to

Stravinsky: *Requiem Canticles*

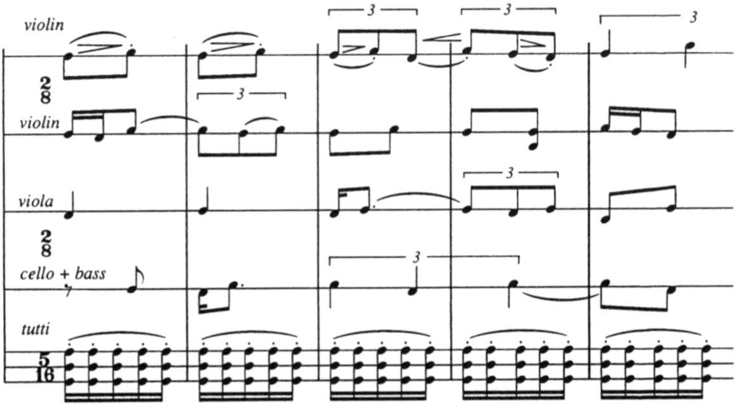

Multiple timelayers for strings in Stravinsky's Requiem Canticles *(1966)*

resemble the quintuple isorhythms of "Liturgie de Cristal" from Messiaen's *Quartet for the End of Time*. In a broader sense however Milhaud's concept looks ahead to Boulez's . . . *explosante–fixe* . . . in memory of Stravinsky, a rondeau originally sketched for chamber ensemble and electronics in 1971. Echoes of his former teacher and *musique concrète* are even detectable in Stockhausen's *Orchester-Finalisten* of 1994–96.

There are important differences all the same between Ives's and Milhaud's multipart music, Messiaen's isorhythmic compositions, and the multilayered orchestral music of Elliott Carter, Stockhausen, and others. The main difference is a relative absence of orthodox tonality of any kind in the later composers. However tonality makes an unexpected reentry in the descent phase of Stockhausen's rotorious *Helikopter-Streichquartett*, a sliding chord sequence to match the return of the musicians to earth.

Late Stravinsky is a rich source of small but perfectly formed studies in multiple time relations. It is as though, having subjected Stockhausen's *Gruppen* and *Zeitmasse* to detailed scrutiny, the Russian master has decided that notational exactness has its limits, both for the sake of the performer mastering the score, and given the uncertainties of musical performance in any circumstance. The schematic reproduced is from the *Requiem* Prelude, a transparent texture with the timbre of viols. Partial rhythms combining 3, 4, and 5, or 5, 6, and 7, are abundant in Stravinsky's scores after *Movements*. Outstanding among them are measures 283–87 for winds, culminating in a "fast rewind" for pizzicato violins and marimbaphone, in the scene "The Building of the Ark" from *The Flood*, the ingenious miniature *Canon* of 1966 on a theme from *Firebird*, and the "Libera Me" from the *Requiem Canticles*, in which the solo singers persevere in even quarter-notes over the inchoate parlando murmur of a chorus in the role of congregation.

Note

1. Darius Milhaud, *Étude Poétique* (MS) and "Konstruierte Musik." *Gravesaner Blätter* V (August 1956), 9–14.

TWENTY

A COCHLEAR IMPLANT

Spectral music is a cult term for a musical aesthetic based on timbre (tone-color) rather than harmonic progression. Music of timbre means that instead of singing or moving from note to note, or chord to chord, away from a home position and back to it, the singer or musician concentrates on varying the color of the same note, i.e. altering the timbre. Spectral music can be regarded as the outcome of a vocal tradition, rather than a natural outgrowth of instrumental music. The principle of varying the timbre is quite normal for a vocalist intoning words, since words in any language consist of linked sequences of spectra (formants, or bandwidths of heightened resonance) that vary from vowel to vowel, and syllable to syllable, and it is only possible to hear formant shifts and diphthongs with ideal clarity by restricting the voice tone to a monotone. In some cultures the monotone is produced mechanically by a jaw harp, and in others its function is taken by a drone. Since it is typically audited out of doors and at a distance, the relationship of melody line to drone in Scots bagpipe music is arguably analogous to the modulation of formant spectrum of a voiced tone.

Monotone chanting is associated with cultures throughout the world: Japan, the medieval orthodox liturgy (Ambrosian chant), Tibetan Buddhism, Gregorian chant, Central Asian and Hebridean mouth music, and jaw harp music from Africa to China, India, Indonesia, and the midwest. The jaw harp is a device inserted into the mouth to provide a constant twanging fundamental tone in place of a carrier tone from the larynx. Why anybody whould want to do this is an interesting question. In New Zealand Maori culture, a form of jaw harp was employed by young people of both sexes to transmit covert messages to the ear of one's beloved, in the guise of making innocent music. As a completely independent tone mechanism, the jaw harp is an anonymous substitute for the player's personal tone of voice, and therefore unidentifiable with the individual by anybody who happens to overhear, a useful security measure for lovers whose parents may well not approve. In addition to anonymity, the device is an energy-saver, freeing the musician from the draining task of voicing a constant tone after the fashion of a mouth musician. The jaw harp's constant drone provides a reliable (indeed, transferable) reference against which the formant resonances produced by changing the shape of the mouth cavity can be heard. On the evidence of a distinction being made between a fixed artificial mechanism responsible for the carrier frequency (the jaw harp), and a living mechanism for modulating the formant resonances to create meaning (the airways and tissues of the throat, mouth, and nose), clearly these early cultures were conscious of tone generation and modulation as functionally separate processes, and aware of speech as the modulation of an inflexible carrier tone by alteration of timbre by varying the cavity resonances of the vocal tract. Were it not already recognized as a musical instrument, a jaw harp would be open to interpretation as a speech enhancer, and certainly as an aid to teaching the proper incantation of a culturally significant ritual, which is as much about exact pronunciation as about singing in tune.

Along with anonymity (or impersonality) and transferability, the advantages of delegating the role of tone generator from a person to a separate instrument include conservation of energy, ability to sustain a performance beyond the duration of a breath, and potential for more elaborate ornamentation of the carrier tone. Most of all, the mechanism is a guarantee of objectivity, reliability, and consistency of intonation, since being inflexible in pitch, the instrument is more accurate in reproducing the partial tone or overtone resonances that correspond to the vowel formants of a spoken text. There is an echo of jaw harp tradition in the curious mnemonic of medieval plainchant that reduces the Latin text of the Doxology *Et in saecula saeculorum Amen* ("Glory be to the Father") to the string "e u o u a e." What makes it interesting as a memory aid is its manifest function as a visual reminder of the vowels and their audible tone colors.

Musical instruments and their "voices" can be passed from one generation to another and in that way ensure the uncorrupted continuity of sacred ritual within the extended life of the tribe. In the west that role is attached especially to Stradivari and Guarneri violins. It is no coincidence that these instruments are valued for their voicelike qualities and beauty of tone. Here again the values of an instrument over the living custodian are reliability, permanence, and transferability of voice to another executant. These advantages are offset by a loss of intelligibility. At best, intonation can only handle vowels, not consonants. Loss of consonants is loss of the elements of speech that give definition and meaning to individual words. When only timbre and melody are preserved, it is likely to lead over time to a loss of cultural memory of the "speech" content the instrument was designed to perpetuate. When a text is assigned to a musical instrument, over time inevitably the melody takes on a life of its own as an abstract shape, and any memory of the original meaning is lost. In *Art and Illusion* Ernst Gombrich observes the same tendency for stylized formulae to mutate over time into abstract stereotypes, a process exemplified with particular vividness in the coinage of Roman Britain.[1] Over generations of repetition the textual references of melodies originally intended to preserve the actual words and inflection of a speaker's voice are worn away, leaving abstract melody shapes of purely symbolic meaning. Similar processes are traced in the evolution of written alphabets from relatively intelligible pictograms to abstract shapes, and in the evolution of number systems from ancient Egypt and Mesopotamia. There is however a residue of significance to be read into the high cultural value attached in the west to famous violins, a trait implicitly assigning a higher value to tone of voice than the information content of what is said. The same bias in favor of tone of voice as an authenticator of meaning underlies the eighteenth-century preoccupation with the power of rhetoric, and survives to the present day in the significance attached to the camp accent and mannerisms of the British stereotype of the Thespian actor.

To *compose* spectral music, as distinct from cultivating a music that is spectral in implication, implies a prior conception of tone quality or timbre as a variable rather than a fixture. Tone color as a steady state, and timbre (the acoustic consistencies of an individual voice or instrument across its range) are normally understood as distinct and indivisible *qualia* sharing a common source and modulated in an identical manner. The ability to distinguish vowel timbre (what somebody is saying) from tone of voice (the person saying it) is acquired in infancy as children learn to modulate and exploit their own voices as instruments of command and control. Though played for laughs by Shakespeare in *Coriolanus*, Menenius's tale of the rebellion of the organs of the body against the belly, for all its scatological connotations, is a lesson in critical deconstruction of an organized body and its effects on corporate health. In order to rebel against the belly, the other organs are required to become aware of themselves as independent agents, a major leap of faith for service personnel. In taking action to assert their specialist functions, and assigning separate and equal value to each one, the organs imagine themselves to be "empowered" to rebel against one of their number, ignoring the relationship of mutual support that binds them all into a functioning system. The lesson of Menenius is a variation of the Garden of Eden myth, which is also about the painful consequences of perceiving an organic whole as a collection of parts, and using that perception to act selectively, assume control, and disrupt the system. The same morality informs ancient and modern myths of humankind creating artificial life, from the Golem to Frankenstein, via Hollywood fantasies *Terminator*, *Blade Runner*, and *Robocop*, through to *The Wizard of Oz*. In all of these tales an inorganic creature is assembled by a human creator out of foreign materials, and every story carries the identical moral that it is wrong, based on a perception of the body as a collection of separate parts, to imagine that it is possible to reconstruct a being out of separate parts and then expect it to act with integrity or conscience.

Building musical unity from separately manufactured components is all the same the subtext of perhaps the greatest invention in western musical history, the grand organ. A significant name, *organ*. What the jaw harp and mouth music are able to achieve within the limitations of the vocal tract, the organ is designed to effect by combinations of pipe resonances set in vibration and controlled by a uniform airflow. The pipe organ evolved to its essential form over more than a thousand years. That its development as a mechanism for the synthesis of complex timbres was sanctioned by

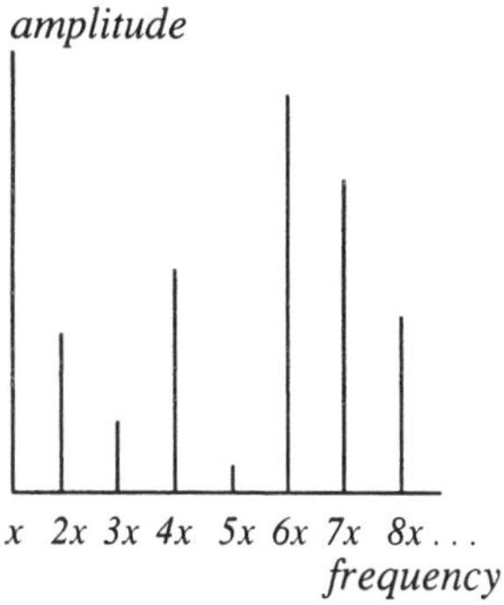

Initial spectrum

Spectrum A

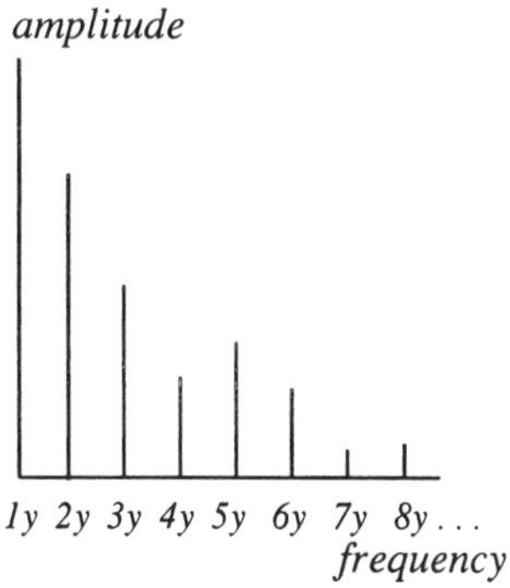

Transformed spectrum

Spectrum B

the church is an indication that the controversial implications of creating a mechanism to imitate the human voice had been debated and were justified doctrinally.

As a development of contemporary music, spectral music is perceived as a specifically French alternative to electronic and serial music, emphasizing the expressive implications of timbre in contrast to the dynamic implications of Austro-German atonality. Among French composers the trend emerges with Messiaen's organ music after 1951 which experiments with unorthodox combinations of mixture stops to produce strange new timbres. The aesthetic of timbre was adopted in 1952 by Jacques Lasry and François and Bernard Baschet, whose *Structures sonores*, "sound sculptures" created in vinyl, metal, and Plexiglas, produced a limited range of resonant tones and noises evocative of space travel. The same aesthetic of shimmering *frisson* would reemerge in the late 1970s as computer generated sound by Jean-Claude Risset, Andrew Gerzso, and Pepino di Guigno, in hybrid live-electronic works by Boulez that include *Répons*, *. . . explosante-fixe . . .*, and *Anthèmes 2*.

In spectral music every sound is defined as a simple harmonic spectrum, after the theory of Joseph Fourier (another Frenchman). Applied to vibration analysis, and from there to music synthesis, Fourier's insight that any waveform is capable of reduction to a spectrum of sine waves has led to the curious misconception that sounds in nature can be represented as amplitude variations of a universal harmonic spectrum of sine tones, and in consequence that

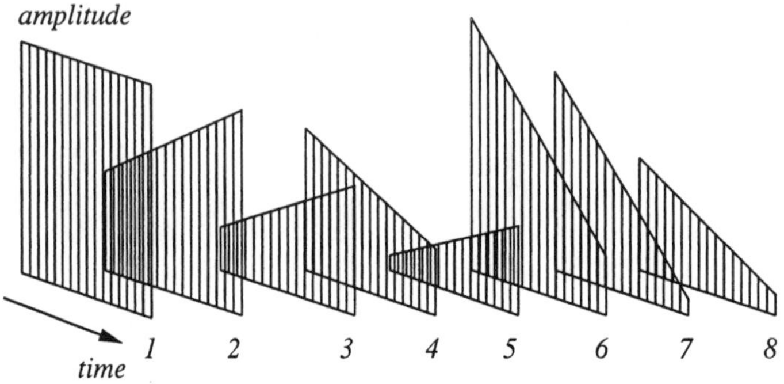

Transformation of spectrum A to spectrum B by interpolation

every sound, considered as a sample spectrum, has the potential to be transformed into any other sound by a process of interpolation between amplitudes. The flaw is in confounding a waveform and its analysis with the definition of a sound and its synthesis. It implies that all sounds are static, whereas we know that all are dynamic by nature, and that they evolve in accordance with the structure and material of the resonating body. The finesse of explaining away the difficulty by pretending that a sound can be accurately characterized as an initial set of starting conditions exploits the Cartesian fallacy (another Frenchman) of a world consisting of states adjacent in space and time, and not a continuum. The same fallacy is further reinforced by the movies' representation of motion in time and space as a succession of discrete timeframes (more Frenchmen: the Lumière brothers and Étienne Marey). An iconic example of spectrum interpolation is audible in Jonathan Harvey's *Mortuos plango, vivos voco*, in which the live sound of a boy's voice is transformed, with the aid of Xavier Rodet's "Chant" software, into the dead timbre of a bell.

The larger objection to computer-generated spectral music is that it all sounds metallic, which is not only unnatural but inevitable given its initial terms of reference, defining a timbre in effect as an instantaneous microphone sample of a spectrum located in a sound field that is essentially anechoic. The metallic quality of computer-generated timbres, by turn matt and lustrous, more antiseptic than real, persists even when the sounds are transformed by frequency inversion. The limited reality and static quality of such sounds is a direct expression of the limitations of underlying theory. What is almost as interesting to a music historian is the persistence of the theory, which reaches back beyond Fourier to the voice timbre experiments of Perotin's *Sederunt principes* in the twelfth century (there you go, another Frenchman), to the theory of timbre synthesis embodied in the grand organ.

A cochlear implant is a crude miniature electrophonic device to restore hearing to patients whose inner ear mechanism is damaged but whose cochlea and neural pathways are still functioning. At the time of writing, the surgical implant receives acoustic information from an external microphone and feeds it to eight locations on the basilar membrane corresponding to frequency bands from low to high. Although not designed from a music-theoretical perspective, the implant inevitably incorporates a primitive theory of music as well as a theory of hearing. It implies that even though the brain perceives acoustic images and processes as integral objects in an acoustic field, what the binaural hearing process is actually doing is reconciling time, phase, and amplitude relationships arising from duplicate neural discharges at different frequency bands.

Musicians recognize a musical score as a graphic display of notes representing sounds organized on the page in a vertical order more or less corresponding to pitch, from the highest voices at the top of the treble stave to the lowest on the bass stave. That layout convention is all very well. It corresponds to a distribution of real instrumental voices and is easy to follow. But such a schema does not necessarily correspond to what a listener actually hears, or indeed, to the organization of instrumental qualities a composer may intend. The raw, unprocessed sound picked up by the ears in their capacity as microphones consists of a largely undifferentiated amalgam of overlapping multiple spectra, even though a listener may consciously hear the same as a collection of different instruments sounding together. If a line feed is led from a microphone in front of an orchestra to an oscilloscope, making the fluctuating voltage visible as a modulated waveform, what is being seen is the total sum of a great many waveforms and their reflections, a virtually incomprehensible oscillation in which at best a periodic rhythm might just be discernible.

What this undifferentiated waveform conveys is a dynamic image of the signal normal ears, and the microphones of cochlear implant patients, actually receive. The totality of sound received by the ears passes to a miracle of biological design, the inner ear, in which this combined waveform is literally stretched to form a continuous spectrum of frequency response in a sealed, fluid filled, tapering spiral tube enclosed by a conductive membrane and held rigid within a bony labyrinth, the cochlea. The composite audio signal received at the outer ear is normally transferred to this fluid filled structure as a sequence of impulses by a miniaturized percussive mechanism which might well adopt the name of *le marteau sans maître*. Since musical sounds are periodic by nature, a complex signal passing through the middle ear is reduced to a pattern of impulses that varies in periodicity and intensity according to frequency. The periodicity or repetition rate of a given frequency layer within a complex signal generates a pattern of pressure peaks at a frequency-specific location within the cochlea, and that location is served by dedicated neural sensors firing in synchronization.

The recording studio equivalent of an inner ear is a third-octave filter. When the sound of a full symphony orchestra passes by way of a third-octave filter, a listener is able to monitor the level of activity in relatively fine layers within the total bandwidth, in much the same way perhaps as a surgeon is able to examine a computer tomograph of a patient's body cross-section by cross-section. Whereas the conventional layering of a musical score isolates the actions of specific instruments, the third-octave filter isolates all of the available information from all instruments within a selected bandwidth, and not just a single instrument or group. Virtually all instruments of music generate a range of frequencies from low to high, and brighter timbres such as brass, strings, and metal percussion are able to extend that range beyond the upper threshold of human hearing.

In 1979 a pilot study was undertaken by Vlad Naslas, a student at Surrey University, to examine whether the spectrum of a composer's orchestration might conform to an individual "tone of voice" analogous to a personal speaking voice. Underlying the study was the practical assumption that composers "listen inwardly" as they compose, and that their natural preferences in instrumental balance and combination would tend therefore to be influenced by personal sensitivities, since every person's hearing has a different

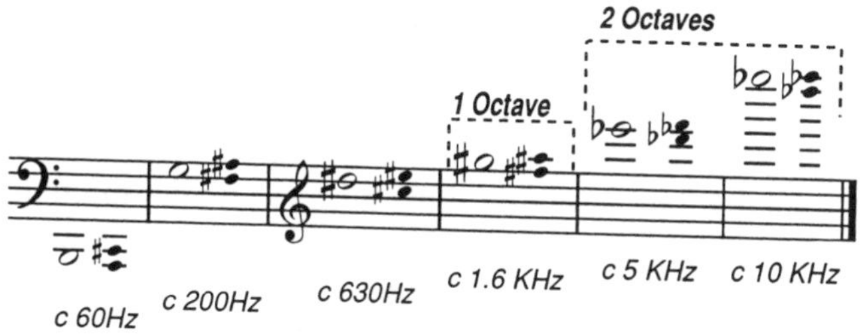

Approximate bandwidths and center frequencies of analyses of Bach, Beethoven, and Stravinsky orchestrations by bandwidth

frequency profile. There is no catch-all standard. A person's "tone of hearing" is affected in a number of ways by factors including age, acuity of hearing, the shape and size of the outer ears, individual stature, and the frequency centers of a person's native language.

Naslas selected three examples of orchestral music, by J. S. Bach, Beethoven, and Stravinsky. The first movements of Bach's Brandenburg Concerto No. 2 in F, Beethoven's Symphony No. 8 in F, and the Symphony in C by Stravinsky are of broadly comparable duration, orchestration, character, tempo, and density. Recordings of the three movements were transferred to tape and analyzed for activity and intelligibility using a studio third-octave filter at six different third-octave frequency bandwidths centered on frequencies ranging from 60 hertz in the bass to 10,000 hertz, near the upper extreme of human hearing, and well beyond the notation range of the highest pitch instruments.

By comparing the cumulative orchestration across the range of bandwidths it was possible to form an impression of the distribution of total information at different bandwidths and evaluate the degree of internal coherence between bandwidths of the same movement. The exercise aimed to identify areas of potential difference that might relate either to the composer's manner of orchestration, to the historical period (baroque, classical, modern), or to a personal center of attraction within the audible spectrum.

This may well have been the first study of its kind. A similar but inconclusive study of vocoder recordings of spoken translations of the same English text in various languages, had been undertaken by Bell Labs researchers in the 1940s in an attempt to determine centers of activity and zones of attraction specific to different languages, an exercise hampered to some extent by a technical ceiling of 4,000 hertz in the vocoder recordings.[2]

Like visible light emerging from the infrared (which we cannot see, but can feel as heat) and passing through the spectrum to disappear into the ultraviolet (which we likewise cannot see, but which gives the skin a tan), so the range of audible frequencies also emerges from a subaudio domain responding to the body's internal rhythms, passes into the range of music and speech, and discernible pitch through to 4,000 hertz, into an ultrasound region in which a perception of absolute pitch dissolves into a range of tone qualities synesthetically identified with brightness, crispness, harshness, etc. The same processes that allow a listener to distinguish the vowels [a] or [o] from [ee] or [oo] also identify the characteristic tone color of a flute as being different from an oboe, and a violin from a soprano saxophone. Extremes of audible range, where hearing is less sensitive to frequency, are typically occupied by percussion of indistinct pitch, for example bass drum, cymbals, and triangle. By analogy, the role of the drummer in a rock band is to play consonants to the vowel melodies of vocalists and guitars.

When a recording of orchestral music is filtered into separate frequency bands, the global sound material in each band is audited as a mass and not as distinct instruments. This is because when we listen to music, a totality of sound information is received all at once. It is the brain matching and integrating left-ear and right-ear inputs that enables a listener to identify different components of a complex signal as recognizable voices or musical instruments, and locate them in space. The matching process is harder to achieve for limited bandwidths. At the lowest bandwidth, for example, there is nothing in principle to distinguish a bass drum from a bassoon or a double bass: all are melded together in a pattern of bumps. In the midrange corresponding to the tone of a normal speaking or singing voice, different instruments are easier to identify because we have more experience. Above the upper tone threshold of 4,000 hertz, a listener is mostly aware of an indistinct noise. The physiological reasons for these frequency-related associations are well documented. What is not so well known is the functional role of these zones in auditory cognition.

FREQUENCY ANALYSIS OF MUSIC BY BANDWIDTH ACTIVITY

Vlad Naslas

The basic aim of this project was to seek preliminary answers to the question "Can the examination of discrete layers in the frequency spectrum tell us anything about the inherent characteristics of a piece of music?" If so, then can the process be taken a step further and the information used to discover new meanings in the music that would otherwise be hidden to an intuitive investigation? Can the psychological effect of music be correlated with the activity of these various frequency bands?

The first movements of three works were chosen: the Brandenburg Concerto No 2 in F by J. S. Bach; Symphony No. 8 in F by Beethoven; and the Symphony in C by Stravinsky. The chosen compositions mark important phases in the evolution of western music. The movements are of similar orchestral weight and comparable length.

The method used was to take a signal from a gramophone record and then pass it through a third-octave filter. The output from the filter was recorded on a tape and also on a graph using a pen recorder, for visual monitoring. Third-octave bands around six frequency values were extracted, centered on 60, 200, 630, 1,600, 5,000, and 10,000 hertz.

The following results were obtained from listening to the tape. What we were mainly looking for is evidence of particular kinds of information contained in the various bands.

BACH
Brandenburg Concerto No. 2 in F

60 hertz This band mainly seemed to respond to the tonic F. Although it sounds very muddy, the basic meter and structure are just about discernible.

200 hertz Only a small range of about four notes are clearly exposed, but definite contrapuntal lines are heard. Meter and rhythm are quite clear and the music is surprisingly even and full in this low band. The harmony can just be made out.

630 hertz A wider range of notes, but no definite orchestral coloring. Instruments enter the range and then disappear in a continuous criss-cross fashion. This probably reflects the strongly contrapuntal nature of the music.

1.6 kilohertz Woodwind are very prominent here. Little else seems to be going on.

5 kilohertz Apart from the presence of strings and trumpet harmonics, the sound is decidedly empty.

10 kilohertz This bandwidth is picking up the accents of every instrument. The graph showed definite tendencies to map out the subjective loudness of the music. The probable explanation is that when instruments play loud or accented they project a higher proportion of high harmonics.

BEETHOVEN

Symphony No. 8 in F, first movement

60 hertz Although the music is in the key of F like the Bach, this band seems to have a completely different feel. Very little can be made out and certainly even the tonic Fs that we would expect to hear do not appear.

200 hertz This band is very confused, and the music comes in uneven blocks. It tells us very little about key or rhythm. The meter is much less well defined.

630 hertz Once again no particular instrument dominates, but a greater number of instruments weave in and out of the band than in the Bach. There is less of a block feeling than before, and the key can just about be made out.

1.6 kilohertz This is again woodwind territory, but unlike the Bach there is much more happening besides. The strings are more prominent. The sound is much less static (or block-like) and there is a greater sense of movement. Only at this level has the music taken on any real meaning (compared to the lower bands).

5 kilohertz Once again the strings are prominent, and there is less trumpet than in the Bach. There is a curious absence of other information.

10 kilohertz Unfortunately the recording did not contain much signal in this bandwidth, but perhaps this is meaningful in itself because the music may not rely so much on high frequency definition.

STRAVINSKY

Symphony in C, first movement

60 hertz There is absolutely nothing meaningful in this band. We have plenty of signal, but the ear just cannot detect where it is coming from or what purpose it serves.

200 hertz Only unrecognisable sounds, which cannot be associated with instrumental timbres. There is a curious rhythmic content, but it is definitely not a reflection of the meter of the music, that is, what we are hearing is a hidden rhythm. The key is very indistinguishable.

630 hertz Unlike the two previous examples we cannot hear particular instruments weaving in and out. What we hear sounds musical, but it does not seem to come from the same music. This band would make a much more meaningful entity by itself than the other two. It has a rhythm of its own, with a meter just happening somewhere in the background.

1.6 kilohertz This band is not as wind-orientated as previous examples. The strings are more prominent. The music makes very good sense harmonically and rhythmically.

5 kilohertz Unlike previous examples, strings and wind are on more equal terms. The texture is even more transparent. There is not much brass to be heard, but Stravinsky tends to use brass just for highlighting anyway.

10 kilohertz This is much more irregular than the Bach, although the subjective loudness does come into it again.

From the results obtained, the activity patterns revealed in the chosen works of music do appear to reflect idiomatic trends that one would expect these three pieces of music to show.

The Bach, even though it is the most contrapuntal, is made up of definite layers, resting firmly on a strong harmonic and metric bass. The 200 hertz band is thus full of information and meaning, and even at 60 hertz we can make out elements of the music. In the Beethoven we need to go to at least 630 hertz, and in the Stravinsky up to 1.6 kilohertz to obtain the equivalent information.

We see that the Bach concerto defines its operational layers (1.6 kilohertz for winds, 5 kilohertz for strings) and mainly sticks to them without much interpenetration. Beethoven is more flexible and Stravinsky even more, in that his instruments are free to appear anywhere at any time thus creating the strange effect at 630 hertz whereby a pattern is created by viewing the whole at a different angle, as it were.

It is significant that the 10 kilohertz curve, which as mentioned earlier appears to follow the accent distribution, is very regular in the Bach, and highly irregular, by comparison, in the Stravinsky.

The project shows quite clearly that the examination of discrete layers in the frequency spectrum can tell us something about the inherent characteristics of a piece of music. A more sophisticated and thorough approach is needed to provide detailed theoretical models, but the indications are promising. It would be interesting to apply this technique to other forms of

> music where the message itself is different, to see if there is any correlation between the message and the pattern of information transmitted within the various frequency bands.

Orchestral works are hard to audit analytically as spectra in the way a gong or bell timbre can be heard as a combination of distinct partials. Nevertheless, what this research by Vlad Naslas suggests, and the theory and practice of cochlear implants also implies, is that at a primitive level of brain function the world of sound is monitored in frequency strata, each of which conveys information of a particular kind: rhythm, color, dynamics. It is from the integration of such patterns of information across the range of frequency bands that an impression of a total sound field is acquired. Perhaps the closest examples of such a type of organization in western music are the "tone color melodies" of Webern.

We associate small instruments with higher pitch and large instruments with lower pitch, likewise small speakers ("tweeters") in a hifi system with the upper extreme, and large ("woofers") with bass and sub-bass frequencies, longer wavelengths which demand more power.

That the resonator of a musical instrument can be too small for its ostensible range of pitches was shown by Jan Schouten in 1940.[3] Schouten filtered violin tones into frequency bands and was surprised to discover that the wavelength of the fundamental tone and nominal pitch of the instrument, corresponding to the length of the string, was extremely weak, indeed all but inaudible. His remarkable discovery indicated two things: first that the resonant cavity of the violin was too small to accommodate the fundamental wavelength of the lowest string; second, the fact that it is all the same audible had to mean that it is generated as a consequence of the higher harmonics vibrating in step at a periodicity corresponding to the fundamental, and perceived as the lower tone by default. A third intriguing implication asking for further inquiry is that the violin may therefore knowingly have been invented in the first place as an instrument of coloration rather than as a leading voice.

In practical terms it means that when a violinist is recorded playing a firm steady tone on the open G string, the fundamental frequency can be filtered out electronically and the listener will not notice any change in pitch, or alteration in timbre. A more extreme proof is audible if the violin is exchanged for a *pochette* or dancing-master's kit, a miniature instrument that plays like a violin but sounds like a bumblebee. Schouten's discovery of upper partial integration as a determinant of pitch perception explains how it is possible for a listener to recognize voices and music on the limited bandwidth of a portable radio or telephone. Coherence of upper frequency information is perceived as low frequency activity and presence. The effect is like hearing music performed at first in the same room, and then from outside: the music remains audible, but appears thinner and weaker.

Notes

1. E. H. Gombrich, *Art and Illusion: A Study in the Psychology of Pictorial Representation* 5th edition. Oxford: Phaidon, 1991, 64–65.
2. "Foreign Language Interests." In Ralph K. Potter, George A. Kopp, and Harriet Green Kopp, *Visible Speech.* New York: Dover Publications, 1966, 343–75.
3. Jan F. Schouten, "The Perception of Pitch." *Philips Technical Review* Vol. 5 No. 10 (1940), 286–294.

TWENTY-ONE

SERIALISM

Serialism (sometimes called *total serialism*) is a postwar development in musical thinking associated with the European avant-garde of Boulez and Stockhausen, with electronic music, and with the influential periodical *die Reihe*. It is often cited as an example of extreme determinism in music, arising from developments in science up to and including the Second World War of 1939–1945, and representing a European way of thinking at an opposite remove from the improvisatory and indeterminist trends in new music associated with American fifties jazz and the New York avant-garde of Cage, Feldman, Brown, and Wolff. At a time when American jazz was promoting an aesthetic of free improvisation and the American composer Aaron Copland was attempting, in his music and in his written criticism, to make classical music more accessible to the general public, serialism in the sense articulated by the authors of *die Reihe* was perceived as high intellectualism, elitist and authoritarian. More to the point, however, serialism coincided with the rapid rise of information science, artificial intelligence, and set theory in the United States, developments in postwar cybernetics arguably even more intellectual than European serialism.

Serialism is often mentioned in the same context as Schoenberg's twelve-tone method, a mistake arising from the term "series" being loosely employed as a synonym for a note-row in twelve-tone music. The difference between twelve-tone music and serialism was vigorously asserted by the serialists themselves, and with spectacular finality by Boulez in his 1952 manifesto "Schoenberg est mort" (Schoenberg is dead) declaring that Schoenberg's method was obsolete, that it perpetuated the romantic notion of the primacy of the theme, and that it applied only to melody and harmony, leaving time relations, tone color, dynamics, and other variables of expression unaccounted for. That the composer had continued to compose "neoclassical" works such as the Op. 31 *Variations for Orchestra* in the twelve-tone method was proof enough, according to Boulez, that for all its originality and importance in breaking with conventional tonality, Schoenberg's method ultimately did not go far enough.

The published writings on serialism and its aesthetic by Boulez, Stockhausen, and Herbert Eimert betray little awareness of the history of serial thinking, other than genuflecting to Webern's constructivist purity and attachment to magic squares, in particular the Latin acrostic

S A T O R
A R E P O
T E N E T
O P E R A
R O T A S

—which while of a piece with Webern's training in renaissance music under Guido Adler, and doctoral thesis on the music of Heinrich Isaac, does not itself add up to much.[1] Fifty years on, it is clear that the serial agenda was largely directed by political interests outside music, in instrument manufacturing, language, and information science, inquiring into the possible applications of a science of language to research in artificial intelligence and voice recognition by computer. Studios for electronic music in Cologne, and computer music at the University of Illinois, were set up with government assistance as research posts in speech science: at Illinois, to study the deep structure of speech melody and the grammar and syntax of simple songs, and in Cologne from 1952, to focus with particular emphasis on the syllabic repertoire and connecting rules of speech. Musicians were chosen for the task not because they were speech experts or information scientists, and certainly not on account of their political views, but because they had the best ears, and because music was considered by those in authority to be an expression of speech in its most abstract and essential form.

Sadly for conspiracy theorists, the study of music in relation to speech as an abstract determinant of meaning, personality, and cultural identity, is far from new and certainly not a cold war invention.

Some of the earliest studies in this area come from the ancient Greek writers, in particular Aristoxenus. The tetrachord and theory of temperaments were developed as formulae of speech intonation by which the Greek philosophers sought to classify the expressive and personality traits of speech in order to understand the intentions of diplomatic and trading partners of barbarian tribes whose languages were unfamiliar to them. The implications of such a science extended beyond intertribal relations to the diagnosis and treatment, on the evidence of their speech, of individuals whose states of mind had come under the influence of malign spirits.

For a science of speech and intonation to progress, speech itself had to be anatomized into a repertoire of distinct sounds, and the sounds classified. Such a process is an inevitable consequence of the development of a written alphabet of the western type, though perhaps not quite so inevitable among cultures employing pictograms, such as ancient Egyptian and Chinese civilizations.

By medieval times European science had developed to a point where a limited symbolic language for the pronunciation of Latin was available. This symbolic language is still in use as *neumata* or plainchant notation, from which modern accents, diacriticals, and punctuation marks are derived, and from which by another route western music notation is also descended.

Throughout the seventeenth and eighteenth centuries, philologists across Europe, and as far away as China and Japan, pursued the holy grail of a primeval or original speech, in order to rediscover how to pronounce ancient writings of cultural importance. These scholars were recognizing for the first time that without a clear understanding of how their language was originally spoken, and with what emphases and inflections, the meaning of surviving ancient texts could not be known with certainty, and might indeed have become corrupted or lost. In western Europe this scholarly and historical inquiry was accompanied by a burgeoning public interest in the cultural messages of contemporary regional dialects, their history and meaning. It brought into being the standard joke about the Englishman, the Scotsman, and the Irishman who, faced with an identical situation, are made to respond in words and actions that identify their national characters and embedded cultural priorities. Musicians and publishers bought into the folk music revival as an aspect of the identity politics of the time. Italian and French opera, especially the volatile Italian genre, was cultivated in England and across Europe as a suitable medium for a quasi-scientific examination of classical, hence archetypal character types and relationships presented in controlled dramatic situations: male against female, older and younger, aggressive and passive, and so on.

A PERILOUS JOURNEY

The most obvious objection to serial music is that it is incoherent and fragmented. In place of themes and melodies and harmony, the music presents to the listener as a scatter of random data points without apparent connection.

This is as if to say that the conventional music with which we are most comfortable is continuous like a journey or a routine; that the pleasure we take in it arises from a secure sense of controlled movement within a recognizable landscape, and sense of arrival once we reach the end.

These primal anxieties toward serial music are very ancient and very real. They tap into the old functions of music in primitive culture, to aid memory, to coordinate movement, and to maintain confidence in the execution of routine tasks.

Consider the hunter-gatherer out hunting, or the traveler (say, Little Red Riding Hood) going from home to another place by way of the woods, or anybody on the highway on a bicycle or in a car. In all of these cases a journey through time is a journey into the relatively unknown. The hunter-gatherer and Little Red Riding Hood are on the alert for wild beasts, and the driver or cyclist is looking out for traffic coming in the opposite direction.

A person venturing into unfamiliar territory looks out for landmarks or signs to navigate by. Part of the point of being a hunter or making a journey is to be as unobtrusive as possible: you do not want to become the target of a highway policeman or wild animal. What this implies is that the journey is played out in a series of encounters with landmarks or signs, people passing by, or prey. These events are momentary impacts that guide the traveler toward a destination and are not intended to divert the traveler from a chosen path. If a farmer takes a dog to round up his sheep in hill pastures, or a hunter takes a dog along on the hunt, the dog is there as a silent companion on the journey, to bark only when necessary. A dog that barked continuously would not be of much use. Barking is a form of signposting. The art of barking effectively is of suddenly making a noise without previously being noticed.

The nursery rhyme as a journey: "Jack and Jill" sung to the harmonics of a monochord in C. Harmonics 4 – 10 are signposts on the journey up the hill and down again. However harmonic 7 is a "false note" and is substituted by the note A. The words of the rhyme that fall on the "false note" — "broke his crown" and "mend his head" — connote a painful experience

Learning a song, like learning to read, is a kind of journey, but one in which letters and notes are the signposts. The song "Jack and Jill" is especially interesting, because it follows the harmonics of an open string. The message of the rhyme is about stumbling on the journey and getting a bump on the head. The subtext of the message, however, is about avoiding the seventh harmonic, a false note: hence, take care what signposts you follow, if you want to avoid getting hurt or being led astray.

In normal life human activity is largely silent. Personal silence allows us to attend to the world at large and monitor what we are doing from the incidental sounds our actions make. Attending to the sounds of the world at large is a relaxing, even philosophical occupation, provoking the listener to make sense of an environment of intermittent and more or less chaotic signals, some of which are continuous and easily located, like a waterfall or stream, but most of which are momentary and uncertain.

A journey without encounters would not be a real journey. Also, most encounters in a journey are by definition transitory and unexpected: we deal with them as they occur, acknowledge them, use them, or evade them, as they pass by. A journey is not the same as a procession. In a journey other people are going in the opposite direction—meaning, they are coming from the place you are going toward. In a primitive sense, for that reason, they are coming from a location in your immediate future, and are headed toward a location in your immediate past. So one of the indications to look out for in passing traffic is of impending disaster. If everyone you encounter is hurrying by in panic, the signs are not good.

Because serial music in general and pointillist music in particular deal with transitory phenomena, it will tend to arouse the same alarm responses as an experience of high-speed traffic racing by in the opposite direction, with horns blaring and headlights flashing. The appropriate response, as for a hunter-gatherer, is to stay calm and observe any consistencies in the direction and pattern of flow. When Handel was asked, late in life, to compose music for a park exhibition of the Royal Fireworks, he could easily have produced a baroque equivalent of Tchaikovsky's *1812 Overture*, the standard accompaniment, complete with cannon fire, to Fourth of July celebrations in the United States. Today firework displays are timed to the second, but the eighteenth century experience of airborne detonations was exciting, random, and dangerous. Handel's *Music for the Royal Fireworks* is designed to be performed simultaneously with a firework display, and to reassure the watching crowd by sending out strong signals, and matching detonations on multiple drums, that are in control and demonstrate leadership.

THE PARAMETERS OF SERIAL MUSIC

Serialism, unlike Schoenberg's method of composing with twelve notes related only one with another, was intended to take organization all the way. Be advised that a series is not a row but a sequence of terms forming a scale of values (the modes of Messiaen's *Mode de valeurs* are not series but "rows"). The music of Webern was embraced by the serialists because of evidence of serial thinking in the domains of tone color (instrumentation), attack (legato, staccato, accents etc.), and dynamics (*pp, p, mp, mf, f, ff*), in works such as the *Symphony* and the *Piano Variations* Op. 27. The aesthetic of serialism envisaged by the generation of Boulez was intentionally abstract, not music as entertainment involving melody and harmony illustrating emotions and telling stories to please an audience, but rather music as a kind of science, or coded message, or even a kind of alchemy, a discipline of methodically working under laboratory conditions to discover new elements and how to combine them. In this regard serialism turns away from the musical tastes of nineteenth-century bourgeois romanticism and assumes once again the mantle of the Enlightenment artist like Goethe, a poet and visionary who was also a self-professed scientist.

According to American specialists, the order-relationships of twelve-tone music are *numbers signifying pitches*, while for others (including Schoenberg and Stravinsky) the ordering is essentially intervallic: of ratios between consecutive pitches. In traditional music we understand a theme as a shape able to be transposed at will into a different key. The internal contradictions of postbaroque music have to do with recognizing that the intervals of a particular scale are in fact unequal, hence a modulation or transposition of key implies subtle alterations of intervallic tensions within a theme and its associated harmonies. These perceived *changes in nature* have persisted from the era of Frescobaldi, who employed meantone temperament, to the time of Chopin, who employed a piano tuned in a version of just intonation that favored certain exotic keys while making others unusable. Even J. S. Bach, who promoted his own compromise system, based loosely on Werckmeister, found the key of D minor hard to get on with, on account of some ugly and prominent major thirds. The violin family, with long fingerboards and absence of frets, was invented in part to allow players to adjust the tuning of every harmony to the best possible consonance, rather than be bound to the perhaps conflicting ratios of a keyboard tuned in advance to a scale of fixed pitches.

In the context of the atomic age, a new era of mutually assured destruction, the rise of serialism can be read in part as signaling a determination to embrace an international language of music, and rid art music of the familiar Napoleonic connotations of nationalism and heroic sacrifice that had led nations to colonize and conquer the world at will in the name of progress. In simple terms, the aim was to create a music of facts and to discover a different set of values, in a musical language of functional design pared down to universal bare essentials. Despite its proponents' outward show of disdain for neoclassicism and its connotations of irrational adherence to tradition and national pride, the new serialism was clearly an aesthetic of objectivity and manifestly classical in spirit. As art and science crossed national boundaries, so music should be released from any political obligation to bolster partisan ideologies.

On the other hand, the nuclear age had ushered in an awareness of the awesome power of the atom, and focused attention on the musical potential of creating new music from atoms of music, just as physics was seeking to create new elements by combining atomic particles. The musical task was to define the smallest elements or building blocks of music, from which should come a better understanding of the forces that hold them together, and allow them to form stable structures. After Messiaen criticized the lack of rigor in Schoenberg's method, in not including dynamics and timbre in the matrix, his own students challenged him to come up with an example of a music in which every variable is scaled and organized. Messiaen responded with the 1949 composition *Mode de valeurs et d'intensités*, a breakthrough concept based on a limited "alphabet" or code of musical characters.

In later years Messiaen revisited the notion of a musical alphabet in *Le Mystère de la Sainte-Trinité* for organ, for which he devised a system extending beyond the A–H and S of traditional musical code to include the entire alphabet, including definite and indefinite articles, to render passages from the Bible as abstract melodies. This however is not serialism but cryptography in the sense made famous by Schumann in his Op. 1 *Abegg Variations*, dedicated to Meta Abegg (the name encoded as a musical motif A – B flat – E – G – G). The *Chamber Concerto* by Alban Berg uses the same method to conceal the names of Schoenberg (in German notation E flat – C – B natural – B flat – E – G), Webern, and himself in their respective themes. Boulez himself employs the code with admirable economy, in . . . *explosante–fixe*. . . centered on E flat (S for Stravinsky), and in the sextet *Messagesquisse* dedicated to Paul Sacher (S A C H E R).

To see serialism merely as cryptography however is to miss the point. Serialism exists as it were in three guises:

1. as a theory of permutations of *note values* ordered in sets or hierarchies specific to each work;
2. as a music of preordained *interval ratios* applying equally to pitch, duration, intensity, harmonic density, etc.; and
3. as a theory or preordained *law of generation* by which an entire composition may be derived from a single cell or formula.

Of the three, the simplest is the first. In Webern's classic acrostic

S A T O R
A R E P O
T E N E T
O P E R A
R O T A S

—a magic square of words forms a meaningful if obscure statement ("The sower Arepo holds the wheels at work") that can be read in four different orders: the words formed left to right and down the page; in reverse: right to left and up the page; vertically: down the page, left to right; and vertically in reverse: up the page and right to left. Webern sought by this example to prove that Schoenberg's twelve-tone method, which recognizes four versions of the row: O, R, I, and IR or original, retrograde, inversion, and retrograde inversion (terms vary from composer to composer), belonged to a much older tradition of combinatorial poetics.

Webern's interest in the contrapuntal music of Isaac may have brought him into contact with the writings of Scaliger the Elder (1484–1558), inventor of the Proteus poem, a line of Latin verse the order of words of which can be permutated without the meaning being affected.[2] The possibilities of word permutation opened up by movable type provoked an early literary and philosophical interest in combinatorics, pursued in the seventeenth century among others by Georg Philipp Harsdörffer.[3]

Literary antecedents of permutational serialism include the detective story, invented by Edgar Allan Poe, a narrative puzzle involving the permutation of actions of a number of characters. An interest in the possible origins of serialism in magic number squares and palindromes led Mauricio Kagel to base a composition on the reversible Latin text *In girum imus nocte et consumimur igni* ("Into the circle we venture by night and are consumed by fire"). Serial practices have a special affinity with ritual and coded messages, especially in wars of the twentieth century, out of which emerged the first number-crunching devices for decoding enemy messages, and also the machine code for programming them. Machine code is essentially a system of moving information from one place to another, a theme popularized shortly after the end of World War II in Hermann Hesse's novella *Magister ludi* (or *The Glass Bead Game*). As in wartime code, the significance of a serial composition lies in a sequential displacement of the elements in an original order to conceal its message, and of reversing the sequence to reveal it.

In music, the archetypal serial device is the set of wind chimes suspended from a tree, at the entrance to the house, or above a baby's cot; a half dozen plates or tubes that chime in distinct pitches forming a scale or mode (or hexachord). Blown by the breeze they move about and chime at random, bumping against one another. The gentle music produced has the effect of calming the occupants and is believed by some to ward off evil spirits, so there is a magic component to permutation as well.

When there are only half a dozen notes for the wind to play with, and the notes form a scale or set with one another, the real magic consists of (a) making audible the random energy of normally silent air currents, and (b) the possibility of random natural motion producing crystalline melodies that resemble the melodies of a real composer or musical box. Given a scale of only six notes already in diatonic relationship, the appearance of melody is not all that hard to find in a random process, but for wind chimes there is also a rhythmic component arising from the random motion of the wind. An infinite variety of melodic shapes is thus produced out of a random natural impulse (the breeze) interacting with a carefully tuned sounding device of limited range (the chimes). Although its patternmaking is only random to western ears, gamelan music from Indonesia attracted the attention of a number of twentieth-century western composers, among them Debussy, Poulenc (*Concerto for two pianos*), Britten (*The Prince and the Pagodas*), Colin McPhee, and John Cage and Lou Harrison (*Double Music*), for its resemblance to wind chimes, and partly for its tranquil connotations as a natural activity projected onto a resonant keyboard.

The implications of considering the tempered scale as a higher form of wind chimes lead inevitably to either a music of chance, in which notes are selected at random by a performer or by an external device such as a computer, or alternatively to a music of pure patternmaking according to some cabbalistic code or mathematical formula. The latter approach embraces Xenakis, serialism, and also fractal music, which is computer generated. In the case of chance music, the ostensible source of inspiration is the performer's subconscious, so what is alleged to arise in the absence of any externally imposed order is the musical equivalent of seance, dream, or spontaneous self-analysis. In serial, stochastic, or computer music, however, the selection process is usually assigned to some other intelligence, so what is being revealed is a translation into musical terms of a mathematical selection process for which the tempered scale may be more or less adequate. That natural processes normally expressed as numerical relationships on a graph may reveal hidden patterns when translated into music is an interesting idea put to the test by Charles Dodge in *Earth's Magnetic Field*, a realization in music of the fluctuation in terrestrial magnetism under the sun's influence. Since the human ear is a powerful analyzer of acoustic data, the question is not really about perceiving melodic tendencies in a stream of momentary samples taken many hours apart, but rather about detecting harmonic constants in a natural turbulence or noise generated continuously across the entire range of hearing.

In a permutational music of a simple kind, such as the traditional chiming of the hours by a chiming clock (first introduced in the fifteenth century) an array of four pitches is permutated:

A F G C   F G A F   A G F C   C G A F

1 2 3 4	A F G C	
2 3 1 2	F G A F	[strictly: C F G A]
1 3 2 4	A G F C	
4 3 1 2	C G A F	

It is clearly imperfect: group 2 is missing a C, in order to enable the groups to end alternately in C and F (dominant and tonic). C F G A would make the sequence symmetrical. But it is near enough. There are twenty-four order permutations of four bells, one for every hour of the day, so in theory a chiming clock should be able to progress through a complete sequence in a day, with a new order for every hour. Perhaps this is why a series of four bells was chosen. In practice—for whatever reason, perhaps because the mechanical challenge was too complicated or expensive to implement—only four chosen permutations are traditionally assigned to the quarter hours, accumulating to all four on every hour.

Change ringing of a peal of bells ranges in complexity from a Plain Bob of four bells to changes and peals involving eight, ten, and even twelve bells. The composed element in a course of ringing changes or peals lies in the variation in order of successive rounds, which is composed somewhat like a dance in which each bell steps back and forth through the order in a more or less regular sequence. Two chamber works by Peter Maxwell Davies, *Stedman Doubles* and *Stedman Caters*, composed in 1968, are based on a method of change-ringing discovered around 1680 by the Englishman Fabian Stedman, for five bells and nine bells respectively. Stedman's art (published as *Tintinnalogia* in 1668) is described by Percy Scholes as "not so much a branch of music as mathematics athletically applied to the making of a merry noise." [4]

Change-ringing meets the detective story in Dorothy L. Sayers's novel *The Nine Tailors*, in which the villain of the piece is finally revealed to be the bells themselves. The title of John Cage's *Music of Changes* for piano also alludes to change-ringing as setting a precedent for a method of composing by number permutation. The poet Stéphane Mallarmé dreamed of writing a *Livre* or Book of Changes the content of which could be read in more than eight hundred permutations (he was probably predicting the internet).

Serial thinking in the avant-garde sense is predicated on the twelve fixed notes of the keyboard, a reason why some of the major works of serial music are composed for piano. *Structures I* (1951) for two pianos by Boulez is a masterpiece, a rigorous example of serial composition whose wit, energy, and exuberance are equally character traits of the composer. Stockhausen's *Kreuzspiel* (1951, revised 1959) is another work in similar vein. Both are referenced to their teacher Olivier Messiaen: Boulez's series for *Structures* is derived from Messiaen's *Mode de valeurs*, whereas Stockhausen's series permutations in *Kreuzspiel* are based on Messiaen's method of *interversion*, according to which the notes in successive orders change places in an orderly manner that in turn relates to change-ringing and is quite different from the linear permutations of the twelve-tone system (really a system of intervals rather than notes).

In change-ringing practice, each number corresponds to one bell (the order of bells 1–6 forming a descending scale). The following example is from a Plain Bob Major, of six bells.

5	3	6	1	4	**2**	
3	**5**	1	6	**2**	4	
3	1	**5**	**2**	6	4	
1	3	**2**	**5**	4	6	
1	3	**2**	**5**	6	4	
3	1	**5**	**2**	4	6	
3	**5**	1	4	**2**	6	
5	3	4	1	6	**2**	etc.[5]

This is the beginning of a Maximus (twelve bells) peal of 576 changes, titled Cambridge Surprise.

1	2	3	4	5	6	7	8	9	**10**	11	12	
2	**1**	4	3	6	5	8	7	**10**	9	12	11	
1	2	4	6	3	8	5	**10**	7	12	9	11	
2	**1**	6	4	8	3	**10**	5	12	7	11	9	
2	6	**1**	4	3	8	5	**10**	7	12	9	11	
6	2	4	**1**	8	3	**10**	5	12	7	11	9	
6	3	**1**	4	8	**10**	3	12	5	11	7	9	etc.[6]

By comparison, the rotation table sampled overleaf, governing the percussion parts of Stockhausen's *Kreuzspiel* (1951) is treated as a precompositional resource and only selected orders are employed in the score. The method of pattern derivation is modeled on another composition by his teacher Messiaen, the movement "Reprises par Interversion" from the *Livre d'Orgue*, a serially permutated but non-twelve tone composition also dating from 1951:

2	8	7	4	**11**	1	**12**	3	9	6	5	10	
8	7	4	**11**	1	10	2	**12**	3	9	6	5	
7	4	**11**	1	5	2	10	8	**12**	3	9	6	
4	**11**	1	6	8	10	2	5	7	**12**	3	9	
11	1	9	10	7	5	8	6	2	4	**12**	3	
1	3	2	4	5	6	7	8	9	10	**11**	**12**	etc.[7]

According to Allan Forte, set theory in the United States is based on analogous principles.

> A *pitch-class set* . . . is a set of distinct integers [i.e., no duplicates] representing pitch classes. . . . An ordering of a set is called a permutation, and the number of distinct permutations of a set depends upon the number of elements in the set. . . . To determine the normal order of a set, however, it is not necessary to consider all of its permutations, but only those called *circular permutations*. . . . Hence, by definition, an ordered set is a circular permutation of itself, and, in general, there are n circular permutations of a set of n elements. . . . Of the 220 distinct pc sets only 4 have vectors in which each entry is unique:

6 – 1	[5 4 3 2 1 0]
6 – 32	[1 4 3 2 5 0]
7 – 1	[6 5 4 3 2 1]
7 – 35	[2 5 4 3 6 1][8]

Set theory in the United States evolved as a primarily analytical method, initially applied to identify hidden patterns of relationship in atonal music of which the composer is presumed to have been unaware. It may be regarded as an esoteric code-breaking technique based on the recognition of note collections of equivalent interval content (called pitch-class sets or pc sets). Since octave relations are defined as identical (C is always C, whatever the octave, as in twelve-tone music), there are always and only twelve pitch classes. This of course is a concept based on a keyboard of fixed tuning; it does not recognize enharmonic relations as different (A sharp and B flat are identical, likewise E sharp and F), and it also does not recognize refinements of interval that arise from meantone or just intonation, or indicate preferential tonal affinities.

Of interest is the set theorist's definition of an ordered set as "a circular permutation of itself" which sounds very much like an oversimplification of change-ringing. The rules of an ordered set are designed to establish a hierarchy limiting the range of valid permutations to a manageable number (very convenient given that the possible number of order permutations of twelve tones is numbered in the hundreds of millions). Even so, the possibilities of set theory appear primitive and arbitrary compared to the more elaborate permutations available to twelve-tone music, and their antecedents in acrostics, poetics (the Proteus poem), and change-ringing.

Arbitrary choices, on the other hand, lend themselves more readily to automation, for example by a codebreaking computer of the early postwar era. The rationale underlying identification of key clusters of pitch-classes in a musical score as pc sets specific to the composition is directly comparable, therefore, to designing a codebreaking mechanism to monitor a telephone line or scan a printed page of code and look for collections of data that recur with above average frequency and might therefore correspond to identifiable words or names. In the long run this entire US initiative (extending to Chomsky and Minsky and others in the field of artificial intelligence) has to do with uncovering the "deep structure" of an outwardly unnatural and thus "foreign" *musical* language—atonal music—in order to isolate any subliminal organizational properties (grammar) that distinguish it as music despite its lack of orthodox tonal references. In turn, that deep structure might provide either a template for the analysis of classically tonal music, or perhaps music of other ethnicities, or the basis of a code of universal traits representing basic linguistic patterns rather than preferences specific to a particular culture. Such considerations in the musical domain link up directly, and are still relevant, to developments in artificial intelligence including computer speech recognition.

Set theory looks for patterns in the written notes of a musical score, but only those notes corresponding to notes of the tempered scale, omitting percussion parts for triangle, side drum, or cymbals, that are only of relative pitch or are merely rhythmic in function, ignoring glissandi or inflected pitches, and treating all timbres as equivalent. A theory with this degree of reductionism has its intellectual roots in eighteenth-century rationalism. As a theory of music it has features in common with the image of music as data patterns in time expressed in mechanical devices such as musical boxes and mechanical organs. Such devices of course are more than just for entertainment. They embody a perception of the universe and life in general as complex machines and of the disembodied music produced by mechanical means as somehow closer to the pure essence of musical relationships, uncontaminated by human error.

A less restrictive approach was advocated by the eighteenth-century forerunners of serialism. Writing in 1779, philologist Joshua Steele, member of the Society of Arts, author of *Prosodia Rationalis*, and inventor of a notation for dramatic speech, identified the parameters of speech as *sound*, *stress*, *quantity*, and *quality*, affecting every syllable. Such thinking is serial in essence. A century later, in *The Principles of Psychology*, Herbert Spencer classified the variables of voice expression, and by inference, of all music, under the headings of *loudness*, *quality*, *timbre*, *pitch*, *intervals*, and *rate of variation*. This is serial thinking on precisely the same wavelength.

Serialism as practiced by European composers recognized the expressive significance of tempo, rhythm and accent, dynamics, and spatial (tone color) effects. As in the case of set theory, the motivation for developing scales of subjective properties can be traced back to mechanical devices, including the classic metronome, invented to codify tempo, the musical box, and the barrel organ. Early in the twentieth century, piano manufacturers devoted a great deal of energy to improving piano roll technology to capture and reproduce a famous performer's style of playing with great realism. The application of science to physical performance brought to light previously unknown subtleties of technique and also helped to establish the principle of serial thinking in other areas of music.

In *The Physical Basis of Piano Touch and Tone*, published in 1925, Otto Ortmann summarizes studies into the relationship of the weight with which a key is struck, and the resulting dynamic, and offers the following rough approximations: *ppp* = 3 oz.; *pp* = 3½ oz.; *p* = 4½ oz.; *mp* = 6 oz.; *mf* = 10 oz.; *f* = 17+ oz.; and *ff* = "several pounds to many pounds." In a later chapter, however, the tone quality is modified by speed of attack, introducing variations in the mode of vibration that are peculiar to *sf* and *sfff* notations. A dynamic scale based on Rachmaninov's piano *Prelude in C minor*, for example, is not a world away from Messiaen's scale of dynamics in *Mode de valeurs et d'intensités*. [9]

sfff – fff – ff – f – mf – mp – p – pp

The dynamic levels of a reproducing piano roll were keyed by a live performer, not punched by hand, so for a reproduction to convey a convincing impression of a live performer, something essential of the quality of a real personality had to be captured. The development of reproducing piano technology can thus be seen as a process the ultimate purpose of which was not simply to reproduce the artistry of living musicians, but potentially to isolate and codify the elements in which personality and artistry reside, in order to enable future owners of a reproducing piano to program the instrument to simulate a range of different personalities and performance styles at will.

A similar approach was taken for an optical sound graphics system developed during the 1940s by Norman McLaren for use in animated movies. "Op art" templates or cards corresponding to waveforms of fixed or variable pitch, overlaid by masks to give the resulting tone a particular shape and quality: abrupt, smooth, lingering, etc., could be linked or superimposed to create a synthesized music track to an exact timeframe without requiring live musicians. Unlike natural sound effects and voices, which come readymade with dynamics and harmonic shaping, McLaren's artificial sounds proved to be relatively inert and organ-like, and conscious decisions had to be made concerning the relative loudness and timbre of each. In a paper published in 1953 McLaren observed:

> In creating animated music the precise dynamics of every note in the score is the job of the composer; in other words the composer must also be the interpretative artist.
>
> To this end, 24 degrees of dynamic level were used. . . . For instance, 0, 1, and 2 represent three differing degrees of *ppp*; 9, 10, and 11, three shades of *mp*; 12, 13, and 14, three degrees of *mf*; 21, 22, and 23, three degrees of *fff*, and 24 represents a *ffff*.

> The composer has control over pitch (to the nearest 1/10 of a tone), over dynamics (to at least 1 per cent of the total dynamic range), over rhythm and metric spacing (to thenearest 1/50 of a second). The control over "timbre" (tone-contouring and tone-quality) is less flexible, but a variety of about a half-dozen types of tone-quality and tone-contour is possible, which by cross-combination give quite a range of "instrumental" effects."[10]

Serializing timbre—that is to say, organizing tone qualities in a scale, say from dark to bright, or in terms of waveform, from the simplest sine tone (flute playing softly, without vibrato) to noise (say, a snare drum playing continuously), proved a sticking point for composers, for the simple reason that they were dealing not just with easily programmable wave shapes drawn optically or synthesized electronically, rather they were having to discover a method of classification for historic instruments of often complex timbre—in the case of violin timbre, virtually unanalyzable.[11] It simply was not possible to classify timbres by waveform, as some researchers had earlier imagined (the American Dayton C. Miller, for example). While a synthetic waveform produced directly by tone wheel, or optically from a transparency is bound to be the same every time, the waveform of a musical instrument picked up by a microphone in the atmosphere is subject to infinite variation in relation to where the microphone is placed and in response to any movement of the performer. In reality the harmonic components of a complex timbre are apt to change their alignment in unpredictable ways, one of the reasons that a live performance sounds volatile and alive compared to the steady-state sounds of an electronic oscillator or computer.

Notes

1. "According to some, the acrostic was first used as a mnemotechnic device to endure completeness in the oral transmission of sacred texts. In ancient times mystical significance was attributed to acrostic compositions." Christoph E. Schweizer, "Acrostics." In Alex Preminger ed., *Princeton Encyclopedia of Poetry and Poetics* enl. edn. London: Macmillan, 1974, 4–5.
2. Julius Caesar Scaliger (Giulio Bordone della Scala), *Poetices Libri Septem* II. xxx, 1561.

3. Georg Philipp Harsdörffer, *Mathematische und Philosophische Erquickstunden. Texte der Frühen Neuzeit* (Nürnberg: 1636). Frankfurt: Keip, 1990.
4. Percy Scholes, *Oxford Companion to Music* ed. John Owen Ward. 10th rev. edn. (1970). London: Oxford University Press, 1975, 99. The method of interweaving the order of the bells is also related to the art of knitting or weaving, in turn related to the weaving patterns of folk dance. The ropes, chevrons, and diamond decorations of fishermen's knitted jerseys are manifestations of serial orders in which stitches are carefully permutated, the overall patterns alluding in code to the region and village of the owner, so that if the body of a fisherman were washed up, it could be returned to its place of origin. *See* Rae Compton, *The Complete Book of Traditional Guernsey and Jersey Knitting*. London: Batsford, 1986.
5. E. S. Powell and M. Powell, *Ringers' Handbook*. 5th edn. repr. Leeds: Whitehead & Miller, 1955.
6. Christopher Groome ed., *Diagrams: Based on the Original Work by Jasper and William Snowdon* repr. Burton Latimer, Northants: Christopher Groome, 1974 repr. 1978.
7. Jonathan Harvey, *Music of Stockhausen: An Introduction*. London: Faber and Faber, 1975, 14–20.
8. Allen Forte, *The Structure of Atonal Music*. New Haven CT: Yale University Press, 1973, 3–4, 16.
9. Otto Ortmann, *The Physical Basis of Piano Touch and Tone*. London: Kegan Paul, Trench, Trübner & Co., Curwen & Sons. New York: Dutton, 1925.
10. Norman McLaren, "Notes on Animated Sound." *Hollywood Quarterly* Vol. VII No. 3 (1953) repr. in Roger Manvell and John Huntley, *Technique of Film Music*. London: Focal Press, 1957, 169–77. The McLaren image of a single line of animated music accompanied by small patches of contrasting tone and harmony calls to mind the lively quality and attenuated texture of Stravinsky's *Movements for piano and orchestra* of 1959–1960.

    C. V. Raman, *Scientific Papers of C V Raman*. Volume II: Acoustics ed. S. Ramaseshan. Bangalore: Indian Academy of Sciences, 1988.

TWENTY-TWO

SCHRÖDINGER'S CAT

In this version of the story the box is a violin, the cat is a vibrating string (catgut), and the decaying isotope the choice of key (literally, the key to life and death). The parable of Schrödinger's cat turns on the counterintuitive notion that a system can exist in a superimposition of different, even contradictory states that only resolve into a single state when observed. In a mysterious way the act of observing collapses the possibilities into one. Out of that conception arises the more recent and seemingly more outrageous notion of multiple dimensions, and indeed, of multiple coexistent universes.

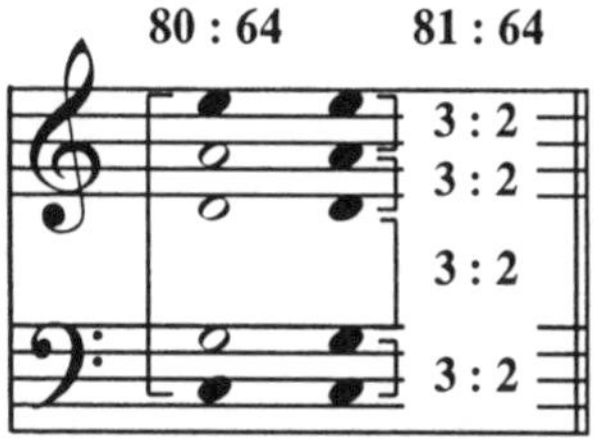

Violin/viola tuning in powers of 2 and 3

In music the issue of superimposed states is relatively familiar. The Cremonese instrument makers who decided to tune their new violins in perfect fifths were certainly aware that the interval span of four perfect fifths of viola and violin superimposed, C – G – D – A – E, covering two octaves and a major third, can be written in two different ways: (1) as superimposed major ninths: $9/8 \times 9/8 = 81/64$; or (2) as a major third and two octaves: $5/4 \times 16 = 80/64$. Clearly 81/64 cannot be the same ratio as 80/64, and yet the two intervals are the same. The only difference is how the relationship is defined. (The implications of an undefinable major third are

Beethoven 'Pastoral' Symphony No. 6, I movement

Beethoven plays on the ambiguity of the 11th natural harmonic and its resolution in the opening movement of his "Pastoral" Symphony

profound, like the square root of 2. I am inclined to think that the reason thirds were excluded from the harmonic canon in early medieval times had something to do with the undefinable nature of the interval.) In music such ambiguities abound. An octave ratio 2 : 1 can be defined as the cube of a major third $(5/4)^3 = 125/64$, somewhat less than an octave; or a minor third to the fourth power $(6/5)^4 = 1296/625$, somewhat greater. Debussy's whole-tone scale $(9/8)^6$ is more than an octave; a scale of 7 minor tones $(10/9)^7$ less than an octave. The paradoxical messages that the identical interval can be expressed by incompatible ratios—and by extrapolation, therefore *no* harmonic interval computes absolutely—bring the world of classical music face to face with relativity theory.

At the heart of the story of Pandora's Box (or Schrödinger's Cat) are the ideas (1) that knowledge is a matter of personal choice;

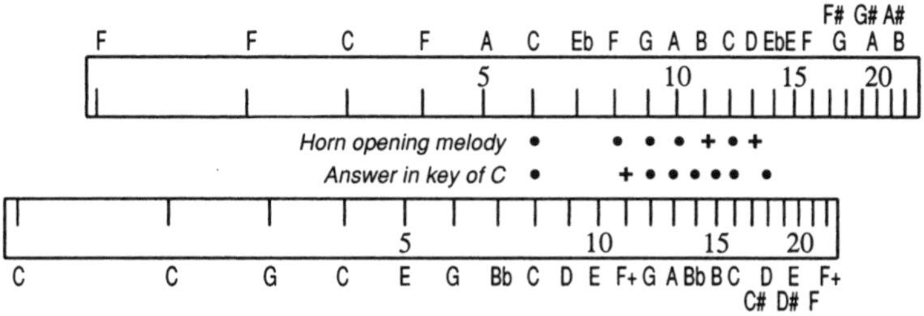

On this "slide rule" of harmonic scales the ambiguous note relations of Beethoven's theme can be easily identified

(2) that the will to find something out (open the box) determines the outcome; and (3) that the world order created by one person co-exists with, and is different from, the world order created by anyone else. That sounds naively like saying that photographs taken from different angles at a public unveiling of a monument are not of the same object, and properly belong to different world views. A world view, however, is an expression of editorial choice. Views from different angles are taken to suit alternative viewpoints. Schrödinger imagined a box containing a cat that could either be alive or dead, and furthermore had to be considered, in the absence of visible proof (opening the box) to be both alive and dead at the same time. That the cat is both alive and dead until the box is opened is a way of saying that for the time being it makes no difference whether the value assigned to an unknown is positive or negative.

On the one hand it resembles the fairy tale form in which the suitor of a princess has to make a choice between three caskets, of gold, silver, or lead. In such stories there are different outcomes, and they actually do depend on the predispositions of the person making the choice. It is an added sophistication to have only one casket and the issue whether or not to open it, that is, the option of choosing knowledge rather than ignorance. That the cat once out of the bag—or box—is alive or dead carries an additional layer of implication that the outcome may be open or closed. That the outcome in Schrödinger's version of the story turns on an uncertain quantum of radioactive decay introduces a gratuitous whiff of contemporary (1930s) angst to the discussion.

Inquiring into the nature of things without understanding the complications that may arise is a tale as old as Adam and Eve in the Garden of Eden. This is the second interpretation brought to this particular puzzle in the present book, so the story itself can be read as a superposition of possible states. In a historical context the story is a metaphor of the potential for good or evil waiting to be released from the resonant container of a musical instrument (bandoura) or family radio ("Pandora's Box"); in this sense a myth of information disclosure (not objective knowledge but stuff you are told which has to be believed). In its new guise as a systemic ambiguity lurking at the heart of music itself, the analogy is still acoustical, but more specifically musical. Hiding beneath the mystery that a distant (or merely detached) observer can somehow interfere with the state of a system merely by looking at it, is the more prosaic inference that by observation we mean measurement, and to measure something depends on an observer establishing a time, location, and unit of measurement, and that the choices of time and unit of measure can actually influence the dimensions of a system (which we know to be the case from fractal mathematics). This is normal. For an airplane passenger there is no longer any puzzle in the time of day having to depend on how fast you are moving and what time zone you happen to be passing through at that moment.

That musicians are familiar with ambiguity in tonal relations is easily demonstrated. We begin with a thematic example from the first movement of the "Pastoral" Symphony No. 6 by Beethoven. That the duality is openly discussed in the music itself means that the composer was aware of it.

Beethoven's message in the exposition of the first movement of the Sixth Symphony is that the identity of the ambiguous partial F^{11} (a quasi B flat) becomes a matter of choice, not of actual frequency (here shown as 484 hertz). This is not a statement of an inherent ambiguity in the note itself, since the eleventh harmonic in the key of F is a natural harmonic, and thus a stable state. Rather, the issue turns on the set of perceptions a listener brings to resolving the identity of the pitch, in relation to either the tonic or dominant key. What the note signifies—indeed, what it *is*—becomes a matter of personal choice and not an issue of its intrinsic nature. In changing key from F to C the problematic F^{11} (484 hertz) is split into adjacent harmonics B flat (C^{14}, 462 hertz) and B natural (C^{15}, 495 hertz). The composer is able to deal with a noncomputable ratio by a change of key, because in other respects the two tonalities are alike in scale at this region. Here the harmonic F^{12} (528 hertz) is defined as identical in frequency with the harmonic C^{16} (also 528 hertz), whereas F^{11} is neither C^{14} nor C^{15} but somewhere between the two. The irony of the present case is that B flat (a perfect fourth above, and perfect fifth below F) is a critical determinant for the key of F, and yet is not a natural harmonic of F, whereas A (the major third) is critical for the key of F but an irrational harmonic in the key of C (C^{13}), being somewhat flat. The theme is presented in the strings, but a listener recognizes it immediately as a natural F horn melody, in keeping with the pastoral nature of the symphony.

By coincidence, the third movement of Leopold Mozart's *Sinfonia Pastorella* in G (1755) incorporates a solo for alphorn that plays amusingly on the ambiguity of the same eleventh harmonic, a note mysteriously consonant and dissonant at the same time. This obscure rococo pastoral was revived by the British horn virtuoso Dennis Brain in a suitably rustic version for hosepipe and strings, in the Hoffnung Interplanetary Concert of 1958. The same eleventh harmonic is employed to haunting effect in the Introduction and Epilogue of the *Serenade for Tenor, Horn and Strings* by Benjamin Britten, a work dating from the early 1940s and first performed by tenor Peter Pears and Dennis Brain.

Beethoven's purpose in assigning a natural horn melody to the violins is richly ambiguous. The composer may be alluding to the natural harmonic series of the *tromba marina*, an antique portable monochord formerly used for teaching and perhaps also for calculating interval ratios. In assigning the melody and its working out to the string orchestra, however, Beethoven has in mind that the violin family had been designed in Renaissance Italy precisely to allow such tonal ambiguities to be glossed over or concealed. Violins are ideally equipped to expose the ambiguous nature of F^{11} and then resolve it either to B flat or to B natural. Opening in the tonality of F, the theme begins with a statement based purely on harmonics, as for a natural horn, deliberately drawing attention to the eleventh harmonic, a natural number even though it sounds out of key. The continuation goes on to alter the melody's tonal frame of reference from F to C major, and restyle (with emphasis, in a phrase repeated over and over again) the ambiguous region between A and C as a zone of continuous transition in which the location

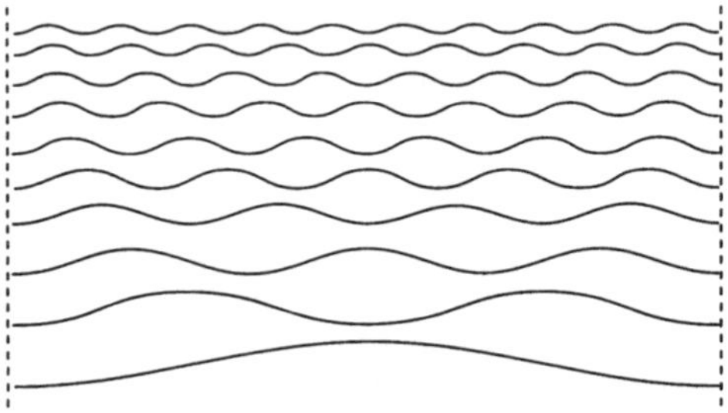

A vibrating string oscillates simultaneously in a variety of standing waves at harmonic frequencies. The paradox of multiple waveforms occupying the same vibrating string at the same time suggests that the string is able to exist simultaneously in multiple states and even to be moving both up and down at a given point at the same time

occupied by F^{11} is split and redefined as B flat and B natural (C^{14} and C^{15}) played in succession, not simultaneously.

Was Beethoven inspired by the earlier Pastoral Symphony by Leopold Mozart? The existence of two "pastoral" symphonies by significant composers, in which the pastoral landscape is characterized by the same authentic, but implicitly "uncivilized" harmonic series for natural horn, suggests that both were employing a musical cliché of eighteenth-century urban perceptions of country life, the wild and uncivilized hierarchies of nature in the raw.

In the Beethoven movement, the question being asked is, what "state" is represented in the key of F by the 11th harmonic? Is the note a B flat, or a B natural? Or neither? Or both at once? The listener is faced with the reality that the aberration is neither one nor the other, and possibly both—a note that is nevertheless valid and represents a stable state. That the composer is aware of the dilemma is easily understood, because Beethoven sets about resolving the ambiguity without delay, first by modulating to B flat, then transposing the harmonic base from F 44 hertz to C 33 hertz, a fourth below. In doing so, however, the assigned frequency of A 440 hertz (major third, 10 : 9, F^{10}) diminishes to A 429 hertz in the key of C (13 : 12, C^{13}). This exchanges one set of ambiguities for another. Faulty intonation never becomes a serious issue, however, because the passage is assigned to the violins which are capable of subtly misrepresenting tonal relations, and also because the ear is more tolerant of variant intonation at intervals approximating the major third, than for example at the augmented fourth, the tritone or "blue" note of jazz. It is interesting to note that the varieties of intonation debated by the ancient Greeks are framed strictly within the tetrachord 4 : 3, the interval of the fourth, and this issue is open to be read as an ongoing and unresolved controversy on the moral and religious implications of the ambiguous third. The difference between major and minor diatonic scales is essentially a difference in order of thirds in the triad. Thus the uncertainty attaching to the interval of the third may account for its delayed acceptance as a harmonic interval in the medieval era.

Underlying the ambiguity is the larger issue of identifying a note of distinct pitch as a location within a continuum, like a major scale or mode, or its frequency as an energy state, which is how the reality of a harmonic of a string or air column is defined. Comparing Beethoven's conundrum with the myth of Schrödinger's cat is a way of saying that we cannot assign a scale value to F^{11} even though the latter corresponds to a stable state. In a "real"—that is, diatonic—musical context (a scale or key) the note has to be either B flat or B natural.

LIFE ON A CAROUSEL

Plane rotation has long been a source of controversy in astronomy in relation to the motion of the planets, and more recently of galaxies and accretion discs. That accounting for the speed of rotation at different locations on a disc remains problematic is indicated by a reference by Stephen Hawking in *The Universe in a Nutshell.*

> The Einstein universe is like a cylinder: it is finite in space and constant in time. . . . Consider matter in an Einstein universe that is rotating about some axis. If you were on the axis, you would remain at the same point in space, just as you do when standing at the center of a children's carousel. But if you were not on the axis, you would be moving through space as you rotated about the axis. The further you were from the axis, the faster you would be moving. So if the universe were infinite in space, points sufficiently far from the axis would have to be rotating faster than light.[1]

Just a minute. Are we talking about a solid disc, and if so, why does it have to be solid? Does Pluto orbit faster than Jupiter or Mercury, because it is farther away? I don't think so. A solar system or spiral galaxy is no more solid than an accretion disc around a black hole, or Saturn's rings, or the waste water spiraling into the plughole of the kitchen sink. This is clearly a figure of speech. Then why say it? We could just as well be arguing the respective merits of cylinder

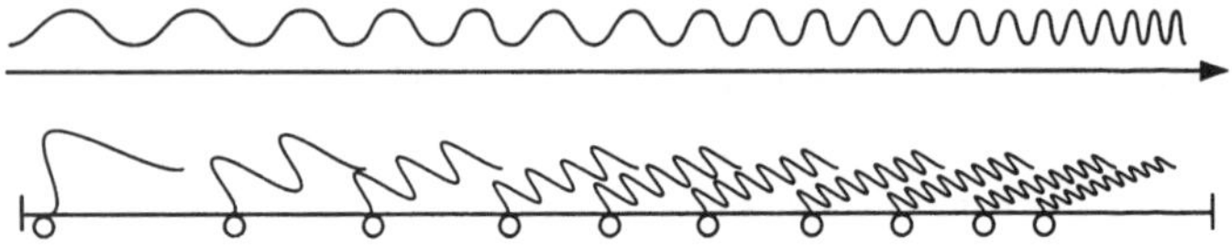

The density of information in the groove of a disc recording is compressed, and time is compressed, as the turntable arm moves toward the center (top). As a player's finger moves along the fingerboard the note frequency increases in a similar way (bottom). Some may be tempted to assign frequency values to locations on the open string, when in fact they are due to alterations in length of the string

and disc recording as Einstein might have considered them in his role as a junior in the Swiss Patent Office. Edison's cylinder recordings had the merit of constant speed tracking, but were difficult to mass produce; Berliner's platters, on the other hand, were easy to manufacture but information on the disc became progressively compressed and degraded toward the center. It almost seems that public debate over the respective information handling properties of cylinder and disc recording has spilled over into theoretical astrophysics. In the early years of the twentieth century the Andromeda nebula and other distant star systems were discovered to be disc-shaped and rotating, provoking discussion of the implications of galaxies behaving as solid objects. Not for the first time: in *The Dream of Scipio* Cicero, an able politician but indifferent astronomer, had declared that distant stars revolve faster, for the reason that they are more distant: "The outermost sphere, the star-bearer, with its swifter motion gives forth a higher-pitched tone, whereas the lunar sphere, the lowest, has the deepest tone."[2] Here, too, orbital velocity is identified fancifully with frequency.

If a disc is rigid like a wheel, all parts complete one rotation in the same period, from which it follows that those parts that are more remote from the axis will cover a greater distance within the period of rotation than points closer to the center of the disc. But they will not be *rotating* any faster. The issue for science has to do with the notional velocity of a body at points along a radius extending from the hub to the circumference of a rotating disc, such that if it is moving at near light speed at a point half way, then at the rim it will have to be moving faster than light, which of course is not possible. It is a bit like asking whether the pickup arm of a turntable

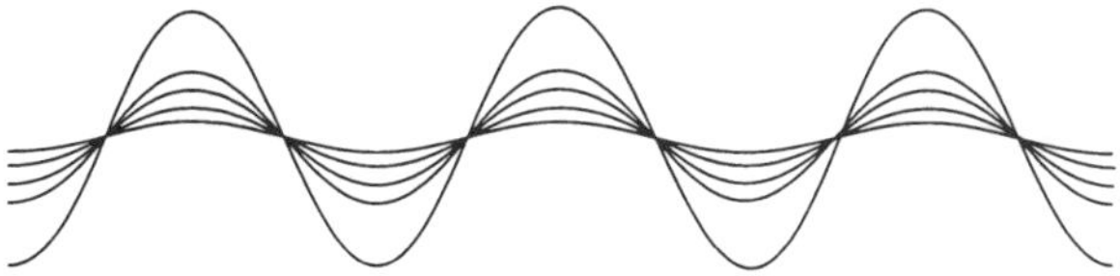

The rotational speed of a rotating disc is said by Professor Hawking to increase as one moves from the center to the edge; but what varies is not the speed of rotation (which is constant) but the amplitude

is traveling faster at the edge of a record, and getting slower as it tracks inward toward the center.

A disposition to argue from mechanical invention to natural causes is a normal, if illogical, feature of western science. This is a paradox attracting the attention of scholars in the early 1900s, when Edison's cylinder phonograph was beginning to compete in the marketplace with Berliner's disc gramophone. Learned names in philosophy and psychology argued just as fiercely over the truth to nature of Étienne Marey's chronophotographs of birds in flight, and moving pictures in general. They seemed to be wondering whether the mechanisms of motion capture—movie or sound recording—embodied principles that might be extrapolated to the physics of natural processes. Discussion over the relative merits of cylinder and disc recording centered on the fact that the speed of tracking is constant from start to finish on a cylinder recording, whereas the tracking speed of a disc recording is several orders of magnitude faster when it begins than when it ends.

In the early twentieth century violin-playing Einstein was the musician, not Niels Bohr; and yet it was Bohr who came to the musical intuition that the permitted velocities (that is, periodicities) of electrons orbiting around a nucleus in a stable state could not vary freely but were bound to correspond to cyclic steady states or harmonic periodicities of a fundamental. Since the motion of a stretched string is an expression of resistance to applied force,

Blues intonation

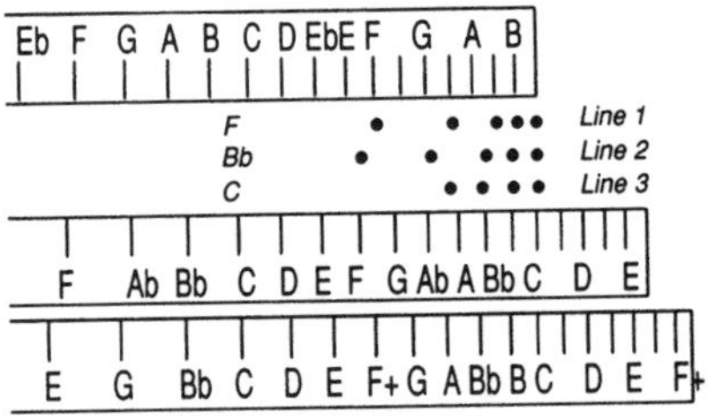

"Oh, I hate to see the evenin' sun go down." Like Beethoven, W. C. Handy in 1912 plays on the ambiguous interval ratios of a melody against a backdrop of changing harmonies

independent of the applied force, the permitted velocity of an orbiting electron, as a partial frequency, might also be interpreted as an expression of resistance.

The information engraved on a cylinder recording is constant in density from start to finish, compared to the information on a disc recording, engraved in a spiral path on a plane surface, the density of which becomes increasingly compacted as the stylus tracks toward the center. Differences arise from a recording process in which time is converted to space. Pressure fluctuations in time are transferred to a moving wax surface, but in the case of a cylinder recording, the speed of the moving surface at the point of contact with the stylus remains constant, whereas for a disc blank passing beneath a cutting head on an inward tracking spiral, the relative speed of the surface is constantly decelerating.

The commercial implications of the cylinder versus disc debate were qualitative: whether the gradual change in density of recorded data in a disc recording affected the sound quality in comparison to a cylinder. A more general question was whether real-world events, considered as information, might also be subject to unsuspected time-compression and dilation effects. The twins paradox is one outcome. Another is the inconstant motion of a pendulum or point on a wheel rim, resolved when the pattern of motion is projected along a time dimension perpendicular to the plane of motion.

For some theoretical physicists the debate proved particularly fruitful. In 1909, Max Born sought to account for the distortion of time and space at the perimeter of a hypothetical rotating disc of cosmic proportions by redefining the nature of a solid disc. Born proposed a Lorentz-invariant definition of a rigid body according to which "the perimeter must contract, while the radius remains the same . . . [hence] there is no way to define simultaneity for the spinning disc as a whole." (This is not to say that because such a disc does not exist, it cannot exist, but rather that if it did exist we would be unable to verify its existence as a disc, which is not quite the same thing.) The same year, 1909, Paul Ehrenfest drew attention to an internal contradiction in Special Relativity Theory arising from this very matter. Defining a disc as "a many-particle system" rather than a solid body enabled Ehrenfest to claim that "there is no relative motion among different points on a rotating disc, each *point* belonging to a different noninertial frame."[3]

To a layperson this is like redefining a time continuum as a movie. A disc made up of an infinity of points each belonging to a separate frame of reference is by definition no longer solid, or rather its solidity, or continuity in time and space, is accounted for by an occult property such as gravitational attraction that behaves differently from a vortex, such as a pirouetting ballet dancer or whirlpool, where the various points are nonetheless connected and the speed of rotation remains constant, leading to a gradual increase in the frequency of rotations as the radius diminishes. For an imaginary rotating superdisc the issue to be adjudicated is a distortion of reality arising from the alteration in speed of motion at the rim relative to the center and intermediate points. The Ehrenfest paradox relates specifically to movement along the spoke of the wheel, relative motion at points along an imaginary radius, visualized perhaps as the movement of a pickup arm across a spinning 78 rpm platter.

Since a record groove is continuous and arguably stringlike in implication, we can reformulate the issue as a problem related to a vibrating string. As the stylus tracks from edge to center the density of vibratory information increases, however during the same time the speed of rotation past the stylus decreases to maintain a constant ratio between the density of information and the rate at which the information is picked up. The issue for relativists is whether the stylus is regarded as moving *across* the disc or *along* the groove. Since it can be raised and lowered at will onto different points of an imaginary radius, it is tempting to consider the speed of rotation at a given point on the radius as specific to the distance of the radius from the center, when in fact it is specific to a location along the groove as a whole. And to speak of velocity as specific to a given point is also a mistake, since velocity is dependent on the speed of rotation of the disc as a whole. All we can say is that the density of information at a given region is greater or lesser than at another region, since there is no movement at any point, only a succession of displacements as the stylus tracks along the groove.

In 1909 gramophone recordings were mono, and it was problematic enough to conceive how a point on a groove could be said, in the absence of rotational motion, to represent a state of vibration, or a voice or instrument, an up or down motion etc. It could in context convey all of these. With the arrival of stereo, a further lateral dimension would add further complication. How does one define the state of vibration at a cross-section of a groove? The issue can only be resolved, if at all, as a transitional datum or cross-section of a continuum. With movies the same issues were under lively discussion, the difference being that each frame of a movie could be seen to represent a timeframe, separated from the next by a fixed time interval. One could vary the speed of a movie in the same way as the speed of a piano roll, by altering the spacing between events, frames and notes, the latter remaining the same.

TIME TRAVEL IN LITERATURE

When Oscar Wilde published *The Picture of Dorian Gray* in 1890 the idea of an image of a person ageing while the living person remained forever in the flower of youth was unusual and thought-provoking. That year, Florence Nightingale recorded a message for posterity on an Edison cylinder in which she said “When I am no longer even a memory, just a name, I hope *my voice* may perpetuate the great work of my life. . . " The novel and the recorded message are indicators of a perception of new technology—for Wilde the camera, for Nightingale the cylinder phonograph—as media of an alternate existence. The fictional Dorian Gray's soul enters the picture and it assumes his living identity as a being in time, subject

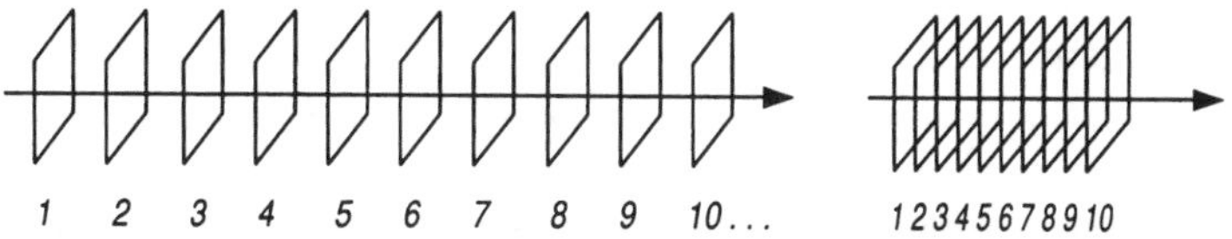

The information in a movie consists of timeframes in succession, each a cross-section of a continuous action. By decreasing the size of the gap between them, the timescale of events in the movie can be speeded up relative to the viewer

to the ageing process. He meantime enters the limbo of an ageless present: a photograph, an Elvis, or the age-defying movie star in a cosmetics ad. The mystery presence in Schrödinger's casket could well be the voice of Florence Nightingale, and the paradox, whether her voice still lives.

More astutely, Florence Nightingale understands the potential of the new recording medium to continue to address generations in the future in her voice when her physical body has ceased to exist and even her name is forgotten. In *The Time Machine* H. G. Wells portrayed an inventor traveling back and forward in time on a fabulous machine, but not altering the flow of time on his arrival in the future; in the short story "The New Accelerator" first published in 1903, he imagined being able to view the world in slow motion, like a science movie, by chemical means. In the world of scientific moviemaking, the speed of the movie camera was increased or slowed down to reveal the dynamics of natural processes to the naked eye for the first time.

These flights of imagination from the turn of the twentieth century converge on the same bizarrely relativistic notion that the time dimension of experience is somehow separate from external reality; that for us, as for Buridan in the fourteenth century, time is a clock that may run fast or slow, that the world as we experience it is intimately related to the speed we move through time, and that under certain conditions time may stop and personal time cease: "and there shall be Time no longer" as Messiaen's epigraph from Revelations reads on the title page of the *Quartet for the End of Time*.

In his defence of the General Theory Einstein proposes that a person (or cat) trapped inside a windowless elevator (or box) that is accelerating upward at a constant rate may experience a sensation indistinguishable from gravity, and for that reason gravity and acceleration are the same. The information engraved in a continuous groove on a disc is also subject to constant acceleration, but is experienced within a matching timeframe of constant deceleration. The "time continuum" of a disc, unlike a cylinder recording, is delivered not uniformly (the rotational speed of the turntable) but as the interaction of two processes, one accelerating (that is, increasing in density) and the other in constant deceleration.

That a person's subjective awareness of temporal sequence in real life is variable and different from chronometric time, and may be sensed as faster or slower depending on one's mood, medication, or degree of sensory overload, is an uncontroversial and legitimate topic of study. That on the contrary, human temporal experience is of *being conveyed through time* rather than time as being inferred in terms of a person's varying ability to process information, is a very different proposition. It is like saying that different notes of a violin melody (different frequencies) are the same note subject to different degrees of acceleration, or that a change of key from F major to C major is precisely analogous to a change of speed, neither of which is true. The difficulty here is discriminating frequency information from elapsed time, since both perceptions are time-dependent. What that means is for a person to be aware of a sound as being musical, and of a certain pitch, a certain time must already have elapsed—more precisely, a minimum number of cycles—for its periodicity to register on the ear. The *onset time* of a musical tone is one thing; its apparent duration quite another. One is apprehended as virtually instantaneous, the other an estimate, subject to conscious measurement.

The late Arthur C. Clarke nurtured a dream of a cosmic elevator connecting the earth with a space station in geostationary orbit. To attain escape velocity, all one had to do was go up in the lift.

Once again we are faced with the concept of a stringlike link from earth to sky up which an astronaut ascends, as in Einstein's sealed box, in which one is subject to a constant acceleration that is no more irksome than the normal force of gravity. This is a version of Jack and the Beanstalk combining the same ingredients as ancient myth: a magic stringlike connection linking earth and the heavens, acceleration or change of frequency as our hero ascends the string, and a realm of untold wealth waiting at the top.

MUSIC OF VARIABLE SPEED

Because early wind-up gramophones came equipped with varispeed slide controls, the public quickly grew accustomed to the delights of altering the turntable speed at will between limits of ca. 65 to 80 rpm for discs of nominal 78 rpm playback speed. Ravel's *La Valse*, composed in 1920 but a concept dating from 1906, draws upon the reproducer's ability to vary the playback speed of a disc to recreate —in real life and in real time—a manic parody of Viennese waltz spinning out of control and ending in disaster. Of interest in this context is that the waltz is not only a declaration of opposition to the enemy forces of World War I, but also emblematic of the culture's adoption of industrial rotary motion as a national dance. The music's tortuous distortions of tempo (heard to particular effect from the tenth minute) would be inconceivable in any other era than the age of the gramophone. For the Vienna of Johann Strauss II the waltz was a celebration of survival and a necessary antidote to the sufferings of war and deprivation. In Ravel's hands the emotion is highly strung and on the edge; the waltz's speed of rotation (suggesting the pace at which life in Vienna is lived) directly related to an impression of the emotional stability of the culture and its middle class.

Stravinsky's ballet *The Firebird* dating from 1910 is affected —though more benignly—by a similar varispeed aesthetic, the music starting low and gradually rising from a cyclical tritone figure in the deep bass to reach a plateau of lightness and energy in the Firebird's Dance in the Enchanted Garden. Here the change of temperament is aptly conveyed, in mechanical terms, in the transition from low to high registers, and corresponding alteration of tone quality from sluggish and congested ostinato to a brusque staccato texture. *Firebird* ends on a slightly different tack, this time borrowing from the mechanical action of a calliope or musical box. The Finale is presented as a slowing-down process, as though winding down, but the broadening of tempo is unexpectedly coupled with a gradual crescendo and stretching of note values from short to long.

Schoenberg's "mystery chord" from No. III of the Op. 16 *Five Pieces for Orchestra* (1909), is a particularly genial example of a temporal shift and compression of frequency ratios occurring in the absence of any outward sign of alteration of timescale. An "endless

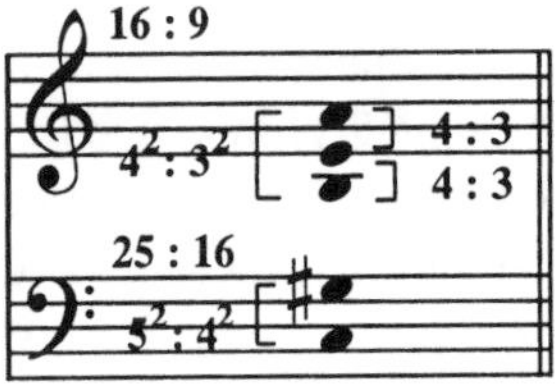

The "mystery chord" from Schoenberg's Op. 16 Five Orchestral Pieces *(1909): No. III "Farben"*

chord" is by definition timeless, but a chord of indefinite duration is still of indefinite duration even when it is accelerated. So the fact that the chord is unending does not mean that it is not subject to acceleration all the same.

We note that the mystery chord is based on viola C—the note shared between bass and solo viola on the open string—and extends up to the A corresponding to the viola highest open string. (Schoenberg played viola as a student.) It is as though the ascending chain of natural fifths of viola and violin tuning has been compressed by acceleration so that the fifths have become fourths, and the G natural a G sharp. The ratios of this chord are intriguing, alluding to the Pythagorean 3 : 4 : 5 triangle and theorem. In his choice of instrumental pairings Schoenberg sets high and low registers in subtle opposition to create an impression of the orchestra alternately "speeding up" or "slowing down": the viola at its lowest note in exchange with the contrabass close to its upper extreme of range. Flutes, clarinets, and trumpets are relatively "low" in pitch, cor anglais, horns, and bassoons relatively "high." Elsewhere, momentary gestures by bass clarinet, harp, celesta, and string harmonics highlight the extremes of a frequency space extended to its limits, while the climax is marked by a delicate and complex evocation of a gradual deceleration and decline in pitch.

When a sampled long note of slow onset and decay is subjected to acceleration, its information content is compressed, causing it to gain in percussiveness and loudness, as well as rise in frequency. In compiling the three modes of *Mode de valeurs* for piano Messiaen generally assigns longer, heavier, and louder values to lower notes, and shorter and lighter dynamics to higher, indicating a familiarity with the varispeed aesthetic of Pierre Schaeffer's *musique concrète*, an art of montage of concrete sounds recorded on disc.

Stockhausen's *Kontakte* marks a high point of tape era electronic music in which entire vocabularies of timbres are generated by acceleration of loops of simple tones and impulse patterns. This genuinely relativistic aesthetic reveals unforeseen identity relations between outwardly different timbres. For example, the sound of a sampled sine tone of very short duration and low frequency resembles a tom-tom or wood drum, whereas a similar tone of medium duration and midrange frequency resembles a flute, while another of short duration and high frequency, with added reverberation, is virtually indistinguishable from the sound of a greek finger cymbal.

The unanswered conundrum is whether frequency and elapsed time are in any way interchangeable. Since the perceived reality of the temporal image (movie, voice recording) depends on the speed at which the recorded information is transferred to the consciousness of the observer, the notion arises of the transfer of information being dependent on the timeframe of the observer: in other words, on how fast the twin in Einstein's paradox is moving through time. The original events are supposed to take place in real time, subject to the speed of the recording device, and recoverable only when the speed of the playback (reading) device conforms to the speed at which the information was captured. We view a slow-motion replay as taking place in a virtual time that the observer is at liberty to experience as real life in slow motion. The concept of experiencing events in virtual time easily spills over to a perception of events in real time as existing in a special state of virtual time that just happens to correspond to real time. Anecdotal evidence is plentiful of people in situations of stress experiencing time as suspended, or faster than real.

Notes

1. Stephen Hawking, *The Universe in a Nutshell*. New York: Bantam, 2001, 150–51.
2. Robin Maconie, *The Concept of Music*. Oxford: Clarendon Press, 1990, 85–86.
3. Michael Weiss, "The Rigid Rotating Disk in Relativity." http://math.ucr.edu/home/baez/physics/relativity/SR/rigid_disk.html (02.04.07)

TWENTY-THREE

PREPARED PIANO

From any rational standpoint, John Cage's prepared piano doesn't add up. Since the effects of preparation are directly related to the piano design and layout of the strings, the composer's meticulous instructions for inserting foreign objects between the strings only produce the sonorities he originally intended when applied to a certain make and model of piano. (In his notes to a 1998 recording of the *Sonatas and Interludes* Aleck Karis offers the additional insight that screws, nuts, and bolts of the 1942 era produce acoustically more satisfying results than those available today, which contain too much zinc.) The inevitable consequence of inserting objects between the piano strings is that the instrument's natural timbre is taken apart from a sonorously uniform tone from bass to treble, to sound like a loose assortment of defective timbres. The relationship of notated pitch values to the keys and tones normally associated with them is also displaced, so from the performer's point of view (the audience being none the wiser) the normal direct transference of data on the printed page to fingers on the keys, and music emerging into the air, no longer obtains. In addition, since the instrument is disintegrated in all three aspects of touch, tone, and timbre, conventional techniques of expression no longer apply either. Finger technique is another casualty, since continuity of flow on the page is doomed to appear broken up in performance. The sound quality itself is odd, like a toy instrument. That in itself implies a criticism of the end of classical music and civilization as we know it.

And yet it worked. The prepared piano created a huge impact, even though Cage's music for prepared piano is rarely performed in concert. (There is surely a market for a digital piano with optional "original" prepared piano tuning, saving the home pianist from the messy business of preparation, which in the case of an electronic instrument is impossible anyway.) Why so seemingly ramshackle a contrivance was ever taken seriously is the million-dollar question. The answer lies in the nature of the instrument, its conceptual and philosophical associations, and the counter-implications of Cage's act of subversion.

All keyboard instruments from the pipe organ to the spinet and midi make the claim of representing a multi-octave pitch universe of uniform tone quality, expressed as an orderly continuum of keys separated by more or less equal semitonal intervals, and played at arm's length from the fingertips. Compare a spinet to a lute and the differences and advantages of a keyboard are immediately obvious: ease of performance (you do not have to find the note, all possible notes are available in front of you), logical correspondence of the layout of the keyboard with music notation on the stave, democratization of the pitch space—in other words, absence of hierarchy in pitch that invites the keyboardist to roam freely at will from tonality to tonality, along with a mechanical design deliberately engineered to ensure that every note is sounded in an identical manner and perceived from the same objective viewpoint (at a distance, from the fingertips).

Keyboards are the first instruments to be designed specifically for *reading* music from a printed score. In the sense popularized by Marshall McLuhan, the uniformity of the keyboard compares with the uniform texture of print, and linear disposition of the alphabet. Like a musical box, which it resembles mechanically and philosophically (a plucked array of vibrating bodies of graduated length, producing tones of uniform quality) the spinet is intended to eliminate expressive distinctions of accentuation and inflection from the presentation of a musical pattern. It was in reaction against the idealized imagery of an emotionally neutral, disembodied, robotic baroque keyboard style that the French school of d'Anglebert, Couperin, and Rameau introduced a range of notated special effects, graces, or ornaments—accents, inflections, hesitations, tremors, stumbles, and so on—as expressive markers. These evolved to assist the keyboardist in coordinating an ensemble of players, and in solo performance to allow the performer to apply a figurative makeup and invest a plain musical score with life and character. The notion of a piano score as an emotional blank sheet can be compared to the absence of expression of classical ballet or mime. Avoiding the distractions of facial or emotional mannerism allows the audience to focus on the expressive content of the music. The aesthetic would return with Satie in the late nineteenth century, as a protest against the unstable rhetoric of romanticism, and thereafter in the silent movie era of Chaplin and Buster Keaton, and again in the neoclassicism of the twenties and thirties.

The modern piano or midi keyboard is a keyboard instrument of artificially tempered pitch. It is structured in the image of a pitch continuum, and the idea of each note as an equally valid position within the continuum. That perception is already controversial, since a historic distinction of rank is drawn between the civilized diatonic scale of seven white notes—a historically magic number recognized even by Isaac Newton—on which is superimposed the rustic black five-note or pentatonic scale of folk music. Both are reconciled in the 12-note chromatic scale, a number symbolizing the twelve hours of day, and twelve of night.

Not all keyboard instruments are triangular in shape. A central European cymbalom may be rectangular, its strings interlaced and in a different order compared to a spinet or clavichord. The left to right disposition of a baroque keyboard, and triangular shape of the instrument, are signs of a commitment to Pythagorean principles of pitch as a continuum of point locations. The new technology combination of a notated sheet music and keyboard, both reading from low to high, reinvents the ancient art of memorized and intuitive performance as a mechanical task of reading and key selection from a printed score. Those who supported the development of keyboard instruments and their music were self-evidently representatives of a newly visual and scientific culture, a development implying in turn that the objective of music-making had changed from spontaneous invention to the accurate reproduction of a preexisting text.

The aesthetic goal of a musical box is to produce music of a disembodied or crystalline beauty from which any contamination of subjective will has been eliminated. This sense of detachment is akin to the impersonal character of the bar-room player piano and aesthetic of ragtime (affecting an Apollonian nonchalance to offset the Dionysian chaos of fight scenes of classic cowboy movies) and can also be related to Cage's philosophical quest for a music of no-mindedness, not forgetting Stravinsky's dictum that music is incapable of expressing anything, and that his own music at least is not for interpreting but to be objectively realized. In consequence of its engineered uniformity of tone in so many dimensions, even a recording of a piano performance of the classical repertoire will tend by default to give the impression of an *objet trouvé*, a finished article, and not a live performance event undertaken as an act of self-discovery. It raises the significant question whether music is divine or human in implication, dealing in transpersonal perfection, or suffering human experience.

Japanese calligraphy and art attract qualities of connoisseurship that appreciate a work that is at one and the same time an object of beauty and also a demonstration and perpetual reminder of the process: the hand gesture, the tools, the quality and interaction of materials, of pigments on surfaces, or fingers on clay. Along with many of his contemporaries, Cage was drawn to oriental art for reasons including an instinctive dissatisfaction with the intellectual goal of manufactured perfection of western music, extending even (bizarrely) to the music of Schoenberg. In its place Cage sought an art of ritual, and he found it in situations carefully contrived to generate unexpected epiphanies, in place of the "Czerny exercises" ridiculed by Henry Miller: featureless exercises in harmony and counterpoint created by rote and relying on limited and prescriptive rules of tone association.

The world of the prepared piano is discontinuous and unpredictable, and gains a particular edge from confounding the normal expectations of the listener. Cage's charming music reinvents the renaissance concept of a "broken consort," reminding a classical audience that keyboards were invented not to create harmony, but to impose order and uniformity on a tonal universe previously dominated by hierarchies: the god of trumpets, the god of strings, the god of panpipes, the gods of bells and reeds, etc. The idea of imposing unity on a sound universe previously ruled by competing hierarchies is characteristic of a culture motivated by an idea of universal order, in which everything is understood as related to everything else. The same is true of Greek science, aiming to express every aspect of creation in terms of varying ratios of the same basic constituents of air, earth, fire, and water, and explaining transitions as alterations in the balance. The idea that each species or member of creation is a more or less perfect example of an archetype or "ideal form" is fundamental to classical aesthetics, and remains locked in the notion of a hierarchical society to the present day. Accordingly, perfection is embodied in the notion of a stable state, and of transitional forms as imperfect or unstable, or otherwise disabled or diseased (all of these terms implying loss of ability to function, and loss of composure).

That in fact the world of creation is a dynamic environment in which species can be selected and crossbred to develop new and desirable traits is a perception reflected in the arts of plant and animal husbandry from the dawn of agriculture. It was not even true, even in Plato's or Parmenides' day, to insist that the world and its species were perfect and unchanging, or immune to human interference. The idea of changelessness as an ideal traces back to Parmenides. That change in form is still to be feared is shown in the term *chimera* which shares the same root as alchemy and chemistry: the science of change affecting inert substances. That life is change, and therefore chemical, was considered fanciful. The only reasonable excuse in making the assumption of ideal types was in order to be able to discuss the world at all. Argument, conflict, and learned discussion were evidence that individuals did indeed differ in their interpretations of the world, and understanding of one another, to the extent of imagining that the resolution of difference, whether by arms, logic, or definition of terms, would be bound to lead to a change of state (sense of identity, belief, and state of mind) among the vanquished in favor of the victor. It would not be until the renaissance that the concept of change of mind would be reinvented as a tactic of political or material expediency unfettered by moral or religious constraint.

The modern keyboard is itself a renaissance invention, one incorporating a number of sophisticated compromises with the ideal world of natural sound. A knowledge of harmony, arising from observation of the behavior of vibrating strings and air columns, leads to the idea of a natural hierarchy of permitted tonal states, or tonal relationships, based on ratios of perfect fifths. We recognize a natural hierarchy of interval relationships in music incorporating a drone, including mouth music. For scientists in the age of Galileo, a new age of exploration, contradictions arose in deciding between a scale of perfect interval relationships but restricted modulation, and a standard system of tuning allowing for unrestricted movement from key to key, but at a cost of harmonic imperfection. To eliminate imperfection would require a keyboard of infinite length. The decision to limit the chromatic octave to twelve fixed pitches was significant, like limiting the alphabet to a fixed number of letter forms. It made practical sense from the point of view of notation, execution, and instrument design, and was intuitively realistic in terms of human fallibilities in pitch discrimination, memory, and the acoustics of performance.

Standardization of the keyboard, and its associated imagery of equal temperament, came about in response to the invention of a standardized music notation. It led to the popularization of a range of domestic and portable keyboard instruments playable by non-professionals, in particular the ladies of the house. The baroque keyboard owes its form and characteristic deficiencies of expression to the prior limitations of a system of music notation which is unique to western civilization. Bach's well-tempered keyboard was the musical typewriter of its day, an instrument that reduced the skills of playing a real musical instrument to reading a text and pressing the right keys in the right order.

The piano or harpsichord keyboard organizes pitch in a linear fashion to assist a *reader* to *reproduce* information on a music stand. In printed music the data is organized in a pitch continuum from bass to treble, and in time from left to right, as for a printed text. By comparison, the arrangement of letters on a modern keyboard, varying from language to language, is designed to assist a *typesetter* to *compose* a finished communication from handwritten or shorthand notes, or from a dictaphone recording, or straight from memory. For the keys of a typewriter to be arranged in alphabetical order makes typing more difficult, since as with playing the piano, the task is executed more efficiently through the fingers acting independently of vision. The typist is also typically producing a new article from scratch, whereas the task of the keyboard is typically of reproducing an existing article.

Cage's prepared piano can also be interpreted in another sense as a casualty of war. An instrument emblematic of romantic idealism during the Second World War, associated with images of heroic aspiration and high culture under fire in Richard Addinsell's *Warsaw Concerto* for the 1941 movie *Dangerous Moonlight*, and Charles Williams's *The Dream of Olwen*, composed for Anthony Asquith's *The Way to the Stars* of 1945, is rendered a victim at the war's end, its heroic voice reduced to a whisper as a consequence of pieces of shrapnel lodged in its body, victim of its own heroics. The mortally wounded grand piano of Stockhausen's *Samstag aus LICHT* ("Lucifer's Dream") tells a similar story.

The imagery of disintegration works on a number of levels. Unlike the weirdly eroticized samurai aesthetic of *Crash* some fifty years later, the meaning of Cage's fractured wholeness may also have to do with healing and recovery: calling to mind the concert pianist Paul Wittgenstein, brother of the philosopher, who lost his right arm in the trenches of World War I, but went on to resume his concert career and commissioned concert works for the piano (left hand) by Ravel, Richard Strauss, Prokofiev, Britten, and others. Perhaps the prepared piano of Cage, a pacifist, may be construed as a transferred epithet of human and musical survival.

Boulez was attracted to Cage for his formal methods, but as a recent apprentice to Schaeffer's *musique concrète* studio he had encountered the prepared piano as a useful extension of the limited range of effects available to an art of prerecorded sound then in its infancy. Schaeffer's 1948 series of concrete études had been based on prerecorded train sounds, pots and pans ("casseroles"), and "tourniquets," a reference to turntables. After Cage's visit in 1949 the prepared piano was added to the studio's repertoire of sonic effects. Pierre Henry plays prepared piano in Schaeffer's slight but amusing *Bidule en ut* (Thingummyjig in C) of 1950. The instrument had become a fixture by 1952 when Stockhausen arrived in Paris, and provided the tonal material on which the *Konkrete Etüde*, his first exercise in tape composition, is based.

If the image of Cage preparing his instrument before a fashionable Paris audience calls to mind an eighteenth-century keyboardist tuning the instrument provided by his host before entertaining the guests, the same image is evoked, with a hint of malice, in Pierre

Schaeffer's account of the high society soirée in 1949 at which the young American first performed in Paris:

> The scene unfolded at the home of Mme Tezenas some time prior to 1950. Before an invited public of indolent and insatiable pleasure-seekers, a tall young American, at the time virtually unknown, could be seen bent over and fishing about in the interior of a grand piano. Armed with erasers, nails, morsels of wood, rubber and suchlike, he executed a series of criminal acts upon the strings and the sound-board, the hammers and the felts, in a rite of preparation which, he said, should ideally be implemented with the utmost precision over two or three hours. Then, seated at the keyboard, he performed with exquisite classicism the *Sonatas and Interludes* of 1946–1948, followed by the *Bacchanale* of 1938, the piano transformed into a percussion orchestra, a music strangely reminiscent of Asia.[1]

Cristofori's invention in 1700 of the hammer-action fortepiano, combining the efficient layout of the baroque keyboard with the touch-sensitivity of the cymbalom, reminds us not only that the harpsichord was not designed for expression on a human scale, but also that it was not *intended* as an instrument for continuously modifying the dynamics of a performance, by expressive crescendos and diminuendos. This was in effect a new instrument to give expression to the perceptions of a volatile humanism, a product of the same Italian sensibility that already sanctioned the *crescendo* in operas by Monteverdi, and the violin family.

Dynamics on the harpsichord, an instrument designed for mechanical consistency of attack, could only be varied, if at all, by a change of register from loud to muted, audible as a change of timbre (the same as the soft pedal on a modern piano). Cristofori's new touch-sensitive keyboard responded to subtle differences of finger pressure, and in doing so abandoned the older virtues of tonal consistency and objectivity, ceding control of timbre to the whim of the performer. At this time Antonio Vivaldi, also Italian, was perfecting the concerto grosso, a keyboard-based ensemble from which the classical symphony orchestra would eventually evolve. Ignoring their relative merits as concert works, concertos for mandolin by Vivaldi, and for lute, guitar, and mandolin by J. S.

Bach, can be understood as using the solo instruments as variable attack instruments to impose an expressive dimension on the bland tone quality of the harpsichord in anticipation of Cristofori's fortepiano.

The onset, or attack, of a note largely determines its tone quality. If the onset of a recorded trumpet note is edited away, what is left sounds more like a flute. If a tape recording of a piano is reversed, it sounds like a harmonium with motion sickness. The initiative taken by Cristofori in inventing the hammer-action keyboard is predicated on a significant awareness of the difference between the onset of a tone and its continuation, equivalent in language terms to understanding the distinct effects of different consonants on vowel tone in song. In his treatise on architecture, published in the first century AD, Vitruvius refers to the natural variety of consonantal sounds, and their classification as abrupt, gradual, diffuse, etc. Vitruvius acknowledges Aristoxenus as his source of acoustics information, so we are free to assume that Cristofori was also basing his concept of a touch-sensitive keyboard on classical sources. After the harpsichord had been superseded by the fortepiano as a solo instrument it was possible not only to play soft and loud on the same keyboard, merely by varying the touch, but also to move continuously from loud to soft and back, opening the door to a new performance style, raised to a high degree of sophistication by Mozart and Haydn, of continuous modulation of tone and loudness. In the nineteenth century, music of primarily emotional contour began to take precedence over earlier values of objectivity, leading to the temporary eclipse of all but a few composers and items of the classical repertoire. The objective idiom persisted all the same in mechanical instruments such as the musical box, orchestrion, and pianola.

A monument to typographic culture, the modern grand piano is incapable by design of continuous melody or expression of any kind. It cannot bend the note. It cannot make a crescendo on a note. It cannot glide from one note to the next, like a normal voice, or guitar, or violin. Over the years Cristofori's keyboard has been systematically modified to address inherent inadequacies: changing the hammer action, changing the hammer material, varying the leg design and transfer of energy to the floor, making the casework larger, deeper, and more resonant, introducing stronger bracing to support heavier and more powerful strings, and raising the tuning from A 384 hertz in Haydn's day to A 432 hertz by the time of Beethoven—a huge increase in tension, all of it to create the effect of a singing tone. Cage's extraordinary achievement in reverse engineering has deconstructed the intellectual apparatus and prejudices of three centuries to remove any pretense to singing quality, and reassert the piano's original nature as a percussion instrument.

Cage is not the only American composer of his generation to invent new keyboard instruments. More varied, more grounded in theory, more consistent in tone, and for the same reasons arguably more interesting in the long run, are the keyboards of Harry Partch, starting with a pair of modified quarter-tone and sixth-tone harmoniums, and gradually extended over the composer's working lifetime to encompass a range of quasi-ethnic instruments (a giant marimba, cloud chamber bowls, and the *Zymo-xyl*, a set of tuned and eviscerated lightbulbs), and drawing on radio special effects. According to Henry Brant, who was friendly with both Cage and Partch during the forties when all three were living in New York, Partch saw a future in new timbres, and has been proven right. Few synthesizer patches are as authentically interesting, however, as the genuinely "acoustic" sounds of Partch's invented instruments.

Whether the inventor of the prepared piano was as interested in new timbres for their own sakes is not quite so clearcut. Cage was driven by a different imperative of total disconnection, like the serialists in Europe, according to which notes in sequence would no longer be heard as necessarily connected, either logically or in any other way. This was an aesthetic not so much of new sounds, as of accidental encounters. The fact that a method of preparing a piano, so painstakingly laid out in the score of *Sonatas and Interludes*, would be likely to produce completely different results on pianos of different manufacture, would in that sense be as much an advantage as a criticism.

By changing the distribution of forces within the strings, damping the strings with a variety of materials at different locations has the effect of suppressing certain partials of a normally complex overtone structure, and enhancing or distorting others. Messiaen may not have approved of the crudity of Cage's interventions, but along with Boulez he must have appreciated the underlying motive —and perhaps the wit—of converting the instrument of Brahmsian and Rachmaninov rhetoric into a vehicle of crystalline arabesque. In fact Messiaen does two things by way of acknowledgement: one, he composes *Mode de valeurs et d'intensités*, in effect a thirty-six-tone prepared piano (only previously specified keys are employed, and each is always sounded at previously specified loudness, attack, and duration values); two, he invents the "prepared organ," an instrument in which normally dissonant mixture stops are employed as sonorities in their own right.

Although outwardly offended by any suggestion of influence, Stockhausen takes up and greatly improves on Cage's original idea of transformed piano tone in *Mantra* for two pianos of 1970. In this work, without mechanical intervention, the piano timbre is modulated electronically by tunable sweep frequency oscillators that in the course of the piece impose a higher-order tonality on constituent sections corresponding to original and inverted series. In addition to enriching the piano tone in a variety of attractive ways, Stockhausen's modulation of piano tone by sinewave control frequencies has the effect of "critiquing" their respective tunings: the "scientific" frequency scale of a signal generator pitted against the traditionally imperfect equal-tempered tuning of a piano. Right before an audience's ears the medieval canon of perfect harmony meets and clashes with the Galileian heresy of tempered tuning. The audible consequences are a succession of pulsating, glistening, fascinating, and occasionally haunting sonorities, distorting and shadowing the two pianos, and at times appearing even to interact in the space between them.

Stockhausen is right to be outraged, of course. His method is richer in consequence and more systematic than Cage, and the acoustic results are also more predictable and controllable in effect. Here the piano sound is shadowed and alienated, but not abused. All the same, the two composers' methods of preparation express a certain reciprocity of view: Cage, that the piano is no more than a keyboard interface with potential applications in other sonic directions than the selection of combinations from a uniform sound mass; Stockhausen drawing attention to the fact that the sounds of a piano, while seemingly uniform, in fact differ considerably in timbre and in tuning across registers, and react in very different but characteristic ways to frequency measures applied at any one time to the *entire range of the piano*, and not just to selected keys.

At the heart of both modes of transformation the same critical concepts remain: (1) the concept of a closed, homogeneous system or universe of acoustic possibilities arranged in an order of discrete step values accessed individually by keys; and (2) the idea of an enticing alternative world of acoustic possibility that has been persistently suppressed by, and lies beyond, that rational structure. That other, mystical world can nevertheless be revealed by tuning the piano in unorthodox ways.

Cage's music for prepared piano is perfect for callers waiting for a connection, as I discovered when calling the head office of Naxos USA some years ago, when their recordings of Cage by Boris Berman were fresh off the press. That the new sounds created by preparing the piano tend to resemble gongs and cymbals and give an overall impression to western ears of a vaguely oriental percussion orchestra should come as no surprise. The piano is a percussion instrument after all. That an oriental percussion orchestra might conceivably sound like a prepared piano is an insight perhaps more provocative than the trivial notion of the prepared piano conforming to a wishful orientalism on Cage's part. It hints at as yet unexamined possible correspondences between the oriental percussion ensemble as a composite instrument of musical speech, in opposition to the analogous principles of western musical speech embodied in the keyboard mechanism. For example, we may intuit a connection between the uninflected tones of the western prepared piano and absence of inflection in modern western (i.e., New York, Parisian) speech, in comparison with the inflections or bending tones available to nonwestern music, and the implications of rising and falling syllables in Asian speech as indicators of meaning.

The use of a sampler keyboard to coordinate sound effects is now regular practice in Hollywood, for example the space combat sequences in the *Star Wars* series, timed and executed from a midi keyboard to a musical score. Cage's inspired notion of a keyboard interface controlling a choreography of sound effects makes sense, even though viewers remain unaware of the musical systems underlying such exuberantly destructive imagery.

That the pianist of a prepared piano is the one in control, and the instrument simply responds passively, is perfectly clear. If the piano were suitably prepared, the pianist could even play speech sounds. And one would have attained a situation where notation is reinvented as a mystery code for connecting syllables into words. Disconnecting notation from musical sound is another version of the symbolist ideal of disconnecting the verbal music of poetry from printed words and their ordinary meanings.

Stockhausen's *Mikrophonie I* takes the non-western approach of using a tam-tam, an organic sound source, as an alternative to the fragmented continuum of the piano keyboard. A composition where the preparation is applied in real time and in organic gestures to a single resonating source is bound, or so the theory goes, to produce a range of alien sounds that are not merely "different" in a philosophical sense, but fundamentally *continuous* as gestures, and organically *related* as sonorities, by virtue of being derived from the same body of vibration.

Note

1. Pierre Schaeffer, *La Musique Concrète*. Paris: Press Universitaires de France, 1967, 65.

TWENTY-FOUR

ALEATORY

Un coup de dés n'abolira jamais le hasard.

STÉPHANE MALLARMÉ

The composition we live in changes but what happens does not change. We inside us do not change but our emphasis and the moment in which we live changes. That it is never the same moment it is never the same emphasis at any successive moment of existing. Then really what is repetition. It is very interesting to ask and it is a very interesting thing to know.

GERTRUDE STEIN

From the Latin "alea" (dice): aleatory is a method of composition practiced by composers after 1950 that allows a limited randomization in the performance ordering of precomposed segments. Throwing dice in a game of chance is a ritual in which the player allows crucial decisions to be made by fate, and is prepared to bet on the outcome. In practice, as any gambler will acknowledge, good decision-making can influence a person's success even in a game of chance.

The term is associated with Pierre Boulez and related to his admiration of the poet Stéphane Mallarmé, in particular the poem *Un coup de dés* ("A throw of the die will never [totally] eliminate chance") from *Poésies complètes* (1887). Consisting of a main statement and appositional subordinate clauses in parentheses, the poem is designed and laid out on the page in such a way that it can be read in a variety of orders without its sense being affected.

The chance element in an aleatoric composition has to do with the ordering of precomposed elements, which are fully composed, and not to the spontaneous invention of musical content. In an ideal world such a reordering process would lead in each case to a different meaning, but this is not the case with classical aleatoric music, even though the reordering may lead to differently nuanced interpretations of the same basic text.

Monet's celebrated studies of Rouen Cathedral and parts of London under differing light conditions are contemporary with Mallarmé, and may be regarded as aleatoric in the sense that the accidents of time of day and associated light conditions are able to transform a viewer's perception of the same object viewed from precisely the same vantage point.

Most western music is through-composed, meaning it has a beginning, a middle, and an end. That order never changes, though at times elements may be edited out. Musically speaking, the western world seems far too obsessed with continuity of experience and musical argument and oblivious to the possibilities of a music created in modules that can be assembled in any number of different orders. This is why the sudden surge of interest in aleatoric music in the 1950s—in Europe by *die Reihe* advocates Boulez, Pousseur, Stockhausen, and Berio; in the United States by Morton Feldman, Cage, and Earle Brown—was welcome and interesting, and its premature demise in the 1960s such a disappointment.

For many composers, the prototype and model of aleatoric process was music for the movies. From the silent movie era musicians were employed to play along with the screen action to cover the noise of the projector and set a more or less appropriate mood. Only on rare occasions was this music through-composed. Most silent movie pianists or ensembles relied on a basic repertoire of music-hall songs and popular classics, snatches of which were edited together to follow the screen action. A few publishers compiled guidebooks and theme albums for house musicians, copious selections of familiar themes classified by mood, temperament, and pictorial imagery. The music assembled by an ensemble paid by a movie house to accompany silent movies was totally subordinate to the visual image, was not intended to make any independent sense, and its use of already familiar materials was a way of ensuring that its emotional references were instantly and subconsciously understood and did not distract attention from the visual action.

The use of quasi-improvised musical illustration as background to a slide show presentation predates the movies and sets the tone for the genre of musical montage that follows no internal logic of thematic development or continuity. Aleatory was fashionable even in the eighteenth century. The first movement of Mozart's *Eine kleine Nachtmusik* deconstructs into a succession of phraselike frames or gestures with very little in common other than being in the same key and sharing the same pulsation. The Introduction to Rossini's Overture to *La Cenerentola* is a brilliant assembly of isolated gestures chosen seemingly at random.

As a frequent moviegoer Erik Satie devised a movie score for René Clair's *Entr'acte* out of a deliberately composed miscellany of fragments in familiar styles to be juxtaposed with scenes in the movie but to convey the same sense of incongruity he had experienced at the movies from musical choices made on the spur of the moment out of a limited repertoire of popular items. Satie's friend and collaborator Jean Cocteau, who devised the surrealist scenario of *Parade* in 1917, based on European perceptions of American newsreels as bizarre kaleidoscopes of inconsequential images, would himself eventually become a director of surreal romances in the making of which it delighted him to take music composed by Georges Auric for certain scenes and transpose them to completely different scenes.

> What I like is accidental synchronism. I provoke it . . . by reshuffling. I've been using that method ever since *Le Sang d'un Poète*, when I shifted and reversed the order of the music in every single sequence. . . . I took the most irreverent liberties with [Auric's music]. I recorded the music [for *Orphée*] without the images, and for example put the scherzo he had composed for the comic home-coming scene into the chase through the deserted house. Or, even better, I recorded "Eurydice's Lament" by Gluck, meaning to use it only for the wireless in the cottage. But when I cut into Auric's music at the first shot of Heurtebise's entrance, I noticed that the first and last notes of Gluck's music fitted exactly with the first and last images of the scene, and I shamelessly took advantage of that little miracle.[1]

In doing so Cocteau was building on Satie's instinct for dissociation and avoiding the dangers of "mickey-mousing" encountered by

Hollywood composers, Korngold in particular, that are apt to occur when movie music is choreographed too intimately with the screen action, so that the action suddenly becomes less real.

Anticipating radio and piped music, which were some decades away from impacting on popular culture, Satie and Darius Milhaud had previously experimented in creating a *musique d'ameublement* or music to be treated as part of the furniture, at a picture exhibition in 1920 at which a quintet of piano and winds played "fragments of popular refrains from *Mignon* and *Danse Macabre* and isolated phrases repeated over and over again, like the pattern of wallpaper" as a background, not to be listened to and not intended to interfere with the visitors' conversation in any way. Unfortunately the Paris audience did not perceive themselves as actors in a newsreel and persisted in standing still and listening to the music.

In *Entr'acte*, a movie interval entertainment for the ballet *Relâche* (a title meaning "Performance canceled"),

> the action on the screen is accompanied by musical phrases cut, as it were, into lengths, constantly repeated and juxtaposed without any attempt at illustration and quite dissociated from the meaning of the images presented to the eye. The role of the music in fact is deliberately confined to underlining the action indirectly without calling attention to itself.[2]

The aleatoric elements in Satie's conception of incidental music are (1) a selection process from an existing repertoire of composed fragments of music, (2) a selection process relatively indifferent to the expressive content of the music in relation to the narrative it accompanies, and (3) a selection process equally indifferent to any impression of incoherence or inconsequentiality that may be created by the juxtaposition of musical items.

These contribute to an aesthetic manifesto that some may interpret as not too far removed from Schoenberg's "music of twelve tones related only one to another." Underlying both Satie and Schoenberg can be detected a Freudian, or at least surrealist, belief in the subliminal power of artistic intuition to imbue otherwise randomly selected materials with narrative meaning. The same aesthetic of willful dissociation reemerges, in more subtle guise, in Messiaen's birdsong rhapsodies.

RULES OF ASSOCIATION

The first puzzle of aleatoric music is the idea of a musical sequence assembled by a random selection process, from a repertoire of fragments, having meaning; the second, third, and subsequent mysteries are that different sequences from the same repertoire will also have meaning, but different meanings from each other.

The puzzle is a key to Artificial Intelligence research. John von Neumann, a key figure in the history of computer science, game theory, and information science, was fascinated by Tristan Tzara's idea in the 1930s that poetry could be composed by taking words at random out of a hat. Neumann's previous history involved wartime codemaking and codebreaking, the application of reversible mathematics to number sequences representing letters of the alphabet, from which serialism in music is also partly derived.

Game theory was developed to learn from war strategies and apply the same principles to business and economic practice. It is about making the "right choice" from a number of options available at any one time. The right choice is one that confers a decisive advantage in a contest that only one opponent can win. The development of game theory coincided with a period of intensive research into a theory of language organization that transcended national language differences: a theory of how ideas are formed and articulated. It relied on a conception of knowledge as a selection and ordering of terms from a preexisting vocabulary to preexisting rules of association that guarantee meaning. For a statement to have meaning it had to be understood by others in the sense intended; the critical resemblance of game theory to battlefield strategy being that orders are conveyed verbally and the success of any campaign depends on those orders being successfully carried out. (We will overlook the logical weaknesses embedded in both these positions: namely, that campaign strategies rely on a conception of a *fixed* limited number of options available to both sides at any time, and that orders are obeyed *without question*, i.e. without appreciation of their full human consequences.)

The information scientist's extensively documented inquiries into text encryption and deconstruction, including breaking up of a text into arbitrary groups of two, three, four, five, or more letters (as depicted by Raymond Queneau in *Exercices de Style*), aimed at discovering and exploiting fundamental properties of language, and of the language of different cultures—for example, letter formations corresponding to frequently used words, and frequency distributions of individual letters corresponding to their pattern of incidence in English or the target language—that a mechanical reading device might be programmed to recognize. Both Tzara's suggestion of taking words at random from a hat, and Queneau's fragmentation of a text into units of a few letters, presuppose an original text that has meaning and is coherent: a poem or message, and not just a page from a dictionary. The prototype of such a text is the *Proteus poem* of Julius Caesar Scaliger (1484–1558), a form of words the order of which can freely rearranged.

Sit pax da pacis tu Rex peto tempore nostro.
Sit pax da pacis tu tempore Rex peto nostro.
Sit pax da pacis Rex tu peto tempore nostro.
Sit pax da pacis Rex tempore tu peto nostro.
Sit pax da pacis nostro peto tempore tu Rex.

. . .

Nostro pacis tempore Rex sit pax peto da tu.
Nostro pacis tempore Rex sit da peto tu pax.
Nostro pacis tempore Rex sit da peto pax tu.
Nostro pacis tempore Rex sit tu peto da pax.
Nostro paCIs teMpore ReX sIt tV nostro Da paX.

From an anonymous chronogram in hexameter the 24,480 permutations of which run to 346 manuscript pages and encode the date of composition MDCXXVII or 1627. An example of a selection of words that may be drawn from a hat at random and always make sense

Born into the same central European culture that produced Scaliger and the Proteus poem, von Neumann was interested in discovering the point at which meaning could be perceived in a word sequence randomized from a coherent text. If an original text is randomized, its totality is preserved as a set of limits: vocabulary, language (alphabet, letter distribution), subject matter, and even tone of voice and personality. If a given vocabulary is intact but randomized, much of a text's original meaning can be grasped without a reader having to restore it to its original order.

Poets routinely arrange words and phrases in orders different from normal speech. Sometimes this is done for rhythm and rhyme, and sometimes to create ambiguities of contiguity, the same phrase referring back as well as forward in context to set up potential differences of construction and meaning. Naturally this is deeply irritating to AI researchers, though it has led to a small portfolio of interesting computer-generated poems. Fridge magnet poetry is a recent and slightly more sophisticated application.

A related issue affecting semiotics and information science has to do with the implications of language as a system and vocabulary as a resource. If all that a speaker can do is use words from a common vocabulary, and order them according to rules that enable them to convey meaning, how then is it possible for anyone, especially a child, to say something new? And since language is the instrument of thought, how is it possible for anything new to be imagined? If words are the only medium for sharing information, and all words are already classified, then the only new information that can be created has to be a rearrangement of existing information. Compared to the ruminations of a Scaliger, Dylan Thomas's word permutations seem a little tame. But they make new conjunctions and are evocative, which is quite an achievement.

> Dead men naked they shall be one
> With the man in the wind and the west moon . . .

from the elegy "And Death shall have no Dominion" is more than a reordering of "man in the moon and the west wind" which is what a listener expects and what gives the phrase a sudden sense of familiarity and potency. The permutation is truly surreal, certainly aesthetically more satisfying than T. S. Eliot's or Oliver Wendell Holmes' "patient etherized upon a table" for whom the universe is merely suffused with the smell of turpentine.

Paul Valéry complained that poets, unlike composers of music, were forced to use words, regarding words as snares of the imagination and music as a blissful transcendence of grammar and the dictionary. Since it is not bound by the same rules of association as language, in principle it should be possible for any random order of musical phrases to make sense. A large part of the physical impact —perhaps even, moral impact—of the Sacrificial Dance that brings Stravinsky's *Le Sacre du Printemps* to a shattering climax, arises from the composer's constantly varying, asymmetrical reiteration of a limited number of fragmentary rhythmic modules, an image intended to reflect the physical deterioration of the victim, and in effect astonishingly similar to the distorted arrhythmia of a patient in terminal cardiac failure. In this case the emotional impact is created less by the juxtaposed material than the violence of juxtaposition itself.

News editors counsel their reporters to write in short sentences. Such a style is easy to edit, and in the news media where space is constantly at a premium, the ability to edit a report without loss of sense or coherence is a vital consideration. The implications of a prose that can be edited, and hence "read," in abbreviated form, are as interesting as Mallarmé's poem. In the terms of artificial intelligence, they ask questions like: "Is grammar a form of logic?" Or, "Is math a grammar?" Since so much popular music is set to words, it is easy to fall into an assumption that music is also narrative in implication, and that the order in which a music unfolds is the same as a grammatical or logical order on which its meaning depends.

Events that happen in an order are normally described in the same order, and their significance is normally inferred from the order in which they occurred, or are reported to have occurred. But being in a certain order does not always mean that the events make sense, for instance (a) because the prior objective of a course of events does not always require that a certain order be followed, or (b) because in a dynamic real environment unforeseen obstacles may arise to influence the order in which events are executed. The pattern that insists on a particular order of events being followed on every occasion is identified as a pathological symptom of autism and not as normal behavior.

That grammar and syntax influence the order of words in a sentence so that the latter has meaning, or that the terms of a mathematical equation are arranged in a certain sequence to converge on an equals sign and answering term, suggests a relationship between grammatical order and causality: that meaning not only requires that data be presented in a certain order, but that there is a necessary causal relation between reading data in the correct order and being informed, getting the point, and above all *being changed* by the content transforming a state of ignorance of something into a state of knowledge of the same thing.

That this is an old controversy is revealed by the Cartesian dictum "I think, therefore I am" conveying an impression that such formulations are necessarily logical, that the operation of logic leads to an alteration of consciousness, and by extension that the roles of grammar and syntax in the formulation of statements in a particular order are necessarily logical as well, because they induce a change in the mind of the thinker. Descartes is surmising that the act of thinking resembles a chemical reaction in which thoughts in close proximity interact to generate a new compound and a certain amount of heat. For the period, coinciding with the foundation of the Royal Society, it is a fashionable line for the philosopher to take. But it does not make sense. It is a futile attempt to draw a causal significance from the juxtaposition of two statements, one of which "I think" is a personal observation, the other "I am" merely superfluous. The weasel word is "therefore." It has no place. The experience of being may have impressed Descartes as a personal epiphany, but its inference is hardly a tribute to logic. "Sir, I refute it thus!" cried Dr. Johnson later and in another context, stubbing his toe. *I hurt*, therefore I am.

Since being is a necessary condition of thinking, but does not entail the power to think or the act of thinking as a consequence, it is misleading to infer, or even suggest, that to be aware of oneself thinking (which is what Descartes is really saying) is a prior condition, let alone the only prior condition, of determining that one is existing. The "I" who puts thoughts into my head may be the author of a book I am reading, and not myself; or my beloved spouse summoning me to table for a meal, or the parson's voice from the pulpit breaking into my Sunday morning reverie. That I may be spontaneously aware of the thoughts of others does not make them my thoughts or validate my existence as a thinking being.

That a statement makes sense does not mean that it has to be grammatical. That a statement is grammatical does not mean that it has to be logical. That a statement is logical does not mean that it has to be true.

It is of course essential for Descartes and his successors in AI to make thought commensurate with speech, or rather a text, since we cannot know that a person is thinking unless something is said or written, and hearing is unreliable. Speech is the missing element in the Cartesian dictum, which being fully expressed says "I say and hear myself saying that I am thinking, for which reason I am objectively aware of myself in the act of saying something, and must therefore exist as a being capable of hearing, of knowing what is being said, and of recognizing the person saying it as myself."

That language is stored in the memory as vocabulary and figures of speech, and retrievable at random in order to give effect to ideas and directions in everyday life, is part of the explanation of the Cartesian fallacy, if we can call it that. In order to say what he claims to think, the philosopher draws on his knowledge of language. That he employs the present tense, or present participle ("I am thinking") is a ploy to give an impression of thinking aloud and of a logical inference occurring in real time. We are not fooled by this. In speech as in real life, objects and images are retrieved from memory in random order and according to rules of association that even Freud understood to have more in common with face recognition than the alphabet.

Likewise a grammar in AI intends to define language rules in functional terms allowing for the substitution of subject, verb, adjective, adverb, and object components. Accordingly a new sentence is not aleatoric since (a) words can only be employed in their "proper function," and (b) the order of terms is subject to rules. Aleatoric music makes no such rules. Terms from its repertoire of words or phrases are truly interchangeable. And in an ideal world, every new ordering should give rise to a statement of new meaning. Here Descartes meets Chomsky. Where do the rules come from? Cage's *mesostics* are an interesting consideration; Samuel Beckett's and Helmut Heissenbüttel's reiterative verses another; still another is William Burroughs's invention of the cut-up.

COMPOSING BY DICE

In 1757 Johann Kirnberger, a pupil of J. S. Bach, published an *Allzeit fertiger Polonaisen- und Menuettenkomponist* (loosely translated as "a ready reckoner for composing polonaises and minuets." At about the same time one Johannes Kade, town musician and ballet repetiteur of Kassel, published tables by which "anybody, whether musically trained or not, is able to make up as many minuets as they like." Since the duties of a repetiteur can become rather boring, and the musical quality of a repetiteur performance is less important to the practicing dancers than keeping time, one can readily understand why Kade would be interested in the idea of automating the composition of minuets and eventually handing over the task to a mechanical player. Stravinsky had much the same idea in mind when he collaborated with the Pleyel Piano Company to publish piano roll versions of his Russian Ballets, scores of a complexity far beyond the average underpaid repetiteur.

Dozens of "recipe books for music" were published, some by distinguished names. *Tables from which a person can compose minuets and trios by throwing dice* was published in Vienna in 1781 by the theorist and historian Maximilian Stadler, a friend of Haydn and Mozart. *Le Toton Harmonique* or "Harmonic teetotum"—named after a spinning top of six or more sides, on which letters of the alphabet, in this case, measures of music are inscribed—was published in 1762 by the Marquis de la Chevardière. A *Gioco Filarmonico* ("Music-lovers' Joke") for two violins or flutes and bass, allegedly by Haydn, was published in Naples in 1790, with the subtitle "an easy method of composing an endless number of minuets and trios, even for those unlearned in counterpoint." Methods for composing waltzes (the word *Walzer* in German means "a barrel" as in a bran tub, lottery or lucky dip) were published anonymously by Carl Philipp Emanuel Bach, the son of J. S. Bach, and over the name of Mozart himself after the composer's death. Numerous editions of the Mozart *Anleitung* were published: by Hummel, Simrock, Goetz, and Kreitner in Germany, by Henning in Amsterdam, and in 1806 by Wheatstone in London, under the title *Mozart's Musical Game*, where it is described rather fancifully as "An easy system for composing an endless number of Waltzes, Rondos, Hornpipes & Reels."

All of these compositional methods work in a similar way. The basic composition is in two parts, in binary form. In the first part the music modulates from tonic to dominant, and in the second part it modulates back from the dominant to the tonic. There are eight measures in each part, numbered alphabetically A to H. The number thrown by the dice (all of the methods demand at least two dice, or two throws of a die added together) is referred to a table, one for each part, ordered in columns A to H numbered vertically from 2 to

12. Suppose the aspiring composer begins by thowing a 10. One looks up the part I table at column A, square 10. Box A-10 contains the number 98. We then consult measure 98 in the accompanying look-up table of measures of music, and write it down as measure 1. The next throw is a 7. Table I, column B, box B-7, contains the number 157. Find the corresponding measure in the look-up table, and write it in as measure 2. And so on, until the eight measures of part I are completed. The same procedure follows for part II, this time using the part II table. When sixteen measures are written out, the composition is complete.

Although to an amateur the generation of seemingly coherent if uninspired pieces of music by throwing a pair of dice might seem magical, in practice the well-shuffled music tables of written-out measures and the numbers assigned to them only look random at first glance. A careful scrutiny of the Mozart *Anleitung* shows that measures bearing the numbers 5, 24, 30, and 33 are in fact the same music, and are all allocated to the same position in the composition, part I, measure 8. Throwing the dice merely gives the appearance of randomness to a selection process that has been contrived to make rudimentary sense in every possible configuration.

That more than just Mozart's name was involved in this early form of aleatoric composition is indicated by surviving manuscript sketches, for example of the Adagio KV 516, with each measure identified by a letter—lower case *a* to *z* (omitting *c*, *q*, *x*, and *y*), and upper case in sequence B D F G K L M N P Q S T W Z—that is, amounting to a matrix or magic square of 36 (6 × 6) letters.

Attention was drawn to the existence of the Mozart *Anleitung* in a 1952 article by Henry Cowell in which the veteran American composer sought to establish a connection between modern musical developments in chance processes and the classical tradition.[3] Cage had begun employing dice to order items from a table of musical elements. He would soon go on to embrace the I-Ching, a traditional Chinese method of throwing yarrow-reeds, one that generates a larger range of hexagrams, or sixfold possibilities, than a pair of dice. Later still, in collaboration with Lejaren A. Hiller, composer and codeveloper of the pioneer ILLIAC computer language for generating melodies, Cage employed a computer-generated 10,000 random number set to aid in the composition of HPSCHD for a maximum of seven harpsichords and fifty-one tapes (1967–1969). US purchasers of the Nonesuch longplaying disc were rewarded with segments of the printout inserted in the record sleeve.

In pointing out that the name of Mozart, of all people, was connected with a late-eighteenth century fashion for creating music by the throw of a pair of dice, neither Cowell, nor anyone since, thought to ask: (1) why the fashion might have arisen in the first place, and (2) whether there might be any evidence of serious music in the public domain being composed by such means. From the dire quality of waltzes obtained by this procedure it would seem highly unlikely to find reputable composers taking it seriously. However the invention of a system for composing simple musical forms for pleasure is already a good fit with an eighteenth-century aristocracy obsessed with mechanical automata and devoted to the Cartesian doctrine of human beings as machines. After two decades of experimentation and development, in 1791 the Hungarian Wolfgang von Kempelen published a treatise on his invention of a Heath Robinsonian contraption, assembled from bits of various musical instruments, that could actually be programmed to speak.[4]

A few years ago, reviewing the tape composition *Hymnen* by Karlheinz Stockhausen, I noted that the composer's idea of taking national anthems apart and reassembling them into new melody sequences was similar to, and may even have been inspired by, AI researches conducted in the United States that sought to transform one melody into another by computer recognition and interpolation between melody shapes and tone resources (scales). For a time I assumed the choice of national anthems by both parties was simply coincidental. It now appears that national anthems are more suitable for computer randomizing operations of this kind because they have been composed in such a way to begin with.

GOD SAVE THE KING

Of uncertain origin, the melody "God Save the King"—in Europe, the British national anthem and in the United States a patriotic song sung to alternative lyrics as "My Country 'tis of Thee"—is claimed to have been composed by Henry Carey and first published around 1743. The military context of its composition cannot be overlooked. A variant form, "God Save Our Lord the King," also by Carey, is said to have become popular as a loyalist anthem at the time of the Scottish Rebellion of Bonnie Prince Charlie in 1745. Shortly thereafter the same tune was simultaneously published as an English anthem in different harmonizations by Charles Burney and Thomas Arne. It also appeared as a minuet to an anonymously composed country dance titled "Long Live the King" in a collection published in London in 1748.

The term *country dance* incidentally is English and applied to dances in which male and female partners line up face to face, like opposing armies. On mainland Europe the same is translated as *contredanse* (French) and *Kontretanz* (German), implying opposition, a difference in interpretation that British music dictionaries continue to ascribe, naively in my view, to false etymology. Indeed, the version of the *Anleitung* reproduced in Henry Cowell's article for the *Musical Quarterly* advertises it as a method "to compose, without the least knowledge of music, Country-dances, by throwing a certain Number with two Dice."

The traditional view is that country dances developed in Elizabethan England, and the practice is uncontaminated by continental influences. In defending the reputation of country dances as harmless English rural folk dances adopted by the nobility as a pastoral conceit, Frank Kidson nevertheless conceded the peculiarity that "it was not confined to any special figure or step, and its music was never limited by any special time-beat or accent. . . [and adding] It is fortunate that country dances were so elastic as to permit the use of almost any air."[5] Elizabethan England had faced rebellion from the Scots, and Mary Queen of Scots was apprehended and brought to trial on the basis of intercepted coded messages indicating her guilt. The revival of country dances in the mid-eighteenth century coincided with renewed opposition to the monarchy from Scottish forces loyal to Bonnie Prince Charlie. Published dances passed freely throughout the land and excited no suspicion, providing a perfect vehicle for the transmission of secret messages. That the dance might have served as a means of conveying coded messages from place to place, or as a way of covertly expressing loyalty to a particular political or religious group, is an intriguing possibility.

Composing by throwing a die offers the protection, on the one hand, of conferring anonymity on the composer if that is desired:

such a music has no identifiable personal traits and may not be identified as the work of any one person. The subtext of a method of composing music "without having to know anything about music" is that it can be adopted as a form of codemaking by anybody. It provides the perfect cover. Any coded message in musical form is excused for lapses of musical taste on the grounds of having been composed by an amateur. Another implication, more philosophical and scientific, is that such compositions offer insight into "units of musical speech" that are universal: this aspect is perhaps closer to accounting for the interest of American information scientists in programming early computers to compose melodies in the period immediately after the end of the war in 1945.

This is not to say that "God Save the King," or any other melody composed in a similar way, contains a coded message. It is simply to say that they conform to dice composed melodies, that such melodies enjoyed wide circulation as loyal anthems, and that the method was sufficiently ingenious and widespread to allow for the sending of coded messages in musical form if necessary. The conditions of a dice melody, after all, are seriously restrictive and easy to apply, and the anonymity and lack of distinct identity of the term "country dance" allows a melody of any and every form to pass muster without question.

The melody of "God Save the King" was adopted in Germany, and served for a time as the national song of Denmark. Beethoven composed a set of variations, and it was a favorite of Weber who harmonized it for voices on at least two occasions. A number of features make this melody a suitable candidate for a musical dice-game. First, it is in triple time. Second, it is constructed largely in three-note segments. Third, the variation of segments suggests a serial order. In other words, in order to compose such a melody only a very small number of variables is required.

1. Every measure except the last in each part has three notes.
2. The threes are alternately even (1:1:1) or odd (3:1:2).
3. There are 1, 2, or 3 different pitches in each measure.
4. Each measure is stepwise and most joins between measures are also stepwise.
5. A melody can move only up or down within a measure.

6. Since a dotted measure can be read as dividing the measure in two, each measure is either 1, 2, or 3 divisions.
7. The melody is composed on a six note scale, F sharp – G – A – B – C – D.

(In the Carey version published in 1743, the E in the penultimate measure is omitted.) A further curiosity of this melody is that the first part is only of six measures instead of the usual eight: another clue that the composition was created by a system organized in sixes.

GOD SAVE THE KING

Melody of "God Save the King." The words are a later addition to the melody, the rhythm of which is more suited to the Latin "lau - da - te Do - mi - num"

This is a melody to which different lyrics have been written from the outset. Carey's 1747 version is different in melodic shape and in words, and other contemporary versions have different words as well. So it is fair to surmise that the words did not come first, but rather they were written for or adapted to the melody. One also notices that without exception the various lyrics, including the British Anthem and the US national song, add nothing to the melody. In fact, both surviving versions sound lumpen and graceless. One is bound to reflect that these are anthems requiring an audience to stand still not so much out of respect, but because as the lyrics define them rhythmically they are wooden and undanceable. This is strangely at odds for a melody identified in at least one early context as a *minuet*. And, if the lyrics are stripped away and the melody considered on its own terms, it is eminently danceable, but with very specific accentuation. The reasons for paying attention to the rhythmic organization of the melody are its consistency, unlike a song but very like a waltz, and the role of alternate even and odd rhythms in Viennese waltz.

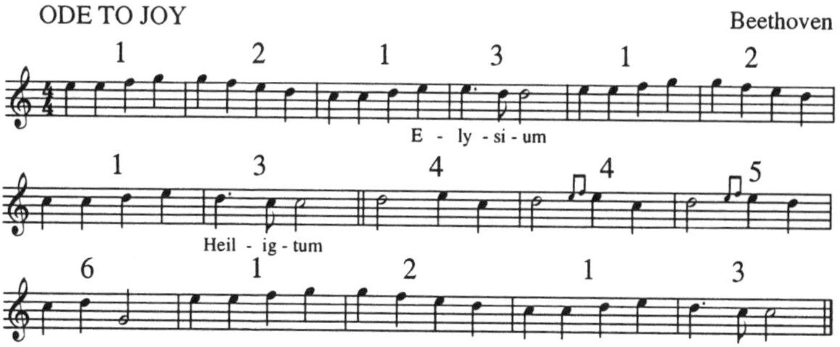

Beethoven's setting of Schiller's "Ode to Joy" could also be a dice melody

Beethoven's "Ode to Joy" from the Ninth Symphony, and the opening subject of Schubert's Great C major Symphony (also the composer's Ninth) are melodies that could have been composed by a throw of dice. Both are constructed, like "God Save the King" out of a table of possibilities reducing to *the same* simple register of melodic and rhythmic units: equal or unequal rhythms, stepwise movements up or down, or rotations of them, and an expressive cadence related to the predominance of equal or unequal rhythms. In the first movement of the Schubert Ninth Symphony, equal rhythms representing stability alternate with unequal rhythms representing freedom of movement but also instability, a dangerous mix with relevance to the turbulent times of postrevolutionary Europe in the Napoleonic era. In Beethoven's melody for "Ode to Joy"—also reducible to only six units of movement, if decorations are ignored —the preponderance is even rhythms and stability, the rhythm only unlocking for the emotionally insecure words "Elysium" and "Heiligtum" (holiness).

Modern examples of aleatoric practice include Stockhausen's *Piano Piece XI*, in which random order-permutations are combined with transformational rules, Boulez's *Troisième Sonate* for piano, a work of strictly limited rules of association, and a number of works by Witold Lutoslawski and Berio that acknowledge the influence of Mallarmé. Strictly a throw of dice allows for the same number to be thrown more than once, or (where multiple dice are thrown at once) for the same total to be reached by different combinations (though it should be pointed out that throwing a pair of dice weighs the probabilities toward median values, since there are only single possibilities of throwing 2 or 12). The six-sided dice could be seen as an influence on the serialists, whose method favours a breakdown of the twelve-tone series into sets of six, known as *hexachords*, though Webern persisted in reducing a twelve-tone series into set divisions as small as four- and three-note groups. A method of permutation involving six dice to decide a six-digit array could be said to correspond more closely with the free rotational set theory of J. M. Hauer.

Notes

1. Jean Cocteau, *Cocteau on the Film* tr. Vera Traill. London: Dennis Dobson, 1954, 73.
2. Rollo Myers, *Erik Satie*. London: Dennis Dobson, 1948, 60–61.
3. Henry Cowell, "Current Chronicle." *Musical Quarterly* Vol. XXXVIII No. 1 (1952) repr. in Richard Kostelanetz ed., *John Cage*. London: Allen Lane, 1971, 94–105.
4. Bernd Pompino-Marschall, "Von Kempelen et al. – Remarks on the history of articulatory-acoustic modelling." *ZAS Papers in Linguistics* 40 (2005), 145–59. *See also* Hartmut Traunmüller, "Wolfgang von Kempelen's speaking machine and its successors." (http://www.ling.su.se/staff/hartmut/kemplne.htm) (06/29/2007)
5. Frank Kidson, "Country Dance" in J. A. Fuller-Maitland ed., *Grove's Dictionary of Music and Musicians*. Volume I. London: Macmillan, 1910, 624–25. "God Save the King." *Grove* Volume II, 188–191.

TWENTY-FIVE

SATIE'S CAPTIONS

> Water-fleas, cheesemites, badgers and seabirds all seem to have more star value in their films when their movements are emphasized by simple original music and not overshadowed by great works.
>
> MARY FIELD AND PERCY SMITH

One of the unsolved puzzles of modern music is the whimsical captions that Erik Satie inserted into his piano pieces from early on in his career, among them the 1913 set with the slightly disturbing collective title *Embryons desséchés*, meaning "dried out embryos," with the connotation of "laboratory specimens"—in the spirit, if not the gross substance, perhaps, of an embalmed artwork by Damien Hirst, though on a much smaller scale. Satie's captions themselves are benign commentaries on the tranquil lives of more or less imaginary sea creatures. In his biography of Satie, Rollo Myers quotes the composer's friend and advocate, pianist Alfred Cortot, insisting on the seriousness of these ascriptions and their significance. That is all very well, but it explains nothing. The captions are interpreted as private jokes, parodies of the extravagant directions beloved of romantic composers, whimsical gestures of a harmless eccentric. All the same, if they are to be taken seriously, one asks what they mean, and then how they are to be interpreted. They are not to be read aloud—that was strictly forbidden—so the only person to witness them is the pianist.

Satie began inserting aphoristic directions to the player in 1890 in characteristically brief piano scores composed without barlines or tempo or key signatures, evoking a deliberately blank spacetime that in one sense recalls the action-space of a French unmeasured prelude for harpsichord, and in another alludes to the relativistic continuum of a perforated piano roll, anticipating not only Conlon Nancarrow's studies in musical turbulence, but also looking ahead to Cage's *Music of Changes*. A perception of time as a blank sheet on which objects with their own internal rhythmic proportions are inserted at will is typically French.

> From 1908 to 1916, his fantasy became more exuberant. To the pieces he now began to issue he gave more and more grotesque titles and a regular "running commentary" of quips and nonsensical remarks was often superimposed upon the music. . . . Alfred Cortot . . . maintains that the prose commentaries which accompany all the piano pieces of this period (1897–1915) are an essential part of Satie's intentions and not merely added to put the critics off the scent. . . . Satie was absolutely opposed to any reading aloud of his verbal texts during performance, and specifically stated his objection to this in a "Warning" which serves as a Preface to his *Heures séculaires et instantanées* written in June and July, 1914.[1]

Woven into the *Gnossiennes* (1890) are enigmatic expressions to suggest states of mind in which the music has been composed, or as it should be performed. *Très luisant* (Very gleaming) evokes the innocence of Sunday school: "Jesus bids us shine/With a pure clear light"; elsewhere *Du bout de la pensée* (From the edge of thought), and *Sur la langue* (About language—or perhaps, On the tip of the tongue) seem to refer to a meaning of music just beyond the reach of words, a perception reinforced by *Être visible un moment*, from the *Danse de travers* (1897) suggesting a fleeting epiphany or momentary glimpse. More sardonic and self-aware are *Un peu cuit* (A bit overdone) and *En y regardant à deux fois* (Thinking twice about it). In works of an overtly Rosicrucian persuasion some indications acquire Gnostic overtones, for example *Très sincèrement silencieux* (In very sincere silence), or *Avec un grand oubli du présent* (In a state of great forgetfulness of the present—or perhaps, Without any sense of time). Phrases suspended in the page like parentheses out of Mallarmé, they are there to distract the performer from the purely mechanical enterprise of reading the notes, and in that sense may be interpreted as a subtle anticipation of Stockhausen's text pieces *Aus den sieben Tagen*.

Satie's captions appear eccentric on the surface, and have never been taken very seriously. They are sometimes referred to Rossini's *Péchés de Vieillesse*, a collection of musical images of a photographic ordinariness treating unorthodox subjects including the infirmities of age. On their own account Satie's texts offer a subversive commentary on the wordily effete epigraphs of some of Debussy's own pieces, a preciousness extending to the *Préludes* of Olivier Messiaen. That Satie's captions are surreal and unexpected may make them appear pointless and trivial to musicians of taste. On the other hand, there is an element of puzzle-setting, in keeping with the parlor games of the period, along with the contemporary fashion for nonsense and the surreal in works of literature. Rossini kept his *Sins of Old Age* to himself, so the possibility remains that what appear humorous or in bad taste in the spirit of the times may have been as serious to him as Satie's eccentricities were to the younger composer. The idea of composing vignettes on nothing in particular, or on normally inappropriate subjects, may have been Rossini's way of signaling his rejection of the sentimental middle-class taste into which nineteenth-century music had declined. But it is not enough simply to write off Satie's captions as inscrutable private jokes. In order to be jokes, they have to have a point. That point may be found in the use of captions elsewhere.

The first issue to resolve is whether Satie's captions allude to the use of captions, surreal or otherwise, in music or any other contemporary context. There are three aspects to consider: first, a public and scientific interest in movement capture, specifically images of people or animals in motion; second, the role of captions in relation to such images; and third, the role of music in relation to both. An obvious starting-point is the practice of captioning silent movies. Satie's pieces from 1890 are on the very cusp of the era of the movies. Marey's chronophotographic gun was developed in 1882, and Edison's first movies date from about 1888. The first screenings of the Lumière brothers' short movies on trivial subjects (feeding the baby, leaving the factory) took place in 1895. But Satie may well have imagined his earlier captioned piano works in the role of character pieces to accompany magic lantern shows. Traveling magic lantern entertainments, involving the projection of images or paintings on glass on a wall or screen, had become very popular during the nineteenth century. Satie's *Embryons desséchés* are easy to interpret as music to accompany an imaginary magic lantern lecture in the spirit of Jules Verne, on the subject of obscure marine life encountered by submarine explorers. Such entertainments have a history going back at least to the 1600s, but increased in popularity following the advent of photography.

> About 1660 the Dutch physicist, Christian Huygens, made what was probably the first magic lantern. . . . It was introduced into England by an acquaintance of Huygens, John Reeves, a manufacturer of optical instruments to the then recently formed Royal Society. A demonstration of the lantern in 1665 was described in Pepys's Diary. . . . The heyday of the magic lantern was reached in the 19th century. Dissolving views, consisting of the simultaneous and alternate projection of several slides, enables a greater range of effects to be produced. . . . Moving slides were known from early days and the Victorians made full use of them to make the slides tell a story with moving pictures. . . . The lantern was also used for education. . . . When moving picture films appeared at the end of the 19th century they were often shown in the same programme as magic lantern slides.[2]

Augustus Voigt's *The Battle of Navarino* for piano is a musical scenario to accompany a lecture presentation or dramatic reenactment and slide show of the famous naval engagement of 1827. Published in the early 1830s, well in advance of the silent movie era, the score exhibits all the features of a spontaneous piano improvisation to a story in pictures, including captions inserted in the score as expression marks to alert the pianist to each change of scene. The convention of captioning static photoengraved images at magic lantern shows continued into the silent movie era.[3]

Voigt's piece is clearly music to accompany a narrative account of the battle as it actually happened, and not just a retrospective evocation based on the emotions of the event. Any doubts that the music is strictly narrative in intention are put to rest by the messages of the captions ornamenting every episode and change of pace, explaining what the music is describing: "Moans of the wounded," "Continued firing of Marines," "Rejoicing of the Greeks" etc. Unspoken, they add nothing to an otherwise loose

From Augustus Voigt, The Battle of Navarino *(c.1830)*

sequence of formally unrelated episodes galloping to a triumphant but pointless conclusion. The only way this genre can make any sense is as the accompaniment to a nineteenth-century PowerPoint presentation depicting the famous victory, with master of ceremonies and narrator, as a guest item in a music-hall entertainment.

The question then arises whether Satie's use of captions is an allusion to a magic lantern show, and whether magic lantern shows on the subject of bottom-feeding sea creatures might have existed. In his autobiography *Came the Dawn* the pioneer British film-maker Cecil Hepworth recalled going as a child in the 1870s to public lectures at the Royal Polytechnic Institution in Upper Regent Street in central London. These lectures on the mysteries of science were often illustrated by magic lantern shows of the most advanced kind, where successive images could be faded in and out to give an impression of movement. He recalled

> I think some of the lantern slides were photographic, but the majority of them were hand-painted and many were of great size, eight or ten inches in diameter. There were any number of trick slides too, of the *Sleeping Man Swallowing Rat* description, and revolving geometrical patterns which gave some very fine effects upon the screen. Also there was a Beale's "Choreutoscope," a curiously interesting anticipation of a modern cinematograph though not the least like it in effect. It had a cut-out stencil of a skeleton figure in about a dozen different positions which changed instantaneously from one to another. . . . The means of

> that quick movement was practically the same as the movement of a modern film projector . . . ten or fifteen years before anyone had a film to show.[4]

Similar presentations were employed as interval entertainments at concerts of music. By the 1890s, these presentations included moving pictures. To liven up his 1896 summer season of promenade concerts at Queen's Hall, Henry Wood and his manager engaged a provider of animated pictures, to be presented in the intervals between music-making. These pictures, the programme maintained, would be "reproduced with all the actual movements of real life." The 1896 selection included:

Outside the Houses of Parliament
A Wedding Procession
Chirgwin's Comicalities
A Peep at Paris
Music Hall Sports, 1896
Bill Stickers, Beware!
Rough Sea—Cornish Coast
David Devant, Conjuring with Rabbits
Factory Gates at Dinner-Time
Mr. Maskelyne's Plate-Spinning
Young Ladies Drilling (performing synchronized exercises)
A Gallant Rescue

—of which at least one, *Factory Gates at Dinner-Time*, is identifiable as a classic Lumière short.[5]

The early history of the silent movies contains a significant scientific film component that, perhaps for lack of star appeal, is often overlooked. Scientific movies were of particular interest to artists, especially in the Paris of Satie, Picasso, and Duchamp, since they provided a point of departure for cubism, simultaneism, and surrealism, new kinds of pictorial realism incorporating movement and image transformation in space and time. Breton and the surrealist movement (to which Satie was affiliated) conceived the movies after the prevailing interpretations of Hugo Münsterberg and Sigmund Freud, as a symbolist art and medium of dreams, subliminal fantasies ranging from the charmingly fanciful, as in René Clair's *Entr'acte*, to music by Satie, to the morbidly grotesque visions of *Un Chien Andalou* by Luis Buñuel and Dalí.

Satie was an avid moviegoer in wartime Paris and experienced with fresh eyes the fantastic world of black and white moving images of an unassuming and indeterminate meaning, interspersed with white on black captions of an unsettling prosaic quality, and accompanied by a patchwork of music incorporating familiar melodies and gestures. He was attracted to the humble, microscopic, magical reality of blood cells, diatoms, and amoebas depicted larger than life in black and white on a flickering screen. And we also know, both from his writings and from the character of his music, that Satie was averse to theatrical showmanship for its own sake. It surfaces in his collaboration with the young Darius Milhaud to introduce "furniture music" to a Paris art gallery, music in the background, introduced for the sake of atmosphere, familiar and banal, ideally to be ignored, and intended to transform ordinary life into art exactly like the silent movies of the 1914–1918 era. The same aesthetic of transcending the ordinary also emerges in the newsreel-like juxtapositions of *Parade* in 1918, and to notable effect in the heart-wrenching reserve with which Satie depicts the philosopher drinking from the poisoned chalice in *La Mort de Socrate*. As the equivalent of a small red corpuscle in the bloodstream of Parisian society, Satie identified with the dignity of these seemingly insignificant specks of life in science documentaries going about their designated duties without exaggeration or ostentation, as he also respected the care and precision of the scientists and their apparatus dedicated to observing them.

So to the question, what are the captions about? Since the "seeds of life" (*embryons*) are "dried out" (*desséchés*) the title can be taken to refer either to photographic images on film, or actual specimens on a slide, that either way implicitly are now lifeless. As descriptions of living creatures, Satie's captions speak to the score reader and performer as affirmations of the living reality of these fascinating, unknown life forms preserved by science. And they are more than that, too. In effect the composer is saying that music has the divine gift of restoring living movement to inanimate matter, an awesome power to be administered with an appropriate sense of the sacred by the musician at the keyboard.

Satie, Cocteau, Stravinsky, and the entire surrealist generation perceived the movies as adding new dimensions of time and motion to a pictorial art hitherto confined to a flat surface enclosed by a frame. They were aware of the fractured continuity and clumsy patchwork of most cheap movies and music providers, butchering familiar clichés of music-hall and opera to create musical labels for flickering images of exaggerated action and sentimental emotion. In such a theater Satie's quietly controlled and understated music can be understood as asserting an alternative set of values, in part neoclassical, in part environmentalist in sympathy.

In French the term *embryon* (embryo) is also slang for a small person or life form. Satie's title *Embryons desséchés* refers to dried specimens under glass, perhaps projections of demonstration slides prepared for microscopy. Paradoxically, dried specimens do not move, so the allusion would seem to be to a magic lantern display rather than moving pictures. In actual fact Satie's music and his captions hint at magical transformation of these exotic creatures back to life, or at least an intention for the music to evoke how these creatures lived.

Behind the paradox is the larger question whether the photographic image (for which "dried embryos" is the metaphor) is capable of *representing life*. Along with many artists the sculptor Rodin famously denied that the action photography of Muybridge and Marey could be able to represent movement faithfully. Satie would seem here to be responding to those skeptics, or claiming a lifegiving power for music that was absent from the photographic image. Related to the artist's disbelief that realistic motion capture is ever possible is the implied futility of a science pretending to inquire into the nature of living creation through depriving innocent creatures of life and observing them preserved on film or pickled in formalin. Satie comes to the rescue. Music, he implies, has the power of life, whereas science can only contemplate death. And by extension, all movie images acquire the fascination of specimens of innocent life invaded, captured, and preserved as transparencies for public wonder and entertainment. Their life is not real, but simulated. It is the role of music to restore them to genuine movement.

POETRY IN MOTION

A classical likeness in bronze or oils is understood as a local example of an ideal physical and character type in a state of arrested development. Absence of motion is vested in the ideal. The lesson of nineteenth-century photography is that real people are physically —and perhaps also morally—far from ideal, do not easily strike attitudes, and find it difficult to keep still.

Because real people tend to look unattractive compared to oil paintings or statues, public attention shifts from discerning beauty in visual appearance to admiration of the person as the living exemplar of virtuous action or achievement. At this point absence of movement becomes a disadvantage. Emphasis on action, absence of speech, and mistrust of facial expression as an indicator of moral character all meet in the blank faced anti-heroes of the silent movie era: Chaplin, Buster Keaton, Harold Lloyd, and Harry Langdon. The paradigm of likeness alters from the idealized portrait or still photograph to the movie dynamic of a real object in motion—motion in the full sense of conveying motivation and planning as well as movement in space and physical grace in execution. The same virtues are caricatured with total understanding by Chaplin in the silent era, his tramp the epitome of innocent grace trapped in a bleak and inert Garden of Eden of photographic reality (caught thereafter, in the era of sound, in the serpentine voice and slithering movements of a distinctly less innocent Groucho Marx). Moving pictures introduced doubt and skepticism into the old world of static ideal types, bringing excitement and trust, but also a new sense of risk, into figures and images of movement to be understood not as examples of morality, but as images of the realities of life and survival in an ever-changing environment. Today's dystopian fixation of computer games on survival to be achieved not by dialogue but by shooting down the opposition, is symptomatic not just of the limitations of the game plan, but of the perverse consequences of a rationalism grounded in eighteenth-century imperialist culture that sees security in absence of change, the presence of strangers as a constant threat, and the possibility of change as a challenge to be eliminated rather than negotiated. We see it in the comic inadequacies of the Keystone Cops, figures of authority whose role is to maintain order and limit the freedom of action of others, but whose attempts to chase down an offender reveal their inability to cope with a world in constant motion.

The whimsical, melancholy nature of Satie's captions to his

later pieces post-1914 corresponds to the early heyday of the silent movie, so refer directly to the film medium's representation of living movement. His insistence that they be read silently rather than aloud is in keeping with the role of captions in the movies as silent, prosaic descriptions of moving images caught in an imaginary limbo between life and not-life. That the words should not be spoken in the performance of a piece might readily be understood as implying that the texts are not for public knowledge, which is what his biographer appears to suggest. However, if that were the case, they could then only be explained as a private affectation shared with the pianist and intended perhaps to introduce an ironic air into a musical interpretation. But since movie captions are also read in silence, it seems more likely that they represent a poetic response—particularly meaningful for movie audiences watching silent battle-line newsreel footage at a time of terrible war—to a medium capable of evoking the same poignant reflection on life in general as Plato's famous description of reality as shadows on the wall of a cave.

The interest of moving pictures is an interest in motion itself. A moving picture in which nothing moves is a contradiction in terms—though highly dramatic also: think of René Clair's *Paris qui dort*, a movie divertissement about a group of tourists arriving by small aircraft in a Paris in which time has stopped and the city and its inhabitants have become elements in a three-dimensional snapshot. Or, fifty years later, Chris Marker's *La Jetée*, a narrative of time travel into the future, told in agonizing stills except for a magical interlude where the time-traveler's lover is seen waking, and her eyelids momentarily tremble. Or Antonioni's *Blow-Up*, in which David Hemmings plays a photographer in a chaotic pop culture who thinks he has discovered an Oswald-like assassin hiding in the background vegetation of a fashion shoot set on Hampstead Heath. The idea of the power of life being trapped, or somehow suspended, in a photographic image is taken for granted and yet very different from the tradition of sculpture or portraiture.

After essaying classical four-movement form in the Second String Quartet (1907), Schoenberg returned to shorter forms, as did Webern. The new medium of disc recording imposed severe limitations on duration (a maximum of three to four minutes for every movement) and ensemble (only a small number of instruments). Out of this self-imposed discipline emerged the masterpieces *Herzgewächse* and *Pierrot Lunaire*. He later reflected

> Although I did not dwell very long in this style, it taught me two things: first, to formulate ideas in an aphoristic manner, which did not require continuations out of formal reasons; secondly, to link ideas together without the use of formal connectives, merely by juxtaposition.[6]

Early scientific films employed all the tricks of cinematography to "make visible" (Paul Klee's phrase) the beauty and delicacy of natural movement. Mary Field and Percy Smith, makers of the documentary series *Secrets of Nature*, brought microphotography, magnification, and time-compression and dilation (fast motion, slow motion) to the understanding of natural phenomena during the very same period that Einstein and his colleagues were ruminating on the implications of a universe of relative motion.

> The *Secrets of Nature*, in their silent days, usually had special musical settings arranged for them and, when they became "sound-films," the greatest attention was devoted to their accompanying music. At first well-known works were used, but, after a time, the policy of using original music written for the picture was adopted. . . . There were two reasons for the change. The first was that first-class music is too good to be an accompaniment to anything. It challenges notice; detracts from the importance of the film; and, for many people, has associations which interfere with the interest of the picture. The second reason was that the *Secrets* are full of short sequences and changes of rhythm; and to select extracts from classical music to synchronize with all of these changes of mood meant to make a potpourri from the work of masters which was not acceptable even to elementary students of music.[7]

Such movies as *To Demonstrate How Spiders Fly* (1909), *The Birth of a Flower* (1910), and *The Strength and Agility of Insects* (1911) have no narrative content in the traditional sense. These are not miniature civilizations in the sense of Jonathan Swift's Lilliputians: tiny, argumentative editions of gross humankind. Nor are they inhabitants of a virtual internet reality. Their stories as such subsist in actions driven by survival that are seen by turns as touching, determined, elegant, and resourceful, at times demonstrating an aptitude for aesthetic creation that is the more impressive for its total absence of self-consciousness. One is inclined to think that Cage would have intended the performers of his improvisations to approach their actions in the same spirit as diatoms under glass. In *Orchester-Finalisten* (1995–1996) Stockhausen's musicians enact similar roles as human plankton floating in a tape-recorded sea, caught twitching from time to time in the camera lens.

Science photography and the movies elevated the previously unnoticed and the superficially banal to a realm of fantasy, and drew attention to exotic new realities in distant realms, outer space, and below the surface. Satie's wry take on scientific demonstrations and movies conveys a serious and innocent wonder in the face of new technology that—for his piano pieces at least—remains invisible. The seriousness of his respect for these images of a previously unknown reality is conveyed both in his surtitles and in the calm deliberation of the accompanying music, which often appears to inhabit a different time world (perhaps of the player-piano). An ideal way of experiencing these pieces by Satie might be in semi-darkness, the pianist out of sight, against a backdrop of silent newsreel footage.

Ballet is an art of accompanied movement. Movements in ballet are lifesize and heavily stylized. In nature movies, by contrast, movements are natural, unscripted, and nevertheless continuous; furthermore, most actions of plant and animal life (walking, flying, swimming, stampeding) are self-evidently cyclical. For an accompanying music to mimic nature, as in the Disney movie *The Living Desert*, is briefly amusing but essentially caricature, since it reduces living creatures or people to cartoon animations, hence the description "mickey-mousing." A practical man, Thomas Edison opted for nonsynchronized music for his earliest movies, though he did on occasion experiment with miming to a prerecorded sound track when precise synchronization was required, as for pop stars today. (The perils of failed synchronization are delightfully exposed in the movie *Singin' in the Rain*.)

An interesting distinction is observed between sound effects and music as accompaniments to movie action. According to Walter Leigh, properly synchronized sound effects emphasize the realism of the imagery, whereas appropriate but nonsynchronized music conveys an idealized perception of animal or plant life as manifestations of a creation that is essentially benign. Whether the sound effects in a scientific movie are authentic, or even appear realistic, makes little difference as long as synchronization with the visual action is exact. To me this says something profound. On the other hand, music has the power to link together and give emotional continuity to adjacent images in a movie sequence that have nothing in common and are not organically connected in any way. In this regard music came to assume responsibility for attributing not only life and momentum in action, but also continuity in logic and narrative.

Notes

1. Rollo Myers, *Erik Satie*. London: Dennis Dobson, 1948, 43–45.
2. David B. Thomas, *The Origins of the Motion Picture*. London: Her Majesty's Stationery Office, 1964, 3–4.
3. Augustus Voigt, *The Battle of Navarino. See* Robin Maconie, *The Second Sense: Language, Music, and Hearing*. Lanham MD: Scarecrow Press, 2002, 287.
4. Cecil Hepworth, *Came the Dawn: Memories of a Film Pioneer.* London: Phoenix House, 1951, 17–18.
5. Henry J. Wood, *My Life of Music*. London: Gollancz, 1938, 93.
6. Arnold Schoenberg, "A Self-Analysis." In *Style and Idea: Selected Writings of Arnold Schoenberg* ed. Leonard Stein tr. Leo Black. London: Faber and Faber, 1975, 78.
7. Mary Field and Percy Smith, *Secrets of Nature*. London: Faber and Faber, 1934; cited in Roger Manvell and John Huntley, *The Technique of Film Music*. London and New York: Focal Press, 1957, 39.

TWENTY-SIX

MINIMALISM

> If you think anything over and over and eventually in connection with it you are going to succeed or fail, succeeding and failing is repetition because you are always either succeeding or failing but any two moments of thinking it over is not repetition. . . . As I said it was like a cinema picture made up of succession and each moment having its own emphasis that is its own difference and so there was the moving and the existence of each moment as it was in me.
>
> GERTRUDE STEIN

Minimalism refers to a music of perpetual motion and seemingly incessant repetition of neutral melodic/rhythmic figures over an extended duration during which time imperceptibly slow alterations of pattern, rhythm, and color are introduced. Technically speaking it is a music of extremely limited but disciplined patternmaking paradoxically directed toward numbing the mind rather than awakening the perceptions of the audience. The listener is lured into a false sense of saturation or boredom and only wakes up from time to time upon realizing that the music has changed from what it was before. In a number of ways the repetitive and disciplined nature of this music suggests the repetitive rhythms of mass production, an imagery previously linked to the music of Varèse, though the style of the latter is more heroic. In other ways minimalism alludes to nonwestern traditions of ritual music that to western ears appear repetitive, for example the traditional gamelan music that inspired Debussy and other composers at the 1889 Exposition in Paris, and also the whirling Dervish and mantric traditions that employ cyclic repetition to attain a state of higher contemplation, for the relief of pain, or to induce the ecstasy of dizziness and loss of equilibrium. Steve Reich, one of the founders of minimalism, has claimed that his music of shifting patterns is inspired by the study of African music.

There are alternative sources of inspiration exemplified in the poetry of Gertrude Stein, which by her own admission is modeled on the physical process of the movies (repeated images that change imperceptibly from frame to frame), the art of the Futurists, whose images imitate the photographic studies of birds in flight of Jean-Étienne Marey, and the sixties op art of Bridget Riley, dizzying moiré patterns of intersecting geometric patterns in black and white that tease the eye and fool the brain into seeing dancing shapes and fringe color effects. In all of these examples the artwork acts as a stimulus that interferes with the perceptions of the observer or listener, so that conscious attention is shut down and other normally subliminal perceptions are released. The effect may be loosely compared to being caught unawares by a bright flashing light and then becoming aware of a shadowy or colored afterimage darting about in the field of view.

Based on pioneer research into random-dot stereograms by Béla Julesz for Bell Labs in the late 1950s, the more recent fashion for computer-generated multiple images that reveal hidden secondary images when the eyes are focused on a plane behind the surface of the page, is another example of the application of the science of optics to art in which the superficial object of awareness is trivial and repetitious, but can be transcended through cultivation of the right degree of disciplined awareness to reveal a hidden imagery or process. Essentially stereographic art and minimalist music share the objective of instructing the participant in how a transcendent state may be attained among western industrial cultures historically devoted to time-dependent models of delivering a text or organizing a workforce to create a complex structure. It is no coincidence that an aesthetic of minimalism came to be launched in the United States at the same time in the mid-1960s that the Beatles and others embraced transcendental meditation.

For minimalism to interact with natural perceptual rhythms it has to be composed on a human scale. Ligeti's *Atmosphères*, which on the printed page is composed of bands of tiny repeating structures, might qualify as an early European example of minimalism if it were performed at a slower tempo, but because of the speed and density of writing, the work is interpreted more impressionistically, as a cloud or group event like a swarm of locusts or shoal of fish in a natural history movie. And because it has to engage and interlock with the perceptual rhythms of the listener, and depends for its effect on its ability to distract, this music is of some scientific and therapeutic interest as a source of information on auditory processes in normal listeners, and potentially on the perceptions of listeners who are suffering from an attention disorder. Like Julesz, Ligeti was a Hungarian exile uprooted by the 1956 Soviet invasion, so the composer's attraction to the musical equivalent of random dot stereograms may have a strong cultural component. (This is not to say that Ligeti's *Atmosphères* or his work for 100 metronomes hide subliminal images, though the idea is intriguing. If stroboscopic lighting may induce a heart attack in the susceptible, there may be interesting consequences to be mined in a strobophonic music—at least, of more interest than hallucinating or mindwandering. For a music of precision random dot displacement to be truly effective, it would have to be recorded in an anechoic chamber and the recorded image manipulated under studio conditions.)

For such works representing the aesthetics of the laboratory to qualify as art may challenge conventional ideas of what art is about. When the music of John Adams or Philip Glass is compared to the title music for the *Superman* movies by John Williams (or Aaron Copland's influential if patronizing *Fanfare for the Common Man*, not to mention the punch-drunk repetitiveness of Shostakovich's wartime Seventh Symphony), what the Williams score stands for in style as well as subject matter is the tradition of the superhero and of music celebrating physical power, loyalty, and determination to protect the civilian population against the fear of change in a dynamic and unstable environment. Hippie era minimalism on the other hand is outwardly devoted to medication—oops, meditation—and higher consciousness. It is easy and trivial to identify minimalism as just another byproduct of a deteriorating western culture embracing nonwestern philosophies, given the holistic tradition among European and American intellectuals, from as far back as the eighteenth century, of embracing Chinese, Indian, or Tibetan religious beliefs as a vital corrective to a western commitment to relentless progress and ruthless competition.

To discover a European precedent for American minimalism one need go no further afield than the baroque. In Handel's popular "The Arrival of the Queen of Sheba," the orchestral Sinfonia to Act III of the oratorio *Solomon,* the baroque aesthetic of repeated and broken-chord figures subject to gradual transformation and displacement in tonality is associated with the new technology of mechanical time (the pocket watch) and its implications for personal identity and freedom. Clock time transcended the individual and brought all things under the jurisdiction of a universal legislator. The dotted rhythms embraced by Louis XIV and redirected by Handel toward his royal patron King George III were a sign and reminder that the monarch in his stately processional gait, resembling the pendulum action and slow tick of a majestic clock, was the earthly representative of a divine power controlling the cogs and wheels of the universe. The same dotted rhythms are reserved in modern times for public funeral processions of the great and good, or at least the great.

American composers of the minimalist generation grew up in a postwar era when the popular image of modern music—of Bartók, Schoenberg, Berg, Shostakovich—was associated overwhemingly with themes of post-traumatic stress affecting an entire culture, popularly expressed in movie narratives of anxious minds altered by alcoholism, haunted by threats of invasion from outer space, or threatened with betrayal by enemies within: spies, fifth columns, government intelligence agencies, and the Communist menace. One is tempted to observe that not much has changed, at least in Hollywood. The habit of associating musical modernism with the consumption of psychotropic drugs coincides with, but outwardly should have very little to do with, attraction to holistic beliefs, or Zen Buddhism, or indeed, religion of any kind. However a wider perception of classical music as a form of state mind control, and of modern music (electronic or otherwise) as an assertion of individual freedom, is alive and kicking in today's physically and psychologically more dangerous world of rave music and party pills, a culture of mind-emptying recreation far removed, one might suppose, from transcendental meditation of any kind, even if arguably connected to Plato's dystopian vision of a world of partying, drink, and the pleasures of self medication.

The defining ingredients of any hypnotic process include overcoming the resistance of the listener, inducing an altered perception of relationship of the mind to the body, persistence, indifference to the effect on the listener (so, absence of dialogue), and resistance to interrogation or negotiation (i.e., to avoiding action on the part of the victim or listener) other than to reinforce the reaction stimulated in the listener. Under exposure to the dangerous, intensely saturated music experienced in club settings enhanced by strobe lights and party pills, the most effective way of dealing with sensory overload is by strenuous dancing without any respite, and even then the cumulative effects of exposure can and do cause permanent physical damage to hearing and cognitive function in the long term.

Minimalist music is more benign in its effects, though its effects are intentionally therapeutic in much the same way. This is a music designed to eliminate a sense of time passing and to allow the thinking mind to rest and recuperate, for example at the wheel during a long drive along the turnpike to a business meeting in the next state, or on a long flight. These are everyday situations where the individual has relinquished control over the timing of events, and where the goal is to find ways of dealing with long periods of inertia. In space movies the problem is met by putting passengers unwanted on the voyage into suspended animation: for the business class traveler the remedy is less drastic, though alcohol remains part of the mix.

How musicians and audiences alike are expected to deal with a music of constant repetition in a conventional live concert setting is an interesting question. The answer may be surprising. Beethoven used motif repetition as a rhetorical device, to hammer a point home. The endless repetitions of "Augures Printaniers" from Stravinsky's *Le Sacre* are minimalist *avant la lettre*, and may even have inspired Gertrude Stein's epigraph cited above describing repetition as constant renewal. Ravel's *Bolero*, to take a famous example of music that requires a performance of military precision and does nothing but repeat itself for fifteen minutes, getting louder all the while, has proved immensely popular with the general public, to even the composer's surprise. Nobody seems to mind, neither performers in the orchestra nor members of the audience, that the music expresses no personality at all, or that it tells no story other than evoking the image of an approaching and overwhelming force. Presumably something in the nature of city-dwellers actually enjoys being made to feel like a hedgehog caught in the headlights of an approaching vehicle. That the piece itself (which Ravel described as "anti-music") relies on arousing a mesmerizing sense of imminent doom, and is very successful in doing so, probably has something useful to tell us about human nature and the cathartic function of artistic expression.

The absent message of minimalism is a reminder of the western tradition of linking music to storytelling, to mass persuasion, to the values of social cooperation and interaction, and to reinforcing belief in a benign social and transpersonal reality. In other words, of music as a corrective to anarchy or the sense of being permanently isolated in a prison of individual impressions the reality of which can never be known for certain. The more complex and impenetrable a music, the greater confidence a listener may feel in the reality and meaning of life as a member of society, and in the ability of society to defend itself. For minimalist composers of the hippie era, society had become overindustrialized and the balance had to be restored. That the minimalist idiom itself was intended to liberate individual perception through the contemplation of mechanistic formulae that, on the surface at least, evoke the tireless and soulless rhythms of industrial production, and require performers to take on the roles of impersonal robots, is yet another irony.

Taking his cue from the habit among movie musicians in the silent movie era to repeat a phrase over and over while waiting for the scene to change, Erik Satie devised an appropriately titled work called *Vexations* to be repeated over and over again over the course of a twenty-four hour day. It has been performed a few times, and is reported by those taking part to have had temporarily mind-altering effects.

The paradox of timelessness in a music of ceaseless time is a feature of minimalism that attaches to philosophy along with the mind-body enigma of classical dualism. The endless motion of a river, inspiration of Smetana's *Vltava* (The Moldau), Johann Strauss II's *Beautiful Blue Danube*, and the emblematic "endless chord" of Wagner's opera *Das Rheingold*, express the same enigma, to human perceptions, of an object of contemplation in constant movement and flow that all the same is constantly the same: an image of transience in nature recognized by astronomers and religions alike as a metaphor of the continuity and transience of human life.

Time itself is the hidden subject of western classical music from the baroque era. In the unyielding clockwork beat of Bach, or Vivaldi's *The Seasons*, or the Introduction to the first movement of Beethoven's Symphony No. 4, perceptions of "slow" and "fast" alike derive much of their emotional force, in the absence of any expressive interventions, pauses, ritardandos or accelerandos, from a sense of the invincible onward pressure of time itself. Of course this is not minimalist music in any modern sense. Rather it is music of a period in western culture struggling to come to terms with the new idea of time as an absolute measure independent of the actions of the individual, and music as a measure and objective description of particular qualities of the experience of time as slow or fast. Minimalist music derives its title of minimalism in part from a concern to expose the experience of time if anything more directly to the attentive listener.

As with the op art of moiré and Bridget Riley, the stimulus of minimalist music is designed to act on the observer at the receptor stage (eyes, ears), that is, ideally before the brain has time to interpret what is going on. In an ideal world perhaps fringe color effects corresponding to the visual interference illusions of op art would appear spontaneously from music as well. The word "phase" in the title of Steve Reich's *Piano Phase* for two pianos (1967) refers loosely in the first instance to the sensation of one pianist moving out of synch with the other, and more precisely to the interference vibration generated when tape copies of the same loop of music begin simultaneously and move gradually out of synchronization because one loop is a millimeter longer than the other, or the other machine is running fractionally slower. Music performed live on the concert platform is music heard at a distance, and the sound of two pianos is clouded by concert hall ambience, so the "phasing" of Reich's title has to do with the players moving out of synch with one another over a period of time, something very demanding technically and deserving of enthusiastic applause. However the more interesting and transforming effect of waveform interference implied by two signals moving gradually "out of phase" in the conventional sense of the term, is only likely to arise between two performances that are literally identical with one another, that is, where not only the notes but the *waveforms* are identical in intensity, frequency, and harmonic infrastructure, because only then does the conjunction and displacement of the two relative to one another produce audible changes of intensity, stereo location, and timbre at the level of fine detail. A special effect made famous by The Small Faces in the sixties hit *Itchykoo Park* (an effect to be perceived as linked to the mid-altering consequences of smoking pot), phasing (or flanging) is created when a musical signal is doubled through an auxiliary studio tape deck the speed of which can be varied continuously. When the two signals are added together, the time delay between them creates a peak of reinforcement of the voice timbre at a frequency directly related to the delay (an effect also heard in the vocals of the Beatles hit "Strawberry Fields"). By this means the tonality of the voice is continuously altered to produce psychedelic effects of color and movement within the sound.

In mundane reality phasing is a normally unwanted effect that dogs apprentice audio engineers. The effect is not normally noticed in the absence of microphones, but can be recognized for example in the atmospheric wow and flutter in propellor tone of the sound of a light aircraft passing overhead. Phasing is the means by which a moving voice or instrument can be tracked across a small enclosed studio (less so on the operatic stage). Concert items such as Berio's *Circles*, Boulez's *Domaines*, and Stockhausen's *Harlekin*, in which the principal soloist moves back and forth, or rotates at speed on the platform, present serious challenges for recording in stereo because the consequences of moving in space are exaggerated in the presence of microphones, which are point samples. For essentially the same reasons, the simulation of continuous movement in space in electronic music remains an impossible task because much more is involved in synthesizing movement than changing levels: the entire harmonic structure of the musical signal is effectively warped, and the degree of warp varies with the frequency of each harmonic.

Phase relations are what happen when a car drives by as you are waiting to cross the road: what we hear as the Doppler effect is an approaching sound changing in tone as the vehicle passes by and moves away. The inner harmonic structure of the sound is warped and stretched in audible ways by virtue of moving in space in relation to the listener. Reich may be signaling an interest in phase relations of this delicate kind, by giving his piece that title, but *Piano Phase* is not really about phasing at all, since all a listener hears is two players moving gradually out of synch with one another. To hear real phasing in action one should listen to *Refrain* by Stockhausen (1959), chiming superimposed harmonies by piano, celesta, and glockenspiel caught on close microphone, that are heard to ripple and dance as their sounds die away.

A complication is that pianos are multi-string instruments: apart from the lowest octave, each key on the keyboard strikes two, three, or at the highest register as many as four strings at once. Multiple strings in the midrange and above are designed to balance the stronger tone of bass register strings, which are massive and very long, and may carry a tension of several tons. If the multiple strings are exactly in tune, however, the tone is thin and does not reverberate for very long. To improve the piano tone and give it body, a specialist tunes the pairs, threes, or fours of strings very slightly out of tune with one another. The warmth and liveliness of piano tone that result are genuine *phase effects* produced by discreet distuning of the strings within a key group, and by adjusting the pitch at extremes of pitch to compensate for the disparities in weight and density of strings at lowest and highest registers.

If Steve Reich had really wanted to illustrate phase effects for two pianos, he would simply have them play long unisons, in the manner of Stockhausen's *Refrain*, or Boulez's *Le vierge, le vivace et le bel aujourd'hui* and let the chiming vibrations interact freely. But no, Reich is American and a man of action. There is a competitive streak in the character of a composer creating a piece in which one player overtakes the other. So this is really a piece about winning.

To achieve the subtle effects of genuine electronic phasing a number of options are available, none of which involve two pianos and two pianists. To obtain an acoustic effect analogous to op art in the visual domain it is necessary to eliminate natural reverberation entirely, take two images of the same complex waveform and change their alignment in very subtle ways. Perhaps surprisingly, there are a number of ways of doing so.

1. For a live performance, one piano and one performer, close-miked, going to the left channel; the *same* signal, routed via a varispeed tape machine (or digital delay) to the right channel. The speed of the second tape machine is varied electronically so that the signal from the replay head is progressively delayed, so both channels remain in tune, but move out of synch. This is in keeping with the Reich prescription in that both signals remain in tune. What changes in this case is the timbre. The piece begins as a single piano, gradually the tone quality hardens, then the two audio signals slowly draw apart until one hears two distinct images. If the delayed image is simultaneously faded and artificial reverberation slowly added, a spatial impression will be created, like an imaginary tunnel. This is what echo is about. A combination of signals that are out of phase leads to selective cancellation and reinforcement of different harmonics within the same signal, determined by the relationship of the harmonic wavelength to the length of the delay. This is a naturalistic effect since our two ears hear different versions of the same external signal and compute distance, position, and other variables from those differences in input.

2. Take two copies of the same prior recording (or tape loop); set them up to begin synchronously on two machines, one of which is variable in speed. The two tapes begin in synch after which the varispeed machine is slowed down by infinitesimal degrees. In this case the phase shift effect is accompanied by a change of frequency relations, both of which are interesting. However since the two signals will no longer be identical in frequency, simultaneous amplitude and harmonic interferences will lead to sideband distortion or spurious harmonics (similar to tuning a shortwave radio) as well as selective reinforcement of frequency components of both signals where they coincide.

3. As above (2) but in this case the second tape is digitally slowed down without varying the pitch. This would be an ideal version of *Piano Phase* omitting any distortions arising from the two pianos being not exactly in tune, and the two players not performing perfectly in (or out of) synch. In subtle effects of this claimed nature, the human contribution is invariably distorting, arguably to such a degree that no reasonable conclusions can be drawn. The sweep frequency phasing of Stockhausen's *Mantra* for

two pianos and electronics (1970) is in principle superior, controllable, and audible (though the composer is not completely above a bit of judicious faking from time to time).

4. In this variation the tape copy is digitally distuned, but without varying the speed: that is, the two instruments remain in synch. In this very interesting case the acoustic effect is as though one instrument is gradually moving out of tune with itself. The nearest real composition I know of that examines such an effect (which is most interesting at the most subtle degrees of difference) is Boulez's *Sur Incises* (1998) for three pianos, three harps, and three percussion including (horror of horrors) tuned metal pans. The composer admits that the piece is an exercise in deconstructing piano tone, after the fashion—way after—of Cage's prepared piano. The piece is characteristically turbulent, so phase effects are difficult to hear or keep up with, but the concept is real.

An even more fascinating possibility (which to my knowledge has not yet been attempted as an artistic device) would be to invert the first signal electronically before adding it to the delayed signal, meaning that as long as the two remain exactly synchronized, they will tend to cancel one another out (the audience would only hear the live piano, and nothing from the speaker). Phase inversion is the secret of Blumlein stereo, and implicit in the two-channel formation of Stockhausen's *Mikrophonie I* for solo tam-tam, left and right channels of which are from opposing sides of the tam-tam and therefore out of phase. In this variation of *Piano Phase* the tape signal is initially inaudible and gradually emerges as the prime and inverted signals move out of synch. All of the above interactions are potentially interesting, aesthetically and scientifically, to some degree since most correspond in some way with familar auditory illusions in nature. All are hinted at in Reich's approach to phasing, but none are obtainable in the manner he prescribes.

Andy Warhol's movie *Empire* (1964), an image of the Empire State Building changing in real time over twenty-four hours—imagery that speeded up has since become a television cliché to illustrate the passing of time—is phase transition movie style, but with an edge: an illusion relying on the power of mechanical devices to register change without falling prey to any human aftereffects of fatigue or emotion. Any music involving multiple microphones, stereo or surround-sound, or computer interaction such as sampling, is subject to mechanical operations of which a poetic intention might be claimed "to go beyond surface appearances to reveal a hidden vision or process." In ordinary life, however, the very same processes of interpreting complex and subtle phase and time interactions are normal and essential functions of human hearing and vision. We do these things all the time without thinking. That modern art seeks to reveal hidden mysteries of perception in the life we take for granted is arguably its real function, and that art seeks to do so intuitively, without fully understanding the processes involved, is perhaps a reflection of its historic mission.

Reich's *Piano Phase* at least has the merit of drawing attention to the difference between mechanical and human accuracies of repetition—the mechanical experience essentially timeless, since uncoordinated with human action, compared to which the human performance is nevertheless real *by virtue of* its natural inconsistencies and lapses arising from fatigue or loss of concentration. A merely electromechanical transformation, such as Reich's tape loop composition *It's Gonna Rain* (1965) or Alvin Lucier's *I am Sitting in a Room* (1970), while interesting as studies in "weathering" or eroding tape samples of speech to reveal their underlying melodic content, are too easily dismissed as relatively trivial exercises in degradation corresponding to the reprographic imagery of flower power: there is not enough interrogation of the process to make it interesting.

Minimalist techniques of this kind might have transformed *musique concrète* which, ahead of its time, was forced to rely on the closed loop or *sillon fermé* of acetate disc recording rather than tape. Instead, it was left to Stockhausen in the late fifties to develop an extended typology of taped sound materials based on waveforms painstakingly edited together from prerecorded pure tones and impulses, and accelerated up to thousands of times. Unlike the efforts of minimalism, which remain firmly locked in the mediocre timescale of human actions, and thus to the classical perception of human actions as essentially robotic in motivation, Stockhausen's tape sounds, above all in *Kontakte*, are both able to escape the connotations of clock time and domestic rhetoric and move into other realms of association and perception: timbre, texture, color, and so on. Such a technique relegates the minimalism of Reich, Adams, Glass, Michael Nyman, and others into a narrow stratum of temporal experience (on the scale of a daily exercise regime) from which it has no intention nor indeed conscious means of escape.

More sympathetic, and even a little mysterious, is Morton Feldman's four-minute orchestral study *Madame Press Died Last Week at Ninety*, composed in 1970. In an interview with Paul Griffiths Feldman claimed the title was given by his mother, but what he neglected to add was that the piece was already about repetition, and practice making perfect, and already consisted of ninety repetitions of the same phrase, or something very similar, chiming like the sound of a cuckoo-clock. This is minimalism with a moral, repetition in a telescoped real time, complete with mistakes. After sixty-one of the ninety repetitions, something happens: there is a gap, a moment of reflection before the music resumes, a little more confidently in tone. A listener is led to imagine that this momentary break in transmission represents the passing of his piano teacher, Madame Maurina-Press, a former pupil of Busoni. One is left pondering how the composer could have known in 1970 that the sixty-first repetition was a prediction of his own passing, in 1987, in his sixty-first year.

TWENTY-SEVEN

GRAPHIC MUSIC

> A single blot on a paper by my friend Eugene Berman I instantly recognize as a Berman blot. What have I recognized—a style or a technique? Are they the same signature of the whole man?
>
> IGOR STRAVINSKY

Graphic music—a music of drawings rather than notes on the page, to be interpreted intuitively by a performer or mechanically translated into sound by a photoelectric device—enjoyed a temporary vogue during the 1950s and 1960s. The first graphic scores to be published as serious art music were American, associated with the New York school of Cage, Feldman, and Earle Brown. Their influence spread to Europe with Cage in the 1950s and attracted many admirers and some imitators. At this time the Australian-born Percy Grainger created his "Kangaroo-Pouch Free Music machine" with the help of American Burnett Cross, one of a series of prototype photocell devices for reading and converting graphic images on a moving transparent strip into sound. In the world of experimental movies the Canadian animator Norman McLaren led the way in 1955 with the amusing visually pointillist short *Blinkety Blank*, a vitalist essay in handmade image and sound drawing on a hidden tradition of abstract movie-making pursued by Hans Arp, Hans Richter, Piet Mondrian, and Fernand Léger in the early twentieth century, and consolidated by Len Lye, Carl Robert Blum (inventor of the click track), Rudolf Pfenniger, and Oskar Fischinger in the 1930s. As well as playing with abstract animated shapes resembling diatoms under the microscope, early animators, including McLaren, were involved in the theory and synthesis of musical sounds by optical means.

In an overview published in 1953 McLaren traces the concept

of hand-drawn sound on film to the era of silent film. The principle of optical sound reproduction by photoelectric means had been established in the early years of the twentieth century: what had hitherto been missing from the production chain were suitable microphones and amplification for optical recording, which became available in 1927. In 1922 photographer Lázló Moholy-Nagy and composer Ernst Toch published articles advocating the production of sound by writing directly on film. Experiments in Holland and Germany had been aimed at developing abstract animated films *in color* as a new art of visible music, inspired by the improvisations of Kandinsky and the de Stijl group of painters. Although not originally intended to be directly reproduced as sound or music, the growth of abstract animation in the period leading up to the arrival of optical sound was focused on the potential of simple geometrical shapes—rectangles, triangles, circles, ellipses—as graphic material, a trend also reflected in Kandinsky's tendency toward more rigidly formal geometric shapes in his own art. Some of the first frame by frame experiments in sound animation undertaken at the Leningrad Scientific Experimental Film Institute by Arseny Avzaamov, N. Y. Zhelinsky, and N. V. Voinov were also employing simple geometric figures as basic units for sound synthesis.

Avzaamov, who had set as his goal the freeing of music from the restrictions of the twelve-tone tempered scale, and the creation of new tonal systems assimilating many of the scales of traditional folk music of the Eastern and Southern Republics, managed to achieve very accurate control over pitch and volume. His range of timbres was limited, however, doubtless due to his self-imposed restriction to Pythagorean geometric forms. Avzaamov's methodical approach to tone-quality required the discipline of simple graphic shapes for ease of classification and reproduction.[1] Of interest in this respect is the fact that Stockhausen's *Elektronische Studie II*, the most famous graphic score of electronic music, consists only of rectangular and triangular shapes, albeit not for any aesthetic goal (though the score is very beautiful to look at) as much as for practical reasons relating to the pitch content and dynamic evolution of the notated material.

Hans Richter's earlier forays into abstract animation of rectangular colored shapes as a member of de Stijl, for instance the movie

Rhythm 21 of 1921, and his 1923 sketch *Orchestration of Color*, are likely to have influenced not only Mondrian's development toward a severely formal abstraction, but also the distinctly more animated style of his later *Broadway Boogie-Woogie* 1942–1943 and the unfinished *Victory Boogie-Woogie* of 1943–1944.[2] Though not trained in music, Mondrian shared a love of dixieland and big band jazz with many experimental film makers of the period, including New Zealanders Len Lye and Jack Ellitt, among the first to draw a soundtrack directly on film.

An intimate relationship between graphic animation and music had therefore already developed in the silent movie era, and was ready to flourish during the 1930s of early optical sound, a time when movie music (both classical and popular) was proving more robust, more easily comprehended, and more marketable internationally than actors' voices speaking local languages. The development of visible speech recording (the vocoder) by Bell Labs in the early 1940s was a remarkable advance. Visible speech generated enormous optimism as a truly scientific—and readable—graphic notation for recording dynamic natural sounds in real time. Early vocoder analyses were made of famous voices, taken from mono 78 rpm recordings of Caruso, Lily Pons, Lawrence Tibbett, Giovanni Martinelli, Luisa Tetrazzini, and others from the world of opera, and Bing Crosby, Frank Sinatra, Judy Garland, and Ethel Waters from popular music.[3] That research did not progress can be attributed to a number of factors including US involvement in the European conflict, the low fidelity and limited frequency range of commercial music recording at the time, and a sudden postwar boom in new technology leading to the introduction of German magnetic tape as a replacement for the acetate disc, and the launch by Columbia of the high fidelity, silent surface vinyl longplaying disc as a substitute for shellac in the marketplace, to be followed in 1956 by the first stereo discs.

Grainger's primitive optical readers (which would go on to influence the design of the Australian Fairlight synthesizer, the first of its kind to allow shapes to be freely drawn by light pen onto a computer screen) were based on a probably naive inference from the technology of optical movie sound, a process by which the complexity and depth of meaning of speech and orchestral music are reduced to a barcode-like variable density or plain variable area black on transparency optical sound track, the variation in each case corresponding to a fluctuating signal from a microphone. There are curious parallels with the invention of the phonautograph in the 1850s, an earlier sound recording technology which many also believed at the time to have the potential to render speech not only as a visible waveform, but as a kind of sign language that would also be easily readable (and perhaps, hand-writable as well).

News of Grainger's free music machines reached Britain in the 1950s, where composer and BBC balance engineer Daphne Oram saw an opportunity to develop and improve Grainger's homespun device at a time when optical sound was being rapidly superseded by magnetic tape. Her hopes for BBC research support were overruled and she was forced, like Grainger, to pursue her interest in "Oramics" hand-drawn sound privately. In London, as in the leading experimental music centers of Paris and Cologne radio, tape was accredited as the medium of choice, and because magnetic tape is a nonvisual medium the graphic visualizations of tape music were able to remain clinically objective and relatively uncontaminated by optical fantasy, unlike subsequent avant-garde scores of the sixties that would be purely visual in inspiration.

Among the European avant-garde, music transparency based optical imaging took a backseat until Cage's visits to Europe in 1958. Along with visually intriguing early scores by Feldman and Earle Brown, Cage's chance music in the 1950s, in both its graphics and timing, is clearly conceived with machine-readable protocols in mind. The sparse 1955 score *26'1.1499" for a String Player*, for example, can be seen to follow the same principles and multi-track layout as Oram's Oramics, including notations.[4] In 1958 Cage unveiled a number of works, such as *Cartridge Music*, that involve the superimposition (and variation) of multiple layers of graphic transparencies, introducing the possibility of "reading" the resulting configurations from any number of directions. Like so many initiatives in this domain of musical possibility, Cage's was inspired play and way ahead of the knowledge required for its realization in musical terms. (Of interest to ethnomusicologists is the observation that mythical imagery of snakes and ladders, which already make an appearance in Miró's iconic and musically inspired painting

Harlequin's Carnival (1924–1925), can also be detected, albeit surreptitiously, in a Cage graphic for *Fontana Mix* in which a dense grid or ladder of rationalism is laid over a tangle of serpentine curves and a single straight line.)

Compared to Cage's tentative experiments with transparencies, Stockhausen's graphic compositions of the period are models of visual logic and coherence (*Zyklus*, *Refrain*, *Kontakte*). His friendship with Cage at this time, and the fact that Cage's ideas were taken seriously by Stockhausen's mentor, Werner Meyer-Eppler, make it likely that word of Grainger's work in optical music would have reached Cologne and been communicated to Stockhausen by Meyer-Eppler prior to Stockhausen's 1958 lecture tour of the United States. Though there is no record of the two composers meeting, Grainger was among the audience at Stockhausen's lecture on "New Instruments and Electronic Music" given at McMillin Theater, Columbia University, on November 3, 1958, early in the tour, and was suitably impressed.[5]

The essence of graphic music is completely rational. Optical recording devices, beginning with the phonautograph of Léon Scott in the 1850s, a mechanism for inscribing samples of atmospheric pressure waves as a wavy line on waxed paper, and its successors the barograph, oscilloscope, sound on film and the vocoder, had all rendered sound visible in ways very different from conventional notations of music and sound. These devices inspired a revival of interest in the relationship of sound and sign on a scale previously associated in the history of western music with the development of music notation itself from the tenth-century era of Hucbald and Guido d'Arezzo.

Though plainchant notation evolved as "tactile reading," a sense of reading time rather than feeling time is alien to most musicians, with the exception of gracenotes and ornamental figurations that are contained within a rhythm structure but otherwise unconditioned by it, for instance in some piano music of Beethoven and Chopin. The unmeasured preludes of Louis Couperin place deliberately ambiguous note values within an open pitch space to be interpreted relatively freely, in sequence, as though occurring in a timeless present.

Graphic scores serve as a reminder of the arbitrary nature of music notation in general. In medieval illumination and classical art sounds of nature and also human noises of varying politeness are characteristically represented as surreal gremlins or animations of musical instruments, most strikingly in artists of the anticlerical Flemish tradition of Hieronymus Bosch and Martin de Vos. In England from the early maritime era keyboard studies were regarded as virtual maps of longitude (time) and latitude (pitch) within which small identifiable craft (musical figures) could be heard to navigate in time and space. These readily identifiable musical figures moved up and down the scale, their inner shapes adjusting to the intervals of the chosen key. When your musical world is one of constantly varying tuning, either because instruments go out of tune rather too quickly, or the idea of freely navigating from key to key has become a paramount issue, part of the purpose of abstract music for keyboard is the pursuit of the elusive goal of a universal temperament suitable for every available key. Hence the attraction to graphic objects that look the same as they progress across the great stave, but are heard to be subtly or curiously deformed the more they stray from a limited number of safe keys.

The development of a standard graphic notation for music had been an outstanding achievement of western civilization. Not only did it allow music to be freely sight read in different countries speaking different languages, but the high status of music meant that the implications of an international notation were perceived not merely as an aid to courtly entertainment, but potentially as an international medium of information exchange. Its legacy includes not only punctuation marks, but the money market graph. Since in other respects music is an expression of dynamic processes evolving in tonality and time, the development of reliable graphic notation had significant implications for science as a whole.

In the mid-nineteenth century a prevailing aesthetic of natural expression combining with scientific research in voice synthesis by Scott, Bell, Helmholtz, and others, along with the development of new technologies of recording and transmission, provoked a surge of interest in the acoustics of the voice and hitherto hidden variables of voice expression, as indicators of meaning, temperament, social and cultural origin, and the human condition. During this time morse telegraph and telephone voice communication were already creating a need among the business community for faster than longhand, preferably automated methods of transcription of accelerated messages sent by wire.

The need for an adequate symbolic representation of pausation and inflection in natural speech, both melodic and occurring within the syllable, had also been recognized by educationists and speech therapists, including Alexander Melville Bell, whose instructional methods were designed to improve habits of speech and assist the hearing impaired to communicate. Bell's primitive notation of syllabic inflection would be taken over and improved by Daniel Jones in the early twentieth century, to surface in *Carré*, *Momente*, and other Stockhausen vocal scores fifty years later. Working apparently without reference to musical practice, early twentieth-century speech scientists based their notations of inflection on what they perceived to be the essential features of articulate speech. These did not include a sense of key or timing, simply moment to moment locality, succession rather than rhythm, and movement within the syllable. Especially close attention was paid to syllable definition and discrimination, in particular between vowels. We can describe these priorities as harmonic or timbre oriented, since the distinctions of vowel timbre are perceptions of harmonic (formant) resonance within the syllable. What is fascinating about this practical but essentially naive development of a graphic for speech is that precisely the same issues are self-evidently being addressed as those considered a thousand years earlier by the European medieval scholars who originally developed music notation. Both sets of priorities and solutions are in essence the same, though of the two, music notation is undoubtedly the more versatile.[6]

Nineteenth-century children's puzzles employed pictograms in rebus messages whose meaning depended on the sounds associated, usually punningly, with the images. For example an eye, a knee, a D, and an ewe could stand for the phrase "I need you." During the 1930s Kurt Schwitters created stories for children with letter shapes as characters. Taking their cue from the graphics of poster art, from Mallarmé, from calligrams such as the Dormouse's song in *Alice in Wonderland*, and manifestos of symbolism, futurism, and surrealism, poets such as Marinetti, Apollinaire, e e cummings and others experimented freely with words as elements of a graphic imagery both reflecting the content of the verbal message, and as abstract composite letterforms available to be "read" in the manner of an abstract language.

The transformation of an outline female profile into a waveform, a scientific trick illustrated by the American Dayton C. Miller in his authoritative *Science of Musical Sounds*, published in 1916, is a fanciful but altogether practical example of the possibilities of harmonic synthesis by Fourier's method. We are not told how the lady's profile sounded as a waveform, but in the spirit of the times Miller comments, just a little mischievously, "If mentality, beauty, and other characteristics can be represented in a profile portrait, then it may be said that they are also represented in the equation of the profile." In other words, if the outline is repeatable, you can make a waveform out of it.[7]

A major motivation of experimental filmmakers in the 1930s was to develop reliable and quick methods of tone synthesis by optical means adapted from the movies, and working directly on film, without the intervention of live performers, microphones, or other recording media. The plan was clearly driven by economic as well as quality issues, since money was tight and live musicians were expensive and not always reliable. The graphics employed by workers in the movie profession were exact representations of wave forms executed by the variable density method, which would then be painstakingly photographed frame by frame using a range of masks representing characteristic envelopes of onset, evolution, and abrupt or gradual termination. Though cumbersome, these methods were aligned to contemporary procedures in phonological research conducted by Abbé Rousselot and Harold R. Stetson, and took account of experiments in electrical tone synthesis undertaken in the 1920s and 1930s by Givelet, Hammond, and other inventors of electrical keyboard instruments employing tone wheels and voltage generating circuits.

Optical tone synthesis was intended to simplify the production of music tracks for short films, as well as improve the audio quality of film music of the period. It had the effect of putting control of the music track of a movie in the hands of graphics artists rather than musicians. Other factors implicated in the development of a culture of graphic music included the piano roll, reinvented as a graphics tablet in the forties by Conlon Nancarrow. For Eisenstein's *Alexander Nevsky* (1939) Sergei Prokofiev created a music directly inspired by the continuity visuals of the movie, shot by shot, reading from left to right.[8] The Brazilian composer Heitor Villa-Lobos devised a graphics process called "symphonic millimetrization" allowing him to transcribe visual outlines into melodic shapes, most famously in the composition *New York Skyline*, broadcast from Rio de Janiero to mark the opening of the Brazilian Pavilion at the New York World's Fair on April 7, 1940. Part of Stockhausen's score of *Gruppen* (1955–1957) is shaped after the outline of a Swiss mountain range.

Hollywood animated film composers were less concerned with the abstract representation of music—a rare exception being the Kandinsky-inspired, Oscar Fischinger-directed visualization of the Bach-Stokowski Toccata and Fugue for *Fantasia* (1940)—than with music exactly synchronized to animated gesture, a technique known as "mickey-mousing." The gestural exaggerations of postwar music animations up to and including the 1950s, culminating with comic realizations of familar classics including Liszt's *Hungarian Rhapsody* played by Bugs Bunny on a rebellious piano, and a pocket version of Wagner's *Ring* cycle starring Elmer Fudd as Brunnhilde, can be seen as part of a larger tendency to seek comic relief from the bravura tactics of a classical repertoire perceived in retrospect as a form of cultural imperialism. Spike Jones's celebrated deconstructions of classical music were another, non-graphic expression of the same trend, but with the added bonus that classical music originals were ingeniously recreated as montages of high art and stereotype sound effects (car horns, cowbells etc.) from the silent movie and early radio eras. In some respects at least the musicalization of incidental noises can be seen to validate the concept of a conventional music interpreted with the aid of unconventional noisemakers for which a notation did not exist and appropriate graphics of one sort or another might one day be invented.

The use of graphics to visualize sound in the modern era is associated most directly with comics, notably action picture stories of war and humor. The typography and naming of sounds reached a height of inventiveness in the 1950s, an era dominated by radio and captured for posterity in iconic publications such as Wallace

Wood's parody strip "Sound Effects" in MAD No. 20, 1955, and Roy Lichtenstein's artworks such as *Whaam!* 1963. Joining in the fun, in 1966 mezzo-soprano Cathy Berberian published *Stripsody*, a performance art graphic bagatelle of the comic strip genre in which imagery of sprocketed film stock is clearly visible.

That most "graphic" avant-garde music is of little or no consequence does not mean that graphics is a dead end, or an unsuitable or invalid area of musical inquiry, only that it is more difficult to do well. Published compilations of musical graphics such as Erhard Karkoschka's *Notation in New Music: A Critical Guide*[9] or *Notations*, a collection by John Cage published in 1969,[10] are of theoretical use as studies in the possibilities of notation, but in the absence of musical proof of functionality in most cases, discussion is likely to remain largely academic. Simple graphic effects, for example the chord glissandi in Bartók's *Sonata for Two Pianos and Percussion*, or clusters, as in some early scores of Penderecki, can serve a useful purpose in easing the task of a reader or conductor, as long as the content of a cluster is as undifferentiated in performance as the sign purports to show it on paper. Microtonal inflections can often be more effectively notated by line graphics than by modified sharp or flat signs. Classical graphics from the past: ornamental signs such as the trill, mordent, and turn, have survived because they are economical and effective. Stockhausen's graphic scores for the electronic music of *Kontakte*, *Hymnen*, and *Telemusik* are readable and apt representations of electronic sounds that do not have to be interpreted but at best merely followed. The same composer's instrumental graphics for *Zyklus* and *Mixtur* are likewise attractive, serviceable, and explanatory in ways outside the scope of traditional music notation. Their exceptional quality arises directly from the composer's training in phonetics.

In the broader sense graphic music asks the question of how graphics in general, including orthodox notations, actually function. When a musician reviews a graphic score for the first time, what is looked for is evidence of an intention behind the graphics that justifies both the unconventional notation and the preparatory effort required to master it. If the evidence is not readily discernible, what is left is likely to be interpreted as wilful deception or masquerade. Feldman's graphic scores, such as *Projection I*, *Intersection I*, and

The King of Denmark, convey a fundamental lucidity, discipline, and seriousness of vision, though the same is not always true of his associates. An unexpected endorsement of Feldman's approach is offered by Maurice Blackburn, Norman McLaren's composer for *Blinkety-Blank*. This little-known score employed a conventional but purely rhythmic three-line notation for a quintet of flute, oboe, clarinet, bassoon, and cello, the three lines representing notes to be improvised in high, middle, or low registers. The idea was to create spontaneous but coordinated patterns of musical notes from which McLaren would later select the best takes. Feldman's early graphic scores are identical in all significant respects. No less interesting, from a "method acting" perspective, is Blackburn's applied psychology of performance:

> The best results of this semi-free improvisation were achieved by taking the orchestra practically by surprise and recording without rehearsals, thus ensuring as complete a divergence of inspiration in each musician as possible, [and] a complete disregard for all consciously agreed key signatures. . . . To create additional percussive effects, synthetic sounds were scratched directly on the film afterwards.[11]

Graphic scoring revives interest in the musical act of reading aloud as an art of making signs into tangible entities. As medieval neumata are drawings of the shapes of speech, and not merely visual, in the same way the action of reading a music of graphics draws on a buried physical sense of, or curiosity toward, what might be called the involuntary tone and texture of vocalization as a Cartesian epiphany of being. If that sounds grandiose, consider a situation of suddenly being aware of catching yourself in the act of speaking, as though listening from another place. When consciousness of the *meaning* of what one is saying is switched off, as it were, what is left is an abstract and possibly intriguing pattern of vocal tones and noises in the present tense. That sense of detachment combined with tactile immediacy is also conveyed in the arts of Chinese and Japanese calligraphy, and also pottery. In adopting graphics in preference to standard notation, some composers in the 1960s may have wished to draw a line between the imaginative world of the artist and the functional, clichéd world of the virtuoso performer. There is more than a touch of this willfully romantic alienation to be found in Cage as well.

Likewise a return to conventional notation after a long period of graphic composition, as Feldman reverted to conventional notation, and Cage and Stockhausen also, should not be taken to signify a denial of the former, and reversion to neoclassical ways and interpretative practices. The same awareness of musical sounds as "sound objects" in the sense of *musique concrète*: as tactile shapes and processes, can be heard to exceptional effect in the instrumental choreography of Stravinsky's late serial works. Technically and spiritually, Stravinsky's composing career began in ballet, which is virtual animation, the cat-and-mouse score of *Petrushka* inspiring and leading the way for two generations of Hollywood composers; among them the great Carl Stalling, whose score for the Warner Bros. cartoon *There They Go Go Go* (1956), orchestrated by Milt Franklyn, is a genial parody and tribute to the Russian composer's 1912 ballet of a puppet brought magically to life. (A Hollywood citizen from 1940, Stravinsky returned the compliment in 1962 with the comedic and supremely animated "Building of the Ark" sequence from *The Flood*.) Like Matisse in old age, the veteran composer's connoisseur's delight in new taste and texture combinations, still awaiting notice in the review pages, can be appreciated in some of the strangest instrumental combinations ever devised: they include the scrape of double-bass harmonics in *Canticum Sacrum* and *Agon*, fricative violas in *Abraham and Isaac*, and block sonorities of multiple flutes and timpani in *Requiem Canticles*, the last without question based on the sonorities of Stockhausen's *Electronic Study II*, and to this listener sounding like the acoustical equivalent of a Sierpinski sponge in Mandelbrot's *Fractals*.[12]

Notes

1. Norman McLaren, "Notes on Animated Sound." *Hollywood Quarterly* Vol. VII No. 3 (1953) repr. in Roger Manvell and John Huntley, *The Technique of Film Music*. London: Focal Press, 1957, 169–77.
2. Standish D. Lawder, *Cubist Cinema*. Anthology of Film Archives Series 1. New York: New York University Press, 1975.
3. "Vocal Music Interests," chapter 17 of Potter, Kopp, and Kopp,

Visible Sound, 376–409.

4. Daphne Oram, *An Individual Note: Of Music, Sound, and Electronics*. London: Galliard; and New York: Galaxy, 1972, 105.
5. The laconic entry in Grainger's diary: "Good." John Bird, *Percy Grainger*. London: Elek, 1976, 233.
6. Emil Naumann, *The History of Music* tr. Frederick Praeger, ed. F. A. Gore Ouseley. 2v. Vol I. London: Cassell & Company, n.d. (1886), 182–200.
7. Dayton C. Miller, "Analysis and Synthesis of Harmonic Curves." From *The Science of Musical Sounds*. New York: Macmillan, 1916, 119–20.
8. Sergei Eisenstein, *The Film Sense* tr. ed. Jay Leyda. London: Faber and Faber, 1943, 137–168.
9. Erhard Karkoschka, *Notation in New Music: A Critical Guide* tr. Ruth Koenig. London: Universal Edition, 1972.
10. John Cage ed. and Alison Knowles ed., *Notations*. West Glover, VT: Something Else Press, 1976.
11. Cited in Roger Manvell and John Huntley, *The Technique of Film Music*, 168–69.
12. Benoît B. Mandelbrot, *Fractals: Form, Chance, and Dimension*. San Francisco: W. H. Freeman, 1977, 166–67.

TWENTY-EIGHT

CLUSTER MUSIC

A cluster in music is the effect of playing simultaneously and without emphasis all the notes within a chosen interval. Claimed by the American composer Henry Cowell to have been introduced in his piano piece *Banshee* 1925, applying a ruler to the keyboard, keyboard clusters are employed by Varèse in *Ionisation* 1934, glissando clusters in Bartók's *Sonata for Two Pianos and Percussion* in 1936 and Stockhausen's *Piano Piece X* of 1961, armfuls of clusters for grand organ in Ligeti's *Volumina* 1962 and for electric organ in Stockhausen's *Momente* 1964–1972. Cluster writing for string orchestra is a feature of Penderecki's *Threnody* 1960, and for full orchestra in Ligeti's *Atmosphères* 1961, Scelsi's *Konx–Om–Pax* 1969, Stockhausen's *Trans* 1971 and several works of Feldman, for example *Coptic Light* 1986. Stravinsky's *The Flood* of 1962 opens and closes with a cluster-like representation of chaos in the form of a twelve-tone curtain of superimposed fifths for tremolo strings, out of which trumpet and trombone motifs emerge. In the *Symphonic Variations* of 1964 a coruscating twelve-part variation for twelve solo violins has clusterlike properties even though each part is fully worked out.

In the movement "Gagaku" from the 1960 *Sept Haï-Kaï* (Seven Haiku—strictly a misnomer, as the individual pieces are admittedly edits of much longer workplans, like tape samples. But let that pass) Messiaen transforms the Japanese *shô* or "mouth organ" into clusterlike sonorities of solo strings. Like Stravinsky's twelve-part variation, this very interesting sonority is limited to a narrow bandwidth in the treble, avoiding the overpowering connotations of full spectrum white or colored electronic noise. The traditional Japanese instrument is played by blowing into a gourd-shaped chamber held in the hands out of which numerous reed pipes of different lengths project in a bunch. Unlike a conventional woodwind, where the fingers select the notes to play one at a time, the *shô* sounds all at once, similar to a cluster on harmonium, and the player's fingers are employed to close off a selection of pipes from sounding at any one time. Acoustically, the effect is at first somewhat akin to having a migraine, but a listener quickly accustoms to the sonority as a constant presence, stimulus, and also mask to obscure other distractions and enable the attention to be fully focused on the musical ritual. Japanese traditional music made a grand reappearance in Europe in 1959, and left a definite impression on Messiaen, Boulez, Stockhausen, and other composers. In one sense Ligeti's *Volumina* for organ can be read as the composer's typically Transylvanian tongue-in-cheek response to the oriental sonority. In *Der Jahreslauf* (1977) Stockhausen pays tribute to the *shô* with cluster sonorities on harmonium.

The defining, and to some, psychologically disturbing characteristic of cluster music is a lack of internal definition. A cluster is a mass of sound. It is perceived as a presence. The repeating patterns of some minimalist music are cluster-like in effect, in that they occupy pitch space without appearing to define it, and because they change imperceptibly. A cluster is intentionally lacking in clearly defined boundaries but is permitted to vary perceptibly in color and brightness. Essentially a keyboard concept, it relies on evenness of tone across an interval of pitch space, and can thus be construed as a subliminal critique of the mind-numbing consequences of embracing a music of tonal invariance. In electronic music clusters are associated with noise generators the sound of which resembles vocal hissing and shushing. The functional implications of hissing and shushing in ordinary speech are precisely the same: to mask unwanted acoustic information and persuade those making it to be silent. Sound effects of a speeding arrow or knockout punch are represented in the movies by bursts of white or colored noise.

Clusters for keyboard instruments are difficult to shape internally, though it can be done if two players and instruments are combined. For an orchestra the greater challenge is to maintain evenness of tone, a reversion to the aesthetics of the age of viol consort playing. For greater density of effect, the use of vibrato is best avoided. The static and striking effect of surface texture and sheen arising from cluster formations by the Europeans Xenakis, Ligeti, Penderecki, and others to a certain extent resembles the resinous textures of early music, even though in principle a symphony orchestra offers greater potential to modify the shape, color, and texture of a cluster in subtle ways. In works by Ligeti and Scelsi coloration of the cluster by changes of instrumentation is highly developed and very effective.

Since the main objective of cluster composition is to dazzle, overload, or in other ways distract an audience from a perception of line, harmony, rhythm, and direction in the conventional way, the listener is left in a disorientated frame of mind that may be more or less disturbing emotionally. Unlike a background noise in the environment, such as the sound of air conditioning or the hum of a refrigerator, which can easily be ignored, cluster music is intentionally obtrusive and occupies too much of a listener's frequency space to be set aside. The only option is to scan the sound mentally in search of distinctive cues, in the same way as a person caught in fog peers into the indistinctness in search of familiar objects.

Use of an organ cluster as a musical metaphor for disorientation or dream arose as early as the 1940s, as a radio and movie cliché appropriate for dramas dealing with the subconscious and with altered mental states (less so with the supernatural, which was assigned to the wailing theremin and ondes martenot). During the 1950s notorious experiments in sensory deprivation, as a means of "softening up" prisoners for interrogation, were undertaken in Britain, the US, and Canada, and despite wide condemnation have continued in use during the Northern Ireland troubles, in the Middle East, and more recently at Guantanamo. Prominent among the armory of sensory deprivation is the use of piped white noise, electronically generated noise filling the entire audible range, in an effort to deplete a subject's normal sensory cues for orientation and sense of reality. It is probably not a coincidence that Ligeti, himself a refugee from Soviet invasion and occupation, should embrace cluster music in *Atmosphères*, a relatively benign experience of sensory overload but with uncomfortable political overtones, at the same time as contemporary analogues in color field painting, for example Clyfford Still, Mark Rothko, and Barnett Newman.

If conventional harmony is compared to the vowels of human speech, cluster music resembles the diffuse consonants [ss], [ssh], [ff], and [kh] in speech. Since western music employs a chromatic mesh of discrete pitches, cluster music is heard as music rather than noise, but it shares with noise the property of filling a bandwidth rather than resolving into harmonies. Like consonants in speech—a function imitated in jazz and pop music by cymbals and drums—clusters are defined by the boundaries of the pitch space they occupy, rather than a perception of internal structure. Depending on its instrumentation and dynamics, a cluster can be more or less dazzling and more or less colored. In the comfort of a concert hall environment, despite lacking the usual signposts of melody and pulse, a great deal of cluster music can be heard with satisfaction as an immersion experience of therapeutic interest. Listeners with the presence of mind to pay attention to what is going on inside the cluster may be rewarded with the appearance of a seemingly intelligent presence within the sound field.

Something very like a searing cluster, assisted by percussion, introduces the "Montagues and Capulets" sequence (Suite 2, No. 1) of Prokofiev's ballet music *Romeo and Juliet* 1935–1936. It is clearly a wake-up call. In this case the dramatic significance of the sonority is unclear, though bound to jolt an audience to attention just as the opening "Dies Irae" of Verdi's *Requiem* is calculated to frighten the living daylights out of an unsuspecting congregation.

Cluster music invites the listener to consider the field of experience rather than objects within a field. It resembles the painterly effect called *impressionism* as in the late studies of Claude Monet, or *pointillism* as we understand it in Seurat, a world of appearances reduced to the juxtaposition of points of color that a viewer's eye and brain endeavor to discern as indistinct shapes and images. The reality of such an experience resides not in the contemplation of recognizable signs placed in an order, but in the mental exercise of coming to terms with an apparently chaotic or formless sense impression that will not go away. Some of the same nervous apprehension associated with cluster music is recognizable in the weather paintings of Turner and Constable, the nocturnes of Whistler, and analogous movie devices of darkness, mist, fog, and gaslight in stories of detective fiction from the Victorian era. They remain familiar in classic murder mysteries of the Hitchcock and Pabst era between the wars, and the use of CO_2 fog at heavy metal concerts from the seventies; they are still effective in the hands of Ridley Scott and other masters of sci-fi and horror movies of the *Alien* genre. Such apprehensions toward the dark and the unknown are deeply embedded in the human psyche, and exploited by the "black arts" in myth and legend.

In the early atmosphere studies of J. M. W. Turner the viewer comes face to face with the depiction of natural forces of wind and weather in which the detail of reality is reduced to a few scattered hints. In these paintings, coinciding with the earliest atmospheric studies of Louis Daguerre—and experiments in nitrous oxide ingestion by Humphry Davy—the power of art to draw attention to, and even capture, the mental and physical act of perception is perhaps closer to the intention of cluster music than at any other time. In that sense cluster music can be considered "realistic," since the art draws on a heightened awareness of normally subconscious behavior and is not about illusions or visions induced by some form of narcotic. Turner's atmospheric studies are about the hidden beauty revealed in perfectly natural experiences when essential light and color relationships are accurately depicted but the natural appearance of objects is only partially revealed. The late canvases of Renoir draw their compelling beauty from a deliberate suppression of surface detail in favor of forms and color relationships apprehended subliminally. Photography introduced a range of aesthetic options based on out of focus imagery and the distortions of images in motion. The unsettling impressions of Francis Bacon's willfully smeared wrestlers and mirror-like interiors are enhanced by a visual sense of mystery and suspense, of resisting resolution, along with intense color associations.

Cluster music in general asks to be performed without emotion, allowing the interpretation to arise spontaneously in the listener. To convey an impression of passivity is a dramatic option in itself, suggesting a response of helplessness in the face of some imminent doom. Passivity is equally characteristic of sleep, during which the memory releases strange half-formed images that in the twilight world of clinical psychiatry are supposed to betray normally suppressed anxieties. The sense of leaving each member of an audience to his or her own devices is both a legitimate response to a music experience perceived as a species of psychoanalysis, as well as a reminder of the extent to which conventional music relies on guiding and directing the listener's attention to specific patterns and gestures, and the corresponding value attributed to the conductor and performer as interpreters.

Because it draws on meanings from the listener's subconscious —"monsters from the Id," that is, images already existing in the mind of the listener—cluster music differs in principle from highly chromatic music, such as Scriabin, that pretends to lead the listener to visions of a transcendental kind. The operative criterion presumably is the degree to which an interpretation has to rely in practice on the acting talent of an interpreter as distinct from a detached reading of the music itself.

Since it deals with broad bands of sound, cluster music is open to invention in notation, for keyboards with the further options of choosing white-note (diatonic) or black-note (pentatonic) as well as both combined (the full chromatic). Naturally white- or black-note clusters tend to sound more harmonious than the full chromatic. Notation can be avoided if the chosen instrument is a player piano, for which the required collections of notes can be simply punched on piano roll. Among the earliest and liveliest are the exuberant up and down gliding clusters of *Sea Song Sketch* composed by Percy Grainger in 1907 and punched directly to piano roll in 1933 in order to bring its complexities accurately to life. This startling automatic performance, in which the piano keys ripple and surge like a tide of their own accord, would become a cartoon animation cliché in following decades.

Cluster music is also a recognizable equivalent of crowd noise, a usually unacknowledged presence in opera and an often forgotten but essential ingredient of music from earlier times. Handel's *Music for the Royal Fireworks*, devised for a public fireworks display in the open air in London's Vauxhall Gardens, is arguably incomplete if the sound of fireworks (today prerecorded, of course) is not heard along with the music. A music conceived in part as a means of crowd control, especially an event involving fireworks in celebration of a military victory at which the public attendance is likely to be both numerous and excitable, can only be truly appreciated against a background of crowd noise at ground level and random detonations high in the air.

That the function of a great deal of classical music is ceremonial in nature and includes formulae for calming an audience and cueing exits and entrances is logical and self-evident. The sound of numerous side drums plays its part. A military or school band on parade does not choose to play complicated music that is hard to listen to or understand. A noisy crowd does not have the degree of attention or concentration required to figure out a music of any subtlety or complexity; likewise the members of a band on parade are marching and playing instruments at the same time in an outdoor context where making yourself heard and keeping to the beat and in tune are already problematic enough. It is different in the closed and disciplined environment of a concert hall where classical and modern music is performed that demands much higher levels of individual skill. Even in the concert hall, however, at an event like the BBC Promenade concerts, crowd noise is a fact of life and audience attention is liable to wander, to cope with which classical music comes equipped with signals and admonitions to listen up and take heed, in which loud noises and cymbal clashes perform a useful role.

Until the mid-twentieth century classical music and musicians regarded percussion instruments with a certain disdain. That percussion ensembles such as gamelan sound beautiful and exciting was a key discovery of the late nineteenth century, and the arrival of portable Edison sound recording in the 1890s and its impact on the new discipline of ethnomusicology introduced the sounds of gongs and ceremonial drumming from the African continent and elsewhere to European cultures already puzzling over the aesthetic influence of primeval artifacts on the art of Picasso, Braque, and Modigliani. The "primitive" appeal of jazz to twenties European society was as much about identifying with the visceral rhythms of percussion, as with embracing the supposedly less inhibited lifestyles of less industrialized cultures. Jazz was music to be enjoyed in a relaxed, informal, and inebriated context far removed from the stiffness of the traditional concert hall.

The power of noise is the power of numbers, and also the image of chaos: an image ominously realized in early news footage of political rallies. Among European cultures, a fear of noise is a fear of infinite possibilities. When Lewis Carroll writes

> The Walrus and the Carpenter
> Were walking hand in hand;
> They wept like anything to see
> The beaches full of sand. . . .

—the author is alluding as a mathematician to the impossibility of numbering the grains of sand, an ancient and resonant image of infinity. (The Carpenter is a professional whose livelihood depends on quantity and measure.) Likewise the mixed emotions conjured up by cluster music tap into the same anxieties that attend images of innumerable crowds—sights and sounds of mass demonstrations from Fascist and National Socialist rallies of the newsreel era (to music by Wagner) through to Woodstock (and musical graphics by Jimi Hendrix) in the late 1960s.

DISTURBING THE PEACE

Noise is defined paradoxically as any sound—including music—that disturbs the peace. Since disturbing the peace is also what music is about, though in a context of general agreement that the peace should be disturbed, by inquiring into the definition of noise it is possible to clarify what features of music make it more acceptable in general terms.

The first (and true) definition of noise is unstructured sound. As with all such definitions, the description "unstructured" is subjective, varying from person to person, and with the rider "as far as I am concerned." Work noises, animal noises, and other familiar noises may be unstructured in the sense of uncoordinated, but all the same tolerable. Common definitions of white noise in nature include the sound of the Niagara Falls, heavy rain on the roof, and audience applause. People do it. At the beach we do not require the seagulls to call in rhythm to feel comfortable. Lack of structure in background noise can in fact be restful, since it screens out a range of distractions, such as the conversation of others nearby, that call attention to themselves by the very fact that they are coherent and have meaning. When background noise is something you do not want to pay attention to, for instance the sound of air conditioning in a library, it can still be appreciated as a means of providing a sense of a personal private space.

That music along with talk radio fulfills a role of screening a listener from consciousness of reality puts a somewhat sinister gloss on the notion of individual freedom, using the themes you identify with as a means of shielding yourself from the needs or concerns of others. Fountains in public places, the original cluster music, have a primary function of cooling the atmosphere and a secondary function of providing acoustic privacy zones in which people can meet and talk without being overheard. A fountain is close to white noise in a technical sense, a broadband noise that is both undifferentiated and undistracting. Crowd noise in the foyer of a concert hall creates a similar enveloping environment, but one that the listener is free to explore and select from. Cage's *Variations IV*, a reality recording of what appear to be guests circulating during the interval of a concert, or at an art exhibition reception, is about that freedom, and also the boredom it may entail. The analogous function of cluster music, to pursue the crowd metaphor, given that a performance occurs in a public place or alternatively can be listened to in private, might also be to fill the space with outwardly amorphous musical noise the effect of which is to allow the listener to daydream. An equivalent orchestral sound that allows the listener maximum freedom to daydream could also have therapeutic value, perhaps the reason why some concertgoers betray a tendency to fall asleep. Sound resembling industrial noise, that outside the concert hall might prevent a listener from thinking clearly, in a concert hall might provide an opportunity to study a saturation experience and even learn how to deal with it.

Naturally cluster music is created by musicians and their instruments, so in much the same way as a performance for prepared piano creates a sense of dislocation between what the listener sees and what is actually heard, the visual appearance of an orchestra performing anti-music in a perfectly normal way is offset or dislocated by an aural imagery that might appear to suggest that the audience's hearing has suddenly deteriorated, or as if one were listening underwater, or through a haze of radio static.

If the definition of western music is actions composed by an artist for musical instruments, written out in classical notation and performed before paying guests in a concert hall, then in outward respects cluster music is conventional music. If a video were made of such music being performed, and viewed without the sound being audible, it would appear to all intents and purposes indistinguishable from a classical performance. If the criterion is what it sounds like rather than how it looks, cluster music is not in the least conventional, lacking in line, harmony, and sense of direction. Many sounds in nature and of human activity are noisy, but what we have come to expect of music is melody, harmony, action, and direction, so music omitting these basic qualities is not music in that sense, and can even be interpreted as an attack on the conventional view of what music is about.

Cluster music is far from easy to compose. The density of part writing is normally several orders of magnitude greater than a normal orchestral score, which means more notes for a composer to write. In addition there is the challenge of making the noise last, and of maintaining consistency. The positive qualities that can be expected of a cluster composition include a consistently nebulous quality, absence of outline, and—strangely enough—that it sustain interest, in the same way as it takes a great deal of talent to paint a townscape in mist or fog, as Monet did, or in shimmering heat, as did Van Gogh, and it also takes time to adjust to the way the artist is seeing the world, as well as attempting to represent it in color and form. There is as much of a poetry to indistinctness as to hard-edged definition.

Cluster music is rare and special in music for its ability to draw a listener's attention to the act of listening itself in real time. Other music has leading motifs, rhythms, and movements that guide the audience. One could say that cluster music is for the imagination of seated listeners what a Johann Strauss II waltz is for the bodies of dancers on the dance floor: an opportunity to enjoy the sensation of being guided on autopilot as it were, in real time and space.

Why has more cluster music not been composed? Perhaps one reason is that it is invincibly mono in a world that has embraced stereo and surround-sound. To exploit cluster music in a dimensional sense (rather than in the earlier role of sensory deprivation) would probably require electronics, and for maximum effect, computer sound generation, if the idea were to achieve a kind of holographic imagery which, like Julesz's random dot visuals, is three-dimensional in perception but at the same time lacking in outline or source definition of any kind.

Having defined the problem, it comes as a surprise to identify the experience as commonplace in nature and also in urban life. A chorus of cicadas, for example, or the swarm of bees imitated in Ligeti's *Atmosphères*, the rush of sound as a flock of birds suddenly takes flight, or the turbulence of a crowd of children shouting and splashing in a crowded swimming pool—all of these are relatively familiar and benign in implication, but would appear less so if they were to be reproduced in the enclosed space of a concert hall. Events in the open air benefit greatly from being in the open. There we do not have to pay attention. In the absence of a containing structure, dense and complex sounds are free to float away. For an acceptable alternative sensation in an enclosed space, ambient noise in a cathedral or temple is ideal and can be genuinely comforting to listen to.

In stereophonic recording the same sound field is captured by separate microphones facing in different directions, at times from the same point in space, at other times from separated locations. The resulting two channels, omitting any further intervention, are recorded to disc or tape as left and right channels. These are the same music but from different perspectives. They are identical in most respects but significantly different in microcosm, and it is in the microcosmic differences that spatial depth is encoded: in the relative loudness and timing, not of the whole ensemble—since the gross volume is the same—but of every individual particle.

To create an acoustic hologram of discernible shape but no outline *in stereo* after the manner of Ligeti's *Atmosphères* or even Steve Reich's *Piano Phase*, some way of simulating phase and amplitude difference information is required. Impressionist painting shows that the brain is quite capable of interpreting incomplete data, and the example of a score such as Stockhausen's *Carré* for four orchestras, in which turbulent noises are heard to rotate around the audience in different directions, suggests an answer. Unlike the brass choirs of *Gruppen*, which exchange fixed chords among three orchestras—an effect equivalent to panning the same chord from side to side in a three-channel mix—the effect of depth would be created in a matched stereo pair of orchestras by employing Ligeti's tactic of micropolyphony or uncertainty at the fundamental level, where instead of well-defined lines and patterns in antiphonal opposition, as for example in a polychoral composition by Heinrich Schütz, each point in the composite image is reduced to a shimmer of notes. Imagine a Seurat painting reproduced in duplicate, but where left and right images are subtly modified in accordance with a stereoscopic composite visual field. In the absence of firm outlines, the spectator is forced into tactics of mental approximation based on low-definition correlation that is scrupulously consistent in a gross sense but relatively indeterminate at the level of fine detail. This is essentially the approach taken by Louis Lumière, whose successful stereoscopic autochrome photographs amount in effect to stereo pairs in Seurat-style pointillist technique. To achieve the same result is possible in a musical sense, but would imply duplicate ensembles performing from the same impressionist score.

REALITY CHECK

White noise is defined in the technical literature as thermal noise occupying a transmission bandwidth and undifferentiated in frequency—meaning that there is interference at every point in the frequency spectrum. Noise limited to a particular bandwidth, like a snare drum or the sound of hissing, is called colored noise, and electronic noise that is biased to match the sensitivity of human hearing is called pink noise. These are technical definitions that properly relate to the inspection of random samples in a laboratory. These samples are invariably monaural. The technical implication of noise on the line is that it interferes with any message trying to get through. The sinister implications of the use of white noise in sensory deprivation torture are that it disorientates a victim by removing the means of selflocation in space.

In real life however, exposure to broadband noise does not have to be disorientating. People live and work for long periods within hearing of the Niagara Falls, and tourists are not put off visiting such landmarks by any fear of going out of their minds. There are two reasons. One, people are free to move around, and in moving around they are exercising control over the noise as they hear it. With every move of the head there is a corresponding change in shape of the source sound. Second, human beings are binaural creatures. The fact that the same "undifferentiated" dense bandwidth of sound is listened to by two ears rather than one means that two images of the same continuous sound are constantly being monitored and matched, rather than just one. The situation is comparable to a Julesz random dot stereo image, since the *same* random dot pattern is presented to each ear, but the two inputs vary subtly in amplitude and phase at every level of frequency. These variations are perceived internally as the two input signals are matched, and translate into awareness of the sound coming from the left or right, and phase differences, shadowy peaks and troughs in the overall texture of the noise, that vary precisely with every movement of the listener. I mow the back lawn with an old hand mower which makes a characteristic clatter, and can hear phase changes rising within the sound as the mower approaches a reflecting surface such as a fence or shed wall, caused by the noise from the mower interacting with its own reflection at a rapidly closing distance.

Architects and record producers clap hands to test the acoustic of a concert hall. Some engineers fire a starting pistol and record the resulting reverberation on tape. These test signals are like short bursts of noise, and are intended to excite a broadband response within the structure of sufficient intensity to isolate any peaks—wiry, trembling effects also called *eigentones*—that might interfere with an audience's enjoyment of music. What this shows is that the noise quality of a piece of cluster music, or music for percussion by Varèse, is colored not only by head movement on the part of the listener, but also by the concert environment. The oppressive nature of white noise is largely due to an enclosed environment adding subliminal structure and intensity to the noise signal, and to other restrictions on the listener's freedom of movement.

A further irony emerging from the idea of cluster music in stereo has to do with the expansion of the symphony orchestra to its present size in the nineteenth century. At the speed of sound, 1,120 feet per second, the area occupied by an orchestra introduces significant delays within the ensemble that invariably lead to loss of distinction in the total sound (this is why a modern orchestra relies on *visual* rather than aural cues to stay synchronized). Since a typical concert platform is already 0.1 to 0.85 second in width, it is apparent that a modern symphony orchestra is unable to keep perfect time. It is simply not possible for music produced over so broad an area to be perfectly synchronized, either in itself, or to members of the audience sitting on opposite sides of the auditorium. The chaos is already with us. The challenge facing a new generation of composers is to exploit natural delays of the order of a sixteenth-note in duration—well within the compass of a rank and file orchestra musician—to create musical effects of a novel and fascinating spatiality, either by precise calculation and execution, or with the aid of electronics.

TWENTY-NINE

FRACTAL MUSIC

Can a computer be programmed to compose melody? The short answer is, well, yes it can, though that is no guarantee that the melodies it composes will be totally satisfying musically. The composition of melody by computer is of interest because it aims at simulating a product of human thought. A successful program might serve as a model of the creative process; in addition it may be relied upon to improve our understanding of the many unconscious as well as conscious rules that guide a composer in searching for a memorable musical theme. For a program to be judged successful the software must be allowed some freedom of choice, otherwise it could hardly be said to have invented a melody. It also follows that certain preconditions have to be set if the resulting invention is to be regarded as a plausible melody, and not just a string of notes.

The origins of melody, some would argue the origins of music, lie in the rise and fall of ordinary human conversation. The meaning of a spoken sentence is affected by the melody in which it is said. In European languages a melody can be imposed on a sentence without altering its meaning, but in tonal languages, as in China, the precise meaning of a word or phrase can depend on the starting pitch and direction of intonation within a syllable. A composer is constrained by the need to incorporate the inflection pattern in the melody as a necessary part of the setting of a Chinese text. In most languages the contextual meaning of a sentence or phrase (distinct from the dictionary meaning of a word) is likely to be influenced by additional modalities of inflection expressing agreement, doubt, surprise, anger, and so forth. Translators of opera libretti are bound to take these features into account. In other traditions, such as India, the choice of a mode amounting to a limited range of notes (or more accurately, interval steps) has emotional significance related to a text or improvisation. In devising software for melody composition one is brought face to face with previously hidden criteria that in turn may throw light on expressive mannerisms of speech and music in general, a metalanguage of subliminal processes and attitudes to be allowed for along with latent cultural associations of form and expression.

That the mode or scale of a speech melody can be understood as a grammatical indicator independent of the word content is demonstrated in the formulaic utterances of plainchant. A melody is understood as a shape rather than as a sequence of notes; stored in memory in a form robust enough to be recognized in a different key, distorted rhythm, and different tempo from the template originally committed to memory. The conditions of recall of a melody evidently rely, as the Greek philosophers would have said, on a memory for relationships rather than precise values. This is perhaps unexpected given that music is notated in a prototype graph form as data points on a grid.

In a remarkable feat of lateral thinking the British writer Denys Parsons published a book on the classification of melody *incipits* (opening gambits) showing beyond doubt that the "deep structure" of melody resides not in their exact pitches, nor even in interval or rhythmic relationships, but can be reduced to a formula of *changes of direction*, ignoring the metrical or durational value of individual notes. After ten or twelve changes of direction, Parsons discovered, a melody has defined itself so completely that it can be identified uniquely in terms of its pattern of directional changes (up, down, or repeat).[1] That a melody can be recognized as "out of tune"—that is, as a distortion of a known melody rather than as a new melody in its own right—is one of the paradoxical features of oral memory that is accounted for by Parsons's discovery. In the world of classical music as well as jazz and pop music, musical forms are commonplace in which an original melody configuration is repeatedly modified by decoration or reduction of content. The existence of such idioms also tells us something about the way essential identities of form and pattern are recognized.

When fractal music came on the scene in 1977 everything changed. For the first time in history it seemed that a mathematical description of music might finally be possible. Not only that, but the same terms might be applied to the Cage world of chance music, as to the determinist aesthetic of a Boulez or Xenakis. One would then be able to map and explore a continuum of probability between the extremes of indeterminacy and total serialism.

The discoverer of fractals, Benoît Mandelbrot, describes his work as a science of roughness.[2] An understanding of the mathematics of indeterminacy is of value in a great many fields, from measuring coastlines and mountain ranges to predicting population fluctuations and share price trends in the stock market from their pattern of fluctuation in the past. Mandelbrot noticed not only that there were consistencies in natural fluctuations in space and time to which a numerical value could be assigned, but that many of these exhibited the same degree of fluctuation irrespective of the size of the sample. For example, the distribution of stars in one part of the sky is roughly the same (or similarly rough) to that of another segment, and when a small portion of one segment is magnified and more stars revealed, again the same degree of roughness is found.

Mandelbrot extended his study from natural phenomena to patterns of human activity, and was excited to discover that works of art exhibited the same degrees of instinctive self-similarity, from which he deduced that the quality of roughness in nature might also coincide with the aesthetic sense of human beings. When the message of fractals in nature was eventually announced to the public in an article by Martin Gardner in the *Scientific American*, it was the musical implication of fractals, researched by Richard F. Voss, to which Gardner drew special attention.[3] There was a reason for this. Voss's discovery of a fractal number for melody was the first major contribution to the theory of probabilistic music since the pioneer researches of Hiller and Isaacson at Illinois in the 1950s,[4] and Mathews and Rosler at MIT in the 1960s.[5]

Mandelbrot's mathematics of roughness is a way of describing the controlled irregularities of nature in terms that account for them as manifesting a tension between total disorder and an opposing tendency toward total connectedness. In music we understand disorder as fragmentation and total order as monotony, for example a Shinto monotone chant without any rhythm.[6] In mathematics however the extreme positions are described a little differently. An illustration of total disorder (also known as white noise, or a spectral density of $1/f^0$) might be to drop a quantity of ball bearings onto the strings of an open grand piano. The resulting succession of tones, written as a melody, would have little to no correlation, every note being the result of a separate encounter between a ball bearing and a string. At the other extreme, if a single small bouncing ball were dropped onto the piano strings and the sequence of tones recorded, even though it might not make a very catchy melody, it would be highly correlated, since only one ball would have been involved, and where it bounced next would have depended on where it bounced previously. Such a sequence would also be heard as coherent for reasons of the pattern consistently accelerating in time and making a gradual decrescendo as the bouncing ball lost energy. A bouncing ball melody is closer to the extreme predictability of Brownian motion, assigned a spectral density of $1/f^2$. (Brownian motion will even account for the ball bouncing out of the piano and onto the floor.)

The excitement of such a discovery was that previous efforts in computer generation of melody could now be fairly and properly compared and critiqued. The consequent objection to stochastic music, as practiced by Xenakis using an IBM computer in the early sixties, was that it is composed to rules of selection that do not exhibit the same degree of roughness at every scale: there is not enough correlation, the result is more like white noise. The objection to probabilistic computer melody generating and interpolation routines based on Markov chains and note-groups derived from existing melodies, as practiced by Hiller and Isaacson in the 1950s, and modified by Mathews and Rosler in the 1960s, is that the results are frankly bland and not varied enough. There is too much correlation and not enough unpredictability: the results are closer to Brownian motion.

Voss's discovery that melodies of every type and culture of music conform to the same degree of self-similarity or roughness, in spectral terms assigned a value of $1/f$ noise, located the secret of music somewhere between the two extremes. This was a significant breakthrough, even though the music examples cited in Gardner's article were exclusively melodic (and not very inspiring melody either), and had nothing to say about rhythm, or harmony, or formal repetitions, all of which are important elements of western conventional music.

Burt Bacharach: "Do you know the way to San José?"

Beethoven: Symphony No. 5

Denys Parsons: Directional method of encoding melody

MELODIC SUCCESSION

We begin with the proposition that a melody is a fluctuation of pitch (singular) and not a succession of notes (plural) exhibiting movement in pitch. A fluctuation or *movement of pitch* defines a melody as the discontinuous expression of a continuous curve: an implicit connection from one note to the next. The problem of melody generation is to establish predictive rules that govern the movement of a melody from one momentary value to the next in line.[7] The same kind of reasoning underpins Parsons's definition of a melody as a sequence of moves from a starting-point where the choice is reduced to up, down, or repeat. The alternative view of a melody as a *succession of notes* exhibiting a pattern of changes of location is equally legitimate, but requires a different approach. In this case the melody is understood as a shape projected onto a raster or scale of pitches. The tuning of the scale can be varied in advance to correspond to alternative expressive modalities, the melody shape remaining the same. A computer melody program of the simplest kind determines both the *movement* of a melody up or down on a note-by-note basis, and also the *pitches* assigned to the movement. What this implies is that the pitch content of such a melody is essentially arbitrary: in some scales the pattern of fluctuation may not sound especially musical, while in other scales—pentatonic, major, minor etc.—it may appear more satisfactory. In his *Scientific American* article Gardner outlines simple methods of generating "white" and "brown" melodies using dice or spinners. The melodies illustrating these differences were unconvincing in a musical sense. To me they did not say anything about real melodies in the real world. I decided to investigate further using a simple computer program, based on Gardner's game, to make the decisions and play back the resulting melodies. Although the concept of a tempered or chromatic scale is more scientific than natural, I decided to accept as a starting-point the idea of a fractal program operating within a tempered chromatic scale.

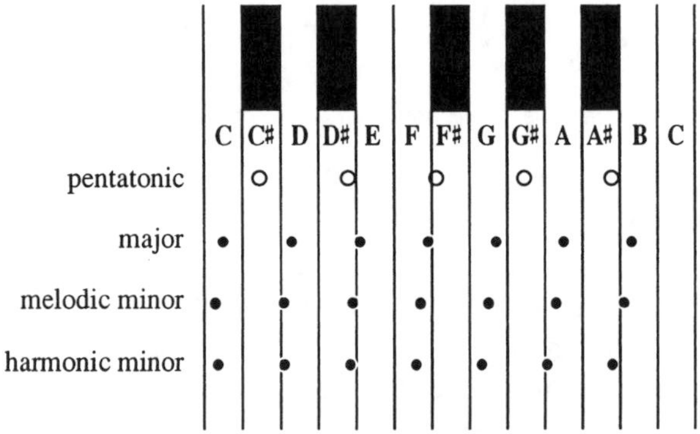

Computer generation of major, minor, and pentatonic scales from equal-interval series by approximation

The reason for choosing the twelve-tone chromatic scale was that it is made up of relatively equal steps of the twelfth root of 2. A classical diatonic major or minor scale, by comparison, moves up and down in an inconsistent sequence of whole steps and half steps: tone, tone, semitone, tone, tone, tone, semitone (2, 2, 1, 2, 2, 2, 1) for a major scale, and tone, semitone, tone, tone, tone, tone, semitone (2, 1, 2, 2, 2, 2, 1) for an ascending minor scale, for example (there are other variant forms). For a pentatonic scale as formed by the black notes of the piano, the interval sequence is tone, minor 3rd, tone, tone, minor 3rd (2, 3, 2, 2, 3). The first question was whether a simpler method could be found of generating a major or minor scale, than of storing the interval sequence, or note sequence, in computer memory. Since melodies are shapes first and note sequences afterward, I wanted if possible to avoid specifying a scale regime in advance. I subsequently discovered that the irregularities of major, minor, and pentatonic scales could in fact be computed as equal-interval number sequences rounded down to the nearest values in the chromatic scale, as shown above.

The determining parameters of a randomly generated melody, omitting rhythm and dynamics, are *scale*, *interval*, *range*, and *bounce*. Scale defines the size of an interval step, e.g., five, seven, twelve, or more than twelve steps to the octave. (Alternatively, it may be defined as a harmonic series, for bugle or natural horn, in which case the steps are of *equal frequency number* e.g., 400, 500, 600, 700, 800, 900, 1000 hertz etc.)

Interval signifies the leap or number of steps up or down from note to note. A zero value interval corresponds to a repeated note. The range of a melody is defined as how far it may rise or fall in absolute pitch. A voice or musical instrument can be broadly categorized by a combination of range and interval. At the core of the original (and primitive) Fractal Melody program is a formula by which the software decides the movement of a melody up or down; at each stage the new note becomes the zero point for calculating the following interval step. The user enters a number to determine the range of the melody in octaves, and a second number to specify the maximum range in semitones a melody may rise or fall.

```
10   Q = 0                          [Set bounce value to zero]
20   INPUT "RANGE IN OCTAVES? ";R
30   IF R > 6 THEN 20               [Range not to exceed 6 octaves]
40   R = R * 24
50   INPUT "INTERVAL RANGE IN 1/2 TONES ";W
60   W = W * 2                      [Converts step size]
70   INPUT "SPEED ";D               [Sets duration in cycles]
80   INPUT "BOUNCE FACTOR; 1 TO 5 [Large bounce]
90   Y = (160 - R)/2                [Splits the difference between
                                     pitch and melody range]
100 P = (R / 2)+ Y: POKE PITCH, P [Chooses starting note in mid-
                                     range, plays it]
110 FOR S = 1 TO D: NEXT S         [Sustains it for duration D]
120 LEAP = INT(W * RND (1) + 1)    [Chooses a random interval in
                                     range W, rounded up]
130 LEAP = (LEAP + 2) - (W + Q)    [Converts to up or down]
140 P = P + LEAP                   [Adds to previous pitch]
150 P = INT (P / 2) * 2            [Rounds down to nearest semitone]
160 IF P < Y THEN P = Y; Q = Q - B
170 IF P > (160 - Y) THEN P = (160 - Y); Q = Q + B
                                   [If the added interval exceeds the
                                   chosen range, it "sticks" at the
                                   limit while the balance of
                                   probability changes in favour of a
                                   return within range. NB: Here the
                                   bounce is cumulative]
180 POKE PITCH, P                  [Plays the new pitch]
190 FOR S = 1 TO D: NEXT S         [Sustains it for duration D]
200 GOTO 120                       [Returns to repeat process]
```

As long as the generated melody remains within its stipulated range, its motion in principle will reflect an equal probability of upward or downward movement. In practice however the melody will tend to drift in a particular direction and if left unchecked would end by wandering "off the keyboard." It is to ensure that a melody remains within range (and thus within the believable limits of a voice or instrument) that a program has to incorporate some means of detection when a melody reaches either limit, and to nudge it back toward mid-range. In the version of the program detailed above, if a melody drifts to either extreme of range it "sticks" there until the altered bias of interval choice takes effect to bring the melody back within range.

In the following example the combination of an octave range and maximum leap of up to a minor third (four semitones) leads to a melody in the character of a Middle-Eastern chant:

Fractal Melody
Range 1 Interval 4 Bounce 1

As the interval size limit is increased, so the character of the resulting melody becomes less vocal and smooth, more "jagged" and instrumental. If the interval size limit nears the absolute melody range, however, the two dimensions will begin to interfere with one another and the melody will begin to oscillate back and forth. This could in fact be a way of modeling the timbre of a wind instrument.

The angle of drift of a fractal melody can be shallow or steep. It will be shallow if consecutive intervals are small, and steep where they tend to be larger. Here the size of bounce plays a role. In an early form of the program, when a melody reaches an extreme of range, it waits there for a choice of interval to take it back from the extreme toward the center. The longer it waits, the more bounce accumulates, increasing the likelihood of a steeper angle of return. A gentle rise to a high note, followed by a sudden drop, or its inversion, a gentle descent followed by a sharp rise, are traits that

Bounce as observed in traditional melody

can actually be observed in some familar melodies, for instance the folk song "Oh Danny Boy," or the hymn "Jerusalem" by Hubert Parry.

All the same, bounce should not normally be an obtrusive feature of a melody, since it is designed to act not as a mechanical barrier, but as a natural brake or constraint on melodic movement as a vocalist would feel when reaching the limits of normal range. If a bounce value of less than 1 is chosen, the effect is a good deal more subtle, and the melody is able to linger in a naturalistic way (like the theme from Ravel's *Bolero*, which lingers at extremes of range). The next example, but with a bounce set at 0.1 rather than 1.0, for some reason is noticeably more diatonic—a little like Bach's "Air on the G string."

Fractal Melody
Range 1 Interval 4 Bounce 0.1

A fractal melody incorporating range and bounce conditions has to reconcile three separate oscillations:

1. A fluctuation of interval size within the set limit;
2. A slower oscillation between upper and lower limits of range; and
3. An oscillation of bounce, i.e. the weighting of movement up or down.

The amplitude and frequency of bounce oscillation will vary as the melody and interval parameters are varied, and also according to the mode of range-sensing built into the program. If for example the program instructs a melody to stick at the extremes of range until sufficient bounce has accumulated to dislodge it, a slow climb will be followed by a precipitous drop. In other situations the two may interact to reinforce one another, creating a forced sawtooth or ramp wave oscillation between extremes of range.

Normally, of course, a melody doesn't bob to the top of its range and wait there, like a toy diver at the surface of a glass of water. Extremes of range are difficult for voices and instruments to sustain, so there is a built-in tendency for voice and instrumental melodies to gravitate toward the mid-range. (Notable exceptions are the keyboards, which in this context can once again be recognized as scientific pitch and interval measuring devices.) The absence of a "bell-curve" tendency for pitches to gravitate toward the center is likely to have contributed to the perceived strangeness of early serial and chance music in the mid-twentieth century. The tendency of a melody is to veer away, or at least slow down, as it approaches an extreme of range. When the program is modified so that instead of cutting an overreaching interval to fit (which causes the melody to stick at the extremes, and is unnatural) the exceeding interval is cancelled, the melody pauses at whatever note it last reached, so is heard to rise more naturally to a range of peaks of various heights instead of to a level plateau.

As interval and range limits are expanded, the character of a synthetic melody changes from vocal to instrumental, and from modal to diatonic, eventually advancing to an idiom recognizably closer to the atonal expressionism of a Berg or Boulez. To achieve an effect comparable to avant-garde "pointillism," however, the limit of note to note progression has to be expanded to leap in octaves rather than semitones. A fair approximation to Xenakis is achieved if the instrument range is set at six octaves, while the maximum interval leap from note to note is allowed to *exceed* that range. The result is that more notes are generated outside the range than within. When notes that fall outside the range are replaced by silence, a texture of wide intervals and erratic durations is produced, of a character not unlike Xenakis's *Eonta* for piano, or Boulez's *Structures I* for two pianos. This particular aesthetic takes octave register into account as a compositional determinant, exactly as for early Stockhausen. The interesting conclusion to be drawn from the fractal program is the thought that the difference between plainchant and pointillism is ultimately a matter of scaling.

Up to this point we have been proceeding on the basis that a melody is "the discontinuous expression of a single continuous curve." However, the stepwise progression of a melody in western music is affected by other tonal relations than simple proximity, for example movement between notes of a common triad, octave leaps, and chord relations, as well as more nuanced inflections such as "bending the note." To do justice to established conventions of harmony and classical tonal progression would seem to imply a program of some complexity, as well as implying that natural melodies are not free at all.

Johann Strauss II: "Beautiful Blue Danube"

Kurt Weill: "Mack the Knife"

Examples of well-known melodies incorporating harmonic leaps (octave, major third, fourth) as natural progressions in place of note to note transitions up and down the scale

Numerous attempts have been made to incorporate textbook rules of harmony into composition software. This is to miss the point that while a melody may be made to conform to harmonic rules, and may be harmonized in different ways, it does not necessarily mean that it was composed with those rules in mind. Since melody is preserved in memory as shape rather than specific pitch and time values, the harmonization of a melody to *any* given set of rules does not address the meaning behind the shape—or even, as Parsons has shown, the meaning encoded in its pattern of directional changes. One may suppose that melodies arise initially out of a sense of movement up and down within a uniform pitch space, and are only afterward pinned down, with the aid of a keyboard or guitar, into a particular key or set of key relations.

Western melody moves with equal ease between harmonic intervals of a third or fifth as to an adjacent tone or semitone.

Examples are Johann Strauss II's "Beautiful Blue Danube," and the persistent triadic formations of Kurt Weill's "Mack the Knife" in *The Threepenny Opera*: melodies that strictly speaking should be unsingable, but in practice are not at all difficult to reproduce. In classical music, shifts between notes of a common chord, or melodic "faults" that suddenly shift a melody up or down by an octave (as in the preceding examples) give the lie to the definition of a melody as a single continuous curve. The opening phrases of Strauss's famous melody draws a curve as points on a plane of pitch and time, but harmonically speaking all the notes in each phrase are degrees of the same chord, so the movement is spatial (changes of state within the chord) rather than dynamic (tending toward change of key). A conventional tonal melody is subject therefore to "change of state" movement within the same chord, as well as "progression" through degrees of a scale, or within an absolute pitch space. Whether a melody interval is perceived as a degree change or as a chord change depends to a large extent on how the listener imagines it to be harmonized. In the absence of explicit harmonization, melody intervals that share a common chord tend to be perceived as degrees of the same chord, whereas intervals of a semitone, tone, tritone, or major seventh, are more likely to be signaling a change in chord or key. When the "missing notes" from these imaginary triads are correlated, latent tonalities may emerge. This can even apply to the high serialism of Stockhausen's pointillist *Piano Piece I*, the note collections of which can be seen to gravitate around implicit tonal centres of D and A, like atoms around a black hole:

Stockhausen: D and A interval ratios ending Piano Piece I

Paradoxically, it is from an analysis of vocal melodies from the Op. 10 Second String Quartet by Schoenberg, melodies intended to

Arnold Schoenberg: String Quartet No. 2 Op. 10, fourth movement

Schoenberg: atonal melodies in diatonic intervals over a sinking bass-line. From the String Quartet Op. 10 No. 2, fourth movement, at score number [59] *shown above, and at* [74] *below*

celebrate the liberation of music from classical tonality, that a new method of computing melodies is derived. The analysis shows that each melody derives its atonal character and late Romantic sense of yearning from what might be described as a "sinking bassline" or sliding tonality that shifts downward in key with nearly every note.

The soprano melody can now be described as lying atop a kind of figured bass in which the actual pitch sung is the tonic, major third, or perfect fifth of an implied moving bassline. This lends itself to a simple program that computes the drifting tonic and then adds a harmonious interval to that computed pitch. For the purposes of the program, and in line with the examples illustrated, the added values are limited to the unison, major third, perfect fifth, or octave.

A melody generated by the Schoenberg 2 variant program consists of a drift or element to which is added an upward interval corresponding to unison, major third, fifth, or octave. In the harmonized example, the melody and associated rhythm are computer-generated

The structure of a melody generated by the Schoenberg 2 program is non-symmetrical, since the second-stage tonal interval is always added over the underlying "drifting tonic" and never subtracted from it. The most visible feature of a Schoenberg program melody is its greater interval bandwidth compared to a plain fractal melody. An interesting feature is the ease with which melodies lie within the programmed limits, indicating a nice equilibrium between the drift and harmonic curves. Octave displacement to bring a melody back into range is already a feature of atonal as well as tonal melody, as is seen from the authentic Schoenberg melodies reproduced overleaf.

In a variant Schoenberg 2 program, when the generated melody reaches an extreme of range, the *drift* interval is subtracted, but the added *harmonic* interval is left intact. This allows a melody to exceed the preset upper limit, while preventing it from drifting away altogether. A charming quality of hesitancy as it reaches for the top notes is brought out in a finished example of a Schoenberg 2 melody, harmonized opposite in idiomatic fashion.

Both Fractal Melody and Schoenberg programs are simple to a fault. But for all their simplicity they do point to quantifiable differences in melody types, as well as indicating ways of simulating melodies of specific character (early, modern, vocal, instrumental, serial, etc.). One would not expect key autocorrelation in a randomly generated melody, but spontaneous key relations are surprisingly good in both programs: the melodies seem to hover in the same key for quite plausible lengths of time. Perhaps this says more about our human propensity to hear key relationships than anything else: if so, that would be interesting in itself. Overall the experience suggests that not only may Parsons be right after all, but rhythmic and tonal conventions may also eventually be shown to contribute only cosmetically to the satisfaction communicated by a particular melody.

Although iconic moving images of accelerating into a Mandelbrot set—a kind of reverse black hole expanding to infinity and constantly seeding new strands and constellations seemingly out of nowhere—offer a slightly terrifying glimpse of falling toward eternity in a film of oil on the surface of an antediluvian dark ocean, fractals are perhaps the most exciting development in aesthetics for some generations. In a controversial recent case, fractal analysis has been employed to determine that a number of paintings purporting to be by Jackson Pollock may have been faked.[8] To paraphrase Mallarmé, however, the coup of fractal analysis does not eliminate aesthetic intuition. Mandelbrot himself identified a subtle fractally quantifiable difference between an older genre of classical Chinese landscape art depicted from nature, and a later urban landscape genre based on stereotyped images copied from the earlier style. Fractal analysis offers a self-sufficient and independent numerical basis for aesthetic judgements based on human instinct.

From a musical perspective, the simplicity of fractal programming, and its constraints, offer a way ahead and out of the dead end that has been reached in music synthesis and analysis. In the domain of timbre or instrument simulation, we can look ahead to replace the metallic synthetic tones of the past, which are based on rigid mathematical data and are unable to convey any sense of tonal expression (like the Italian harpsichord of Cristofori's day, three centuries ago), by simple and easily manipulated recursive formulae that interact with their own boundary conditions to produce tones of a complexity and controlled variability analogous to real musical instruments, like the violin and oboe. These algorithms will behave "like minimalism with a human face," much faster and with agreeably approximate results. The basis for creating synthetic sounds is likely to shift from exactly specifying a result, to simulating the conditions of operation of real instruments functioning as transducers, taking in incoherent information (energy, random numbers) and converting it to structured energy (musical tones).

Mandelbrot's work has drawn attention to fractal relations in other musical domains than melody and timbre. We can now begin to appreciate the fractal dimension of an acoustic interior in relation to the music associated with it: of plainchant and polyphony related to the complex fractal interior surfaces of a Gothic cathedral, or music of tonality in relation to the eigentones of rectangular spaces in harmonic proportions of a mansion by Palladio, or the acoustic messages of tonal freedom implied by the warped curves and voids of baroque architecture, and of levitation implied by the domes of religious interiors.[9]

Notes

1. Denys Parsons, *A Directory of Tunes and Musical Themes.* London: Spencer Brown, 1975.
2. Benoît Mandelbrot, *Fractals: Form, Chance, and Dimension.* San Francisco: W. H. Freeman, 1977.
3. Martin Gardner, "White, Brown, and Fractal Music." *Scientific American* Vol. 238 No. 4 (1978) repr. in *The Night is Large: Collected Essays 1938–1995*. New York: St Martin's Press, 1996, 375–93.
4. Lejaren A. Hiller and Leonard M. Isaacson, *Experimental Music.* New York: McGraw-Hill, 1959.
5. Max V. Mathews and Lawrence Rosler, "Graphical Language for the Scores of Computer-generated Sounds." 84–114 in Heinz von

Foerster ed. and James W. Beauchamp ed., *Music by Computers*. New York: Wiley, 1969.

6. *Kagura: Japanese Shinto Ritual Music* rec. János Kárpáti, Hungaroton SPLX 18193, 1988. Robin Maconie, *The Second Sense: Language, Music, and Hearing*. Lanham MD and London: Scarecrow Press, 2002, 73–74.
7. Robin Maconie and Chris Cunningham, "Computers Unveil the Shape of Melody." *New Scientist* Vol. 94 No. 1302 (1982), 206–9.
8. R. P. Taylor, R. Guzman, T. P. Martin, G, D. R. Hall, A. P. Micolich, D. Jonas, and C. A. Marlow, "Authenticating Pollock Paintings Using Fractal Geometry." (www.uoregon.edu/~msiuo/taylor/art/TaylorSubmission.pdf) (08/07/2008)
9. Rudolf Wittkower, *Architectural Principles in the Age of Humanism* 4th edn. London: Academy Editions, 1988.

THIRTY

SIMULTANEITY

Toward the end of his life, having composed celebrations of the year (*Sirius*) and the week (*LICHT*), Stockhausen expressed an intention to address the hour, the minute, and eventually the second. He indicated that a music celebrating the second would be, as always, of major length. And in his final years John Cage devoted attention to a personal style of blank verse that he called *mesostics*, a selection of chance-determined cuttings of text, drawn from a single source or a limited number of sources, taken as it were out of a hat in the sense made famous by Tristan Tzara, and arranged on the page in an order dictated by a vertical spelling of one or more code words which remain unspoken. Although they look as though they are only visual in intention and significance, Cage insisted on reading such arranged texts aloud, and to listen to the tapes of his Harvard lectures, *I – VI*, is quite an intriguing experience.[1]

These two statements are of interest as propositions by intelligent musical minds in the flower of their wisdom about what music is, how it is experienced, and where the art of music goes next. They are also, in a curious way, related. They are also relatable to a vital thread of intelligence in the music of Pierre Boulez. To a majority of musicians these propositions are likely to appear totally off the wall. I am persuaded that they not only make sense, but also connect with the oldest paradoxes considered in the present narrative. They ask the same questions about existence, consciousness, beauty, and communication as were being asked in ancient Greece.

How can a music of "one second" be conceived? On the internet for a start. The music of chance encounters envisaged by Cage in the aftermath of war is a poetic device for representing a music that is allowed to emerge spontaneously from a data resource. In the normal course of events, the data resource is memory, and the act of recall is called *inspiration.* We all know what inspiration is. It comes unbidden, at the wrong time, or refuses to come when we most need it. The universal perception in the west of a work of art as a coherent and finished article allows most people who are not artists to discount the imaginative training necessary for inspiration to develop in the first place, let alone the practical craft of putting a work together. A music of a second, in Stockhausen's terminology, might well be conceived, like *Gruppen*, as a waveform originally of a second's duration that has been stretched electronically, in time and perhaps also in frequency, so that its inner proportions remain the same but its evolution is transformed from a single note of a particular timbre into a modulated and airy monotone, like a religious chant. Such a foundation in exquisitely slow motion could be imitated and decorated by live performers in ways designed to highlight, and possibly develop in new directions, features in the original sound. In this sense the concept links up to Stockhausen's plus-minus compositions of the 1960s—which are programs for transforming samples of music retrieved from memory or the airwaves—and beyond them to Pierre Schaeffer's *musique concrète* of the early 1950s. One could also imagine the original sound for a one-second composition recorded on multiple tracks by multiple microphones facing up, left, right, and toward the rear in a classic tetrahedral array. This would provide a means of manipulating the sound and its transformations in a coherent original ambient space, allowing for rotation and elevation.

On such a basic framework a music of infinite variety could be devised. In addition to resources of optional instrumental sound, there exist a range of other possibilities: punctuation, interruption, inversion, reflection, augmentation, and diminution of the original, like a fugue by J. S. Bach or a note-row by Schoenberg. Gaps are okay. A cheese with holes is still a cheese. The original sound on which this variation is based may be a time-condensed version of a melody formula for one or more instruments, or the same melody formation played simultaneously in slow- and fast motion. These techniques are all familiar from the composer's earlier works, but would differ from them in the respect that the new composition would retain the feeling of the work of a moment in time.

That is what Stockhausen might have done. It is a guess, but in relation to his earlier music it makes a kind of sense. There are other options that spring to mind, of which the most interesting would be a kind of musical kaleidoscope, lasting a minute at a time, based on precomposed material that can be combined in an infinite number of ways, but is always beautiful in a classical sense of "well made," all parts fitting together and making pleasing and graceful gestures. This idea has many attractions. It allows every performance to be a premiere, which is good for business. It allows a certain freedom of choice of instruments, like baroque music. It can be combined with a variety of intuitive instructions, like the text pieces *Aus den sieben Tagen*, but avoiding some problems associated with the latter. Unlike method acting, where the performer's intuition is focused on recreating an authentic character within a preexisting dramatic context and script outline, Stockhausen's text compositions oblige a performer to be inspired spontaneously on a number of levels at once: imaginatively, in relation to the text; technically, in relation to the music one utters; and socially, in terms of integrating with other players. Each of the above requires skill; to do all at once is asking a lot of classically trained musicians. Ideally the result would resemble a cadenza, or series of cadenzas variously superimposed (like Cage's transparencies), produced by performers from a common set of musical samples which are open to be embroidered and modified in a variety of ways. The players can therefore dispose of the problematic invention element of the exercise, and focus (like practiced jazz players) on adapting the items they have to a mood or theme as if it were arising from a spontaneous interaction, like a conversation among friends. Such a method of group composition already has elements in common with the improvisatory music of other traditions.

VARIABLE SIMULTANEITY

The idea of a music that does not go anywhere is not new. The idea of a process that appears to be going somewhere but actually stays in the same place is familiar from nature, in imagery of the river, in the metaphor of time as a river, and also of the sea and the movement of celestial bodies, among the most ancient of mysteries.

It follows that the idea of a music celebrating a second in

duration, or momentary glimpse of eternity, alludes philosophically to a perception of experience as fleeting, and aesthetic appreciation as transitory. To the ancients the constellations were fixtures of the night sky; today we understand that the view from earth is also a view back in time, and that the light of each star making up a sign of the zodiac is remote from every other in time and space: the observer is a mere point of convergence of information timelines

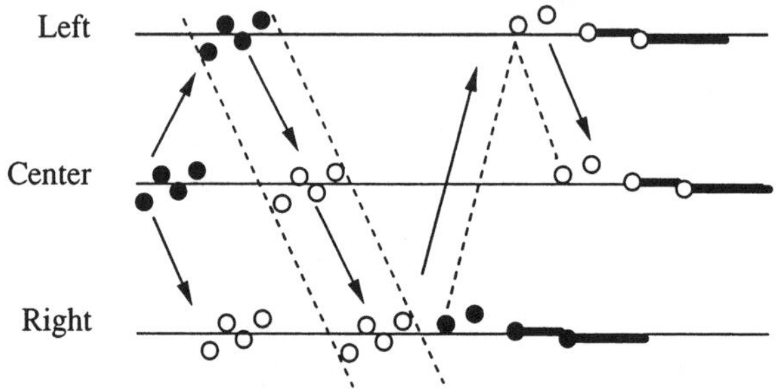

Because sound travels relatively slowly, separated musicians are unable to synchronize precisely. This accounts for the development of echo canon in music of the Venetian school of Gabrieli

traveling unimaginable distances at the speed of light. Simultaneity ultimately has to do with where we happen to be at a particular moment.

The paradox of variable simultaneity was considered at length by the Venetian school of composers that included Andrea and Giovanni Gabrieli, Heinrich Schütz, and Giovanni Priuli. Their new line of inquiry into a spatialized art of music challenged the earlier principle of ensemble unity—the unified musical space of religious observance—by experimenting in distributing a group of players to various locations at the midpoint and periphery of the performing space. What began as instrumental music in call and answer mode evolved into something much more mysterious. When players are within earshot of each other but widely separated in spatial terms, they are unable to play in time any longer. Visual synchronization may be instantaneous, at the speed of light, but widely separated players cannot synchronize their playing because of the time it takes for a signal to travel from player to player, and from end to end of a performing space of any size.

The implications are startling. They remain startling today for orchestra audiences. Depending on where you are located, in a cathedral or concert environment, a music involving widely separated players will sound more or less synchronized, and coordinated in different ways. This discovery can only have been disturbing to the church authorities in the early seventeenth century. It was bad enough that composers were experimenting with purely instrumental music, abandoning music's conventional role as servant of a sacred text. Now the fundamental unities of space and time were being literally blown apart, not only by Galileo and his wretched telescope, but musically as well by the Gabrielis and their bands of wind instruments. How was a listener to know which came first, the trumpets on the left or those on the right? If the answer depended on where a listener was standing, what was that saying about the church speaking with one voice?

In the realm of hifi there is a concept of "the sweet spot." This is a point in the midst of a super-expensive audio system where the stereo or surround sound image is ideally balanced. In almost every case, there is only one spot in the room where the balance of left, centre, right and rear speakers is as good as it can be. Radio broadcasts of classical music and opera aim to replicate not any seat, but the best seat in the house. In fact there is only one "best seat" in the house. What Gabrieli and his friends discovered was that there was only one place in St Mark's Basilica where their spatialized music was perfectly balanced. What that implied was that everywhere else, the balance was skewed. The consequences of losing not only a sense of unity of place, which has theological implications, but losing the sweet spot (unless it happened to be a point below the central dome), are quixotic and fascinating. In place of the traditional unified space, a congregation would have to grapple with the new baroque concept of a space containing multiple equally valid points of view.

The time delays involved in antiphonal polyphony, even in a large cathedral, are less than a second, which is tolerable if the music is sung in unison and slow-moving, as church music usually is. For composers like Gabrieli and his peers who wanted to compose fast-moving and competitive music, they threatened disaster. They were able to work around the problem of synchronization at speed by avoiding it altogether and building on the ancient call and answer tradition of mountain cultures. When delays are already built in to the musical argument, as it were, the natural delays in transmission from point to point are no longer critical, or critically exposed. Similar tactics of question and answer are employed in satellite newscasting from remote parts of the world for precisely the same reason, to disguise unavoidable delays in signal transmission and reception.

Setting up what in effect is a communications network in a religious space is challenging enough in its own terms, which are spiritual and moral as well as technical in implication. In a majority of canzonas by the Venetian school the call and answer exchanges are scripted for identical or similar sonorities: cornetts, trombones. This makes sense because the tactic eliminates all other variables from the musical equation than space and time. In a few rare cases, however, the idea of *multiple coexistent spaces* can be heard to intrude on the Gabrielian concept of *one space* enclosing *multiple points of view*. Among the most provocative is Monteverdi's setting of "Deposuit potentes" from the *Magnificat* in the *Vespers* of 1610. Here in addition to defining the cardinal dimensions of length, breadth, and height by carefully staged echo canons, Monteverdi plays with more subtle oppositions of instrumental timbres: cornetts (wind) against violins, contrasting external (real) and internal (imaginary) space, as well as traditional plainchant, representing timeless unity, and the renaissance dynamic of canonic imitation, representing displacement in space and time. To these refinements of musical symbolism Monteverdi's contemporary Priuli brought a novel innovation of distributed color in a breathtaking *Canzona prima a 12* for a trio of spaced quartets of woodwinds (treble), brass (bass), and strings (midrange). In this enchanting piece, by adding timbre and register to the directional equation, it is as though Priuli is attempting to create holographic effects through separating and combining three-color images.

RONDEAU

The medieval rondeau *Sumer is icumen in* can be regarded as a musical game of pass the parcel in which a short verse of melody is started by one singer and taken up successively by further singers in a circle, and continuously repeated, like a series of echoes that in puzzling fashion eventually return to the point where they began. The implications of a round in full swing are surprisingly modern. They include the startling images of a random access memory in a computer, information in constant circulation, of primeval chaos, or turbulence. Finally, a melody that loops back on itself is an image of a universe in stable orbit, and of time as a closed loop.

Loop formations in the micro domain are already familiar in the concept of the tone wheel as a waveform generator in the Hammond organ, Stockhausen's synthesis of waveforms on tape, and even the cyclical figurations of minimalist music. In the macro or formal domain, the most innovative recent developments are the 1966 *Canon* by Stravinsky, an endless loop for orchestra based on the composer's *Firebird*, and Boulez's . . . *explosante–fixe* . . . dating from 1971, in commemoration of Stravinsky's death, a concept that has undergone numerous transformations and generated a range of "spin-off" compositions in subsequent years. There is, too, a hint of the endless loop in some compositions by Webern which appear to exhaust the order-possibilities of a chosen series at the expense of describing a classical development or narrative process toward a specific conclusion. In turn, Boulez's initial concept may have been provoked by the examples of Milhaud's Op. 333, a notional planetary system in which multiple themes orbit at different periodicities, and Messiaen's isorhythms, such as the "Liturgie de Cristal" from the *Quartet for the End of Time*. Both Milhaud and Messiaen drew inspiration from the revolving turntables and closed circuit disc recorded sounds of *musique concrète*. One might suppose that an intellectual fascination with loops in time is a peculiarly French phenomenon, stretching back to Guillaume de Machaut.

A traditional *rondeau* alternates a refrain sung by everyone in the circle, and verses newly invented by individual members in succession. The implication of the form is of corporate unity in the chorus, and individual personality and freedom of choice in the verse. But inasmuch as the verses are all invented to the same basic melody, the underlying implication is of everybody in principle singing their verses at the same time, creating a fractal noise, a thousand years in advance of dixieland, in which certain structural consistencies are nevertheless audible within the chaos.

Robin Maconie: Mozart-Kugel

This diatonic round for multiple violins is an illustration of the complexity possible in a round for instruments. Up to 14 violins can take part, at half measure intervals, so at full swing all of the theme above is simultaneously audible in the timespan of one second

A *Kugel* in German is a sphere. The music above is diatonic, hence *Mozart*, and more than a simple round—in fact, a round in three dimensions, hence *Kugel* in the title. It is a "sphere" because it can be approached from any direction. The piece, like all rounds, is of indefinite length in performance, and of specific length in melodic terms. However, since the melodic length can be coiled on itself like a strand of DNA, as more voices are added, a time zone is reached in performance when the entire music is pulsating at the frequency of half a measure, around a second in duration. Here then is an example of a music of a second's duration having indefinite length.

In principle one might consider the above piece as an example of a magic square in the sense admired by Webern. If one were to divide the score vertically into sixteenth-note squares, it should be theoretically possible to derive alternative note sequences after the manner of a Cantor set, reading the first of line 1a, the second of

1b, the third of line 2a, the fourth of line 2b, and so on, preserving the positional status of the note within each half measure, but moving diagonally through the stack rather than laterally in order. The possibilities are endless. Alternatively, such a number sequence of sixteenth-note segments could be rotated, like the combination lock of serialism; or some notes replaced by silence in a structured or random way. A performance beginning from a randomized or pulverized version of the text would then be heard to condense out of chaos as more and more instrumental voices were added to the flux. It is all very exciting.

The counterargument to such treatment is the same routinely opposed to twelve-tone or serial music, as would be raised to any code scrambling of information: that the meaning of the original text is lost in the process. For codemakers, that of course is the whole point. It entails in any case the assumption that "meaning" is embodied, as Schoenberg observed of his method of composition, not in the notes themselves but in their sequence and interval relations. Accordingly, the current meaning of *Mozart-Kugel* lies in the present shape and rhythm and movement in time of the melody line, and is lost when the line is taken apart. In other words, the piece has *meaning* in the same way as a DNA sequence, and also *potential* when reduced to a collection of DNA fragments. While there may be scientific interest in breaking the original sequence into fragments and trying them out in different orders, the only aesthetic merit of such a practice, one might suppose (other than to conceal its information in coded form) would be the curious sensation of creating a work in which the parts mysteriously join together again, like Humpty Dumpty in reverse. That this is precisely the sensation that appeals to change-ringers in rural England, and that European pointillist composers in the early fifties were also trying to achieve, cannot entirely be ruled out.

From the composer's and performer's perspective, however, a rondeau theme defines itself as a *reading* of a data set, rather than the plain set itself (which is where a Schoenberg differs from, say, a Milton Babbitt or Allen Forte). By calling it a *reading* one is saying that the information is modified in performance by virtue of being delivered as a continuous inflected melody by the same instrument, on a human timescale and with expressive continuities of tempo and dynamic curvature. It is not a computer voice putting together words from a data bank, but the expression of a human gesture and quality of execution, an important element of which is *integrity.* This is what banks look for in a specimen signature, for example: not correct spelling or letter formation, but a distinctive continuity of gesture.

Having said that, there is no reason why a randomized version of the *Kugel* melody could not also be interpreted in a similar way, so as to make different sense; it is simply that for it to make sense might entail spreading out the fragments over a longer timespan, and interpolating new material to give the new construction shape and form, like an archaeologist reconstructing a monster body shape from only a few small skeletal fragments, a task requiring considerable imagination, coupled with a knowledge of bodies and how they work.

To take such a thematic formula and extend it over a longer duration, as Stockhausen has done in *Mantra*, *Musik im Bauch*, *Jubiläum*, and *LICHT*, and Boulez also in *. . . explosante–fixe . . .* and its many derivatives, does not necessarily imply that the result of an expansion process is bound to be an experience of perpetual slow motion. Renaissance composers who built complete masses for the church out of musical "found objects" and popular tunes, were doing precisely the same thing. They understood self-similarity in their music in the same terms as Mandelbrot understands changes of scale in a mountain range, or the curvature of Australia, or the growth of a silver fern: that when the same pattern is enlarged, more detail emerges; when reduced, detail is suppressed. Medieval scholars and composers were at ease with the idea of magnification, in their music as in their illuminated manuscripts, understanding the enlarged letter forms and extended syllables of plainchant as acknowledgments of the greatness of the Almighty, and the magnitude of creation and eternity. Greatness in musical terms includes harmony, repetition, and alteration of instrumental color. The closer one examines the skin of a freshly-caught fish, or a piece of woven Harris tweed cloth, the brighter and more varied the colors.

In the past generation, from the time humanity walked on the moon, a kind of *horror vacui* has descended as people begin to comprehend the implications of interplanetary travel, especially the loss of connection arising from maintaining radio contact over vast distances. A hint of the experience is conveyed by Kubrick in the movie *2001: A Space Odyssey*, in the deceptively banal greetings sent by proud parents to one of the astronaut crew on the probe heading toward Jupiter. These domestic and slightly embarrassing endearments are perceived as messages in a bottle cast into a void from which an answer may come in twenty minutes to an hour, or not at all. The obstacle to realizing Charles Ives's dream of multi-orchestra music performed on opposing mountain peaks—or more logically, of a music linking a number of cities in different continents via satellite, in celebration of a major political or cultural event—is that, even on earth, when information is sent and received at light speed, the various ensembles could never be synchronized. It is the Gabrieli phenomenon all over again.

In space the isolation is total, so the emotional implications of a musical speech are especially profound. Of course there are options of transmitting and receiving speech and music information in highly compressed bursts, as already happens on the internet, in which case at least the receipt of messages can be acknowledged in real time, and their return can be anticipated, like emails, with comments and answers interpolated.

Over a distance of light-years, however, even that expedient becomes irrelevant. Distance in space and time becomes indistinguishable from distance in time here on earth. We wonder about the messages left behind by composers long dead, of Schubert's tenth symphony, or Beethoven's, or Mahler's: what they might have said, whether the sketches have any meaning, and whether that meaning can ever be recovered. And having made that imaginative leap, from dialogue in real time to the idea of connection across time, the issue of devising a form of simultaneous music for performance by orchestras on different continents begins to resolve as a new species of rondeau on a world scale in which the same primary data is individually elaborated, passed back and forth between orchestras, and subject to commentary expressing degrees of approval.

The added dimension of such a form of discourse, unique to music, is the ability to design a structure in which, as for Gabrieli, time delays become manageable and spontaneous combinations, as in Bach, assured of making musical sense even when they do not coincide in the same way at either end. The restoration of an aesthetic of spontaneity to symphonic music of the western tradition is likely to appeal to nonwestern industrialized cultures that have embraced western music, but retain their own traditions and beliefs in respect of intuition and the accidental conjunction in art.

PARTICLES AND WAVES

That Cage's mesostics are also statements about intuition and the accidental conjunction in real life may be true, and perhaps even sufficient, in the way Messiaen's celebrations of birdsong may be justified as imitations of natural disorder, or randomness, or even communication as the avian community understands it. That the composer's message is also about codes, and cut-ups, and information theory of a postwar era deeply involved with the power of the subconscious and deeply suspicious of the power of language, is also to the point. But it is not enough, on that basis, to conclude that Cage's fragmented but not-quite-disordered ruminations are no more than a mission statement of a postwar intellectual community in denial of reason, though they are that too. That listening to Cage reading his mesostics can be sleep-inducing may be a criticism, or maybe not. If audence members at a classical concert are put to sleep by Brahms or Schumann, there is perhaps something to be learned from that. And with modern music also. Going to sleep could be a response to information that a listener has difficulty in following. In a relaxed state the mind works differently. Faced with an abnormal density of information, instead of trying to read it sequentially, in real time, a listener may resort to a form of random processing, seeking underlying consistencies of pattern and shape that might not be obvious on the surface.

Such a way of listening may appear to contradict the values of coherence and order identified with classical music or rational discourse. On the other hand, it has its advantages, obvious even —or indeed, to give them credit, *especially*—to an audience of Harvard academics. First, it is never boring, because while the material may be drawn from familiar sources, disorder is always interesting because of the unexpected element. Since academic speeches tend to be boring, this is welcome. Second, and more significantly, what Cage is saying is that what interests him is not how people say things, since what people say is what they have already decided, and what has already been decided is already beyond discussion, a point of no return. What Cage's mesostics deliver is not what people say, but how people actually think: not connectedly, but by opening the mind to a search and rescue process in which things that were lost can sometimes be found, and questions asked a long time ago may suddenly be answered.

Whether music is wave or particle, or both at once, is not the point. For most of my adult life I have wondered about the twin slit experiment. This is the test where single photons of laser light are fired through a slit in an opaque barrier and registered on a surface behind it. When there is only one slit, the light accumulates in a zone opposite the slit, as one might expect. However if another slit is open in the plate, at a distance far enough away to ensure no light from the laser passes through, something very strange occurs. The light accumulating behind the slit changes into an interference pattern of alternate light and dark vertical lines, peaks and troughs of illumination. This experiment convinced the world of physics that light energy exhibits both particle and wavelike properties.

I have no idea what the answer is from a scientific perspective. But as a musician, the answer is obvious. If a person listens with only one ear, the other being disabled, the world is heard in mono. Such a listener may hear a sound clearly enough, but be unable to appreciate, other than by educated guesswork, where the sound is coming from or how far away it may be. For a similar experience, one has only to compare listening to a mono recording with the same in stereo.

Remove the earplug, and suddenly the acoustic world regains depth and direction. It is the same for the twin slit experiment. As soon as a second slit is opened, an interference pattern forms even though no light is passing through it. And that is the point. In opening the second slit, *absence of light* is allowed to pass through. It is absence of light interacting with direct light from the other channel that creates the interference pattern. In turn, that shows that the dual slit apparatus has suddenly acquired a sense of location in space.

❦

Note

1. John Cage, *I–VI* (The Charles Eliot Norton Lectures 1988–1989). Cambridge MA: Harvard University Press, 1990.

BIBLIOGRAPHY

Adorno, Theodor. *Negative Dialectics* tr. E. B. Ashton (1973). Repr. London: Routledge & Kegan Paul, 1990.

Anderson, Alan Ross ed. *Minds and Machines*. Englewood Cliffs: Prentice-Hall, 1964.

Armitage, Merle ed. *Schoenberg*. New York: Schirmer, 1937 repr. Westport CT: Greenwood Press, 1977.

Auden, W. H. "The Word and the Machine." *Encounter* Vol. II, No. 2 (April 1954).

Bailey, Winston J. *Acoustic Behaviour of Insects: An Evolutionary Perspective*. London: Chapman and Hall, 1991.

Ballantine, Deborah. *Handbook of Audiological Techniques*. London: Butterworth-Heinemann, 1990.

Barnsley, Michael. *Fractals Everywhere*. San Diego CA: Academic Press, 1988.

Barrow, John. *The Book of Nothing: Vacuums, Voids, and the Latest Ideas about the Origins of the Universe*. New York: Pantheon Books, 2000.

——. *New Theories of Everything: The Quest for Ultimate Explanation*. New York and Oxford: Oxford University Press, 2007.

——. *Theories of Everything: The Quest for Ultimate Explanation* n.e. London: Vintage, 1992.

Battcock, Gregory ed. *Minimal Art: a Critical Anthology*. New York: E. P. Dutton, 1968.

Bell, David Charles and Alexander Melville Bell. *Bell's Standard Elocutionist: Principles and Exercises* (1860) rev. edn. London: Hodder and Stoughton, 1892.

Bell, E. T. *Men of Mathematics* 2v. (1937) repr. Harmondsworth: Penguin Books, 1953.

Bell, John L. "Continuity and Infinitesimals." *The Stanford Encyclopedia of Philosophy* (2005). (http://plato.stanford.edu/entries/continuity/) (04/03/2008)

Berlin, Isaiah. *Concepts and Categories: Philosophical Essays* ed. Henry Hardy. Oxford: Oxford University Press, 1980.

Bird, John. *Percy Grainger*. London: Elek, 1976.

Bragg, Sir William. *The World of Sound: Six Lectures Delivered at the Royal Institution*. London: G. Bell and Sons, 1933.

Bronowski, Jacob. *The Ascent of Man*. London: British Broadcasting Corporation, 1973.

Buchanan, Andrew. *Films: The Ways of the Cinema*. London: Pitman, 1932.

Burn, A. R. *Pelican History of Greece*. Harmondsworth: Penguin Books, 1966.

Burnet, J. "Philosophy." 57–96 in R. W. Livingstone ed. *The Legacy of Greece*. Oxford: Clarendon Press, 1921.

Burrow, J. A. *Mediaeval Writers and Their Work: Middle English Literature and Its Background 1100–1500*. Oxford: Oxford University Press, 1982.

Cage, John. *I–VI*. The Charles Eliot Norton Lectures 1988–1989. Cambridge MA: Harvard University Press, 1990.

——. "Lecture on Nothing" (1950) repr. *Incontri Musicali* (April 1959). 109–27 in *Silence: Lectures and Writings*. Cambridge MA: M. I. T. Press, 1966.

——. *Silence: Lectures and Writings*. Cambridge MA: M. I. T. Press, 1966.

Cage, John ed. and Ruth Knowles ed. *Notations*. West Glover VT: Something Else Press, 1976.

Calder-Marshall, Arthur. *The Innocent Eye: The Life of Robert J. Flaherty*. New York: Harcourt, Brace, & World, 1963.

Chevalier, Jean ed. and Alan Gheerbrant ed. *Dictionary of Symbols* (2nd edn., 1982) tr. John Buchanan-Brown. London: Penguin Books, 1996.

Chomsky, Noam. *Modular Approaches to the Study of the Mind*. San Diego CA: San Diego State University Press, 1984.

——. *Syntactic Structures*. The Hague: Mouton, 1957.

Cocteau, Jean. *Cocteau on the Film* tr. Vera Traill. London: Dennis Dobson, 1954.

Coelho, Victor ed. *Music and Science in the Age of Galileo*. Dordrecht:

Kluwer, 1992.

Compton, Rae. *The Complete Book of Traditional Guernsey and Jersey Knitting*. London: Batsford, 1986.

Coveney, Peter and Roger Highfield. *The Arrow of Time: The Quest to Solve Science's Greatest Mystery*. London: Flamingo, 1990.

Cowell, Henry. "Current Chronicle." *Musical Quarterly* Vol. XXXVIII No. 1 (1952) repr. in Richard Kostelanetz ed., *John Cage*. London: Allen Lane, 1971.

Crevier, Daniel. *AI: The Tumultuous History of the Search for Artificial Intelligence*. New York: Basic Books, 1993.

Crombie, A. C. *Science, Optics, and Music in Medieval and Early Modern Thought*. London: Hambledon Press, 1990.

Dennett, Daniel C. *Consciousness Explained*. Boston and New York: Little, Brown, 1991.

Dickinson, G. Lowes. *The Greek View of Life*. 13th edn. New York: Doubleday, Page & Co., 1920.

Dilke, O. A. W. *Mathematics and Measurement*. London: British Museum Press, 1987.

Eisenstein, Sergei. *Film Form: Essays in Film Theory* tr. ed. Jay Leyda. New York: Harcourt Brace & Company, 1949.

——. *The Film Sense* tr. ed. Jay Leyda. London: Faber and Faber, 1943.

Farrington, Benjamin. *Greek Science*. Rev. ed. Harmondsworth: Penguin Books, 1963.

Field, Mary and Percy Smith. *Secrets of Nature*. London: Faber and Faber, 1934.

Foerster, Heinz von ed. and James W. Beauchamp ed., *Music by Computers*. New York: Wiley, 1969.

Forte, Allen. *The Structure of Atonal Music*. New Haven CT: Yale University Press, 1973.

Gardner, Martin. "Mathematical Games: White, Brown, and Fractal Music." *Scientific American* Vol. 238 No. 4 (1978).

——. *The Night is Large: Collected Essays 1938–1995*. New York: St Martin's Press, 1996.

Gimpel, Jean. *The Cathedral Builders* tr. Teresa Waugh. London: Pimlico, 1983.

Gingerich, Owen. "Kepler, Galileo, and the harmony of the world." 45–63 in Victor Coelho ed., *Music and Science in the Age of Galileo*. Dordrecht: Kluwer, 1992.

Gombrich, E. H. *Art and Illusion: A Study in the Psychology of Pictorial Representation*. 5th edn. Oxford: Phaidon, 1991.

——. *The Sense of Order: A Study in the Psychology of Decorative Art*. Ithaca NY: Cornell University Press, 1979.

Gott, J. Richard. *Time Travel in Einstein's Universe: The Physical Possibilities of Travel Through Time*. Boston: Houghton Mifflin, 2001.

Gottlieb, Gilbert ed. and Norman A. Krasneger ed. *Measurement of Audition and Vision in the First Year of Postnatal Life: A Methodological Overview*. Norwood NJ: Ablex Publishing Corporation, 1985.

Groome, Christopher. *Diagrams: Based on the Original Work by Jasper and William Snowdon* (1972) repr. Burton Latimer, Northants: Christopher Groome, 1978.

Gunderson, Keith ed. *Mentality and Machines: A Survey of the Artificial Intelligence Debate* 2nd edn. London: Croom Helm, 1985.

Haldane, J. B. S. *The Inequality of Man*. Harmondsworth: Penguin Books, 1937.

Hale, Terry ed. *The Automatic Muse: Surrealist Novels by Robert Desnos, Michel Lievis, Georges Limbour & Benjamin Péret* tr. Terry Hale and Iaian White. London: Atlas Press, 1994.

Haren, Michael. *Mediaeval Thought: The Western Intellectual tradition from Antiquity to the Thirteenth Century*. London: Macmillan, 1985.

Harsdörffer, Georg Philipp. *Mathematische und Philosophische Erquickstunden. Texte der Frühen Neuzeit* (Nürnberg: 1636). Frankfurt: Keip, 1990.

Harvey, Jonathan. *Music of Stockhausen: An Introduction*. London: Faber and Faber, 1975.

Hawking, Stephen W. *A Brief History of Time: From the Big Bang to Black Holes*. London: Bantam Press, 1988.

——. *The Universe in a Nutshell*. New York: Bantam Books, 2001.

Heller, Erich. *The Disinherited Mind: Essays in Modern German Literature and Thought*. Cambridge: Bowes & Bowes, 1952.

Hepworth, Cecil. *Came the Dawn: Memories of a Film Pioneer*. London: Phoenix House, 1951.

Hiller, Lejaren A. and Leonard M. Isaacson. *Experimental Music*. New York: McGraw-Hill, 1959.

Hobson, J. Allan. *Consciousness*. New York: Scientific American Library, 1999.

Hogben, Lancelot. *Mathematics for the Million* 3rd rev. edn. London: George Allen & Unwin, 1951.

Holmes, Oliver Wendell. *Mechanism in Thought and Morals*. Boston: J. R. Osgood and Company, 1871. (www.druglibrary.org/schaffer/Library/studies/cuCU43.html) (06/07/2006)

Hoover, Cynthia A. *Music Machines—American Style*. Exhibition catalog. Washington DC: Smithsonian Institution, 1971.

Huffman, Carl A. *Philolaus of Croton: Pythagorean and Presocratic*. Cambridge: Cambridge University Press, 1993.

Ionesco, Eugene. *The Lesson*. In *Plays Volume I* tr. Donald Watson. London: John Calder, 1958.

Jeans, Sir James. *The Growth of Physical Science*. Cambridge: Cambridge University Press, 1950.

——. *The Mysterious Universe*. Cambridge: Cambridge University Press, 1930.

——. *Science & Music*. Cambridge: Cambridge University Press, 1937.

Jevons, W. Stanley. *Elementary Lessons in Logic: Deductive and Inductive*. London: Macmillan, 1925.

Joad, C. E. M. *Philosophic Aspects of Modern Science*. London: George Allen & Unwin, 1932.

——. *Return to Philosophy: Being a Defence of Reason, An Affirmation of Values, and a Plea for Philosophy*. London: Faber and Faber, 1935.

Jones, Daniel. *The Pronunciation of English* (1909) 4th rev. enl. edn. Cambridge: Cambridge University Press, 1956.

Karkoschka, Erhard. *Notation in New Music: A Critical Guide* tr. Ruth Koenig. London: Universal Edition, 1972.

Kidson, Frank. "Country Dance." 624–25 in J. A. Fuller-Maitland ed., *Grove's Dictionary of Music and Musicians*. 2nd edn. Vol. I. London: Macmillan, 1910.

——. "God Save the King." 118–19 in J. A. Fuller-Maitland ed., *Grove's Dictionary of Music and Musicians*. 2nd edn. Vol. II. London: Macmillan, 1910.

Kitto, H. D. F. "That Famous Greek 'Wholeness.'" 54–59 in R. B. McConnell ed., *Art, Science, and Human Progress: The Richard Bradford Trust Lectures given between 1975 and 1978 under the auspices of the Royal Institution*. London: John Murray, 1983.

Kostelanetz, Richard ed. *John Cage*. London: Allen Lane, 1971.

Kultermann, Udo. *Art-Events and Happenings* tr. John William Gabriel. London: Mathews Millar Dunbar, 1971.

Lawder, Standish D. *Cubist Cinema*. Anthology of Film Archives Series 1. New York: New York University Press, 1975.

Lindgren, Ernest. *The Art of the Film*. London: George Allen & Unwin, 1948.

Ling, Daniel. *Speech and the Hearing-Impaired Child: Theory and Practice*. Washington DC: Alexander Graham Bell Association for the Deaf, 1975.

Livingstone, R. W. ed. *The Legacy of Greece* (1921). Oxford: Clarendon Press, 1947.

London, Kurt. *Film Music: A Summary of the Charcteristic Features of its History, Aesthetics, Technique: and Possible Development* tr. Eric S. Bensinger. London: Faber and Faber, 1936.

Low, Rachel and Roger Manvell. *The History of the British Film 1896–1906*. London: George Allen & Unwin, 1948.

Maconie, Robin. *The Concept of Music*. Oxford: Clarendon Press, 1990.

——. "Musical Acoustics in the Age of Vitruvius." *Musical Times* Vol. 146, No. 1890 (2005).

——. *Other Planets: The Music of Karlheinz Stockhausen*. Lanham MD and Oxford: Scarecrow Press, 2005.

——. *The Second Sense: Language, Hearing, and Music*. Lanham MD: Scarecrow Press, 2002.

——. *The Way of Music: Aural Training for the Internet Generation*. Lanham MD: Scarecrow Press, 2006.

Maconie, Robin and Chris Cunningham. "Computers Unveil the Shape of Melody." *New Scientist* Vol. 94 No. 1302 (1982).

Mandelbrot, Benoît B. *Fractals: Form, Chance, and Dimension.* San Francisco: W. H. Freeman, 1977.

Manvell, Roger and John Huntley. *The Technique of Film Music.* London: Focal Press, 1957.

Mathews, Max V. and Lawrence Rosler. "Graphical Language for the Scores of Computer-generated Sounds." 84–114 in Heinz von Foerster ed. and James W. Beauchamp ed., *Music by Computers.* New York: Wiley, 1969.

McConnell R. B. ed. *Art, Science, and Human Progress: The Richard Bradford Trust Lectures given between 1975 and 1978 under the auspices of the Royal Institution.* London: John Murray, 1983.

McLaren, Norman. "Notes on Animated Sound." *Hollywood Quarterly* Vol. VII No. 3 (1953) repr. in Manvell and Huntley, *Technique of Film Music.*

McLuhan, H. Marshall. *The Gutenberg Galaxy: The Making of Typographic Man.* London: Routledge and Kegan Paul, 1967.

Milhaud, Darius. "Konstruierte Musik." *Gravesaner Blätter* V (August 1956).

Miller, Dayton C. *The Science of Musical Sounds.* New York: Macmillan, 1916.

Minsky, Marvin. *The Emotion Machine.* New York: Simon and Schuster, 2006.

——. "Once more with feelings." Interview with Amanda Gefter. *New Scientist* Vol. 193 No. 2592 (2007).

Moles, Abraham A. *Informationstheorie und Ästhetische Wahrnehmung* tr. Hans Ronge, Barbara Ronge, Peter Ronge. Cologne: DuMont Schauberg, 1971.

Myers, Rollo. *Erik Satie.* London: Dennis Dobson, 1948.

Naumann, Emil. *The History of Music* tr. Frederick Praeger ed. F. A. Gore Ouseley. 2v. London: Cassell and Co., n.d. (1886).

Negroponte, Nicholas. *Being Digital.* New York: Vintage, 1996.

Olson, Harry F. *Music, Physics and Engineering* (formerly *Musical Engineering*). 2nd edn. New York: Dover, 1967.

Oram, Daphne. *An Individual Note: Of Music, Sound, and Electronics.*

London: Galliard; and New York: Galaxy, 1972.

Ortmann, Otto. *The Physical Basis of Piano Touch and Tone*. London: Kegan Paul, Trench, Trübner & Co., Curwen & Sons. New York: Dutton, 1925.

Palisca, Claude. *Humanism in Italian Renaissance Musical Thought*. New Haven CT: Yale University Press, 1985.

Parsons, Denys. *A Directory of Tunes and Musical Themes*. Cambridge: Spencer Brown, 1975.

Pater, Walter. *Appreciations: With an Essay on Style*. London: Macmillan, 1892.

Penrose, Roger. *The Emperor's New Mind*. London: Vintage, 1990.

Pettit, Philip. "Parmenides and Sartre." 161–84 in *Philosophical Studies* Vol. XVII (1968).

Philip, Robert. *Early Recordings and Musical Style: Changing Tastes in Instrumental Performance*. Cambridge: Cambridge University Press, 1992.

Pierce, John R. *The Science of Musical Sound*. New York: Scientific American Library, 1983.

Pinker, Steven. *How the Mind Works*. London: Allan Lane, The Penguin Press, 1998.

——. *The Language Instinct: The New Science of Language and Mind*. Harmondsworth: Penguin Books, 1994.

Plato. *The Republic of Plato* tr. Francis Macdonald Cornford. Oxford: Clarendon Press, 1944.

Pompino-Marschall, Bernd. "Von Kempelen et al.—Remarks on the history of articulatory-acoustic modelling." 145–59 in *ZAS Papers in Linguistics* 40, 2005.

Popper, Karl R. *Conjectures and Refutations: The Growth of Scientific Knowledge* 4th edn. London: Routledge and Kegan Paul, 1972.

——. *Quantum Theory and the Schism in Physics* ed. W. W. Bartley, III (1982) repr. London: Routledge, 1995.

Potter, Ralph K., George A. Kopp, and Harriet Green Kopp. *Visible Speech*. New York: Dover, 1966.

Powell, E. S., and M. Powell. *Ringers' Handbook*. 5th edn. repr. Leeds: Whitehead & Miller, 1955.

Preminger, Alex ed. *Princeton Encyclopedia of Poetry and Poetics* enl.

edn. London: Macmillan, 1974.

Preston, John. *The Created Self: The Reader's Role in Eighteenth-century Fiction.* London: Heinemann, 1970.

Pritchett, James. *The Music of John Cage.* Cambridge, Cambridge University Press, 1993.

Raman, C. V. *Scientific Papers of C. V. Raman* ed. S. Ramaseshan. Vol. II: Acoustics. Bangalore: Indian Academy of Sciences, 1988.

Randall, Brian A. ed. *The Origins of Digital Computers: Selected Papers* 3rd edn. Berlin, Heidelberg, and New York: Springer-Verlag, 1982.

Rastall, Richard. *The Notation of Western Music.* London: J. M. Dent & Sons, 1982.

Read, Herbert. *Art & Industry: The Principles of Industrial Design* (1941) 3rd rev. edn. London: Faber and Faber, 1953.

Rock, Irvin. *Perception.* New York: Scientific American Library, 1984.

Ronan, Colin A. *Cambridge Illustrated History of the World's Science.* Cambridge: Cambridge University Press, 1983.

Rothstein, Edward. *Emblems of Mind: The Inner Life of Music and Mathematics.* New York: Avon Books, 1995.

Sabaneev, Leonid. *Music for the Films: A Handbook for Composers Conductors* tr. S. W. Pring. London: Pitman, 1935.

Sachs, Curt. *Rhythm and Tempo: A Study in Music History.* London: Dent, 1953.

——. *The Wellsprings of Music* ed. Jaap Kunst. New York: McGraw-Hill, 1965.

Sanouillet, Michel ed. and Elmer Petersen ed. *The Essential Writings of Marcel Duchamp.* London: Thames and Hudson, 1975.

Sawyer, W. W. *Mathematician's Delight.* Harmondsworth: Penguin Books, 1943.

Scaliger, Julius (Giulio Bordone della Scala). *Poetices Libri Septem.* 1561.

Schaeffer, Pierre. *La Musique Concrète.* Paris: Presses Universitaires de France, 1967.

Scherchen, Hermann. *The Nature of Music* tr. William Mann. London: Dennis Dobson, 1946.

Schlain, Leonard. *Art & Physics: Parallel Visions in Space, Time, and*

Light. New York: William Morrow, 1991.

Schoenberg, Arnold. "Problems of Harmony" tr. Adolph Weiss. In Merle Armitage ed., *Schoenberg*. New York: Schirmer (1937) repr. Westport CT: Greenwood Press, 1977.

——. *Style and Idea: Selected Writings of Arnold Schoenberg* ed. Leonard Stein tr. Leo Black. London: Faber and Faber, 1975.

Scholes, Percy A. *Oxford Companion to Music*. 10th rev. edn. (1970) ed. John Owen Ward. London: Oxford University Press, 1975.

Schon, Donald A. *Invention and the Evolution of Ideas* (formerly *Displacement of Concepts*). London: Tavistock, 1963.

Schouten, Jan F. "The Perception of Pitch." *Philips Technical Review* Vol. 5 No. 10 (1940).

Schweizer, Christoph E. "Acrostics." In Alex Preminger ed., *Princeton Encyclopedia of Poetry and Poetics* enl. edn. London: Macmillan, 1974.

Seashore, Carl E. *Psychology of Music*. New York and London: McGraw-Hill, 1938.

Spencer, D. A. and H. D. Waley. *Cinema Today* (1939) 2nd edn. London: Oxford University Press, 1956.

Spencer, Herbert. *A System of Synthetic Philosophy*. Vol. I. 5th rev. edn. London: Williams & Norgate, 1884.

Statham, H. Heathcote. *My Thoughts on Music and Musicians*. London: Chapman and Hall, 1892.

Stein, Gertrude. *How to Write* (1931) repr. with a new Preface and Introduction by Patricia Meyerowitz. New York: Dover, 1975.

Storr, Anthony. *Music and the Mind*. London: HarperCollins, 1992.

Strathern, Paul. *Hawking & Black Holes*. London: Arrow, 1997.

Stravinsky, Igor and Robert Craft. *Conversations with Igor Stravinsky*. London: Faber and Faber, 1959.

Sullivan, J. W. N. *Aspects of Science*. London: Jonathan Cape, 1923.

Taylor, R. P., R. Guzman, T. P. Martin, G. D. R. Hall, A. P. Micholich, D. Jonas, and C. A. Marlow. "Authenticating Pollock paintings using fractal geometry." (www.uoregon.edu/~msiuo/taylor/art/TaylorSubmission.pdf) (08/07/2008)

Thomas, David B. *The Origins of the Motion Picture*. London: Her Majesty's Stationery Office, 1964.

Traunmüller, Hartmut. "Wolfgang von Kempelen's speaking machine and its successors." (http://www.ling.su.se/staff/hartmut/kemplne.htm) (06/29/2007)

Turing. Alan M. "Computing Machines and Intelligence." *Mind* Vol. LIX No. 236 (1950) repr. in Alan Ross Anderson ed., *Minds and Machines*. Englewood Cliffs: Prentice-Hall, 1964.

Valle, Ronald S. ed. and Rolf von Eckartsberg ed. *Metaphors of Consciousness*. New York and London: Plenum Press, 1989.

Vermeule, Emily. *Aspects of Death in Early Greek Art and Poetry*. Berkeley, Los Angeles CA, London: University of California Press, 1981.

Vitruvius [Marcus Vitruvius Pollio]. *Ten Books on Architecture* tr. Morris Hickey Morgan. Cambridge MA: Harvard University Press (1914) repr. New York: Dover, 1960.

Waldrop, M. Mitchell. *Complexity: The Emerging Science at the Edge of Order and Chaos*. London: Viking, 1993.

Walker, D. P. *Studies in Musical Science in the Late Renaissance*. London: Warburg Institute, University of London; Leiden: E. J. Brill, 1978.

Weiss, Michael. "The Rigid Rotating Disk in Relativity." (http://math.ucr.edu/home/baez/physics/relativity/SR/rigid_disk.html) (02/04/2007)

Whitehead, Alfred N. *A Philosopher Looks at Science*. New York: Philosophical Library, 1965.

——. *Science in the Modern World*. Cambridge: Cambridge University Press, 1926.

Wittkower, Rudolf. *Architectural Principles in the Age of Humanism* 4th edn. London: Academy Editions, 1988.

Wood, A. B. *A Textbook of Sound* 3rd. rev. edn. London: G. Bell and Sons, 1960.

Wood, Sir Henry J. *My Life of Music*. London: Gollancz, 1938.

Wozencraft, John M. and Barney Reiffen. *Sequential Decoding*. Cambridge MA: M. I. T. Press, 1961.

Young, J. Z. *Doubt and Certainty in Science* new edn. New York: Galaxy Books, 1960.

INDEX

1/*f* noise 459–60
3–4–5 triangle 86, 87, 129, 131–32, 134, 148, 366
1939–1945 war 7, 211, 279, 375

absence 10, 117, 273, 371, 420, 487
absolute zero 8
absorption line 130
abstract art 17, 62, 65, 71, 98, 243, 269, 275, 294, 317, 429–30
absurdity 175–76
accelerated motion 364, 366
accentuation 223, 226, 296, 304, 333, 346, 370
accretion disc x, 357–58, 361
accuracy 70, 103, 296, 306, 371
Achilles, 163
Achilles and the tortoise xiii, 119–22, 137–42, 150, 158–59, 176
acoustic 59, 62, 202, 291, 472
acrostic 339, 348n, 482–83
act, musical 26, 27, 30, 53 *see* performance
action at a distance 24, 37, 47, 64, 69, 168, 182, 183
Adam and Eve 33–34, 39, 193, 353
Adams, John 417, 427
Addinsell, Richard 375
—*Warsaw Concerto* 375
Adler, Guido 332
Adorno, Theodor 5–6, 68, 283
aeolian harp 67
aerodynamics 95, 96
Aesclepius, staff of 39
Aeschylus 175
—*Oresteia* 175
Aesop x, xii, 121, 159
aesthetics 204, 232–33, 249, 272, 274, 308, 315, 319, 338, 365, 371, 375, 378, 386, 412, 430, 434, 447, 449, 459, 466, 471, 478, 483, 486
affect 21, 79, 175, 248
affirmation 70
agreement 69, 70, 71, 239, 251, 263
air column 90, 93, 108, 135, 148–49, 160, 178–80, 357, 373
alarm signal 66, 287
aleatory 251, 383–400
algebra 70
alienation 62, 440
allegory 101
alpha and omega 88, 89, 93, 123
alphabet 231, 317, 333, 338, 370, 374, 392, 393
alteration 100, 112, 116, 119, 126, 128, 144, 145, 148, 240, 242–43, 277, 281–82, 294, 364, 373, 391, 415, 418
ambience 61, 86
ambiguity 41, 91, 244, 249, 253, 352–56, 389, 433
Ambrosian chant 315
Amis, John 205
amphitheater 211
amplitude 52, 171, 187n, 203, 319, 453, 455
anesthesia 281–82
analytical engine (Babbage) 258
anarchy 76, 420
Andersen, Hans Christian 283
anechoic chamber 13, 61, 320, 417
Anglebert, Jean-Henri d' 370
animation, movie 231, 241, 264, 440
anthropic principle 13
anti-music 420, 451
Antonioni, Michelangelo 410
—*Blow-Up* 410
Apocrypha 16n
Apollo 134, 150, 183
Apollodorus 133
apposition 100
Aquinas, Thomas 235–37, 240, 263
—*On the Unity of the Intellect* 235
archery 134, 150–60, 175, 183 *see* bow and arrow
Archimedes, death of xv–xvi
architecture 131–33, 143
Arezzo, Guido d' 433
Ariadne 162

Aristotle, 93, 102, 103, 137, 157, 174, 235–36, 307
—*De Anima* 236
Aristoxenus 225, 226, 333, 377
arithmetic 133, 135, 138, 139, 142, 160, 254
Arne, Thomas 396
Arp, Hans 429
arrow of time 183, 197, 478
arrow paradox (Zeno) 140, 150–60, 220
Arroyo, Martina 283
ars nova 185, 304, 484
art nouveau 272, 308
artificial intelligence 209, 244, 245, 247–48, 250–54, 257–67, 305, 318, 331–32, 345, 387, 389, 391–92, 457–72
artlessness 296
Asquith, Anthony 375
—*Way to the Stars* 375
association, rules of 387–92
astronomy 130, 271–72, 303, 358, 478–79
astrophysics 48, 165, 201–9, 357–62
asymmetry 97, 102, 389–90
atonality 220, 269–84, 296, 319, 334, 466, 469–70
attack instrument 377
Auden, W. H. 201, 217n
audience 61, 62, 239, 249, 264, 289, 296, 337, 447–48, 452
auditory field 24, 66, 249, 328
auditory perception 58, 85, 138, 186, 202, 236, 255, 324, 452
Augustine of Hippo, St 43, 83, 173
Auric, Georges 385
authenticity 293, 296
autism 390
autochrome (stereoscopy) 454
automata 207–9, 274, 276, 305, 318, 346, 393–95
avant-garde 7, 331, 432, 466
Averroes 235–37
Avzaamov, Arseny 430

Babbage, Charles 258, 266n
Babbitt, Milton 230, 483
Bach, Carl Philippe Emanuel 393
Bach, J. S. 52, 61, 62, 97, 216, 217, 219–20, 238, 271, 273, 275, 277, 285–86, 301, 305, 323, 325–28, 337, 374, 376, 393, 465, 476, 486
—*Air on the G string*
—*Brandenburg concertos* 97, 305
—*Brandenburg concerto No. 2* 323, 325–28
—*Chromatic fantasy* 219–20
—*"Durch Adams Fall"* organ prelude 301
—*St Matthew Passion* 278, 285–86
—*"Vom Himmel Hoch" Variations* 271
—*Well-Tempered Clavier* 273, 374
Bacharach, Burt 311, 461
—*Do You Know the Way to San José* 461
—*Trains and Boats and Planes* 311
Back to the Future movies 197
Bacon, Francis artist 447
Bacon, Roger 155
bagpipe music 292, 315
balance 99
ballet 28, 98, 361, 412, 440
bandoura 193, 354
bandwidth 150, 315, 321–28, 329, 443, 446, 448, 454, 470
Barraud, Francis 82, 283
—*His Master's Voice* painting ("Nipper the dog") 82, 283
barrel organ 306, 346
Barrow, John 164n, 176n
Barry, John 305
Bartók, Bélà 237, 292, 418, 438, 443
—*Sonata for two pianos and percussion* 438, 443
Baschet, Bernard 319
Baschet, François 319
basilar membrane 321
BBC English 228
Beatles, The 416
—"Strawberry Fields" 422
beauty 30, 409, 475
Beauvais cathedral 184–85
Beckett, Samuel 12, 62, 173, 250, 392
—*Waiting for Godot* 62, 250
Beethoven, Ludwig van xi, 61, 80, 97, 119, 205, 207–8, 215, 238, 252, 278–81, 301, 304–6, 323, 325–28, 352–56, 378, 397, 399, 419, 433, 485
—*Ode to Joy* (Symphony No. 9) 399
—*Piano Concerto No. 4* xi
—*Piano Sonata No. 14 "Moonlight"* 119,

278–80, 304–6
—*Symphony No. 4* 207, 281, 305, 421
—*Symphony No. 5* 23, 61, 97, 205, 238
—*Symphony No. 6 "Pastoral"* 207–8, 352–56
—*Symphony No. 8* 323, 325–28
being, state of 20, 76, 87, 94, 100, 130, 171, 175, 195, 206, 333, 390–91, 418–19, 439, 445
Bell, Alexander Graham 84, 434
Bell, Alexander Melville 287, 435
Bell, David Charles 287
—*Bell's Standard Elocutionist* 287
Bell, E. T. 95, 113n
bell curve 466
Bell Laboratories 323, 416
belly dance 30
Beowulf 198
Berberian, Cathy 438
—*Stripsody* 438
Berg, Alban 63, 65, 193, 269, 275, 283, 290, 291, 303, 308, 338, 418, 466
—*Altenberg Lieder* 281, 290
—*Chamber concerto* 338
—*Lulu* 193, 269
—*Wozzeck* 269
Berio, Luciano 23, 197, 289–91, 384, 399, 422
—*Circles* 289–90, 422
—*Sinfonie* 23
Berkeley, Bishop 8
Berlin, Isaiah 220–21, 233n
Berliner, Émile 358–59
Berman, Boris 380
Berman, Eugene 429
Bernstein, Leonard 311
—*West Side Story* 311
bicycle 80, 96, 271
big bang 17, 22, 165
Big Ben 305
binaural hearing 46, 47, 203, 321, 424, 455
Bingen, Hildegard von 228
binocular vision 46, 47
birdsong 486
black hole 36, 48, 49, 184, 214, 358, 468, 471
Blackburn, Maurice 439
Blake, William 89, 281, 305
blindness 33, 58, 85, 161
blot 429
blues 74, 282, 360
Blum, Carl Robert 429
Blumlein, Alan 425
Boccherini, Luigi 42n
—*Cello concerto No. 9 in B flat* 42n
Boethius 177–83
—*De institutione musica* 177–83
Bohr, Niels 156, 359
bonding, social 64, 71
Born, Max 361
Bosch, Hieronymus 434
Boston Legal tv series 295–96
Botticelli, Alessandro 18
—*Primavera* 18
Boulez, Pierre 5–6, 14, 27, 68, 180, 209, 230, 262, 282, 290, 291, 298, 307, 319, 331–32, 336, 338, 342, 375, 378, 383, 384, 399, 422, 423, 425, 444, 459, 466, 475
—*Anthèmes* 319
—*Domaines* 422
—*. . . explosante-fixe . . .* 312, 319, 338, 481, 484
—*Improvisations sur Mallarmé* 290
—*Le marteau sans maître* 180, 290
—*Le vierge, le vivace et le bel aujourd'hui* 298, 423
—*Messagesquisse* 338
—*Répons* 27, 319
—"Schoenberg is dead" article 14, 331
—*Structures I* 342, 466
—*Sur Incises* 425
—*Troisième Sonate* 399
bounce 460, 463, 465
boundary condition 52, 53, 71, 76, 89, 93, 108, 109, 110, 162, 163, 165–68, 171, 320, 391, 444, 446, 463, 470, 472
bow and arrow 44–46, 50, 55–56, 95, 105, 112, 113, 118, 125–27, 133–34, 142–45, 148–60, 171–72, 175, 182–83, 240
Brahms, Johannes 64, 237, 307, 379, 486
—*Hungarian Dances* 64
Brain, Dennis 355
brane 201, 212–15
Brant, Henry 310, 378
Braque, Georges 449
Brawardine, Thomas 105

Breton, André 406
bridge, movable 86, 141
Britten, Benjamin 340, 355, 375
—*Prince and the Pagodas* 340
—*Serenade for Tenor, Horn, and Strings* 355
broken consort 372
Bronowski, Jacob vii
Brooks, Louise 200n
Brown, Earle 331, 384, 429, 432
Brownian motion 460
Bryn-Julson, Phyllis 283
Bugs Bunny 437
Buñuel, Luis 406
—*Un Chien Andalou* 406
Bunyan, John 196
—*Pilgrim's Progress* 196
Buridan, Jean 4, 185, 228, 363
Burn, A. R. 176n
Burnet, John 165, 176n
Burney, Charles 396
Burroughs, William 392
Busoni, Ferruccio 307, 427
butterfly effect 165
Byron, Lord 274

cabaret 282, 291
cacophony 63
cadenza 61, 477
Caduceus 33
Cage, John 8–15, 20, 26, 62, 65, 66, 76, 85, 208, 247–65, 266n, 267n, 295, 303, 310–11, 331, 340, 342, 369–81, 384, 392, 394–95, 402, 412, 425, 429, 432–33, 438, 440, 451, 459, 475, 486–87, 488n
—*I – VI* Harvard Lectures 475
—*4'33"* silent composition 8–15
—*26'1.1499" for a string player* 432
—*Cartridge Music* 432
—*Double Music* (with Lou Harrison) 340
—*Fontana Mix* 433
—*HPSCHD* (with Lejaren A. Hiller) 394–95
—*Imaginary Landscape IV* 310
—*Lecture on Nothing* 247–67
—*Music of Changes* 62, 208, 342, 402
—*Sonatas and Interludes* 369, 376, 378
—*Variations IV* 451
Calder-Marshall, Arthur 189, 200n
calligraphy 371, 435, 439
canon cancrizans 216
Cantor, Georg 95, 157–58, 483
cantus firmus 263, 300
Caraël, Michel 5–6
Carey, Henry 395–96, 398
carillon 62
carrier frequency 149, 315–16
Carroll, Lewis 165, 295, 435, 450
—*Alice in Wonderland* 435
Carter, Elliott 301, 303
Caruso, Enrico 431
Casimir, Hendrik 14, 209–12, 213
Casimir effect 14, 209–12
causation 80, 100, 390
cavity resonance 150, 209–12, 256, 315–16
cello (violoncello) 136, 158
chance music 26, 66, 100, 195, 341, 432, 475
change 43, 44, 76, 115, 147, 156–57, 159, 171, 173, 184, 220, 236–37, 240–44, 273, 275, 279, 281, 294, 362, 364, 373, 383, 390–91, 409, 458, 467, 468
change ringing 342–445, 483
changes, Book of 342
Chanson de Roland 200
Chant software (Rodet) 320
chaos 21, 23, 25, 53, 63, 66, 68, 148, 160, 162, 165, 201, 220, 255, 299, 302, 308, 335, 410, 446, 449, 456, 483
Chaplin, Charles 371, 409
Char, René 180
character 174–75, 238, 281, 334 *see* temperament
Chaucer, Geoffrey 196
—*Canterbury Tales* 196
Chevalier, Maurice 291
Chicken Licken 37–38
chimes, clock 341
China, art music of 64
Chomsky, Noam 71, 345, 392
Chopin, Frédéric 81, 208, 301–2, 305, 307, 337, 433
—*Grand Valse* 302
—"Minute Waltz" 302
chromatic scale 219, 374, 430, 446, 462
Chuang Chou 20, 25
Churchill, Winston 294
Cicero, Marcus Tullius 157, 358

—*Dream of Scipio* 157, 358
circle, squaring the 55, 131–32, 143–44
circular permutation 344–45
Clair, René 385, 406, 410
—*Entr'acte* 385–86, 406
—*Paris qui dort* 410
clap test 455
clarinet 92, 93
Clarke, Arthur C. 364–65
clavecin 219
click track 429
clock time 184–85, 224–25, 281, 303–5, 364, 418–19, 426–27
Clooney, George 259
cluster 438, 443–56
cochlea 322
cochlear implant 315, 321–29
cocktail effect 300
Cocteau, Jean 385, 399n, 407
—*Orphée* 385
—*Sang d'un Poète* 385
cognition, auditory 324, 487
coherence 50, 51, 122, 220, 223, 323, 329, 433, 460, 476, 486
Colby, K. M. 258
Cold War 7
Coleridge, Samuel Taylor 281–82, 305
—*Kubla Khan* 281
Columbus, Christopher 78, 304
combinatorics 339
comics, action 437
community 64
compass point 98
complexity 65, 67, 68, 202, 276, 301–2, 472, 482
compression, time 307, 358, 360–61, 362–63, 366–67, 411
compromise 69
computer games 42, 136, 185, 196–200, 220, 257, 409
computer modeling 166, 207, 223, 231, 251, 265, 279, 286, 332, 387, 395, 457–72, 481
computer music 67, 279, 319, 320, 332, 341, 348, 394–95, 426, 431, 452–53, 460, 461–72
concert hall acoustic 23, 291, 446, 449, 453, 455
concerto grosso 376
conductor 63, 448
connectedness 459, 461–72, 487
consciousness 4, 21, 30, 73, 79, 206, 209, 228, 242, 253, 265, 279, 281–82, 305, 318, 391, 475
consecration 60
consistency 53, 60, 111, 157, 204, 236, 300, 304, 316, 370, 376, 444, 452, 486
Constable, John 63, 446
constancy 59, 96, 104, 112, 116, 118, 127, 130, 144–45, 149, 236, 304, 341, 359
contest 142
continuity ix, 21, 24, 28, 36, 38, 43, 57, 76, 77, 78, 79, 85–87, 90–95, 100, 103, 106, 107, 109, 111, 115, 116, 119, 130, 147, 150, 156, 158–59, 186, 202, 206, 208, 219–21, 229–30, 236, 262–63, 274–75, 279, 281, 304, 317, 357, 370, 381, 384, 413, 421, 459, 483
contredanse 396
Copland, Aaron 331, 417
—*Fanfare for the Common Man* 417
correlation 460, 471
Cortot, Alfred 401–2
cosmic elevator 364–65
cosmology viii–ix, 4, 22, 36, 89, 165, 184, 201–4, 214, 271–72
country dance 396
Couperin, François 370
Couperin, Louis 433
course 137, 140, 142
Cowell, Henry 394–95, 399n, 443
—*Banshee* 443
Craft, Robert 237, 298
Crash movie (Cronenberg) 375
creation, act of xv, 20
creation, continuous 27, 94, 172
creation myth 22–23, 25, 36, 48, 89
creation, preconditions of 22, 25
creativity, artistic 17, 18, 19, 25, 52, 245, 457
Cristofori, Bartolomeo 376–77, 472
Crombie, A. C. 113n, 164n
Cros, Charles 81
Crosby, Bing 291, 431
Cross, Burnett 429
cryptography, musical 338, 345
cummings, e e 290, 435

Cunningham, Chris 473n
Cupid's bow, arrow 151–52, 154
Curtis, Tony 195
curvature 45, 46
cut-up (Burroughs) 392, 486
cybernovel 197
cycle 108, 109, 160, 216
cyclical motion 53, 99, 100, 106, 108, 144, 145, 148, 182, 216, 223, 274, 304, 412, 415
cycloid 101, 103, 106, 107, 108, 109
cylinder recording 120, 216, 282–83, 286, 291, 357–60, 362–64
cymbalom 371
Czerny, Carl 372

dada 85, 295
Daguerre, Louis 447
Dahlhaus, Carl 5–6
Dalí, Salvador 406
—*Un Chien Andalou* 406
dance notation 223, 230
dance suite, baroque 97, 119, 223, 274
Danton movie (1921: Buchowetski) 191–92
Darmstadt, music festival 5
Darwin, Charles 79, 173, 221, 275
—*On the Origin of Species* 79, 221
data point 91, 106, 203, 205
David, King 33, 182–83
Davies, Peter Maxwell 342
—*Stedman Caters* 342
—*Stedman Doubles* 342
Davy, Humphrey 281, 447
Debussy, Claude 60, 97, 237, 288, 292, 308, 340, 352, 403, 415
—*Pelléas et Mélisande* 288
—*Prélude à l'Après-midi d'un Faune* 60, 97
deceptive cadence 261–62
Dedekind, Richard 95
deep structure 345, 458
Defoe, Daniel 57
—*Robinson Crusoe* 57
Dehmel, Richard 281–82
delay in transmission 478–80
Dennett, Daniel 251, 253, 257–58, 265, 266n
Descartes, René vii, 21, 25, 82, 91, 100, 207, 220, 229, 251, 276, 305, 320, 391–92, 395, 438
des Prez, Josquin 238
—*Missa L'Homme Armé* 238
de Stijl 430
detective story 192–93, 196, 339
deviation 46, 77, 222
dialogue 60–62, 64, 239, 244, 247, 251, 253, 256–60, 262, 264, 279, 409, 480, 485
diatonic scale 291, 357, 371, 462
dice game 383, 461
Dickens, Charles 196, 276
—*Nicholas Nickleby* 196
Dietrich, Marlene 291
difference 57, 182, 236, 323, 353, 373, 381, 387
difform motion 106, 360, 364
digeridu 149
Dikë, goddess 171, 173
Dilke, O. A. W. 131, 145n
diphthong 230–32
direction 51, 97, 99, 109, 116, 118, 154–55, 163, 171, 183, 452, 458
director's cut 189–200
disc recording *see* gramophone
disc rotation 357–65
disconnection 485
discontinuity 24, 156, 186–87, 372, 378
disharmony 66, 77, 108, 282, 450
Disney Corporation, Walt 241, 412, 437
—*Fantasia* 437
disobedience 37, 77, 102, 245
disorder 63, 65, 66, 67, 68, 276, 450, 459–60, 486
disorientation 445, 451, 454
dissonance 220, 275, 297, 355, 379
distortion 43, 44, 46, 148, 150, 253, 309, 361, 422–24, 447
division 141–42, 158–59
dixieland jazz 300, 431, 481
Dodge, Charles 341
—*Earth's Magnetic Field* 341
Doppler effect 157, 422
Dowland, John 61
Doxology 316
Doyle, Arthur Conan 282
dragon 40, 44
Drake, Francis 78, 304
drama, Greek 77, 174–75, 254, 334
drift (melody) 464, 469–70

drone 58, 59, 150, 292, 315–16
duality 354
Duchamp, Marcel 117, 119, 259–60, 406
—*Three Standard Stoppages* 117
dulcimer 219
duration 119, 147, 364

ear mechanism 322
early music viii, 130, 445
eating, act of 35, 37, 48, 241
Ebbinghaus, Hermann 295
echo effect 25, 253, 256, 424, 478, 480–81
Eden, Garden of 33, 35–36, 48, 318, 353, 409
Edison, Thomas Alva 216, 282, 307, 309, 358–59, 363, 403, 412, 449
eigentone 210, 212, 455, 472
Ehrenfest, Paul 361
Eimert, Herbert 332
Einstein, Albert 85, 109, 117, 120, 138, 216, 307–8, 357–59, 364–65, 367, 411
Eisenstein, Sergei 11, 191, 196, 200n, 437
—*Alexander Nevsky* 437
—*Film Form* 191
El Greco 18
elapsed time 367
electric recording 232–33
electricity 80, 279
electroacoustic music 58, 286, 289, 319, 332, 367, 422, 430, 433, 438
electrostatic speaker 213
elements, the four 54, 79, 172, 373
Eliot, T. S. 282, 389
Ellis, Alexander 74
Ellitt, Jack 431
Emerson, Ralph Waldo 303
Emett, Rowland x
Eminem 293
emotion 99, 116, 128, 130, 154, 174, 175, 183, 222, 248, 252, 265, 275–77, 281, 287, 292, 296, 447
emotion, stave of 287
empathy 57, 150
enclosure 59, 455
endless chord 366, 420
endless melody 269
endpoints 89, 108, 109, 111–13, 116–22, 139, 147, 151, 166–71, 173, 186, 189, 194, 216–17
energy conservation 45, 55, 126, 128, 130, 143, 145, 163, 172, 182, 316
energy conversion 22, 52, 56, 115, 144, 148–49, 154, 157, 168, 172, 182, 472
energy, excess 51, 52, 89, 94, 112, 123, 142–43, 145, 148–49, 170, 171, 201
energy state 92, 128, 156, 169, 210, 214, 357
energy, structured 53, 182, 472
English language 287
enharmonic modulation 273
entertainment 29, 136, 195, 259, 337, 434
environment 57, 58, 197, 245, 335, 453
epic 197–200
epicycle 102, 271
epiphany 99, 147, 242, 439
epithet, transferred 156, 375
equal temperament 138, 143, 272, 371, 374, 462
equilibrium, melodic 470
error 43–56, 237, 251, 253
error, margin of 46
Escher, Maurits 18
ethnomusicology viii, 449
Eudoxos 95
event horizon 184
existence 22, 115, 148, 216, 245, 248, 254, 263, 363, 475
experiential time 363–64
expression, modes of 75, 205–6, 226, 229, 232, 248, 252, 304, 319, 346, 370, 409, 434, 484
extension 45, 47, 48, 49, 56, 89, 106, 166, 205, 216

facts, music of 337
Fairlight synthesizer 431
Fall of Man 36
fallibility 173
falsifiability (Popper) 48, 204
Fantasound (RCA-Bell) 309–10
fantasy, fantasia 28
Faraday, Michael 279
Farrington, Benjamin 55, 56n
Fascism 261, 450
fear of music 1
feedback 27, 51, 68, 84, 149, 210, 243
Feldman, Morton 63, 331, 384, 427, 429, 432, 438–40, 443

—*Coptic Light* 443
—*Intersection I* 438
—*King of Denmark* 439
—*Madame Press Died Last Week at Ninety* 427
—*Projection I* 438
Feynman, Richard 111, 120, 122, 166–67, 169, 174, 175, 186, 198
fiddle, bow 52
Field, Mary 401, 411
—*Secrets of Nature* 411
fiery breath 41, 42
figure-ground relation 59
figured bass 74, 469
film 156, 187 *see* movies
filter 323–28, 329
fire 41
Fischinger, Oskar 213, 429, 437
Flaherty, Robert A. 189, 191
—*Man of Aran* 191
—*Nanook of the North* 191
flamenco dance 244
fluctuation, melody 460
fluctuation, natural 459
flute 52, 58, 60, 74, 75, 77, 178–81
folk music xiv, 237–39, 293, 333, 349n, 396
forbidden fruit 33, 35–37, 40
force, applied 44, 89, 93, 101, 124, 126, 129, 142, 143–44, 148–49, 157, 171, 172, 174–75, 177–83, 185, 346–47, 359
force field 79
forked tongue 40
formant resonance 149, 150, 230, 315–16
formulae, language 69, 458
Forster, E. M. 260
Forte, Allen 344, 349n, 483
fortepiano 307, 376–77
Foucault, Michel 109
found object 238, 372, 484 *see* readymade
Fourier, Joseph 214, 319–21
Fourier Theory 214, 319–21, 436
fractal dimension 116, 212, 354, 457–72
fractal geometry 117–18, 212, 458–59
Fractal Melody program (BASIC) 463–66
fractal music 341, 457–72
fractal noise, 481
fractions, computation by 134–36, 138, 140, 158, 159
Frame, Janet 57
frame, still *see* stop motion
Franklin, Benjamin 279
Franklyn, Milt 440
free music machine 429, 432
free will 76, 98, 113, 137, 172, 194, 228, 276–77, 305
freedom of action 97, 100, 175, 226, 277, 279, 282, 418, 451, 454–55
freedom of expression 19, 227, 229, 244–45, 249, 277, 282, 289, 418, 481
frequency 47, 52, 60, 93, 109, 111, 119, 127, 141–42, 147, 215, 217, 320, 324, 358, 367
frequency analysis 320, 325–28
Frescobaldi, Girolamo 273, 337
Freud, Sigmund 34, 83, 84, 162, 283, 297, 386, 392, 406
fugue 28, 217, 476
Fuller, Buckminster 9
fundamental 88, 89, 109, 118, 119, 124, 132, 149, 170, 329
furniture music 386, 407
futurism 85, 167, 295, 435

Gabrieli, Giovanni 478–79, 485
Gaffurio, Franchino 178–81
—*Theorica musice* 178–81
Galilei, Vincenzo 138, 272
Galileo (Galilei) 39, 78, 100, 102, 111, 138, 157, 199, 220, 229, 245, 271, 272, 379, 479
Gama, Vasco da 78, 304
game theory 387
gamelan 340, 415, 449
garage band 69
Garbo, Greta 10
Garden of Eden *see* Eden, Garden of
Gardner, Martin 459–61, 472n
Garland, Judy 431
Gauss, Karl Friedrich 158
generation 339
geometry 38, 55, 56, 65, 87, 117, 130, 133–34, 138, 148, 430
George, Stefan 281
Gershwin, George 311
—*I Got Rhythm* 311
Gerszo, Andrew 319

gestalt 228, 238
Gesualdo, Don Carlo 79, 272
Giacometti, Alberto 271
Gibson, J. J. 48
Gingerich, Owen 233n
Givelet, Armand 436
Glass, Philip 209, 417, 427
gliding tone 75, 92, 147, 156, 219, 221–22, 229–30, 345, 367, 377, 435, 438, 448
glissando *see* gliding tone
glossolalia 295
Gluck, Christoph Willibald 385
—*Eurydice's Lament* 385
goal-directed activity 99, 100, 199, 262
"God Save the King" anthem 273, 395–98
Goethe, Johann Wolfgang von 281, 305, 337
Goliath, David and 182–83
Golem 318
Gombrich, Ernst 317, 329n
—*Art and Illusion* 317
gospel music 283, 295
Gott, J. Richard 217n
Grainger, Percy 62, 429, 432–33, 441n, 448
—*Sea Song Sketch* 448
gramophone x, 38, 116, 120, 193, 216, 325, 357–60, 364–65, 426, 431
graph, scientific 91, 106, 110, 321, 341, 434, 458
graphic music 429–40
great stave 78
Gregorian chant 315
Grierson, John 66
Griffith, D. W. 309
Griffiths, Paul 427
Grosseteste, Robert 155
groove, recording 215–16, 357–67
Groundhog Day movie 197
group formation 68
Grützmacher, Friedrich 42n
Guarneri, Giuseppe 317, 351
Guigno, Pepino di 319
guitar 87, 126, 127, 132, 136, 163, 167, 170, 377
gyroscope 96

hair, wavy 31–33, 253, 266n
hammer action 377
Hammond, Laurens 436
Hammond organ 436, 481
Handel, Georg Frideric 225, 226–27, 275, 336, 418, 448–49
—*Messiah* 225
—*Music for the Royal Fireworks* 336, 448–49
—*Semele* 226–27
—*Solomon* 418
Handy, W. C. 282, 360
—*Memphis Blues* 282
—*St Louis Blues* 282, 360
happening, art form 14, 65, 310
hare and tortoise fable 121
Haren, Michael 245n
harmonic 85, 86, 87, 88, 89, 109, 110, 128, 130, 132, 134–36, 139, 144, 147, 158, 179, 210, 212, 301, 319, 335, 422
harmonic series 132, 134–35, 139, 142, 145, 147, 158–59, 182, 202, 216, 316, 335, 352–55, 467, 468
harmonic telegraph (Edison) 309
harmony 66, 67, 68, 70, 77, 90, 132, 148, 150, 157, 168, 182, 221, 224, 269, 277, 303, 331, 379, 446, 467, 472
harp 33, 36, 46, 47, 77, 91, 128, 130, 136, 137, 151, 183
harpsichord 61, 212, 376, 472
Harrison, Lou 340
—*Double Music* 340
Harrison, Rex 285
Harsdörffer, Georg Philipp 339, 348n
Harvard University 13, 156, 475, 486
Harvey, Jonathan 320, 349n
—*Mortous plango, vivos voco* 320
Hauer, Josef Matthias 399
Hawking, Stephen x, 18, 166–67, 176n, 216, 217n, 357, 359, 368n
—*Brief History of Time* x
—*Universe in a Nutshell* x, 167, 216, 357
Hawking radiation 184
Haydn, Joseph 80, 208, 281, 304, 377, 378, 393
Haydn, Michael 42n
—*Trumpet Concerto in D major* 42n
hearing 54, 85, 322–24
hearing, philosophy of 8, 321
heaven and earth 30–34, 77, 129, 365

Hector, humiliation of 163
Hegel, Georg Wilhelm Friedrich 3, 68
Heissenbüttel, Helmut 392
Helmholtz, Hermann 4, 74, 434
Hendrix, Jimi 293, 450
Henry, Pierre 375
Hepworth, Cecil 405–6
—*Came the Dawn* 405–6
Herbert, George 85
—*Easter Wings* 85
Hesse, Herrmann 153, 340
—*The Glass Bead Game* 153, 340
heterophony 150
hexachord 340, 342–43, 399
hierarchy 60, 69, 80, 85, 87, 129, 261, 370–73, 380
hifi 328–29, 479
Hiller, Lejaren A. 394, 459–60, 472n
—*HPSCHD* 394–95
Hindenburg disaster 294
hiphop 295
Hirst, Damien 401
history 220–21
Hitchcock, Alfred 254–57, 447
—*Blackmail* 254–57
Hoffnung, Gerard 98, 355
Hofstadter, Douglas 18
—*Gödel–Escher–Bach* 18
Hogben, Lancelot 145n
Holmes, Oliver Wendell 282, 284n, 389
Homer 198
Honegger, Arthur 305
honey tree 35, 39
honky-tonk piano 307
Hucbald 223–25, 304, 433
Huffmann, Carl A. 93, 94n
human nature 40, 276
hurdy-gurdy 112
Huygens, Christian 111, 211, 404

Icarus 31
I-Ching 394
identity 64, 68, 71, 74, 82, 116, 171, 236, 238, 240–42, 277, 279, 289, 290, 333, 351, 355, 370, 373, 397
ideology 71, 337–38
illusion 44, 107, 115, 171, 172, 184, 213, 308, 329, 416
imaginary number 107
imbalance 81, 95, 97, 270
imitation 247, 290, 299, 305
Imitation game (Turing) 247, 250–52, 305
impetus 185
impressionism 446, 452–53
improvisation 100, 244, 252, 263, 293, 295, 297, 384, 412, 439, 477
impulse, creative 52
impulsion 45, 46, 56, 126, 144, 148, 149, 182, 183, 280
incantation 60, 75, 80, 128, 225, 287
incipit 290, 458
incoherence 77, 334, 386, 455–56, 472
incompleteness 97, 253, 453
incongruity 385
inconstancy 67, 74, 131, 229, 360–61
independence 299–313
indeterminacy 76, 107, 187, 260, 459
India, music of 64, 78, 219, 457–58
Indian rope trick 31–32
indifference 62, 222, 386, 419
induction, reverse *see* reverse induction
inertia 96, 101, 129, 142, 174, 419
inevitability 76, 185, 194, 199
infinite sets 157–58, 202
infinity xv, 50, 67, 88, 95, 103, 107, 111, 122, 139, 142, 153, 158, 169–70, 175, 186, 204, 357, 361, 450, 471
inflection 75, 91, 222–24, 226–30, 292, 294–97, 333, 345, 377, 380, 435, 457, 483
information science 331–49, 387–400, 434, 486
innocence 39, 409
inspiration 28, 244, 341, 439, 476–77
instability 52, 80, 81, 95, 96, 97, 98, 99, 101, 108, 115, 222, 269–70, 273–75, 279, 365, 373
instantaneity 119, 171, 173, 364, 402
instrument *see* musical instrument
integration 318, 321, 326–29
integrity 149, 209, 243, 279, 299, 484
intelligibility 69, 75, 150, 206, 209, 251
intention 22, 27, 52, 71, 99, 100, 199, 208, 244, 306, 333
interaction 57, 64, 65, 252–53, 258, 455
interference 182, 213, 421, 423–24, 487
interjection 231, 296
internet 194, 249, 342, 412, 475, 485
interpolation 207, 230–31, 245n, 320,

395, 460, 484
interval 75, 80, 119, 136, 140–41, 143, 158, 169, 179, 186, 225–26, 240, 263, 290, 337, 339, 374, 463, 464, 468
interversion (Messiaen) 342–44
intonation 206, 222, 224, 232, 248, 292, 295, 316, 333, 356, 457
invariant tempo 305
invasion 61, 249
Ionesco, Eugene 250, 254–57, 266n
—*The Lesson* 250, 254
irrational number 40, 67, 80, 103–4, 107, 108, 138, 139, 142, 148, 158, 175–76, 355
Isaac, Heinrich 332, 339
Isaacson, Leonard 459–60
isolation 57, 68, 71, 269, 279–80, 420, 451, 485
isorhythm 312, 481
Ives, Charles 300, 302–3, 309, 310, 485

Jack and the beanstalk 32, 162, 365
Jack and Jill 335
James, William 156, 295
Janáček, Leoš 292
Janequin, Clément 185
Jannings, Emil 191–92
Japan, music of 25, 230, 315, 443–44
jaw harp 67, 206, 315–16, 318
jazz 17, 244, 252, 257, 269, 293, 295, 297, 300, 331, 449, 458, 477
Jeans, Sir James 145n, 175–76, 176n
Johnson, Samuel 391
joined-up thinking 229
Jones, Daniel 435
Jones, Spike 437
Joplin, Scott 209
Jourdan, Louis 291
Joyce, James 83, 232
—*Finnegans Wake* 232
Julesz, Béla 316–17, 453, 455
Jupiter 193
just intonation 221, 337, 344

Kade, Johannes 392
Kafka, Franz 71, 250
—*The Trial* 71
Kagel, Mauricio 197, 310, 339–40
—*In girum imus nocte* 339–40
kaleidoscope 477
Kandinsky, Wassily 430
Kangaroo-Pouch Free Music Machine (Grainger) 429
karaoke 15, 243
Karis, Alick 369
Karkoschka, Erhard 438
Keaton, Buster 371, 409
Kelly, Gene 412
Kempelen, Wolfgang von 82, 381, 395, 399n
Kennedy, John F. 215, 294
Kepler, Johannes 4, 111, 229, 303
key 71, 99, 119, 157, 219, 221, 240, 282, 309, 326–28, 337, 352–55, 434, 435, 458, 467
keyboard instrument 91, 97, 219, 283, 344, 370–71, 373–81, 436, 444
Keystone Cops 409
Kidson, Frank 399n
King, Martin Luther Jr 294
Kirnberger, Johann 392
kit, dancing-master's 329
kithara 74, 136
Kitto, H. D. F. 176n
klangfarbenmelodie 205, 239
Klee, Paul 411
Klingon language (*Star Trek*) 295
knitting pattern 349n
knowledge, absolute 48, 105
knowledge, definition of vii, xiv, 7, 15, 37, 129, 156, 235–36, 245, 332, 352–53, 387
knowledge, music as 5, 150–51, 156, 201–09
knowledge, tree of 33–36, 39, 193
Koenig, Rudolph 83, 84
Korngold, Erich Wolfgang 305, 386
koto 126
Kreisler, Fritz x
Kubrick, Stanley 13, 485
—*2001: A Space Odyssey* 13, 485

La Fontaine xii, xiv
labyrinth 160–62
ladder 29–31, 43, 92
La Mettrie, Julien de 251
—*L'Homme Machine* 251
Lancelot, Sir 200
Langdon, Harry 409

language 5, 57, 63, 64, 68, 69, 70, 173, 240–41, 245, 247–49, 257, 324, 345, 387, 389–92, 457, 486
Laplace, Pierre-Simon 166
laser 50, 149
Lasry, Jacques 319
latent energy 94, 127, 128
latent tonality 468
latitude 106, 272, 434
leadership 69, 82, 129, 168, 293
leading instrument 24
Le Corbusier (Charles-Édouard Jeanneret) 131, 133
—*Le Modulor* 133
Léger, Fernand 429
Leigh, Walter 413
leitmotiv 221, 238
length 49, 92, 94, 107, 108, 116–25, 130, 132, 133, 136, 138, 141–42, 147, 159, 166
Lenya, Lotte 291
Lichtenstein, Roy 438
—*Whaam!* 438
life force 172
lifeline 113, 174, 184, 192, 194
Ligeti, György 23, 63, 416, 443, 445, 453–54
—*Atmosphères* 23, 416, 443, 445, 453
—*Volumina* 443
light 51, 236, 308, 447
light ray 49
light speed 308, 357, 478
likeness 409
limit 53, 76, 89, 90, 93, 94, 95, 113, 141, 163, 248, 387–88, 463–66, 460
line 48, 49, 79, 80, 84, 86, 91, 92, 93, 112, 113, 116–25, 153, 166, 169, 175, 232
line of sight 50
Ling, Daniel 206, 217n
linguistics xv, 70, 237, 248, 332, 345
Lissajous curve 201
Liszt, Franz 307, 437
—*Hungarian Rhapsòdy* 437
literacy 15
Little Red Riding Hood 334
Livy xv–xvi
Lloyd, Harold 409
location 73, 106, 122, 124, 140, 147, 151, 167–70, 173, 202–3, 221, 240, 348, 354, 357, 362, 435, 454, 478, 487
locomotion 80, 112, 126, 144
logic 24, 79, 80, 100, 142, 150, 186, 209, 235, 239, 260, 262, 370, 385, 387, 390–92, 413, 433
logos 36
London, Kurt 217n
long line 80 *see* melody
longitude 106, 434
loop 201–2, 311, 421, 481
loudness 288
Louis XIV 223, 418
Lovelace, Ada Lady 245, 258, 261, 266n
Lucier, Alvin 426
—*I Am Sitting in a Room* 426
Lulu (Louise Brooks) 200
Lumière brothers (Auguste, Louis) 320, 403, 406
lute 61, 137, 163, 193, 201, 370, 454
Lutoslawski, Witold 399
Lye, Len 429, 431
lyre 36, 74, 77, 90, 128, 130, 136, 183, 244

Machaut, Guillaume de 185, 216, 225, 481
—*Ma fin est mon commencement* 216
Machiavelli, Niccolò 79, 229, 240, 261
machine code 340
machine intelligence 264–65, 395
machine readable score 429, 431–32
Maconie, Robin 4, 164n, 215, 217n, 284n, 368n, 473n, 482–83
—*Concept of Music* 215, 368n
—*Mozart-Kugel* 482–84
—*Second Sense* 217n, 413n
—*Way of Music* 4
MAD magazine 438
Maelzel, Johann Nepomuk 208
magic lantern 403–5, 408
magic square *see* acrostic
magnetism 80
magnification 484
magnitude 206
Mahabharata 200
Mahler, Gustav 485
Mallarmé, Stéphane 85, 342, 383–84, 390, 399, 402, 435, 471
—*Livre* 342
—*Un coup de dés* 85, 383

managed instability 270–71, 274, 281
management 68, 69, 195, 250, 306
Mandelbrot, Benoît 116, 440, 457–72, 472n, 484
Mandelbrot set 471
Mannheim School 83
many-particle system 361
many-worlds hypothesis 265
mapmaking 65, 78, 272, 304, 434
Marey, Étienne-Jules 167, 320, 359, 403, 408, 416
Marker, Chris 410
—*La Jetée* 410
Martinelli, Giovanni 431
Marx, Groucho 409
masque, 277
mathematics 65, 76, 78, 133–36, 139, 157–58, 166, 201–2, 253, 266n, 341, 342, 387, 390, 450, 457–72
Mathews, Max 459, 472n
Matisse, Henri 440
Maurina-Press, Madame 428
Mayer, Louis B. 309
maze 41, 161, 198, 201 *see* labyrinth
McCarthy, Joseph 259–61
McLaren, Norman 347–48, 349n, 429, 439, 44n
—*Blinkety Blank* 429, 439
McLuhan, Marshall 9, 11, 260, 274, 370
meantone tuning 337, 344
measure 89, 91, 92, 93, 103, 107, 116–19, 122–23, 125, 128, 131, 132, 138, 156, 170, 173, 204, 220, 351, 354, 450, 480
mechanical motion 97, 184–85, 208–9, 281, 283, 303–4, 366, 418, 420
medium is the message, 11
Medusa 32–33
megaphone 291
melisma 205
melody 58, 60, 61, 64, 67, 71, 74, 80, 81, 92, 97, 116, 168, 205, 221, 223, 230, 232, 237–39, 269, 290, 294, 297, 304, 317, 331, 340, 397, 457, 461–72, 483
memory 24, 28, 74, 75, 127, 128, 191, 221, 236, 255, 262, 317, 374, 392, 447, 458, 467, 476
Mendelssohn, Felix 80, 205, 273
Menenius's tale 318
Mercator, Gerardus 272
Mersenne, Marin 4
mesostics 85, 295, 392, 475, 486
Messiaen, Olivier 305, 312, 319, 336, 338, 342, 347, 364, 367, 378–79, 386, 403, 443–44, 481, 486
—*Livre d'Orgue* 343
—*Mode de valeurs* 336, 338, 342, 347, 367
—*Mystère de la Saint-Trinité* 338
—*Quartet for the End of Time* 312, 364, 481
—*Sept Haï-Kaï* 443
method acting 293, 296–97, 439, 477
metronome 62, 208, 280–81, 346, 417
Meyer-Eppler, Werner 433
Michelangelo 195
mickey-mousing 385, 412, 437
microphone 58, 202–3, 210, 214, 255–56, 291, 320–21, 348, 422, 425, 453
microphotography 408–11
Midas, King 242
midi keyboard 371, 380
Milhaud, Darius 237, 309–12, 313n, 386, 407, 481
—*Étude poétique Op. 333* 310–12, 313n
—*Serenade* 309
Miller, Dayton C. 348, 436
—*Science of Musical Sounds* 436
Miller, Henry 372
mind-body paradox 280, 420
minimalist music 100, 415–27, 444
Minotaur 41, 201
Minsky, Marvin 264–65, 267n, 345
Miró, Jean 432–33
—*Harlequin's Carnival* 433
mixture stop (organ) 379
mobility 99
Möbius strip 260
mode 60, 74, 75, 77, 78, 99, 128, 175, 222, 277, 280, 293, 357, 458
modern music 7, 239, 248, 252, 275, 296, 308, 319, 418, 486
Modigliani, Amedeo 449
modulation 52, 78, 97, 149–50, 157, 219, 221, 240, 270, 273–74, 288, 290, 294, 315–16, 321, 355, 374, 377, 434
modulation, electronic 379
Moholy-Nagy, Lázló 430
momentum 38, 47, 80, 89, 97, 106, 140,

157, 413
Mondrian, Piet 429, 430
—*Broadway Boogie-Woogie* 431
—*Victory Boogie-Woogie* 431
Monet, Claude 384, 446, 452
mono (one channel) 202, 362, 452, 454, 487
monochord 35, 38, 39, 40, 43, 84, 95, 113, 117, 124–25, 129, 131, 132, 135, 137–39, 150, 156, 158–59, 179, 181, 194, 335, 355
monotony 459
montage 11, 189–200, 260, 384–86, 389–90, 404–5, 411, 413, 426, 437
Monteverdi, Claudio 23, 215, 229, 304, 376, 480
—*Magnificat* 215, 480
—*Vespers* 23, 480
Morrison, Herbert 294
Moszkowski, Moritz 307
motion 44, 49, 53, 54, 58, 59, 78, 87, 96, 97, 98, 100, 101, 104–6, 142, 151, 153, 160–64, 173, 182, 186, 203, 210, 216, 222, 271, 273–74, 307, 361, 409, 415–16, 461, 477
motion capture 80, 93, 150, 155, 156, 173, 186–87, 207, 223, 231, 274, 308, 320, 359, 403, 408, 410 *see* stop motion
motionless arrow 150–60 *see* arrow paradox
motivation xiv, 47, 76, 129, 163, 171–72, 244, 274, 289, 296–97, 409
mouth 36, 48, 49, 184
mouth music 149, 206, 315, 318
movies 11, 60, 79, 80, 93, 155, 156, 186, 189–200, 254–57, 273, 276, 304–5, 308, 320, 361, 363, 384, 403–13, 415, 429–31
moving arrow paradox (Zeno) 140 *see* arrow paradox
moving bassline 270, 273, 469–70
Mozart, Leopold 355–56
—*Sinfonia Pastorella* 355
Mozart, Wolfgang Amadeus 80, 92, 209, 238, 275, 276, 277, 281, 288, 295, 302, 305–6, 377, 385, 393–96, 482
—*Adagio KV 516* 394
—*Anleitung* (method of composing by dice, attr.) 393–94, 396
—*Clarinet concerto in A* 92
—*Don Giovanni* 302, 306
—*Eine kleine Nachtmusik* 281, 305, 385
—*Magic Flute* 288
—*Mozart's Musical Game* 393–94
multiple coexistent spaces 480, 485
multiple (higher) dimensions 202–4, 215–17
multiple histories 192, 197, 265, 276, 321, 353, 356, 425, 479–80
multiple timescales 299–313, 423–25, 475–76
Munch, Edvard 71
—*The Scream* 71
Münsterberg, Hugo 156, 406
Murrow, Edward R. 259
music, definition of 451–52
music, existence of vii, 4
music of the spheres 303, 358
music, power of 41, 162
musical box 75, 207, 306–8, 346, 366, 371, 377
musical instrument 51, 52, 60, 74, 75, 76, 93, 117, 126–28, 151, 157, 182, 193, 306, 316–17, 321, 324, 472
musique concrète 238, 311–12, 367, 375, 426, 440, 476, 481
musique d'ameublement 386, 407
Mussorgsky, Modest 292
Muybridge, Eadweard 79, 408
"My Country 'tis of Thee" song 273, 395–98
Myers, Rollo 401–2, 410
mystery chord (Schoenberg) 366
myth vii–xvi, 8, 17, 18, 30, 37, 38, 45, 51, 101, 160–64, 168, 183, 193, 196, 201, 318, 353

Nancarrow, Conlon 301, 303, 401–2, 437
Napier, Sir Charles 205
Napier, John 135
Naslas, Vlad 322–29
National Socialism 193, 237, 450
natural disposition 250–51
natural law 98, 356, 459
navigation 78, 79, 85, 91, 161, 304, 434
Neumann, John von 387
neumata 224, 226, 333, 439
Newman, Barnett 445
Newton, Isaac 4, 30, 54, 82, 111, 157,

212, 216, 371
Nightingale, Florence 276, 282, 362–63
Nijinsky, Vaslav 154
Nixon, Marni 283
node 86, 87, 88, 132, 142, 169
noise 66, 341, 348, 437, 443, 445, 448–52, 454, 455
—definition of 450–51, 454–55
no-mindedness 371
nonsense 69, 266n, 295, 403
notation, music 4, 65, 70, 73, 74, 78, 79, 81, 85, 91, 106, 110, 156, 184, 204, 213, 217, 219, 222–25, 228, 230, 298, 301–2, 304, 321, 333, 371, 374, 433–34, 437–39, 451
note-row 339, 476
nothing 8, 9, 88
number 87, 95, 317, 337, 449, 459
numerals, Roman 85
Nuremberg trials 237
Nyman, Michael 427

object, sound 440
observer 50, 51, 61, 120–22, 142, 171, 192, 196, 209, 251, 257, 354, 367, 447, 478
Occam's razor 202
octave 139, 140, 263, 344, 352, 374
Odysseus 175, 200
Oedipus and the Sphinx xiii–xv
Olivier, Laurence 195, 252
Olson, Harry 230
ondes martenot 445
onset 377, 436
op art 213, 347, 423
opera 82, 185, 197, 221, 229–30, 238, 274, 275–77, 281, 292, 334, 448, 457
optical sound 213, 347, 429–31, 436
oral culture viii, x, 7, 18, 194, 229, 299, 316, 334, 458
Oram, Daphne 432
Oramics 432
orbital motion 38, 78, 102, 111, 145, 157, 201, 243, 263, 271, 274, 303, 357–59, 468, 480–82
orchestra, symphony 52, 322–24
order 53, 66, 67, 68, 77, 148, 189, 299, 370, 372, 383, 390, 459
Oresme, Nicole 4, 105, 106, 185, 228
organ *see* pipe organ
organum 263
orientation 96, 203, 270
original sin 29, 39, 45, 47
ornamentation 74, 222–23, 228–29, 232, 292, 304, 316, 370, 433, 438
Ortmann, Otto 346, 349n
—*Physical Basis of Piano Touch and Tone* 346
Orwell, George 71
—*1984* 71
oscillation 51, 93, 106, 112, 145, 149, 169, 321, 348, 464, 465–66
overload *see* sensory overload
Ovid 226

Pabst, G. W. 193, 200n, 447
—*Pandora's Box* movie (1929) 193, 200n
Pachelbel, Johann 28
pain 248, 254–59
Palisca, Claude 177–81, 187n
Palladio, Andrea 15, 29, 472
Pan 90
Pandora's box 193–94, 352, 354
panpipes 74, 77, 90
paradigm shift 77
paradox ix, 8, 26, 30, 47, 69, 88, 90, 101, 103, 104, 109, 119, 120, 131–45, 150–60, 186, 204, 228–29, 245, 369, 475
parameter 336–37, 346, 463
Parmenides ix, 43, 44, 45, 46, 47, 48, 83, 106, 107, 147, 171, 172, 176, 184, 186, 373
Parry, Hubert 465
—*Jerusalem* 465
Parsons, Denys 290, 298n, 458, 461, 467, 471, 472n
Pärt, Arvo 28
Partch, Harry 378
partial vibration 43, 85, 124, 132, 147, 159, 167, 170, 316, 360
particle-wave duality *see* wave-particle duality
path integral 165–76
patter song 285
pattern 66, 99, 100, 191, 201, 204, 206, 223, 292, 340–45, 370, 415, 439, 444, 448, 458, 460–61, 467, 486
Penderecki, Krzysztof 63, 438, 443
—*Threnody* 443

pendulum 22, 35, 37, 38, 53, 95, 97, 106, 109, 118, 168, 223, 361, 418
Penrose, Roger 18, 258
—*Emperor's New Mind* 258
pentatonic scale 291–92, 371, 461
percussion 66, 177–83, 345, 378, 380, 449
performance 26, 51, 53, 59, 65, 73, 76, 98, 208–9, 223, 252, 257, 347, 448
Peri, Jacopo 229
periodicity 107, 108, 303, 321–22, 359, 481
permutation 338–45, 388, 483
Perotin 205, 321
—*Sederunt Principes* 321
—*Viderunt Omnes* 205
persistence 79, 124, 127, 130, 163, 172, 317, 419
personality 226, 242, 297, 346–47, 371, 388, 419 *see* temperament
Pfenninger, Rudolf 213, 429
phase 203, 215, 348, 421–25, 453, 455
Philip, Robert 233n
Philolaus of Croton ix, 93, 178–79
philology 254, 276 *see* linguistics
philosophy xv, 4, 73, 76, 130, 173, 247, 420, 475
philosophy of language xv, 332–33, 458
phonautograph 81, 83, 307, 432, 433
phonemes 25
phonograph 120, 216, 282–83, 286, 291, 357–59
phonography (shorthand) 81
phonology 436
photoelectric sound 429, 430
photography 18, 93, 156, 213, 363, 408–11, 447
pi (π), value of 40, 108, 123, 148
Piaf, Edith 291
piano, acoustic 91, 181, 244, 307, 371, 377
piano, prepared 26, 369–81, 425
piano, reproducing 26, 187n, 208, 306, 308, 346–47, 371, 377, 412, 448
piano roll 301, 306–7, 346, 347, 362, 393, 401, 436, 448
Picasso, Pablo 17, 18, 161, 406, 449
pickup arm (gramophone) 361
Pinter, Harold 12
pipe organ 75, 105, 214, 318, 321, 370, 443–44
pirouette 98, 361
piston motion 154
pitch 52, 56, 74, 86, 92, 112, 123, 127, 143, 149, 159, 181, 206, 225, 248, 288, 296, 337, 357, 366, 371, 461
pitch class 344–45
pitch space 129, 130, 215, 217, 223, 273, 321, 323, 357, 366, 370, 371, 433–34, 463–71
Pitman, Isaac 81
Plain Bob Major 342–43
plainchant 205–6, 222–24, 226, 228–29, 263, 292, 304, 315, 333, 433, 458, 484
plane 91, 357
planetary motion 78, 82, 108, 111, 145, 157, 172, 185, 223, 229, 263, 271, 303, 357–58, 477, 481
Plato 1–3, 38, 53, 55, 76, 171, 214, 373, 410, 418
—*Timaeus* 53
Platonic essences 3–4, 102, 171, 214, 240, 338
player piano *see* piano, reproducing
Pleyel Piano Company 393
pochette 329
Poe, Edgar Allan 12, 280, 339
—*The Raven* 280
poetry 248, 249, 259, 295, 297, 388–89
point 48, 49, 50, 91, 92, 93, 103, 110, 139, 147, 153, 173, 202–3, 207–8, 361, 446
pointillism 336, 446, 466, 483
Polder, Dirk 14
poll, opinion 14
Pollock, Jackson 17, 471
polytonality 309–10
Pons, Lili 431
Pope, Alexander 226–27
Popper, Karl 43, 44, 47, 48, 56n, 172, 204
portamento 221, 229, 232–33
possession 261
potential energy 45, 94, 118
Poulenc, Francis 292, 340
—*Concerto for two pianos* 340
Pousseur, Henri 197, 384
—*Votre Faust* 197
prayer 69
precision, false 91, 165–66, 169, 203,

248, 293, 352
predestination 76, 113, 174–75, 194, 195, 196, 217
prediction 77, 97, 99, 100, 102, 108, 165, 170, 193, 203, 244, 245, 299, 460
Presley, Elvis 215, 363
Princeton-Columbia Mk I and Mk II synthesizers 230
prism 236
Pritchett, James 261–62, 266n
Priuli, Giovanni 478, 480
—*Canzona prima a 12* 480
probability 166, 169, 170, 460, 464
problem solving 99, 100, 189, 486
process 196, 221, 426
progression 92, 99, 239, 271, 315, 342–44, 466–67
Prokofiev, Serge 23, 375, 437, 446
—*Alexander Nevsky* 437
—*Romeo and Juliet* 23, 446
prolongation 112
pronunciation 228, 333
proof by audition 179
proportion 15, 36, 46, 85, 131, 132, 300, 472, 476
propulsion 113, 126, 143–44, 152
Proteus poem 339, 345, 388
psychoanalysis 83, 84, 244, 258, 283, 341, 447–48
Ptolemaus 111
Pudovkin, Vsevolod 66
punctuation marks 224, 228, 333, 434
Purcell, Henry 270, 305
—*Dido and Aeneas* 270, 305
Pythagoras, 30, 133, 176, 177–83
Pythagoras, School of ix, 2, 44, 45, 53, 54, 55, 86, 90, 93, 95, 105, 134, 138, 141, 148, 168, 175–76, 184, 186, 201, 371, 430
Pythagoras, Theorem of 55, 86, 87, 88, 132–33, 143–44, 366

quality 106, 139, 321, 324, 348, 484
quantity 87, 91, 106, 108, 147, 156, 160, 221, 303, 450
Queneau, Raymond 387–88
—*Exercices de Style* 387
Quincey, Thomas de 282
—*Confessions of an English Opium Eater* 282
quiz games 15, 259

Rachmaninov, Sergei 346–47, 379
—*Prelude in C minor* 346–47
Racine, Jean 293
radiant energy 22, 48, 51, 52, 54, 89, 155, 168, 182
radio 58, 62, 150, 168, 193, 228, 256, 310, 386, 437, 445
ragtime 209, 371
Raman, C. V. 349n
Rameau, Jean-Philippe 274, 370
random activity 99, 201, 210, 340–41, 448–49, 486
random dot stereogram 416–17, 453, 455
randomness 24, 67, 68, 201, 383, 387–88, 392, 394–95, 399, 449, 463, 471, 481, 483, 486
range (fractal melody) 463–72
rap 295
Rapunzel 32, 162, 266n
ratio 36, 46, 110, 119, 129, 131, 132, 134, 136, 138–39, 142, 145, 147, 157, 178–83, 216, 290, 301, 337, 351, 354, 373
Ravel, Maurice 297, 307, 308, 365, 375, 419–20, 465
—*Bolero* 419–20, 465
—*Daphnis et Chloé* 297
—*La Valse* 365
RCA-Bell 309
reading aloud 223, 439
readymade 259–60
real number 95, 158, 160, 176, 357
real time 91, 381, 427
reality, external 21, 37, 43, 53, 65, 77, 79, 100, 148, 201, 203, 257, 447
reason 36, 40, 80, 199, 236, 486
rebus 435
reciprocal 141
recitative 281, 285–86, 295
recording, sound 58, 61, 202, 232–33, 276, 292, 307, 322, 357–59, 449
recurrence 24, 419
redundancy 253
reflection, sound 210–11
register 150, 379–80 *see* tessitura
Reich, Steve 415–16, 421, 423–27, 453
—*It's Gonna Rain* 426
—*Piano Phase* 421, 423–26, 453

Reihe, die music periodical 331, 384
relation 77, 89, 96, 106, 108, 109, 195, 240–42, 354, 372, 447
relativity theory 85, 109, 117, 120, 138, 173, 216, 271, 307–8, 352, 357–58, 361, 364, 367, 401, 411
Ren and Stimpy 264
Renoir, Pierre-Auguste 447
repetition 415–27
resemblance, terms of 3
resistance 46, 47, 52, 61, 62, 78, 88, 89, 94, 100, 111, 118, 125, 126, 144, 149, 163, 166, 280, 359, 419, 447
Resnais, Alain 197
—*Last Year at Marienbad* 197
resonance 50–51, 118, 148, 149, 150, 168, 178–82, 210, 256, 280, 286, 289, 315–16, 320, 381
retrospection 21, 196
revelation 100
reverberation 22, 59, 60, 61, 130, 149, 212, 423–24, 455
reverse induction vii, 48, 81, 192, 212–13, 339–40
rhetoric 19, 37, 61, 75, 80, 82, 168, 206, 209, 241, 294, 297, 317, 379
Rhind papyrus 134
rhythm 64, 68, 74, 99, 150, 168, 185, 223, 248, 292, 294, 296, 297, 346, 389–90, 411, 415, 458
Richter, Hans 429, 430–31
—*Rhythm 21* 431
right angle triangle 55, 129, 143–44, 148
Riley, Bridget 213, 347, 416, 421
risk 195
Risset, Jean-Claude 319
ritual 52, 53, 59, 60, 61, 63, 65, 74, 80, 161, 184, 231, 241, 247, 277, 317, 372, 383
Robinson, W. Heath 82, 395
robotics 245, 279, 370, 420 *see* artificial intelligence
Rodet, Xavier 320
Rodin, Auguste 271, 408
Ronan, Colin A. 176n
rondeau 74, 97, 216, 312, 480–85
rosette 201
Rosler, Lawrence 459, 472n
Rossini, Gioachino 385, 402–3
—*La Cenerentola* 385
—*Péchés de Vieillesse* 403
rotary motion 54, 95, 96, 98, 101, 102, 103, 108, 110, 111, 126, 182–83, 274, 357–65, 415, 422, 481
Rothko, Mark 445
roughness 459–60
Rousselot, Abbé 436
routine 100
Roy, Claude 311
Royal Society 279, 391, 404

Sabaneev, Leonid 1, 11, 16n
Sacher, Paul 338
Sachs, Curt 246n, 302
St George and the dragon 40, 197
St Mark's basilica Venice 479
Samson and Delilah 33, 161, 162, 266n
Satie, Erik 209, 292, 371, 385–86, 401–13, 420
—*Danse de travers* 402
—*Embryons desséchés* 401, 403, 407–8
—*Gnossiennes* 402
—*Gymnopédies* 209
—*Heures séculaires et instantanées* 402
—*Parade* 385, 407
—*Relâche* 386
—*Socrate* 407
—*Vexations* 420
Saussure, Ferdinand de xv, 71
Sauveur Joseph 276
Sayers, Dorothy L. 342
—*Nine Tailors* 342
scala 43, 92 *see* ladder
scale 60, 74, 75, 77, 78, 92, 128, 131, 143, 170, 175, 219, 272, 283, 293, 336–37, 341, 346, 357, 380, 458, 462, 463, 476, 484
Scaliger, Julius Caesar 339, 348n, 388
—*Poetices* 348n
Scarlatti, Domenico 59
Scelsi, Giacinto 63, 443, 445
—*Konx-Om-Pax* 443
Schaeffer, Pierre 367, 375–76, 381n, 476
—*Bidule en ut* 375
Schenker, Heinrich 68
Schiller, Friedrich 399
Schoenberg, Arnold 14, 58, 65, 97, 235, 237–39, 246n, 260, 269, 275, 279, 281–83, 290, 291, 298, 303, 308, 331–32, 337, 338, 366, 371, 386,

410–11, 418, 468–70, 483
—*Buch der Hängenden Gärten* 281
—*Erwartung* 269, 290
—*Five Orchestral Pieces* 58, 366
—*Herzgewächse* 290, 411
—*Pierrot Lunaire* 282, 283, 291, 298, 411
—*String quartet No. 2* 281–82, 410, 468–69
—*Style and Idea* 413n
—*Survivor from Warsaw* 298
—*Three Pieces for piano* 280
—*Variations for orchestra* 298, 332
Schoenberg program 470–72
Scholes, Percy 342
Schopenhauer, Arthur 3, 68
Schouten, Jan 329, 330n
Schrödinger, Erwin xiv, 51, 156, 192–93, 351–57, 363
Schrödinger's cat xiv, 192–93, 351–53, 357
Schubert, Franz 252, 278, 399, 485
—*Der Erlkönig* 278
—*Symphony No. 9* 399
Schumann, Robert 338, 486
—*Abegg variations* 338
Schütz, Heinrich 454, 478
Schwarzenegger, Arnold 197
Schwitters, Kurt 295, 435
science, Greek 89, 104, 106, 129, 138–39, 145, 156–57, 276, 372
science, medieval 155–56, 333
Scott [de Mandéville], Léon 79, 81, 83, 84, 307, 433, 434
Scott, Ridley 447
—*Alien* 447
Scriabin, Alexander 307, 448
selection process 386–400, 460–61, 475
self-awareness 21, 25, 175, 245, 318, 391, 454
self-determination 276, 282
self-expression 69
self-organizing process 51, 99, 101, 115, 123, 145, 148, 460, 463, 465, 471
self-similarity 459–60, 484
sense organs 46, 47, 54, 155
sensory deprivation 445
sensory overload 419, 445
separation awareness 26, 57, 235, 478, 485
sequence 189, 221
serialism 230, 319, 331–48, 378, 397, 468, 483
serpent 33–34, 36, 38, 44, 409 *see* snake
set theory 331, 340–41, 344–45, 483
Seurat, Georges 446, 454
Seven ages of Man 107
Shakespeare, William 8, 11, 16n, 78, 195, 241, 293, 296, 297, 318
—*Coriolanus* 318
—*Hamlet* 195, 252
—*King Lear* 8, 16n
Shaw, George Bernard 231, 283, 285–86
—*My Fair Lady* movie 285
—*Pygmalion* 231, 283, 285–86
Shelley, Mary 266n, 279
—*Frankenstein* 266n, 279, 318
shô (mouth organ) 443–44
shock wave 151
shorthand, Pitman's 81
Shostakovich, Dmitri 237, 417, 418
—*Seventh Symphony* 417
sideband distortion 424
Sierpinski sponge 440
silence 5–16, 20, 41, 46, 51, 61, 148, 228, 335
silence, degrees of 12
silence, rituals of 9–10
silent majority 14
silent movie 10, 255, 309, 371, 384, 403–5, 407, 410, 430–31, 437
sillon fermé 426, 481
simultaneity 119, 167, 169, 171, 236, 309, 361, 477–80, 485–87
sin 39–40, 46 *see* original sin
Sinatra, Frank 291, 431
Singin' in the Rain 412
sinuousness 41
sinusoidal motion 38, 43, 106
Sirens 41
Sistine Chapel 195
Sitwell, Edith 291
slide rule 134, 135, 353
slide show 384
sliding scale 272, 469
slingshot 38, 50, 102, 111, 126, 182–83
slow motion 363, 367, 476
Small Faces 422
—*Itchykoo Park* 422
Smetana, Bedrich 420

—*Vltava* 420
Smith, Percy 401, 411
—*Secrets of Nature* 411
snake 29–36, 39, 45, 48, 92
snake charmer 30–32
snakes and ladders 29–31, 43, 44, 206, 432–33
sociology of music 5–6
Socrates 7, 39, 45
solid 91
soloist 58, 61, 63, 225–26, 263, 269, 370
song, power of 41, 42, 285
sonometer 95
Sophocles 77, 175, 293
—*Oedipus Rex* 77, 175, 293
sound, propagation of 51, 152–56
sound-bite 294
sound effects 255, 413, 437, 444, 445
sound recording 156, 187, 212–15, 276, 310, 453 *see* gramophone
sound typography 437
spectral music 315, 317, 319–20
speech 41, 48, 57, 75, 149, 206, 222, 231, 232, 282, 287, 289, 298, 332, 345, 432, 485
speech act 25, 36, 37, 69, 70, 82, 128, 206, 225, 228, 249, 286, 333
speech, cockney 232
speech, elements of 25, 66, 81, 223–24, 226–27, 286, 289–92, 295, 297, 317, 324, 332–33, 345, 346, 377, 397, 435, 444, 446
speech synthesis 82, 83, 206, 345, 380, 395
Spencer, D. A. 186, 187n, 299
Spencer, Herbert 73, 79, 84, 85, 93, 94, 94n, 109, 221, 346
—*Principles of Psychology* 346
sphere 49, 50, 54, 90, 108, 154, 303, 482
spider web 161–62, 203
spin 95, 96, 174
spinet 370
spinning top 80, 95, 96, 98, 101, 271, 361, 393, 461
sprechstimme 282, 285–98
square root of 2 40, 175, 272
stability 95, 96–99, 145, 149, 233, 273, 357, 373
Stadler, Maximilian 393
Stalling, Carl 440
—*There They Go Go Go* 440
standing wave 89
starlight 49, 50
starting point *see* endpoints
state, mental *see* being
stave, music 74, 78, 79, 90, 374
steady state 46, 52, 76, 80, 106, 173, 201, 207–8, 229, 265, 273, 317, 320, 348, 357, 359, 373, 468
stealth fighter 80, 96
Stedman, Fabian 342
—*Tintinnalogia* 342
Steele, Joshua 346
—*Prosodia Rationalis* 346
Stein, Gertrude 83, 294–95, 383, 415, 416, 419
step structure 43, 60, 92, 211, 458, 462–63
stepwise motion 80, 97, 103, 120, 123, 170, 186, 208, 229, 271, 458, 462
stereo (two channel) 202, 213, 215, 362, 422, 425, 452–53, 487
stereoscopy 416, 454
Sterne, Laurence 198–99
—*Tristram Shandy* 198
stethoscope 83
Stetson, Harold R. 436
Still, Clyfford 445
stochastic music 341, 460
Stockhausen, Karlheinz 12, 13, 58, 63, 68, 119, 208, 209, 224, 246n, 263, 301, 303, 310, 312, 331–32, 342–44, 367, 375, 379, 380, 384, 395, 399, 402, 412, 422–26, 430, 435, 437, 438, 440, 443–44, 453, 466, 468, 475–77
—*Aus den sieben Tagen* 402, 477
—*Carré* 435, 453
—*Elektronische Studie II* 430, 440
—*Gruppen* 312, 437, 453, 476
—*Harlekin* 422
—*Helikopter-Streichquartett* 312
—*Hymnen* 13, 310, 395, 437
—*Inori* 263
—*Jahreslauf* 444
—*Jubiläum* 484
—*Konkrete Etüde* 375
—*Kontakte* 367, 426, 433, 438
—*Kreuzspiel* 342–44
—*LICHT* opera cycle 295, 375, 475, 484

—*Mantra* 379, 424, 484
—*Mikrophonie I* 381, 425
—*Mixtur* 438
—*Momente* 197, 283, 435, 443
—*Musik im Bauch* 484
—*Orchester-Finalisten* 312, 412
—*Piano Piece I* 119, 468
—*Piano Piece IV* 209
—*Piano Piece X* 443
—*Piano Piece XI* 399
—plus-minus compositions 476
—*Refrain* 423, 433
—*Samstag aus LICHT* 375
—*Sirius* 475
—*Stimmung* 58, 224
—*Telemusik* 438
—*Trans* 12, 63, 443
—*Zeitmasse* 301, 312
—*Zyklus* 433, 438
stop motion 93, 150, 155, 173, 186, 273, 320, 362–63, 410, 415–16
Stradivari, Antonio 317, 351
straightness 117, 118, 123, 198, 233
strange attractor (chaos theory) 160–62, 201
Strauss, Johann II 365, 420, 452, 467
—*Blue Danube* waltz 420, 467
Strauss, Richard 23, 375
—*Also sprach Zarathustra* 23
Stravinsky, Igor 6, 19, 60, 62, 69, 97, 154, 160, 209, 237, 261, 262, 264, 292, 303, 307, 308, 323, 325–28, 337, 365–66, 389, 393, 407, 419, 429, 440, 443, 481
—*Abraham and Isaac* 440
—*Agon* 440
—*An Autobiography* 261
—*Canon* 313, 481
—*Canticum Sacrum* 440
—*Duo Concertant* 309
—*Firebird* 313, 365–66, 481
—*Flood* 313, 440, 443
—*Movements* 313
—*Nightingale* 283
—*Petrushka* 300, 440
—*Piano Sonata* 62, 209
—*Requiem Canticles* 312–13, 440
—*Sacre du Printemps* 60, 97, 154, 160, 389, 419
—*Symphonic Variations* 443
—*Symphony in C* 323, 325–28
—*Threni* 289
stream of consciousness 11, 255, 269
stress 74, 130, 174, 221–22, 226, 243, 367, 418
stretched string *see* vibrating string
string theory ix, 88, 115–30, 136, 156, 165, 201–2, 216–17
string vibration *see* vibrating string
structures sonores (Lasry-Baschet) 319
stylus (recording) 38, 82, 215, 362
sum over histories (Feynman) 111, 166–67, 175
Sumer is icumen in 480
superposition of states 351–54
surrealism 11, 18, 202, 255, 282, 297, 385–86, 403, 406, 407, 434, 435
surround-sound 202, 215, 426, 452, 479
Suzuki, Daihetzu 9
swearing 231
sweet spot 479
Swift, Jonathan 411
syllable, components of 226–27
syllogism 99, 100
symbolist poetry 297, 298, 381, 389, 435
sympathetic vibration 151, 168, 182
synaesthesia 324
synchronicity 67, 68, 118, 280, 386, 411–13, 421, 423–24, 455–56, 478–80, 485
synchronism, accidental 385
synthesizer 91, 213, 318, 348, 431, 436, 472

tablature 74
Tallis, Thomas 63, 300
—*Spem in Alium* 63, 300
Tao 171
Tchaikovsky, Peter Ilyich 307, 336
—*1812 Overture* 336
temperament 74, 75, 76, 77, 82, 83, 116, 127, 128–29, 143, 174–75, 183–87, 194, 226, 275, 277, 283, 333, 337, 365, 379, 434, 458, 461
tempo 99, 119, 300–13, 346, 421, 458
temptation 39, 41, 42, 76
tension, 38, 40, 51, 56, 74, 75, 87, 88, 89, 90, 93, 94, 100, 108, 117, 123–25, 127–29, 134, 136, 140–43, 147, 157, 159, 170, 175, 183, 194–95, 217,

244, 275, 459
tension ratio 56, 58, 90, 204
termination 117, 173, 195, 228 *see* endpoints
Terminator movies 197, 318
tessitura 74
tetrachord, Greek 225, 333, 357
Tetrazzini, Luisa 431
texture 445
Thales 174
theme 97, 237–38, 337, 483
theoi 174, 175
theology 53
theory, scientific 43
Theory of Everything 87, 88, 157, 160
theremin 297, 445
Theseus and the Minotaur 160–64, 213
third dimension 46, 85, 91, 201, 214
third-octave filter 322–23, 325–28
Thomas, Dylan 389
Thomson, Virgil 295
—*Four Saints in Three Acts* 295
thunder, clap of 152
Tibbett, Lawrence 431
Tibetan Buddhism 58, 63, 315
timbre 52, 53, 149, 174, 205, 215, 288, 317, 319, 324–28, 348, 367, 369, 379, 426, 430, 476
time travel 362–67, 410
timekeeping 305, 308, 393
timeline 113, 174, 194, 196, 198, 217, 334, 361, 478
Toch, Ernst 430
Tolkein, J. R. R. 295
—*Lord of the Rings* 295
Tom and Jerry 264
tonality 68, 71, 78, 92, 211, 261, 269, 271–73, 277–78, 282, 309, 345, 355, 370, 468
tone color 52, 74, 127, 204, 205, 215, 315–17, 324, 331, 444
tone language 228, 380, 457
tone, musical 27, 53, 66, 118, 125, 147, 149, 179, 182, 348, 472
tone of voice 75, 76, 82, 127, 174, 252, 277, 288, 317–18, 322–23, 388
tone wheel 436, 481
touch 73, 79, 84, 90, 94, 124, 151, 161, 163, 187n, 208, 215, 242, 370, 433, 439, 445
touch-sensitive keyboard 376
tragedy, Greek 76, 89, 113, 162, 174–75, 185, 194, 217, 264–65, 270
transaction 70, 243, 244
transcendental meditation 416, 448
transcendental numbers 139
transducer 52, 182, 472
transference 235–245, 316–17, 367, 389
transformation 76, 115, 220, 238, 320, 380, 390 , 395, 476 *see* change
transience 7, 171, 173, 336, 421, 478
transition 76, 79, 83, 90, 92, 169–71, 204–5, 219–33, 273, 277–78, 355–56, 373, 467
translation 54, 240, 292–98
transmutation 240–43, 279
tromba marina 132, 355
truth 47, 48, 70, 171, 195, 201, 203, 251, 253, 261, 283, 293, 391
tuning 61, 74, 75, 76, 78, 131, 136, 140–41, 175, 194, 211, 219, 221, 280, 316, 337, 351, 370, 378, 379–80, 423–25, 430, 461
tuning fork 118
turbulence 67, 152, 341, 402
Turing, Alan 209, 250–52, 261, 266n
Turing test 209, 214
Turner, J. M. W. 446–47
twelve-tone composition 14, 269, 283, 291, 331, 339, 344, 386, 483
twin slit experiment 487
twins paradox 109–111, 121, 122, 361, 367
Tzara, Tristan 387–88, 475

Uccello, Paolo 40, 197
—*St George and the Dragon* 40, 197
Ulysses 200
Un-American Activities Committee 259
uncertainty 28, 41, 46, 47, 48, 77, 80, 81, 94, 122, 162, 169, 171, 195, 196, 199, 222, 229, 233, 245, 250, 260, 263, 269, 276, 281, 357, 454, 460
undulation 41, 43, 155, 162
unexpected 260, 276, 460
uniform motion 106
unison 136, 137, 150, 263, 479
universal law 98, 108, 164, 173, 177, 180, 182, 337–38
universe 76, 77, 82, 370, 372, 418

unknown 353
unlimiteds 93
unmeasured prelude 61, 401, 433
unsteadiness 97 *see* imbalance
upbeat 7, 205

Valéry, Paul 389
Van Gogh, Vincent 452
Varèse, Edgar 63, 415, 443, 455
—*Ionisation* 443
variable density 432, 436
varispeed 216, 306, 309, 365–67, 424
velocity 106, 109, 110, 138, 140, 142, 157, 159, 306–7, 346–47, 358–59, 362
Verdi, Giuseppe 446
—*Requiem* 446
Verne, Jules 404
vibrating string 36, 41, 43, 46–48, 51, 53, 85, 86–90, 106, 108–10, 112, 119, 120, 122, 124–30, 132–36, 144, 147, 149, 150–52, 159, 162, 163, 167–70, 181–83, 194, 202, 212, 216, 217, 356, 359, 362, 373
vibrato 52, 232, 291, 298, 348
Vienna 282–83, 295, 365, 393
Villa-Lobos, Heitor 437
—*New York Skyline* 437
Vinci, Leonardo da 131–32, 219–20
—*Mona Lisa* 219–20
vine 34
viol consort 444
viola 136, 351, 366
violin 74, 85, 112, 126, 127, 136, 147, 158, 170, 229, 317, 329, 337, 351, 355, 364, 376, 377
virtual space 58, 214
virtual time 367
virtue 40, 409
visible music 430
visible speech *see* vocoder
visual culture 23, 156, 371
visual field 24
visual memory 21
visual perception 20, 21, 48, 54, 58, 85, 138, 148, 156, 186, 215, 236, 447
Vitruvian figure 131–32
Vitruvius 29, 211, 226, 233n, 377
Vitry, Philippe de 185
Vivaldi, Antonio 185, 376, 421
—*The Seasons* 421
vocalization 59, 206, 226–28, 281, 285, 287, 289, 315–18, 323, 434, 439
vocoder 323–24, 431, 433
voice recognition 332
void 94, 272, 485
Voigt, Augustus 404–5
—*Battle of Navarino* 404–5
Voinov, N. V. 430
vortex 361
Vos, Martin de 434
Voss, Richard F. 459–60

Wagner, Richard 221, 238, 276, 281, 420, 437, 450
—*Das Rheingold* overture 420
Waley, H. D. 186, 187n, 299
Walton, William 291
—*Façade* 291
waltz 274, 302, 365, 393–95, 398, 420, 452
Warhol, Andy 425
—*Empire* 425
Waters, Ethel 431
wave function, collapse of 51, 122, 169
wave motion 36, 41, 152–53, 155, 167–71, 266n
waveform 30, 31, 132, 213, 214, 320–21, 348, 356, 421–23, 426, 432, 436, 476, 481
wavelength 52, 108, 119, 132–33, 136, 142, 210, 211
wave-particle duality 156, 204–9, 213, 486–87
Weber, Carl Maria von 397
Webern, Anton 6, 62, 205, 275, 283, 291, 332, 336, 338–39, 399, 411
—*Piano Variations* 336
—*Symphony* 336
Wedekind, Franz 193
—*Lulu* 193
Weierstrass, Karl 95
weight 140–42, 159, 181, 185, 304, 346–47
Weill, Kurt 467–68
—*Threepenny Opera* 467–68
Weiss, Michael 368n
Weizenbaum, Joseph 258
Wells, H. G. 363
—*New Accelerator* 363

—*Time Machine* 363
Werckmeister, Andreas 337
wheel 84, 95, 101–13, 121, 147, 153, 361
whispering 288–89
Whistler, James A. McNeill 446
white noise 445, 450–51, 454–55, 460
whiteboard 202
Whitehead, Alfred North 73, 94n
whole-tone scale 60, 352
Wilde, Oscar 362–63
—*Picture of Dorian Gray* 362–63
William I the Conqueror 231
Williams, Charles 375
—*Dream of Olwen* 375
Williams, John composer 305, 417
wind chimes 340–41
Winograd, Terry 257
wisdom, definition of 5, 7
Wittgenstein, Ludwig 9, 10–11, 193, 375
Wittgenstein, Paul 375
Wolff, Christian 331
Wood, Henry 406
Wood, Wallace 438
Woodstock 450
world order 353
world, phenomenal 54, 85
world soul 54
wormhole 48
wow and flutter 422
writing 228–29, 252, 287, 432
wrong note 92
wrong number 254
Wyatt, Thomas 163

X-files tv series 196
Xenakis, Iannis 68, 341, 459–60,
—*Eonta* 466
xylophone 91, 181

Young, J. Z. 248–49, 266n

Zacharias, Magister 301
Zarlino, Gioseffo 138, 272
Zen Buddhism 9, 260, 418
Zeno of Elea ix, xiii, 95, 119, 121, 122, 137–38, 140–45, 147, 150–60, 163, 176, 186, 220
zero 36, 67, 88, 122, 184
Zeus 162
Zhelinsky, N. Y. 430
zither 219
Zymo-xyl (Partch) 378

ABOUT THE AUTHOR

Born in Auckland, New Zealand, in 1942, Robin Maconie studied piano with Christina Geel and majored in English literature and contemporary music at Victoria University under Don McKenzie, Frederick Page, and Roger Savage. As a graduate he studied under Olivier Messiaen at the Paris Conservatoire during 1963–1964, and the following year in Cologne as a DAAD scholar with composers Karlheinz Stockhausen, Herbert Eimert, Bernd-Alois Zimmermann, the pianist Aloys Kontarsky, and other distinguished tutors. He has held teaching appointments at the universities of Auckland, Sussex, Surrey, Oxford, and The City University, London, and for five years led a course in music appreciation and critical listening at Savannah College of Art and Design.

As a London music columnist for *The Daily Telegraph, The Times Educational Supplement*, and *Literary Supplement* during the 1970s he gained a reputation as a trenchant advocate of new music while also gaining experience as editorial assistant to John Mansfield Thomson in the formative years of *Early Music*. His wider reputation as a writer and music is as a specialist in the philosophy of music and the avant-garde aesthetic of Karlheinz Stockhausen, on whom he has written and collaborated in a succession of titles, most recently *Other Planets*, published in 2005 by Scarecrow Press.

In his journalism and other writings including *The Second Sense* (2002) and *The Way of Music* (2006), Maconie delights in defending modern music and aesthetics against the doctrinaire criticisms of philosophy, music education, linguistics, and cognitive science. His books are praised for their conceptual boldness, clarity, and freedom from jargon.

Maconie has been married twice and has a daughter of whom he is very proud. He returned to New Zealand in 2002 to live and work in Dannevirke.